A Complete Record
1878-1985

A Complete Record
1878-1985

IAN ROSS & GORDON SMAILES

BREEDON BOOKS SPORT

Editor: Anton Rippon

Compiled by Ian Ross and Gordon Smailes
Additional research by Tony Matthews and Andrew Ward

First published in Great Britain by
The Breedon Books Publishing Company Limited
44 Friar Gate, Derby DE1 1DA

ISBN 0 907969 10 0

Printed by Butler and Tanner Ltd, Frome.
Jacket designed by Graham Hales

CONTENTS

ACKNOWLEDGEMENTS

The authors wish to thank Everton Football Club, the Football League and Colin Hunt of the Liverpool Post and Echo for their assistance.

Photographs supplied by the Liverpool Post & Echo, Colorsport, BBC Hulton Picture Library, Illustrated London News Picture Library, Steve Hale and Dennis Clareborough.

INTRODUCTION

EVERTON FOOTBALL CLUB was one of the first big names in soccer. Founded, like several of today's Football League clubs, as a humble church team, Everton grew quickly and were natural founder-members of the League in 1888. Their Goodison Park ground was the first major football stadium in England, and in the 1890s, Everton were one of the richest clubs in the country.

Over the century, Everton FC has maintained its position as one of the big clubs. Even when playing fortunes have been at a low ebb, the name of Everton has still ranked alongside the best clubs in the game.

In 1985, Everton again proved themselves a big name in every way. On the field they won the Canon League Championship and the European Cup-winners' Cup, as well as the Charity Shield; twelve months earlier they had lifted the FA Cup at Wembley, and only the incredible pressures of trying to attain such a feat ultimately denied them a much-vaunted treble when they fell at the final hurdle at Wembley in May 1985.

There can, therefore, be no more appropriate time to look at the history of this great club. The statistics have been collected over a number of years, a task which has involved long hours poring over dusty, crumbling Victorian and Edwardian newspapers, and visiting Football League headquarters at Lytham.

Football facts and figures can be a minefield of error for the unwary, and in the compilation of this book, mistakes have been uncovered which have been perpetuated down the years, repeated in books and newspaper articles. Indeed, it will be surprising if this book itself is without a single error, for the primary sources of information have been those ancient newspaper reports which often failed to give teams and scorers in precise detail.

However, we believe that diligent research has produced a more complete and accurate record of Everton's competitive games than anything else previously published.

Note: All statistics are up to the end of the 1984-5 season. In the season-by-season results section, the progressive points total and League position are shown in the columns following the scorers. In Players' Career Records *signifies that the player was still on Everton's books at the end of 1984-5; **signifies the player joined Everton from local junior football; # signifies that the player's contract was cancelled. An asterisk before a player's name (eg *Gray) shows that additional appearances are to be found in the Everton in Europe section.

Where it is known, the date of signing and leaving (eg Apr 1925) is given; where this is not known, the first and last seasons in which the player appeared are shown (eg 1925 means 1925-26). Often, players who made only a handful of appearances, especially in the earlier years, came and went without comment in newspapers and so in some cases it has not been possible to discover a player's previous and post-Everton clubs. Similarly, birthplaces are given, although it has proved impossible to provide a fully comprehensive list.

THE EVERTON STORY

WHEN Liverpool's Stanley Park was officially opened to the public in the summer of 1870, football was taking its first faltering steps towards the game we know today.

The Football Association, which had been formed in 1863, was still concerned with unifying the various sets of rules which held sway in different regions, but clubs like Notts County, Nottingham Forest, Sheffield Wednesday, Stoke and Chesterfield were already in existence. And the FA Cup competition, and the first official England-Scotland international, were only two years away.

As the game grew, so working-class sides would eventually take over from the public school, university and army teams as the dominant force. And the young Scotsmen who were drifting south in search of employment would have much to do with that change. They were to prove adept players and dedicated administrators.

Many of the early football clubs were associated with churches and chapels, and were named after them. Cricket clubs in the summer, they turned to football as the days grew shorter. One such organisation can claim the distinction of having been the cradle of Everton Football Club.

The youngsters connected with St Domingo's Church formed a cricket club and in 1878 they added a football section to the rapidly-expanding organisation. The origins of Everton FC can be traced back to that day.

St Domingo's Football Club soon attracted members from outside the Church and in November 1879, at a meeting in the Queen's Head Hotel, Village Street, it was decided to adopt the name of the district of Everton.

The first pitch was situated at the south-east corner of Stanley Park, opposite Stanley House, the home of John Houlding JP, a brewer who was later to become Lord Mayor of Liverpool, and a man who was to become one of the new club's most influential patrons.

From the Park Lodge in Mill Lane, the first Everton players carried the goal posts, fixed them into hand-crafted sockets and marked out the lines. There was no admission charge and, indeed, those few who gathered to watch the forerunners of some of the game's elite were at the mercy of the notoriously inclement North-West weather. Dressing-room facilities were simply non-existent.

For the first few seasons only a handful of dedicated spectators watched them, the Stanley CC cricketers being a conspicuous group among the meagre gathering. Football at that time relied heavily on the art of dribbling. The passing game was something that they would learn from the Scots.

Everton's first-ever match was played in Stanley Park on 20 December 1879, against St Peter's. Everton had the happiest possible start, celebrating their inaugural game with a 6-0 victory. The local newspapers reported the score only — no teams or scorers — so the names of the men who played in that historic match are lost forever.

On 24 January 1880, Everton met St Peter's again, this time winning 4-0. Again, no scorers were mentioned but we do know that the men named for Everton's second match were: W. Jones, T. Evans, J. Douglas, C.Chiles, S. Chalk, R.W. Morris, A. White, F. Brettle, A. Wade, Smith, W. Williams.

Everton's success meant that they were attracting players from rival clubs and in 1880-81 Everton were admitted as members of the newly-formed Lancashire Football Association, an early recognition of merit within the county.

In the draw for the Lancashire Cup, Everton were paired with Great Lever, a side from the Bolton area and one of the better teams in the North of England. It was the first time Everton had travelled to a fixture by train and they returned in great spirits after holding Great Lever to a 1-1 draw. In the replay at Stanley Park, however, the Merseysiders were unceremoniously crushed 8-1.

Notwithstanding this embarrassing reversal, Everton's general play in this period was highly encouraging. Victories over Birkenhead (7-0) and Liverpool (5-0) were important contributors to the club's growing stature in Lancashire, although the Liverpool club was no relation to the one we know today.

Everton's team was greatly strengthened by the arrival of Jack McGill, a former Glasgow Rangers player who proved to be a brilliant player and tireless coach. He was elected captain and the quality of his play was such that he added Lancashire representative honours to those he had won with his native Ayrshire.

Everton's colours have seen several changes down the years. Originally they were blue and white stripes, although new players often wore the shirts belonging to their former clubs. This led to a cry for uniformity which was made more pressing when Everton became affiliated to the Lancashire FA.

Short of money themselves, and worried about embarrassing the less affluent playing members, Everton officials decided to dye all the shirts black, a two-inch wide scarlet sash being added as an afterthought to brighten up the morbid strip. The shirts led to the club's first nickname, 'the Black Watch'.

Later, Everton adopted salmon shirts with blue shorts, and later still, ruby shirts with blue trimmings and dark blue shorts. The famous royal blue was introduced much later.

The 1881-2 season opened in quite disastrous fashion, Bolton Wanderers burying Everton under an avalanche of class and style to win 13-1. Yet fortunes improved quickly and by the end of that season Everton had won 15 of their 22 matches. There were big wins over Burscough (8-0) and Halliwell (6-0), and on 22 October, a hat-trick from W. Gibson and two goals from McGill earned 'the Moonlight Dribblers', as they had become known, a 5-0 win in the Lancashire Cup. Everton went out 3-1 at Turton in the next round, but by the end of the season one local newspaper declared them 'the premier Association club in South-West Lancashire'.

But financial problems were an inescapable fact. In March 1882, at a meeting at John Houlding's Sandon Hotel, Everton officials agreed that they had to find a private ground where they could charge for admission. At some of the more important matches at Stanley Park, attendances of 2,000 were not uncommon; there had to be some way of tapping this interest.

After much discussion it was decided to accept the offer of a Mr J. Cruitt of Coney Green, who offered the club use of a field off Priory Road.

The 1882-3 season was Everton's fourth and last at Stanley Park. They reached the semi-final of the Liverpool Cup before losing 3-1 to Bootle who went on to become the first winners.

At Priory Road, Everton built primitive dressing rooms and a sort of stand for officials, but the opening game, between Liverpool & District and Walsall & District, did not live up to expectations. Only fourteen shillings (70p) was taken at the gate and officials set about raising money by other means. Some £20 was raised by a concert given by Sam Crosbie's Teachers' Choral Society at the Hand-in-Hand Club, Foley Street.

On the field, Everton's fortunes soared and in 1883-4 they won their first-ever trophy — the Liverpool Cup. They beat Bootle 5-2 in the semi-final, then won a dramatic Final, again at Bootle, when they emerged 1-0 victors of Earlestown. On 29 March 1884 their new president, John Houlding, already known as 'King John of Everton', held the Cup aloft.

But Everton's joy was shortlived and within weeks they were homeless. Mr Cruitt, tired of the club's vociferous and often over-exuberant supporters, withdrew his support and told them to find another ground. They did, moving to a field in Anfield Road, a site which was to become one of the most famous football grounds in the world.

John Houlding assumed the tenancy — his Sandon Hotel was now the club's headquarters — and club members set to work. The field was one of two pastures owned by the Orrell Brothers, well-known local brewers. It was hired out on the following conditions: 'That we, the Everton Football Club, keep the existing walls in good repair, pay the taxes, do not cause ourselves to be a nuisance to Mr Orrell and other tenants adjoining, and also pay a small sum of rent or subscribe a donation each year to the Stanley Hospital in the name of Mr Orrell'.

Having readily agreed, Everton's officials and players — helped by supporters — took up spades, hammers and nails, and barrows. They set about turning the Anfield Road field into a football ground and Everton's first match there was played on 27 September 1884 when Earlestown provided the opposition.

Everton won 5-0, fielding the following players: Joliffe, McGill, Pickering, Preston, Parry, Berry, W.Richards, Whittle, Finlay, Higgins, Gibson.

Earlestown were also the opponents in the Liverpool Cup Final when Everton were controversially beaten 1-0. They claimed that they had scored a goal, but the referee, who in those days was on the touchline and only intervened when there was an appeal against the umpires' decision, ruled that the ball had drifted past the wrong side of the post. It was one of the many such arguments that eventually led to the introduction of goal-nets.

For six seasons Everton players had been, in name at least, amateurs, but by 1885 the leading English clubs favoured open professionalism. They knew that success meant bigger attendances and greater income. Players who could devote their time solely to training and playing, without the often tiring distractions of a job in trade or industry, would have the best chances to succeed.

Everton were not slow at falling into line with this thinking. George Dobson, a full-back from Bolton Wanderers, and George Farmer, a forward from Oswestry, became Everton's first official professionals for the 1885-6 season. Alec Dick, a daring, often reckless full-back from Kilmarnock, followed. Dick's wild play was to earn him a two-month suspension.

Everton lifted the Liverpool Cup in 1886, beating their fierce rivals, Bootle, 2-1; and the following season they won the Cup again, this time defeating Oakfield 5-0.

Such successes encouraged the club to enter the FA Cup for the first time. In 1886-7 they were drawn against Glasgow Rangers, but on the eve of the game at Anfield, Everton found that they could not hope to beat the Scots unless they fielded players who were ineligible for the competition. They decided to play their strongest team — they lost 1-0 — but scratched from the competition. So the match that was eventually played on 30 October 1886 was only a prestigious friendly.

The following season Everton tried again. They played no less than four FA Cup-ties against Bolton Wanderers. After losing the first game Everton raised a successful objection to the eligibility of a Bolton player; there followed two drawn matches before Everton won the fourth, whereupon Bolton claimed that seven Everton 'amateurs' had been offered money to play. Everton lost 6-0 to Preston in the next round before they were told that the FA had eliminated them anyway.

Bolton met Preston in a rearranged match — and lost 9-0 — and the 'Everton seven' were declared professionals and the whole club suspended for a month from 5 December 1887. The Liverpool FA decided that they too would act, and they confiscated the Liverpool Cup which had, for two seasons, stood proudly in the Sandon Hotel. The experience chastened Everton, who did not appear in the 1888-9 FA Cup competition.

By then, however, the club had a new competition to consider. Everton's fixture list had been improving all the time, with matches against teams like Aston Villa, Wolves, Notts County and Derby County. It was obvious, however, that friendly matches did not offer the same attraction — and therefore did not bring in as much cash — as the cup competitions. In 1888, some of the leading clubs in the North and Midlands founded the Football League.

Everton were one of the 12 original members and in September of that year they played their first League match, against Accrington at Anfield. Their record in that first season was disappointing — eighth place with nine wins in 22 matches. But the following season saw a marked improvement and at the end of the season Everton were only two points adrift of Preston North End, who won the League Championship for the second time.

Everton now had some of the best footballers in the land including three players who would all win England caps, half-back Johnny Holt, and forwards Edgar Chadwick and Alf Milward.

In 1890-91 Everton overcame the challenge of Preston to become the second club to win the League title. They won 14 matches and took a particular liking to Derby County, who the previous season they had beaten 11-2 in the FA Cup. In League games, Everton scored 13 goals against Derby. Burnley were hit for seven at Anfield and although Preston took all the points off Everton, it was the Merseysiders who stood two points clear at the end of the season.

In Everton's first ten years in the League they scored 324 goals, a figure topped only by Aston Villa (326). But off the field a crisis was looming, a smouldering fire which burst into flames after being fanned by committee-room discontent. At the centre of the row was John Houlding, one of the club's early benefactors.

Houlding, once the tenant of Anfield, was now its owner and therefore Everton's landlord. The row had festered for some time because there were Everton committee members who disliked their club's HQ and dressing rooms being on licensed premises, namely the Houlding-owned Sandon Hotel.

Houlding responded by telling Everton Football Club that, as their success brought more money through the turnstiles, so he would expect to raise the club's rent. And between 1887-8 and 1888-9 the rent was indeed raised, by 150 per cent.

On 25 January 1892, at a special general meeting, George Mahon, organist at St Domingo's and one of Liverpool's leading accountants, told disenchanted members that he had 'a new ground in his pocket'.

Mahon, at one-time a self-confessed hater of football, had been converted after watching a particularly entertaining match between Everton and Preston, and he was now one of the Anfield club's greatest supporters.

Now he had an option on Mere Green Field. It was situated on the north side of Stanley Park, near Goodison Road, and was later described as having 'degenerated from a nursery into a howling desert'. Some members expressed a view that it might be better to live with Houlding at Anfield than to gamble everything on another move, but Mahon and his supporters were adamant.

It was agreed that: 'The club be formed into a limited company under the name of *The Everton Football Club Limited*, with a capital of £500 in £1 shares, each member to be allowed one share, ten shillings to be called up in monthly instalments of two shillings and sixpence. Such shares as are not taken up to be allotted as the directors may determine.'

For a time it appeared that there would be two Everton Football Clubs, when Houlding insisted that he would keep the name alive at Anfield. But it was ruled that the name belonged to the majority of members — who were now installed by the Goodison Road — and so Houlding called his club 'Liverpool FC'. Thus began one of football's greatest local rivalries, although even then, Liverpool RFC objected to Houlding's new club name. Eventually 'Liverpool AFC' was agreed.

Meanwhile, Everton's first season at Goodison ended on a high note. The team fought back from a poor start to finish third in the League — now the First Division after members of the Football Alliance had formed a second section — and there was a record Goodison attendance of 30,000 for the visit of Preston. Gate receipts for the season topped £8,000 — a far cry from the Priory Road days when £45 was taken in the first season there.

By 1895 Everton's stature was such that no fewer than 12 players had been capped by their respective countries. That year Everton finished runners-up behind Sunderland, and the following season they were third behind Aston Villa and Derby County.

These were eventful days, both on and off the field. At the 1895 annual meeting, after reporting a profit in excess of £6,000 over the previous three years, chairman

Everton's first FA Cup Final appearance was marred by the crowd spilling on to the pitch at the Manchester Athletic Club ground at Fallowfield. The venue was inadequate for such a big game and, as this picture shows, many of the 45,000 crowd could not see. At one stage the game looked unlikely to begin.

14

George Mahon and four of his fellow directors resigned 'owing to acute administrative difficulties'. Of six new directors elected, one was Wilf Cuff, a man who was to serve them for over 50 years and who was to become one of the most influential figures in Everton's history.

The reasons behind the boardroom upheaval have never been made clear, but it must have been a clash over the way the club was being run financially. Ground improvements — a new stand and new covered accommodation — were not unanimously agreed; and there was even a police investigation concerning gatekeepers. It led to improved turnstiles being installed at Goodison.

On the playing side, Everton continued to prosper, reaching the FA Cup Final in 1893 and again four years later. In 1893 they met Wolves at Fallowfield, Manchester, and the game will be best remembered for the totally inadequate facilities which almost led to the match being abandoned. Wolves won when their centre-half, Allen, put in a high ball and Everton's goalkeeper, Williams, was blinded by the sun. The ball found the net and Everton were on their way to defeat.

In 1897 there was the prospect of an all-Merseyside Cup Final, but Liverpool could not overcome Aston Villa in the semi-final. Nor could Everton in the Final at the Crystal Palace. It was a classic match, Villa triumphing 3-2 with all five goals coming in the first-half, and John Bell being voted the outstanding player.

Everton 'celebrated' their 21st birthday by slumping to 11th position in 1899-1900, their lowest League placing at that time. Yet there were to be two important personnel changes. 'Sandy' Young made his debut at centre-forward, and to the delight of Everton's fans, John Bell returned to play outside-left. Everton finished runners-up in 1901-02, but the inconsistency which had become a hallmark of their play, returned and next season they were twelfth in a First Division of 18 clubs.

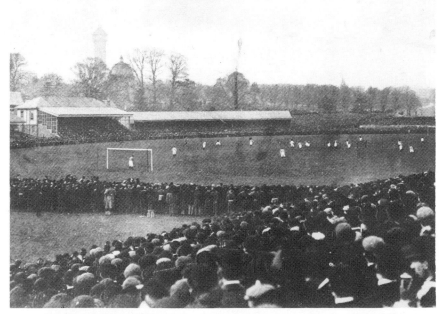

General view of the 1897 Cup Final at the Crystal Palace between Everton and Aston Villa.

Everton goalkeeper Billy Muir and the rest of his defenders look on anxiously as Aston Villa mount an attack during the match at Villa Park in September 1901. Everton were happy with the eventual 1-1 draw.

Everton infuriated their supporters during the ensuing years with a confusing mixture of fine performances and downright disappointing displays. In some seasons they were dazzlingly successful; in others frustratingly mediocre. But always there were magnificent players to watch, and spectacular incidents to be recounted.

Sheffield Wednesday were League Champions in successive seasons, 1902-03 and 1903-04, as Everton finished 11th and then third, one point behind runners-up Manchester City and four points adrift of Wednesday.

The following season Everton signed the eccentric Welsh intellectual and international goalkeeper, Dr Leigh Richmond Roose. They had thoughts of doing the League and Cup double that year — First Division runners-up and FA Cup semi-finalists — and Roose's sometimes outrageous antics between the posts made a lasting impression on those who saw him.

Everton were at the summit of the First Division when they defeated Liverpool in the FA Cup first round in 1904-05. A Harry Makepeace penalty ensured a draw at Anfield, and the replay was won 2-1 with the decisive goal coming five minutes from time.

Everton cantered to a 4-0 win over Stoke in the second round, and Southampton fell by the same score before Everton met Aston Villa in the semi-final.

Some 35,000 people at Stoke's Victoria Ground saw a close-fought 1-1 draw. But Villa were easily the better side in the Nottingham replay, winning 2-1 before going on to defeat Newcastle United 2-0 in the Final.

Everton's title hopes were not helped when a game against Woolwich Arsenal, which they were winning 3-1, was abandoned because of bad weather. When the match was replayed — as the penultimate game of the season — Everton lost 2-1. They found themselves agonizing over the outcome of Newcastle's final match, against Middlesbrough. The Magpies won 3-0 — and with 48 points lifted the title one point ahead of Everton.

The following season quite literally belonged to Merseyside. Everton at last won the FA Cup, while Liverpool took the League Championship.

Everton's path to the Crystal Palace saw them beat West Brom, Chesterfield, Bradford City and the formidable Sheffield Wednesday — and Liverpool. A goal by Abbott — whose shot was diverted over the line by Dunlop — and a moment of sheer inspiration by Hardman were more than enough to end Liverpool's dream of the double. The Final against Newcastle United was settled by a solitary goal from Young.

Season 1906-07 saw Everton swoop to another FA Cup Final and mount a sustained challenge for the title. To reinforce the team they signed Stevenson from Accrington;

Fans outside St Paul's Cathedral before the 1906 FA Cup Final against Newcastle United at the Crystal Palace.

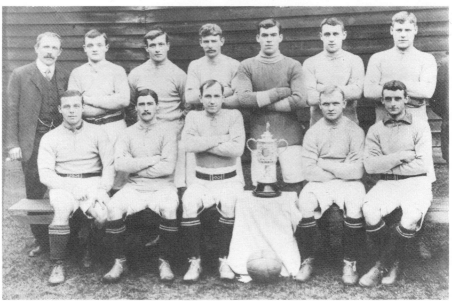

Everton's FA Cup-winning team 1906. Back (l to r): J.Elliott (trainer), Makepeace, W.Balmer, Taylor, Scott, Crelley, Abbott. Front: Sharp, Bolton, Young, Settle, Hardman. Note the former trophy.

Jack Sharp (hidden) scores Everton's goal in the 1907 FA Cup Final.

Settle, a local boy; and three skilful Scots, the Wilson brothers and Graham from Third Lanark.

By the end of November, Everton were top of the table before losing ground and finishing third behind Newcastle and Bristol City. Sheffield Wednesday, who had enjoyed good fortune to overcome Liverpool in the fourth round, stood between Everton and a second successive FA Cup Final. But there was no glory and the Merseysiders lost 2-1 in one of the poorest Finals for years.

It took a full season for Everton to readjust. Full-backs Walter Balmer and Jack Crelley, and Settle who went to Stockport, were phased out; in came players like full-back Maconnachie of Hibs and half-back Adamson of Lochgelly. Morale was low and results disappointing as Everton finished 1907-08 in 11th place.

The arrival of forwards Bertie Freeman and Tim Coleman from Woolwich Arsenal added a new dimension to Everton's goalscoring potential and in 1908-09 the club finished runners-up again.

That close season Everton helped the development of football in South America by playing two exhibition games against Tottenham Hotspur in Buenos Aires. They also tested the local strength with victories over a club side, Alumini, and representative teams of the Argentinian League and Uruguayan League.

Everton's second League Championship success, which came 24 years after the first, was the last to be achieved before the First Division was extended from 20 to 22 clubs. Their success came in football's twilight season of 1914-15, when many people felt that

Everton defenders prepare to tackle a Southampton corner during the 1908 FA Cup quarter-final replay at The Dell. The first match was drawn 0-0 at Goodison, but Everton went down 3-2 in the second game.

Everton 1909. Back (l to r): Harris, R.Balmer, Scott, Maconnachie, Taylor, Makepeace. Front: Sharp, Coleman, White, Freeman, Young, Turner.

Billy Scott is beaten as Swindon net their second goal in the 1912 FA Cup match at the County Ground.

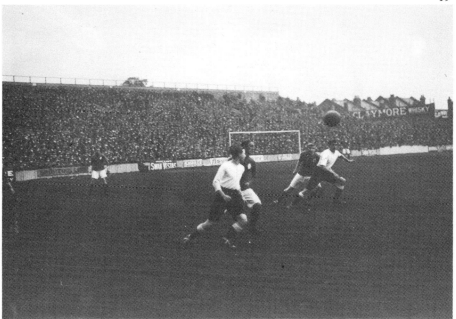

Everton at White Hart Lane for a First Division match against Spurs in 1912.

it was immoral — even treasonable — to continue professional football while the flower of England's youth was preparing to die on the Western Front.

The title was won with several new signings, men like Bobby Parker who solved a goalscoring problem, Tom Fern, who had replaced the seemingly indestructible Billy Scott in goal, and Jimmy Galt, a centre-half from Glasgow Rangers who skippered the side. Outside-right Sam Chedgzoy had his best season, laying on many of Parker's 36 goals.

After several seasons of wartime regional football, Everton, like almost every other club, were forced to make 'perpetual changes' and dropped to 16th place in 1919-20. Their fortunes took a turn for the better in 1920-21, although Liverpool won both derby games within the space of seven days. They triumphed 1-0 at Anfield and 3-0 at Goodison, watched by an aggregate attendance of 100,000 spectators. It unsettled Everton's hitherto consistent form that season and title hopes were forgotten.

It was Liverpool who won the Championship the following season as Everton narrowly avoided the drop to Division Two. The title was again bound for Anfield in 1922-3, while the Goodison club survived the embarrassment of having four goals shot past them in five minutes by McIntyre of Blackburn Rovers, at Ewood Park in September. Everton went on to finish fifth, and made the important signings of Alec Troup, Jack Cock and Neil McBain.

The quality of Everton's play in the early '20s, while widely acknowledged by the game's critics, was not always reflected in results. The influential *Athletic News* was adamant that 'no team in the country has served up more delightful football'.

But, well aware that the club's supporters would never settle for second-best, new chairman, Wilf Cuff, knew that in spite of such flattery, Everton needed something

Everton 1922-3. Back row (l to r): Hart, Brewster, Peacock, Fern, McDonald, Chedgzoy. Front: Harrison, Downs, Irvine, Forbes, Williams.

special to underline their superiority.

The time was right for a hero to emerge, and emerge he did. His name was Billy 'Dixie' Dean, a man who was to become one of the most potent forces that football has ever known, though it is most unlikely that even Cuff could have realised just what sort of a player he was signing when he completed the transfer of Dean from Tranmere Rovers on 16 March 1925, for £3,000.

In personal terms Dean made an immediate impact, scoring 33 League and Cup goals in his first season, but collectively Everton still struggled to find the blend and rhythm which would transform individual talents into a successful team.

The cohesion was not far away, however. In 1927-8, with a new double-decker stand bursting at the seams, Everton won the title for the third time and on occasions it seemed that Dean was taking them to it almost single-handed.

New signings, winger Ted Critchley and full-back Warney Cresswell, were key figures, of course, but it was Dean who captured all the headlines. In 39 League games the muscular scoring-machine hammered home 60 goals — 31 in 15 away games, 29 in 14 at home; 40 shots and 20 headers. It was an astonishing feat, and should have paved the way to seasons of glory at Goodison. that it did not is a mystery which puzzles Evertonians to this day.

An alarming slump in 1928-9 resulted in Everton — Dean and all — finishing fifth from bottom of Division One. The following season Everton finished rock-bottom and were relegated for the first time in their history.

Unmoved by wholesale criticism, the Goodison board refused to implement drastic 'panic' measures and their attitude paid huge dividends. There followed an amazing transformation in both attitudes and results as Everton swept to the Second Division Championship, the League title and the FA Cup in successive seasons. The 1931-2 season saw the emergence of goalkeeper Ted Sagar who was to clock up a record 463 League appearances for Everton.

The club's overall fortunes took a dip in the mid-'30s when Arsenal's great side, under Herbert Chapman, held centre-stage while the highest Everton could manage

Everton 1928-9. Back row (l to r): Hart, Cresswell, Davies, Griffiths, Virr. Front: O'Donnell, Ritchie, Forshaw, Dean, Martin, Troup.

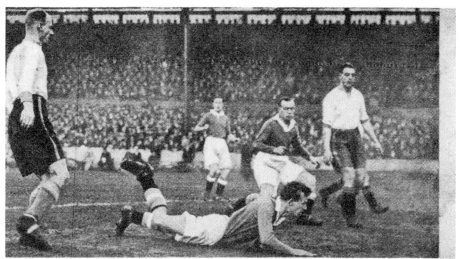

Warney Cresswell (left) watches as Chelsea raid Everton's goal in 1932. Hughie Gallacher is the Chelsea player in the centre of the picture.

Dixie Dean dives bravely during the 1931 FA Cup semi-final match against West Brom at Old Trafford. As always, Dean is oblivious to personal danger, ignoring the flying boots of fellow striker Tommy Johnson and the Albion goalkeeper.

Everton players admire the wax figure of Dixie Dean at Madame Tussaud's in 1929.

Dixie Dean holds aloft the FA Cup at Wembley's front door in 1933.

Post-Wembley smiles. Dixie Dean and his wife with good-luck mascots after the 1933 FA Cup Final.

Everton's 1933 FA Cup-winning team. Back (l to r): H. Cooke (trainer), Britton, Cresswell, Sagar, Cook, White, Thomson. Front: Geldard, Dunn, Dean, Johnson, Stein, Critchley.

Ted Sagar punches clear during the 1937 FA Cup replay at White Hart Lane. Spurs won by the odd goal in seven.

Everton's Championship side, 1938-9. Back row (l to r): Lawton, Jones, Sagar, Cook (trainer), Mercer, Greenhalgh. Front: Cook, Gillick, Bentham, Thomson, Stevenson, Boyes. Mascot is Billy Shannon.

Everton players inspect the pitch before a wartime regional league game.

Harry Catterick hammers an Everton goal during a wartime match against Newcastle United.

between 1934 and 1938 was eighth in 1935.

But they were re-fashioning their side around the skills of young players like Joe Mercer, while the 17-year-old Tommy Lawton had been bought from Burnley for the princely sum of £6,500 in 1936. The forward line was further strengthened by the signing of Bobby Bell from Tranmere Rovers.

Supervised by Dean, young Lawton became the focal point of an attack which led Everton to a fifth title in 1939.

Everton were one of the last major English clubs to appoint a manager. Their first such appointment was made in 1939 when they gave the job to club secretary Theo Kelly. Although a hard-working and efficient administrator who had superb organising ability, Kelly was never particularly popular with the players.

World War Two erupted shortly after Kelly had taken office and for seven years, Britain's soccer fans were sustained by a diet of regional league and cup football. International matches, though not counting towards official caps, provided some magnificent football and England had one of her strongest-ever teams during this spell. At wing-half in many of them were the Everton pair, Cliff Britton and Joe Mercer.

Attendances boomed when sanity was restored to a grateful world, but for Everton it meant a nose-dive in playing fortunes. Champions for seven years, they surrendered the title to Liverpool in 1946-7, and by the following season they were 14th in Division One. Mercer and Lawton had long since departed for London clubs.

Action was needed and in 1948, Cliff Britton returned as manager. Britton had steered Burnley into Division One and to the FA Cup Final; and he was widely respected by the Everton club, players, officials and supporters alike. Kelly stayed on as secretary, but one face was sadly missing. In 1949, Wilf Cuff, the man who had

Everton 1954-55. Back row (l to r): Cliff Britton (manager), Grant, Moore, Jones, O'Neill, Donovan, Lello, Leyfield (trainer). Front: McNamara, Fielding, Wainwright, Farrell, Eglington, Hickson, Parker.

guided them through triumphs and ills, died.

Britton, meanwhile, went on the look-out for players. He brought centre-forward Dave Hickson from Ellesmere Port, and at the other end of the scale paid an Everton club record fee of £20,000 for Burnley inside-forward Harry Potts.

Hickson, in particular, played well for Britton, but the widely-predicted revival failed to materialise and after finishing 18th in successive seasons, Everton were relegated for only the second time in the club's history.

Two indistinguished seasons of Second Division football were highlighted only by a run to the FA Cup semi-finals in 1953, before promotion was gained in 1953-4. There was the inevitable joy of returning to the big time, yet the spark was still missing and during the second half of the '50s, Everton hovered in the lower reaches of Division One with remarkable consistency.

The monotony was somewhat relieved by an exciting FA Cup run in 1956, before Manchester City ended Everton's gallop in the quarter-final. Everton's board gave Britton the broadest hint when they announced that they would like to appoint a caretaker manager while he was abroad with the team. Inevitably, he left and Everton's playing affairs were run by a three-man committee until the appointment of former Scottish amateur international, Ian Buchan, as team coach.

Britton's successor as manager was not appointed until October 1958 when Johnny Carey arrived to breathe new life into the club. Carey found Bobby Collins already on the pay-roll and he added players like Derek Temple, Albert Dunlop, Brian Labone and Mick Meagan.

Towards the end of the '50s, there emerged a man who was to steady the club's erratic course. John Moores, millionaire football fanatic, former amateur player, and a member of the family which founded the massive Littlewoods football pools and mail-order organisation, became chief benefactor of a club he had supported from childhood.

With additional cash at his disposal, Carey signed up some fine players with Alex Young, Roy Vernon and Jimmy Gabriel topping the list.

In 1960-1, Carey's team took Everton to fifth place in the First Division, their highest post-war placing. Yet the manager was not allowed to finish the job he had started and chairman Moores decided that a new face was needed.

In came Harry Catterick, a quietly-spoken disciplinarian who had played centre-forward for Everton in the immediate post-war era. In 1961-2 they finished fourth, while across Stanley Park, Liverpool under Shankly were winning the Second Division title.

The following season was one of the worst in terms of weather — the season was extended after hundreds of games had been postponed — but for Everton it was a glorious campaign. They swept to the title, remained unbeaten at home, and set a new club record points total.

Having taken their first steps into European competition (losing a Fairs Cup match on aggregate to Dunfermline) Everton prepared for the European Cup.

They were drawn against Inter Milan, experts at the art of a two-legged tie, and went out to a solitary goal in Italy after a goalless stalemate at Goodison. Everton's consolation was the performance of debutant Colin Harvey, who survived a baptism of fire to launch his illustrious career.

Having bought Tony Kay to add steel to an already impressive midfield department, Catterick was badly shaken when Kay, along with others was sent to prison and banned from the game for life after being found guilty of accepting bribes to affect the results of matches during his days as a Sheffield Wednesday player.

In 1966, Everton went back to Wembley and one of the most memorable Finals of modern times. Two goals down to Sheffield Wednesday, they hauled themselves back from the brink with two goals from unsung Mike Trebilcock, and won a sensational victory with a Temple goal.

In August 1966, Catterick won the race to sign Alan Ball; seven months later he secured the services of Howard Kendall, and another title-winning side was in the making. In 1968, Everton reached another FA Cup Final, this time losing to West Brom in extra-time at Wembley, and a year later they were losing semi-finalists.

But the 1969-70 season capped anything that had gone before. Driven on by the midfield trio of Harvey, Kendall and Ball, a seventh title was secured with a new record points tally (for Everton) of 66. The power and the passion of Everton's play set them well apart from their contemporaries and Catterick's blend of precocious young talent and great experience looked like giving Everton the stage for seasons to come.

Only months later they were struggling to beat even an average First Division side. The Goodison faithful looked on in disbelief as a slide of epic proportions left Everton in 14th place. A brave European Cup bid ended when the Greek side, Panathinaikos, went through on the away goals rule.

West Brom's Kaye heads clear as Everton's Hurst challenges during the 1968 FA Cup Final.

Everton skipper Alan Ball with the 1970 FA Charity Shield after the win over Chelsea.

Chairman Sir John Moores and manager Billy Bingham admire the skills of their new signing, Bob Latchford.

Catterick's men returned from Athens to face Liverpool in an FA Cup semi-final and saw the last avenue of success that season closed down by a 2-1 defeat.

Catterick, baffled as to why his side had fallen apart, spent the best part of two seasons 'remoulding', but with four years of his contract still to run, and suffering from illness, he was moved into an executive position in April 1973.

Another former Everton player, Billy Bingham, was given the job of steering Everton back on course, his job made even more difficult by the astonishing success that Liverpool were experiencing under the forceful management of Bill Shankly.

Everton finished a respectable, if unspectacular seventh in Bingham's first season in charge, after he had tried to solve the scoring problem by smashing the British transfer record, paying £350,000 for Bob Latchford. The big striker repaid Bingham's faith with goals in plenty.

But still there was no trophy and in January 1977, with Everton drifting in mid-table, Bingham was fired and Gordon Lee appointed. That year, Lee led the side out at Wembley, for the League Cup Final against Aston Villa. It took three games before Villa emerged victorious to break Evertonian hearts.

That was also the year of the FA Cup semi-final against Liverpool, when Welsh referee Clive Thomas disallowed what looked like a perfectly good goal by Bryan Hamilton. It had looked as though Everton had secured a famous victory. Thomas felt otherwise and Liverpool won the replay 3-0.

Season 1977-8 saw Everton finish third with 76 goals to become the First Division's leading scorers. The future looked bright and Lee had built a side which combined flair with commitment. But in 1979-80, things turned sour and after losing an FA Cup semi-final replay to West Ham, the Merseysiders finished 19th, only four points clear of relegation. After a month of speculation, Lee was sacked on 6 May 1981, after Everton had improved marginally to finish 15th.

The new manager was a familiar face — Howard Kendall, one of the stars of the great 1970 Championship-winning side. In his first season as manager, Kendall guided Everton to eighth place. Twelve months later, despite a catastrophic 5-0 Goodison drubbing by Liverpool, Everton finished seventh.

But the real turning point came in the New Year of 1984. After surviving calls for his dismissal, Kendall saw the team he had moulded begin to climb. On the way to seventh place in the League they met Liverpool in the Milk Cup Final — the first-ever Merseyside Wembley Final — and fought their way to an FA Cup Final meeting with Watford.

The Milk Cup turned sour in a Maine Road replay but, after a 14-year wait, Everton landed a trophy when they beat Watford to lift the FA Cup.

A Charity Shield victory over Liverpool in August 1984 raised the curtain on a magnificent season. The Canon League Championship was lifted in tremendous style; the European Cup-winners' Cup came to Goodison after the destruction of Rapid Vienna in the Final in Rotterdam; and there was honour in defeat when Manchester United, playing bravely with ten men, ended Everton's hopes of what would have been an astonishing treble by winning the 1985 FA Cup Final.

Howard Kendall was named Manager of the Year; Neville Southall was the Football Writers' Association Footballer of the Year; Peter Reid was honoured by his fellow professionals as the PFA's Player of the Year.

Reid, Trevor Steven, Gary Stevens, Paul Bracewell, Graeme Sharp and Pat Van den Hauwe all won their first international caps to underline the coming of age of arguably Everton's greatest-ever side.

Those Victorian footballers who played the first matches on Stanley Park would be proud to see the progress of the club they founded more than a century ago.

Howard Kendall and Everton chairman Philip Carter look particularly thoughtful on the day Kendall became manager at Goodison.

Adrian Heath turns away after scoring the winning goal against Southampton in the 1984 FA Cup semi-final.

Derek Mountfield takes the salute for the goal against QPR that ensured Everton's 1985 Canon League title.

Andy Gray opens the scoring in the 1985 European Cup-winners' Cup Final.

EVERTON'S FOOTBALL LEAGUE RECORD
1888-9 to 1984-5 INCLUSIVE

			HOME				AWAY					
SEASON	P	W	D	L	F	A	W	D	L	F	A	Pts	Pos

FOOTBALL LEAGUE

SEASON	P	W	D	L	F	A	W	D	L	F	A	Pts	Pos
1888-9	22	8	0	3	23	14	1	2	8	12	32	20	8th
1889-90	22	8	2	1	40	15	6	1	4	25	25	31	2nd
1890-91	22	9	0	2	39	12	5	1	5	24	17	29	1st
1891-2	26	8	2	3	32	22	4	2	7	17	27	28	5th

FIRST DIVISION

SEASON	P	W	D	L	F	A	W	D	L	F	A	Pts	Pos
1892-3	30	9	3	3	44	17	7	1	7	30	34	36	3rd
1893-4	30	11	1	3	63	23	4	2	9	27	34	33	6th
1894-5	30	12	2	1	47	18	6	4	5	35	32	42	2nd
1895-6	30	10	4	1	40	17	6	3	6	26	26	39	3rd
1896-7	30	8	1	6	42	29	6	2	7	20	28	31	7th
1897-8	30	11	3	1	33	12	2	6	7	15	27	35	4th
1898-9	34	10	2	5	25	13	5	6	6	23	28	38	4th
1899-1900	34	11	1	5	30	15	2	6	9	17	34	33	11th
1900-01	34	10	4	3	37	17	6	1	10	18	25	37	7th
1901-2	34	11	2	4	31	11	6	5	6	22	24	41	2nd
1902-3	34	10	2	5	28	18	3	4	10	17	29	32	12th
1903-4	34	13	0	4	36	12	6	5	6	23	20	43	3rd
1904-5	34	14	2	1	36	11	7	3	7	27	25	47	2nd
1905-6	38	12	1	6	44	30	3	6	10	26	36	37	11th
1906-7	38	16	2	1	50	10	4	3	12	20	36	45	3rd
1907-8	38	11	4	4	34	24	4	2	13	24	40	36	11th
1908-9	38	11	3	5	51	28	7	7	5	31	29	46	2nd
1909-10	38	8	6	5	30	28	8	2	9	21	28	40	10th
1910-11	38	12	3	4	34	17	7	4	8	16	19	45	4th
1911-12	38	13	5	1	29	12	7	1	11	17	30	46	2nd
1912-13	38	8	2	9	28	31	7	5	7	20	23	37	11th
1913-14	38	8	7	4	32	18	4	4	11	14	37	35	15th
1914-15	38	8	5	6	44	29	11	3	5	32	18	46	1st
1919-20	42	8	6	7	42	29	4	8	9	27	39	38	16th
1920-21	42	9	8	4	40	26	8	5	8	26	29	47	7th
1921-2	42	10	7	4	42	22	2	5	14	15	33	36	20th
1922-3	42	14	4	3	41	20	6	3	12	22	39	47	5th
1923-4	42	13	7	1	43	18	5	6	10	19	35	49	7th
1924-5	42	11	4	6	25	20	1	7	13	15	40	35	17th
1925-6	42	9	9	3	42	26	3	9	9	30	44	42	11th
1926-7	42	10	6	5	35	30	2	4	15	29	60	34	20th
1927-8	42	11	8	2	60	28	9	5	7	42	38	53	1st
1928-9	42	11	2	8	38	31	6	2	13	25	44	38	18th
1929-30	42	6	7	8	48	46	6	4	11	32	46	35	22nd

SECOND DIVISION

1930-31	42	18	1	2	76	31	10	4	7	45	35	61	1st

FIRST DIVISION

1931-2	42	18	0	3	84	30	8	4	9	32	34	56	1st
1932-3	42	13	6	2	54	24	3	3	15	27	50	41	11th
1933-4	42	9	7	5	38	27	3	9	9	24	36	40	14th
1934-5	42	14	5	2	64	32	2	7	12	25	56	44	8th
1935-6	42	12	5	4	61	31	1	8	12	28	58	39	16th
1936-7	42	12	7	2	56	23	2	2	17	25	55	37	17th
1937-8	42	11	5	5	54	34	5	2	14	25	41	39	14th
1938-9	42	17	3	1	60	18	10	2	9	28	34	59	1st
1946-7	42	13	5	3	40	24	4	4	13	22	43	43	10th
1947-8	42	10	2	9	30	26	7	4	10	22	40	40	14th
1948-9	42	12	5	4	33	25	1	6	14	8	38	37	18th
1949-50	42	6	8	7	24	20	4	6	11	18	46	34	18th
1950-51	42	7	5	9	26	35	5	3	13	22	51	32	22nd

SECOND DIVISION

1951-2	42	12	5	4	42	25	5	5	11	22	33	44	7th
1952-3	42	9	8	4	38	23	3	6	12	33	52	38	16th
1953-4	42	13	6	2	55	27	7	10	4	37	31	56	2nd

FIRST DIVISION

1954-5	42	9	6	6	32	24	7	4	10	30	44	42	11th
1955-6	42	11	5	5	37	29	4	5	12	18	40	40	15th
1956-7	42	10	5	6	34	28	4	5	12	27	51	38	15th
1957-8	42	5	9	7	34	35	8	2	11	31	40	37	16th
1958-9	42	11	3	7	39	38	6	1	14	32	49	38	16th
1959-60	42	13	3	5	50	20	0	8	13	23	58	37	16th
1960-61	42	13	4	4	47	23	9	2	10	40	46	50	5th
1961-2	42	17	2	2	64	21	3	9	9	24	33	51	4th
1962-3	42	14	7	0	48	17	11	4	6	36	25	61	1st
1963-4	42	14	4	3	53	26	7	6	8	31	38	52	3rd
1964-5	42	9	10	2	37	22	8	5	8	32	38	49	4th
1965-6	42	12	6	3	39	19	3	5	13	17	43	41	11th
1966-7	42	11	4	6	39	22	8	6	7	26	24	48	6th
1967-8	42	18	1	2	43	13	5	5	11	24	27	52	5th
1968-9	42	14	5	2	43	10	7	10	4	34	26	57	3rd
1969-70	42	17	3	1	46	19	12	5	4	26	15	66	1st
1970-71	42	10	7	4	32	16	2	6	13	22	44	37	14th
1971-2	42	8	9	4	28	17	1	9	11	9	31	36	15th
1972-3	42	9	5	7	27	21	4	6	11	14	28	37	17th
1973-4	42	12	7	2	29	14	4	5	12	21	34	44	7th
1974-5	42	10	9	2	33	19	6	9	6	23	23	50	4th
1975-6	42	10	7	4	37	24	5	5	11	23	42	42	11th
1976-7	42	9	7	5	35	24	5	7	9	27	40	42	9th
1977-8	42	14	4	3	47	22	8	7	6	29	23	55	3rd
1978-9	42	12	7	2	32	17	5	10	6	20	23	51	4th
1979-80	42	7	7	7	28	25	2	10	9	15	26	35	19th
1980-81	42	8	6	7	32	25	5	4	12	23	33	36	15th
1981-2	42	11	7	3	33	21	6	6	9	23	29	64	8th
1982-3	42	13	6	2	43	19	5	4	12	23	29	64	7th
1983-4	42	9	9	3	21	12	7	5	9	23	30	62	7th
1984-5	42	16	3	2	58	17	12	3	6	30	26	90	1st

1888-89

1	Sep	8	(h)	Accrington	W	2-1	Fleming 2	2	
2		15	(h)	Notts Co	W	2-1	E.Chadwick, Ross	4	
3		22	(a)	Aston Villa	L	1-2	Watson	4	3
4		29	(a)	Bolton W	L	2-6	Lewis, Watson	4	6
5	Oct	6	(h)	Aston Villa	W	2-0	Farmer, Waugh	6	4
6		13	(a)	Notts Co	L	1-3	Ross	6	6
7		20	(a)	Derby C	W	4-2	Costley 2, E.Chadwick, McKinnon	8	5
8		27	(h)	Derby C	W	6-2	McKinnon 3, Ross 2, Watson	10	4
9	Nov	3	(h)	Bolton W	W	2-1	Brown, Ross	12	3
10		10	(a)	Blackburn R	L	0-3		12	4
11		17	(a)	Burnley	D	2-2	E.Chadwick, Watson	13	4
12		24	(h)	Burnley	W	3-2	E.Chadwick, Costley, Coyne	15	4
13	Dec	1	(a)	West Brom A	L	1-4	E.Chadwick	15	4
14		15	(a)	Stoke C	D	0-0		16	4
15		22	(a)	Preston N E	L	0-3		16	6
16		29	(a)	Accrington	L	1-3	Brown	16	7
17	Jan	12	(h)	Stoke C	W	2-1	Davies, Milward	18	7
18		19	(h)	Preston N E	L	0-2		18	7
19		26	(a)	Wolves	L	0-4		18	7
20	Feb	9	(h)	Wolves	L	1-2	E.Chadwick	18	7
21		23	(h)	West Brom A	L	0-1		18	7
22	Mar	30	(h)	Blackburn R	W	3-1	Davies, Milward, Waugh	20	8

League Appearances
League Goals

EVERTON'S PRE-LEAGUE FA CUP RECORD

1886-7

Entered for the first time and drawn against Glasgow Rangers but scratched
because some of the players used in the eventual 1-0 defeat by Rangers would
have been ineligible for the FA Cup.

1887-8

Oct	15	(a)	Bolton W*	L	0-1		Rd 1
	29	(h)	Bolton W	D	2-2	Farmer, Watson	Replay
Nov	12	(a)	Bolton W	D	0-0		Replay
	19	(h)	Bolton W**	W	2-1	Goodie, Watson	Replay
	26	(a)	Preston N E	L	0-6		Rd 2

FA Cup Appearances
FA Cup Goals

*Everton lodged an appeal that Bolton centre-forward Struthers was ineligible. Appeal upheld.

**Bolton lodged an appeal that seven Everton players were ineligible. Everton suspended
for one month and Bolton Wanderers then met Preston North End

1888-9

Everton did not compete in FA Cup.

Angus J	Briscoe W	Brown W	Chadwick A	Chadwick E	Costley J	Coyne	Davie	Davies J	Dick A	Dobson G	Farmer G	Fleming G	Higgins M	Holt J	Joliffe C	Jones R	Kelso R	Keys	Lewis W	McKinnon A	Milward A	Ross N	Smalley R	Stevenson G	Sugg F	Warmby	Watson R	Waugh D	Weir J	Wilson W	Match
				10					2	6	11	7		4	5				9			3	1					8			1
				10					2	6	11	7		4					9	5		3	1					8			2
				10					2		11			6				9				3	1			5	7	8	4		3
				9					2	6	10										11	3	1				7	8	5		4
				11					2	6				5						7		3	1		9		8	10	4		5
	10			11					2	6				5						7		3	1		9		8		4		6
				10	11					2	6			5	1					7		3			9		8		4		7
				10	11					2	6			5						7		3	1		9		8		4		8
		11		10					2	3	6			5						7		9	1				8		4		9
		11		10						2	7			6							9	3	1		5		8		4		10
		11		10	9					2	6	7		4								3	1		5		8				11
				10	11	8	9				6	7		5								3	1		2				4		12
		3		10	11	8	9	7		2	4												1		6				5		13
				10	11			7		2	6			5								3	1				8		4		14
11	8	9		10						2	6			5								3	1				7		4		15
11	7	9		10						2						1						3			5		8		4		16
9				10				7		2	6			5	1						11	3					8		4		17
11				10				7		2	6			5	1		4				9	3					8				18
11				10				7		2	6			5							9	3	1	4			8				19
	11		6	10				7	3	2	4										9		1				8				20
				10				7	3	2	4			5								9	1				8	11	6		21
				10				7		2	4		9	5									1				8	11	6	3	22
5	3	6	2	22	6	2	2	8	9	18	21	4	1	17	4	1	1	1	3	6	6	19	18	1	9	1	18	7	16	1	
	2			6	3	1		2		1	2								1		4	2	5				4	2			

Morris played number 9 in Match 14; H.Parkinson played number 6 in Match 16;
Pollock played number 4 in Match 4; Roberts played number 5 in Match 20.

Briscoe W	Cassidy	Dick A	Dobson G	Farmer G	Fleming G	Gibson A	Goudie	Higgins M	Izatt	Joliffe C	Murray	Richards R	Smalley R	Watson R	Weir J
	7	2	3	8		5	9	4	11	1	6			10	
	7	2	3	8		5	9	4	11	1	6			10	
		2	3	8	11	5	9	4	7				1	10	6
11		2	3	8		5	9	4	7				1	10	6
		2	3	8		5	9	4	7			11	1	10	6
1	2	5	5	5	1	5	5	5	5	2	2	1	3	5	3
			1				1							2	

1889-90

1	Sep	7	(h)	Blackburn R	W	3-2	Geary 2, Parry		2	
2		14	(h)	Burnley	W	2-1	Geary, Parry		4	
3		16	(a)	Wolves	L	1-2	Parry		4	2
4		21	(a)	Bolton W	W	4-3	Geary 2, Chadwick, Milward		6	1
5		28	(h)	Bolton W	W	3-0	Geary 2, Latta		8	1
6		30	(h)	Wolves	D	1-1	Chadwick		9	1
7	Oct	5	(a)	Derby C	D	2-2	Chadwick, Orr		10	1
8		19	(a)	Notts Co	L	3-4	Milward 2, Geary		10	2
9		26	(h)	Accrington	D	2-2	Chadwick, Geary		11	2
10	Nov	2	(h)	Stoke C	W	8-0	Geary 3, Brady 2, Latta 2, Milward		13	1
11		9	(a)	Stoke C	W	2-1	Geary, Latta		15	1
12		16	(h)	Preston N E	L	1-5	Geary		15	2
13		23	(a)	Aston Villa	W	2-1	Geary 2		17	2
14	Dec	7	(h)	Notts Co	W	5-3	Latta 3, Chadwick, Parry		19	2
15		21	(a)	Preston N E	W	2-1	Geary, Milward		21	2
16		28	(a)	Blackburn R	W	4-2	Milward 2, Brady, Latta		23	2
17	Jan	4	(h)	Aston Villa	W	7-0	Brady 2, Chadwick 2, Geary 2, Latta		25	2
18	Feb	8	(a)	Burnley	W	1-0	Chadwick		27	2
19		22	(a)	Accrington	L	3-5	Brady 2, Geary		27	2
20	Mar	8	(h)	West Brom A	W	5-1	Milward 2, Brady, Chadwick, Holt		29	2
21		15	(h)	Derby C	W	3-0	Milward, opp.og 2		31	2
22		22	(a)	West Brom A	L	1-4	Geary		31	2
								League Appearances		
								League Goals		
23	Jan	18	(h)	Derby C	W	11-2	Brady 3, Geary 3, Milward 3, Doyle, Kirkwood	FA Cup Rd 1		
24	Feb	3	(a)	Stoke C	L	2-4	Geary, Milward			2
								FA Cup Appearances		
								FA Cup Goals		

Brady A	Cain R	Chadwick E	Cox W	Doyle D	Farmer G	Geary F	Hammond H	Hannah A	Holt J	Jamieson R	Joliffe C	Jones R	Kirkwood D	Latta A	Milward A	Orr	Parry C	Smalley R	Sugg F	Weir J	
		10		3	4	9		2	5					7	11		8	1		6	1
		10		3	4	9		2	5					7	11		8	1		6	2
		10		3	4	9		2	5					7	11		8	1		6	3
		10		3	6	9		2	5		1	8		7	11		4				4
		10		3	6	9		2	5				8	7	11		4	1			5
		10		3	6	9		2	5				8	7	11		4	1			6
		10		3	6			2	5				8	7	11	9	4	1			7
		10		3	6	9		2	5				8	7	11		4	1			8
		10		3	6	9		2	5				8	7	11		4	1			9
8	6	10		3		9		2	5					7	11		4	1			10
8	6	10		3		9		2	5					7	11		4	1			11
8		10		3	6	9		2	5					7	11		4	1			12
8	6	10		3		9		2	5					7	11		4	1			13
8	4	10		3		9		2	5					7	11		6	1			14
8	4	10		3		9		2	5					7	11		6	1			15
8	4	10		3				2	5				6	7	11		9	1			16
8		10		3		9		2	5				4	7	11		6	1			17
8		10		3		9		2	5				4	7	11		6	1			18
8	4	10	1	3		9		2	5					7	11		6				19
8	4	10	1			9	3	2	5					7	11		6				20
8	4	10	1	3				2		9				7			6		5		21
8	4	10	1	3		9		2	5					7	11		6				22
13	10	22	4	22	10	18	1	22	21	1	1	1	11	19	22	1	22	17	1	3	
8		9				21								9	10	1	4				opp.og 2
8		10		3		9		2	5				4	7	11		6	1			23
8		10		3		9		2	5				4	7	11		6	1			24
2		2		2		2		2	2				2	2	2		2	2			
3				1		4							1	4							

1890-91

1	Sep 6	(a)	West Brom A	W	4-1	Geary 2, Brady, Campbell	2	
2	13	(h)	Wolves	W	5-0	Geary 2, Milward 2, Chadwick	4	
3	20	(a)	Bolton W	W	5-0	Geary 2, Milward 2, Latta	6	1
4	27	(a)	Accrington	W	2-1	Geary, Milward	8	1
5	Oct 4	(h)	Derby C	W	7-0	Geary 2, Milward 2, Brady, Chadwick, Kirkwood	10	1
6	11	(a)	Aston Villa	D	2-2	Geary 2	11	1
7	18	(h)	Bolton W	W	2-0	Brady 2	13	1
8	25	(h)	West Brom A	L	2-3	Holt, Latta	13	1
9	Nov 1	(a)	Notts Co	L	1-3	Geary	13	1
10	8	(a)	Blackburn R	L	1-2	Chadwick	13	1
11	15	(h)	Sunderland	W	1-0	Robertson	15	1
12	22	(a)	Preston N E	L	0-2		15	2
13	29	(h)	Blackburn R	W	3-1	Geary 2, Brady	17	2
14	Dec 6	(a)	Wolves	W	1-0	Geary	19	1
15	13	(a)	Derby C	W	6-2	Wylie 4, Brady, Geary	21	1
16	20	(a)	Sunderland	L	0-1		21	2
17	26	(h)	Accrington	W	3-2	Milward 2, Chadwick	23	1
18	27	(h)	Burnley	W	7-3	Chadwick 3, Latta 2, Brady, Milward	25	1
19	Jan 1	(h)	Aston Villa	W	5-0	Brady 2, Chadwick, Geary, Milward	27	1
20	3	(h)	Notts Co	W	4-2	Chadwick 2, Geary, Milward	29	1
21	10	(h)	Preston N E	L	0-1		29	1
22	Mar 14	(a)	Burnley	L	2-3	Geary 2	29	1
							League Appearances	
							League Goals	
23	Jan 17	(a)	Sunderland	L	0-1		FA Cup Rd 1	
							FA Cup Appearances	
							FA Cup Goals	

Angus J	Brady A	Campbell W	Chadwick E	Doyle D	Elliott J	Geary F	Gordon P	Hannah A	Holt J	Jardine D	Kirkwood D	Latta A	Lochhead A	McLean D	Milward A	Parry C	Robertson H	Smalley R	Wylie T	
1	8	6	10	3		9		2	5		4	7			11					1
1	8	6	10	3		9		2	5		4	7			11					2
1	8	6	10	3		9		2	5		4	7			11					3
1	8	6	10	3		9		2	5		4	7			11					4
1	8	6	10	3		9		2	5		7				11	4				5
1	8	6	10	3		9		2	5		7				11	4				6
1	8		10	3		9	7	2	5		6				11	4				7
1	8	2	10	3		9			5		6	7			11	4				8
1	8	5	10	3	7	9		2						4	11	6				9
	8		10	3		9		2	5					6	11	4	7	1		10
1	8	6	10	3		7		2	5		4				11	9				11
1	8	4	10	3		9	7	2	5		6				11					12
	8	6	10	3		9	7	2	5	1	4				11					13
	8		10			9		2	5	1	4			3	11	6			7	14
	8	6	10			9		2	5	1	4			3	11				7	15
	8	6	10	3		9		2	5	1	4				11				7	16
	8		10	3		9		2	5	1	4				11	6			7	17
	8		10	3		9		2	5	1	4	7			11	6				18
	8		10	3		9		2	5	1	4	7			11	6				19
			10	3		9		2	5	1	4	7			11	6	8			20
	8		10	3		9		2	5	1	4	7			11	6				21
	8		10	3		9			5	1		7	4	2	11	6				22
11	21	13	22	20	1	22	3	20	21	10	19	10	1	5	22	13	3	1	4	
	9	1	10			20			1		1	4			12		1		4	
1			10	3		8			5		4	7		2	11	6	9			23
1			1	1		1			1		1	1		1	1	1	1			

1891-92

1	Sep	5	(a)	West Brom A	L	0-4		0	
2		7	(h)	Darwen	W	5-3	Geary 2, Milward 2, Latta	2	
3		19	(h)	Blackburn R	W	3-1	Geary, Kelso, Latta	4	7
4		26	(a)	Accrington	D	1-1	Gordon	5	5
5	Oct	3	(a)	Sunderland	L	1-2	Geary	5	10
6		10	(h)	Preston N E	D	1-1	Thomson	6	7
7		17	(a)	Bolton W	L	0-1		6	11
8		24	(a)	Derby C	W	3-0	Latta 2, Chadwick	8	7
9		31	(a)	Preston N E	L	0-4		8	8
10	Nov	7	(h)	West Brom A	W	4-3	Latta 3, Milward	10	8
11		14	(a)	Darwen	L	1-3	Latta	10	8
12		21	(a)	Wolves	L	1-5	Latta	10	9
13		28	(h)	Aston Villa	W	5-1	Chadwick 2, Latta, Maxwell, Wylie	12	9
14	Dec	5	(a)	Blackburn R	D	2-2	Latta, opp.og	13	9
15		12	(h)	Wolves	W	2-1	Chadwick, Latta	15	5
16		25	(h)	Sunderland	L	0-4		15	8
17		28	(a)	Aston Villa	W	4-3	Chadwick 2, Maxwell 2	17	7
18	Jan	2	(h)	Burnley	D	1-1	Milward	18	7
19		9	(a)	Notts Co	W	3-1	Latta, Maxwell, Milward	20	5
20	Feb	13	(a)	Burnley	L	0-1		20	6
21	Mar	5	(h)	Stoke C	W	1-0	Chadwick	22	6
22		12	(h)	Stoke C	W	1-0	Chadwick	24	6
23		19	(h)	Accrington	W	3-0	Chadwick 2, Latta	26	5
24	Apr	15	(h)	Derby C	L	1-2	Kelso	26	6
25		16	(h)	Notts Co	W	4-0	Latta 3, Geary	28	5
26		18	(h)	Bolton W	L	2-5	Geary, Milward	28	5
							League Appearances		
							League Goals		
27	Jan	16	(h)	Burnley	L	2-4	Chadwick, Robertson	FA Cup Rd 1	
							FA Cup Appearances		
							FA Cup Goals		

Campbell W	Chadwick E	Collins J	Earp F	Elliott J	Geary F	Gordon P	Holt J	Howarth R	Jardine D	Jones R	Kelso R	Kent J	Kirkwood D	Latta A	Lochhead A	McClean D	Marsden J	Maxwell A	Milward A	Murray J	Parry C	Robertson H	Thomson S	Williams R	Wylie T	#
5	10				8			1			4			7		3	2		11		6	9				1
5	10		2		8			1			4			7	6	3			11			9				2
	10	3	9		8	5		1			4			7	6	2			11							3
	10	3	9		8	5		1			4				6	2			11						7	4
3	10		9		8	5		1			4			7	6	2			11							5
3	10				8	5		1			4			7		2			11			6	9			6
	10		9				5	1			2		4	7		3			11	8		6				7
	10						5				2		4	9		3			11	8		6		1	7	8
	10						5	1			2		4	9		3		8	11			6			7	9
	10						5				2		4	9		3			11	8		6		1	7	10
	10		2				5	1				3	4	9					11	8		6			7	11
	10		2				5	1					4	7	6	3		9	11						8	12
	10	3	2				5						4	7				9	11			6		1	8	13
	10						5				2		4	7		3		9	11			6		1	8	14
	10						5				2		4	7		3		9	11			6		1	8	15
	10						5				2		4	7		3		9	11			6		1	8	16
	10						5				2		4	7		3		9	11			6		1	8	17
	10						5				2		4	7		3		9	11			6		1	8	18
	10						5				2		4	7		3		9	11			6		1	8	19
	10						5	1			2		4	7		3		9	11			6			8	20
	10	3					5	1			2		4	7				9	11			6			8	21
	10						5	1	8		2		4	7		3		9	11			6				22
	10						5	1	8		2		4	7		3		9	11			6				23
							5	1	8		2		4	7		3		9	11			6		10		24
	10	3					5	1	8		2		4	7				9	11			6				25
	10	3					5	1	8		2		4	7				9	11			6				26
4	25	6	9	1	10	4	21	11	17	3	23	1	5	25	5	20	1	16	26	4	1	20	3	9	16	
	10				6	1					2			17				4	6				1	1		opp.og 1
	10	3	9				5	1	8		2		4	7					11			6		1	8	27
	1		1				1	1	1		1			1								1		1	1	
	1																					1				

1892-93

1	Sep 3	(h)	Nottingham F	D	2-2	Geary, Milward	1	
2	10	(a)	Aston Villa	L	1-4	Geary	1	
3	17	(a)	Blackburn R	D	2-2	Latta, Maxwell	2	13
4	24	(h)	Newton Heath	W	6-0	E.Chadwick 2, Geary 2, Maxwell, Milward	4	8
5	Oct 1	(h)	Aston Villa	W	1-0	Maxwell	6	4
6	8	(h)	Sunderland	L	1-4	Latta	6	9
7	15	(a)	West Brom A	L	0-3		6	10
8	19	(a)	Newton Heath	W	4-3	Latta 4	8	8
9	22	(h)	Accrington	D	1-1	Milward	9	8
10	29	(a)	Bolton W	L	1-4	Latta	9	9
11	Nov 5	(a)	Derby C	W	6-1	Geary 3, Latta 3	11	7
12	12	(h)	Stoke C	D	2-2	Geary, Milward	12	7
13	26	(h)	Sheffield W	L	3-5	E.Chadwick 2, Milward	12	9
14	Dec 3	(a)	Preston N E	L	0-5		12	10
15	10	(h)	Wolves	W	3-2	E.Chadwick, Geary, Gordon	14	10
16	17	(a)	Notts Co	W	2-1	Geary, Latta	16	9
17	24	(h)	Burnley	L	0-1		16	9
18	Jan 3	(a)	Sunderland	L	3-4	Milward 2, Latta	16	13
19	7	(h)	Notts Co	W	6-0	Geary 2, E.Chadwick, Latta, Maxwell, Milward	18	12
20	12	(a)	Nottingham F	L	1-2	Stewart	18	13
21	14	(h)	West Brom A	W	1-0	Geary	20	8
22	28	(a)	Stoke C	W	1-0	Milward	22	8
23	Feb 11	(h)	Preston N E	W	6-0	Maxwell 2, E.Chadwick, Gordon, Latta, Milward	24	4
24	13	(a)	Sheffield W	W	2-0	E.Chadwick, opp.og	26	3
25	25	(a)	Accrington	W	3-0	E.Chadwick 2, Kelso	28	3
26	Mar 18	(a)	Wolves	W	4-2	Geary 2, Elliott, Hartley	30	3
27	Apr 1	(h)	Blackburn R	W	4-0	Geary, Jones, McMillan, Maxwell	32	3
28	3	(h)	Bolton W	W	3-0	Latta 2, Geary	34	3
29	8	(h)	Burnley	L	0-3		34	3
30	15	(h)	Derby C	W	5-0	Geary 2, Latta 2, Milward	36	3

League Appearances
League Goals

31	Jan 21	(h)	West Brom A	W	4-1	Geary 2, Latta, Maxwell		FA Cup Rd 1
32	Feb 4	(h)	Nottingham F	W	4-2	Milward 2, E.Chadwick, Geary		2
33	18	(h)	Sheffield W	W	3-0	E.Chadwick, Geary, Maxwell		3
34	Mar 4	(n)	Preston N E	D	2-2	E.Chadwick, Gordon (Bramall Lane)		SF
35	16	(n)	Preston N E	D	0-0	(Ewood Park)		Replay
36	20	(n)	Preston N E	W	2-1	Gordon, Maxwell (Trent Bridge, Nottingham)		Replay
37	25	(n)	Wolves	L	0-1	(Fallowfield, Manchester)		F

FA Cup Appearances
FA Cup Goals

Bell J	Boyle R	Chadwick A	Chadwick E	Collins J	Dewar J	Elliott J	Geary F	Gordon P	Hartley A	Holt J	Howarth R	Jamieson R	Jardine D	Jones R	Kelso R	Latta A	McMillan J	Maxwell A	Milward A	Murray J	Parry C	Pinnell A	Rennie A	Robertson H	Stewart A	Thomas W	Thompson R	Williams R	No.
	4		10	3			9			5	2		1			7		8	11					6					1
	4		10	3			9			5	2		1		6	7		8	11										2
	4		10	3			9			5	2					7		8	11			1		6					3
	4		10	3			9			5	2					7		8	11			1		6					4
	4		10	3			9			5	2		1			7		8	11					6					5
	4		10	3			9			5	2					7		8	11			1		6					6
	4		10	3			9			5	2		1			7		8	11					6					7
	4		10	3			9			5	2				6	7		8	11									1	8
	4		10	3		7	8			5	2				6			9	11									1	9
	4	3				7	8			5	2				6			9	11		10							1	10
	4	3	10				9			5	2				6	7		8	11									1	11
	4	3	10				9			5	2				6	7		8	11									1	12
	4	3	10				9			5	2				6	7		11	8									1	13
	4		10				9	8		5	2				6	7			11		3							1	14
			10				9	8		5	3	6		1	2	7			11						4				15
			10				9	8		5	3	6		1	2	7			11						4				16
			10				9	8		5	3	6			2	7	1		11						4				17
			10				9			5	2	6				7	1	8	11		3				4				18
			10				9			5	2	6				7		8	11		3		1		4				19
			10				9			5	2	6				7		8	11		3		1		4				20
	5		10				9				2	6				7		8	11		3		1		4				21
	4		10				9			5	3				2	7		8	11					6				1	22
	4		10					8		5	3				2	7		9	11					6				1	23
	4		10					8		5	2	6				7		9	11		3							1	24
	4		10			7	8			5	2							9	11		3			6				1	25
	4					11	9	8	1	5					2	7		10			3			6					26
	6					11	9			5					2	7		8	10						4			1	27
7	4		10				9			5	3		1		2			8	11					6					28
8	4		10					11		5	3		1		2	7		9						6					29
8	4		10				9			5	3		1		2	7			11					6					30
3	25	3	27	9	1	4	24	11	1	26	26	14	8	2	14	28	2	23	27	4	10	3	4	6	12	1	1	11	opp.og 1
	4		10				9			5	2						3	11		10	7			6				1	31
	4		10				9			5	3				2	7		8	11					6				1	32
	4		10				9			5	3				2	7		8	11					6				1	33
	4		10					8		5	3				2	7		9	11					6				1	34
	4		10					8		5	3				2	7		9	11					6				1	35
	4		10					8		5	3				2	7		9	11					6				1	36
	4		10					8		5	3				2	7		9	11					6				1	37
	7		7				3	4		7	7					7		7	7					7				7	
	3						4	2								1		3	2										

1893-94

#	Date		Venue	Opponent	Res	Score	Scorers	League Apps	League Goals
1	Sep	2	(h)	Sheffield U	L	2-3	Latta, Milward	0	
2		4	(h)	Nottingham F	W	4-0	McMillan 2, Boyle, Milward	2	
3		9	(a)	Derby C	L	3-7	Chadwick, Milward, Southworth	2	11
4		16	(h)	Aston Villa	W	4-2	Bell, Kelso, McMillan, Walker	4	10
5		23	(a)	Aston Villa	L	1-3	Southworth	4	13
6		30	(h)	Sunderland	W	7-1	Chadwick 3, Latta 2, Milward, Southworth	6	7
7	Oct	7	(a)	Burnley	L	1-2	Stewart	6	10
8		14	(h)	Blackburn R	D	2-2	Milward, Southworth	7	7
9		21	(h)	Darwen	W	8-1	Latta 2, Maxwell 2, Southworth 2, Bell, Chadwick	9	6
10		28	(h)	Preston N E	L	2-3	Southworth 2	9	9
11	Nov	4	(a)	Sheffield W	D	1-1	Milward	10	9
12		11	(h)	Derby C	L	1-2	Latta	10	11
13		25	(h)	Burnley	W	4-3	Bell 2, Chadwick, Geary	12	11
14	Dec	2	(a)	Newton Heath	W	3-0	Geary 2, Chadwick	14	9
15		4	(a)	Wolves	L	0-2		14	9
16		9	(a)	Sheffield U	W	3-0	Southworth 2, Milward	16	8
17		16	(a)	Blackburn R	L	3-4	Bell, Chadwick, Southworth	16	9
18		23	(h)	Sheffield W	W	8-1	Southworth 4, Bell 2, Chadwick, Latta	18	8
19		30	(h)	West Brom a	W	7-1	Southworth 6, Bell	20	8
20	Jan	1	(a)	Darwen	D	3-3	Chadwick, Southworth, opp.og	21	8
21		6	(h)	Newton Heath	W	2-0	Chadwick, Southworth	23	6
22		13	(a)	Preston N E	W	4-2	Chadwick, Milward, Southworth, opp.og	25	6
23		18	(a)	Nottingham F	L	2-3	Geary, opp.og	25	6
24	Feb	3	(a)	West Brom A	L	1-3	Bell	25	7
25		6	(a)	Sunderland	L	0-1		25	7
26	Mar	3	(a)	Stoke C	L	1-3	Southworth	25	8
27		24	(h)	Wolves	W	3-0	Geary 2, Southworth	27	10
28		26	(h)	Bolton W	W	3-2	Chadwick, Hartley, Southworth	29	10
29	Apr	7	(h)	Stoke C	W	6-2	Geary 2, Latta 2, Hartley, McMillan	31	8
30		16	(a)	Bolton W	W	1-0	Reay	33	6

League Appearances
League Goals

| 31 | Jan | 27 | (a) | Stoke C | L | 0-1 | | FA Cup Rd 1 |

FA Cup Appearances
FA Cup Goals

Arridge S	Bell J	Boyle R	Chadwick E	Elliott J	Geary F	Hartley A	Holt J	Howarth R	Jardine D	Kelso R	Latta A	Lindsay W	McMillan J	Maxwell A	Milward A	Parry C	Reay H	Southworth J	Stewart W	Storrier D	Walker J	Whitehead J	Williams R	
	8	4	10				5	3		2	7			9	11				6				1	1
	8	4		11			5	3		2	7	10			9				6				1	2
	8	4	10				5	3		2	7				11			9	6				1	3
	8	4		11				3		2	7	10						9	6		5		1	4
	8	4		11				3		2	7	10						9	6		5		1	5
	8	4	10				5	3		2	7				11			9	6				1	6
	8	4	10				5	3		2	7				11			9	6				1	7
	8	4	10				5	3		2	7				11			9	6				1	8
	11	4	10				5	3		2	7		8					9	6				1	9
	11	4	10				5	3		2	7		8					9	6				1	10
	11	4	10				5	2			7	3	9	8					6				1	11
	8	4	10				5	3		2	7				11			9	6				1	12
	9		10	8			5			2	7	3			11				6		4		1	13
	8	4	10	9			5	2			7	3			11				6				1	14
	8	4	10	9			5	2			7	3			11				6				1	15
	8		10				5	2		4	7	3			11			9	6				1	16
	8		10				5	2		4	7	3			11			9	6				1	17
	8		10				5			4	7	3			11	2		9	6				1	18
3	8		10				5			4	7				11	2		9	6				1	19
3	8		10				5			4	7				11	2		9	6				1	20
	8	4	10				5			6	7	3			11	2		9					1	21
	8	4	10				5			3	7				11	2		9	6				1	22
	8	4	10	7			5			3					11	2		9	6				1	23
	8		10				5	2		4	7				11	3		9	6				1	24
			10	8			5	2		4	7				11	3		9	6	5			1	25
			10	8						4	7	2			11	3		9	6		5		1	26
		4	10	11			8	5	3	1	2	7						9	6					27
		4	10	11			8	5	3	1	2	7						9	6					28
	5				9	8	2			4	7	10			11	3	7		6				1	29
		4	10		9		5	2					8		11	3	7		6				1	30
2	24	21	24	3	9	6	26	22	2	26	29	9	4	4	24	11	1	22	29	1	3	2	26	opp.og 3
	9	1	13		8	2				1	9		4	2	8	1		27	1				1	
	8		10				5	2		4	7				11	3		9	6				1	31
	1		1				1	1		1	1				1	1		1	1				1	

1894-95

1	Sep	1	(h)	Sheffield W	W	3-1	Bell, Chadwick, McInnes	2	
2		3	(h)	Small Heath	W	5-0	Southworth 3, Bell 2	4	
3		8	(a)	Stoke C	W	3-1	Chadwick, Latta, McInnes	6	1
4		15	(h)	Nottingham F	W	6-1	Southworth 3, Bell, Latta, McInnes	8	1
5		22	(a)	Nottingham F	W	3-2	Bell, Chadwick, Southworth	10	1
6		29	(h)	West Brom A	W	4-1	Bell, Chadwick, McInnes, Southworth	12	1
7	Oct	6	(a)	Bolton W	W	3-1	Bell, Latta, McInnes	14	1
8		13	(h)	Liverpool	W	3-0	Bell, Latta, McInnes	16	1
9		20	(a)	Blackburn R	L	3-4	Chadwick, Hartley, Southworth	16	1
10		27	(h)	Sunderland	D	2-2	Boyle, McInnes	17	1
11	Nov	3	(a)	Small Heath	D	4-4	Latta 3, Bell	18	1
12		17	(a)	Liverpool	D	2-2	Kelso, Latta	19	1
13		24	(h)	Blackburn R	W	2-1	Bell, Milward	21	1
14	Dec	1	(a)	West Brom A	W	4-1	Chadwick, Latta, Milward, Stewart	23	1
15		8	(h)	Bolton W	W	3-1	Chadwick, Latta, McInnes	25	1
16		15	(a)	Preston N E	W	2-1	Hartley, Milward	27	1
17	Jan	1	(a)	Sheffield W	L	0-3		27	3
18		5	(a)	Wolves	L	0-1		27	3
19		7	(h)	Stoke C	W	3-0	Chadwick, Geary, W.Williams	29	3
20		12	(a)	Derby C	D	2-2	Geary, Parry	30	3
21		17	(h)	Aston Villa	W	4-2	Milward 2, Bell, Geary	32	3
22		26	(h)	Sheffield U	D	1-1	McInnes	33	3
23	Feb	23	(h)	Preston N E	W	4-2	Bell, Chadwick, Hartley, Milward	35	3
24		26	(a)	Sheffield U	L	2-4	Hartley, McInnes	35	3
25	Mar	16	(a)	Burnley	W	4-2	Bell, Chadwick, Milward, Stewart	37	2
26		21	(h)	Burnley	W	3-2	Bell, Latta, Milward	39	2
27	Apr	8	(h)	Wolves	W	2-1	Bell, Milward	41	2
28		13	(h)	Derby C	L	2-3	Geary, Milward	41	2
29		20	(a)	Sunderland	L	1-2	Chadwick	41	2
30		24	(a)	Aston Villa	D	2-2	Boyle, Hartley	42	2

League Appearances
League Goals

31	Feb	2	(a)	Southport	W	3-0	Bell 3	FA Cup Rd 1	
32		16	(h)	Blackburn R	D	1-1	Chadwick		2
33		20	(a)	Blackburn R	W	3-2	Chadwick 2, Hartley	Replay	
34	Mar	2	(a)	Sheffield W	L	0-2			3

FA Cup Appearances
FA Cup Goals

Adams J	Arridge S	Bell J	Boyle R	Cain T	Chadwick E	Elliott J	Geary F	Hartley A	Hillman J	Holt J	Kelso R	Latta A	McInnes T	McMillan J	Milward A	Parry C	Reay H	Southworth J	Stewart W	Storrier D	Sutton W	Williams R	Williams W	
2		11	4		10					5		7	8			3		9	6			1		1
2		11	4		10					5		7	8			3		9	6			1		2
2		11	4		10			9		5		7	8			3			6			1		3
2		11	4		10					5		7	8			3		9	6			1		4
2		11	4		10					5		7	8			3		9	6			1		5
2		11	4		10					5		7	8			3		9	6			1		6
		11	4	1	10					5	2	7	8			3		9	6					7
2		11	4	1	10					5		7	8			3		9	6					8
2		11	4	1	10		8			5		7				3		9	6					9
			4	1	10					5	2	7	8		11	3		9	6					10
2		11	4	1	10			9		5		7	8			3			6					11
		11	4	1	10			9		5	2	7	8			3			6					12
		11	4	1	10					5	2	7	8		9	3			6					13
		11	4	1	10					5	2	7	8		9	3			6					14
		11	4	1	10					5	2	7	8		9	3			6					15
			4	1	10			9		5	2	7	8		11	3			6					16
2		11	4	1	10		8			5		7			9	3			6					17
		11	4		10	7				5	2		8		9	3			6			1		18
			4		10			9		5	2		8		11	3			6			1	7	19
		11	4		10			9		5	2		8			3			6	1			7	20
		11	4		10			9		5	2		8		7	3			6			1		21
		11	4		10			9			2		8		7	3			6		5	1		22
2		11	4		10					5		7	8			3		9	6			1		23
	3	11	4			6		9		5	2		8		10			7				1		24
		8	4		10			9	1	5	2		7		11	3			6					25
		9	4		10				1	5	2	7	8		11	3			6					26
		8	4		10			9	1	5	2		7		11	3			6					27
	3	8	5		10	4		9	1		2				11				6				7	28
	3	8	4		10			9	1	5	2				11				6				7	29
2		8	4		10	6		9	1	5					11	3							7	30
12	3	27	30	11	28	4	8	11	6	27	19	20	23	1	18	27		9	27	1	1	12	5	
		15	2		11		4	5		1		11	10		10	1		9	2			1		
		11	4		10			9		5	2		8		7	3			6			1		31
		11	4		10			9		5	2		8		7	3			6			1		32
			4		10	7		9		5	2		8		11	3			6			1		33
		11	4	1	10	6		9			2		8		7	3				5				34
		3	4	1	4	1		1		4	3		4		4	3			4	1	3	1	3	
		3			3			1																

1895-96

1	Sep	2	(h)	Sheffield W	D	2-2	Boyle, Milward	1
2		7	(h)	Nottingham F	W	6-2	Chadwick 2, Milward 2, Bell, Flewitt	3
3		9	(h)	Bury	W	3-2	Bell, Chadwick, Milward	5	2
4		14	(a)	Bolton W	L	1-3	McInnes	5	3
5		21	(h)	Blackburn R	L	0-2		5	6
6		28	(a)	Wolves	W	3-2	McInnes 2, Milward	7	6
7		30	(a)	Aston Villa	L	3-4	Bell 3	7	6
8	Oct	5	(h)	Sheffield U	W	5-0	Chadwick 3, Latta, Milward	9	2
9		12	(a)	Nottingham F	L	1-2	Chadwick	9	4
10		19	(h)	West Brom A	D	1-1	Milward	10	5
11		26	(a)	Burnley	D	1-1	Hartley	11	5
12	Nov	2	(h)	Wolves	W	2-0	Chadwick, Milward	13	4
13		9	(a)	Sheffield U	W	2-1	Hartley, Milward	15	4
14		16	(h)	Sunderland	W	1-0	Milward	17	3
15		23	(a)	West Brom A	W	3-0	Hartley, McInnes, Milward	19	2
16		30	(h)	Burnley	W	2-1	Adams, Boyle	21	1
17	Dec	7	(a)	Small Heath	W	3-0	Milward 3	23	1
18		14	(h)	Stoke C	W	7-2	McInnes 3, Bell 2, Cameron, Milward	25	1
19		21	(h)	Aston Villa	W	2-0	Bell, McInnes	27	1
20	Jan	1	(a)	Blackburn R	W	3-2	Bell, Chadwick, opp.og	29	1
21		11	(a)	Bury	D	1-1	Milward	30	3
22		25	(a)	Preston N E	D	1-1	Chadwick	31	3
23	Feb	3	(h)	Small Heath	W	3-0	Hartley 2, Goldie	33	2
24		18	(a)	Sheffield W	L	1-3	Cameron	33	2
25		22	(a)	Sunderland	L	0-3		33	3
26	Mar	7	(h)	Preston N E	W	3-2	Boyle, Hartley, Milward	35	3
27	Apr	3	(h)	Derby C	D	2-2	Cameron 2	36	3
28		6	(h)	Bolton W	D	1-1	Chadwick	37	3
29		7	(a)	Derby C	L	1-2	Williams	37	3
30		11	(a)	Stoke C	W	2-1	Hartley, Schofield	39	3
							League Appearances	
							League Goals	
31	Feb	1	(a)	Nottingham F	W	2-0	Chadwick, Milward	FA Cup Rd 1
32		15	(h)	Sheffield U	W	3-0	Bell, Cameron, Milward	2
33		29	(a)	Sheffield W	L	0-4		3
							FA Cup Appearances	
							FA Cup Goals	

Adams J	Arridge S	Bell J	Boyle R	Briggs H	Cameron J	Chadwick E	Elliott J	Flewitt A	Goldie H	Hartley A	Hillman J	Holt J	Kelso R	Latta A	McInnes T	Milward A	Parry C	Robertson J	Schofield A	Stewart W	Storrier D	Williams W	No.
	3	8	4			10				9	1	2				11				6	5	7	1
	3	8	4			10		9			1	5	2			11				6		7	2
	3	8	5			10		9	4		1	2				11				6		7	3
	3	8	4			10		9			1	5	2		7	11				6			4
	3	8	4			10				9	1	5	2			11				6		7	5
	3		4			10				9	1	5			8	11			2	6		7	6
	3	9	4			10					1	5			8	11			2	6		7	7
2	3	8	4		9	10					1	5		7		11				6			8
2	3	8	4		9	10					1	5		7		11				6			9
2	3	9	5			10			4		1			7	8	11				6			10
2	3	8	5			10			4	9	1			7		11				6			11
2	3	8	5			10			4	9	1			7		11				6			12
2	3	7	5			10			4	9	1				8	11				6			13
2	3	7	5			10			4	9	1				8	11				6			14
2	3	7	5			10			4	9	1				8	11				6			15
2	3	7	5		9	10			4	8	1					11				6			16
2	3	7	5		9	10			4		1				8	11				6			17
2	3	7	5		9	10			4		1				8	11				6			18
2	3	7	5		9	10			4		1				8	11				6			19
2	3	7	5		9	10	6		4		1				8	11							20
2	3	7	5		9	10				6	1		4		8	11							21
2	3	7	4		9	10					1	5			8	11				6			22
2	3	7	4			10			8	9	1	5				11				6			23
2	3	7	4			10				9	1	5			8	11				6			24
2	3		4			10				9	1	5			8	11				6		7	25
2	3	7	4							10	1	5			8	9		11		6			26
2	3	7	4		9	10					1	5			8	11				6			27
2	3	7	4		9	10					1	5			8	11			5	6			28
	3		5			10			4	9	1				8	11				6	2	7	29
2		7	4	1	9	10			8			5				11				6	3		30
28	23	27	30	1	13	28	1	3	15	15	29	14	6	5	19	29	2	1	2	28	3	8	opp.og 1
1		9	3		4	11			1	1		7		1	8	17				1		1	
2	3	7	4		8	10				9	1	5				11				6			31
2	3	7	4		9	10					1	5			8	11				6			32
2		7	5		8	10			4		1	3				11				6	9		33
3	2	3	3		3	3			1	1	3	2	1		1	3				3	1		34
		1			1	1										2							35

1896-97

1	Sep	5	(h)	Sheffield W	W	2-1	Cameron, Taylor		2	
2		12	(a)	Wolves	W	1-0	opp.og		4	
3		19	(h)	Aston Villa	L	2-3	Milward, Taylor		4	9
4		26	(a)	Aston Villa	W	2-1	Hartley, Stewart		6	6
5	Oct	3	(h)	Liverpool	W	2-1	Hartley, Milward		8	3
6		10	(a)	Burnley	L	1-2	Stewart		8	6
7		17	(h)	Sheffield U	L	1-2	opp.og		8	7
8		24	(a)	Sheffield W	l	1-4	Milward		8	9
9		31	(h)	Wolves	D	0-0			9	8
10	Nov	14	(h)	Bolton W	L	2-3	Chadwick, Milward		9	11
11		21	(a)	Liverpool	D	0-0			10	11
12		28	(h)	Burnley	W	6-0	Cameron 3, Bell, Chadwick, Milward		12	11
13	Dec	7	(a)	Bolton W	L	0-2			12	11
14		12	(a)	Sunderland	D	1-1	Holt		13	10
15		19	(h)	Stoke C	W	4-2	Bell 2, Cameron, Taylor		15	9
16		26	(h)	Sunderland	W	5-2	Bell 2, Chadwick, Hartley, Milward		17	8
17	Jan	1	(a)	Sheffield U	W	2-1	Taylor 2		19	7
18		2	(a)	Stoke C	W	3-2	Bell, Hartley, Taylor		21	7
19		9	(h)	Nottingham F	W	3-1	Bell 2, Taylor		23	5
20		16	(a)	West Brom A	W	4-1	Taylor 3, Bell		25	4
21	Feb	6	(h)	Preston N E	L	3-4	Chadwick, Hartley, Taylor		25	6
22	Mar	2	(a)	Bury	L	1-3	Milward		25	7
23		6	(a)	Blackburn R	L	2-4	Bell, Taylor		25	8
24		10	(a)	Nottingham F	L	0-3			25	8
25		13	(h)	Blackburn R	L	0-3			25	8
26	Apr	3	(a)	Preston N E	L	1-4	Campbell		25	8
27		16	(h)	Derby C	W	5-2	Chadwick 2, Bell, Hartley, Milward		27	9
28		17	(h)	West Brom A	W	6-3	Bell 3, Chadwick, Milward, Taylor		29	8
29		20	(a)	Derby C	W	1-0	Stewart		31	7
30		24	(h)	Bury	L	1-2	Bell		31	7
								League Appearances		
								League Goals		
31	Jan	30	(h)	Burton W	W	5-2	Bell, Chadwick, Holt, Milward, opp.og		FA Cup Rd 1	
32	Feb	13	(h)	Bury	W	3-0	Taylor 2, Milward			2
33		27	(h)	Blackburn R	W	2-0	Hartley 2			3
34	Mar	20	(n)	Derby C	W	3-2	Chadwick, Hartley, Milward	(Victoria Ground, Stoke)	SF	
35	Apr	10	(n)	Aston Villa	L	2-3	Bell, Boyle	(Crystal Palace)		F
								FA Cup Appearances		
								FA Cup Goals		

#	Arridge S	Banks H	Barker G	Bell J	Boyle R	Briggs H	Cameron J	Campbell W	Chadwick E	Goldie H	Hartley A	Holt J	Maley W	Meecham P	Meiklejohn G	Menham R	Milward A	Molyneux G	Palmer J	Patrick J	Robertson J	Schofield A	Stewart W	Storrier D	Taylor J	Williams W	Notes
1	3			7	4	1	9		10			5					11						6	2	8		
2		3		7	4	1	9		10			5					11						6	2	8		
3		3		7	4	1	9		10			5					11						6	2	8		
4	3			7	4	1			10		9	5					11						6	2	8		
5	3			7	4	1			10		9	5					11						6	2	8		
6	3			7	4	1			10		9	5					11						6	2	8		
7	3			7	4	1	9		10			5					11						6	2	8		
8	3	2		11	4	1		8	10			5					9						6		7		
9	3			7		1	9		10	4		5					11						6	2	8		
10	3			8	4	1	9		10			5					11						6	2	7		
11	3			8	4		9		10			5				1	11						6	2	7		
12	3			8	4		9		10			5					11		1				6	2	7		
13	3			8	4		9		10			5				1						11	6	2	7		
14	3			8	4		9		10			5				1	11						6	2	7		
15	3			8	4		9		10			5				1	11						6	2	7		
16				8	5				10	4	9					1	11	3					6	2	7		
17	3				4				10		9	5	8			1	11						6	2	7		
18	3			8	4				10		9	5				1	11						6	2	7		
19	3	2		8	4				10		9	5				1	11						6		7		
20	3			8	4				10		9	5				1	11						6	2	7		
21	3				5			8	10	4	9			2		1	11						6		7		
22	3			7	4				10		9	5		2			11	1					6		8		
23	3			7	4		9		10			5		2			11						6	2	8		
24	3			8	4				10							1	11				5		6	2	7	9	
25		11			4		9		10				8	2	5	1							6	3	7		
26				8	4				10		9	5		2		1	11						6	3	7		
27	3			8	4				10		9	5		2		1	11						6		7		
28				8	4				10		9	5		2		1	11						6	3	7		
29		11		8	4		9		10					2		1					5		6	3	7		
30	23	2	4	27	29	10	15	3	28	3	14	25	2	7	1	18	27	1	1	1	3	1	29	25	30	1	
		15			5	1	7					6	1				9							3	13		opp.og 2
31	3			8	4				10		9	5				1	11				6			2	7		
32	3			8	4				10		9	5		2		1	11						6		7		
33	3			8	4				10		9	5		2		1	11						6		7		
34				8	4				10		9	5		2		1	11						6	3	7		
35				8	4				10		9	5		2		1	11						6	3	7		
	3			5	5				5		5	5	4			5	5				1		4	3	5		
				2	1				2		3	1					3								2		opp.og 1

1897-98

1	Sep	4	(h)	Bolton W	W	2-1	L.Bell 2	2	
2		11	(a)	Derby C	L	1-5	Divers	2	
3		18	(h)	Wolves	W	3-0	Hartley 3	4	7
4		25	(a)	Liverpool	L	1-3	Taylor	4	10
5	Oct	2	(h)	Blackburn R	D	1-1	Divers	5	11
6		9	(a)	Wolves	W	3-2	L.Bell, Cameron, Divers	7	7
7		16	(h)	Liverpool	W	3-0	Williams 2, L.Bell	9	3
8		23	(a)	Bury	W	1-0	Divers	11	3
9		30	(h)	Sheffield U	L	1-4	L.Bell	11	5
10	Nov	6	(a)	West Brom A	D	2-2	Divers, Taylor	12	6
11		13	(a)	Aston Villa	L	0-3		12	8
12		20	(a)	Preston N E	D	1-1	Taylor	13	9
13		27	(h)	West Brom A	W	6-1	Chadwick 2, Divers 2, J.Bell, L.Bell	15	7
14	Dec	11	(h)	Notts C	W	1-0	Divers	17	6
15		18	(a)	Sunderland	D	0-0		18	6
16		25	(h)	Aston Villa	W	2-1	Chadwick, Robertson	20	5
17	Jan	1	(a)	Blackburn R	D	1-1	Chadwick	21	6
18		8	(h)	Sheffield W	W	1-0	Chadwick	23	3
19		15	(a)	Notts Co	L	2-3	J.Bell, opp.og	23	6
20		17	(h)	Stoke C	D	1-1	Cameron	24	5
21	Feb	5	(a)	Sheffield W	L	1-2	Cameron	24	7
22		22	(a)	Sheffield U	D	0-0		25	6
23	Mar	5	(h)	Bury	W	4-2	J.Bell, L.Bell, Chadwick, Divers	27	6
24		12	(a)	Nottingham F	D	2-2	L.Bell 2	28	6
25		21	(h)	Preston N E	D	1-1	J.Bell	29	6
26		26	(a)	Bolton W	L	0-1		29	6
27	Apr	2	(h)	Nottingham F	W	2-0	L.Bell, Divers	31	6
28		8	(h)	Derby C	W	3-0	L.Bell 2, Divers	33	3
29		9	(a)	Stoke C	L	0-2		33	4
30		11	(h)	Sunderland	W	2-0	Chadwick 2	35	4
								League Appearances	
								League Goals	
31	Jan	29	(h)	Blackburn R	W	1-0	Williams	FA Cup Rd 1	
32	Feb	12	(a)	Stoke C	D	0-0		2	
33		17	(h)	Stoke C	W	5-1	L.Bell 2, Cameron, Chadwick, Taylor	Replay	
34		26	(a)	Burnley	W	3-1	Taylor 2, L.Bell	3	
35	Mar	19	(n)	Derby C	L	1-3	Chadwick	(Molineux) SF	
								FA Cup Appearances	
								FA Cup Goals	

Balmer W	Barker G	Barlow J	Bell J	Bell L	Boyle R	Cameron J	Chadwick E	Divers J	Gee E	Hartley A	Holt J	Keeley S	McFarlane R	Meecham P	Muir W	Robertson J	Stewart W	Storrier D	Taylor J	Williams W	Wolstenholme S	
		11	9	4	8	10					5		1	2		6		3	7			1
			9	4	8	10	11				5		1	2		6		3	7			2
	3			4	8	10	11			9	5		1	2		6			7			3
	3	11		4	8	10				9	5		1	2		6			7			4
			8	4		10	11			9	5		1	2		6		3	7			5
			9	4		10	11				5		1	2		6		3	7	8		6
			9	4		10	11				5		1	2		6		3	7	8		7
			9	4		10	11				5		1	2		6		3	7	8		8
			9	4		10	11				5		1	2		6		3	7	8		9
3	2		9	4		10	11				5				1	6			7	8		10
	2		9	4		10	11				5				1	6		3	7	8		11
2			8	9	4	10	11				5				1	6		3	7			12
			8	9	4	10	11				5			2	1	6		3	7			13
			8	9	4	10	11				5			2	1	6		3	7			14
			8	9	4	10	11				5			2	1	6		3	7			15
			8	9		10	11				5			2	1	6	4	3	7			16
			8	9		10	11				5			2	1	6	4	3	7			17
			8	9		10	11				5			2	1	6	4	3	7			18
			8	9		10	11				5			2	1	6	4	3	7			19
			8			9	11	10			5			2	1	6		3	7	4		20
2			9		8		11	10			5				1	6	4	3	7			21
2			9		8		11	10			5				1	6	4	3	7			22
2	3		9		8	5	11	10							1	6	4		7			23
2	3		9		8	5	11	10							1	6	4		7			24
2			9	4	8		11	10			5				1	6		3	7			25
2			9	4		8	11	10			5				1	6		3	7			26
2			9	4			11	10	8	11	5				1			3	7			27
2			9	5	8	7	11	10							1	6		3	4			28
2					8	7	11	10			5	9			1	6		3	4			29
2			9	4	8		11	10			5				1	6		3	7			30
12	6	2	22	23	22	14	22	26	3	3	27	1	9	17	21	26	9	25	30	9	1	
			4	12	3	8	11	3								1		3	2		opp.og 1	
2			9		8		11	10			5				1	6		3	4	7		31
2			9		8		11	10			5				1	6	4	3	7			32
2			9		8		11	10			5				1	6	4	3	7			33
2			9		8		11	10			5				1	6	4	3	7			34
2			9		8		11	10			5				1	6	4	3	7			35
5			5	5		3	5	2			5				5	5	4	5	5	1		
				3		1	2											3	1			

1898-99

1	Sep	1	(h)	Blackburn R	W	2-1	Clarke, Proudfoot	2	
2		3	(a)	Sheffield U	D	1-1	Proudfoot	3	
3		10	(h)	Newcastle U	W	3-0	Clarke, Owen, opp.og	5	1
4		17	(a)	Preston N E	D	0-0		6	1
5		24	(h)	Liverpool	L	1-2	Proudfoot	6	4
6	Oct	1	(a)	Nottingham F	D	0-0		7	4
7		8	(h)	Bolton W	W	1-0	Oldham	9	3
8		15	(a)	Derby C	D	5-5	Oldham 2, Owen 2, Bell	10	5
9		22	(h)	West Brom A	W	1-0	Oldham	12	4
10		29	(a)	Blackburn R	W	3-1	Bell, Oldham, Proudfoot	14	2
11	Nov	5	(h)	Sheffield W	W	2-0	Bell, Kirwan	16	2
12		7	(a)	West Brom A	L	0-3		16	2
13		12	(a)	Sunderland	L	1-2	Bell	16	2
14		19	(h)	Wolves	W	2-1	Bell, Kirwan	18	2
15		26	(h)	Bury	L	0-1		18	2
16	Dec	3	(a)	Notts Co	W	1-0	Proudfoot	20	2
17		10	(h)	Stoke C	W	2-0	Chadwick, Oldham	22	2
18		17	(a)	Aston Villa	L	0-3		22	3
19		24	(h)	Burnley	W	4-0	Proudfoot 2, Kirwan, Oldham	24	2
20		31	(h)	Sheffield U	W	1-0	Proudfoot	26	2
21	Jan	2	(h)	Nottingham F	L	1-3	Kirwan	26	2
22		7	(a)	Newcastle U	D	2-2	Proudfoot 2	27	2
23		14	(h)	Preston N E	W	2-0	Crompton, Kirwan	29	2
24		21	(a)	Liverpool	L	0-2		29	3
25	Feb	25	(a)	Bolton W	W	4-2	Oldham 2, Proudfoot, Taylor	31	3
26	Mar	4	(a)	Sheffield W	W	2-1	Chadwick, Oldham	33	3
27		11	(h)	Sunderland	D	0-0		34	3
28		18	(a)	Bury	L	1-3	Taylor	34	3
29	Apr	1	(h)	Notts Co	L	1-2	Proudfoot	34	4
30		3	(h)	Derby C	L	1-2	Taylor	34	6
31		8	(a)	Stoke C	L	1-2	Boyle	34	6
32		15	(h)	Aston Villa	D	1-1	Oldham	35	7
33		22	(a)	Burnley	D	0-0		36	6
34		29	(a)	Wolves	W	2-1	Schofield, Toman	38	4
								League Appearances	
								League Goals	
35	Jan	28	(h)	Jarrow	W	3-1	Chadwick, Proudfoot, Taylor	FA Cup Rd 1	
36	Feb	11	(h)	Nottingham F	L	0-1			2
								FA Cup Appearances	
								FA Cup Goals	

Balmer W	Barlow J	Bell L	Blythe J	Boyle R	Chadwick E	Clarke H	Crompton T	Divers J	Eccles G	Gee E	Hughes E	Kirwan J	Kitchen G	Molyneux G	Muir W	Oldham W	Owen W	Proudfoot J	Schofield A	Settle J	Taylor J	Toman W	Turner J	Vaughan A	Wolstenholme S	
2				4	10	7	8			11					3	1	5	9			6					1
2				4	10	7	8			11					3	1	5	9			6					2
2		8		4	10	7				11					3	1	5	9			6					3
2				4	10	7				11	8				3	1	5	9			6					4
2		8		4		7				11					3	1	5	9			6					5
2		9		4		7	8			10					3	1	5		11		6					6
2		8		4		7				11				10	3	1	9	5			6					7
2		8		4		7				10					3	1	9	5	11		6					8
2		8		4		7				10					3	1	9	5	11		6					9
2		7		5								11		10	3	1	9	8			6				4	10
2		7		5								11		10	3	1	9	8			6				4	11
2	11	9		5		7								10	3	1		8			6				4	12
2		7		5								11		10	3	1	9	8			6				4	13
2		7		5								11		10	3	1	9	8			6				4	14
2		7		5								11		10	3	1	9	8			6				4	15
2		9		4	10							11		6	3	1	5	8			7					16
2				4	10							11		6	3	1	9	5	8		7					17
2		9		4	10							11		6	3	1	5	8			7					18
2		7		4	10							11		5	3	1	9	8			6					19
		7		4	10							11		5	3	1	9	8			6		2			20
2				4	10							11		5	3	1	9	8			6					21
2				4	10			9	3	5		11		6		1		8			7					22
2		7		4	10			9				11	1		3			8			6			5		23
2		7		4	10			9			6	11			3	1	5	8								24
			6	5	10				2			11			3	1	9	8			7				4	25
			6	5	10				2			11			3	1	9	8			7				4	26
			6	5	10				2			11			3	1	9	8			7				4	27
			6	5	10				2			11			3	1	9	8			7				4	28
			6	5	10				2			11			3	1	9	8			7				4	29
			6	5	10				2			11			3	1	9	8			7				4	30
	8		6	5	10				2			11			3	1	9				7				4	31
				5	10				2			11			3	1	9	8	7		6		2		4	32
				5	10				2			11			3	1		8	7	9	6				4	33
			6	5	10				2			11			3	1		8		9	7				4	34
23	2	18	8	34	22	12	3	4	10	17	8	24	1	33	33	19	13	28	7	1	34	2	2	1	15	
	5				1	2	2	1			5			11			3	12	1		3	1			opp.og	
2		7		4	10			9				11			3	1	5	8			6					35
2		9		5	10							11		7	3	1		8			6				4	36
2		2		2	2			1	1			2		2	2	2		2			2				2	
					1													1			1					

1899-1900

1	Sep	2	(h)	Sheffield U	L	1-2	Settle		0	
2		9	(a)	Newcastle U	L	0-2		0	
3		16	(h)	Aston Villa	L	1-2	Toman	0	17
4		23	(a)	Liverpool	W	2-1	Settle, Taylor	2	15
5		30	(h)	Burnley	W	2-0	Toman 2	4	11
6	Oct	7	(a)	Preston N E	D	1-1	Settle	5	11
7		14	(h)	Nottingham F	W	2-1	J.Sharp, Toman	7	9
8		21	(a)	Glossop	D	1-1	Toman	8	8
9		28	(a)	Stoke C	D	1-1	Taylor	9	9
10	Nov	4	(a)	Sunderland	L	0-1		9	12
11		11	(h)	West Brom A	L	1-3	J.Sharp	9	13
12		25	(a)	Blackburn R	L	1-3	Settle	9	13
13	Dec	2	(h)	Derby C	W	3-0	Settle, J.Sharp, Taylor	11	13
14		9	(a)	Bury	L	1-4	Toman	11	13
15		16	(h)	Notts Co	L	0-2		11	14
16		23	(a)	Manchester C	W	2-1	Gray, Settle	13	13
17		25	(h)	Stoke C	W	2-0	Settle, Taylor	15	12
18		26	(a)	West Brom	D	0-0		16	11
19		30	(a)	Sheffield U	L	0-5		16	12
20	Jan	1	(h)	Preston N E	W	1-0	Proudfoot	18	9
21		6	(h)	Newcsatle U	W	3-2	Proudfoot 2, Settle	20	9
22		13	(a)	Aston Villa	D	1-1	Taylor	21	9
23		20	(h)	Liverpool	W	3-1	Settle 2, Blythe	23	9
24	Feb	3	(a)	Burnley	L	1-3	Proudfoot	23	9
25		17	(a)	Nottingham F	L	2-4	Balmer, Proudfoot	23	9
26	Mar	10	(h)	Sunderland	W	1-0	Toman	25	9
27		17	(a)	Wolves	L	1-2	Taylor	25	10
28		24	(h)	Wolves	L	0-1		25	10
29		31	(h)	Blackburn R	D	0-0		26	10
30	Apr	7	(a)	Derby C	L	1-2	J.Sharp	26	11
31		14	(h)	Bury	W	2-0	Abbott, Proudfoot	28	12
32		16	(h)	Glossop	W	4-1	McDonald, Proudfoot, J.Sharp, Taylor	30	11
33		21	(a)	Notts C	D	2-2	McDonald, opp.og	31	11
34		28	(h)	Manchester C	W	4-0	Turner 2, Proudfoot, Toman	33	11

League Appearances
League Goals

35	Jan	27	(a)	Southampton	L	0-3	FA Cup Rd 1

FA Cup Appearances
FA Cup Goals

Abbott W	Balmer W	Blythe J	Boyle R	Crelley J	Eccles G	Gee E	Gray R	Kitchen G	McDonald A	Molyneux G	Muir W	Oldham W	Proudfoot J	Schofield A	Settle J	Sharp B	Sharp J	Taylor J	Toman W	Turner J	Watson J	Wolstenholme S	No.
10	2	5			11			3	1					8			7	6	9			4	1
10	2	5			11			3	1					8			7	6	9			4	2
10	2	5			11				1	3				8			7	6	9			4	3
	2	6	5							3	1	11			8		7	10	9			4	4
	3	6	5		2						1	11			8		7	10	9			4	5
	3	6	5		2						1	11			8		7	10	9			4	6
	3	6	5		2	11					1				8		7	10	9			4	7
	3	6	5		2	11					1				8		7	10	9			4	8
	3	6	5		2	11					1				8		7	10	9			4	9
	3	6	5		2	11					1				8		7	10	9			4	10
	3	6	5		2	11					1		9				7	10	8			4	11
	3		5		2	11					1		9		10		7	6	8			4	12
6	3		5				11				1				10	2	7	8	9			4	13
6	3		5				11				1				10	2	7	8	9			4	14
6	3		5				11				1				10	2	7	8	9			4	15
6	3		5		2		11				1		9		10		7		8			4	16
6	3	4	5		2		11				1		9		10		7		8				17
6	3	4	5		2		11				1		9		10		7		8				18
6	3		5		2		11				1		9		10		7		8			4	19
6	3		5		2		11				1		9		10		7		8			4	20
6	3		5		2		11				1		9		10		7		8			4	21
6	3		5		2		11				1		9		10		7		8			4	22
6	3		5		2		11				1		9		10		7		8			4	23
6	2		5				11			3	1		9		10		7		8			4	24
6	2		5				11			3	1		9		10		7		8			4	25
6	2	4	5				11			3	1		9		10		7		8				26
6	2	4	5				11			3	1		9		10		7		8				27
6	2	4	5				11			3	1		9		10		7		8				28
6	2		5	3			11				1		9		10		7		8			4	29
10	6		5		2						1		9				7	11	8		3	4	30
6	3		5		2					10	1		9				7	11	8			4	31
6	3		5		2					10	1		9				7	11	8			4	32
6			5		2					10	1		9				7	11	8		3	4	33
6	2		5							10	1		9				7		8	11	3	4	34
25	32	19	29	1	20	11	15	2	5	9	32	3	20	3	26	3	29	32	25	1	3	29	App
1	1	1			1		1			2			8		10		5	7	8	2		1	Gls *(opp.og 1)*
6	3		5		11						1		9		10		7	8				4	35
1	1	1	1		1						1		1		1		1		1			1	

1900-1901

1	Sep 1	(a)	Preston N E	W	2-1	Proudfoot, Sharp	2	
2	8	(h)	Wolves	W	5-1	Turner 2, McDonald, Proudfoot, Settle	4	
3	15	(a)	Aston Villa	W	2-1	Settle, Turner	6	3
4	22	(h)	Liverpool	D	1-1	McDonald	7	3
5	29	(a)	Newcastle U	L	0-1		7	5
6	Oct 6	(h)	Sheffield U	W	3-1	Abbott, Proudfoot, Turner	9	6
7	13	(a)	Manchester C	L	0-1		9	7
8	27	(a)	Nottingham F	L	1-2	Settle	9	8
9	Nov 3	(h)	Blackburn R	D	0-0		10	9
10	10	(a)	Stoke C	W	2-0	McDonald, Taylor	12	7
11	17	(h)	West Brom A	W	1-0	Taylor	14	7
12	24	(h)	Sheffield W	D	1-1	Proudfoot	15	7
13	Dec 1	(a)	Sunderland	L	0-2		15	9
14	8	(h)	Derby C	W	2-0	McDonald, Wolstenholme	17	7
15	15	(a)	Bolton W	L	0-1		17	9
16	22	(h)	Notts C	L	0-1		17	10
17	25	(a)	Sheffield U	L	1-2	Settle	17	10
18	26	(h)	Bury	D	3-3	Abbott, Proudfoot, Turner	18	10
19	29	(h)	Preston N E	W	4-1	Sharp 2, Abbott, Taylor	20	9
20	Jan 1	(a)	Bury	L	0-3		20	9
21	5	(a)	Wolves	D	1-1	Taylor	21	11
22	12	(h)	Aston Villa	W	2-1	Settle, Wolstenholme	23	8
23	19	(a)	Liverpool	W	2-1	Taylor 2	25	7
24	Feb 16	(h)	Manchester C	W	5-2	Settle 2, Taylor 2, Sharp	27	6
25	Mar 2	(h)	Nottingham F	W	4-1	Proudfoot 2, Abbott, Settle	29	5
26	9	(a)	Blackburn R	L	1-2	Turner	29	6
27	16	(h)	Stoke C	W	3-0	Proudfoot, Settle, Sharp	31	5
28	30	(a)	Sheffield W	L	1-3	Taylor	31	6
29	Apr 6	(h)	Sunderland	W	1-0	Sharp	33	6
30	8	(h)	Newcastle U	L	0-1		33	6
31	9	(a)	Notts Co	L	2-3	Proudfoot, Settle	33	6
32	13	(a)	Derby C	W	1-0	Proudfoot	35	6
33	20	(h)	Bolton W	L	2-3	Sharp, Taylor	35	7
34	22	(a)	West Brom A	W	2-1	Abbott, Taylor	37	7
							League Appearances	
							League Goals	
35	Feb 9	(a)	Southampton	W	3-1	Settle, Taylor, Turner	FA Cup Rd 1	
36	23	(a)	Sheffield U	L	0-2			2
							FA Cup Appearances	
							FA Cup Goals	

Abbott W	Balmer W	Beveridge R	Blythe J	Booth T	Boyle R	Corrin T	Crelley J	Eccles G	Gray R	McDonald A	Muir W	Proudfoot J	Settle J	Sharp J	Taylor J	Turner J	Watson J	Wolstenholme S	
6	2			5						8	1	9	10	7		11	3	4	1
6	2			5						8	1	9	10	7		11	3	4	2
6	2			5						8	1	9	10	7		11	3	4	3
6	2			5						8	1	9	10	7		11	3	4	4
6	2			5						8	1	9	10	7		11	3	4	5
6	2			5						8	1	9	10	7		11	3	4	6
6	2			5						8	1	9	10	7		11	3	4	7
6	2	9		5						8	1		10		7	11	3	4	8
6	2	9		5						8	1		10		7	11	3	4	9
6	2	9		5						8	1		10		7	11	3	4	10
6	2	9		5						8	1		10		7	11	3	4	11
6				5					2	8	1	9	10		7	11	3	4	12
6	2			5	11		10			8	1	9			7		3	4	13
6	2			5	11			10		8	1	9			7		3	4	14
6	2			5					10	8	1	9			7	11	3	4	15
6	2			5		10				9	1		8		7	11	3	4	16
6	2			5							1	9	10	7	8	11	3	4	17
6	2			5							1	9	10	7	8	11	3	4	18
6	2			5							1	9	10	7	8	11	3	4	19
6	2			5							1	9	10	7	8	11	3	4	20
6	2		5							8	1	9	10	7		11	3	4	21
6	2			5							1	9	10	7	8	11	3	4	22
6				5				3	2		1	9	10	7	8	11		4	23
6	2			5		11		3			1	9	10	7	8			4	24
6	2			5				3			1	9	10	7	8	11		4	25
6	2			5				3			1	9	10	7	8	11		4	26
6	2			5				3			1	9	10	7	8	11	3	4	27
6	2			5				3	10		1	9		7	8	11		4	28
6	2			5				3			1	9	10	7	8	11		4	29
6	2			5				3			1	9	10	7	8	11		4	30
6				5					2		1	9	10	7	8	11	3	4	31
6	2			5				3		8	1	9	10	7		11		4	32
6	2			5				3			1	9	10	7	8	11		4	33
6	2			5				3			1	9	10	7	8	11		4	34
34	31	4	1	31	2	3	1	12	5	18	34	29	30	25	25	31	24	34	
		5								4		10	10	7	11	6		2	
6	2			5				3			1	9	10	7	8	11		4	35
6	2			5				3			1	9	10	7	8	11		4	36
2	2			2				2			2	2	2	2	2	2		2	
													1		1	1			

1901-1902

#	Date		Opponent	Res	Score	Scorers	App	Goals
1	Sep 2	(h)	Manchester C	W	3-1	Bell 2, Toman	2	
2	7	(h)	Wolves	W	6-1	Settle 3, Taylor 3	4	
3	14	(a)	Liverpool	D	2-2	Settle, J.Sharp	5	1
4	21	(h)	Newcastle U	D	0-0		6	1
5	28	(a)	Aston Villa	D	1-1	Abbott	7	1
6	Oct 5	(h)	Sheffield U	W	2-1	Abbott, Settle	9	1
7	12	(a)	Nottingham F	L	0-4		9	4
8	19	(h)	Bury	D	1-1	Settle	10	4
9	26	(a)	Blackburn R	L	1-3	Paterson	10	6
10	Nov 2	(h)	Stoke C	W	1-0	J.Sharp	12	5
11	9	(a)	Grimsby T	W	2-0	Settle 2	14	2
12	16	(a)	Sunderland	W	4-2	Settle 2, Abbott, J.Sharp	16	1
13	23	(h)	Small Heath	W	1-0	Bell	18	1
14	30	(a)	Derby C	L	1-3	Settle	18	1
15	Dec 7	(h)	Sheffield W	W	5-0	Settle 2, J.Sharp 2, Young	20	1
16	14	(a)	Notts Co	W	2-0	Settle, Taylor	22	1
17	21	(h)	Bolton W	W	1-0	Settle	24	1
18	25	(h)	Aston Villa	L	2-3	Taylor 2	24	1
19	26	(a)	Wolves	L	1-2	Bell	24	1
20	Jan 11	(h)	Liverpool	W	4-0	Settle 2, Bell, Young	26	2
21	18	(a)	Newcastle U	D	1-1	Young	27	2
22	Feb 1	(a)	Sheffield U	D	0-0		28	2
23	15	(a)	Bury	L	0-1		28	3
24	22	(h)	Blackburn R	L	0-2		28	4
25	Mar 1	(a)	Stoke C	W	2-1	Abbott, Booth	30	2
26	8	(h)	Grimsby T	L	0-1		30	2
27	15	(h)	Sunderland	W	2-0	Taylor, Young	32	2
28	17	(a)	Manchester C	L	0-2		32	2
29	22	(a)	Small Heath	W	1-0	Taylor	34	2
30	29	(h)	Derby C	W	2-0	Settle, Young	36	2
31	31	(h)	Nottingham F	W	1-0	J.Sharp	38	2
32	Apr 5	(a)	Sheffield W	D	1-1	Bowman	39	2
33	12	(h)	Notts Co	L	0-1		39	2
34	19	(a)	Bolton W	W	3-1	Wolstenholme, Young, opp.og	41	2

League Appearances
League Goals

| 35 | Jan 25 | (a) | Liverpool | D | 2-2 | J.Sharp, Young | FA Cup Rd 1 |
| 36 | 30 | (h) | Liverpool | L | 0-2 | | Replay |

FA Cup Appearances
FA Cup Goals

Abbott W	Balmer W	Bell J	Blythe J	Bone J	Booth T	Bowman A	Boyle D	Chadwick T	Clark C	Eccles G	Kitchen G	Muir W	Paterson	Proudfoot J	Rankin G	Roche	Settle J	Sharp B	Sharp J	Singleton B	Taylor J	Toman W	Watson J	Wolstenholme S	Young A	
6	2	11			5	4						1					10		7	8	9	3				1
6	2	11			5	4						1					10		7	8	9	3				2
6	2	11			5	4						1	9				10		7	8		3				3
6	2	11			5	4						1	9				10		7	8		3				4
6	2	11			5							1				7	10				8		3	4	9	5
6	2	11			5							1	8				10		7				3	4	9	6
6	2				5							1	8				10		7	11			3	4	9	7
10	2		6		5						1		8				11		7				3	4	9	8
6	2	11			5						1		8				10		7				3	4	9	9
6	2	11			5				4		1		8				10		7				3		9	10
	2	11	6		5				4	3	1		8				10		7						9	11
6	2	11			5					3	1		8				10		7					4	9	12
6	2	11			5					3	1		8				10		7					4	9	13
6	2	11			5					3	1						10		7		8			4	9	14
6	2	11			5					3	1						10		7		8			4	9	15
6	2	11			5					3	1						10		7		8			4	9	16
6	2	11			5					3	1						10		7		8			4	9	17
6	2	11			5					3	1						10		7		8			4	9	18
6	2	11			5						1						10		7		8		3	4	9	19
6	2	11			5						1						10	3	7		8			4	9	20
	2	11	6		5					3	1						10		7		8			4	9	21
6	2				5						1			10	8			3	7	11				4	9	22
6	2	11			5						1		8				10	3	7					4	9	23
6	2			10	5			11			1							3	7		8			4	9	24
6	2	11			5						1						10	3	7		8			4	9	25
6	2			10	5				4		1							3	7	11	8				9	26
6	2	11			5					3	1						10		7		8			4	9	27
6					5					2	1						10		7	11	8		3	4	9	28
10	2		6		5		11			3	1								7		8			4	9	29
			6		5		11			2	1						10		7		8		3	4	9	30
6					5		11			2	1						10		7		8		3	4	9	31
10			6		5		11			2	1								7		8		3	4	9	32
6		11			5					2	1						10		7		8		3	4	9	33
6		11			5					2	1						10		7		8		3	4	9	34
31	28	24	6	2	34	4	7	1	3	14	27	7	5	7	1	1	29	6	32	3	26	2	17	27	30	
4	5				1	1							1				18		6	8	1		1		6	opp.og 1
6	2	11			5		10			3	1								7		8			4	9	35
6	2	11			5		10				1							3	7		8			4	9	36
2	2	2			2		2			1	2							1	2		2			2	2	
																			1						1	

1902-03

1	Sep	1	(a)	West Brom A	L	1-2	Young		0	
2		6	(a)	Middlesbrough	L	0-1			0	
3		13	(h)	Newcastle U	L	0-1			0	17
4		20	(a)	Wolves	D	1-1	Rankin		1	17
5		27	(h)	Liverpool	W	3-1	Abbott, Brearley, Young		3	14
6	Oct	2	(a)	Nottingham F	D	2-2	Sharp 2		4	13
7		4	(a)	Sheffield U	W	2-0	Abbott, Booth		6	11
8		11	(h)	Grimsby T	W	4-2	Bowman 2, Abbott, Brearley		8	8
9		18	(a)	Aston Villa	L	1-2	Bell		8	10
10		25	(h)	Nottingham F	D	1-1	Young		9	11
11	Nov	1	(a)	Bolton W	W	3-1	Bell 2, Sharp		11	7
12		8	(a)	Blackburn R	L	2-3	Bell, Brearley		11	10
13		15	(a)	Sunderland	L	1-2	Young		11	11
14		22	(h)	Stoke C	L	0-1			11	11
15		29	(h)	Derby C	W	2-1	Bell, Settle		13	10
16	Dec	6	(a)	Sheffield W	L	1-4	Settle		13	12
17		13	(h)	West Brom A	W	3-1	Brearley, Settle, Wolstenholme		15	10
18		20	(a)	Notts Co	L	0-2			15	13
19		25	(a)	Grimsby T	D	0-0			16	12
20		27	(h)	Bolton W	W	3-1	Sheridan 2, Sharp		18	12
21	Jan	1	(a)	Bury	L	2-4	Taylor 2		18	12
22		3	(h)	Middlesbrough	W	3-0	Brearley 3		20	11
23		17	(h)	Wolves	W	2-1	Abbott, Settle		22	11
24		31	(h)	Sheffield U	W	1-0	Rankin		24	11
25	Feb	14	(h)	Aston Villa	L	0-1			24	13
26		28	(h)	Bury	W	3-0	Sharp 2, Clark		26	12
27	Mar	14	(h)	Sunderland	L	0-3			26	12
28		21	(a)	Stoke C	L	0-2			26	12
29		28	(a)	Derby C	W	1-0	Booth		28	12
30	Apr	1	(a)	Newcastle U	L	0-3			28	12
31		4	(h)	Sheffield W	D	1-1	Settle		29	10
32		10	(a)	Liverpool	D	0-0			30	13
33		13	(h)	Blackburn R	L	0-3			30	13
34		18	(h)	Notts Co	W	2-0	Taylor, Young		32	12
								League Appearances		
								League Goals		
35	Feb	7	(h)	Portsmouth	W	5-0	Bell 2, Abbott, Bearley, Sharp	FA Cup Rd 1		
36		21	(h)	Manchester U	W	3-1	Abbott, Booth, Taylor			2
37	Mar	7	(a)	Milwall	L	0-1				3
								FA Cup Appearances		
								FA Cup Goals		

Abbott W	Balmer R	Balmer W	Bell J	Booth T	Bowman A	Brearley J	Clark C	Crelley J	Dilly T	Henderson W	Kitchen G	Lee J	Makepeace H	Rankin G	Russell J	Settle J	Sharp J	Sheridan J	Taylor J	Whitley J	Wolstenholme S	Young A	No.
6		2	11	5		8					1	3				10	7		4			9	1
6		2	11	5		8					1	3				10	7		4			9	2
6		3	11	5		8		2			1					10	7		4			9	3
6			11	5		8		3	2		1						7	10	4			9	4
6		3	11	5		8		2			1						7	10	4			9	5
6		2	11	5		8					1						7	10	4	3		9	6
6		3	11	5		8					1					10	7		4	2		9	7
6		3	11		9	8	5				1						7	10	4	2			8
6		3	11	5	9	8					1						7	10	4	2			9
6		3	11	5		8					1						7	10	4	2		9	10
6		3	11			8		2			1		5				7	10	4			9	11
6		2	11	5		8		3			1						7	10	4			9	12
6		2	10	5		8		3		11	1						7		4			9	13
6		2	11	5		8				3	1						7	10	4			9	14
6		2	11	5	9			3			1					10	7	8	4				15
6		2		5	9			3		11	1					10	7	8	4				16
6		2		5	9			3			1			11		10	7	8	4				17
6		2		5	9			3			1			11		10	7	8	4				18
6				5	9			3	2					11		10	7	8		1	4		19
6				5	9			3						11		10	7	8	4	1	2		20
6		3		5	9			2			1			11		10	7	8	4				21
6	3	2	11	5	9						1					10	7	8	4				22
6		3		5				2		11	1					10	7	8	4			9	23
6		3		5	9			2						11		10	7	8	4	1			24
6		3	11	5	9			2								10	7	8	4	1			25
6		3	11	5				2		4	1		10				7	8				9	26
			11	5				3	2				6	9		10	7	8	4	1			27
6			11	5				3	2		1					10	7	8	4			9	28
6		2		5				3		11	1					10	7	8	4			9	29
6		2						3		11	1				5	10	7	8	4			9	30
6		2						3		11	1				5	10	7	8	4			9	31
6		2	11	5				3			1					10	7	8	4			9	32
6			11	5				3	2		1					10	7	8	4			9	33
6		2	11	5				3			1					10	7	8	4			9	34
33	1	28	23	29	5	22	3	18	6	13	26	2	3	13	3	20	27	17	33	8	22	19	
4		5	2	2		7	1						2			5	6	2	3	1		5	
6		3	11	5	9			2								10	7	8		1	4		35
6		2	11	5	9			3								10	7	8		1	4		36
6		3	11	5				2	4						8		7		9	1	10		37
3		3	3	3	2		1	1			2				1	1	2	2	3	3	2	1	
2			2	1			1									1					1		

1903-04

1	Sep	1	(h)	Blackburn R	W	3-1	Hardman, Sharp, Young	2	
2		5	(h)	Notts Co	W	3-1	McDermott, Settle, Sharp	4	
3		12	(a)	Sheffield U	L	1-2	Young	4	7
4		19	(h)	Newcastle U	W	4-1	Booth, Hardman, Settle, Young	6	5
5		26	(a)	Aston Villa	L	1-3	Settle	6	6
6	Oct	3	(h)	Middlesbrough	W	2-0	Sharp, Wolstenholme	8	6
7		10	(a)	Liverpool	D	2-2	Sheridan 2	9	5
8		17	(h)	Bury	W	2-1	McDermott, Wolstenholme	11	3
9		24	(a)	Blackburn R	W	2-0	Booth, Wolstenholme	13	3
10		31	(h)	Nottingham F	L	0-2		13	3
11	Nov	7	(a)	Sheffield W	L	0-1		13	5
12		14	(h)	Sunderland	L	0-1		13	7
13		21	(a)	West Brom A	D	0-0		14	7
14		28	(h)	Small Heath	W	5-1	Abbott, Booth, Sharp, Taylor, Young	16	7
15	Dec	5	(a)	Wolves	D	2-2	McDermott 2	17	6
16		12	(a)	Stoke C	W	3-2	Taylor 2, Corrin	19	4
17		19	(h)	Derby C	L	0-1		19	7
18		26	(a)	Manchester C	W	3-1	McDermott, Settle, Taylor	21	6
19	Jan	2	(h)	Notts Co	W	3-0	Booth, McDermott, Sharp	23	6
20		9	(h)	Sheffield U	W	2-0	Abbott, Settle	25	5
21		16	(a)	Newcastle U	L	0-1		25	6
22		23	(h)	Aston Villa	W	1-0	Settle	27	6
23		30	(a)	Middlesbrough	L	0-3		27	7
24	Feb	13	(a)	Bury	D	0-0		28	7
25		27	(a)	Nottingham F	W	4-0	Sharp 2, Rankin, Taylor	30	7
26	Mar	12	(a)	Sunderland	L	0-2		30	8
27		26	(a)	Small Heath	D	1-1	McDermott	31	8
28	Apr	1	(h)	Liverpool	W	5-2	Young 4, Wolstenholme	33	8
29		2	(h)	Wolves	W	2-0	Hardman, Settle	35	6
30		4	(h)	Sheffield W	W	2-0	Hardman 2	37	4
31		9	(h)	Stoke C	L	0-1		37	5
32		16	(a)	Derby C	W	1-0	Abbott	39	5
33		18	(h)	West Brom A	W	4-0	Abbott, Rankin, Settle, Young	41	4
34		25	(h)	Manchester C	W	1-0	Taylor	43	3
								League Appearances	
								League Goals	
35	Feb	6	(h)	Tottenham H	L	1-2	Taylor	FA Cup Rd 1	
								FA Cup Appearances	
								FA Cup Goal	

Abbott W	Balmer R	Balmer W	Booth T	Corrin T	Crelley J	Hardman H	Henderson W	Kitchen G	McDermott T	Murray D	Rankin G	Settle J	Sharp J	Sheridan J	Simpson T	Taylor J	Whitley J	Wolstenholme S	Young A	
6		2	5		3	11		1	8			10	7					4	9	1
6		2	5		3	11		1	8			10	7					4	9	2
6		2	5		3	11		1	8			10	7					4	9	3
6		2	5		3	11		1	8			10	7					4	9	4
6		2	5		3	11		1	8			10	7					4	9	5
6			5		3	11	2	1	8			10	7					4	9	6
6			5		3	11	2	1	8					10		7		4	9	7
6		2	5		3	11		1	8			10	7					4	9	8
6		2	5		3	11		1	8			10	7					4	9	9
6		2	5		3	11		1	8			10	7					4	9	10
6		2	5			11		1	8	3		10	7					4	9	11
6		2	5	9		11		1	8	3			7	10				4		12
6		2	5		3	11		1	8			10	7					4	9	13
6		2	5	11	3			1	10				7			8		4	9	14
6		2	5	11	3			1	10			9	7			8		4		15
6		2	5	11	3			1	10			9	7			8		4		16
		2	5	11	3			1	8			9	7	10		6		4		17
6		2	5	11	3			1	10			9	7			8		4		18
6		2	5	11	3			1	10				7			8		4	9	19
6	2	3	5	11				1	10			9	7			8		4		20
6		2	5		3			1	10			9	7		11	8		4		21
6		2	5		3	11		1	10			9	7			8		4		22
6		2	5		3	11		1	10			9	7			8		4		23
6		2	5		3	11		1	10			9	7			8		4		24
6		2	5		3	11		1	10				7			8		4	9	25
6		2	5		3	11		1	8			10	7			4			9	26
6		2	5		3	11		1	10			9	7			8		4		27
6		2	5		3	11		1	10				7			8		4	9	28
6		2	5		3	11		1	10			9	7			8		4		29
	2	3	5			11		1	8			10	7			6		4	9	30
6		2	5		3	11		1	8			10	7			4			9	31
6		2	5		3	11			7			10				8	1	4	9	32
6		2	5		3	11			7			10				8	1	4	9	33
6	2	3	5			11			7			10				8	1	4	9	34
32	3	32	34	8	29	26	2	31	29	2	3	29	31	3	1	22	3	32	22	
4		4	1	5		7			2			8	6	2		6		4	10	
6		2	5	11	3			1	10			9	7			8		4		35
1		1	1	1	1			1	1			1	1			1		1		

1904-05

1	Sep	3	(a)	Notts Co	W	2-1	McDermott, Settle	2	
2		10	(h)	Sheffield U	W	2-0	Hardman, Young	4	
3		12	(a)	Aston Villa	L	0-1		4	4
4		17	(a)	Newcastle U	L	2-3	Hardman, Settle	4	7
5		24	(h)	Preston N E	W	1-0	McDermott	6	5
6	Oct	1	(a)	Middlesbrough	L	0-1		6	7
7		8	(h)	Wolves	W	2-1	Sharp, Young	8	5
8		15	(a)	Bury	W	2-1	McDermott, Young	10	4
9		22	(h)	Aston Villa	W	3-2	Abbott, Hardman, McDermott	12	3
10		29	(a)	Blackburn R	L	0-1		12	4
11	Nov	5	(h)	Nottingham F	W	5-1	Young 4, Taylor	14	4
12		12	(a)	Sheffield W	D	5-5	Settle 2, Abbott, Hardman, Young	15	4
13		19	(h)	Sunderland	L	0-1		15	7
14	Dec	3	(h)	Derby C	D	0-0		16	9
15		10	(h)	Stoke C	W	4-1	Sharp 2, Abbott, Young	18	7
16		17	(a)	Small Heath	W	2-1	Makepeace, Taylor	20	3
17		24	(h)	Manchester C	D	0-0		21	4
18		26	(a)	Wolves	W	3-0	McDermott, Settle, Young	23	3
19		27	(a)	Derby C	W	2-1	Hardman, McLaughlin	25	1
20		31	(h)	Notts Co	W	5-1	Abbott, Hardman, McLaughlin, Sharp, Taylor	27	2
21	Jan	7	(a)	Sheffield U	L	0-1		27	4
22		14	(h)	Newcastle U	W	2-1	Rankin, Settle	29	4
23		21	(a)	Preston N E	D	1-1	McDermott	30	2
24		28	(h)	Middlesbrough	W	1-0	Makepeace	32	1
25	Feb	11	(h)	Bury	W	2-0	Hardman, Settle	34	1
26		25	(h)	Blackburn R	W	1-0	Sharp	36	1
27	Mar	11	(h)	Sheffield W	W	5-2	Young 2, Makepeace, Sharp, Taylor	38	1
28		18	(a)	Sunderland	W	3-2	Sharp 2, McDermott	40	1
29	Apr	5	(h)	Woolwich Arsenal	W	1-0	Young	42	1
30		8	(a)	Stoke C	D	2-2	Hardman, Makepeace	43	1
31		15	(h)	Small Heath	W	2-1	Makepeace, Young	45	1
32		21	(a)	Manchester C	L	0-2		45	1
33		22	(a)	Woolwich Arsenal	L	1-2	Settle	45	1
34		24	(a)	Nottingham F	W	2-0	McLaughlin, Settle	47	2
								League Appearances	
								League Goals	
35	Feb	2	(a)	Liverpool	D	1-1	Makepeace	FA Cup Rd 1	
36		8	(h)	Liverpool	W	2-1	Hardman, McDermott	Replay	
37		18	(a)	Stoke C	W	4-0	McDermott 2, Makepeace, Settle	2	
38	Mar	3	(h)	Southampton	W	4-0	Settle 3, McDermott	3	
39		25	(n)	Aston Villa	D	1-1	Sharp (Victoria Ground, Stoke)	SF	
40		29	(n)	Aston Villa	L	1-2	Sharp (Trent Bridge, Nottingham) Replay		
								FA Cup Appearances	
								FA Cup Goals	

Abbott W	Ashworth S	Balmer R	Balmer W	Booth T	Chadwick T	Crelley J	Dilly T	Hardman H	McDermott T	McLaughlin W	Makepeace H	Rankin G	Roose L	Scott W	Settle J	Sharp J	Taylor J	Wildman W	Young A	No.
6			2	5		3		11	8				1		10	7	4		9	1
6			2	5		3		11	8				1		10	7	4		9	2
			2	5		3	11		8	6			1		10	7	4		9	3
			2	5		3		11	8	6		7	1		10		4		9	4
			2	5		3		11	8	6		7	1		10		4		9	5
	4		2			3		11	8	6		7	1		10		5		9	6
	4		2			3		11	8	6			1		10	7	5		9	7
6			2			3		11	8		4	7	1		10		5		9	8
6	4		2			3		11	8			7	1		10		5		9	9
	4		2			3		11	8	6		7	1		10		5		9	10
6	4		2			3		11	8				1		10	7	5		9	11
6	4		2			3		11	8				1		10	7	5		9	12
6	4		2			3		11	8				1		10	7	5		9	13
6	4		2			3		11	8				1		10	7	5		9	14
6			2			3		11	8		4		1		10	7	5		9	15
6			2			3		11	8		4		1		10	7	5		9	16
6			2			3		11	8		4		1		10	7	5		9	17
6	4		2			3		11	8				1		10	7	5		9	18
6			2			3		11	8	9	4	7	1		10		5			19
6	4	3	2					11	8					1	10	7	5		9	20
6			2	4		3		11	8			7		1	10		5		9	21
6		3	2	4				11	8			7		1	10		5		9	22
6	4	3	2					11	9	8				1	10	7	5			23
6		3						11	8		4	7		1	10		5	2	9	24
6		3	2					11	8		4			1	10	7	5		9	25
6			2			3		11	8		4			1	10	7	5		9	26
6			2			3		11	8		4			1	10	7	5		9	27
6			2			3		11	8		4			1	10	7	5		9	28
6			2			3		11	8		4	7		1	10		5		9	29
6		3	2					11	8		4	7		1	10		5		9	30
6		3	2	5				11			4	7		1	10		8		9	31
6			2		4	3		11	8					1	10	7	5		9	32
6			2		4	3		11	8					1	10	7	5		9	33
6		3	2		4			11	8					1	10	7	5		9	34
28	**11**	**11**	**30**	**8**	**3**	**26**	**1**	**32**	**29**	**7**	**19**	**16**	**18**	**16**	**32**	**21**	**34**	**1**	**31**	Tot
4								8	7	3	5	1			9	8	4		14	Gls
6			2			3		11	8		4			1	10	7	5		9	35
6			2			3		11	8		4			1	10	7	5		9	36
6			2			3		11	8		4			1	10	7	5		9	37
6			2			3		11	8		4			1	10	7	5		9	38
6			2			3		11	8		4			1	10	7	5		9	39
6			2			3		11	8		4			1	10	7	5		9	40
6		**3**	**3**			**6**		**6**	**6**		**6**			**6**	**6**	**6**	**6**		**6**	Tot
									1		4				2	4	2			Gls

1905-06

1	Sep	2	(h)	Middlesbrough	W	4-1	Settle 2, Rankin, Young	2	
2		9	(a)	Preston N E	D	1-1	opp.og	3	
3		16	(h)	Newcastle U	L	1-2	Sharp	3	12
4		23	(a)	Aston Villa	L	0-4		3	15
5		30	(h)	Liverpool	W	4-2	Abbott, Hardman, Settle, Sharp	5	11
6	Oct	7	(a)	Sheffield U	L	2-3	McDermott, Young	5	16
7		14	(h)	Notts Co	W	6-2	Oliver 3, Abbott, Hardman, Settle	7	11
8		21	(a)	Stoke C	D	2-2	Hardman, Oliver	8	12
9		28	(h)	Bolton W	W	3-1	Settle 2, Taylor	10	8
10	Nov	4	(a)	Woolwich Arsenal	W	2-1	Settle, Young	12	7
11		11	(h)	Blackburn R	W	3-2	Abbott, Rankin, Settle	14	7
12		18	(a)	Sunderland	L	1-2	Settle	14	11
13		25	(h)	Birmingham	L	1-2	Hardman	14	11
14	Dec	2	(a)	Wolves	W	5-2	Young 2, Hardman, McLaughlin, Makepeace	16	11
15		9	(a)	Derby C	D	0-0		17	10
16		16	(h)	Sheffield W	W	2-0	Settle, Sharp	19	9
17		23	(a)	Nottingham F	L	3-4	Abbott, Makepeace, Young	19	11
18		25	(a)	Bury	L	2-3	Sharp, Young	19	11
19		26	(h)	Bury	L	1-2	McLaughlin	19	11
20		30	(a)	Middlesbrough	D	0-0		20	11
21	Jan	1	(a)	Manchester C	L	0-1		20	12
22		6	(h)	Preston N E	W	1-0	Hardman	22	12
23		20	(a)	Newcastle U	L	2-4	Dilly 2	22	13
24		27	(h)	Aston Villa	W	4-2	Sharp 2, Settle, Taylor	24	13
25	Feb	10	(h)	Sheffield U	W	3-2	Sharp 3	26	12
26		17	(a)	Notts Co	D	0-0		27	11
27	Mar	3	(a)	Bolton W	L	2-3	Cook, Taylor	27	12
28		17	(a)	Blackburn R	W	2-1	Bolton, Cook	29	12
29		21	(h)	Woolwich Arsenal	L	0-1		29	13
30		24	(h)	Sunderland	W	3-1	Young 2, Abbott	31	11
31	Apr	3	(h)	Stoke C	L	0-3		31	12
32		7	(h)	Wolves	D	2-2	Bolton, Young	32	12
33		9	(a)	Birmingham	L	0-1		32	12
34		13	(a)	Liverpool	D	1-1	Taylor	33	12
35		14	(h)	Derby C	W	2-1	Cook, Jones	35	12
36		16	(h)	Manchester C	L	0-3		35	14
37		23	(a)	Sheffield W	L	1-3	Bolton	35	14
38		28	(h)	Nottingham F	W	4-1	Bolton 2, Young 2	37	11
								League Appearances	
								League Goals	
39	Jan	13	(h)	West Brom A	W	3-1	Hardman, Makepeace, Sharp	FA Cup Rd 1	
40	Feb	3	(h)	*Chesterfield	W	3-0	Settle, Taylor, Young		2
41		24	(h)	Bradford C	W	1-0	Makepeace		3
42	Mar	10	(h)	Sheffield W	W	4-3	Bolton, Booth, Sharp, Taylor		4
43		31	(n)	Liverpool	W	2-0	Abbott, Hardman	(Villa Park)	SF
44	Apr	21	(n)	Newcastle U	W	1-0	Young	(Crystal Palace)	F
								FA Cup Appearances	
								FA Cup Goals	

*Chesterfield were drawn at home but agreed to the match being played at Goodison Park

Abbott W	Balmer R	Balmer W	Birnie A	Black W	Bolton H	Booth T	Chadwick T	Collins H	Cook H	Crelley J	Dilly T	Donaldson J	Donnachie J	Grundy H	Hardman H	Hill P	Jones T	McDermott T	McLaughlin W	Makepeace H	Oliver F	Rankin G	Scott W	Settle J	Sharp J	Taylor J	Young A	Match
6	2									3					11			8		4		7	1	10		5	9	1
6		2								3					11			8	10	4			1		7	5	9	2
6		2	4							3					11			8					1	10	7	5	9	3
		2		6						3					11					4	8		1	10	7	5	9	4
6	2									3					11			8		4			1	10	7	5	9	5
6	2									3					11			8		4			1	10	7	5	9	6
6	2						4	1		3					11			8			9			10	7	5		7
6	2					5				3					11					4	9		1	10	7	8		8
6	2	3				5									11					4	9		1	10	7	8		9
6	2									3					11			8		4			1	10	7	5	9	10
6	2									3					11			8		4		7	1	10		5	9	11
6	2									3					11					4	9		1	10	7	5	8	12
6	2					5				3					11					4			1	10	7	8	9	13
6	3					5									11	2		10	8				1		7	4	9	14
6	2					5				3					11					8			1	10	7	4	9	15
6	2					5									11					8			1	10	7	4	9	16
6	2					5				3					11					8			1	10	7	4	9	17
	2			6		5				3					11					8			1	10	7	4	9	18
9		2			7	6	5								11				10				1			4	8	19
	3	2				6	5								11					8			1	10	7	4	9	20
	3					6	5								11	2				8			1	10	7	4	9	21
6	3						5						9		11	2				8			1	10	7	4		22
6	3				8								9		11	2		10	4				1		7	5		23
	3			4	8										11	2				6			1	10	7	5	9	24
	3				8							6			11	2				4			1	10	7	5	9	25
6	2				8					3	7				11					4			1	10		5	9	26
		7			8		4		10	3					11	2				6			1			5		27
	2				8		4		10	3					11					6			1		7	5	9	28
	3						4		8		7				11	2				6			1	10		5	9	29
6	2				8		4			3					11								1	10	7	5	9	30
6	2				8		4			3	7				11								1	10		5	9	31
6	3			4	8	5									11	2							1	10	7		9	32
				4			6	1	10	3					11	2				8					7	5	9	33
6	3	2		4	8				10						11								1		7	5	9	34
6				4	8	5			10	3	7				11	2		9					1					35
	3				7		4	1	10			6			11	2		9	8							5		36
6	3			4	8										11	2							1	10	7	5	9	37
6	2				8					3					11					4			1	10	7	5	9	38
27	20	18	3	13	13	17	4	3	7	23	2	2	8	2	31	13	2	6	8	27	4	4	35	28	29	36	30	
5					5					3	2				6			1	1	2	2	4	2	11	9	4	12	opp.og 1
6	3					5									11	2				4			1	10	7	8	9	39
6	3				8										11	2				4			1	10	7	5	9	40
6	2				8				10	3					11					4	9		1		7	5		41
	2	3			8		4								11					6			1	10	7	5	9	42
6	2				8					3					11					4			1	10	7	5	9	43
6		2			8					3					11					4			1	10	7	5	9	44
5	2	5					4	2		2	3				6	2				6		1	6	5	6	6	5	
1							1	1			2				2									1	2	2	2	

J.Hannan played number 3 in Match 19; W.Wildman played number 3 in Match 16;
R.Wright played number 9 in Match 27.

1906-07

#	Date		Opponent		Score	Scorers		
1	Sep 1	(a)	Middlesbrough	D	2-2	Bolton, Young	1	
2	3	(h)	Manchester C	W	9-1	Young 4, Settle 2, Abbott, Bolton, Taylor	3	
3	8	(h)	Preston N E	W	1-0	Hardman	5	1
4	15	(a)	Newcastle U	L	0-1		5	7
5	17	(h)	Notts Co	D	2-2	Abbott, Young	6	3
6	22	(h)	Aston Villa	L	1-2	Abbott	6	6
7	29	(a)	Liverpool	W	2-1	Young 2	8	5
8	Oct 6	(h)	Bristol C	W	2-0	Bolton, Sharp	10	4
9	13	(a)	Notts Co	W	1-0	Young	12	4
10	20	(h)	Sheffield U	W	4-2	Young 2, Bolton, G.Wilson	14	2
11	27	(a)	Bolton W	W	3-1	Bolton, Sharp, Young	16	1
12	Nov 3	(h)	Manchester U	W	3-0	Settle, G.Wilson, Young	18	1
13	10	(h)	Stoke C	L	0-2		18	1
14	17	(h)	Blackburn R	W	2-0	Settle, Young	20	1
15	24	(a)	Sunderland	L	0-1		20	1
16	Dec 1	(h)	Birmingham	W	3-0	Young 2, Sharp	22	1
17	8	(h)	Derby C	W	2-0	Bolton, G.Wilson	24	1
18	15	(a)	Woolwich Arsenal	L	1-3	Sharp	24	1
19	22	(h)	Sheffield W	W	2-0	Sharp, Young	26	1
20	25	(a)	Bury	W	2-1	Sharp, Young	28	1
21	26	(a)	Manchester C	L	1-3	Bolton	28	1
22	29	(h)	Middlesbrough	W	5-1	Bolton 3, Hardman, Young	30	1
23	Jan 1	(h)	Bury	W	1-0	Young	32	1
24	5	(a)	Preston N E	D	1-1	Young	33	1
25	19	(h)	Newcastle U	W	3-0	Young 2, Sharp	35	1
26	26	(a)	Aston Villa	L	1-2	Bolton	35	1
27	Feb 9	(a)	Bristol C	L	1-2	Young	35	2
28	Mar 2	(h)	Bolton W	W	1-0	Hardman	37	2
29	4	(a)	Sheffield U	L	1-4	Rouse	37	2
30	16	(h)	Stoke C	W	3-0	Abbott, Bolton, Young	39	2
31	29	(h)	Liverpool	D	0-0		40	2
32	30	(h)	Sunderland	W	4-1	Jones 2, Bolton, Settle	42	2
33	Apr 6	(a)	Birmingham	L	0-1		42	2
34	8	(a)	Blackburn R	L	1-2	Settle	42	2
35	10	(h)	Woolwich Arsenal	W	2-1	Young 2	44	2
36	13	(a)	Derby C	L	2-5	Booth, Couper	44	2
37	22	(a)	Manchester U	L	0-3		44	3
38	27	(a)	Sheffield W	D	1-1	Young	45	3
							League Appearances	
							League Goals	
39	Jan 12	(h)	Sheffield U	W	1-0	opp.og	FA Cup Rd 1	
40	Feb 2	(a)	West Ham U	W	2-1	Settle, Sharp	2	
41	23	(h)	Bolton W	D	0-0		3	
42	27	(a)	Bolton W	W	3-0	Abbott, Settle, Taylor	Replay	
43	Mar 9	(a)	Crystal Palace	D	1-1	Taylor	4	
44	13	(h)	Crystal Palace	W	4-0	Settle 2, Hardman, Young	Replay	
45	25	(n)	West Brom A	W	2-1	Sharp, G.Wilson	(Burnden Park) SF	
46	Apr 20	(n)	Sheffield W	L	1-2	Sharp	(Crystal Palace) F	
							FA Cup Appearances	
							FA Cup Goals	

Abbott W	Balmer R	Balmer W	Black W	Bolton H	Booth T	Chadwick T	Couper G	Crelley J	Depledge R	Donnachie J	Graham R	Hardman H	Hill P	Jones T	Makepeace H	Rouse F	Scott W	Settle J	Sharp J	Sloan D	Strettle S	Taylor J	Wilson D	Wilson G	Young A	
6		2		8				3				11			4		1	10	7			5			9	1
6		2		8	4			3									1	10	7			5		11	9	2
6	3			8	4					7		11	2				1	10				5			9	3
6		2		8				3							4		1		7			5	10	11	9	4
6		2		8	4			3									1		7			5	10	11	9	5
6		2		8				3							4		1		7			5	10	11	9	6
6		2		8				3				11			4		1		7			5		10	9	7
6		2		8				3				11			4		1		7			5		10	9	8
6		2		8				3		7					4		1					5	10	11	9	9
	3	2		8	4							11			6		1		7			5		10	9	10
6	3	2		8	4												1	10	7			5		11	9	11
6	3	2		8	4												1	10	7			5		11	9	12
6		2		8	4			3				11					1	10	7			5			9	13
6	3	2	4	8								11				7	1	10				5			9	14
6	3	2	4													8	1	10	7			5		11	9	15
6	3	2		8											4		1	10	7			5		11	9	16
6	3	2		8								11			4		1		7			5		10	9	17
6	3	2													4	8	1	10	7			5		11	9	18
6	3	2		8								11			4		1		7			5		10	9	19
6	3	2		8											4		1	10	7			5		11	9	20
	3	2	6	8								11			4		1		7			5		10	9	21
	3	2		8	4	6				7		11					1					5		10	9	22
		2		8	4	6			3	7		11					1					5		10	9	23
	3	2		8	4	6				7							1	10				5		11	9	24
6	3	2		8								11			4		1		7			5		10	9	25
6	3	2		8								11			4		1		7			5		10	9	26
6	3	2	4	5						11						10	1	8	7						9	27
	3						6			7	8	11			4	9	1				2	5		10		28
		3					6			11	8				4	9	1				2	5		10		29
6	3	2		8					1	7		11			4			10				5			9	30
6	3	2										11			4		1	8	7			5		10	9	31
	3	2		8	5	6				7				9	4		1	10						11		32
6		2		8				3				11			4		1	10	7			5			9	33
		2	8	5	6	7		3				11		9	4			10		1						34
	2	3	4	8	6	7						11					1					5		10	9	35
6		2	4	5			9	3									1	8	7				11	10		36
		2		8	6			3				11			4		1	10	7			5			9	37
		2	4	8	6			3				11					1	10	7			5			9	38
26	25	33	7	31	14	10	3	15	1	13	2	19	1	2	23	6	35	21	27	2	2	34	5	28	33	
4				13	1		1					3		2	1			6	7			1		3	28	
	3	2		8	6					7					4		1	10				5		11	9	39
6	3	2										11			4		1	8	7			5		10	9	40.
6	3	2										11			4	10	1	8	7			5			9	41
6	3	2										11			4		1	8	7			5		10	9	42
6	3	2								7		11			4		1	8				5		10	9	43
6	3	2										11			4		1	8	7			5		10	9	44
6	3	2	8									11			4		1	10	7			5			9	45
6	3	2	8									11			4		1	10	7			5			9	46
7	8	8	2	1						2		7			8	1	8	8	6			8		6	8	
1										1								4	3			2		1	1 opp.og 1	

1907-08

#	Date		Venue	Opponent	Res	Score	Scorers		
1	Sep	2	(a)	Bristol C	L	2-3	Bolton, Hardman	0	
2		7	(h)	Manchester C	D	3-3	Young 2, Rouse	1	
3		9	(h)	Preston N E	W	2-1	Abbott, Makepeace	3	6
4		14	(a)	Preston N E	D	2-2	Bolton, Sharp	4	9
5		21	(h)	Bury	W	6-1	Bolton 2, Young 2, Hardman, Taylor	6	4
6		28	(a)	Aston Villa	W	2-0	Settle, Sharp	8	4
7	Oct	5	(h)	Liverpool	L	2-4	Makepeace, Settle	8	6
8		12	(a)	Middlesbrough	W	2-0	Bolton, Young	10	4
9		19	(h)	Sheffield U	W	2-1	Young 2	12	3
10		26	(a)	Chelsea	L	1-2	Booth	12	5
11	Nov	2	(h)	Nottingham F	W	1-0	Mountford	14	3
12		9	(a)	Manchester U	L	3-4	Bolton, Hardman, Settle	14	4
13		16	(h)	Blackburn R	W	4-1	Settle 2, Bolton, Young	16	3
14		23	(a)	Bolton W	L	0-3		16	5
15	Dec	7	(a)	Newcastle U	L	1-2	Settle	16	7
16		14	(a)	Sunderland	W	2-1	Jones, Mountford	18	5
17		21	(h)	Woolwich Arsenal	D	1-1	Jones	19	6
18		25	(a)	Notts Co	L	1-2	Young	19	6
19		26	(h)	Bristol C	D	0-0		20	7
20		28	(a)	Sheffield W	W	2-1	Bolton, Young	22	6
21	Jan	4	(a)	Manchester C	L	2-4	Bolton, Taylor	22	8
22		18	(a)	Bury	L	0-3		22	9
23		25	(h)	Aston Villa	W	1-0	Sharp	24	8
24	Feb	8	(h)	Middlesbrough	W	2-1	Young 2	26	7
25		15	(a)	Sheffield U	L	0-2		26	9
26		29	(a)	Nottingham F	L	2-5	Mountford, opp.og	26	11
27	Mar	14	(a)	Blackburn R	L	0-2		26	16
28		18	(h)	Birmingham	W	4-1	Young 2, Coleman, Settle	28	12
29		21	(h)	Bolton W	W	2-1	Coleman, Sharp	30	10
30		28	(a)	Birmingham	L	1-2	Coleman	30	11
31	Apr	1	(h)	Chelsea	L	0-3		30	12
32		4	(h)	Newcastle U	W	2-0	Coleman, Young	32	11
33		8	(h)	Manchester U	L	1-3	Young	32	12
34		11	(h)	Sunderland	L	0-3		32	15
35		17	(a)	Liverpool	D	0-0		33	14
36		18	(a)	Woolwich Arsenal	L	1-2	Coleman	33	16
37		20	(h)	Notts Co	W	1-0	Freeman	35	15
38		25	(h)	Sheffield W	D	0-0		36	11

League Appearances
League Goals

#	Date		Venue	Opponent	Res	Score	Scorers	
39	Jan	11	(h)	Tottenham H	W	1-0	Young	FA Cup Rd 1
40	Feb	1	(a)	Oldham A	D	0-0		2
41		5	(h)	Oldham A	W	6-1	Bolton 4, Abbott, Young	Replay
42		22	(a)	Bolton W	D	3-3	Settle 2, Bolton	3
43		26	(h)	Bolton W	W	3-1	Young 2, Settle	Replay
44	Mar	7	(h)	Southampton	D	0-0		4
45		11	(a)	Southampton	L	2-3	Bolton, Young	Replay

FA Cup Appearances
FA Cup Goals

Abbott W	Adamson H	Balmer R	Balmer W	Bolton H	Booth T	Chadwick T	Coleman J	Crelley J	Donnachie J	Freeman B	Hardman H	Harris V	Jones T	Maconnachie J	Makepeace H	Mountford H	Rafferty D	Rouse F	Scott W	Settle J	Sharp J	Sloan D	Stevenson W	Taylor J	Winterhalder A	Woods L	Young A	Match
6		2	3	8	4				7		11							10	1					5			9	1
6		2	3	8							11				4			10	1		7			5			9	2
6		2	3	8							11			5	4			10	1		7						9	3
6		2	3	8											4				1	10	7			5	11		9	4
6		2	3	8							11				4				1	10	7			5			9	5
6			3	8		2					11				4				1	10	7			5			9	6
6		3	2	8							11				4				1	10	7			5			9	7
6		3	2	8	5	4					11								1	10	7						9	8
6		3	2	8	5				7		11				4				1	10							9	9
6		3	2	8	5						11				4				1	10	7						9	10
		3	2	8	6						11				4	10			1		7			5			9	11
6		3	2	8							11				4				1	10	7			5			9	12
6		3	2	8											4				1	10	7			5	11		9	13
6		3	2	8							11				4				1	10	7			5			9	14
6				8				3			11		9	5	4				1	10	7		2					15
6		3		8									9	5	4	10			1		7		2		11			16
6	4	3		8									9	5					1	10	7		2		11			17
6	4	3							7					8	5	10			1				2		11		9	18
	4		2	8							11			5	6				1	10	7		3				9	19
				8					7		11				4	6	10		1				2	5			9	20
		4	3				8		7						6	10			1				2	5	11		9	21
		3		8				5			11				4	6	10		1		7		2				9	22
6		3	2	8							11				4				1	10	7			5			9	23
6	4	3	2	8					7		11								1	10				5			9	24
6		3	2								11				4	10			1	8	7			5			9	25
6			2		5		8	3	7					9	4	10			1						11			26
6			2		5		8		7					3	4				1	10					11		9	27
6			2		5		8		7		11			3	4				1	10							9	28
6		2					8				11			3	4				1	10	7			5			9	29
6		2					8				11			3	4				1	10	7			5			9	30
6		2					8				11			3	4				1	10	7			5			9	31
6		2					8		7		11			3	4				1	10				5			9	32
6		2					8		7		11			3	4				1	10				5			9	33
6		2					8				11			3	4				1	10	7			5			9	34
6		2		8					7		11	9		3	4				1	10				5				35
6		2		8					7			9		3	4				1	10				5	11			36
6		2		8					7	11		9		3	4				1	10				5				37
		2		8					7	11		9		3	4	6			1	10								38
21	**16**	**26**	**26**	**27**	**8**	**3**	**13**	**3**	**16**	**4**	**22**	**3**	**5**	**21**	**31**	**10**	**3**	**3**	**34**	**21**	**23**	**4**	**8**	**23**	**4**	**4**	**33**	opp.og 1
1				9	1				5				1	3		2		2	3		1			7	4		16	(goals)
6		3		8							11				4				1	10	7		2	5			9	39
6		3	2								11	9			4				1	10	7			5				40
6		3	2	8							11				4				1	10	7			5			9	41
6		3	2	8							11				4				1	10	7			5			9	42
6		3	2	8							11				4				1	10	7			5			9	43
6		3	2	8							11				4				1	10	7			5			9	44
6		3	2	8							11				4				1	10	7			5			9	45
7		**7**	**6**	**6**							**7**	**1**			**7**				**7**	**7**	**7**			**1**	**7**		**6**	
1											6					3											5	(goals)

J.Borthwick played number 5 in Match 38; G.Couper played number 7 in Match 35;
R.Graham played number 8 in Match 40; S.Strettle played number 3 in Match 20.

1908-09

#	Date		Opponent	Res	Score	Scorers	App	Goals
1	Sep 2	(a)	Woolwich Arsenal	W	4-0	Coleman 2, Freeman 2	2	
2	5	(a)	Bristol C	W	2-0	Freeman 2	4	
3	7	(h)	Woolwich Arsenal	L	0-3		4	3
4	12	(h)	Preston N E	L	0-1		4	5
5	19	(a)	Middlesbrough	W	3-2	Barlow, Coleman, Freeman	6	5
6	26	(h)	Manchester C	W	6-3	Young 3, Sharp 2, Taylor	8	5
7	Oct 3	(a)	Liverpool	W	1-0	Barlow	10	3
8	10	(h)	Bury	W	4-0	Freeman 2, Coleman, Young	12	3
9	17	(a)	Sheffield U	W	5-1	Freeman 3, Coleman, Sharp	14	1
10	24	(h)	Aston Villa	W	3-1	Coleman, Freeman, Sharp	16	1
11	31	(a)	Nottingham F	W	2-1	Freeman, Young	18	1
12	Nov 7	(a)	Sunderland	W	4-0	Freeman 3, Coleman	20	1
13	14	(a)	Chelsea	D	3-3	Freeman 2, Coleman	21	1
14	21	(h)	Blackburn R	D	4-4	Coleman 2, Freeman, opp.og	22	1
15	28	(a)	Bradford C	D	1-1	Freeman	23	1
16	Dec 5	(h)	Manchester U	W	3-2	Freeman 2, Barlow	25	1
17	12	(h)	Sheffield U	W	1-0	Freeman	27	1
18	19	(a)	Leicester C	W	2-0	Sharp, Young	29	1
19	25	(h)	Notts Co	L	0-1		29	1
20	26	(a)	Notts Co	D	0-0		30	1
21	Jan 1	(h)	Newcastle U	L	0-1		30	1
22	2	(h)	Bristol C	W	5-2	Freeman 2, Young 2, White	32	1
23	9	(a)	Preston N E	D	3-3	Barlow, Sharp, White	33	1
24	23	(h)	Middlesbrough	D	1-1	Young	34	2
25	30	(a)	Manchester C	L	0-4		34	2
26	Feb 13	(a)	Bury	D	2-2	Freeman, Sharp	35	2
27	20	(h)	Sheffield U	W	5-1	Freeman 3, Coleman 2	37	2
28	27	(a)	Aston Villa	L	1-3	Freeman	37	2
29	Mar 13	(a)	Sunderland	L	0-2		37	2
30	20	(h)	Chelsea	W	3-2	Freeman 2, Coleman	39	2
31	24	(h)	Nottingham F	D	3-3	Coleman 2, Freeman	40	2
32	27	(a)	Blackburn R	D	0-0		41	2
33	Apr 3	(h)	Bradford C	L	0-1		41	2
34	9	(h)	Liverpool	W	5-0	Freeman 2, Coleman, Turner, White	43	2
35	10	(h)	Manchester U	D	2-2	Coleman 2	44	2
36	12	(a)	Newcastle U	L	0-3		44	2
37	17	(a)	Sheffield W	L	0-2		44	2
38	24	(h)	Leicester C	W	4-2	Coleman 2, Freeman 2	46	2

League Appearances
League Goals

| 39 | Jan 16 | (h) | Barnsley | W | 3-1 | Coleman, Sharp, White | FA Cup Rd 1 |
| 40 | Feb 6 | (a) | Manchester U | L | 0-1 | | 2 |

FA Cup Appearances
FA Cup Goals

Adamson H	Balmer R	Barlow G	Berry C	Bolton H	Borthwick J	Buck H	Clifford R	Coleman J	Dawson H	Donnachie J	Freeman B	Harris V	Jones T	Lacey W	Maconnachie J	Makepeace H	Mountford H	Rafferty D	Scott William	Sharp J	Stevenson W	Strettle S	Taylor J	Turner R	White W	Young A	
	2			10				8	11		9	4			3	6			1	7			5				1
	2			10				8	11		9	4			3	6			1	7			5				2
	2			10				8	11	7	9	4			3	6			1				5				3
	2			10				8	11		9	4			3	6			1	7			5				4
	2	11						8			9	4			3	6			1	7			5		10		5
	2	11						8			9	4			3	6			1	7			5		10		6
	2	11						8			9	4			3	6			1	7			5		10		7
6	2	11						8			9	4			3				1	7			5		10		8
	2	11						8			9	4			3	6			1	7			5		10		9
	2							8	11		9	4			3	6			1	7			5		10		10
	2	11						8			9	4			3	6			1	7			5		10		11
	2	11						8			9	4			3	6			1	7			5		10		12
	2	11						8			9	4			3	6			1	7			5		10		13
	2	11						8			9	4			3	6			1	7			5		10		14
	2	11						8			9	4			3	6			1	7			5		10		15
	2	11						8			9	4			3	6			1	7			5		10		16
	2	11					5				9	4			3	6			1	7					8	10	17
	2	11					5	8			9	4			3	6			1	7							18
	2	11					5				9	4			3	6			1	7					8	10	19
		11					5				9	4			3	6			1	7	2				8	10	20
		11					5	8			9	4			3	6			1	7	2					10	21
							5			11	9	4	7		3	6			1			2			8	10	22
	2	11					5	8			9	4			3	6			1	7						10	23
	2	11					5				9	4	7		3	6			1						8	10	24
	2	11					5	8			9	4	7		3	6			1							10	25
4	2	11			1			8			9				3	6				7			5			10	26
	2							8			9	4			3	6			1	7			5	11		10	27
6	2							8			9	4			3				1	7			5	11		10	28
	2	11						8			9	4			3	6			1	7			5			10	29
	2	11					1	8			9				3	6		4		7			5			10	30
6	2							8			9	4			3		11		1	7			5			10	31
6	2							8			9	4	7		3		11		1				5			10	32
6	2	11				7		8			9	4			3				1				5			10	33
	2							8			9	4			3	6			1	7			5	11		10	34
	2		5					8			9	4			3	6			1	7				11		10	35
	2							8			9	4			3	6			1	7			5	11		10	36
4	2		5					8			9	5			3	6			1	7				11		10	37
	2							8			9	4	7		3	6			1					11		10	38
7	35	23	2	4	1	1	9	33	4	3	37	36	5	1	38	33	2	1	36	31	2	1	27	5	18	23	
	4							20			36										7			1	1	3	9	opp.og 1
	2	11					5	8			9	4			3	6			1	7						10	39
	2							8	11			4			3	6			1	7			5		10	9	40
	2	1					1	2	1	1	1	2			2	2			2	2			1		2	1	

1909-10

1	Sep	1	(h)	Sheffield W	D	1-1	White	1	
2		4	(h)	Tottenham H	W	4-2	Freeman 2, White, Young	3	
3		6	(h)	Newcastle U	L	1-4	Freeman	3	7
4		11	(a)	Preston N E	W	1-0	Freeman	5	6
5		18	(h)	Notts Co	W	2-0	Freeman, Sharp	7	3
6		20	(a)	Sheffield W	W	3-1	Freeman 3	9	1
7		25	(a)	Newcastle U	W	2-1	Freeman, Mountford	11	1
8	Oct	2	(h)	Liverpool	L	2-3	Coleman, Freeman	11	1
9		9	(a)	Aston Villa	L	1-3	White	11	3
10		16	(h)	Sheffield U	L	1-2	Young	11	7
11		23	(a)	Woolwich Arsenal	L	0-1		11	8
12		30	(h)	Bolton W	W	3-1	Freeman 3	13	6
13	Nov	6	(a)	Chelsea	W	1-0	Sharp	15	6
14		13	(h)	Blackburn R	L	0-2		15	10
15		20	(a)	Nottingham F	L	0-1		15	11
16		27	(h)	Sunderland	W	2-1	Coleman 2	17	10
17	Dec	4	(a)	Middlesbrough	D	1-1	Coleman	18	10
18		18	(h)	Bradford C	D	1-1	Freeman	19	11
19		25	(a)	Bristol C	L	1-3	Freeman	19	11
20		27	(h)	Bristol C	W	1-0	Sharp	21	10
21	Jan	1	(a)	Bury	D	2-2	Freeman 2	22	10
22		8	(a)	Tottenham H	L	0-3		22	11
23		22	(h)	Preston N E	W	2-1	Makepeace 2	24	11
24	Feb	12	(a)	Liverpool	W	1-0	Freeman	26	9
25		26	(a)	Sheffield U	L	0-3		26	10
26	Mar	7	(h)	Woolwich Arsenal	W	1-0	White	28	11
27		12	(a)	Bolton W	W	1-0	Freeman	30	10
28		14	(h)	Aston Villa	D	0-0		31	10
29		19	(h)	Chelsea	D	2-2	Gourlay, Makepeace	32	10
30		28	(h)	Bury	W	3-0	Freeman 2, Gourlay	34	10
31	Apr	2	(h)	Nottingham F	L	0-4		34	10
32		6	(a)	Manchester U	L	2-3	Sharp, White	34	10
33		9	(a)	Sunderland	W	1-0	Mountford	36	10
34		11	(a)	Blackburn R	L	1-2	Weller	36	10
35		13	(a)	Notts Co	W	3-2	Coleman, Lacey, Makepeace	38	10
36		16	(h)	Middlesbrough	D	1-1	Freeman	39	10
37		23	(h)	Manchester U	D	3-3	Berry 2, White	40	10
38		30	(a)	Bradford C	L	0-2		40	10
								League Appearances	
								League Goals	
39	Jan	15	(a)	Middlesbrough	D	1-1	White	FA Cup Rd 1	
40		19	(h)	Middlesbrough	W	5-3	Freeman, Makepeace, Taylor, White, Young	Replay	
41	Feb	5	(h)	Woolwich Arsenal	W	5-0	Sharp 2, Barlow, Freeman, Young	2	
42		19	(h)	Sunderland	W	2-0	Makepeace, Young	3	
43	Mar	5	(a)	Coventry C	W	2-0	Freeman 2	4	
44		26	(n)	Barnsley	D	0-0	(Elland Road)	SF	
45		31	(n)	Barnsley	L	0-3	(Old Trafford) Replay		
								FA Cup Appearances	
								FA Cup Goals	

Adamson H	Allan J	Balmer R	Bardsley J	Barlow G	Berry A	Borthwick J	Clifford R	Coleman J	Freeman B	Gourlay J	Harris V	Jones T	Lacey W	Maconnachie J	Makepeace H	Michaels W	Mountford H	Pinkney E	Pratt C	Rafferty D	Scott Walter	Scott William	Sharp J	Stevenson W	Taylor J	Turner R	Weller L	White W	Young A	#
4		2							9					3	6							1	7		5	11		8	10	1
		2							9	4				3	6	11						1	7		5			8	10	2
		2						8	9	4				3	6	11						1	7		5				10	3
		2						8	9	4				3	6							1	7		5	11			10	4
		2						8	9	4				3	6	11						1	7		5				10	5
		2						8	9	4				3	6	11						1	7		5			10		6
		2						8	9	4				3	6	11						1	7		5				10	7
		2					5	8	9	4				3	6							1	7			11			10	8
		2					5	8		4				3	6							1	7			11		10	9	9
		2						8	9	5				3	6	7				4		1				11			10	10
		2					5	8	9	4				3	6							1	7			11			10	11
						5	2		9	4			8	3	6							1	7			11		10		12
						5	2		9	4			8	3	6							1	7			11		10		13
						5	2		9	4			8	3	6							1	7			11		10		14
						5	2		9	4			8	3	6	7	11					1							10	15
6	3						2	8	9	4												1	7		5	11			10	16
	3					5	2	8	9	4					6							1	7			11			10	17
	3	11				5	2	8	9	4					6							1	7					10		18
		11				5	2	8	9	4				3	6							1	7					10		19
							2	8	9	4					6							1	7	3	5			10	11	20
							2	8	9	4				3	6							1	7		5			10	11	21
							2	8	9	4					6							1	7	3	5	11		10		22
		11				5	2		9	4				3	6	7						1						8	10	23
	4	11					2		9					3	6						1		7		5			8	10	24
		11	7			5	2	8	9	4				3						6	1								10	25
	4		7				2		9					3	6	11					1				5			8	10	26
6			7			5	2	10	9	4			8	3		11					1									27
		11				5			9	4				3	6						1	7	2				8	10	28
	4						2		9					3	6	11					1	7		5			8	10	29
6	2					5		8	9	10	4			3		7					1					11				30
6	3		7			5	2	8	10	4	9										1					11				31
							2		9	4				3	6			5			1	7			11		8	10	32
	4	2				5		8	9					3	6	11	7				1							10	33
		2							9	10				3		11	7	5	4		1						6	8		34
	4		7			5	2	8		10				3	6	9					1					11				35
						5	2	8	9	4				3	6		7				1					11		10		36
	2		7			5			9	4				3	6						1					11		8	10	37
	3					5	2		9	4					6						1	7				11		8	10	38
2	8	20	1	6	6	19	23	23	34	4	31	1	6	31	32	3	12	4	2	3	11	27	25	3	14	19	1	23	24	
			2					5	22	2			1		4		2							4				1	6	2	
		11					2		9	4				3	6							1	7		5			8	10	39
		11					2		9	4				3	6							1	7		5			8	10	40
		11					2		9	4				3	6							1	7		5			8	10	41
		11					2		9	4				3	6							1	7		5			8	10	42
		11					2		9	4				3	6							1	7		5			8	10	43
		11					2		9	4				3	6							1	7		5			8	10	44
		11					2		9	4				3	6							1	7		5			8	10	45
						7			7					7	7							7	7		7			7	7	
			1						4						2									2	1			2	3	

1910-11

1	Sep	1	(h)	Tottenham H	W	2-0	Freeman 2	2	
2		3	(a)	Middlesbrough	L	0-1		2	
3		10	(h)	Preston N E	W	2-0	White, A.Young	4	4
4		17	(a)	Notts Co	D	0-0		5	5
5		24	(h)	Manchester U	L	0-1		5	6
6	Oct	1	(a)	Liverpool	W	2-0	Makepeace, A.Young	7	6
7		8	(h)	Bury	W	2-1	Gourlay, R.Young	9	5
8		15	(a)	Sheffield U	W	1-0	Barlow	11	4
9		22	(h)	Aston Villa	L	0-1		11	5
10		29	(a)	Sunderland	L	0-4		11	7
11	Nov	5	(h)	Woolwich Arsenal	W	2-0	Berry, Lacey	13	6
12		12	(a)	Bradford C	L	1-3	A.Young	13	7
13		19	(h)	Blackburn R	W	6-1	A.Young 3, Beare 2, Lacey	15	7
14		26	(a)	Nottingham F	D	1-1	Gourlay	16	7
15	Dec	3	(h)	Manchester C	W	1-0	Gourlay	18	5
16		10	(h)	Oldham A	W	1-0	Berry	20	5
17		17	(a)	Sheffield W	W	2-0	Gourlay, Lacey	22	5
18		24	(h)	Bristol C	W	4-3	Berry 2, Lacey, A.Young	24	3
19		26	(a)	Newcastle U	L	0-1		24	4
20		27	(h)	Liverpool	L	0-1		24	6
21		31	(h)	Middlesbrough	W	2-0	Beare, R.Young	26	3
22	Jan	2	(h)	Newcastle U	L	1-5	Beare	26	4
23		7	(a)	Preston N E	W	2-0	Magner, Pinkney	28	4
24		21	(h)	Notts Co	W	5-0	Lacey 3, Beare, R.Young	30	2
25		28	(a)	Manchester U	D	2-2	Beare, Berry	31	3
26	Feb	11	(a)	Bury	D	0-0		32	3
27		18	(h)	Sheffield U	W	1-0	A.Young	34	3
28	Mar	4	(h)	Sunderland	D	2-2	Magner, R.Young	35	4
29		11	(a)	Woolwich Arsenal	L	0-1		35	4
30		18	(h)	Bradford C	D	0-0		36	4
31		27	(a)	Aston Villa	L	1-2	Lacey	36	5
32	Apr	6	(a)	Blackburn R	W	1-0	Beare	38	6
33		8	(a)	Manchester C	L	1-2	Jefferis	38	6
34		14	(h)	Nottingham F	W	2-1	Gracie, R.Young	40	5
35		15	(a)	Oldham A	L	0-2		40	5
36		17	(a)	Tottenham H	W	1-0	Fleetwood	42	5
37		22	(h)	Sheffield W	D	1-1	Beare	43	4
38		29	(a)	Bristol C	W	1-0	Jefferis	45	4

League Appearances
League Goals

39	Jan 14	(a)	Crystal Palace	W	4-0	Gourlay, Magner, A.Young, R.Young	FA Cup Rd 1	
40	Feb 4	(h)	Liverpool	W	2-1	A.Young 2		2
41		25	(a)	Derby C	L	0-5			3

FA Cup Appearances
FA Cup Goals

Allan J	Balmer R	Barlow G	Beare G	Berry A	Borthwick J	Chedgzoy S	Clifford R	Fleetwood T	Freeman B	Gourlay J	Gracie T	Grenyer A	Harris V	Jefferis F	Lacey W	Maconnachie J	Magner E	Makepeace H	Meunier J	Mountford H	Pinkney E	Scott Walter	Scott William	Stevenson W	Turner R	Weller L	White W	Young A	Young R	
	2								9				4	8	3			6			7	1		11				10	5	1
	2								9				4	8	3			6			7	1		11				10	5	2
	2								9				4		3			6			7	1		11			8	10	5	3
	2	7							9				4		3			6				1		11			8	10	5	4
	2	7								10			4	8	3			6				1		11				9	5	5
	2	7							9	8			4		3			6				1		11				10	5	6
		7							9	8			4		3			6				1	2	11				10	5	7
	2		11	7					9	8			4		3			6				1						10	5	8
	2		11	7					9	8			4		3			6				1						10	5	9
		7					2		9	10			4	8	3			6	11			1							5	10
	3		11	7			2		9	10			4	8				6				1							5	11
	3		11	7			2			10			4		8			6				1						9	5	12
			11	7			2			10			4		8			6	3			1						9	5	13
			11	7	5					10			4		8			6	3				1	2				9		14
			11	7	5					10			4		8			6	3				1	2				9		15
			11	7			2			10			4		8			6					1	3				9	5	16
6	3		11	7						10			4		8								1	2				9	5	17
6	3		11	7						10			4		8								1	2				9	5	18
	3		11			7				10			4		8			6					1	2				9	5	19
	3		11	7						10			4		8			6					1	2				9	5	20
	3		8	7						10			4					6					1	2	11			9	5	21
	3		8	7						10			4					6					1	2	11			9	5	22
6	3		11			7							4				9			8			1	2				10	5	23
	3		11	7									4		8		9	6					1	2				10	5	24
4			11	7						8						3	9	6					1	2				10	5	25
4			11	7						8						3	9	6					1	2				10	5	26
			11		5					8			4		7	3	9	6					1	2				10		27
	3		11	7						8			4				9	6					1	2				10	5	28
	2		11	7					9	8			4		3			6					1					10	5	29
4	2			7						8	9					3		6					1	11				10	5	30
				7						8	9				11	3		6					1	2		4		10	5	31
				7						8	9		4		10	3		6					1	2	11				5	32
				7						8	9		4		10	3		6					1	2	11				5	33
	2			7						8	9		4		10	11		6					1	3					5	34
4				7	5					8	9				10	3		6					1	2	11					35
				7						8	9		4		10	3		6					1	2	11				5	36
				7						8	9		4		11	3		6					1	2				10	5	37
	2			7	5					10	9				8	3		6					1		11	4				38
7	23	5	26	21	4	3	5	8	11	28	7	1	32	5	24	22	6	33	4	1	4	7	31	22	10	5	2	30	31	
	1	8	5					1	2	4	1			2	8			2	1				1				1	8	5	
	3		11	7						8			4				9	6					1	2				10	5	39
			11							8			4		7	3	9	6					1	2				10	5	40
			11	7									4		8	3	9	6					1	2				10	5	41
	1		3	2						2			3		2	2	3	3					3	3				3	3	
			1												1		1						1					3	1	

1911-12

#		Date		Opponent	Res	Score	Scorers		
1	Sep	2	(h)	Tottenham H	D	2-2	Burton, Jefferis	1	
2		6	(a)	Newcastle U	L	0-2		1	
3		9	(a)	Manchester U	L	1-2	Lacey	1	18
4		16	(h)	Liverpool	W	2-1	Beare, Gourlay	3	13
5		23	(a)	Aston Villa	L	0-3		3	17
6		30	(h)	Newcastle U	W	2-0	Burton, Davidson	5	13
7	Oct	7	(a)	Sheffield U	l	1-2	Young	5	15
8		14	(h)	Oldham A	D	1-1	Young	6	16
9		21	(a)	Bolton W	W	2-1	Burton, Lacey	8	14
10		28	(h)	Bradford C	W	1-0	Davidson	10	14
11	Nov	4	(a)	Woolwich Arsenal	W	1-0	Jefferis	12	9
12		11	(h)	Manchester C	W	1-0	Burton	14	6
13		18	(a)	Preston N E	L	1-2	Bradshaw	14	8
14		25	(a)	West Brom A	L	0-1		14	10
15	Dec	2	(h)	Sunderland	W	1-0	Gourlay	16	9
16		9	(a)	Blackburn R	L	1-2	Bradshaw	16	12
17		16	(h)	Sheffield W	W	1-0	Jefferis	18	11
18		23	(a)	Bury	W	2-1	Bradshaw, Jefferis	20	9
19		25	(a)	Middlesbrough	D	0-0		21	8
20		26	(h)	Middlesbrough	W	1-0	Bradshaw	23	4
21		30	(a)	Tottenham H	W	1-0	Beare	25	3
22	Jan	6	(h)	Manchester U	W	4-0	Bradshaw 2, Browell 2	27	3
23		20	(a)	Liverpool	W	3-1	Beare, Browell, Jefferis	29	3
24		27	(h)	Aston Villa	D	1-1	Bradshaw	30	2
25	Feb	10	(h)	Sheffield U	W	3-2	Browell 2, Fleetwood	32	2
26		17	(a)	Oldham A	L	0-3		32	3
27		28	(h)	Bolton W	W	1-0	Bradshaw	34	3
28	Mar	2	(a)	Bradford C	L	0-1		34	3
29		16	(a)	Manchester C	L	0-4		34	5
30		23	(h)	Preston N E	W	1-0	Browell	36	5
31		27	(h)	Woolwich Arsenal	W	1-0	Jefferis	38	4
32	Apr	5	(a)	Notts Co	W	1-0	Browell	40	2
33		6	(a)	Sunderland	L	0-4		40	4
34		8	(h)	Notts Co	D	1-1	Browell	41	3
35		13	(h)	Blackburn R	L	1-3	Davidson	41	4
36		20	(a)	Sheffield W	W	3-1	Browell 2, Jefferis	43	3
37		22	(h)	West Brom A	W	3-0	Browell, Makepeace, Uren	45	2
38		27	(h)	Bury	D	1-1	Browell	46	2
							League Appearances		
							League Goals		
39	Jan	13	(a)	Clapton O	W	2-1	Beare, Browell		FA Cup Rd 1
40	Feb	3	(h)	Bury	D	1-1	Maconnachie		2
41		8	(h)	*Bury	W	6-0	Browell 4, Davidson, Jefferis		Replay
42		24	(a)	Oldham A	W	2-0	Browell 2		3
43	Mar	9	(a)	Swindon T	L	1-2	Makepeace		4
							FA Cup Appearances		
							FA Cup Goals		

*Everton and Bury agreed to stage the replay at Goodison Park.

Allan J	Balmer R	Beare G	Berry C	Bradshaw F	Browell T	Burton A	Davidson W	Fleetwood T	Gourley J	Gracie T	Grenyer A	Harris V	Holbem W	Jefferis F	Jordan W	Lacey W	Maconnachie J	Makepeace H	Meunier J	Scott William	Smith J	Stevenson W	Uren H	Weller L	Young R	#
		7				10	11		9			4		8			3	6		1		2			5	1
		7				10	11		9			4	3	8				6		1		2			5	2
		7						5	10			4		8	9	11	3	6		1		2				3
		7							10			4	3	8	9	11		6		1		2			5	4
		7						5	10	9	6	4		8		11	3			1		2				5
		7				10	11		9			4		8			3	6		1		2			5	6
		7				10	11		9			4		8			3	6		1		2			5	7
		7				10	11		9			4		8			3	6		1		2			5	8
		7				10	11					4		8	9		3	6		1		2			5	9
		7				10	11	5	9			4		8			3	6		1		2				10
4		7				10	11	5	9					8			3	6		1		2				11
4		7	9			10	11	5						8			3	6		1		2				12
		7	9			10	11	5				4		8			3	6		1		2				13
		7	9			10	11	5				4		8			3	6		1		2				14
		7				10	11	5	9			4		8			3	6		1		2				15
		7				10	11	5	9			4		8			3	6		1		2				16
		7				10	11	5	9			4		8			3	6		1		2				17
		7				10	11	5	9			4		8			3	6		1		2				18
		7				10		5	9			4		8		11	3	6		1		2				19
		7				10		5	9			4		8		11	3	6		1		2				20
		7				10	11	5	9			4		8			3	6		1		2				21
		7			9	10	11	5				4		8			3	6		1		2				22
		7			9	10	11	5				4		8			3	6		1		2				23
		7			9	10	11	5				4		8			3	6		1		2				24
4		7		1	9		11	5	10					8			3					2	6			25
		7			9	10	11	5		8	6	4					3			1		2				26
		7			9	10		5				4		8			3	6		1		2	11			27
		7			9	10		5				4		8			3	6		1		2	11			28
					10	9	11	5				4	2	8			3	6		1	7					29
					10	9		5		8	6	4					3			1	7	2	11			30
					10	9	11	5				4	3	8				6		1	7	2				31
					10	9		5				4	3	8				6		1	7	2	11			32
					10	9		5				4	3	8				6		1	7	2	11			33
		7			10	9	11	5				4	3	8			2	6		1						34
	2	7			9		11	5	10			4		8			3	6		1						35
					9			5	10			4	2	8			3	6		1	7		11			36
4					9			5	10				2	8			3	6		1	7		11			37
					9			5	10			4	2	8			3	6		1	7		11			38
4	1	30	1	21	17	12	25	34	16	6	3	34	11	36	2	6	31	34	1	37	8	32	8	1	7	
		3				8	12	4	3	1	2			7	2		1							1	2	
		7				10	11	5	9			4		8			3	6		1		2				39
		7				10	11	5	9			4		8			3	6		1		2				40
		7					11	5	9	10		4		8			3	6		1		2				41
		7				10		5	9			4		8		11	3	6		1		2				42
		7				10	11	5	9			4		8			3	6		1		2				43
		5				4	5	4	5	1		5		5		1	5	5		5		5				
		1				7		1						1						1		1				

1912-13

#	Month	Date		Opponent	Res	Score	Scorers		
1	Sep	2	(a)	Tottenham H	W	2-0	T.Browell, Maconnachie	2	
2		7	(a)	Middlesbrough	D	0-0		3	
3		14	(h)	Notts Co	W	4-0	T.Browell 2, Bradshaw, Harris	5	4
4		18	(a)	Derby C	W	4-1	Maconnachie 2, Beare, Uren	7	1
5		21	(a)	Manchester U	L	0-2		7	4
6		28	(h)	Aston Villa	L	0-1		7	6
7	Oct	5	(a)	Liverpool	W	2-0	T.Browell, Gault	9	4
8		12	(h)	Bolton W	L	2-3	T.Browell 2	9	7
9		19	(a)	Sheffield U	L	1-4	T.Browell	9	9
10		26	(h)	Newcastle U	L	0-6		9	12
11	Nov	2	(a)	Oldham A	L	0-2		9	14
12		9	(h)	Chelsea	W	1-0	Bradshaw	11	14
13		16	(a)	Woolwich Arsenal	D	0-0		12	13
14		23	(h)	Bradford C	W	2-1	Bradshaw, T.Browell	14	11
15		30	(a)	Manchester C	L	0-1		14	13
16	Dec	7	(h)	West Brom A	L	1-3	T.Browell	14	14
17		14	(h)	Sunderland	L	0-4		14	15
18		21	(a)	Sheffield W	W	2-1	Fleetwood, Wareing	16	14
19		25	(h)	Blackburn R	W	2-1	Beare, Uren	18	12
20		26	(a)	Blackburn R	W	2-1	Brannick, Simms	20	12
21		28	(h)	Middlesbrough	W	1-0	Maconnachie	21	11
22	Jan	1	(h)	Tottenham H	L	1-2	Bradshaw	22	12
23		4	(a)	Notts Co	W	1-0	Brannick	24	12
24		18	(h)	Manchester U	W	4-1	T.Browell 2, Jefferis, Wareing	26	10
25		25	(a)	Aston Villa	D	1-1	Beare	27	10
26	Feb	8	(h)	Liverpool	L	0-2		27	10
27		15	(a)	Bolton W	D	0-0		28	12
28	Mar	1	(a)	Newcastle U	L	0-2		28	13
29		12	(h)	Sheffield U	L	0-1		28	13
30		15	(a)	Chelsea	W	3-1	Beare, T.Browell, Jefferis	30	12
31		21	(h)	Derby C	D	2-2	Bradshaw 2	31	12
32		22	(h)	Woolwich Arsenal	W	3-0	Beare 2, Bradshaw	33	10
33		29	(a)	Bradford C	L	1-4	Jefferis	33	12
34	Apr	2	(h)	Oldham A	L	2-3	Bradshaw 2	33	12
35		5	(h)	Manchester C	D	0-0		34	12
36		9	(a)	Sunderland	L	1-3	Bradshaw	34	12
37		12	(a)	West Brom A	D	0-0		35	11
38		26	(h)	Sheffield W	W	3-1	Jefferis 2, Beare	37	11

League Appearances
League Goals

#	Month	Date		Opponent	Res	Score	Scorers		
39	Jan	15	(h)	Stockport C	W	5-1	T.Browell 3, Bradshaw, Wareing		FA Cup Rd 1
40	Feb	1	(a)	Brighton & H A	D	0-0			2
41		5	(h)	Brighton & H A	W	1-0	Jefferis		Replay
42		22	(a)	Bristol R	W	4-0	T.Browell, Fleetwood, Harris, Jefferis		3
43	Mar	8	(h)	Oldham A	L	0-1			4

FA Cup Appearances
FA Cup Goals

Beare G	Bradshaw F	Brannick J	Bromilow W	Browell A	Browell T	Caldwell J	Chedgzoy S	Davidson W	Fleetwood T	Gault W	Gourlay J	Grenyer A	Harris V	Hodge W	Holbem W	Houston J	Jefferis F	Maconnachie J	Makepeace H	Simms S	Simpson R	Smith J	Stevens T	Stevenson W	Uren H	Wareing W	
7	10				9	1			5				4				8	3	6					2	11		1
7	10				9	1			5				4				8	3	6					2	11		2
7	10				9	1			5				4				8	3	6					2	11		3
7	10				9	1			5	8			4					3	6					2	11		4
7	10				9	1			5	8			4					3	6					2	11		5
7	10				9	1			5				4				8	3	6					2	11		6
7	10				9	1		11	5	8			4					3	6					2			7
7	10				9	1		11	5	8		6	4					3						2			8
7	10				9	1		11	5			6	4				8	3						2			9
7	10				9	1		11	5	8			4					3						2		6	10
11	10				9	1			5	8			6					3		7				2		4	11
11	9					1			5		10		6				8	3		7				2		4	12
7	10				9	1			5				6				8	3						2	11	4	13
7	10				9	1			5				6				8	3						2	11	4	14
7				5	9	1					10		6				8	3						2	11	4	15
7	10				9	1			5				6				8	3						2	11	4	16
7	10					1			5	9			4				8	3	6					2	11		17
7	10					1			9				4				8	3	6					2	11	5	18
7	10					1			9			6	4				8	3						2	11	5	19
7	10	8				1						6	4					3	9					2	11	5	20
7	10					1			9			6	4				8	3						2	11	5	21
7	10					1		11	9			6	4				8	3						2		5	22
	10	8			9	1	7	11				6	4					3						2		5	23
7	10				9	1		11				6	4				8	3						2		5	24
7	10				9	1		11				6	4				8	3						2		5	25
7					10	1		11	5				4		2	9	8	3	6					2			26
7					9	1			4		10		6				8	3						2	11	5	27
11					10	1			9			6	4			7	8	3						2		5	28
11	10	8			9							4	6	5	1	3	7							2			29
7	9				10			11	5			4	6		1		8				3			2			30
7	9				10	1		11	5			6	4				8				3			2			31
7	9				10	1						6	4				8				3		11	2		5	32
7	9				10	1						6	4				8				3		11	2		5	33
7	10		1									6	4			9	8				3		11	2		5	34
7	10											4	6		1	9	8				3		11	2		5	35
7	10				9							6	4		1		8				3		11	2		5	36
7	10							11				6	4		1		8		9		3			2		5	37
7	10							11	9			6	4		1		8				3			2		5	38
37	34	3	1	1	26	31	1	13	28	8	6	26	28	6	7	7	27	23	10	2	10	2	5	36	16	24	
7	10				9	1		11				6	4				8	3						2		5	39
7	10				9	1		11				6	4				8	3						2		5	40
7					9	1		11			10		4				8	3	6					2		5	41
11					10	1			9			6	4			7	8	3						2		5	42
11	10				9	1						4	6	5		7	8	3						2			43
	3				5	5		3	2		1	4	5			2	5	5	1					5		4	
	1				4			1				1				2								1			

1913-14

1	Sep	1	(h)	Burnley	D	1-1	Browell	1	
2		6	(h)	Preston N E	W	2-0	Bradshaw, Jefferis	3	
3		13	(a)	Newcastle U	W	1-0	Palmer	5	4
4		20	(h)	Liverpool	L	1-2	Wareing	5	6
5		27	(a)	Aston Villa	l	1-3	Fleetwood	5	10
6	Oct	4	(h)	Middlesbrough	W	2-0	Browell, T.Page	7	7
7		11	(a)	Sheffield U	L	1-4	Houston	7	12
8		18	(h)	Derby C	W	5-0	Nuttall 2, Houston, T.Page, Wareing	9	8
9		25	(a)	Manchester C	D	1-1	Nuttall	10	8
10	Nov	1	(h)	Bradford C	D	1-1	Harrison	11	9
11		8	(a)	Blackburn R	L	0-6		11	11
12		15	(h)	Sunderland	L	1-5	Nuttall	11	15
13		22	(a)	Tottenham H	L	1-4	Johnston	11	16
14		29	(a)	West Brom A	D	1-1	Nuttall	12	16
15	Dec	6	(h)	Sheffield W	D	1-1	Parker	13	16
16		13	(a)	Bolton W	D	0-0		14	16
17		20	(h)	Chelsea	D	0-0		15	17
18		25	(a)	Manchester U	W	1-0	Parker	17	14
19		26	(h)	Manchester U	W	5-0	Parker 3, Nuttall 2	19	11
20		27	(a)	Preston N E	L	0-1		19	12
21	Jan	1	(a)	Oldham A	L	0-2		19	10
22		3	(h)	Newcastle U	W	2-0	Jefferis, Parker	21	12
23		17	(a)	Liverpool	W	2-1	Parker 2	23	11
24		24	(h)	Aston Villa	L	1-4	Clennell	23	12
25	Feb	7	(a)	Middlesbrough	L	0-2		23	15
26		14	(h)	Sheffield U	W	5-0	Clennell 2, Parker 2, Weller	25	12
27		21	(a)	Derby C	L	0-1		25	12
28		28	(h)	Manchester C	W	1-0	Parker	27	11
29	Mar	7	(a)	Bradford C	W	1-0	Jefferis	29	11
30		14	(h)	Blackburn R	D	0-0		30	10
31		21	(a)	Sunderland	L	2-5	Parker 2	30	10
32		28	(h)	Tottenham H	D	1-1	Chedgzoy	31	11
33	Apr	4	(h)	West Brom A	W	2-0	Clennell, Parker	33	9
34		10	(a)	Burnley	L	0-2		33	13
35		11	(a)	Sheffield W	D	2-2	Parker 2	34	13
36		13	(h)	Oldham A	L	0-2		34	13
37		18	(h)	Bolton W	D	1-1	Parker	35	13
38		25	(a)	Chelsea	L	0-1		35	15
								League Appearances	
								League Goals	
39	Jan	10	(a)	Glossop	L	1-2	Bradshaw	FA Cup Rd 1	
								FA Cup Appearances	
								FA Cup Goals	

Beare G	Bradshaw F	Browell T	Chedgzoy S	Clennell J	Fern T	Fleetwood T	Grenyer A	Harris V	Harrison G	Hodge W	Houston J	Jefferis F	Johnston L	Maconnachie J	Makepeace H	Mitchell F	Nuttall T	Page J	Page T	Palmer W	Parker R	Simpson R	Stevenson W	Thompson R	Wareing W	Weller L	
7	10	9					6	4				8		3		1				11				2	5		1
7	10	9					6	4				8		3		1				11				2	5		2
7	10					9	6	4				8		3		1				11				2	5		3
7	10	9										8		3		1								2	5		4
	10					9		4	11		7	8		3	6	1								2	5		5
8	10							4	11		7			3	6	1					9			2	5		6
	8							4	11		7		10	3	6	1					9			2	5		7
								4	11		7		10	3	6	1	8				9			2	5		8
								4	11		7		10	3	6	1	8				9			2	5		9
								4	11	1	7		10	3	6		8				9			2	5		10
						9	6	4	11	1	7		10	3			8							2	5		11
							6	4	11	1	7		10	3			8				9			2	5		12
						5	6	4	11		7		10	3		1	8	2	9								13
7	10					5		4	11	1		8		3	6						9			2			14
7	10				1	5		4	11			8		3	6						9			2			15
		7			1	5		4	11			8		3	6		10				9			2			16
7					1	5		4	11			8		3	6		10				9			2			17
7					1	5		4	11			8	10	3	6						9			2			18
7					1	5		4	11			8		3	6		10				9			2			19
7	4				1	5	6		11			8		3			10				9			2			20
					1	5	10	4	11		7	8			6						9	3		2			21
					1	5	10	4	11		7	8		3							9			2		6	22
	10				1	5		4	11			8		3	6					7	9			2			23
			10		1			4	11			8		3	6					7	9			2	5		24
			10		1	5	6		11		7	8		3							9			2		4	25
			10		1	5	6		11		7	8		3							9			2		4	26
			10		1	5	6		11		7	8		3							9			2		4	27
			10		1	5	6		11		7	8		3							9			2		4	28
			10		1	5	6		11		7	8		3							9			2		4	29
7			10		1	5			11		7	8		3							9			2		4	30
			10		1	5	6		11		7	8									9	3		2		4	31
		7	10		1	5	6		11			8									9	3		2		4	32
		7	10		1		6		11			8		3							9			2	5	4	33
	10	7			1		6		11			8		3							9			2	5	4	34
	10					5	6	4	11		7			3		1	8				9			2			35
	10	7				5			11					3	6	1	8				9			2		4	36
		7	10			5	6	4	11			8		3		1					9			2			37
		7	10		1	5	6	4	11					3			8				9			2			38
11	11	7	7	12	21	27	22	26	35	4	18	27	8	35	16	13	14	1	7	5	24	2	8	30	17	10	
1	2	1	4	1									1	2	3	1				7	2	1	17		2	1	
7	10				1	5		4	11			8		3	6						9			2			39
1	1				1	1		1	1			1		1	1						1			1			
		1																									

1914-15

1	Sep	2	(a)	Tottenham H	W	3-1	Clennell 3		2	
2		5	(a)	Newcastle U	W	1-0	Jefferis		4	
3		7	(a)	Burnley	L	0-1			4	3
4		12	(h)	Middlesbrough	L	2-3	Parker 2		4	8
5		19	(a)	Sheffield U	L	0-1			4	8
6		26	(h)	Aston Villa	D	0-0			5	11
7	Oct	3	(a)	Liverpool	W	5-0	Parker 3, Clennell 2		7	5
8		10	(h)	Bradford	W	4-1	Parker 2, Chedgzoy, Galt		9	4
9		17	(a)	Oldham A	D	1-1	Jefferis		10	4
10		24	(h)	Manchester U	W	4-2	Parker 2, Makepeace, Palmer		12	4
11		31	(a)	Bolton W	D	0-0			13	4
12	Nov	7	(h)	Blackburn R	L	1-3	Parker		13	7
13		14	(a)	Notts Co	D	0-0			14	8
14		21	(h)	Sunderland	W	7-1	Parker 3, Clennell 2, Harrison, Jefferis		16	5
15		28	(a)	Sheffield W	W	4-1	Parker 4		18	5
16	Dec	5	(h)	West Brom A	W	2-1	Clennell, Parker		20	4
17		12	(h)	Manchester C	W	4-1	Parker 3, Clennell		22	3
18		19	(a)	Chelsea	L	0-2			22	5
19		25	(h)	Bradford C	D	1-1	Jefferis		23	3
20		26	(a)	Bradford C	W	1-0	Chedgzoy		25	3
21	Jan	1	(h)	Tottenham H	D	1-1	Kirsopp		26	3
22		2	(h)	Newcastle U	W	3-0	Harrison, Kirsopp, Parker		28	2
23		16	(a)	Middlesbrough	L	1-5	Parker		28	3
24		23	(h)	Sheffield U	D	0-0			29	4
25	Feb	6	(h)	Liverpool	L	1-3	Clennell		29	4
26		10	(a)	Aston Villa	W	5-1	Parker 3, Galt, Kirsopp		31	4
27		27	(a)	Manchester U	W	2-1	Harrison, Parker		33	2
28	Mar	13	(a)	Blackburn R	L	1-2	Kirsopp		33	5
29		17	(h)	Oldham A	L	3-4	Parker 2, Kirsopp		33	5
30		20	(h)	Notts Co	W	4-0	Kirsopp 2, Clennell, Parker		35	5
31		24	(h)	Bolton W	W	5-3	Parker 3, Clennell 2		37	4
32	Apr	2	(a)	Burnley	L	0-2			37	5
33		3	(h)	Sheffield W	L	0-1			37	5
34		6	(a)	Sunderland	W	3-0	Parker 2, Kirsopp		39	4
35		10	(a)	West Brom A	W	2-1	Fleetwood, Harrison		41	4
36		14	(a)	Bradford	W	2-1	Grenyer, Kirsopp		43	2
37		17	(a)	Manchester C	W	1-0	Clennell		45	1
38		26	(h)	Chelsea	D	2-2	Fleetwood, Parker		46	1
								League Appearances		
								League Goals		
39	Jan	9	(h)	Barnsley	W	3-0	Galt 2, Parker		FA Cup Rd 1	
40		30	(h)	Bristol C	W	4-0	Clennell, Kirsopp, Parker, Wareing			2
41	Feb	20	(a)	Q.P.R	W	2-1	Clennell, opp.og	(Stamford Bridge)		3
42	Mar	6	(a)	Bradford C	W	2-0	Chedgzoy, Clennell			4
43		27	(n)	Chelsea	L	0-2		(Villa Park)	SF	
								FA Cup Appearances		
								FA Cup Goals		

	Brown W	Chedgzoy S	Clennell J	Fern T	Fleetwood T	Galt J	Grenyer A	Harrison G	Houston J	Howarth H	Jefferis F	Kirsopp W	Maconnachie J	Makepeace H	Mitchell F	Nuttall T	Palmer W	Parker R	Roberts J	Simpson R	Thompson R	Wareing W	Weller L	Wright W	
		7	10	1	4	5	6	11			8		3					9			2				1
		7	10	1	4	5	6	11			8		3					9			2				2
		7	10	1	4	5	6	11			8		3					9			2				3
		7	10	1	4	5	6						3			8	11	9			2				4
		7	10	1	4	5	6						3			8	11	9			2				5
		7	10	1	4	5					8		3	6			11	9			2				6
		7	10	1	4	5					8		3	6			11	9			2				7
		7	10	1	4	5					8		3	6			11	9			2				8
		7	10	1	4	5					8		3	6			11	9		2					9
		7	10	1	4	5					8		3	6			11	9		2					10
		7	10	1	4	5					8		3	6			11	9		2					11
		7	10	1	4	5					8		3	6			11	9		2					12
		7	10	1	4	5		11				8	3	6				9			2				13
		7	10	1	4	5		11				8	3	6				9			2				14
		7	10	1	4	5		11				8	3	6				9			2				15
		7	10	1	4	5		11				8	3	6				9			2				16
	4	7	10	1		5		11				8	3					9			2	6			17
		7	10	1	4	5		11				8	3	6				9			2				18
		7	10	1	4	5		11				8	3	6				9			2				19
		7	10	1	4	5		11				8	3	6				9			2				20
		7	10	1	4	5		11				8	3	6				9			2				21
	4		10	1		5		11	7			8	3	6				9			2				22
		7	10	1	4	5		11				8	3	6				9			2				23
		7	10	1	4	5	6					8					11		3		2			9	24
		7	10	1	4	5						8	3	6			11	9			2				25
		7	10	1	4	5						8	3	6			9	11			2				26
		7	10	1	4	5		11				8	3	6				9			2				27
		7	10	1	4			11				8	3	6				9			2	5			28
				1	4		6	11			8		3				7	9			2	5		10	29
	4		10					11			8			6	1		7	9			2	5	3		30
			10		4		6	11			8				1		7	9		3	2	5			31
		7	10	1	4	5	6	11			8							9		3	2				32
			10	1	4	5	6	11			8						7	9		3	2				33
			10	1	4		6	11			8						7	9			2	5	3		34
	4		10	1		9	6	11			8						7				2	5	3		35
		7		1	4	5	10	11			8							9			2	6	3		36
			10	1	4	5	6	11			8						7	9			2		3		37
		7	10	1	4	5	6	11			8							9			2		3		38
	4	30	36	36	35	32	14	26	1	1	18	16	28	23	2	5	17	35	1	9	33	8	6	2	
		2	14		2	2	1	4			4	9		1			1	36							
		7	10	1	4	5		11			8		3	6				9			2				39
		7	10	1	4						8			6			11	9		3	2	5			40
		7	10	1	4	5		11			8		3	6				9			2				41
		7	10	1	4	5		11			8		3	6				9			2				42
		7	10		4	5		11			8			6	1			9		3	2				43
		5	5	4	5	4		4			5		3	5	1		1	5		2	5	1			
		1	3			2								1				2			1				opp.og 1

1915-16

1	Sep	4	(h)	Bury	W	5-0	Clennell 2, Kirsopp 2, Grenyer	2	
2		11	(a)	Manchester U	W	4-2	Nuttall 2, Clennell, Kirsopp	4	
3		18	(h)	Blackpool	W	4-2	Chedgzoy 2, Clennell, Kirsopp	6	1
4		25	(a)	Southport	L	1-2	Clennell	6	2
5	Oct	2	(h)	Oldham A	L	2-3	Clennell, Jefferis	6	5
6		9	(a)	Rochdale	W	2-1	Jefferis, Kirsopp	8	5
7		16	(a)	Bolton W	W	4-3	Clennell 2, Grenyer, Kirsopp	10	3
8		23	(h)	Manchester C	W	4-2	Parker 3, Chedgzoy	12	1
9		30	(a)	Stoke C	L	2-3	Clennell 2	12	3
10	Nov	6	(h)	Burnley	L	1-2	Parker	12	4
11		13	(a)	Preston N E	W	2-0	Clennell 2	14	3
12		20	(h)	Stockport C	L	2-5	Clennell, Kirsopp	14	5
13		27	(a)	Liverpool	L	1-4	Clennell	14	7
14	Dec	4	(a)	Bury	W	3-0	Parker 2, Kirsopp	16	5
15		11	(h)	Manchester U	W	2-0	Clennell, Harrison	18	4
16		18	(a)	Blackpool	W	4-1	Clennell 2, Harrison, Wright	20	3
17		25	(h)	Southport	W	2-0	Clennell, Galt	22	3
18	Jan	8	(h)	Rochdale	W	3-2	Chedgzoy, Harrison, Parker	24	2
19		15	(h)	Bolton W	W	2-1	Chedgzoy, Clennell	26	3
20		22	(a)	Manchester C	L	1-2	Clennell	26	3
21		29	(h)	Stoke C	W	4-1	Kirsopp 2, Chedgzoy, Clennell	28	3
22	Feb	5	(a)	Burnley	L	1-2	Clennell	28	3
23		12	(h)	Preston N E	W	2-0	Clennell, Kirsopp	30	3
24		19	(a)	Stockport C	L	1-3	Clennell	30	3
25		26	(h)	Liverpool	L	0-1		30	4
								Appearances	
								Goals	
26	Mar	4	(a)	Manchester U	W	2-0	Kirsopp, Wareing	2	
27		11	(h)	Stockport C	W	2-0	Williamson 2	4	
28		18	(h)	Manchester C	D	1-1	Williamson	5	1
29		25	(a)	Oldham A	W	2-1	Clennell, Harrison	7	1
30	Apr	1	(h)	Liverpool	W	1-0	Clennell	9	1
31		8	(h)	Manchester U	W	3-1	Clennell 2, Rigsby	11	1
32		15	(a)	Stockport C	W	2-1	Clennell, Rigsby	13	1
33		21	(a)	Liverpool	L	2-5	Kirsopp 2	13	1
34		22	(a)	Manchester C	L	4-5	Clennell 2, Williamson, opp.og	13	1
35		29	(h)	Oldham A	L	0-2		13	2
								Appearances	
								Goals	

Matches 1 to 25 inclusive were played in the Lancashire Section Principal Tournament. In that competition, the postponed Oldham Athletic v Everton match was not subsequently played.
Matches 26 to 35 inclusive were played in the Lancashire Section Southern Division Supplementary Tournament.

Baines	Bromilow W	Brown W	Chedgzoy S	Clennell J	Donnachie J	Fern T	Fleetwood T	Galt J	Grenyer A	Harrison G	Howarth H	Jefferis F	Johnson	Kirsopp W	McNeal	Macconnachie J	Mitchell F	Nuttall T	Parker R	Rigsby H	Roberts J	Simpson R	Smith J	Snoddy	Stewart R	Thompson R	Wareing W	Williamson	Wright W	No.
			7	10	11	1	4		6					8		3	9									2	5			1
			7	10	11		4		6					8			1	9				3				2	5			2
		6	7	10	11		4		6					8			1	9				3				2	5			3
			7	10		1	4		6					8		3	9				11					2	5			4
			7	10		1	4		6			9		8		3	1				11					2	5			5
			7	10		1	4		6			9		8		3					11					2	5			6
			7	10		1	4		6		11	9		8		3										2	5			7
			7	10		1	4		6	11				8		3			9							2	5			8
	4		7	10		1			6	11		9		8											3	2	5			9
			7	10		1	4		6	11				8		3			9							2	5			10
			7	10		1	4		6	11		9		8		3										2	5			11
		6	7	10		1	4			11				8		3			9							2	5			12
			7	10		1	4		6	11				8		3			9							2	5			13
1		6	7	10			4			11				8		3			9							2	5			14
1		6	7	10			4			11				8		3										2	5	9		15
			7	10		1	4		6	11				8		3			9							2	5	9		16
			7	10		1	4	5		11				8					9			3				2	6			17
	5		7	10		1	4			11				8	6	3			9				2			2	6			18
	4		7	10		1	5			11				8					9			3				2	6			19
	4		7	10		1	5			11				8	6				9			3				2				20
1	4		7	10			5			11				8										0		2	6	9		21
	4		7	10		1	5		6	11				8		3										2		9		22
9	4		7	10		1			6	11				8		3										2	5			23
	4		7	10		1		9	6	11				8		3										2	5			24
	4		7				5	10		11				8	6		1					3				2		9		25
1	**3**	**13**	**25**	**24**	**3**	**18**	**23**	**1**	**18**	**16**	**1**	**12**		**19**	**3**	**16**	**4**	**5**	**7**		**3**	**6**	**2**	**2**	**1**	**23**	**22**	**4**		Totals (1–25)
			6	24					1	2	3			2					11							2	7	1		goals (1–25)
	4		7			1	5		6	11				8		3			10							2	9			26
1	4		7				5			11				8	6				10			3				2		9		27
	4		7	10		1	5			11				8	6							3				2		9		28
			7	10		1	5			11			4	8								3				2	6	9		29
	4		7	10		1	5							8						11	3					2	6	9		30
	4		7	10		1	5			11				8		3			9							2	6			31
	4		7	9		1	5			11				8		3			10							2	6			32
1	4			9			5			11		8				3			10							2	6	7		33
1	4			10					6	11		7		8	5						3					2		9		34
	4		7	10		1	5			11				8								3				2	6	9		35
3	**9**	**8**	**8**			**7**	**9**		**2**	**9**		**2**	**1**	**9**	**2**	**6**			**5**	**1**	**6**					**9**	**7**	**7**		Totals (26–35)
			7							1		3							2								1	4		opp.og 1 / goals (26–35)

1916-17

1	Sep	2	(a)	Bury	W	3-0	Clennell 3		2	
2		9	(h)	Stoke C	D	1-1	Clennell		3	
3		16	(a)	Southport	L	0-1			3	
4		23	(h)	Blackburn R	L	2-5	Harrison, Sheldon		3	
5		30	(a)	Manchester C	L	1-4	Clennell		3	14
6	Oct	7	(h)	Blackpool	W	3-1	Clennell 2, Kirsopp		5	9
7		14	(h)	Rochdale	W	3-0	Clennell, Harrison, Wareing		7	8
8		21	(a)	Bolton W	W	3-1	Harrison, Kirsopp, Morris		9	7
9		28	(h)	Port Vale	W	3-1	Harrison, Kirsopp, Morris		11	7
10	Nov	4	(a)	Oldham A	W	3-2	Kirsopp 2, Lloyd		13	6
11		11	(h)	Preston N E	W	3-1	Clennell 2, Harrison		15	5
12		18	(a)	Burnley	D	2-2	Clennell 2		16	3
13		25	(h)	Manchester U	W	3-2	Clennell 2, Kirsopp		18	3
14	Dec	2	(a)	Liverpool	L	1-2	Kirsopp		18	3
15		9	(h)	Stockport C	L	0-1			18	5
16		16	(h)	Bury	W	5-0	Blair 2, Clennell 2, Jefferis		20	5
17		23	(a)	Stoke C	W	2-0	Clennell 2		22	3
18		30	(h)	Southport	D	1-1	Clennell		23	3
19	Jan	6	(a)	Blackburn R	W	5-1	Clennell 3, Morris 2		25	3
20		13	(h)	Manchester C	L	0-2			25	4
21		20	(a)	Blackpool	D	1-1	Thompson		26	4
22		27	(a)	Rochdale	L	1-2	Thompson		26	6
23	Feb	3	(h)	Bolton W	W	1-0	Lovelady		28	4
24		10	(a)	Port Vale	D	1-1	Jefferis		29	5
25		17	(h)	Oldham A	W	2-0	Gouldson, Jefferis		31	4
26		24	(h)	Preston N E	D	2-2	Clennell, Cooper		32	4
27	Mar	3	(h)	Burnley	W	5-0	Clennell 2, Gault 2, Jefferis		34	4
28		10	(a)	Manchester U	W	2-0	Gault, Jefferis		36	4
29		17	(h)	Liverpool	D	2-2	Gault 2		37	4
30		24	(a)	Stockport C	L	1-5	Gault		37	5
									Appearances	
									Goals	
31	Mar	31	(h)	Southport	W	4-2	Gault 3, Jefferis		2	
32	Apr	7	(a)	Liverpool	W	4-0	Gault 2, Clennell, Donnachie		4	
33		9	(h)	Stockport	D	1-1	Clennell		5	3
34		14	(a)	Southport	W	1-0	Grenyer		7	2
35		21	(h)	Liverpool	W	5-0	Gault 3, Clennell 2		9	2
36		28	(a)	Stockport C	L	1-2	Gault		9	2
									Appearances	
									Goals	

Matches 1 to 30 inclusive were played in the Lancashire Section Principal Tournament.

Matches 31 to 36 inclusive were played in the Lancashire Section Subsidiary Tournament.

Blair J	Bradbury	Campney	Challinor	Chedgzoy S	Clennell J	Cooper	Donnachie J	Dunn	Fern T	Fleetwood T	Gault W	Gouldson	Grenyer A	Harrison G	Jefferis F	Kirsopp W	Lloyd	Maconnachie J	Merritt	Mitchell F	Morris	Murray	Peet	Simpson R	Smith J	Stewart R	Thompson R	Twiss J	Wareing W	Williams A	Match
9					10				1	4				6	11	8	7							3			2	5			1
	4	9			10				1	5				6	11	8	7							3			2				2
	4	9	5		10				1					6	11	8	7										2		3		3
	4				10				1	5					11	8	7										2		3		4
					8			2	1	6			4	7	10		11				9								3		5
					10					4			6	11		8	7			1	9					2		5	3		6
					10					4			6	11		8	7			1	9					2		5	3		7
					10					4			6	11		8	7			1	9					2		5	3		8
					10					4			6	11		8	7			1	9					2		5	3		9
					10					4			6	11		8	7			1	9					2		5	3		10
	6		4		10			3						11		8	7			1	9					2		5			11
					10		2			4			6	11		8	7			1	9							5	3		12
	4				10		2						6	11		8	7			1	9							5	3		13
9					10					4			6	11		8	7			1						2		5	3		14
					10					4			6	11		8	7	2		1	9							5	3		15
9					10					4			6	11		8	7			1						2		5	3		16
9	6				10					4				11		8	7			1						2		5	3		17
9				7	10					4			6		8			3		1		11				2		5			18
	8				10		11			4			6				7			1	9					2		5	3		19
9					10		11			4			6				7			1	8					2		5	3		20
	10								1	4			6		8		7				9	11				2		5	3		21
			7				11		1	4			6	10							9					2		5	3		22
							11			4			6	10				3	7	1	9					2		5			23
					8		11						6	10			7			1	9				4	2		5	3		24
					8				1	4		11	6	10			7				9					2		5	3		25
					10		8		1	4	9	11	6				7									2		5	3		26
					10		7	11		4	9		6			8				1						2		5	3		27
					10		7	11		4	9		6			8				1						2		5	3		28
				7	10		11			4	9		6			8		3		1						2		5			29
10							11			4	9		6			8	7			1						2		5	3		30
5	10	2	3	2	24	5	9	4	10	25	5	2	27	17	18	13	16	4	5	20	18			2	4	17	4	28	26		
2					25	1							6	1	5	5	7	1			4							2	1		
							11		1	4	9		8					3	7					2			10	5		6	31
					10		11			4	9		6	8						1	7					2		5	3		32
					10					4	9		6	8						1	11	7					3	5			33
					10		11		1	4	9		6	8					7							2		5	3		34
					10		11		1	4	9		6	8					7							2	10	5	3	4	35
							11				9		6	8						1	7					2	10	5	3	4	36
					4	5		3	5	6			5	6				1		3	1	6				4	1	5	2	6	2	
					4	1					9		1	1																	

Elliott played number 8 in Match 22; Hunter played number 5 in Match 5 & number 2 in Match 33; Lovelady played number 8 (and scored once) in Match 23; McNeal played number 6 in Match 4; Sheldon played number 9 (and scored once) in Match 4.

1917-18

No.	Date		Opponent		Result	Scorers	App	Goals
1	Sep	1	(h)	Southport	W 6-1	Clennell 3, Donnachie, Gault, Jefferis	2	
2		8	(a)	Southport	W 2-0	Clennell 2	4	
3		15	(h)	Burnley	W 9-0	Gault 4, Clennell 2, Fleetwood 2, Jefferis	6	1
4		22	(a)	Burnley	W 5-0	Clennell 3, Fleetwood, Jefferis	8	1
5		29	(h)	Liverpool	D 2-2	Clennell, Gault	9	2
6	Oct	6	(a)	Liverpool	L 0-6		9	4
7		13	(h)	Manchester U	W 3-0	Gault 2, Clennell	11	3
8		20	(a)	Manchester U	D 0-0		12	4
9		27	(a)	Stockport C	D 0-0		13	3
10	Nov	3	(h)	Stockport C	L 2-3	Clennell 2	13	4
11		10	(a)	Oldham A	W 3-1	Clennell 2, Jefferis	15	3
12		17	(h)	Oldham A	W 4-2	Clennell 3, Gault	17	3
13		24	(a)	Bury	W 5-2	Gault 4, Jefferis	19	3
14	Dec	1	(h)	Bury	W 7-1	Clennell 4, Wareing 2, Murray	21	3
15		8	(a)	Stoke C	L 0-3		21	3
16		15	(h)	Stoke C	W 3-2	Clennell 2, opp.og	23	3
17		22	(a)	Preston N E	W 1-0	Gault	25	3
18		29	(h)	Preston N E	W 6-0	Clennell 4, Wareing, Wright	27	3
19	Jan	5	(a)	Blackpool	L 0-1		27	4
20		12	(h)	Blackpool	W 7-2	Gault 4, Wright 2, Bain	29	4
21		19	(a)	Manchester C	W 2-0	Gault, Wright	31	3
22		26	(h)	Manchester C	D 0-0		32	3
23	Feb	2	(a)	Rochdale	D 2-2	Bain, Wright	33	3
24		9	(h)	Rochdale	D 2-2	Clennell, Wright	34	4
25		16	(a)	Blackburn R	W 6-0	Gault 3, Wareing 2, Clennell	36	3
26		23	(h)	Blackburn R	W 2-1	Gault, Wright	38	3
27	Mar	2	(a)	Port Vale	W 1-0	Gault	40	3
28		9	(h)	Port Vale	W 7-0	Clennell 4, Gault 2, Jefferis	42	3
29		16	(a)	Bolton W	W 3-2	Gault 2, Wareing	44	3
30		23	(h)	Bolton W	L 2-3	Gault 2	44	3
							Appearances Goals	
31	Jan	1	(a)	Liverpool	L 1-4	Gault	0	
32	Mar	29	(h)	Liverpool	W 3-2	Jefferis 2, Gault	2	
33		30	(h)	Stockport C	W 4-0	Gault 2, Howarth, Wadsworth	4	
34	Apr	6	(a)	Stockport C	W 1-0	Twiss	6	
35		13	(h)	Southport	W 6-1	Gault 3, Clennell 2, Jefferis	8	
36		20	(a)	Southport	W 4-0	Clennell, Gault, Jefferis, Wareing	10	2
							Appearances Goals	

Matches 1 to 30 inclusive were played in the Lancashire Section Principal Tournament.

Matches 31 to 36 inclusive were played in the Lancashire Section Subsidiary Tournament.

Bain G	Bull H	Burgess W	Clennell J	Collins J	Cordall S	Cotter E	Donnachie J	Fern T	Fleetwood T	Gault T	Grenyer A	Guttridge	Jefferis F	Kirsopp W	Mitchell F	Murphy J	Murray S	Redford C	Riley J	Robinson W	Scott	Smith J	South J	Stewart R	Thompson R	Twiss J	Wadsworth	Wareing W	Williams A	Wright W	
		10							11	4	9	6	8		1		7			2					3			5			1
		10							11		9	6	8		1		7			2					3			5	4		2
		10							11	4	9	6	8	7	1					3					2			5			3
		10							11	4	9	6	8		1		7			3					2			5			4
		10							11	4	9	6	8	7	1					3					2			5			5
		10							11	5	9	6	8		1					3					2				4		6
		10				5			11	4	9	6	8		1		7			3				2							7
		10				5			11	4	9	6	8		1		7			3								2			8
		10							11	4	9	6	8		1			7		3		2						5			9
		10								4	9	6	8		1	11		7		3					2			5			10
		10				5			11		9	2	0		1		7			4					3			6			11
		10				6			11	4	9	2	8		1		7								3			5			12
		10							11	4	9	6	8		1					3				7	2			5			13
		10							11	4	9	6	8		1		7			3					2			5			14
		10							11	4	9	6	8		1		7			3					2			5			15
		10							11		9	6	8		1		7			3				3				5			16
		10							11		9	6	4		1				2	3						7		5			17
	2	10							11		8	6	4		1		7			3								5	9		18
	2	10						4	11		8	6			1					3						7		5	9		19
7								4	11		9	6	8		1				2	3								5	10		20
		7						4	11		9	6	8		1					3				2				5	10		21
		7						4	11		9	6	8		1					3				2				5	10		22
7		10						4	11	5		6	8		1				2	3									9		23
7		10							11	4		6	8		1					3								5	9		24
7		10								4	9	6	8		1				2	3								5	11		25
	11		2							4	9	6	8		1		7			3								5	10		26
			2						11	4	9	6	8		1					3								5	10		27
		10	2					7	11	4	9	6	8		1					3								5			28
		10	2						11	4	9	6	8		1					3						7		5			29
								8	11	4	9	6	10		1					3						7		5			30
4	2	1	26	4	4	7	27	22	28	28	2	29	2	30	1	13	2	4	28		4	1	2	12	2	2	27	2	10	
2		35				1	3	30				6				1												6	7		
	2		10				11	1		8	6				7					3							5	9			31
	11	10	2			4				5	9	6	8		1					3							7				32
		7	2					4	9	6					1					3						8	11	5			33
			2			4	11	5	9	6		8			1					3						10	7				34
	11	10	2			4				5	9	6	8		1					3							7				35
		10	2					11		4	9	6	8		1					3						7	5				36
1	3	4	5			3	3	1	5	6	6	4	5	1		3	3		2	5	3	1									
		3						8				4																1	1	1		

Challinor played number 4 in Match 31; Cooper played number 7 in Match 27; Howarth played number 10 (and scored once) in Match 33; Lovelady played number 8 in Match 17; J.Maconnachie played number 2 in Match 16; Newton played number 2 in Match 24.

One opp.og is included in the total for Lancashire Section Principal Tournament.

1918-19

1	Sep	7	(a)	Burnley	W	6-0	Clennell 4, Donnachie, Gault	2	
2		14	(h)	Burnley	W	6-1	Gault 2, Jefferis 2, Fleetwood, Miller	4	
3		21	(a)	Southport	W	3-0	Gault 2, Donnachie	6	1
4		28	(h)	Southport	W	4-0	Clennell 3, Harrison	8	1
5	Oct	5	(a)	Liverpool	W	4-2	Grenyer 2, Gault, Miller	10	1
6		12	(h)	Liverpool	W	4-2	Clennell, Donnachie, Miller, opp.og	12	1
7		19	(a)	Manchester U	D	1-1	Gault	13	1
8		26	(h)	Manchester U	W	6-2	Gault 3, Clennell, Jefferis, Miller	15	1
9	Nov	2	(h)	Stoke C	W	5-1	Gault 3, Donnachie, Miller	17	1
10		9	(a)	Stoke C	W	2-0	Gault, Wareing	19	1
11		16	(h)	Bury	W	5-1	Gault 3, Clennell, Miller	21	1
12		23	(a)	Bury	W	3-0	Clennell, Gault, Jefferis	23	1
13		30	(h)	Blackpool	W	6-0	Clennell 4, Fleetwood, Grenyer	25	1
14	Dec	7	(a)	Blackpool	W	3-1	Clennell 2, Gault	27	1
15		14	(h)	Stockport C	W	2-1	Clennell, Jefferis	29	1
16		21	(a)	Stockport C	D	0-0		30	1
17		28	(a)	Blackburn R	W	4-1	Blair 2, Clennell, Grenyer	32	1
18	Jan	4	(h)	Blackburn R	W	9-0	Gault 5, Clennell 2, Miller, Wareing	34	1
19		11	(a)	Oldham A	W	3-0	Gault 2, Donnachie	36	1
20		18	(h)	Oldham A	W	3-1	Clennell 2, Gault	38	1
21		25	(a)	Manchester C	L	0-1		38	1
22	Feb	1	(h)	Manchester C	W	3-0	Clennell, Gault, Grenyer	40	1
23		8	(a)	Port Vale	W	1-0	Gault	42	1
24		15	(h)	Port Vale	W	3-1	Clennell 2, Gault	44	1
25		22	(h)	Bolton W	W	4-1	Gault 3, Donnachie	46	1
26	Mar	1	(a)	Bolton W	W	6-3	Gault 3, Donnachie, Grenyer, Jefferis	48	1
27		8	(h)	Preston N E	W	3-2	Clennell, Gault, Jefferis	50	1
28		15	(a)	Preston N E	W	3-2	Clennell, Gault, Kirsopp	52	1
29		22	(h)	Rochdale	W	3-1	Rigsby 3	54	1
30		29	(a)	Rochdale	W	3-1	Clennell 2, Kirsopp	56	1
31	May	10	(a)	Nottingham F	D	0-0			
32		17	(h)	Nottingham F	L	0-1			
								Appearances Goals	
33	Jan	1	(h)	Liverpool	L	1-2	Jefferis	0	
34	Apr	5	(a)	Stockport C	W	1-0	Gault	2	
35		12	(h)	Stockport C	L	0-1		2	2
36		18	(a)	Liverpool	D	1-1	Gault	3	3
37		19	(a)	Southport	L	1-4	Rigsby	3	3
38		23	(h)	Southport	L	1-2	Rigsby	3	4
								Appearances Goals	

Matches 1 to 30 inclusive were played in the Lancashire Section Principal Tournament

Matches 31 and 32 were the Championship Decider against the winners of the Midland Section Principal Tournament

Matches 33 to 38 inclusive were played Lancashire Section Subsidiary Tournament

Baker	Blair J	Carlisle	Chedgzoy S	Clennell J	Cotter J	Dagnell	Donnachie J	Evans J	Fern T	Fleetwood T	Gault W	Grenyer A	Harrison G	Howarth H	Jefferis F	Kirsopp W	Maconnachie J	Miller J	Mitchell F	Page J	Peacock J	Pearson	Quinn	Rigsby H	Robinson W	Smith J	Space	Thompson R	Wareing W	Williams A	#
			7	10			11				4	9	6		8				1						2			3	5		1
				10			11				4	9	6		8			7	1						2			3	5		2
				10	5		11				4	9	6		8			7	1						2			3			3
				10			7				4	9	6	11	8				1						2			3	5		4
				10			11				4	9	6		8			7	1						2			3	5		5
				10			11				4	9	6		8			7	1						3	2			5		6
				10	5		11				4	9	6		8			7	1						2			3			7
				10			11				4	9	6		8			7	1						2			3	5		8
				10	6		11				4	9			8			7	1						3	2			5		9
				10			11				4	9	6		8			7	1	3					2				5		10
				10			11				4	9	6		8			7	1						3	2			5		11
				10			11				4	9	6		8			7	1						3	2			5		12
				10	4		11					9	6		8			7	1						3	2			5		13
				10			11				4	9	6		8			7	1						3	2			5		14
				10			11				4	9	6		8			7	1						3	2			5		15
				10			11				4	9	6		8			7	1						3	2			5		16
			9	10			11				4		6		8		8	7	1						3	2			5		17
				10			11				4	9	6		8			7	1	3					2				5		18
				10			11				4	9	6		8			7	1						3	2			5		19
				10			11				4	9	6		8			7	1						3			2	5		20
							11				4	9	6		8			7	1						3	2			5	10	21
				10			11				4	9	6		8	7			1						3	2			5		22
				10			11				4	9	6		8	7			1						3	2			5		23
				10			11				4	9	6		8	7			1						3	2			5		24
								11				9	4		8	7			1					10	3	2			5	6	25
				10			11				4	9	6		8	7			1						3	2			5		26
				10			11				4	9	6		8	7			1						3	2			5		27
				10							4	9	6		8	11		7	1						3	2			5		28
				10							4		6		8	11		7	1					9	3	2			5		29
				10							4	9	6		8	11		7	1	2					3				5		30
				10							4	9	6	11	8			7	1						3	2			5		31
				10							4	9	6		8			7	1				11		3	2			5		32
	1		1	30	4		26	1			31	29	30	2	31	10	1	24	32	3			1	2	30	22		8	31	2	
	2			30			7					9	38	6	1			7	2		7							3		2	
			9	10			11				4	9			8	7			1						3	2			5	6	33
							11					9			8	7			1	2	4			10	3				5	6	34
			9	10									6	11	8			7	1		4				3	2			5		35
				10			11		1			9	6		8			7		2	4				3				5		36
10		5					11								8			7	1		4			9	3	2				6	37
			7	10			11						6		8				1	2					3	9		4	5		38
1	1	2	4	1	1		2	1	1		3	3	2	1	5	1	4	5	3	4	2		3	4	1	1		2	5	3	
												2					1								2						

One opp.og is included in the total for Lancashire Section Principal Tournament

1919-20

1	Aug	30	(h)	Chelsea	L	2-3	Grenyer, Mayson	0	
2	Sep	3	(a)	Bradford	W	2-0	Gault, Rigsby	2	
3		6	(a)	Chelsea	W	1-0	Gault	4	6
4		8	(h)	Bradford	W	2-0	Gault, Miller	6	3
5		13	(a)	West Brom A	L	3-4	Gault, Jefferis, Maconnachie	6	6
6		20	(h)	West Brom A	L	2-5	Gault, Kirsopp	6	13
7		27	(a)	Sunderland	W	3-2	Clennell, Grenyer, Kirsopp	8	10
8	Oct	4	(h)	Sunderland	L	1-3	Maconnachie	8	15
9		11	(h)	Arsenal	L	2-3	Chedgzoy, Gault	8	15
10		18	(a)	Arsenal	D	1-1	Gault	9	17
11		25	(h)	Blackburn R	W	3-0	Clennell, Gault, Kirsopp	11	11
12	Nov	1	(a)	Blackburn R	L	2-3	Clennell 2	11	14
13		8	(h)	Bradford C	W	4-1	Clennell 3, Kirsopp	13	11
14		15	(a)	Bradford C	D	3-3	Clennell 2, Jones	14	12
15		22	(h)	Bolton W	D	3-3	Kirsopp 2, Clennell	15	13
16		29	(a)	Bolton W	W	2-0	Clennell, Gault	17	8
17	Dec	6	(h)	Notts Co	L	1-2	Gault	17	12
18		13	(a)	Notts Co	D	1-1	Chedgzoy	18	9
19		20	(h)	Liverpool	D	0-0		19	10
20		25	(a)	Manchester C	D	1-1	Clennell	20	11
21		26	(h)	Manchester C	W	2-0	Fleetwood, Gault	22	8
22		27	(a)	Liverpool	L	1-3	Parker	22	10
23	Jan	3	(h)	Sheffield W	D	1-1	Chedgzoy	23	13
24		17	(a)	Sheffield W	L	0-1		23	15
25		24	(h)	Newcastle U	W	4-0	Parker 2, Grenyer, Rigsby	25	10
26	Feb	7	(h)	Aston Villa	D	1-1	Parker	26	13
27		11	(a)	Newcastle U	L	0-3		26	14
28		14	(a)	Aston Villa	D	2-2	Gault, Rigsby	27	13
29		18	(h)	Oldham A	L	0-2		27	14
30		28	(a)	Oldham A	L	1-4	Kearslake	27	16
31	Mar	6	(a)	Manchester U	L	0-1		27	17
32		13	(h)	Manchester U	D	0-0		28	16
33		20	(a)	Sheffield U	D	1-1	Kirsopp	29	17
34		27	(h)	Sheffield U	W	3-0	Howarth, Kirsopp, Peacock	31	16
35	Apr	2	(h)	Derby C	W	4-0	Blair 2, Howarth, Kirsopp	33	12
36		3	(a)	Middlesbrough	D	1-1	Kirsopp	34	13
37		5	(a)	Derby C	L	1-2	Grenyer	34	17
38		10	(h)	Middlesbrough	W	5-2	Rigsby 2, Grenyer, Kirsopp, Peacock	36	15
39		17	(a)	Burnley	L	0-5		36	16
40		24	(h)	Burnley	D	2-2	Kirsopp 2	37	15
41		26	(a)	Preston N E	D	1-1	Kirsopp	38	15
42	May	1	(h)	Preston N E	L	0-1		38	16

League Appearances
League Goals

43	Jan	10	(a)	Birmingham	L	0-2		FA Cup Rd 1

FA Cup Appearances
FA Cup Goals

Blair J	Brewster G	Brown W	Chedgzoy S	Clennell J	Donnachie J	Downs R	Evans W	Fern T	Fleetwood T	Gault W	Grenyer A	Harrison G	Howarth H	Jefferis F	Jones G	Kearslake J	Kirsopp W	Leivesley W	Maconnachie J	Miller J	Mitchell F	Page J	Parker R	Peacock J	Rigsby H	Robinson W	Thompson R	Wall A	Wareing W	Weller L	#
				11					4	9	6			8						7	1					3	2		5		1
				11					4	9	6			8						7	1				10	3	2		5		2
		7							4	9	6	11					8		3		1				10		2		5		3
				11					4	9	6			8					3	7	1				10		2		5		4
				11					4	9	6			8					3	7	1				10		2		5		5
			10	11					4	9	6			8						7	1					3	2		5		6
			10	11				1	4	9	6			8					3	7							2		5		7
			10						4	9	6			8			11		2	7	1								5	3	8
		7	10					1	4	9		11		8					2										5	3	9
		7	10					1	4	9	6	11		8					2										5	3	10
			10	11				1	4	9	6			8					2	7									5	3	11
		7	10					1	4	9	6	11		8					2										5	3	12
			4		10	11		1	5					8	7		9		2							6				3	13
			4		10	11		1	5					8	7		9		2							6				3	14
			4		10	11			5					8	7		9				1					6				3	15
			4		10	11		1	5	9	6				7		8		2											3	16
			10	11				1	4	9	6				7		8		2										5	3	17
			4	8	10			1	5	9	6	11			7				2											3	18
			4	8	10			1	5		6	11			7		9		2											3	19
			4	7	10	11		1	5	9	6						8		2											3	20
			4	10				1	5	9		11		8	7				2							6				3	21
			4	7	11			1			6			8										9	10		2		5	3	22
	5		4	7	11			1	10					8			9									6	2		5	3	23
	5	7	10	11				1	2														4	9		6				3	24
	5		4	7	3			1	2		6	11		8										9	10						25
	5		4	7				1	2		6	11		8										9	10					3	26
	5		4	7				1	2		6	11		8										9	10					3	27
			4	7	8			1	5	9	6	11													10					3	28
			4	7				1	5	9	6	11													10		2		8	3	29
			4		3			1	5		6	11		7			9								10		2		8		30
			4	7	2			1	5		6	11							3					9	10				8		31
		7			2			1	5	8		11							3				4	9	10						32
					2			1	5		6	11	10	7			8		3				4	9							33
					2			1			6	11	10	7			8	5	3				4	9							34
9					2			1			6	11	10	7			8	5	3				4								35
					2			1	5		6	11	10	7			8						4	9			3				36
9					2			1			6	11	10	7			8	5	3				4								37
					2			1	4		6	11		7			8	5	3					9	10						38
			4		2			1	5		6	11	10	7			8							9			3				39
		4	7		2			1	5			11		8										9	10		3		6		40
3	5	20	18	18	16	12	2	34	37	21	33	25	7	12	18	1	29	5	16	8	8	8	8	9	14	7	17	3	15	28	41
2				3	12			1	12	5			2	1	1	1	14		2	1			4	2	5						42
		4	7	10				1	5	9	6	11		8					2										3		43
	1	1	1					1	1	1	1	1		1									1							1.	

W.Berwick played number 2 in Match 15;   T.Mayson played number 10 in Match 1(and scored once)
A.Robinson played number 8 in Match 24;   O.Williams played number 6 in Matches 9 and 32

1920-21

1	Aug	28	(a)	Bradford	D	3-3	Parker 2, Kirsopp		1	
2	Sep	1	(h)	Newcastle U	W	3-1	Kirsopp 2, Crossley		3	
3		4	(h)	Bradford	D	1-1	Harrison		4	8
4		8	(a)	Newcastle U	L	0-2			4	11
5		11	(a)	Derby C	W	4-2	Peacock 3, Fleetwood		6	7
6		18	(h)	Derby C	W	3-1	Chedgzoy, Harrison, Kirsopp		8	5
7		22	(h)	Sheffield U	W	3-0	Crossley, Grenyer, Harrison		10	3
8		25	(a)	Blackburn R	D	0-0			11	4
9	Oct	2	(h)	Blackburn R	W	2-1	Chedgzoy 2		13	1
10		4	(a)	Sheffield U	L	0-2			13	2
11		9	(a)	Huddersfield T	W	1-0	Kirsopp		15	2
12		16	(h)	Huddersfield T	D	0-0			16	1
13		23	(a)	Liverpool	L	0-1			16	4
14		30	(h)	Liverpool	L	0-3			16	5
15	Nov	6	(a)	Bradford C	D	2-2	Crossley 2		17	5
16		13	(h)	Bradford C	D	2-2	Crossley, Reid		18	6
17		20	(h)	Sunderland	D	1-1	Parker		19	6
18		27	(a)	Sunderland	W	2-0	Fazackerley, Harrison		21	5
19	Dec	4	(a)	Middlesbrough	L	1-3	Crossley		21	8
20		11	(h)	Middlesbrough	W	2-1	Parker 2		23	5
21		18	(a)	West Brom A	W	2-1	Fazackerley, Parker		25	3
22		25	(h)	Arsenal	L	2-4	Parker 2		25	5
23		27	(a)	Arsenal	D	1-1	Fazackerley		26	8
24	Jan	1	(h)	West Brom A	D	2-2	Fazackerley, Parker		27	7
25		15	(a)	Aston Villa	W	3-1	Harrison 2, Crossley		29	5
26		22	(h)	Aston Villa	D	1-1	Harrison		30	5
27	Feb	5	(h)	Manchester C	W	3-0	Crossley 2, Davies		32	3
28		12	(a)	Manchester U	W	2-1	Parker 2		34	5
29		23	(h)	Manchester C	L	0-2			34	5
30		26	(a)	Chelsea	W	1-0	Crossley		36	4
31	Mar	9	(h)	Manchester U	W	2-0	Crossley, Davies		38	4
32		12	(a)	Tottenham H	L	0-2			38	5
33		25	(a)	Bolton W	L	2-4	Crossley, Davies		38	6
34		26	(h)	Oldham A	W	5-2	Crossley 2, Chedgzoy, Davies, Reid		40	6
35		28	(h)	Bolton W	L	2-3	Crossley, Reid		40	6
36	Apr	2	(a)	Oldham A	W	1-0	Reid		42	6
37		6	(h)	Chelsea	W	5-1	Fazackerley 3, Harrison, Reid		44	6
38		9	(h)	Preston N E	L	0-1			44	6
39		16	(a)	Preston N E	L	0-1			44	6
40		23	(h)	Burnley	D	1-1	Fazackerley		45	6
41		27	(h)	Tottenham H	D	0-0			46	6
42		30	(a)	Burnley	D	1-1	Chedgzoy		47	7
								League Appearances		
								League Goals		
43	Jan	1	(h)	Stockport C	W	1-0	opp.og.		FA Cup Rd 1	
44		29	(h)	Sheffield W	D	1-1	Parker		Rd 2	
45	Feb	3	(a)	Sheffield W	W	1-0	Crossley		Replay	
46		19	(h)	Newcastle U	W	3-0	Crossley 2, Davies		Rd 3	
47	Mar	5	(h)	Wolves	L	0-1			Rd 4	
								FA Cup Appearances		
								FA Cup Goals		

Baker B	Blair J	Brewster G	Brown W	Chedgzoy S	Clennell J	Crossley C	Davies S	Downs R	Fazackerley S	Fern T	Fleetwood T	Grenyer A	Harrison G	Jones G	Kirsopp W	Moffatt A	McDonald J	Parker R	Peacock J	Reid D	Thompson R	Wall A	Weller L	No.
		5	7		10		2		8	1		6				3		9	11				4	1
		5	7		10		2		8	1	4	6		11		3		9						2
		5	7		10		2		8	1	4	6		11		3		9						3
		5	7		10		2		8	1	4	6		11		3		9						4
		5	7		10		2		8	1	4	6		11		3			9					5
		5	7		10		2		8	1	4	6		11		3			9					6
		5	7		10		2		8	1	4	6		11		3			9					7
		5	7		10		2			1	4	6		11		3		9	8					8
		5	7		10		2		8	1	4	6		11		3		9						9
		5	7		10		2		8	1	4	6		11		3		9						10
	5		7				2		8	1	4	6		11		3		9	10					11
	5						2		8	1	4	6	7	11		3		9	10					12
	5								8	1	4	6	7	11		3		9	10		2			13
	5		7				2		8	1	4	6		11		3		9	10					14
			7				2		8	1	5	6		11		3	4	9	10					15
			7				2	9	8	1	5	6		11		3	4		10					16
			7				2		8	1	5	6		11		3	4	9	10					17
			7		10		2		8	1	5	6		11			4	9		3				18
			7		10		2		8	1	5	6		11		3	4	9						19
	5		7		10		2		8	1	4	6		11		3		9						20
	5		7		10		2		8	1	4	6		11		3		9						21
	5		7		10		2		8	1	4	6		11		3		9						22
	5		7		10		2		8	1	4			11		3		9	6					23
	5		7		10		2		8	1	4			11		3		9	6					24
	5		7		10		2		8	1	4			11		3		9	6					25
	5		7		10		2		8	1	4			11		3		9					6	26
	4		7		10		2	9		1	5			11		3						8	6	27
	4		7		10		2		8	1	5			11		3		9					6	28
	5				10		2	9	8	1	4		7			3			11				6	29
1	5		7		10		2	9	8		4					3			11				6	30
	5				10		2	9	8	1	4	6	7	11		3								31
1	5				10	8	2				4		7	11		3		9					6	32
	4		7		10		2	9	8	1	5			11		3							6	33
	5		7		10		2	9		1	4			11		3	8		6					34
	5		7		10		2	9		1	4			11		3	8		6					35
	5		7		10		2			1	4			11	9	3	8		6					36
	4						2	9		1	5		7	11		3	8		6					37
	4						2	9		1	5		7	11		3	8		6		10			38
	4		7		10		2	9		1	5			11		3	8		6					39
	4		7		10		2	9		1	5			11		3	8		6					40
	4		7		10		2	9		1	5			11		3	8		6					41
	5	4	7		10		2	9		1				11		3	8		6					42
2	29	10	35	1	35	10	40	20	40	39	23	38	7	13	1	39	17	28	21	3	2	9		Tot
		5			15	4			8		1	1		8			5		11	3		5		Gls
	5		7		10		2		8	1				11		3		9	6				4	43
			7		10		2		8	1	5	6		11		3	4	9						44
9	5		7		10		2		8	1	4			11		3							6	45
	5		7		10	9	2		8	1	4			11		3							6	46
	5		7		10	9	2		8	1	4			11		3							6	47
1	4		5		5	2	5	5	5	4	1	5		5				5	2	2			4	
			3	1													1							

1 opp.og.

1921-22

1	Aug 27	(h)	Manchester U	W	5-0	Davies 3, Brewster, Fazackerley		2	
2	31	(a)	Newcastle U	L	0-3			2	
3	Sep 3	(a)	Manchester U	L	1-2	Harrison		2	15
4	7	(h)	Newcastle U	L	2-3	Blair, Davies		2	18
5	10	(h)	Birmingham	W	2-1	Fazackerley, Reid		4	13
6	17	(a)	Birmingham	D	1-1	Spencer		5	14
7	24	(h)	Arsenal	D	1-1	Fazackerley		6	15
8	Oct 1	(a)	Arsenal	L	0-1			6	17
9	8	(h)	Blackburn R	W	2-0	Davies, Reid		8	14
10	15	(a)	Blackburn R	D	2-2	Fazackerley, Harrison		9	13
11	22	(h)	Oldham A	D	2-2	Fazackerley 2		10	13
12	29	(a)	Oldham A	D	0-0			11	11
13	Nov 5	(h)	Liverpool	D	1-1	Brewster		12	12
14	12	(a)	Liverpool	D	1-1	Chedgzoy		13	14
15	19	(a)	Cardiff C	L	1-2	Fazackerley		13	16
16	26	(h)	Cardiff C	L	0-1			13	16
17	Dec 3	(h)	West Brom A	L	1-2	Peacock		13	19
18	10	(a)	West Brom	D	1-1	Crossley		14	19
19	17	(a)	Manchester C	L	1-2	Fazackerley		14	20
20	24	(h)	Manchester C	D	2-2	Fazackerley, Irvine		15	20
21	26	(a)	Sunderland	W	2-1	Chedgzoy, Wall		17	20
22	31	(h)	Bolton W	W	1-0	Fazackerley		19	18
23	Jan 2	(h)	Sunderland	W	3-0	Fazackerley, Irvine, Wall		21	15
24	14	(a)	Bolton W	L	0-1			21	15
25	21	(h)	Aston Villa	W	3-2	Irvine 3		23	15
26	Feb 8	(a)	Aston Villa	L	1-2	Irvine		23	15
27	11	(a)	Middlesbrough	L	1-3	Crossley		23	18
28	25	(a)	Tottenham H	L	0-2			23	19
29	Mar 1	(h)	Middlesbrough	W	4-1	Crossley, Fleetwood, Irvine, Spencer		25	17
30	4	(h)	Bradford C	W	2-0	Chadwick 2		27	16
31	11	(a)	Bradford C	L	1-3	Chadwick		27	17
32	15	(h)	Tottenham H	D	0-0			28	15
33	18	(a)	Preston N E	L	0-1			28	17
34	Apr 1	(a)	Chelsea	L	0-1			28	18
35	8	(h)	Chelsea	L	2-3	Reid 2		28	20
36	10	(h)	Preston N E	D	0-0			29	20
37	14	(h)	Huddersfield T	W	6-2	Chedgzoy 3, Irvine 3		31	20
38	15	(a)	Sheffield U	L	0-1			31	20
39	18	(a)	Huddersfield T	W	2-1	Grenyer, Irvine		33	19
40	22	(h)	Sheffield U	D	1-1	Brewster		34	19
41	29	(a)	Burnley	L	0-2			34	20
42	May 6	(h)	Burnley	W	2-0	Fazackerley, Wall		36	20
							League Appearances		
							League Goals		
43	Jan 7	(h)	Crystal Palace	L	0-6		FA Cup Rd 1		
							FA Cup Appearances		
							FA Cup Goals		

Alford F	Blair J	Brewster G	Brown W	Chadwick W	Chedgzoy S	Clennell J	Crossley C	Davies S	Downs R	Fazackerley S	Fern T	Fleetwood T	Grenyer A	Harrison G	Hart H	Irvine R	Jones G	Livingstone D	McDonald J	Peacock J	Reid D	Salt E	Spencer H	Wall A	Weller L	No.
		5	4		7		10	9	2	8	1			11					3	6						1
		5	4		7		10	9	2	8	1			11					3	6						2
			4		7	10		9		8	1	5		11				2	3	6						3
	9				7		10				1	5		11				2	3	6			8		4	4
		5			7			9			1	5	6	11				2	3	4	10		8			5
		5			7			9			1	4	6	11				2	3		10		8			6
		5			7			9	2		1	4	6	11					3		10		8			7
		5			7			9	2	8	1	4	6	11			7		3		10					8
		5			7			9	2	8	1	4		11					3	6	10					9
		5			7			9	2	8	1	4		11					3	6	10					10
11		5						9	2	8	1	4					7		3	6	10					11
		5			7		10	9	2	8	1	4	6	11					3							12
		5			7		10	9	2	8	1	4	6	11					3							13
		5			7		10		2	8	1	4		11				9	3	6						14
		5			7		10		2	8	1	4		11				9	3	6						15
		5			7			9	2		1	4	6	11					3		10		8			16
		5	4				9		2	8	1			11			7		3	6	10					17
		5	4		7		10		2	8	1			11				9	3	6						18
		5	4		7		10		2	8	1			11				9	3	6						19
		5	4		7					8	1			11		9		2	3	6				10		20
			4		7					8	1	5		11		9		2	3	6				10		21
			4		7					8	1	5		11		9		2	3	6				10		22
			4		7					8		5		11		9		2	3	6		1		10		23
					7					8		5		11	6	9		2	3	4		1		10		24
					7		10		2	8		5		11	6	9			3	4		1				25
					7		10		2	8	1	5		11	6	9			3	4						26
		5	4				10		2	8				11	6	9	7		3			1				27
					7		10		2	8	1	5		11	6	9			3	4						28
							10		2		1	5		11	6	9	7		3	4			8			29
				9			10		2		1	5		11	6		7		3	4			8			30
				9			10				1	5		11	6		7	2	3	4			8			31
				9	7		10				1	5		11	6			2		4			8		3	32
			4	9			10				1	5		11	6		7	2					8		3	33
	9		4		7				2		1	5		11		8				6				10	3	34
			4		7				2		1	5	6	11		9			3		10		8			35
		5	4		7						1	2	6	11	10	9			3		8					36
		5			7						1	2	6	11	4	9			3		8			10		37
		5	8		7				2		1		6	11	4	9			3					10		38
		5			7				2	8	1	4	10	11	6	9			3							39
		5			7				2		1		6	11	4	9			3		8			10		40
11		5			7				2		1	4		6		9					8			10	3	41
		5			7				2	8	1	4		11	6	9			3					10		42
2	2	25	16	4	35	1	15	10	28	29	38	33	13	40	17	25	8	24	26	29	16	4	9	8	5	
1	3				3	5		3	5		12		1	2	11					1	4			2	3	
			4		7					8	1	5		11		9		3	2	6				10		43
			1		1					1	1	1		1		1		1	1	1				1		

1922-23

1	Aug 26	(a)	Newcastle U	L	0-2		0	
2	Sep 2	(h)	Newcastle U	W	3-2	Brewster, Irvine, Williams	2	
3	4	(a)	Tottenham H	L	0-2		2	19
4	9	(h)	Blackburn R	W	2-0	Forbes, Irvine	4	13
5	16	(a)	Blackburn R	L	1-5	Harrison	4	19
6	23	(a)	Cardiff C	W	2-0	Williams 2	6	18
7	30	(h)	Cardiff C	W	3-1	Forbes, Hart, Irvine	8	12
8	Oct 7	(a)	Liverpool	L	1-5	Williams	8	19
9	14	(h)	Liverpool	L	0-1		8	19
10	21	(a)	Nottingham F	L	1-2	Chadwick	8	19
11	28	(h)	Nottingham F	W	4-2	Chedgzoy 2, Fazackerley, Williams	10	17
12	Nov 4	(h)	Arsenal	W	1-0	Williams	12	15
13	11	(a)	Arsenal	W	2-1	Chadwick, Williams	14	15
14	18	(a)	West Brom A	D	0-0		15	14
15	25	(h)	West Brom A	L	0-1		15	15
16	Dec 2	(a)	Sunderland	L	1-3	Chadwick	15	18
17	9	(h)	Sunderland	D	1-1	Peacock	16	16
18	16	(a)	Birmingham	D	1-1	Chadwick	17	15
19	23	(h)	Birmingham	W	2-1	Chadwick, Jones	19	15
20	25	(h)	Manchester C	D	0-0		20	14
21	26	(a)	Manchester C	L	1-2	Williams	20	14
22	30	(h)	Huddersfield T	L	0-3		20	16
23	Jan 1	(h)	Tottenham H	W	3-1	Grenyer, Harrison, Peacock	22	15
24	6	(a)	Huddersfield T	L	0-1		22	15
25	20	(h)	Stoke C	W	4-0	Williams 2, Cock, Peacock	24	14
26	27	(a)	Stoke C	L	1-4	Peacock	24	13
27	Feb 10	(h)	Chelsea	W	3-1	Chedgzoy, Cock, Williams	26	13
28	14	(a)	Chelsea	L	1-3	Williams	26	14
29	17	(a)	Middlesbrough	W	4-2	Chadwick 3, Irvine	28	13
30	28	(h)	Middlesbrough	W	5-3	Cock 3, Chadwick, Chedgzoy	30	10
31	Mar 3	(a)	Oldham A	L	0-1		30	13
32	10	(h)	Oldham A	D	0-0		31	13
33	17	(h)	Sheffield U	W	5-1	Irvine 2, Chadwick, Chedgzoy, Cock	33	12
34	30	(a)	Bolton W	W	2-0	Chadwick, Troup	35	11
35	31	(h)	Burnley	W	1-0	Forbes	37	8
36	Apr 2	(h)	Bolton W	D	1-1	Forbes	38	7
37	7	(a)	Burnley	W	1-0	Irvine	40	7
38	14	(h)	Aston Villa	W	2-1	Cock, Troup	42	6
39	16	(a)	Sheffield U	W	1-0	Irvine	44	6
40	21	(a)	Aston Villa	L	0-3		44	7
41	28	(h)	Preston N E	W	1-0	Cock	46	5
42	May 5	(a)	Preston N E	D	2-2	Cock, Williams	47	5
						League Appearances		
						League Goals		
43	Jan 13	(h)	Bradford	D	1-1	Chedgzoy	FA Cup Rd 1	
44	17	(a)	Bradford	L	0-1		Replay	
						FA Cup Appearances		
						FA Cup Goals		

Brewster G	Brown W	Chadwick W	Chedgzoy S	Cock J	Downs R	Fazackerley S	Fern T	Fleetwood T	Forbes F	Grenyer A	Harland A	Harrison G	Hart H	Irvine R	Jones G	Livingstone D	McBain N	McDonald J	Miller H	Parry F	Peacock J	Raitt D	Reid D	Troup A	Wall A	Williams W	
5				2	8	1						11	6	9	7			3				4				10	1
5		7		2		1			9			11	6	8				3				4				10	2
5		7				1			9			11	6	8				3				4	2			10	3
5		7				1			9			11	6	8				3				4	2			10	4
5		7				1			9			11	6	8				3				4	2			10	5
		7					1	5	9			11	6	8				3				4	2			10	6
		7					1	5	9			11	6	8				3				4	2			10	7
		7					1	5	9			11	6	8				3				4	2			10	8
	9	7					1	5				11	6	8				3				4	2			10	9
	9	7					1	5					6					3			8	4	2	11	10		10
	9	7				8	1	5					6					3				4	2	11		10	11
	9	7						5			1		6	8				3				4	2	11		10	12
	9	7						5			1		6	8				3				4	2	11		10	13
	9	7						5			1		6	8				3				4	2	11		10	14
	9	7						5			1		6	8				3				4	2	11		10	15
	9	7						5		6	1		4					3			8		2	11		10	16
	4	9	7					5			1		6					3			8		2	11		10	17
	4	9	7								1		6	5		3					8		2	11		10	18
	4	9						5			1		6		7	3					8		2	11		10	19
	4	9						5			1		6		7	3					8		2	11		10	20
	4	9						5			1		6	8				3	7				2	11		10	21
	4	9						5			1		6	8				3	7				2	11		10	22
	4		7							6	1	11	5	9		3					8		2			10	23
	4		7							6	1	11	5	9		3					8		2			10	24
		9	7	3				4		6	1	11	5								8		2			10	25
		9	7	3				4		6	1		5								8		2	11		10	26
		9	7	3				4		6	1						5				8		2	11		10	27
		9	7	3							1		6	8			5					4	2	11		10	28
	10		7	9	3						1		6	8			5					4	2	11			29
	10		7	9							1		6	8		3	5					4	2	11			30
	10		7	9				5			1		6	8		3						4	2	11			31
	10		7	9							1		6	8		3	5					4	2	11			32
	10		7	9				2			1		6	8		3	5					4		11			33
	10		7	9				2			1		6	8		3	5					4		11			34
	10		7				1	2	9				6	8		3	5					4		11			35
	10		7				1	2	9				6	8		3	5					4		11			36
	10		7				1		9				6	8		3	5					4	2	11			37
	10						1		9				6			3	5		7		8	4	2	11			38
	10		7	9			1						6	8		3	5					4	2	11			39
	10		7	9			1						6	8		3	5					4	2	11			40
	10		7	9			1						6	8		3	5					4	2	11			41
			7	9			1						6	8		3	5					4	2	11		10	42
5	8	27	36	15	9	2	25	23	10	7	17	12	40	32	3	8	15	29	2	3	39	36	13	17	1	28	
	1	13	3	9		1			4	1		2	1	8	1			4				2				13	
	4	9	7					5			1	11	6			2					8	3				10	43
	4		7					5			1		6	9		3					8		2	11		10	44
	2	1	2					2			2	1	2	1		2					2	2	1			2	
			1																								

1923-24

1	Aug 25	(h)	Nottingham F	W	2-1	Hart, Irvine	2	
2	27	(a)	Burnley	D	2-2	Chadwick 2	3	
3	Sep 1	(a)	Nottingham F	L	0-1		3	9
4	3	(h)	Burnley	D	3-3	Chadwick 2, Chedgzoy	4	10
5	8	(h)	Blackburn R	D	0-0		5	10
6	12	(a)	Aston Villa	D	1-1	Peacock	6	11
7	15	(a)	Blackburn R	L	0-2		6	14
8	19	(h)	Aston Villa	W	2-0	Chadwick, Troup	8	8
9	22	(h)	Huddersfield T	D	1-1	Chadwick	9	7
10	29	(a)	Huddersfield T	L	0-2		9	12
11	Oct 6	(h)	Liverpool	W	1-0	Chadwick	11	8
12	13	(a)	Liverpool	W	2-1	Chedgzoy, Cock	13	7
13	20	(a)	Notts Co	D	1-1	Chadwick	14	7
14	27	(h)	Notts Co	W	3-0	Chadwick, Chedgzoy, Irvine	16	5
15	Nov 3	(a)	Sheffield U	L	0-4		16	8
16	10	(h)	Sheffield U	W	2-0	Chadwick 2	18	6
17	17	(h)	West Brom A	W	2-0	Chadwick, Cock	20	6
18	24	(a)	West Brom A	L	0-5		20	7
19	Dec 1	(h)	Birmingham	W	2-0	Cock, Hart	22	5
20	8	(a)	Birmingham	W	1-0	opp.og	24	4
21	15	(a)	Manchester C	L	1-2	Cock	24	7
22	22	(h)	Manchester C	W	6-1	Chadwick 4, Cock, Irvine	26	6
23	26	(h)	Sunderland	L	2-3	Cock, Irvine	26	8
24	29	(a)	Bolton W	L	0-2		26	10
25	Jan 1	(a)	Sunderland	L	0-3		26	10
26	5	(h)	Bolton W	D	2-2	Chadwick, Irvine	27	9
27	19	(h)	Middlesbrough	W	1-0	Cock	29	9
28	26	(a)	Middlesbrough	D	1-1	Cock	30	9
29	Feb 6	(h)	Preston N E	D	1-1	Cock	31	8
30	9	(a)	Preston N E	W	1-0	Cock	33	7
31	16	(h)	Chelsea	W	2-0	Chadwick, Irvine	35	7
32	23	(a)	Chelsea	D	1-1	Chadwick	36	5
33	Mar 1	(h)	Newcastle U	D	2-2	Chadwick, Cock	37	7
34	15	(a)	West Ham U	L	1-2	Irvine	37	8
35	22	(h)	West Ham U	W	2-1	Chadwick, Cock	39	8
36	29	(a)	Cardiff C	D	0-0		40	8
37	Apr 2	(a)	Newcastle U	L	1-3	Chadwick	40	8
38	5	(h)	Cardiff C	D	0-0		41	8
39	12	(a)	Tottenham H	W	5-2	Cock 2, Chadwick, Chedgzoy, Irvine	43	8
40	18	(h)	Arsenal	W	3-1	Chadwick 2, Cock	45	6
41	19	(h)	Tottenham H	W	4-2	Chadwick 3, Irvine	47	6
42	21	(a)	Arsenal	W	1-0	Chedgzoy	49	7
							League Appearances	
							League Goals	
43	Jan 12	(h)	Preston N E	W	3-1	Chadwick, Chedgzoy, Cock	FA Cup Rd 1	
44	Feb 2	(a)	Brighton & H A	L	2-5	Chadwick, Cock	Rd 2	
							FA Cup Appearances	
							FA Cup Goals	

Brown W	Chadwick W	Chedgzoy S	Cock J	Downs R	Fern T	Forbes F	Harland A	Harrison G	Hart H	Irvine R	Kendall J	Livingstone D	McBain N	McDonald J	Parry F	Peacock J	Raitt D	Reid D	Troup A	Williams W	
	10	7		1	9				6	8			5	3		4	2		11		1
4	10			1	9				6	8			5	3	7		2		11		2
4	9	7		1					6	8			5	3			2		11	10	3
4	9	7		1					6	8			5	3			2		11	10	4
	10	7	2	1	9				6	8		3	5			4			11		5
4	10	7	2	1					6	8		3	5			9			11		6
4	10	7	2	1					6	8		3	5			9			11		7
4	10	7	9	1					6	8		3	5	2					11		8
4	10	7	9	1					6	8		3	5	2					11		9
4	10		9	1				11	6	8		3	5	2	7						10
4	10	7	9	1					6	8		3	5	2					11		11
4	10	7	9	1					6	8		3	5	2					11		12
4	10	7	9	1					6			3	5	2	8				11		13
4	10	7	9	1					6	8		3	5	2					11		14
4	10	7	9	1					6	8		3	5	2					11		15
4	10	7	9	1					6	8		3	5	2					11		16
4	10	7	9	1					6	8		3	5	2					11		17
4	10	7	9	1					6	8		3	5	2					11		18
4	10	7	9	1					6	8		3	5				2		11		19
4	10	7	9	1					6	8		3	5				2		11		20
	10	7	9	1					6	8		3	5			4	2		11		21
	10	7	9	1					6	8		3	5			4	2		11		22
	10	7	9	1					6	8		3	5			4	2		11		23
4	10	7	9	1					6	8		3					2	5	11		24
4	10	7	9	1					6	8		3					2	5	11		25
4	10	7	9			1			6	8		3		2				5	11		26
4	10	7	9			1			6	8		3	5	2					11		27
4	10	7	9			1			6	8		3	5	2					11		28
4	10		9			1			6	8		3	5	2	7				11		29
4	10		9			1			6	8		3	5	2	7				11		30
4	10	7	9			1			6	8		3		2				5	11		31
4	10	7	9			1			6	8		3		2				5	11		32
4	10	7	9			1			6			3	5	2				8	11		33
4	10	7	9			1			6	8		3	5	2					11		34
4	10	7	9			1			6	8		3	5				2		11		35
4	10	7	9			1			6	8		3	5				2		11		36
4	10	7	9			1			6	8		3	5				2		11		37
4	10	7	9			1			6	8		3	5				2		11		38
4	10	7	9			1			6	8		3	5				2		11		39
4	10	7	9			1			6	8		3	5				2		11		40
4	10	7	9						6	8	1	3	5				2		11		41
4	10	7	9			1			6	8		3	5				2		11		42
37	42	38	35	3	25	3	16	1	42	40	1	38	37	24	4	8	19	6	41	2	
28	5	15							2	9						1			1		1 opp.og
4	10	7	9			1			6	8		3	5	2					11		43
4	10	7	9			1				8		3	5	2			6		11		44
2	2	2	2			2			1	2		2	2	2			1		2		
	2	1	2																		

1924-25

1	Aug 30	(a)	Birmingham	D	2-2	Chadwick, Cock	1	
2	Sep 6	(h)	West Brom A	W	1-0	Chadwick	3	
3	8	(a)	Burnley	D	0-0		4	10
4	13	(a)	Tottenham H	D	0-0		5	8
5	17	(a)	Leeds U	L	0-1		5	15
6	20	(h)	Bolton W	D	2-2	Chadwick, Chedgzoy	6	15
7	27	(a)	Notts Co	L	1-3	Cock	6	16
8	Oct 4	(h)	Liverpool	L	0-1		6	18
9	11	(h)	Sunderland	L	0-3		6	19
10	18	(a)	Cardiff C	L	1-2	Chadwick	6	20
11	25	(a)	Nottingham F	W	1-0	Troup	8	18
12	29	(h)	Manchester C	W	3-1	Chedgzoy, Cock, Irvine	10	18
13	Nov 1	(h)	Bury	D	0-0		11	17
14	8	(a)	Manchester C	D	2-2	Chadwick, Cock	12	17
15	15	(h)	Arsenal	L	2-3	Hargreaves, Irvine	12	18
16	22	(a)	Aston Villa	L	1-3	Hargreaves	12	18
17	29	(h)	Huddersfield T	L	0-2		12	19
18	Dec 6	(a)	Blackburn R	L	0-3		12	21
19	13	(h)	West Ham U	W	1-0	Cock	14	20
20	20	(a)	Sheffield U	D	1-1	Troup	15	20
21	25	(h)	Newcastle U	L	0-1		15	20
22	26	(a)	Newcastle U	D	1-1	Broad	16	20
23	27	(h)	Birmingham	W	2-1	Broad, Williams	18	19
24	Jan 1	(h)	Burnley	W	3-2	Broad, Irvine, Weaver	20	18
25	3	(a)	West Brom A	L	0-3		20	19
26	17	(h)	Tottenham H	W	1-0	Weaver	22	19
27	24	(a)	Bolton W	L	0-1		22	20
28	Feb 7	(a)	Liverpool	L	1-3	Chadwick	22	20
29	14	(a)	Sunderland	L	1-4	Broad	22	20
30	25	(h)	Cardiff C	L	1-2	Broad	22	20
31	28	(h)	Nottingham F	W	3-1	Broad 2, Irvine	24	20
32	Mar 7	(a)	Bury	L	0-1		24	20
33	18	(h)	Notts Co	W	1-0	Broad	26	20
34	21	(a)	Arsenal	L	1-3	Kennedy	26	20
35	28	(h)	Aston Villa	W	2-0	Dean, Reid	28	20
36	Apr 4	(a)	Huddersfield T	L	0-2		28	20
37	10	(a)	Preston N E	D	1-1	O'Donnell	29	19
38	11	(h)	Blackburn R	W	1-0	Kennedy	31	18
39	13	(h)	Preston N E	D	0-0		32	18
40	18	(a)	West Ham U	L	1-4	Dean	32	19
41	27	(h)	Sheffield U	D	1-1	Reid	33	20
42	May 2	(h)	Leeds U	W	1-0	Kennedy	35	17

League Appearances
League Goals

43	Jan 10	(h)	Burnley	W	2-1	Chadwick 2	FA Cup Rd 1
44	31	(a)	Sunderland	D	0-0		Rd 2
45	Feb 4	(h)	Sunderland	W	2-1	Chadwick, Irvine	Replay
46	21	(a)	Sheffield U	L	0-1		Rd 3

FA Cup Appearances
FA Cup Goals

Bain D	Broad J	Brown W	Chadwick W	Chedgzoy S	Cock J	Dean W	Forbes F	Hargreaves F	Harland A	Hart H	Irvine R	Jones R	Kendall J	Kennedy F	Kerr J	Livingstone D	McBain N	McDonald J	O'Donnell J	Parry F	Peacock J	Raitt D	Reid D	Rooney W	Troup A	Virr A	Wall A	Weaver W	Williams W	#
		4	10	7	9			8		6			1				3	5				2			11					1
		4	10	7	9			8		6			1				3	5				2			11					2
		4	10	7	9			8					1				3	5				2	6		11					3
		4	10	7	9			8		6			1				3	5				2			11					4
		4	10	7	9					6	8		1				3	5				2			11					5
		4	10	7	9			8		6			1				3	5				2			11					6
			10	7	9			8		6			1				3	5			4	2			11					7
		4	10	7	9				1	6	8						3	5				2			11					8
9	4			7					1	6	8						3	5				2			11			10		9
			10	7	9					6	8		1				3	5			4	2			11					10
			10	7	9					6	8		1				3	5			4	2			11					11
			10	7	9					6	8		1				5	3			4	2			11					12
			10	7	9					6	8		1				5	3			4	2			11					13
			10	7	9					6	8	1					5	3			4	2			11					14
			9	7		10				6	8	1					5	3			4	2			11					15
			10	7			8			6	9	1					3	5	2		4				11					16
			10	7	9				1	6	8						3	5	2		4				11					17
5	9			7		10		11	1	6	8					3			2		4									18
			10	7	9				1	6						3			2		4			5	11				8	19
			10	7	9				1	6	8					3			2		4			5	11					20
			10	7	9				1	6						3	5		2		4				11				8	21
	9			7					1	6	8					3		2			4			5	11			10		22
	9			7					1	6	8					3		2			4			5	11			10		23
	9			7					1	6	8					3		2			4			5	11			10		24
	9								1	6	8					3		2		7	4			5	11			10		25
9	4		10						1								5	3		7		2	6	8	11					26
9	4		10	7					1		8						5	3				2	6		11					27
		4	10	7	9				1		8						5	3				2	6		11					28
9	4		10	7					1		8						5	3				2	6		11					29
5	9		10	7					1							4	2	3			6			8	11					30
	9			7					1		8						5	2	3				6	4	11			10		31
	9			7					1		8						5	3				2	6	4	11			10		32
	9			7					1		8			10			5	2	3				6	4	11					33
	9					8			1					10			5	2	3		7		6	4	11					34
		4		7	9				1		8			10			5	2	3				6		11					35
		4		7	9				1		8			10			5	2	3				6		11					36
		4		7	9				1		8			10			5	2	3				6		11					37
		4		7	9				1		8			10			5	2	3				6		11					38
		4		7	9				1		8			10			5	2	3				6		11					39
		4			9	8			1					10			5	2	3		7		6		11					40
9	4			7		8			1					10			5	2	3				6		11					41
9	4			7		8			1					10			5	2	3				6		11					42
3	14	20	27	38	19	7	1	9	27	24	28	3	12	10	2	20	35	29	13	4	17	20	23	4	32	1	2	9	9	
	8		6	2	5	2		2			2			4		3			1		2				2			2	1	
9	4		10						1								5	3		7	8	2	6		11					43
9	4		10						1								5	3				2	6		11					44
		4	10	7	9			8					1				5	3				2	6		11					45
5	9		10	7				8	1							4		3				2	6		11					46
1	3	3	4	3	1				2		3					2	4	4		1	1	4	3		4					
			3														1													

1925-26

1	Aug 29 (h)	Sheffield U	D	2-2	Kennedy, Troup	1	
2	Sep 2 (a)	West Brom A	D	1-1	Irvine	2	
3	5 (a)	Cardiff C	L	1-2	Murray	2	14
4	9 (h)	Birmingham	D	2-2	Kennedy, Troup	3	12
5	12 (h)	Tottenham H	D	1-1	Peacock	4	13
6	16 (h)	West Brom A	W	4-0	Kennedy 2, Irvine, Troup	6	7
7	19 (a)	Manchester C	D	4-4	Kennedy 2, Dean, Irvine	7	8
8	21 (a)	Birmingham	L	1-3	Irvine	7	9
9	26 (a)	Liverpool	L	1-5	Kennedy	7	13
10	Oct 3 (h)	Huddersfield T	L	2-3	Chedgzoy, Troup	7	17
11	10 (a)	Sunderland	L	3-7	Troup 2, Dean	7	19
12	17 (a)	Burnley	W	3-1	Dean 3	9	15
13	24 (h)	Leeds U	W	4-2	Dean 3, Kennedy	11	15
14	31 (a)	Arsenal	L	1-4	McBain	11	18
15	Nov 7 (h)	Manchester U	L	1-3	Dean	11	19
16	14 (a)	Notts Co	W	3-0	Dean 2, Irvine	13	17
17	21 (h)	Aston Villa	D	1-1	Dean	14	16
18	28 (a)	Leicester C	D	1-1	Dean	15	15
19	Dec 5 (h)	West Ham U	W	2-0	O'Donnell, Weaver	17	13
20	12 (a)	Newcastle U	D	3-3	Dean 3	18	14
21	19 (h)	Bolton W	W	2-1	Dean, O'Donnell	20	13
22	25 (a)	Blackburn R	D	2-2	Dean, O'Donnell	21	13
23	26 (h)	Blackburn R	W	3-0	O'Donnell 2, Irvine	23	12
24	Jan 1 (a)	Bury	L	0-1		23	13
25	2 (a)	Sheffield U	D	1-1	Dean	24	13
26	16 (h)	Cardiff C	D	1-1	Dean	25	13
27	23 (a)	Tottenham H	D	1-1	Dean	26	11
28	30 (h)	Leicester C	W	1-0	opp.og	28	11
29	Feb 6 (h)	Liverpool	D	3-3	Chedgzoy, Dean, Irvine	29	11
30	10 (h)	Manchester C	D	1-1	Irvine	30	9
31	13 (a)	Huddersfield T	L	0-3		30	9
32	27 (h)	Burnley	D	1-1	Dean	31	9
33	Mar 6 (a)	Leeds U	D	1-1	Chedgzoy	32	9
34	13 (h)	Arsenal	L	2-3	Chedgzoy 2	32	12
35	17 (h)	Sunderland	W	2-1	Dean 2	34	11
36	20 (a)	Manchester U	D	0-0		35	8
37	27 (h)	Notts Co	W	3-0	Batten, Chedgzoy, Dean	37	6
38	Apr 2 (h)	Bury	D	1-1	Dean	38	6
39	3 (a)	Aston Villa	L	1-3	Dean	38	8
40	17 (a)	West Ham U	L	0-1		38	13
41	24 (h)	Newcastle U	W	3-0	Dean 3	40	11
42	May 1 (a)	Bolton W	W	2-0	Chedgzoy, Dean	42	11
						League Appearances	
						League Goals	
43	Jan 9 (h)	Fulham	D	1-1	Dean	FA Cup Rd 3	
44	14 (a)	Fulham	L	0-1		Replay	
						FA Cup Appearances	
						FA Cup Goals	

M	Bain D	Batten H	Broad J	Brown W	Chadwick W	Chedgzoy S	Dean W	Hardy H	Harland A	Hart H	Irvine R	Kendall J	Kennedy F	Kerr J	Livingstone D	McBain N	McDonald J	Menham C	Murray D	O'Donnell J	Parry F	Peacock J	Raitt D	Reid D	Troup A	Virr A	Weaver W
1		9	4	7							1	6	8		10	5	2			3					11		
2		9	4	7							1	6	8		10	5	2			3					11		
3		9	4	7								6	1		10		2		8	3				5	11		
4		9	4	7								6	1		10		2		8	3				5	11		
5			4			7	9					6	1		10	5				3			8	2	11		
6			4			7	9					6	8	1	10	5				3				2	11		
7			4			7	9					6	8	1	10	5				3				2	11		
8						7	9					6	8	1	10	5				3			4	2	11		
9						7	9				1	6	8		10	5				3			4	2	11		
10			4			7	9				1	6	8		10	5	2			3					11		
11	5	4	10			9						6	8			2	1			3			7		11		
12	5	4	10			9						6	8		3	2	1						7		11		
13	5	4				7	9					6			10	2	1			3			8		11		
14	5	4				7	9	1				6			10					3			8	2	11		
15	5	4				7	9	1				6			10					3			8	2	11		
16	5	4				7	9	1					8							3		10		2	11	6	
17	5	4				7	9	1					8							3		10		2	11	6	
18	5	4				7	9	1					8							3		10		2		6	11
19	5	4				7	9	1					8							3		10		2		6	11
20						7	9	1					8							3		10	4	2	5	11	6
21	5					7	9	1					8							3		10	4	2	11	6	
22	5					7	9	1					8							3		10	4	2	11	6	
23	5					7	9	1					8							3		10	4	2	11	6	
24	5					7	9	1					8							3		10	4	2	11	6	
25	5					7	9	1					8							3		10	4	2	11	6	
26	5					7	9	1					8		11					3		10	4	2		6	
27	5					7	9	1					8							3		10	4	2	11	6	
28	5						9	1					8							3		10	4	2	11	6	7
29	5					7	9	1					8				2			3		10	4		11	6	
30	5					7	9						8	1	10		2	3					4		11	6	
31	5					7	9	1				6	8		10					3			4	2	11		
32	5	10	4			7	9	1					8							3				2	11	6	
33	5	8	4			7	9	1				6								3		10		2	11		
34	5	8	4			7	9					6		1						3		10		2	11		
35	10		4			7	9	1				6	8							3			2	5	11		
36	10		4			7	9	1				6	8							3			2	5	11		
37	10		4			7	9	1				6	8							3			2	5	11		
38	10		4			7	9	1				6	8							3			2	5	11		
39	10		4				9	1				6	8							3	7		2	5	11		
40	8		4			7	9	1				6			10					3			2	5		11	
41	8		4			7	9	1				6			10					3			2	5	11		
42	8		4			7	9	1				6			10					3			2	5	11		
Apps	23	11	4	28	2	38	38	27	4	26	31	8	19	1	5	10	37	3	2	27	1	18	30	11	38	16	4
Gls		1				7	32					8	8			1				1		5		1	6	1	
43	5					7	9	1					8							3		10	4	2	11	6	
44	5					7	9	1					8							3		10	4	2	11	6	
Apps	2					2	2	2					2							2		2	2	2	2	2	
Gls							1																				

opp.og 1

1926-27

#	Date		Opponent	Result		Scorers		
1	Aug 28	(a)	Tottenham H	L	1-2	O'Donnell	0	
2	Sep 1	(a)	Bury	L	2-5	Dominy, Irvine	0	
3	4	(h)	West Ham U	L	0-3		0	21
4	6	(a)	West Brom A	L	2-3	Dominy, O'Donnell	0	22
5	11	(a)	Sheffield W	L	0-4		0	22
6	15	(h)	West Brom A	D	0-0		1	22
7	18	(h)	Leicester C	L	3-4	Irvine 2, Bain	1	22
8	20	(a)	Birmingham	L	0-1		1	22
9	25	(h)	Liverpool	W	1-0	O'Donnell	3	22
10	29	(h)	Bury	D	2-2	Bain, Hart	4	21
11	Oct 2	(a)	Blackburn R	D	3-3	Dominy 2, Irvine	5	21
12	9	(h)	Huddersfield T	D	0-0		6	22
13	16	(h)	Newcastle U	L	1-3	Troup	6	22
14	23	(a)	Leeds U	W	3-1	Dean, Dominy, Irvine	8	21
15	30	(h)	Arsenal	W	3-1	Dean, Irvine, Troup	10	19
16	Nov 6	(a)	Sheffield U	D	3-3	Dominy 2, Dean	11	20
17	13	(h)	Derby C	W	3-2	Dean, Irvine, Virr	13	17
18	20	(a)	Manchester U	L	1-2	Dean	13	18
19	27	(h)	Bolton W	D	1-1	opp.og	14	18
20	Dec 4	(a)	Aston Villa	L	3-5	Dean, Dominy, Irvine	14	20
21	11	(h)	Cardiff C	L	0-1		14	20
22	18	(a)	Burnley	L	1-5	Kerr	14	21
23	25	(h)	Sunderland	W	5-4	Dean 4, Irvine	16	19
24	27	(a)	Sunderland	L	2-3	Bain, Dean	16	21
25	Jan 1	(h)	Burnley	W	3-2	Dean 2, Irvine	18	21
26	15	(h)	Tottenham H	L	1-2	Dean	18	21
27	22	(a)	West Ham U	L	1-2	Irvine	18	21
28	Feb 5	(a)	Leicester C	L	2-6	Dean 2	18	21
29	12	(a)	Liverpool	L	0-1		18	21
30	19	(h)	Blackburn R	W	1-0	Dominy	20	21
31	26	(a)	Huddersfield T	D	0-0		21	21
32	Mar 2	(h)	Sheffield W	W	2-1	Dean, Dominy	23	20
33	5	(a)	Newcastle U	L	3-7	Dominy 2, Forshaw	23	21
34	12	(h)	Leeds U	W	2-1	Dean, Weldon	25	20
35	19	(a)	Arsenal	W	2-1	Troup, Weldon	27	20
36	26	(h)	Sheffield U	W	2-0	Forshaw, Weldon	29	20
37	Apr 2	(a)	Derby C	D	0-0		30	19
38	9	(h)	Manchester U	D	0-0		31	20
39	16	(a)	Bolton W	L	0-5		31	20
40	18	(h)	Birmingham C	W	3-1	Troup 2, Dean	33	20
41	23	(h)	Aston Villa	D	2-2	Dean 2	34	20
42	30	(a)	Cardiff C	L	0-1		34	20

League Appearances
League Goals

#	Date		Opponent	Result		Scorers	
43	Jan 8	(h)	Poole T	W	3-1	Dean, Irvine, Troup	FA Cup Rd 3
44	22	(a)	Hull C	D	1-1	Virr	4
45	Feb 2	(h)	Hull C	D	2-2	Dean, Troup	Replay
46	7	(n)	Hull C	L	2-3	Dean, Dominy	(Villa Park) 2nd Replay

FA Cup appearances
FA Cup Goals

Bain D	Baker B	Batten H	Brown W	Cresswell W	Critchley E	Davies A	Dean W	Dominy A	Forshaw R	Hardy H	Hart H	Irvine R	Kelly J	Kennedy F	Kerr J	McDonald J	Millington T	Moffatt H	O'Donnell J	Parker T	Peacock J	Raitt D	Reid D	Rooney W	Taylor E	Troup A	Virr A	Weaver W	Weldon A	Woodhouse R	No
	1		4					8			6	7	10			3			9			2	5					11			1
	1	10	4					8			6	9				3				7		2	5					11			2
	1	10						8			6	9				3				7	4	2	5					11			3
	1	10	4					8			6					3			9	7		2	5					11			4
	1	10	4					8			6					3			9	7		2	5					11			5
5	1		4								8		10			3	7					2				11	6				6
9	1		4							5	8		10			3				7		2				11	6				7
9	1		4							5	8		10			2	7					3				11	6				8
9	1		4							5	8					3	2	10	7							11	6				9
9	1		4							5	8					3	2	7	10							11	6				10
	1		4						9	5	8					3	2			7						11	6			10	11
			4			1		10		5	8					3	2		9	7						11	6				12
			4			1	9			5	8		10			3	2			7						11	6				13
			4			1	9	10		5	8					3	2			7						11	6				14
			4			1	9	10		5	8					3	2		7							11	6				15
			4			1	9	10		5	8					3	2			7						11	6				16
			4			1	9	10		5	8					3	2			7						11	6				17
5			4			1	9	10			8					3	2			7						11	6				18
			4				9	10	1	5	8					3	2			7			6			11					19
			4				9	10	1	5	8					2	7			3						11	6				20
			4			1	9	10		5	8					3	2			7						11	6				21
			4			1	9	10		5	8					3	2									11	6			7	22
5			4		7	1	9	10				6	8			3						2				11					23
5			4		7		9	8	1	6						3			10			2				11					24
5			4		7		9	10	1			6	8			3						2				11					25
5					7		9	10	1			6	8			3										11	4				26
					7		9	10	1	5	8					3	2				4					11	6				27
			4	2	7		9	10	1		8					3										11	6				28
				2	7			8			5	9	10		4	3								1		11	6				29
				2	7		9	10			5	8			4	3								1		11	6				30
				2	7		9	10			5	8			4	3								1		11	6				31
				2	7		9	10			5	8			4	3								1		11	6				32
				2	7		9	10	8		5				4	3								1		11	6				33
				2			9	8			5	7			4	3								1		11	6		10		34
				2	7		9	8			5				4	3								1		11	6		10		35
				2	7		9	8			5				4	3								1		11	6		10		36
				2	7		9	8			5				4	3								1		11	6		10		37
				2	7		9	8			5				4	3								1		11	6		10		38
				2			9	8			5	7			4	3								1		11	6		10		39
				2			9	8			5	7			4	3								1		11	6		10		40
				2			9	8			5	7			4	3								1		11	6		10		41
				2			9	8			5	7			4	3								1		11	6		10		42
10	11	4	25	15	15	10	27	28	10	7	39	34	14	6	15	24	13	2	24	6	3	11	7	14		37	32	5	9	2	
3							21	12	2			1	11			1			3							5	1		3		
5							9	10	1		8					3			7			2	4			11	6				43
							9	10	1	5	8					3	2		7				4			11	6				44
8							9	10	1	5	7					3	2						4			11	6				45
						1	9	10		5	8					3	2		7				4			11	6				46
2						1	4	4	3	3	4	3	2	1	1	2	1	1	1	3						4	4	4			
3	1						1																			2	1				

T. P. Griffiths played number 5 in Match 28; H. Hamilton played number 2 in Match 26;
D. Murray played number 9 in Match 6

League includes 1 opp. og

1927-28

#	Date		Opponent		Score	Scorers		
1	Aug 27	(h)	Sheffield W	W	4-0	Dean, Forshaw, Troup, Weldon	2	
2	Sep 3	(a)	Middlesbrough	L	2-4	Critchley, Dean	2	
3	5	(a)	Bolton w	D	1-1	Dean	3	12
4	10	(h)	Birmingham	W	5-2	Dean 2, Troup 2, Forshaw	5	8
5	14	(h)	Bolton W	D	2-2	Dean, Forshaw	6	4
6	17	(a)	Newcastle U	D	2-2	Dean 2	7	7
7	24	(h)	Huddersfield T	D	2-2	Dean 2	8	7
8	Oct 1	(a)	Tottenham H	W	3-1	Dean 2, Troup	10	5
9	8	(h)	Manchester U	W	5-2	Dean 5	12	3
10	15	(h)	Liverpool	D	1-1	Dean	13	3
11	22	(h)	West Ham U	W	7-0	White 2, Critchley, Forshaw, O'Donnell, Weldon, opp.og	15	2
12	29	(a)	Portsmouth	W	3-1	Dean 3	17	1
13	Nov 5	(a)	Leicester C	W	7-1	Dean 3, Weldon 2, Critchley, Troup	19	1
14	12	(a)	Derby C	W	3-0	Dean 2, Weldon	21	1
15	19	(h)	Sunderland	L	0-1		21	1
16	26	(a)	Bury	W	3-2	Dean 2, Critchley	23	1
17	Dec 3	(h)	Sheffield U	D	0-0		24	1
18	10	(a)	Aston Villa	W	3-2	Dean 3	26	1
19	17	(h)	Burnley	W	4-1	Critchley, Forshaw, Kelly, Troup	28	1
20	24	(a)	Arsenal	L	2-3	Dean, Troup	28	1
21	26	(h)	Cardiff C	W	2-1	Dean 2	30	1
22	27	(a)	Cardiff C	L	0-2		30	1
23	31	(a)	Sheffield W	W	2-1	Dean 2	32	1
24	Jan 2	(a)	Blackburn R	L	2-4	Dean 2	32	1
25	7	(h)	Middlesbrough	W	3-1	Dean 2, Irvine	34	1
26	21	(a)	Birmingham C	D	2-2	Irvine 2	35	1
27	Feb 4	(a)	Huddersfield T	L	1-4	Dean	35	1
28	11	(h)	Tottenham H	L	2-5	Troup 2	35	1
29	25	(a)	Liverpool	D	3-3	Dean 3	36	1
30	Mar 3	(a)	West Ham U	D	0-0		37	1
31	10	(h)	Portsmouth	D	0-0		38	2
32	14	(a)	Manchester U	L	0-1		38	2
33	17	(a)	Leicester C	l	0-1		38	2
34	24	(h)	Derby C	D	2-2	Dean 2	39	2
35	31	(a)	Sunderland	W	2-0	Easton, Virr	41	2
36	Apr 6	(h)	Blackburn R	W	4-1	Dean 2, Hart, Martin	43	2
37	7	(h)	Bury	D	1-1	Dean	44	1
38	14	(a)	Sheffield U	W	3-1	Dean 2, Martin	46	2
39	18	(h)	Newcastle U	W	3-0	Critchley, Dean, Weldon	48	1
40	21	(h)	Aston Villa	W	3-2	Dean 2, Weldon	50	1
41	28	(a)	Burnley	W	5-3	Dean 4, Martin	52	1
42	May 5	(h)	Arsenal	D	3-3	Dean 3	53	1
						League Appearances		
						League Goals		
43	Jan 14	(a)	Preston N E	W	3-0	Dean, Irvine, opp.og	FA Cup Rd 3	
44	28	(a)	Arsenal	L	3-4	Dean 2, Troup	4	
						FA Cup Appearances		
						FA Cup Goals		

Bain D	Brown W	Cresswell W	Critchley E	Davies A	Dean W	Dominy A	Easton W	Forshaw R	Hardy H	Hart H	Houghton H	Irvine R	Kelly J	Martin G	Meston S	O'Donnell J	Raitt D	Rooney W	Taylor E	Troup A	Virr A	Weldon A	White T	
		2			9			8		5	7		4			3			1	11	6	10		1
		2	7		9			8		5			4			3			1	11	6	10		2
			7		9			8		5			4			3	2		1	11	6	10		3
			7		9			8		5			4			3	2		1	11	6	10		4
		2	7		9			8		5			4			3			1	11	6	10		5
		2	7		9			8		5			4			3			1	11	6	10		6
		2	7		9			8		5			4			3			1	11	6	10		7
		2	7		9			8		5			4			3			1	11	6	10		8
		2	7		9			8		5			4			3			1	11	6	10		9
		2	7		9			8		5			4			3			1	11	6	10		10
		2	7					8		5			4			3			1	11	6	10	9	11
		2	7		9			8		5			4			3			1	11	6	10		12
	4	2	7		9			8		5						3			1	11	6	10		13
		2	7	1	9			8		5			4			3				11	6	10		14
		2	7	1	9			8		5			4			3				11	6	10		15
		2	7		9			8		5		10	4			3			1	11	6			16
		2	7		9			8		5			4			3			1	11	6	10		17
		2	7		9			8		5			4			3		6	1	11		10		18
		2	7		9			8		5			4			3			1	11	6	10		19
		2	7		9			8		5			4			3			1	11	6	10		20
			7		9			8		5			4			3	2		1	11	6	10		21
			7		9							8	4			3	2	6	1	11	5	10		22
			7		9					5		8	4			3	2		1	11	6	10		23
			7		9					5		8	4			3	2		1	11	6	10		24
		2	7		9					5		8	4			3		6	1	11		10		25
		2	7		9	10				5		8	4			3		6	1	11				26
		2	7		9					5		8	4			3			1	11	6	10		27
	4	2	7		9					5		8				3			1	11	6	10		28
		2	7		9			8	1	5			4			3				11	6	10		29
		2	7		9			8	1	5			4			3				11	6	10		30
		2	7				8		1	5		10	4			3				11	6	9		31
		2	7		9		8		1	5			4			3				11	6	10		32
		2	7		9				1	5			4	8		3				11	6	10		33
8		2	7	1	9					5			4	10		3				11	6			34
9		2	7	1			8			5			4	10		3				11	6			35
		2	7	1	9					5			4	8		3				11	6	10		36
		2	7		9				1	5			4	8		3				11	6	10		37
		2		1	9					5			4	8	7	3				11	6	10		38
		2	7	1	9					5			4	8		3				11	6	10		39
		2	7	1	9					5			4	8		3				11	6	10		40
		2	7	1	9					5			4	8		3				11	6	10		41
		2	7	1	9					5			4	8		3				11	6	10		42
2	2	36	40	10	39	1	3	23	6	41	1	9	40	10	1	42	6	4	26	42	39	38	1	
			6		60	1		5		1		3	1	3		1				10	1	7	2	opp.og 1
		2	7		9					5		8	4			3		6	1	11		10		43
		2	7		9					5		8	4			3			1	11	6	10		44
		2	2		2					2		2	2			2		1	2	2	1	2		
					3								1							1				opp.og 1

1928-29

#	Date		Opponent	Res	Score	Scorers	App	Goals
1	Aug 25	(a)	Bolton W	W	3-2	Dean 3	2	
2	29	(h)	Sheffield W	D	0-0		3	
3	Sep 1	(h)	Portsmouth	W	4-0	Dean 3, Ritchie	5	1
4	3	(a)	Sheffield W	L	0-1		5	2
5	8	(a)	Birmingham C	W	3-1	Critchley, Dean, Dunn	7	2
6	15	(h)	Manchester C	L	2-6	Dunn, Weldon	7	5
7	22	(a)	Huddersfield T	L	1-3	Troup	7	13
8	29	(h)	Liverpool	W	1-0	Troup	9	8
9	Oct 6	(h)	Arsenal	W	4-2	Dean 2, Ritchie 2	11	5
10	13	(a)	Blackburn R	L	1-2	Dean	11	10
11	20	(a)	West Ham U	W	4-2	Dean 2, Dunn, Weldon	13	6
12	27	(h)	Leeds U	L	0-1		13	7
13	Nov 3	(a)	Burnley	L	0-2		13	10
14	10	(h)	Cardiff C	W	1-0	Weldon	15	7
15	17	(a)	Sheffield U	L	1-2	Martin	15	9
16	24	(h)	Bury	W	1-0	Dean	17	7
17	Dec 1	(a)	Aston Villa	L	0-2		17	13
18	8	(h)	Leicester C	W	3-1	Dean, Martin, Troup	19	9
19	15	(a)	Manchester U	D	1-1	Troup	20	9
20	22	(h)	Newcastle U	W	5-2	Dean 3, Martin, Ritchie	22	8
21	25	(h)	Sunderland	D	0-0		23	9
22	29	(h)	Bolton W	W	3-0	Dean 3	25	7
23	Jan 1	(h)	Derby C	W	4-0	Dean 3, Dunn	27	4
24	5	(a)	Portsmouth	L	0-3		27	7
25	19	(h)	Birmingham	L	0-2		27	9
26	26	(a)	Manchester C	L	1-5	Forshaw	27	9
27	Feb 2	(h)	Huddersfield T	L	0-3		27	10
28	9	(a)	Liverpool	W	2-1	Griffiths, White	29	9
29	23	(h)	Blackburn R	W	5-2	Martin 2, White, opp.og 2	31	8
30	Mar 9	(a)	Leeds U	L	1-3	Dean	31	8
31	16	(h)	Burnley	W	2-0	White 2	33	9
32	23	(a)	Cardiff C	W	2-0	Easton, White	35	8
33	29	(a)	Sunderland	D	2-2	Easton, Martin	36	8
34	30	(h)	Sheffield U	L	1-3	Troup	36	8
35	Apr 2	(a)	Derby C	L	0-3		36	11
36	6	(a)	Bury	W	2-1	Dean 2	38	11
37	10	(h)	West Ham U	L	0-4		38	11
38	13	(h)	Aston Villa	L	0-1		38	11
39	20	(a)	Leicester C	L	1-4	White	38	13
40	22	(a)	Arsenal	L	0-2		38	14
41	27	(h)	Manchester U	L	2-4	Cresswell, Griffiths	38	15
42	May 4	(a)	Newcastle U	L	0-2		38	18
						League Appearances		
						League Goals		
43	Jan 12	(a)	Chelsea	L	0-2	FA Cup Rd 3		
						FA Cup Appearances		
						FA Cup Goals		

Attwood A	Common E	Cresswell W	Critchley E	Davies A	Dean W	Dunn J	Easton W	Forshaw R	Griffiths T P	Hart H	Kelly J	Kennedy A	Lewis T	Martin G	O'Donnell J	Ritchie H	Rooney W	Stein J	Troup A	Virr A	Weldon A	White T	No.
		2		1	9	8				5	4				3	7			11	6	10		1
		2		1	9	8				5	4				3	7			11	6	10		2
		2		1	9	8				5	4				3	7			11	6	10		3
		2	7	1	9					5	4			8	3				11	6	10		4
		2	7	1	9	8				5	4				3				11	6	10		5
		2	7	1	9	8				5	4				3				11	6	10		6
		2	7	1		8		9		5	4				3				11	6	10		7
		2		1	9	8				5	4				3	7			11	6	10		8
		2		1	9	8				5	4				3	7			11	6	10		9
		2		1	9	8				5	4				3	7			11	6	10		10
		2		1	9	8			4	5					3	7			11	6	10		11
		2		1	9				4	5				8	3	7			11	6	10		12
		2	7	1	9	8			4	5		3							11	6	10		13
		2	7	1	9	8			4	5					3				11	6	10		14
		2		1		8				5				9	3	7			11	6	10	4	15
		2		1	9	8			4	5					3	7			11	6	10		16
		2		1	9			8	4	5				10	3	7			11	6			17
		2	7	1	9			8		5				10	3				11	6		4	18
		2		1				8		5	4			10	3	7			11	6	9		19
		2		1	9	8				5				10	3	7			11	6		4	20
		2		1	9	8				5				10	3	7			11	6		4	21
		2	7	1	9	8				5				10	3			11		6		4	22
		2	7	1	9	8			4	5				10	3			11		6			23
		2	7	1	9	8			4	5					3			11		6	10		24
		2		1	9	8			4	5					3	7		11			10	6	25
		2	7	1	9	8			4	5				10	3		6		11				26
		2	7	1	9	8			4	5				10	3		6		11				27
	2			1			8		4	5	6			10	3	7			11		9		28
	2		7	1			8		4	5	6			10	3				11		9		29
	2		7	1	9				4	5	6			10	3				11			8	30
	2		7	1			8		4	5	6			10	3				11		9		31
	2		7	1			8		4	5	6			10	3				11		9		32
	2		7	1			8		4	5	6			10	3				11		9		33
	2		7	1		6	8		4	5				10	3				11		9		34
	2		7	1			8		4	5	6			10	3				11		9		35
	2		7	1	9		8		4	5	6				3				11		10		36
9	2		7	1			8		4	5	6				3				11		10		37
		2	7	1						5	6				3	8	4		11		10	9	38
		2		1			8			5	6				3	7	4		11		10	9	39
		2	7	1	9					5	4			10	3	8	6		11				40
		2	7	1	9					5	4		6	10	3				11			8	41
		2	7	1	9	8			4	5	6				3				11		10		42
1	10	32	25	42	29	24	12	8	26	40	21	1	1	18	41	19	5	4	38	24	20	21	
		1	1		26	4	2	1	2					6		4			5		3	6	opp.og 2
		2		1	9	8			4	5					3	7			11	6	10		43
		1		1	1	1			1	1					1	1			1	1	1		

1929-30

1	Aug 31	(h)	Bolton W	D	3-3	Dean 2, Stein	1	
2	Sep 2	(a)	Burnley	D	1-1	Stein	2	
3	7	(a)	Liverpool	W	3-0	Dean 2, Martin	4	6
4	11	(h)	Leeds U	D	1-1	Dean	5	6
5	14	(a)	Derby C	L	1-2	Dean	5	9
6	16	(a)	Leeds U	L	1-2	Dean	5	11
7	21	(h)	Manchester C	L	2-3	Dean, Martin	5	16
8	28	(a)	Portsmouth	W	4-1	Dean 3, Stein	7	14
9	Oct 2	(a)	Sunderland	D	2-2	Dean, Martin	8	10
10	5	(h)	Arsenal	D	1-1	Ritchie	9	9
11	12	(a)	Aston Villa	L	2-5	Martin, Stein	9	17
12	19	(h)	Middlesbrough	W	3-2	Dean, Martin, White	11	8
13	26	(a)	Blackburn R	L	1-3	Dean	11	14
14	Nov 2	(h)	Newcastle U	W	5-2	Martin 2, Critchley, Dean, White	13	8
15	9	(a)	West Ham U	L	1-3	Dean	13	13
16	16	(h)	Huddersfield T	L	0-2		13	17
17	23	(a)	Birmingham	D	0-0		14	16
18	30	(h)	Leicester C	L	4-5	Rigby 2, Martin, White	14	18
19	Dec 7	(a)	Grimsby T	W	3-0	Griffiths, Rigby, Troup	16	15
20	14	(h)	Manchester U	D	0-0		17	14
21	21	(a)	Sheffield U	L	0-2		17	17
22	25	(h)	Sheffield W	L	1-4	White	17	19
23	26	(a)	Sheffield W	L	0-4		17	20
24	28	(a)	Bolton W	L	0-5		17	21
25	Jan 4	(h)	Liverpool	D	3-3	Dean 2, Critchley	18	21
26	18	(h)	Derby C	W	4-0	Dean 2, Critchley, Stein	20	20
27	Feb 1	(h)	Portsmouth	D	1-1	Dean	21	20
28	5	(a)	Manchester C	W	2-1	Griffiths, Rigby	23	19
29	8	(a)	Arsenal	L	0-4		23	19
30	22	(a)	Middlesbrough	W	2-1	Martin, Stein	25	19
31	Mar 1	(h)	Blackburn R	D	2-2	Dean, Martin	26	19
32	5	(h)	Aston Villa	L	3-4	Dean, Griffiths, Stein	26	19
33	8	(a)	Newcastle U	L	0-1		26	20
34	15	(h)	West Ham U	L	1-2	Stein	26	21
35	29	(h)	Birmingham	L	2-4	Johnson, Stein	26	21
36	Apr 5	(a)	Leicester C	L	4-5	Martin 2, Critchley, Johnson	26	22
37	12	(a)	Grimsby T	L	2-4	Johnson, Martin	26	22
38	18	(h)	Burnley	W	3-0	Griffiths, Rigby, White	28	22
39	19	(a)	Manchester U	D	3-3	Martin, Stein, White	29	22
40	26	(h)	Sheffield U	W	3-2	White 2, Martin	31	22
41	28	(a)	Huddersfield T	W	2-1	Rigby 2	33	22
42	May 3	(h)	Sunderland	W	4-1	White 3, Johnson	35	22
							League Appearances	
							League Goals	
43	Jan 11	(a)	Carlisle U	W	4-2	Critchley 2, Dean 2	FA Cup Rd 3	
44	25	(a)	Blackburn R	L	1-4	Martin		4
							FA Cup Appearances	
							FA Cup Goals	

Attwood A	Coggins W	Common E	Cresswell W	Critchley E	Davies A	Dean W	Dunn J	Griffiths T P	Hart H	Johnson T	Kelly J	McClure	McPherson L	Martin G	O'Donnell	Rigby A	Ritchie H	Robson T	Rooney W	Sagar E	Stein J	Thomson J	Troup A	Virr A	Weldon A	White T	Wilkinson J	Williams B	
			2		1	9	8		6		4			10	3		7				11					5			1
9			2		1		8		6					10	3		7	4			11					5			2
			2		1	9	8		6		4			10	3		7				11					5			3
			2	7	1	9	8		6		4			10	3						11					5			4
			2		1	9	8		6		4			10	3		7				11					5			5
			2		1	9	8		6		4			10	3		7				11					5			6
			2		1	9	8		6		4			10	3						11					5	7		7
			2		1	9	8		6					10	3		7	4			11					5			8
			2		1	9	8		6					10	3		7	4			11					5			9
			2		1				6					10	3		7	4			11				8	5	9		10
			2	7	1				5					10	3			4			11				8	6	9		11
		2		7	1	9			5	6				10	3			4			11					8			12
			2	7	1	9			5	6				10	3			4			11					8			13
		2		7	1	9			5	6				10	3			4			11					8			14
			2	7	1	9			5	6				10	3			4			11					8			15
			2	7	1	9			5	6				10	3			4			11					8			16
			2	7	1				5					8	3	10		4			11					6	9		17
			2	7	1				5					8	3	10		4			11					6	9		18
			2	7	1				5					8	3	10		4			11	6				9			19
			2	7	1				5					8	3	10		4			11	6				9			20
			2		1			8	5					7	3	10		4			11		6			9			21
		2		7	1	9			5					10	3	11		4					6			8			22
		2			1					6		5		8	3	11	7	4					10			9			23
		2		7	1								6	8	3	10		4					11			5	9		24
			2	7	1	9		8	5				6		3	10		4			11								25
				7		9			5				6	8	3	10		4		1	11							2	26
			2	7	1	9		8	5				6		3	10		4			11								27
				7	1	9			5					8	3	10		4			11					6		2	28
9				7	1				5					8	3	10		4			11					6		2	29
				7		9			5					8	3	10		4		1	11					6		2	30
				7		9			5					8	3	10		4		1	11					6		2	31
				7		9			5					8	3	10		4		1	11					6		2	32
				7		9			5				10	8	3	11		4		1						6		2	33
						9			5				10	8	3	11		4		1	7	6			4			2	34
		3		7		9			5					8		10		4		1	11	6						2	35
			2	7		9					4		10	8	3	11				1	5								36
	1		2	7		9			5				10	4	8	3					11					6			37
	1		2	7					5				10	4	8	3					11	6						9	38
	1		2	7					5				10	4	8	3					11	6						9	39
	1		2	7					5				10	4	8	3					11	6						9	40
	1		2	7					5				10	4	8	3					11	6						9	41
	1		2	7					5				10	4	8	3					11	6						9	42
2	6	4	30	30	28	25	12	26	20	10	6	2	10	40	41	25	9	27	1	8	29	9	4	5	3	35	6	9	
				4		23		4		4				15		7	1				10		1			11			
			7		1	9	8		5	6					3	10		4			11							2	43
			7			9			5				6	8	3	10		4		1	11							2	44
				2	1	2	1		1	2			1	1	2	2		2		1	2							2	
				2		2								1																

1930-31

#	Date			Opponent		Score	Scorers	App	Goals
1	Aug 30	(a)	Plymouth A	W	3-2	White 2, Martin	2	
2	Sep 3	(h)	Preston N E	W	2-1	Griffiths, White	4	
3	6	(h)	Swansea T	W	5-1	Dean 2, White 2, Martin	6	3
4	8	(a)	Cardiff C	W	2-1	White 2	8	2
5	13	(a)	West Brom A	W	2-1	Dean, White	10	1
6	17	(h)	Cardiff C	D	1-1	Dean	11	1
7	20	(h)	Port Vale	L	2-3	Rigby, White	11	2
8	27	(a)	Bradford C	W	3-0	Critchley, Griffiths, Rigby	13	1
9	Oct 4	(h)	Charlton A	W	7-1	Critchley 2, Dean 2, Dunn 2, Griffiths	15	1
10	11	(a)	Barnsley	D	1-1	Johnson	16	1
11	18	(a)	Nottingham F	D	2-2	Dean, Dunn	17	2
12	25	(h)	Tottenham H	W	4-2	Dean, Dunn, Johnson, Rigby	19	1
13	Nov 1	(a)	Reading	W	2-0	Critchley, Dunn	21	1
14	8	(h)	Wolves	W	4-0	Dean, Johnson, Rigby, Wilkinson	23	1
15	15	(a)	Millwall	W	3-1	Dunn, Stein, Wilkinson	25	1
16	22	(h)	Stoke C	W	5-0	Dean 3, Johnson 2	27	1
17	29	(a)	Bradford	L	1-4	Johnson	27	1
18	Dec 6	(h)	Oldham A	W	6-4	Dean 4, Critchley, Dunn	29	1
19	13	(a)	Burnley	L	2-5	Dean, Stein	29	1
20	20	(h)	Southampton	W	2-1	Dean 2	31	1
21	25	(a)	Bury	D	2-2	Dean, Dunn	32	1
22	27	(h)	Plymouth A	W	9-1	Dean 4, Stein 4, Johnson	34	1
23	Jan 1	(h)	Bury	W	3-2	Dean, Gee, McPherson	36	1
24	3	(a)	Swansea T	W	5-2	Dean 2, Critchley, Johnson, Stein	38	1
25	17	(h)	West Brom	W	2-1	Dean, Martin	40	1
26	26	(a)	Port Vale	W	3-1	Critchley 2, Dean	42	1
27	31	(h)	Bradford C	W	4-2	Dean, Dunn, Gee, McClure	44	1
28	Feb 7	(a)	Charlton A	W	7-0	Dean 3, Critchley, Dunn, Johnson, Stein	46	1
29	18	(a)	Barnsley	W	5-2	Dean 2, Dunn 2, Critchley	48	1
30	21	(h)	Nottingham F	W	2-0	Dunn, Johnson	50	1
31	Mar 7	(h)	Reading	W	3-2	Critchley, Dunn, Johnson	52	1
32	16	(a)	Tottenham H	L	0-1		52	1
33	21	(h)	Millwall	W	2-0	Critchley, Johnson	54	1
34	25	(a)	Wolves	L	1-3	White	54	1
35	28	(a)	Stoke C	L	0-2		54	1
36	Apr 3	(a)	Bristol C	W	1-0	Stein	56	1
37	4	(h)	Bradford	W	4-2	Dean 2, Martin, Stein	58	1
38	6	(h)	Bristol C	L	1-3	Dean	58	1
39	11	(a)	Oldham A	D	3-3	Martin 2, Johnson	59	1
40	18	(h)	Burnley	W	3-2	Critchley, Johnson, opp.og	61	1
41	25	(a)	Southampton	L	1-2	Dean	61	1
42	May 2	(a)	Preston N E	L	1-2	Martin	61	1

League Appearances
League Goals

#	Date			Opponent		Score	Scorers		
43	Jan 10	(a)	Plymouth A	W	2-0	Dunn, Stein	FA Cup Rd 3	
44	24	(a)	Crystal P	W	6-0	Dean 4, Johnson, opp.og.	4	
45	Feb 14	(h)	Grimsby T	W	5-3	Johnson 2, Stein 2, Dean	5	
46	28	(h)	Southport	W	9-1	Dean 4, Critchley 2, Dunn 2, Johnson	6	
47	Mar 14	(n)	West Brom A	L	0-1		(Old Trafford) SF	

FA Cup Appearances
FA Cup Goals

Bocking W	Britton C	Coggins W	Cresswell W	Critchley E	Dean W	Dunn J	Gee C	Griffiths T P	Johnson T	Lowe H	McCambridge J	McClure J	McPherson L	Martin G	Rigby A	Stein J	Thomson J	White T	Wilkinson J	Williams B	No.
		1	3	7	9			5						4	10	11	6	8		2	1
		1	3	7	9			5						4	10	11	6	8		2	2
		1	3	7	9			5						4	10	11	6	8		2	3
		1	3	7	9			5						4	10	11	6	8		2	4
		1	3	7	9			5						4	10	11	6	8		2	5
		1	3	7	9			5						4	10	11	6	8		2	6
		1	3	7				5	10					4	8	11	6	9		2	7
		1	3	7		8		5	10		9			4		11	6			2	8
		1	3	7	9	8		5	10					4		11	6			2	9
		1	3	7	9	8		5	10					4		11	6			2	10
		1	3	7	9	8		5	10					4		11·	6			2	11
	4	1	3	7	9	8		5	10							11	6			2	12
	4	1	3	7	9	8		5	10							11	6			2	13
	4	1	3		9	8		5	10							11	6		7	2	14
	4	1	3		9	8		5	10							11	6		7	2	15
	4	1	3		9	8		5	10							11	6		7	2	16
	4	1	3		9	8		5	10							11	6		7	2	17
		1	3	7	9	8		5	10			2	4			11	6				18
		1	3	7	9	8		5	10			2	4			11	6				19
	4	1	3	7	9	8		5	10			2				11	6				20
		1	3	7	9	8		5	10			2	4			11	6				21
		1	3	7	9	8		5	10					4		11	6			2	22
		1	3	7	9	8		5	10					4		11	6			2	23
		1	3	7	9	8	5		10					4		11	6			2	24
		1	3	7	9		5		10					4	8	11	6			2	25
		1	3	7	9	8	5		10				4			11	6			2	26
		1	3	7	9	8	5		10				4			11	6			2	27
		1	3	7	9	8	5		10				4			11	6			2	28
		1	3	7	9	8	5		10			11	4				6			2	29
		1	3	7	9	8	5		10			11	4				6			2	30
		1	3	7	9	8	5		10			11	4				6			2	31
		1	3		9	8	5		10			11	4				6		7	2	32
	4	1	3	7	9	8	5		10			11					6			2	33
	4	1	3	7		8	5		10			11					6	9		2	34
	4	1	3	7		8	5		10			11					6	9		2	35
		1	3	7	9		5		10			11	4		8		6			2	36
		1	3	7	9		5		10			11	4		8		6			2	37
		1	3	7	9		5		10			11	4		8		6			2	38
		1	3	7	9		5		10	11			4		8		6			2	39
		1	3	7	9		5		10	11			4		8		6			2	40
		1	3	7	9		5		10	2		11	4		8		6				41
2		1	3	7		8	5		10	11			4				-6	9			42
1	10	42	42	37	37	28	20	23	36	4	1	15	17	15	14	28	41	10	5	36	
				13	39	14	2	3	14			1	1	7	4	10		10		2	opp.og. 1
		1	3	7	9	8	5		10					4		11	6			2	43
		1	3	7	9	8	5		10					4		11	6			2	44
		1	3	7	9	8	5		10					4		11	6			2	45
		1	3	7	9	8	5		10					4		11	6			2	46
		1	3		9	8	5		10					4		11	6		7	2	47
		5	5	4	5	5	5		5					5		5	5		1	5	
				2	9	3			4					3							opp.og. 1

1931-32

#	Date		Opponent		Result	Scorers	App	Goals
1	Aug 29	(h)	Birmingham	W	3-2	Dunn 3	2	
2	Sep 2	(a)	Portsmouth	W	3-0	White 3	4	
3	5	(a)	Sunderland	W	3-2	Griffiths, Johnson, Stein	6	2
4	12	(h)	Manchester C	L	0-1		6	7
5	16	(a)	Derby C	L	0-3		6	9
6	19	(a)	Liverpool	W	3-1	Dean 3	8	5
7	23	(h)	Derby C	W	2-1	Johnson 2	10	4
8	26	(a)	Arsenal	L	2-3	Critchley, Dean	10	6
9	Oct 3	(h)	Blackpool	W	3-2	Johnson 2, White	12	3
10	10	(a)	Sheffield U	W	5-1	Dean 3, Johnson, Stein	14	2
11	17	(h)	Sheffield W	W	9-3	Dean 5, Critchley, Johnson, Stein, White	16	2
12	24	(a)	Aston Villa	W	3-2	Critchley 2, White	18	1
13	31	(h)	Newcastle U	W	8-1	Dean 2, Johnson 2, White 2, Critchley, Stein	20	1
14	Nov 7	(a)	Huddersfield T	D	0-0		21	1
15	14	(h)	Chelsea	W	7-2	Dean 5, Johnson, Stein	23	1
16	21	(a)	Grimsby T	W	2-1	Stein, White	25	1
17	28	(h)	Leicester C	W	9-2	Dean 4, Johnson 2, White 2, Clark	27	1
18	Dec 5	(a)	West Ham U	L	2-4	Johnson, Stein	27	1
19	12	(h)	Middlesbrough	W	5-1	White 2, Critchley, Dean, Johnson	29	1
20	19	(a)	Bolton W	L	1-2	Dean	29	1
21	25	(a)	Blackburn R	L	3-5	White 2, Dean	29	1
22	26	(h)	Blackburn R	W	5-0	Dean 3, Johnson, White	31	1
23	Jan 2	(a)	Birmingham	L	0-4		31	1
24	16	(h)	Sunderland	W	4-2	Griffiths 2, Dean, White	33	1
25	27	(a)	Manchester C	L	0-1		33	1
26	30	(h)	Liverpool	W	2-1	Critchley, White	35	1
27	Feb 6	(h)	Arsenal	L	1-3	Johnson	35	1
28	13	(a)	Blackpool	L	0-2		35	1
29	20	(a)	Sheffield U	W	5-1	Dunn 2, Critchley, Dean, Johnson	37	1
30	27	(a)	Sheffield W	W	3-1	Dean 2, Dunn	39	1
31	Mar 5	(h)	Aston Villa	W	4-2	Dean 2, Dunn, Johnson	41	1
32	19	(h)	Huddersfield T	W	4-1	Dean 3, Johnson	43	1
33	25	(h)	West Brom A	W	2-1	Dean, Dunn	45	1
34	26	(a)	Chelsea	D	0-0		46	1
35	28	(a)	West Brom A	D	1-1	Stein	47	1
36	Apr 2	(h)	Grimsby T	W	4-2	Dunn 2, Dean, Johnson	49	1
37	9	(a)	Leicester C	W	1-0	Dean	51	1
38	16	(h)	West Ham U	W	6-1	Dean 3, Johnson 2, Stein	53	1
39	23	(a)	Middlesbrough	L	0-1		53	1
40	30	(h)	Bolton W	W	1-0	Dean	55	1
41	May 4	(a)	Newcastle U	D	0-0		56	1
42	7	(h)	Portsmouth	L	0-1		56	1
							League Appearances	
							League Goals	
43	Jan 19	(h)	Liverpool	L	1-2	Dean	FA Cup Rd 3	
							FA Cup Appearances	
							FA Cup Goals	

Bocking W	Clark A	Coggins W	Cresswell W	Critchley E	Dean W	Dunn J	Gee C	Griffiths P H	Johnson T	Lowe H	McClure J	McPherson L	Martin G	Rigby A	Sagar E	Stein J	Thomson J	White T	Williams B	#
2	4		3		9	8	5	7	10						1	11	6			1
2	4		3			8	5	7	10						1	11	6	9		2
2	4		3		9	8	5	7	10						1	11	6			3
2	4		3		9	8	5	7	10						1	11	6			4
2	4		3		9	8	5	7	10						1	11	6			5
2			3	7	9	8	5		10		4	6			1	11				6
2			3	7	9	8	5		10		4	6			1	11				7
2			3	7	9	8	5		10		4	6			1	11				8
	4		3	7	9		5		10						1	11	6	8	2	9
	4		3	7	9		5		10						1	11	6	8	2	10
	4		3	7	9		5		10						1	11	6	8	2	11
	4		3	7	9		5		10						1	11	6	8	2	12
	4		3	7	9		5		10						1	11	6	8	2	13
	4		3	7			5		10				9		1	11	6	8	2	14
	4		3	7	9		5		10						1	11	6	8	2	15
	4		3	7	9		5		10						1	11	6	8	2	16
	4		3	7	9		5		10						1	11	6	8	2	17
	4		3	7	9		5		10						1	11	6	8	2	18
	4		3	7	9		5		10						1	11	6	8	2	19
	4		3	7	9		5		10						1	11	6	8	2	20
	4		3	7	9		5		10						1	11	6	8	2	21
	4		3	7	9		5		10						1	11	6	8	2	22
	4		3	7			5		10				9		1	11	6	8	2	23
	4	1		7	9		5	11	10	3							6	8	2	24
	4		3	7	9		5	11	10						1		6	8	2	25
3	4			7	9				10		5			11	1		6	8	2	26
	4		3	7	9		5		10					11	1		6	8	2	27
	4		3	7	9				10		5			11	1		6	8	2	28
	4		3	7	9	8	5		10						1	11	6		2	29
	4		3	7	9	8	5		10						1	11	6		2	30
	4		3	7	9	8	5		10						1	11	6		2	31
	4		3	7	9	8	5		10						1	11	6		2	32
	4		3	7	9	8	5		10						1	11	6		2	33
	4		3	7	9	8	5		10						1	11	6		2	34
	4		3	7	9	8	5		10						1	11	6		2	35
	4		3	7	9	8	5		10						1	11	6		2	36
2	4		3	7	9	8	5								1	11	6	10		37
	4		3	7	9	8	5		10						1	11	6		2	38
	4		3	7	9	8	5		10						1	11	6		2	39
	4		3	7	9	8	5		10						1	11	6		2	40
	4		3	7		8			10		5				1	11	6	9	2	41
	4		3	7	9	8			10		5				1	11	6		2	42
10	39	1	40	37	38	22	38	7	41	1	7	3	2	3	41	37	39	23	33	
	1			8	45	10		3	22							9		18		
3	4			7	9		5		10						1	11	6	8	2	43
1	1			1	1		1		1						1	1	1	1	1	
						1														

1932-33

1	Aug 27	(a)	West Brom A	L	1-3	Dunn	0	
2	31	(h)	Sheffield W	W	2-1	Johnson 2	2	
3	Sep 3	(h)	Birmingham	W	4-1	Dean, Dunn, Johnson, Stein	4	8
4	5	(a)	Sheffield W	L	1-3	Dean	4	9
5	10	(a)	Sunderland	L	1-3	Stein	4	13
6	17	(h)	Manchester C	W	2-1	Dean 2	6	9
7	24	(a)	Arsenal	L	1-2	Critchley	6	13
8	Oct 1	(h)	Liverpool	W	3-1	Dean 2, Critchley	8	12
9	8	(h)	Blackpool	W	2-0	Dean, Johnson	10	9
10	15	(a)	Derby C	L	0-2		10	11
11	22	(a)	Leicester C	D	2-2	McGourty, Stein	11	10
12	29	(h)	Portsmouth	D	1-1	Dean	12	10
13	Nov 5	(a)	Newcastle U	W	2-1	Dean, Stein	14	10
14	12	(h)	Aston Villa	D	3-3	Dean, Johnson, Stein	15	9
15	19	(a)	Middlesbrough	W	2-0	Geldard, Johnson	17	9
16	26	(h)	Bolton W	D	2-2	Geldard, Johnson	18	10
17	Dec 3	(a)	Chelsea	L	0-1		18	9
18	10	(h)	Huddersfield T	W	2-0	Dunn, White	20	9
19	17	(a)	Sheffield U	L	2-3	Stein, Thomson	20	9
20	24	(h)	Wolves	W	5-1	Dean 2, Dunn, Johnson, Stein	22	7
21	26	(a)	Blackburn R	L	1-3	Geldard	22	8
22	27	(h)	Blackburn R	W	6-1	Johnson 3, Dunn, Stein, opp.og	24	7
23	31	(h)	West Brom A	L	1-2	Dean	24	8
24	Jan 7	(a)	Birmingham C	L	0-4		24	10
25	21	(h)	Sunderland	W	6-1	Dean 2, Dunn, Johnson, Stein, Thomson	26	10
26	Feb 1	(a)	Manchester C	L	0-3		26	12
27	4	(h)	Arsenal	D	1-1	Stein	27	10
28	11	(a)	Liverpool	L	4-7	Dean 2, Johnson, Stein	27	11
29	22	(a)	Blackpool	L	1-2	Dunn	27	11
30	25	(h)	Derby C	W	4-2	Dean, Dunn, Geldard, opp.og	29	11
31	Mar 8	(h)	Leicester C	W	6-3	Dean 3, Dunn 2, White	31	10
32	11	(a)	Portsmouth	D	2-2	Dean, Stein	32	10
33	25	(a)	Aston Villa	L	1-2	Cunliffe	32	10
34	Apr 1	(h)	Middlesbrough	D	0-0		33	10
35	5	(h)	Newcastle U	D	0-0		34	11
36	8	(a)	Bolton W	W	4-2	Dean 2, McGourty, opp. og	36	10
37	15	(h)	Chelsea	W	3-2	Stein 2, Thomson	38	9
38	17	(h)	Leeds U	L	0-1		38	8
39	18	(a)	Leeds U	L	0-1		38	11
40	22	(a)	Huddersfield T	D	0-0		39	11
41	May 3	(h)	Sheffield U	W	1-0	Stein	41	11
42	6	(a)	Wolves	L	2-4	Geldard, Stein	41	11

League Appearances
League Goals

43	Jan 14	(a)	Leicester C	W	3-2	Dean, Dunn, Stein	FA Cup Rd 3	
44	28	(h)	Bury	W	3-1	Johnson 2, Dean	4	
45	Feb 18	(h)	Leeds U	W	2-0	Dean, Stein	5	
46	Mar 3	(h)	Luton T	W	6-0	Johnson 2, Stein 2, Dean, Dunn	6	
47	18	(n)	West Ham U	W	2-1	Critchley, Dunn	(Molineux) SF	
48	Apr 29	(n)	Manchester C	W	3-0	Dean, Dunn, Stein	(Wembley) F	

FA Cup Appearances
FA Cup Goals

Archer J	Bocking W	Britton C	Cook W	Cresswell W	Critchley E	Cunliffe J	Dean W	Dunn J	Gee C	Geldard A	Griffiths P H	Johnson T	McClure J	McGourty J	Mercer J	Sagar E	Stein J	Stevens G	Thomson J	Turner G	Watson J G	White T	Williams B	No.
				3	7		9	8	5			10	4			1	11		6				2	1
				3	7		9	8				10	4			1	11		6			5	2	2
				3	7		9	8				10	4			1	11		6			5	2	3
				3	7		9	8				10	4			1	11		6			5	2	4
				3	7		9	8				10	4			1	11		6			5	2	5
		4		3	7		9	8				10				1	11		6			5	2	6
		4		3	7		9					10		8		1	11		6			5	2	7
		4		3	7		9					10		8		1	11		6			5	2	8
		4		3	7		9					10		8		1	11		6			5	2	9
		4		3	7		9					10		8		1	11		6			5	2	10
6		4		3	7		9					10		8		1	11		5				2	11
6		4		3	7		9					10		8		1	11		5				2	12
		4		3	7		9					10		8		1	11		6			5	2	13
		4		3	7		9					10		8		1	11		6			5	2	14
		4		3			9			7		10		8		1	11		6			5	2	15
		4		3			9			7		10		8		1	11		6			5	2	16
		4		3			9	8		7		10				1	11		6			5	2	17
		4		3			9	8		7		10				1	11		6			5	2	18
		4		3			9	8		7		10				1	11		6			5	2	19
		4		3			9	8		7		10				1	11		6			5	2	20
	2	4		3			9	8		7		10				1	11		6			5		21
	2	4		3			9	8		7		10				1	11		6			5		22
		4	2	3			9	8		7		10				1			6	11		5		23
		4	2	3			9		5	7		10				1			6	11		8		24
		4	2	3			9	8	5	7		10				1	11		6					25
		4	2	3				8	5	7		10				1	11	9	6					26
		4	2	3			9	8		7		10				1	11		6			5		27
		4	2	3			9	8		7		10				1	11		6			5		28
		4	2	3				8		7	9	10				1	11		6			5		29
		4	2	3			9	8		7		10				1	11		6			5		30
		4	2	3		7	9	8				10				1	11		6			5		31
		4	2	3		7	9	8	5			10				1	11		6					32
		4	2	3			9	8		7		10				1	11		6			5		33
		4	2	3			9	8		7						1	11		6		10	5		34
		4	2	3			9			7		10		8		1	11		6			5		35
		4	2	3			9			7		10		8		1	11		6			5		36
		4	2	3			9	8		7		10				1	11		6			5		37
		4	2	3			9		5	7		10		8		1	11		6					38
6	3		2					8	5	7		10	4			1	11	9						39
		4	2	3			9	8		7		10				1	11		6			5		40
		4	2	3			9	8		7		10				1	11		6			5		41
		4	2	3			9	8		7		10				1	11		6			5		42
3	3	36	20	41	17	2	39	25	7	26	1	40	5	14	1	42	40	2	41	2	1	34	20	
					2	1	24	10		5		13		2			16		3			2	Opp.og 3	
		4	2	3			9	8		7		10				1	11		6			5		43
		4	2	3			9	8		7		10				1	11		6			5		44
		4	2	3			9	8		7		10				1	11		6			5		45
		4	2	3	7		9	8				10				1	11		6			5		46
		4	2	3	7		9	8				10				1	11		6			5		47
		4	2	3			9	8		7		10				1	11		6			5		48
		6	6	6	2		6	6		4		6				6	6		6			6		
				1			5	4				4					5							

1933-34

1	Aug	26	(h)	West Brom A	W	1-0	Dean	2	
2		30	(a)	Derby C	D	1-1	Dean	3	
3	Sep	2	(a)	Birmingham	D	2-2	Dean 2	4	5
4		9	(h)	Sheffield W	L	2-3	Dean, White	4	14
5		16	(a)	Manchester C	D	2-2	Dean, Geldard	5	15
6		23	(h)	Arsenal	W	3-1	Dean, Dunn, White	7	11
7		30	(a)	Liverpool	L	2-3	Johnson, White	7	15
8	Oct	7	(a)	Middlesbrough	L	0-2		7	18
9		14	(h)	Blackburn R	W	7-1	White 3, Dunn, Geldard, Johnson, Stein	9	16
10		21	(h)	Tottenham H	D	1-1	White	10	14
11		28	(a)	Leicester C	L	1-3	White	10	17
12	Nov	4	(h)	Huddersfield T	L	0-1		10	20
13		11	(a)	Sheffield U	D	1-1	Dunn	11	18
14		18	(h)	Wolves	L	1-2	Dunn	11	19
15		25	(a)	Stoke C	W	2-1	Cunliffe, White	13	18
16	Dec	2	(h)	Chelsea	W	2-1	Cunliffe 2	15	16
17		9	(a)	Portsmouth	D	0-0		16	13
18		16	(h)	Sunderland	W	1-0	Critchley	18	11
19		23	(a)	Aston Villa	L	1-2	White	18	13
20		25	(a)	Newcastle U	W	2-1	White, Stein	20	11
21		26	(h)	Newcastle U	L	3-7	White 2, Critchley	20	12
22		30	(a)	West Brom A	D	3-3	Stein 2, Cunliffe	21	13
23	Jan	1	(h)	Derby C	L	0-3		21	14
24		6	(h)	Birmingham	W	2-0	Critchley, Cunliffe	23	14
25		20	(a)	Sheffield W	D	0-0		24	15
26	Feb	3	(a)	Arsenal	W	2-1	Cunliffe, White	26	13
27		7	(h)	Manchester C	W	2-0	Johnson, Stein	28	10
28		10	(h)	Liverpool	D	0-0		29	10
29		17	(h)	Middlesbrough	D	1-1	Stein	30	10
30		24	(a)	Blackburn R	D	1-1	Cunliffe	31	10
31	Mar	3	(a)	Tottenham H	L	0-3		31	11
32		10	(h)	Leicester C	D	1-1	Stein	32	12
33		24	(h)	Sheffield U	W	4-0	Higham 2, Gledard, Stein	34	11
34		30	(a)	Leeds U	D	2-2	Cunliffe, Higham	35	10
35		31	(a)	Wolves	L	0-2		35	10
36	Apr	2	(h)	Leeds U	W	2-0	Cunliffe, Geldard	37	9
37		7	(h)	Stoke C	D	2-2	Geldard, Higham	38	9
38		14	(a)	Chelsea	L	0-2		38	11
39		21	(h)	Portsmouth	D	1-1	Dean	39	11
40		25	(a)	Huddersfield T	L	0-1		39	12
41		28	(a)	Sunderland	L	2-3	Higham 2	39	14
42	May	5	(h)	Aston Villa	D	2-2	Dean, Stevenson	40	14
							League Appearances		
							League Goals		
43		Jan 13	(a)	Tottenham H	L	0-3		FA Cup Rd 3	
							FA Cup Appearances		
							FA Cup Goals		

Archer J	Bocking W	Britton C	Coggins W	Cook W	Coulter J	Cresswell W	Critchley E	Cunliffe J	Dean W	Dunn J	Gee C	Geldard A	Higham N	Johnson T	Jones J E	McGourty J	Sagar E	Stein J	Stevenson A	Thomson J	Watson J G	White T	Williams B	
		4		2		3			9	8		7		10			1	11		6		5		1
		4		2		3			9	8		7		10			1	11		6		5		2
		4		2		3			9	8		7		10			1	11		6		5		3
		4	1	2		3			9	8		7		10				11		6		5		4
		4		2		3			9	8		7		10			1	11		6		5		5
		4		2		3			9	8		7		10			1	11		6		5		6
		4		2		3				8	5	7		10			1	11		6		9		7
		4		2		3				8	5	7		10			1	11		6		9		8
		4		2		3				8	5	7		10			1	11		6		9		9
	3	4		2						8	5	7		10			1	11		6		9		10
		4		2		3				8	5	7		10			1	11		6		9		11
		4		2		3			9	8		7		10			1	11		6		5		12
		4		2		3	7		9	8				10			1	11		6		5		13
		4		2		3	7		9	8							1	11		6	10	5		14
		4		2		3	7			8	5			10			1	11		6		9		15
		4				3	7		9	8	5			10			1	11		6			2	16
		4		2		3	7		9	8				10			1	11		6		5		17
6		4		2		3	7	10		8	5						1	11				9		18
6		4		2		3	7	10		8	5						1	11				9		19
6		4		2		3	7	10		8	5						1	11				9		20
6		4		2		3	7	10		8	5						1	11				9		21
6		4		2		3	7	10		8							1	11	5			9		22
6		4		2		3	7	10		8							1	11	5			9		23
		4		2		3	7		9	8				10			1	11		6		5		24
		4				3	7	10		8	5						1	11		6		9	2	25
		4				3	7			8	5						1	11	10	6		9	2	26
		4		3			7			8	5		10	9			1	11		6			2	27
		4	1	3			7			8	5		9					11	10	6			2	28
		4		3					9	8	5	7	10				1	11		6			2	29
		4		3					9	8	5	7	10				1	11		6			2	30
		4		3					9	8	5	7	10				1	11		6			2	31
		4		3						8	5	7	10				1	11		6		9	2	32
		4		3						8	5	7	9				1	11	10	6			2	33
		4		3						8	5	7	9				1	11	10	6			2	34
		4		3						8	5	7	9				1	11	10	6			2	35
		4								8	5	7	9		3		1	11	10	6			2	36
		4								8	5	7	9		3		1	11	10	6			2	37
		4								8	5	7			3		1	11	10	6		9		38
		4						10		8	5	7	9		3		1	11		6			2	39
		4			7					8	5		9		3		1	11	10	6			2	40
		4			7					8	5		9		3		1	11	10	6			2	41
		4				3				8	5	7	9				1	11	10	6			2	42
6	1	42	2	35	3	25	16	27	12	23	29	24	13	19	5	1	40	42	12	38	1	28	18	
								3	9	9	4	5	6		3			8	1			14		
		4		2		3	7		9	8				10			1	11		6		5		43
		1		1		1	1		1	1				1			1	1		1		1		

1934-35

1	Aug 25	(a)	Tottenham H	D	1-1	Dean		1	
2	29	(h)	Leicester C	W	2-1	Dean, Leyfield		3	
3	Sep 1	(h)	Preston N E	W	4-1	Leyfield 2, Dean, Stein		5	3
4	3	(a)	Leicester C	L	2-5	Dean, Leyfield		5	5
5	8	(a)	Grimsby T	D	0-0			6	7
6	15	(h)	Liverpool	W	1-0	Dean		8	5
7	22	(h)	Huddersfield T	W	4-2	Cunliffe 2, Dean, Stein		10	4
8	29	(a)	Wolves	L	2-4	Leyfield, opp.og		10	6
9	Oct 6	(h)	Chelsea	W	3-2	Dean 2, opp.og		12	4
10	13	(a)	Aston Villa	D	2-2	Cunliffe, Dean		13	5
11	20	(a)	Leeds U	L	0-2			13	8
12	27	(h)	West Brom A	W	4-0	Coulter, Cunliffe, Dean, Stevenson		15	6
13	Nov 3	(a)	Arsenal	L	0-2			15	8
14	10	(h)	Portsmouth	W	3-2	Dean 2, Cunliffe		17	5
15	17	(a)	Stoke C	L	2-3	Dean, Stevenson		17	6
16	24	(h)	Manchester C	L	1-2	Coulter		17	8
17	Dec 1	(a)	Middlesbrough	L	2-3	opp.og 2		17	10
18	8	(h)	Blackburn R	W	5-2	Dean 2, Stevenson 2, Cunliffe		19	10
19	15	(h)	Sheffield W	D	0-0			20	10
20	22	(h)	Birmingham	W	2-0	Coulter, Stevenson		22	7
21	25	(h)	Sunderland	W	6-2	Cunliffe 2, Coulter, Dean, Geldard, Stevenson		24	6
22	26	(a)	Sunderland	L	0-7			24	10
23	29	(h)	Tottenham H	W	5-2	Dean 3, Coulter, Cunliffe		26	7
24	Jan 1	(h)	Derby C	D	2-2	Geldard 2		27	6
25	5	(a)	Preston N E	D	2-2	Cunliffe, Stevenson		28	7
26	19	(a)	Grimsby T	W	3-1	Cunliffe 2, Dean		30	5
27	Feb 7	(a)	Huddersfield T	D	1-1	Coulter		31	6
28	9	(h)	Wolves	W	5-2	Cunliffe 2, Stevenson 2, Coulter		33	5
29	20	(a)	Chelsea	L	0-3			33	7
30	23	(h)	Aston Villa	D	2-2	Dean, Stevenson		34	7
31	Mar 6	(h)	Leeds U	D	4-4	Coulter 2, Cunliffe, Dean		35	7
32	9	(a)	West Brom a	W	1-0	Coulter		37	5
33	16	(h)	Arsenal	L	0-2			37	5
34	20	(a)	Liverpool	L	1-2	Dean		37	6
35	23	(a)	Portsmouth	L	1-5	Coulter		37	7
36	30	(h)	Stoke C	W	5-0	Stein 2, Stevenson 2, Dean		39	5
37	Apr 6	(a)	Manchester C	D	2-2	Leyfield 2		40	5
38	13	(h)	Middlesbrough	D	1-1	Dean		41	5
39	20	(a)	Blackburn R	L	2-6	Geldard, Thomson		41	8
40	22	(a)	Derby C	L	1-4	Dean		41	10
41	May 1	(h)	Sheffield W	D	2-2	Geldard, Stevenson		42	9
42	4	(a)	Birmingham	W	3-2	Stevenson 2, opp.og		44	8

League Apparances
League Goals

43	Jan 12	(h)	Grimsby T	W	6-3	Geldard 3, Stevenson 2, Cunliffe		FA Cup Rd 3	
44	26	(a)	Sunderland	D	1-1	Cunliffe		4	
45	30	(h)	Sunderland	W	6-4	Coulter 3, Geldard 2, Stevenson		Replay	
46	Feb 16	(h)	Derby C	W	3-1	Coulter 2, Dean		5	
47	Mar 2	(h)	Bolton W	L	1-2	Coulter		6	

FA Cup Appearances
FA Cup Goals

Bradshaw G	Britton C	Clark A	Cook W	Coulter J	Cresswell W	Cunliffe J	Dean W	Dickinson	Dunn J	Gee C	Geldard A	Higham N	Jackson G	Jones J E	King F	Leyfield C	Mercer J	Sagar E	Stein J	Stevenson A	Thomson J	White T	Williams B	
	4		3		2	8	9			5	7							1	11		6	10		1
	4		3		2	8	9			5						7		1	11		6	10		2
	4		3		2	8	9			5						7		1	11	10	6			3
	4		3		2	8	9			5						7		1	11	10	6			4
	4		3		2	8	9			5						7		1	11	10	6			5
	4		3		2	8	9			5						7		1	11	10	6			6
	4		3		2	8	9			5						7		1	11	10	6			7
			3		2		9		8	5						7	4	1	11	10	6			8
	4		3		2	8	9			5						7		1	11	10	6			9
	4		3		2	8	9			5						7		1	11	10	6			10
	4		3		2	8	9			5		10				7		1	11		6			11
	4		3	11	2	8	9			5	7							1		10	6			12
	4		3	11	2	8	9			5	7							1		10	6			13
	4		3	11	2	8	9			5	7							1		10	6			14
	4		3	11	2	8	9			5	7							1		10	6			15
	4		3	11	2	8	9			5	7							1		10	6			16
	4		3	11		8	9			5	7							1		10	6		2	17
	4		3	11		8	9			5	7							1		10	6		2	18
	4		3	11		10	9		8	5	7							1			6		2	19
	4		3	11			9		8	5	7							1		10	6		2	20
	4		3	11		8	9			5	7							1		10	6		2	21
	4		3	11		8	9				7							1		10	6	5	2	22
	4		3	11	2	8	9			5	7							1		10	6			23
	4		3	11	2	8	9			5	7							1		10	6			24
	4		3	11	2	8	9			5	7							1		10	6			25
	4			11	2	8	9			5	7			3				1		10	6			26
		2		11		8	9			5	7			3			4	1		10	6			27
	4		3	11		8	9			5	7		2					1		10	6			28
			3	11		8	9			5	7		2				4	1		10	6			29
1	4		3	11			9		8	5	7		2							10	6			30
1	4	2		11		8	9			5	7			3						10	6			31
	8			11			9			5	7		2	3	4			1		10	6			32
	4			11			9			5	7		2	3	8			1		10	6			33
	4			10		8	9			5	7		2	3				1	11		6			34
	4			11		8	9	10		5	7		2	3				1			6			35
	4		3			8	9				7							1	11	10	6	5	2	36
			3			8	9				7						4	1	11	10	6	5	2	37
	4		3			8	9			5	7							1	11	10	6		2	38
	4					8	9			5	7			3				1	11	10	6		2	39
	4		3			8	9			5	7		2					1	11	10	6			40
	5						9		8		7			3	1		4		11	10	6		2	41
	5						9		8		7			3	1		4		11	10	6		2	42
2	36	2	29	24	25	39	38	1	6	37	31	1	8	10	5	11	8	35	19	36	42	5	12	
				11		15	26			5						7			4	15	1			opp.og 5
	4		3	11	2	8	9			5	7							1		10	6			43
	4			11	2	8	9			5	7			3				1		10	6			44
	4			11	2	8	9			5	7			3				1		10	6			45
	4		3	11		8	9			5	7		2					1		10	6			46
1	4			11	2	8	9			5	7			3						10	6			47
1	5		2	5	4	5	5			5	5		1	3				4		5	5			
				6		2	1				5									3				

1935-36

1	Aug	31	(h)	Derby C	W	4-0	Dean, Geldard, Leyfield, Stevenson	2	
2	Sep	4	(a)	Portsmouth	L	0-2		2	
3		7	(a)	Liverpool	L	0-6		2	18
4		11	(h)	Portsmouth	W	3-0	Cunliffe, Geldard, Hartill	4	11
5		14	(a)	Bolton W	L	0-2		4	17
6		18	(a)	Preston N E	D	2-2	Stevenson 2	5	13
7		21	(h)	Huddersfield T	L	1-3	Cunliffe	5	16
8		28	(a)	Middlesbrough	L	1-6	Cunliffe	5	17
9	Oct	5	(h)	Aston Villa	D	2-2	Cunliffe, Stevenson	6	19
10		12	(a)	Wolves	L	0-4		6	21
11		19	(h)	Chelsea	W	5-1	Stevenson 2, Archer, Dean, Miller	8	19
12		26	(a)	Blackburn R	D	1-1	Archer	9	19
13	Nov	2	(h)	Stoke C	W	5-1	Cunliffe 4, Dean	11	16
14		9	(a)	Manchester C	L	0-1		11	19
15		16	(h)	Arsenal	L	0-2		11	21
16		23	(a)	Grimsby T	W	4-0	Bentham 2, Leyfield 2	13	17
17		30	(h)	Sunderland	L	0-3		13	20
18	Dec	7	(a)	West Brom A	L	1-6	Cunliffe	13	20
19		14	(h)	Leeds U	D	0-0		14	20
20		21	(a)	Birmingham	L	2-4	Cunliffe, Gillick	14	20
21		26	(h)	Sheffield W	W	4-3	Bentham, Britton, Cunliffe, Gillick	16	21
22		28	(a)	Derby C	D	3-3	Bentham, Cunliffe, Geldard	17	21
23	Jan	4	(h)	Liverpool	D	0-0		18	21
24		22	(h)	Bolton W	D	3-3	Dean 2, Stevenson	19	21
25		29	(a)	Huddersfield T	L	1-2	Gillick	19	21
26	Feb	1	(h)	Middlesbrough	W	5-2	Dean 2, Cunliffe, Geldard, Gillick	21	20
27		3	(a)	Sheffield W	D	3-3	Cunliffe 2, Dean	22	20
28		8	(a)	Aston Villa	D	1-1	Dean	23	20
29		15	(h)	Wolves	W	4-1	Geldard 2, Cunliffe, White	25	18
30		22	(a)	Chelsea	D	2-2	Dean 2	26	18
31		29	(h)	Manchester C	D	2-2	Gillick 2	27	16
32	Mar	7	(a)	Sunderland	D	3-3	Cunliffe, Dean, Stevenson	28	19
33		14	(h)	Blackburn R	W	4-0	Dean 2, Cunliffe, Mercer	30	13
34		25	(a)	Arsenal	D	1-1	Gillick	31	14
35		28	(h)	Grimsby T	W	4-0	Gillick, Stevenson, White, opp.og	33	13
36	Apr	4	(a)	Stoke C	L	1-2	Stevenson	33	14
37		10	(h)	Brentford	L	1-2	Geldard	33	17
38		11	(h)	West Brom A	W	5-3	Cunliffe 4, White	35	14
39		13	(a)	Brentford	L	1-4	Gillick	35	15
40		18	(a)	Leeds U	L	1-3	Bell	35	18
41		25	(h)	Birmingham	W	4-3	Dean 3, Cunliffe	37	18
42	May	2	(h)	Preston N E	W	5-0	Bell 2, Leyfield 2, Britton	39	16

League Appearances
League Goals

43		Jan	11	(h)	Preston N E	L	1-3	Geldard	FA Cup Rd 3

FA Cup Appearances
FA Cup Goals

Archer J	Bell J	Bentham S	Britton C	Cook W	Cresswell W	Cunliffe J	Dean W	Gee C	Geldard A	Gillick T	Hartill W	Jackson G	Jones J E	King F	Leyfield C	Mercer J	Miller W	Sagar E	Stevenson A	Thomson J	White T	Williams B	No.
			4	3			9		7						11		8	1	10	6	5	2	1
			4		3		9		7						11		8	1	10	6	5	2	2
			4		3		9		7						11		8	1	10	6	5	2	3
			4		3	10		5	7			9	2		11		8	1	6				4
			4		3	10		5	7			9	2		11		8	1	6				5
			4			10		5	7				2	3	11			1	8	6	9		6
			4			10		5	7				2	3	11			1	8	6	9		7
6						10		5	7			9	2	3	11	4		1	8				8
			4			10		5	7			9	2	3	11			1	8	6			9
			4			10		5	7			9	2	3	11			1	8	6			10
11			4				9		7				2	3		6	8	1	10		5		11
11			4	2			9		7				3			6	8	1	10		5		12
11			4	2		10	9		7				3			6	8	1			5		13
11			4	2		10	9		7				3			6	8	1			5		14
			4	2		10	9		7				3		11	6		1	8		5		15
		8	4	2		10	9		7				3		11	6		1			5		16
		8	4	2		10	9		7				3		11	6		1			5		17
		8	4	2		10	9		7				3		11	6		1			5		18
			4			10	9		7			2	3		11	6	8	1			5		19
		8	4				9		7	11		2	3			6	10	1			5		20
		8	4	2			9		7	11			3			6	10	1			5		21
		8	4	2			9		7	11			3			6	10	1			5		22
		8	4	2			9		7	11			3			6	10	1			5		23
			4	2		8	9		7	11			3			6		1	10		5		24
				2		8	9	5	7	11			3			4		1	10	6			25
				2		8	9		7	11			3			4		1	10	6	5		26
				3		8	9	5	7	11			2			4		1	10	6			27
				3		8	9		7	11			2			4		1	10	6	5		28
						8	9		7	11		2	3			4		1	10	6	5		29
				2		8	9		7	11			3			4		1	10	6	5		30
				2		8	9		7	11			3			4		1	10	6	5		31
				2		8	9		7	11			3			4		1	10	6	5		32
				2		8	9		7	11			3			4		1	10	6	5		33
				2		8	9		7	11			3			4		1	10	6	5		34
				2		8	9		7	11			3			4		1	10	6	5		35
				2		8	9		7	11			3			4		1	10	6	5		36
				2		8	9		7	11			3			4		1	10	6	5		37
				2		8	9		7	11			3			4		1	10	6	5		38
						8	9		7	11		2	3			4		1	10	6	5		39
11	9					8			7			2	3			4		1	10	6	5		40
			4			8	9			11		2	3		7	6	10	1			5		41
	9		4			8				11		2	3		7	6		1	10		5		42
6	**2**	**7**	**25**	**25**	**4**	**37**	**29**	**9**	**39**	**23**	**5**	**18**	**34**	**5**	**17**	**33**	**15**	**37**	**29**	**25**	**35**	**3**	
2	3	4	2			23	17		7	9		1	5		1	1			10		3		opp.og 1
		8	4	2			9		7	11			3			6	10	1			5		43
		1	1	1			1		1	1			1			1	1	1			1		
									1														

1936-37

#	Date		Opponent	Res	Score	Scorers	App	Goals
1	Aug 29	(a)	Arsenal	L	2-3	Dean, Stevenson	0	
2	Sep 2	(h)	Sheffield W	W	3-1	Dean, Gillick, Stevenson	2	
3	5	(h)	Brentford	W	3-0	Dean 2, Gillick	4	2
4	10	(a)	Sheffield W	L	4-6	Gillick 2, Miller, Stevenson	4	7
5	12	(a)	Bolton W	W	2-1	Gillick, Stevenson	6	5
6	19	(h)	Liverpool	W	2-0	Dean, Stevenson	8	3
7	26	(h)	Huddersfield T	W	2-1	Dean, Hurel	10	3
8	Oct 3	(a)	Sunderland	L	1-3	Stevenson	10	6
9	10	(h)	Wolves	W	1-0	Dean	12	5
10	17	(a)	Leeds U	L	0-3		12	5
11	24	(h)	Birmingham	D	3-3	Dean, Gillick, Stevenson	13	5
12	31	(a)	Middlesbrough	L	0-2		13	10
13	Nov 7	(h)	West Brom A	W	4-2	Dean 3, Cunliffe	15	8
14	14	(a)	Manchester C	L	1-4	Stevenson	15	12
15	21	(h)	Portsmouth	W	4-0	Coulter 2, Gillick, Stevenson	17	9
16	28	(a)	Chelsea	L	0-4		17	12
17	Dec 5	(h)	Stoke C	D	1-1	Dean	18	13
18	12	(a)	Charlton A	L	0-2		18	14
19	19	(h)	Grimsby T	W	3-0	Dean 2, Gillick	20	11
20	25	(h)	Derby C	W	7-0	Cunliffe 3, Dean 2, Stevenson 2	22	9
21	26	(h)	Arsenal	D	1-1	Gillick	23	8
22	28	(a)	Derby C	L	1-3	Dean	23	10
23	Jan 1	(h)	Preston N E	D	2-2	Gillick, Leyfield	24	9
24	2	(a)	Brentford	D	2-2	Coulter, Cunliffe	25	9
25	9	(h)	Bolton W	W	3-2	Dean 2, Stevenson	27	9
26	23	(a)	Liverpool	L	2-3	Stevenson 2	27	10
27	Feb 3	(a)	Huddersfield T	W	3-0	Bell, Coulter, Cunliffe	29	8
28	6	(h)	Sunderland	W	3-0	Dean 2, Coulter	31	7
29	13	(a)	Wolves	L	2-7	Cunliffe, Lawton	31	10
30	27	(a)	Birmingham	L	0-2		31	10
31	Mar 3	(h)	Leeds U	W	7-1	Dean 2, Stevenson 2, Geldard, Gillick, Lawton	33	9
32	6	(h)	Middlesbrough	L	2-3	Geldard, Stevenson	33	9
33	13	(a)	West Brom A	L	1-2	Gillick	33	10
34	20	(h)	Manchester C	D	1-1	Stevenson	34	10
35	26	(a)	Manchester U	L	1-2	Gillick	34	11
36	27	(a)	Portsmouth	D	2-2	Geldard, Gillick	35	11
37	29	(h)	Manchester U	L	2-3	Lawton, Stevenson	35	11
38	Apr 3	(h)	Chelsea	D	0-0		36	13
39	10	(a)	Stoke C	L	1-2	Cunliffe	36	14
40	14	(a)	Preston N E	L	0-1		36	14
41	17	(h)	Charlton A	D	2-2	Cunliffe, Dean	37	15
42	24	(a)	Grimsby T	L	0-1		37	17
							League Appearances	League Goals
43	Jan 16	(h)	Bournemouth	W	5-0	Gillick 2, Stevenson 2, Cunliffe	FA Cup Rd 3	
44	30	(h)	Sheffield W	W	3-0	Britton, Coulter, Dean	4	
45	Feb 20	(h)	Tottenham H	D	1-1	Coulter	5	
46	22	(a)	Tottenham H	L	3-4	Dean 2, Lawton	Replay	
							FA Cup Appearances	FA Cup Goals

Bell J	Bentham S	Britton C	Cook W	Coulter J	Cunliffe J	Dean W	Gee C	Geldard A	Gillick T	Hurel E	Jackson G	Jones J E	Jones T G	King F	Lawton T	Leyfield C	Mercer J	Miller W	Morton H	Sagar E	Stevenson A	Thomson J	Watson T	White T	#
		4	3	11	8	9	5		7		2						6			1	10				1
		4	3	11	8	9	5		7		2						6			1	10				2
		4	3	11	8	9	5		7		2						6			1	10				3
		4	3	11		9	5		7		2						6	8		1	10				4
		4	3	11		9	5		7	8	2						6			1	10				5
		4	3	11	8	9	5		7		2						6			1	10				6
		4	3	11		9	5		7	8	2						6			1	10				7
		4	3	11		9	5		7	8	2						6			1	10				8
		4	3	11		9	5	7	8		2						6			1	10				9
		4	3			9		7	8		2			5		11	6			1	10				10
		4	3			9	5	7	8	2						11	6			1	10				11
		4				9	5	7	8	2	3					11	6			1	10				12
		4	3		8	9	5	7		2						11	6			1	10				13
		4	3		8	9	5	7		2						11	6			1	10				14
		4	2	11	8	9	5	7			3						6			1	10				15
		4	2		8	9	5		7	11	3						6			1	10				16
		4	2	11	8	9	5	7			3						6			1	10				17
9		4	2	11	8		5	7			3						6			1	10				18
		4	2		8	9	5	7			3				11	6			1	10					19
		4	2		8	9	5	7			3				11	6			1	10					20
		4	2		8	9	5	7			3				11	6			1	10					21
		4	2		8	9	5	7			3				11				1	10	6				22
		4	2		8	9	5	7			3				11	6			1	10					23
		4	2	11	8	9	5	7											1	10	3	6			24
		4	2	11	8	9	5	7			3			1			6				10				25
		4	2	11	8	9	5	7			3						6			1	10				26
9		4	2	11	8		5	7			3						6			1	10				27
		4	2	11	8	9	5	7			3			1			6				10				28
	10	4	2	11	8			7		3				9		6			1				5		29
		4	2			9	5	7	11	3					8		6			1	10				30
		4	3			9	5	7	11	2					8		6			1	10				31
		4	3			9	5	7	11	2			1	8		6				10					32
		4	3		8		5	7	11	2				9		6		1		10					33
		4	3			9	5	7	11	2				8		6		1		10					34
		4	3			9	5	7	11	2				8		6		1		10					35
		4	3		8	9	5	7	11	2						6		1		10					36
		4	3			9	5	7	11	2				8		6		1		10					37
		4	3		8	9	5	7	11	2								1		10	6				38
		4	3		8		5	7	11	2				9		6		1		10					39
	4	3	11			9	5	7		2							6		1	10					40
	4	3	11	8		9	5	7		2							6		1	10					41
		4	3	11	8	9	5	7		2							6		1	10					42
3	2	40	41	21	28	36	40	13	42	5	26	16	1	3	10	10	39	1	10	29	41	2	2	1	
1				5	9	24		3	14		1				3	1	1				19				
		4	2	11	8	9	5	7			3						6			1	10				43
		4	2	11	8	9	5	7			3						6			1	10				44
		4	2	11	8	9	5	7			3						6			1	10				45
		4	2		8	9	5	7	11	3				10		6			1						46
		4	4	3	4	4	4		4	1	4				1		4			4	3				
		1		2	1	3			2								1				2				

1937-38

#	Date		Opponent		Score	Scorers	App	Goals
1	Aug 28	(h)	Arsenal	L	1-4	Dean	0	
2	Sep 1	(a)	Manchester C	L	0-2		0	
3	4·	(a)	Blackpool	L	0-1		0	22
4	8	(h)	Manchester C	W	4-1	Stevenson 2, Dougal, Lawton	2	21
5	11	(h)	Brentford	W	3-0	Cunliffe, Dougal, Stevenson	4	14
6	15	(a)	Derby C	L	1-2	Lawton	4	18
7	18	(a)	Bolton W	W	2-1	Lawton, Stevenson	6	16
8	25	(h)	Huddersfield T	L	1-2	Trentham	6	18
9	Oct 2	(a)	Liverpool	W	2-1	Lawton, Trentham	8	16
10	9	(a)	Wolves	L	0-2		8	16
11	16	(h)	Leeds U	D	1-1	Lawton	9	17
12	23	(a)	Grimsby T	L	1-2	Gillick	9	18
13	30	(h)	Preston N E	L	3-5	Lawton 2, Bell	9	20
14	Nov 6	(a)	Middlesbrough	W	2-1	Lawton 2	11	19
15	13	(h)	Chelsea	W	4-1	Lawton 2, Cunliffe, Trentham	13	19
16	20	(a)	West Brom A	L	1-3	Lawton	13	19
17	27	(h)	Stoke C	W	3-0	Lawton 2, Stevenson	15	17
18	Dec 4	(a)	Charlton A	L	1-3	Cunliffe	15	18
19	11	(h)	Birmingham	D	1-1	Geldard	16	18
20	18	(a)	Portsmouth	L	1-3	Trentham	16	19
21	25	(a)	Leicester C	L	1-3	Trentham	16	19
22	27	(h)	Leicester C	W	3-0	Lawton 2, Trentham	18	17
23	Jan 1	(a)	Arsenal	L	1-2	Cunliffe	18	18
24	15	(h)	Blackpool	W	3-1	Cunliffe, Lawton, Watson	20	17
25	26	(a)	Brentford	L	0-3		20	17
26	29	(h)	Bolton W	W	4-1	Geldard, Gillick, Lawton, Stevenson	22	16
27	Feb 5	(a)	Huddersfield T	W	3-1	Cunliffe, Gillick, Stevenson	24	14
28	16	(h)	Liverpool	L	1-3	Lawton	24	15
29	19	(h)	Wolves	L	0-1		24	17
30	26	(h)	Leeds U	D	4-4	Cunliffe 2, Lawton 2	25	18
31	Mar 5	(h)	Grimsby T	W	3-2	Lawton 2, Stevenson	27	13
32	12	(a)	Preston N E	L	1-2	Cunliffe	27	18
33	19	(h)	Middlesbrough	D	2-2	Bell, Boyes	28	17
34	26	(a)	Chelsea	L	0-2		28	19
35	Apr 2	(h)	West Brom A	W	5-3	Lawton 2, Cunliffe, Geldard, Stevenson	30	16
36	9	(a)	Stoke C	D	1-1	Lawton	31	17
37	15	(h)	Sunderland	D	3-3	Cunliffe 2, Thomson	32	16
38	16	(h)	Charlton A	W	3-0	Geldard 2, Lawton	34	15
39	18	(a)	Sunderland	L	0-2		34	16
40	23	(a)	Birmingham	W	3-0	Boyes, Cunliffe, Stevenson	36	15
41	30	(h)	Portsmouth	W	5-2	Stevenson 3, Boyes, Lawton	38	15
42	May 7	(h)	Derby C	D	1-1	Geldard	39	14

League Appearances
League Goals

#	Date		Opponent		Score	Scorers		
43	Jan 8	(a)	Chelsea	W	1-0	Stevenson	FA Cup Rd 3	
44	22	(h)	Sunderland	L	0-1			4

FA Cup Appearances
FA Cup Goals

Bell J	Boyes W	Britton C	Cook W	Coulter J	Cunliffe J	Dean W	Dougal P	Gee C	Geldard A	Gillick T	Greenhalgh N	Jackson G	Jones J E	Jones T G	Lawton T	Mercer J	Morton H	Sagar E	Stevenson A	Thomson J	Trentham D	Watson T	No.
		4	3	11	8	9		5	7		2					6		1	10				1
		4	3	11	8	9		5	7		2					6		1	10				2
		4	2			9	10	5	7				3		8	6		1			11		3
		4	2				10	5	7				3		9	6		1	8		11		4
		4	2		11		10	5	7				3		9	6		1	8				5
		4	2		11		10	5	7				3		9	6		1	8				6
			2		11		10	5	7				3		9	4		1	8			6	7
			2				10	5	7				3		9	4		1	8		11	6	8
			2				10	5	7				3		9	4		1	8		11	6	9
			2				10	5	7				3		9	4		1	8		11	6	10
		4	2				10	5	7	11			3		9	6		1	8				11
		4				9	10	5	7		2		3		8	6		1			11		12
10		4	2		8			5	7	11			3		9	6		1					13
		4	2		8				7				3	5	9	6	1		10		11		14
		4	2		8				7				3	5	9	6	1		10		11		15
		4	3		8				7		2			5	9	6	1		10		11		16
		4	2		8				7				3	5	9	6	1		10		11		17
		4	2		8				7	11			3	5	9	6	1		10				18
		4	2		8	9			7	11			3	5		6	1		10				19
		4	2		8		10		7				3	5	9	6	1				11		20
8		4	2		10				7				3	5	9	6	1				11		21
8		4	2		10				7				3	5	9	6	1				11		22
		4	2		8				7				3	5	9	6	1		10		11		23
		4	2		8				7				3	5	9	6	1		10		11		24
		4	2		8				7				3	5	9	6	1		10		11		25
		4	2		8				7	11			3	5	9	6	1		10				26
		4	2		8				7	11			3	5	9	6	1		10				27
		4	2		8				7	11			3	5	9	6	1		10				28
		4			8				7	11	2		3	5	9	6	1		10				29
	11	4			8			5	7		2		3		9			1	10			6	30
	11	4			8				7		2		3	5	9			1	10			6	31
	11	4			8				7		2		3	5	9			1	10			6	32
10	11	4			8				7		2		3	5	9			1				6	33
8	11	4							7		2		3	5	9			1	10			6	34
	11		2		8				7				3	5	9	4		1	10	6			35
	11		2		8				7				3	5	9	4		1	10	6			36
	11		2		8				7				3	5	9	4		1	10	6			37
	11	4	2		8				7				3	5	9			1	10	6			38
	11		2		8				7				3	5	9	4		1	10	6			39
	11		2		8				7				3	5	9	4		1	10	6			40
	11		2		8				7				3	5	9	4		1	10	6			41
	11		2		8				7				3	5	9	4		1	10	6			42
5	13	31	35	2	34	5	11	14	34	16	12	4	33	28	39	36	16	26	35	9	15	9	
2	3			13	1	2			6	3				28					13	1	6	1	
		4	2		8				7	11			3	5	9	6		1	10				43
		4	2		8				7				3	5	9	6		1	10		11		44
		2	2		2				2	1			2	2	2	2		2	2		1		
																			1				

1938-39

1	Aug 27	(a)	Blackpool	W	2-0	Lawton, Stevenson	2	
2	31	(h)	Grimsby T	W	3-0	Lawton 2, Gillick	4	
3	Sep 3	(h)	Brentford	W	2-1	Lawton 2	6	1
4	5	(a)	Aston Villa	W	3-0	Stevenson 2, Lawton	8	1
5	10	(a)	Arsenal	W	2-1	Lawton, Stevenson	10	1
6	17	(h)	Portsmouth	W	5-1	Bentham, Boyes, Gillick, Lawton, opp.og	12	1
7	24	(a)	Huddersfield T	L	0-3		12	1
8	Oct 1	(h)	Liverpool	W	2-1	Bentham, Boyes	14	1
9	8	(h)	Wolves	W	1-0	Lawton	16	1
10	15	(a)	Bolton W	L	2-4	Lawton, Stevenson	16	1
11	22	(h)	Leeds U	W	4-0	Bell 3, Trentham	18	1
12	29	(a)	Leicester C	L	0-3		18	2
13	Nov 5	(h)	Middlesbrough	W	4-0	Lawton 3, Stevenson	20	2
14	12	(a)	Birmingham	L	0-1		20	2
15	19	(h)	Manchester U	W	3-0	Lawton 2, Gillick	22	2
16	26	(a)	Stoke C	D	0-0		23	2
17	Dec 3	(h)	Chelsea	W	4-1	Lawton 2, Gillick, Stevenson	25	2
18	10	(a)	Preston N E	W	1-0	Lawton	27	2
19	17	(h)	Charlton A	L	1-4	Gillick	27	2
20	24	(h)	Blackpool	W	4-0	Cunliffe 2, Cook, Gillick	29	2
21	26	(h)	Derby C	D	2-2	Cook, Gillick	30	2
22	27	(a)	Derby C	L	1-2	Cook	30	2
23	31	(a)	Brentford	L	0-2		30	2
24	Jan 14	(h)	Arsenal	W	2-0	Boyes, Lawton	32	2
25	28	(h)	Huddersfield T	W	3-2	Cook, Lawton, Stevenson	34	2
26	Feb 1	(a)	Portsmouth	W	1-0	Lawton	36	2
27	4	(a)	Liverpool	W	3-0	Lawton 2, Bentham	38	1
28	18	(h)	Bolton W	W	2-1	Gillick, opp.og	40	1
29	22	(a)	Wolves	L	0-7		40	1
30	25	(a)	Leeds	W	2-1	Bentham, Cunliffe	42	1
31	Mar 8	(h)	Leicester C	W	4-0	Boyes, Greenhalgh, Lawton, Stevenson	44	1
32	11	(a)	Middlesbrough	D	4-4	Lawton 4	45	1
33	18	(h)	Birmingham	W	4-2	Lawton 2, Bentham, Gillick	47	1
34	29	(a)	Manchester U	W	2-0	Gillick, Lawton	49	1
35	Apr 1	(h)	Stoke C	D	1-1	Lawton	50	1
36	7	(a)	Sunderland	W	2-1	Gillick, Lawton	52	1
37	8	(a)	Chelsea	W	2-0	Gillick, Stevenson	54	1
38	10	(h)	Sunderland	W	6-2	Betham 3, Caskie, Lawton, Stevenson	56	1
39	15	(h)	Preston N E	D	0-0		57	1
40	22	(a)	Charlton A	L	1-2	Gillick	57	1
41	29	(h)	Aston Villa	W	3-0	Bentham, Cook, Gillick	59	1
42	May 6	(a)	Grimsby T	L	0-3		59	1
							League Appearances	
							League Goals	
43	Jan 7	(a)	Derby C	W	1-0	Boyes		FA Cup Rd 3
44	21	(h)	Doncaster R	W	8-0	Lawton 4, Boyes 2, Gillick, Stevenson		4
45	Feb 11	(a)	Birmingham	D	2-2	Boyes, Stevenson		5
46	15	(h)	Birmingham	W	2-1	Cook, Gillick		Replay
47	Mar 4	(a)	Wolves	L	0-2			6
							FA Cup Appearances	
							FA Cup Goals	

Barber E	Bell J	Bentham S	Boyes W	Britton C	Caskie J	Cook W	Cunliffe J	Gee C	Gillick T	Greenhalgh N	Jackson G	Jones T G	Lawton T	Mercer J	Milligan G	Morton H	Sagar E	Stevenson A	Thomson J	Trentham D	Watson T	No.
		8	11			2			7	3		5	9	4			1	10	6			1
		8	11			2			7	3		5	9	4			1	10	6			2
		8	11			2			7	3		5	9	4			1	10	6			3
		8	11			2			7	3		5	9	4			1	10	6			4
		8	11			2			7	3		5	9	4			1	10	6			5
		8	11			2			7	3		5	9	4			1	10	6			6
		8	11			2			7	3		5	9	4			1	10	6			7
		8	11			2			7	3		5	9	4			1	10	6			8
7		8	11						10	3	2	5	9	4			1		6			9
		8	11			2			7	3		5	9	4	6		1	10				10
	9	8				2		5	7	3				4			1	10	11	6		11
		8	11			2			7	3		5	9	4			1	10			6	12
		8	11			2			7	3		5	9	4			1	10	6			13
		8	11			2		5	7	3			9	4			1	10	6			14
		8	11			2			7	3		5	9	4			1	10	6			15
		8	11			2			7	3		5	9	4			1	10	6			16
		8	11			2			7	3		5	9	4			1	10	6			17
		8	11			2			7	3		5	9	4			1	10	6			18
		8	11			2			7	3		5	9	4			1	10	6			19
		8	11			2	10		7	3		5	9	4			1		6			20
	9	8	11			2	10		7	3		5		4			1		6			21
		8	11			2	10		7	3		5	9	4			1				6	22
		8	11			2	10		7	3		5	9	4			1				6	23
		8	11			2			7	3		5	9	4			1	10	6			24
		8	11			2			7	3		5	9	4			1	10	6			25
		8	11			2			7	3		5	9	4			1	10	6			26
		8	11			2			7	3		5	9	4			1	10	6			27
	9	8	11			2			7	3		5		4			1	10	6			28
	9		11			2			7	3		5	8	4		1		10	6			29
7		8	11						10	3	2	5	9	4			1				6	30
		8	11			2			7	3		5	9	4			1	10			6	31
		8	11			2			7	3		5	9	4			1	10			6	32
		8	11			2			7	3		5	9	4			1	10			6	33
		8	11			2			7	3		5	9	4			1	10			6	34
		8	11			2			7	3		5	9	4			1	10			6	35
		8	11			2			7	3		5	9	4			1	10			6	36
		8			11	2			7	3		5	9	4			1	10			6	37
		8			11	2			7	3			9	4			1	10	5		6	38
		8	4	11		2	9		7	3		5					1	10			6	39
		8			11	2			7	3		5	9	4			1	10			6	40
		8			11	2			7	3		5	9	4			1	10			6	41
		8			11	2			7	3		5	9	4			1	10			6	42
2	4	41	36	1	5	40	7	2	40	42	2	39	38	41	1	1	41	36	26	1	16	
	3	9	4		1	5	3		14	1			34					11	1			opp.og 2
		8	11			2			7	3		5	9	4			1	10	6			43
		8	11			2			7	3		5	9	4			1	10	6			44
		8	11			2			7	3		5	9	4			1	10	6			45
		8	11			2			7	3		5	9	4			1	10		6		46
		8	11			2			7	3		5	9	4			1	10	6			47
		5	5			5			5	5		5	5	5			5	5	4	1		
			4			1			2				4						2				

1939-40

1	Aug 26	(h)	Brentford	D	1-1	Lawton	1	
2	28	(a)	Aston Villa	W	2-1	Bentham, Lawton	3	
3	Sep 2	(a)	Blackburn R	D	2-2	Lawton 2	4	5

| | | | | | | | Appearances | |
							Goals	
4	Oct 21	(h)	Stoke C	D	4-4	Boyes, T.G.Jones, Lawton, Stevenson	1	
5	28	(a)	New Brighton	W	1-0	Gillick	3	
6	Nov 11	(h)	Manchester C	W	3-1	Bentham, Gillick, Lawton	5	3
7	18	(a)	Chester	L	2-3	Bell, Stevenson	5	5
8	25	(h)	Crewe A	W	6-2	Bell 2, Simmons 2, Boyes, Johnson	7	4
9	Dec 2	(a)	Liverpool	D	2-2	Davies, Stevenson	8	5
10	9	(h)	Port Vale	W	3-1	Bentham, Mercer, Sweeney	10	4
11	23	(a)	Tranmere R	W	9-2	Lawton 4, Bentham 2, T.G.Jones, Mercer, Stevenson	12	2
12	Jan 6	(a)	Manchester U	W	3-2	Lawton, Stevenson, Sweeney	14	1
13	20	(a)	Wrexham	D	0-0		15	1
14	Feb 10	(a)	Stoke C	L	0-1		15	1
15	24	(h)	New Brighton	W	3-0	Bell, Stevenson, Wyles	17	1
16	Mar 9	(a)	Manchester C	D	2-2	Gillick, Greenhalgh	18	3
17	16	(h)	Chester	W	5-0	Boyes 3, Catterick, T.G.Jones	20	2
18	23	(a)	Crewe A	L	1-2	Stevenson	20	3
19	30	(h)	Liverpool	L	1-3	Lawton	20	3
20	Apr 3	(h)	Stockport C	W	7-0	Stevenson 4, Lawton 2, Wyles	22	3
21	6	(a)	Port Vale	L	1-2	Bentham	22	3
22	17	(h)	Tranmere R	W	5-3	Bentham, Boyes, Lawton, Mercer, Stevenson	24	3
23	May 22	(h)	Wrexham	L	1-2	Lawton	24	5
24	29	(a)	Stockport C	W	2-1	Bentham, Simmons	26	5
25	Jun 1	(a)	Manchester U	W	3-0	Stevenson 3	28	3

| | | | | | | | Appearances | |
							Goals	
26	Apr 20	(h)	Preston N E	W	3-1	Boyes, T.G.Jones, Stevenson		
27	27	(a)	Preston N E	D	2-2	Bentham, Lawton		
28	May 4	(h)	Rochdale	W	5-1	Lawton 3, T.G.Jones, Stevenson		
29	11	(a)	Rochdale	L	2-4	Sumner, Wyles		
30	18	(h)	Stoke C	W	1-0	Lawton		
31	25	(a)	Fulham	L	2-5	Gillick, Lawton		

| | | | | | | | Appearances | |
| | | | | | | | Goals | |

Matches 1 to 3 inclusive were played in the Football League which was abandoned when war broke out. The three games do not count in any record of League appearances and goals.

Matches 4 to 25 inclusive were played in the War Regional League, Western Division.

Matches 26 to 31 inclusive were played in the War League Cup. The first two rounds were played on a home and away two-legged basis. Thereafter, the competition was a sudden-death knockout.

Barber E	Bell R	Bentham S	Boyes W	Burnett G	Caskie J	Catterick H	Cook W	Davies J	Gee C	Gillick T	Greenhalgh N	Jackson G	Johnson A	Jones J E	Jones T G	Lawton T	Lindley W	Lyon J	Mercer J	Sagar E	Saunders G	Sharp N	Simmons S	Stevenson A	Sumner W	Sweeney F	Watson T	Wyles T	
		8	11				2			7	3					5	9		4	1				10			6		1
		8	11				2			7	3					5	9		4	1				10			6		2
		8	11				2			7	3					5	9		4	1				10			6		3
		3	3				3			3	3					3	3		3	3				3			3		
		1															4												
		8	11							7	3	2				5	9	4		1				10			6		4
		8	11							7	3	2				5	9	4		1				10			6		5
		8	11						5	7	3	2					9		4	1				10			6		6
	9	8	11	1					5		3	2					4						7	10			6		7
	9		11								3	2	7			5			4	1			8	10			6		8
	9	8	11					7				2				5	4		1		3			10			6		9
	9	8	11								3	2				5	6		4	1				10		7			10
		8	11								3	2				5	9		4	1				10		7	6		11
		8	11								3	2				9	5		4	1				10		7	6		12
		8	11								3	2				5	9	4		1				10			6	7	13
	9	8	11								3	2				5	4			1				10		7	6		14
	9	8	11								3	2				5			4	1				10			6	7	15
		8	11	1		9				7	3	2					5							10			6	4	16
		8	11			9					3	2				5			4	1				10			6	7	17
7		8	11								3	2				5	9		4	1				10			6		18
			11			8					3	2				5	9	4		1				10			6	7	19
			11								3	2				5	9	8	4	1				10			6	7	20
		8	11			7					3	2				5	9		4	1				10			6		21
		8	11								3	2				9	5		4	1				10	7		6		22
		8	11								3	2				5	9	10	4	1							6	7	23
		8	11									2		3		9	4		5	1				10	7		6		24
		8	11								3	2				5	9	7	4	1				10			6		25
1	6	19	22	2		4	1	2		4	21	21	1	1	16	14	14	1	14	20	1	1	2	20	2	4	21	7	
	4	7	6				1	1			3	1	1		3	12				3			3	15		2	2		
7		8	11								3	2				5	9		4	1				10			6		26
7		8	11								3	2				5	9		4	1				10			6		27
		8	11								3	2				5	9	7	4	1				10			6		28
		8	11								3	2				9	5			1				10	7		6	4	29
		8	11			7					3	2				5	9		4	1				10			6		30
		8	11						5	7	3	2					9		4	1				10			6		31
2	6	6				1			1	1	6	6				4	6	2	5	6				6	1		6	1	
	1	1									1					2	6							2	1			1	

1940-41

1	Aug 31 (a)	Manchester C	D	0-0	
2	Sep 7 (h)	Manchester C	W	1-0	Lawton
3	14 (a)	Preston N E	D	2-2	Bailey, Stevenson
4	21 (h)	Chester	W	4-3	Lawton 3, Stevenson
5	28 (h)	Leeds U	W	5-1	Bentham 2, Lawton, Mercer, Stevenson
6	Oct 5 (a)	Southport	W	1-0	Catterick
7	12 (h)	Stockport C	W	4-2	Catterick 2, Britton, Simmons
8	19 (a)	Chester	L	0-1	
9	26 (h)	Bury	W	3-1	Bentham, Lawton, Stevenson
10	Nov 2 (a)	Bury	L	1-2	Simmons
11	9 (h)	Manchester U	W	5-2	Lawton 4, Stevenson
12	16 (a)	Manchester U	D	0-0	
13	23 (a)	Tranmere R	W	9-0	Lawton 3, Stevenson 3, Simmons 2, Arthur
14	30 (h)	New Brighton	W	2-1	Boyes, Catterick
15	Dec 7 (h)	Southport	W	2-1	Catterick 2
16	14 (a)	Tranmere R	W	8-2	Bentham 3, Lawton 2, Boyes, Cook, Simmons
17	21 (h)	Preston N E	L	0-3	
18	25 (a)	Liverpool	L	1-3	Bentham
19	Jan 4 (a)	Liverpool*	W	2-1	Lawton, Lyon
20	11 (h)	Liverpool*	W	4-1	Jackson 4
21	25 (a)	Burnley*	W	3-2	Lawton 2, Lyon
22	Feb 1 (h)	Barnsley	W	3-1	Lawton 2, T.G. Jones
23	8 (a)	Liverpool	W	3-1	Catterick 3
24	Mar 29 (h)	Chesterfield	L	0-1	
25	Apr 5 (a)	Southport	W	5-3	Catterick 2, Bell, Lyon, Stevenson
26	12 (h)	Manchester U	L	1-2	Catterick
27	14 (h)	Blackpool	D	2-2	Catterick, Lawton
28	19 (a)	Chesterfield	L	1-4	Wyles
29	26 (a)	New Brighton	W	4-0	Catterick, Lyon, Mercer, Wyle
30	May 3 (h)	Burnley*	L	0-2	
31	17 (a)	Oldham A	D	1-1	Owen
32	24 (h)	Sheffield U	D	3-3	Lewis, Mercer, Stevenson
33	31 (a)	Liverpool	D	2-2	Mercer, Stevenson
34	Jun 2 (h)	Liverpool	W	3-1	Boyes 2, Jackson

Appearances
Goals

35	Feb 15 (a)	Manchester U	D	2-2	Lawton 2
36	22 (h)	Manchester U	W	2-1	Catterick, Mercer
37	Mar 1 (h)	Southport	W	5-0	Catterick 2, Lawton 2, T.G. Jones
38	8 (a)	Southport	W	5-0	Lawton 4, Bentham
39	15 (h)	Manchester C	D	1-1	Lyon
40	22 (a)	Manchester C	L	0-2	

Appearances
Cup

Matches 1 to 34 inclusive were played in the League North. Clubs did not all play the same number of matches and the positions were decided on goal average. Everton finished fifth with a goal average of 1.66.

Matches 19, 20, 21 and 30 (marked thus*) were Lancashire Cup matches which also counted towards the League North.

Matches 35 to 40 inclusive were played in the League War Cup. The first two rounds were played on a home and away two-legged basis. Thereafter, the competition was a sudden-death knockout.

Arthur J	Bailey G	Bell R	Bentham S	Boyes W	Britton C	Catterick H	Cook W	Finnis H	Greenhalgh N	Hankin N	Hill	Jackson G	Johnson A	Jones J E	Jones T G	Lawton T	Lewis C	Lovett	Lyon J	Mercer J	Penlington A	Owen W	Sagar E	Simmons S	Stevenson A	Sumner W	Watson T	Wyles T	
			8				2		3							5	9			4	11		1		10	7	6		1
			8				2		3							5	9			4	11		1		10	7	6		2
	11		8		4		2		3								9			5			1		10		6	7	3
			8						3	4		2				5	9	11					1	7	10		6		4
			8	7					3			2				5	9	11			4		1		10		6		5
			8		4	8			3	7		2				5		11					1		10		6		6
			7		4	9			3			2				5		11					1	8	10		6		7
	11		7		4	9			3			2				5							1	8	10		6		8
			8				2		3							5	9			7	11		1		10		6		9
			4				2	6	3			7				5	9		1					8	10		11		10
7			4				2		3							5	9		1		6			8	10		11		11
7			8	11			2		3							5	9		1		4				10		6		12
7				11			2		3							5	9		1		4			8	10		6		13
7			4	11		9	2		3							5			1					8	10		6		14
7				11		9			3			2				5			1				8	4	10		6		15
7			8	11			2		3							5	9				4		1		10		6		16
			4	11		9			3			2	7			5							1	8	10		6		17
7			8				2		3			4				5	9	11					1		10		6		18
7			8	11			2		3							5	9			10	4		1				6		19
7			8				2		3			9	6			5				4	11		1		10				20
7			8	11			2		3			1				5	9			10	4						6		21
7			4	11		8	2		3							5	9			10	6		1						22
7			4	11		9	2		3				6			5							1	8	10				23
			4			8	2		3			9								11	5		7	1	10		6		24
	9		7			8		5	3			2	4						1	11					10		6		25
	9		7			8	2		3			11				5			1	10	4						6		26
	7		4			8	2		3			6			9				1	11	5					10			27
			8						3			2	11						1	10	5						6	7	28
			4			9	2		3							5			1	11	8						6	7	29
			4			9	2		3						11	5			1	10								7	30
			4			9	2		3							5			1	11	8				10		6	7	31
			4				2		3			5	6		9					11	8		1	7	10				32
			4		7	9	2		3							5			1	11	8				10		6		33
			4		7		2		3			6			9	5			1	11					10	8			34
12	2	3	32	12	6	16	25	2	34	2	4	17	1	5	27	17	5	15	14	20	4	4	18	14	23	2	26	7	
1	1	1	7	4	1	14	1					5			1	22			4	4			1	5	11		2		
7			8	11			2		3							5	9				4		1		10		6		35
			8		7		2		3				6			5	9			10	4		1				11		36
7			8				2		3				6			5	9				4		1		10				37
7			8				2		3				6			5	9				4		1		10				38
7						9	2		3							5				11	4		1	8	10		6		39
			8			9	2		3			7				5				11	4		1		10		6		40
1			6	1	5	6	6					1	3			6	4			4	6		6	1	5		3	1	
1			3													1	8				1		1						

E.Barber played number 8 in Match 30; H.Lindeman played number 10 in Match 29;
R.Lindley played number 4 in Match 28; J.Powell played number 9 in Match 28;
Thomson played number 6 in Match 30; D.Trentham played number 11 in Match 38.

1941-42

1	Aug 30	(a)	Stoke C	L	3-8	Boyes, Catterick, Cook	0	
2	Sep 6	(h)	Stoke C	W	3-1	Cook, Cunliffe, Mercer	2	
3	13	(h)	Chester	D	1-1	H.Jones	3	21
4	20	(a)	Chester	L	0-2		3	25
5	27	(a)	Manchester U	W	3-2	Owen 2, Stevenson	5	19
6	Oct 4	(h)	Manchester U	L	1-3	H.Jones	5	23
7	11	(h)	Tranmere R	W	3-2	Stevenson 2, Jackson	7	18
8	18	(a)	Tranmere R	W	4-0	Lyon 2, Owen, Stevenson	9	14
9	25	(a)	Liverpool	L	2-3	Cook, Lyon	9	16
10	Nov 1	(h)	Liverpool	W	5-3	Bentham 3, H.Jones, Lyon	11	12
11	8	(h)	Wrexham	W	3-1	Anderson, H.Jones, Owen	13	12
12	15	(a)	Wrexham	W	4-0	Boyes, H.Jones, Mercer, Stevenson	15	10
13	22	(a)	Manchester C	W	4-3	Lawton 3, Lyon	17	8
14	29	(h)	Manchester C	W	9-0	H.Jones 2, Stevenson 2, Bentham, Cook, Lyon, Mutch, opp.og	19	7
15	Dec 6	(h)	New Brighton	W	4-0	H.Jones 2, T.G.Jones, Stevenson	21	7
16	13	(h)	New Brighton	W	5-1	Jackson 2, Owen 2, Stevenson	23	7
17	20	(a)	Stockport C	D	1-1	Mercer	24	7
18	25	(h)	Stockport C	W	6-0	Lawton 3, Cook, Kinnell, Stevenson	26	6
							Appearances Goals	

19	Dec 27	(a)	Sheffield W	W	3-0	Lawton 3		
20	Jan 3	(h)	Sheffield W	W	2-0	T.G.Jones 2		
21	10	(h)	Blackburn R	D	0-0			
22	17	(a)	Blackburn R	D	0-0			
23	31	(h)	Wolves	W	2-1	Cook 2		
24	Feb 7	(h)	Burnley	W	3-2	Anderson, Boyes, H.Jones		
25	14	(a)	Burnley	L	0-1			
26	21	(a)	Oldham A	L	0-1			
27	28	(h)	Oldham A	W	4-0	Mercer 2, Jackson, Stevenson		
28	Mar 7	(a)	Wolves	L	1-11	Anderson		
29	14	(h)	Blackpool	D	2-2	Owen, Stevenson		
30	21	(h)	Southport*	W	3-1	Mercer 2, Waring		
31	28	(a)	Oldham	W	2-1	T.G.Jones, Wyles		
32	Apr 4	(h)	Preston NE**	D	2-2	Cook, T.G.Jones		
33	6	(a)	Preston N E**	W	2-1	T.G.Jones, Mercer		
34	11	(a)	Liverpool**	W	2-0	Anderson, T.G.Jones		
35	18	(h)	Liverpool**	L	0-1			
36	25	(a)	West Brom A**	L	1-3	Lawton		
37	28	(a)	Southport*	L	1-2	Owen		
38	May 2	(h)	West Brom A**	L	1-5	Bentham		
39	9	(a)	Manchester C*	L	0-2			
40	16	(h)	Manchester C*	W	6-1	Lawton 3, Soo 2, Anderson		
41	30	(a)	Liverpool*	L	1-4	Lawton		15
							Appearances Goals	

Matches 1 to 18 inclusive were played in the League North (First Period).

Matches 19 to 41 inclusive were played in the League North (Second Period). The competition consisted of 38 teams and no team played all the others.

Matches marked thus* were in the Lancashire Cup and matches marked thus ** were in the League War Cup, both of which were played on a two-legged home and away basis in the early rounds. The matches in these cups also counted towards the League North (Second Period).

Anderson A	Bentham S	Boyes W	Burnett G	Caskie J	Cook W	Cunliffe J	Curwen G	Greenhalgh N	Hill M	Jackson G	Jones H	Jones J E	Jones T G	Keen E	Lawton T	Lovett P	Lyon J	Mercer J	Mutch G	Owen W	Sagar E	Stevenson A	Thomson J	Waring T	Watson T	Williams A	
	8	10						2	3	5			6			1	11	4									1
	4						2	8	3	7	9		5				11	6			1	10					2
7	4				2		10	3					5	6	9						1	11					3
7	4		1		2			3			9		5							8		10	6				4
7	4		1		2			3			9		5				11	6		8		10					5
7	4		1		2			3			9	8	5	11								10			6		6
7	4		1		2			3	6		9		5	11						8		10					7
7	4		1		2			3			9		5	11	6					8		10					8
7	4		1		2			3					5	6	9		11			8		10					9
	8		1		2			3			9		5	11	4					7		10			6		10
7	4		1		2			3			9		5	11						8		10			6		11
7	8	11	1		2			3			9		5	6	4							10					12
7	4		1		2			3					5		9		11			8		10			6		13
7					2			3			9		5	11	4					8	1	10	6				14
7	4	11			2			3			9		5	6						8	1	10					15
7	4		1		2			3			9		5	6			11			8		10					16
7	8	11	1		2			3			9		5	6	4							10					17
7	8	11	1		2			3					5	6				4				10					18
14	18	4	12	17	2	18	4	8	13	2	8	9	3	3	13	9	2	9	3	16	2	4					
1	4	2			5	1		3	9		1		6		6	3	1	6		10					opp.og 1		
7	8	11	1		2			3			10		5	6	9			4									19
7	4	6	1		2			3			9		5				11			8		10					20
7	8		1		2			3			9		5	6			11	4				10					21
7	4	6			2			3			9		5				11				1	10					22
11	4				2			3			8		5	6	9					7	1	10					23
7	4	11			2			3			9		5	6						8	1	10					24
7	4	9			2			3			1		5	6						8		10				11	25
11	4							3	2	5	9	8									1	10		6	7		26
11	4							3	9	5				6						8	1	10			7		27
11	4		1		2			3					5	6	9		8	7				10					28
7	4		1		2	6		3					5				11			8		10		9			29
	4	11	1		2			3					5							8		10	6	9	7		30
11	4		1		2		6	3					5	7						8		10					31
7	4	11	1		2		8	3					5	9	6							10					32
7	4		1	11	2			3		5	9			6						8		10					33
11	4		1		2		6	3			9		5		8					7		10					34
7	4		1	11	2		6	3			9		5							8		10					35
7	4	11	1		2		6	3					5		9					8		10					36
11			1		2				4	7			5			10				8					9	6	37
	8	11	1		2			3					5	6	9			4				10					38
11	8		1		2		7	3					5		9							10			6		39
7	8		1		2			3					5	6	9			4		11							40
	4		1		2		5	3			6		9		8					7		10				11	41
20	22	9	17	2	22	1	7	14	2	9	13	3	15	17	8		5	14	1	12	5	19	1	2	5	3	
4	1	1			3			1	1		6		8		5		2	2		1							

G.Bailey played number 11 in Match 4; A.Barber played number 7 in Match 1;
H.Catterick played number 9 (and scored once) in Match 1; N.Higham played
number 8 in Match 22; R.Ireland played number 3 in Match 37; R.Kinnell
played number 9 (and scored once) in Match 18; E.Seddon played number 8 in
Match 3; N.Sharp played number 7 in Match 38; F.Soo played number 10 (and
scored twice) in Match 40; T.Wyles played number 9 (and scored once) in
Match 31.

1942-43

							Appearances	Goals
1	Aug 29	(h)	Manchester U	D	2-2	Anderson, Mutch	1	
2	Sep 5	(a)	Manchester U	L	1-2	Jackson	1	
3	12	(a)	Liverpool	L	0-1		1	
4	19	(h)	Liverpool	D	4-4	H.Jones 2, Jackson, Mutch	2	
5	26	(h)	Burnley	W	2-1	Mutch, Urmston	4	
6	Oct 3	(a)	Burnley	W	4-1	Cook, Higham, Jackson, Lawton	6	
7	10	(h)	Wrexham	W	2-1	Jackson, Urmston	8	
8	17	(a)	Wrexham	W	2-0	Bentham, Dellow	10	
9	24	(h)	Bury	W	9-2	Curran 3, Bentham 2, Dellow 2, Fowler, Mutch	12	
10	31	(a)	Bury	L	1-4	Fowler	13	
11	Nov 7	(a)	Tranmere R	W	3-1	Curran 2, Stevenson	14	
12	14	(h)	Tranmere R	L	3-5	Curran 2, Fowler	14	
13	21	(h)	Crewe A	W	4-0	Fowler, H.Jones, Mutch, Stevenson	16	
14	28	(a)	Crewe A	L	2-4	Curran, Jackson	16	
15	Dec 5	(h)	Chester	W	3-1	Anderson, Bentham, H.Jones	18	
16	12	(h)	Chester	W	3-2	Mutch 2, Curran	20	
17	19	(a)	Manchester C	L	1-7	Mutch	20	
18	25	(h)	Manchester C	W	6-3	Lawton 3, Grant, Stevenson, Wyles	22	15
							Appearances	Goals
19	26	(a)	Tranmere R	L	1-2	Lawton	0	
20	Jan 2	(h)	Tranmere R	W	4-0	Anderson, H.Jones, Mercer, Mutch	2	
21	9	(h)	Liverpool	L	1-3	Mutch	2	
22	16	(a)	Liverpool	L	1-2	Lawton	2	
23	23	(a)	Manchester U	W	4-1	H.Jones 3, Bentham	4	
24	30	(h)	Manchester U	L	0-5		4	
25	Feb 6	(h)	Chester	L	4-5	Dellow 2, Mercer, Stevenson	4	
26	13	(a)	Chester	W	1-0	Fowler	6	
27	20	(a)	Southport	W	8-3	Wyles 3, Mutch 2, Stevenson 2, Fowler	8	
28	27	(h)	Southport	W	10-2	Lawton 4, Mutch 2, Cook, Fowler, Stevenson, opp.og	10	
29	Mar 6	(a)	Blackpool**	L	1-4	Wyles	10	
30	13	(h)	Blackpool**	W	4-3	Lawton 2, Curwen, Stevenson	12	
31	20	(a)	Southport*	L	1-4	Fowler	12	
32	27	(h)	Southport*	W	2-1	Lawton, Mutch	14	
33	Apr 3	(a)	Wrexham	L	1-4	Stevenson	14	
34	10	(a)	Tranmere R***	W	4-1	Lawton 2, Mutch, Stevenson	16	
35	17	(a)	Tranmere R***	W	2-1	Curran, Wyles	18	
36	26	(a)	Liverpool***	L	1-4	McIntosh	18	
37	May 1	(a)	Tranmere R	D	1-1	McIntosh	19	25
							Appearances	Goals

Matches 1 to 18 inclusive were played in the League North (First Period).

Matches 19 to 37 inclusive were played in the League North (Second Period).

There were 48 and 54 teams respectively in the two competitions. No team played all the rest.

Matches 19 to 28 inclusive were in the League War Cup Qualifying Competition.

Matches marked thus* were in the Lancashire Cup; matches marked thus** were in the League War Cup KO competition; matches marked thus*** were in the Liverpool Cup. All three cup competitions were played on a home and away basis in the early rounds and all cup matches counted towards the League North (Second Period).

Anderson A	Bentham S	Birkett W	Boyes W	Burnett G	Carey J	Cook W	Curran F	Curwen G	Dellow	Fairfoull T	Fowler	Grant J	Greenhalgh N	Higham N	Humphreys J	Jackson G	Jones H	Jones J E	Jones T G	Lawton T	Lowe W	Lyon J	McDonnell M	McIntosh J	Mercer J	Mutch G	Stevenson A	Urmston T	Watson T	Wyles T	
11	7			1									3					2	5	9					4	8	10		6		1
11	9			1										4	2	5	3							7		8	10		6		2
11	4			1	2							10				7	9	3	5							8			6		3
11	4			1	2											7	9	3	5							8	10		6		4
	4			1	2								3			5	7							11		8	10	9	6		5
		11		1	2								3	10		7	5		9						4	8			6		6
	4			1	2								3		11	7	5									8	10	9	6		7
11				1	2				7				3				9		5						4	8	10		6		8
	4			1	2			9	7		11		3						5							8	10		6		9
	4			1	2			9	7		11		3											5		8	10		6		10
	7			1	2			9			11		3						5						4	8	10		6		11
	4	7		1	2			9			11		3						5							8	10		6		12
	4			1					7		11		3					2		9				5		8	10		6		13
				1				9	7	4	11		3					2	5							8	10		6		14
11	7			1	2						4		3						5	9		6				8	10				15
	4			1				9	7		11		3					2	5							8	10		6		16
11	4			1	2				7				3				9		5							8	10		6		17
	4			1	2						11	8	3			5				9							10		6	7	18
6	16	2		18	13			6	7	2	8	2	15	2	3	11	14	4	5	3		2	1	5	5	17	16	2	17	1	
2	4				1			9	3		4	1		1		5	4		4	8		3				2			1		
	4					6					11		3				9	2	5							8	10		1	7	19
11	7	1		6	2								3				5		9						4	8	10				20
	4			1	2						11		3				5	7	9						6	8	10				21
	7			1	2	6							3				5	11	9						4	8	10				22
	7			1	2	6							3				5	11	9						4	8	10				23
	7			1	2	6							3				5		9	11					4	8	10				24
	9			1	2	6			7				3				5			11					4	8	10				25
	4			1	2				7		11		3				5								6	8	10				26
	4	1	5		2				7		11		3			6										8	10			9	27
	4	1	5		2				7		11		3			6			9							8	10				28
	4			1	2	6							3				5	11	9							8	10			7	29
				1		6				4	11		3					2	5	9							10				30
		1				6			7		11		3		4			2	5	9						8	10				31
	4			1		6					11		3					2		9				5		8	10				32
	8								7		11		3					2	5	9							10		6	4	33
		1						4					3			5	2		11			9	7			8	10		6		34
		1						9			4		3					2					11	5		8	10		6	7	35
	4			1									3				5	2	11						9		8		6		36
	4			1									3			6	5	2				7			9	8	10				37
1	15	11	3	6	2	10	1	9	6	1	9		19	12	13	6	6	3	9	2		1	2	2	7	16	19		5	5	
1	1				1	1		1	1		1		2	4	4				11					2	2	8	7		5		

L.Ashcroft played number 7 in Match 30; R.Beattie played number 10 in Match 36; R. Dunkley played number 7 in Match 32; J.Linaker played number 7 in Match 36; G.Makin played number 11 in Match 37; W.Owen played number 9 in Match 26; Rosenthall played number 8 in Match 30; E.Williams played number 1 in Match 33.

In Matches 19 to 37 (League North Second Period) the total includes 1 opp.og.

1943-44

							Appearances	Goals
1	Aug 28 (a)	Blackburn R	W	3-1	Lawton 2, McIntosh		2	
2	Sep 4 (h)	Blackburn R	D	0-0			3	
3	11 (a)	Manchester U	L	1-4	Mutch		3	
4	18 (h)	Manchester U	W	6-1	McIntosh 2, Wyles 2, Stevenson, Wainwright		5	
5	25 (a)	Burnley	D	0-0			6	
6	Oct 2 (h)	Burnley	D	0-0			7	
7	9 (h)	Liverpool	L	4-6	Lawton, McIntosh, Stevenson, opp.og		7	
8	16 (a)	Liverpool	L	2-5	McIntosh, Stevenson		7	
9	23 (a)	Wrexham	W	3-1	Lawton 3		9	
10	30 (h)	Wrexham	W	4-2	Wyles 3, Bentham		11	
11	Nov 6 (h)	Tranmere R	W	9-2	Lawton 5, Bentham 2, McIntosh, Stevenson		13	
12	13 (a)	Tranmere R	W	6-2	Bentham 3, Grant, Stevenson, Wyles		15	
13	20 (a)	Crewe A	W	8-0	Lawton 3, McIntosh 2, Stevenson 2, T.G.Jones		17	
14	27 (h)	Crewe A	D	5-5	McIntosh 5		18	
15	Dec 4 (a)	Chester	L	0-1			18	
16	11 (h)	Chester	L	0-1			18	
17	18 (h)	Manchester C	W	4-0	T.G.Jones, Lawton, McIntosh, Stevenson		20	
18	25 (a)	Manchester C	W	5-3	Lawton 3, McIntosh, Stevenson		22	11

							Appearances	Goals
19	27 (a)	Chester	W	5-3	Lawton 2, McIntosh 2, Wainwright		2	
20	Jan 1 (h)	Chester	W	7-0	Stevenson 4, Boothway, McIntosh, Wainwright		4	
21	8 (h)	Crewe A	W	9-1	McIntosh 3, Lawton 2, Stevenson 2, Boothway, Wainwright		6	
22	15 (a)	Crewe A	W	6-2	Lawton 5, Wainwright		8	
23	22 (a)	Liverpool	W	4-1	Wainwright 2, Lawton, Wyles		10	
24	29 (h)	Liverpool	L	2-3	Lawton, Wyles		10	
25	Feb 5 (h)	Wrexham	L	2-3	Lawton 2		10	
26	12 (a)	Wrexham	L	1-2	Catterick		10	
27	19 (a)	Tranmere R	W	1-0	McIntosh		12	
28	26 (h)	Tranmere R	W	5-1	Lawton 2, Grant, T.G.Jones, Stevenson		14	
29	Mar 4 (a)	Blackpool**	L	1-7	Lawton		14	
30	11 (h)	Blackpool**	L	1-3	Jackson		14	
31	18 (h)	Chester *	W	5-2	Stevenson 3, Jackson, McIntosh		16	
32	25 (a)	Chester *	W	9-2	Lawton 4, Stevenson 3, McIntosh 2		18	
33	Apr 1 (a)	Tranmere R***	W	5-0	McIntosh 2, Bentham, Jackson, Wainwright		20	
34	8 (h)	Tranmere R***	W	4-0	Lawton 2, Bentham, Wainwright		22	
35	10 (h)	Liverpool*	W	3-0	Grant, T.G.Jones, McIntosh		24	
36	15 (a)	Liverpool*	L	0-3			24	
37	22 (a)	Liverpool*	L	2-4	T.G.Jones, Wyles		24	
38	29 (a)	Bury	L	0-1			24	
39	May 21 (a)	Southport***	D	1-1	McIntosh		25	12
40	22 (h)	Southport***	L	0-1				

Matches 1 to 18 inclusive were in the League North (First Period).

Matches 19 to 39 inclusive were in the League North (Second Period).
There were 50 and 56 clubs respectively in these competitions and no
club played every other club.

Matches 19 to 28 inclusive were in the League War Cup Qualifying Competition.
Matches marked thus * were in the Lancashire Cup; matches marked thus** were
in the League War Cup KO Competition; matches marked thus*** were in the
Liverpool Cup. All the cup matches, with the exception of Match 40, counted
towards the League North (Second Period).

Bentham S	Boothway J	Boyes W	Burnett G	Catterick H	Grant J	Greenhalgh N	Hallard W	Humphreys J	Jackson G	Jones J E	Jones S	Jones T G	Lawton T	Linaker J	Lowe W	McDonnell M	McIntosh	Mercer J	Mutch G	Scott	Steele E	Stevenson A	Tatters C	Turner P	Wainwright E	Watson T	Wyles T	No.
8					1	3			2	6	5	9				11		7			4	10						1
8					1	3			2	6	5	9				11		4				10						2
8					1	3			2		5	9				11		6	7		4	10						3
4					1	7	3		2	6	5					11						10			8		9	4
					1	7	3		2	6		9				11	5					10			8			5
4					1	7	3		2		5					11		6							8		9	6
4					1	7	3		2		5	9				11		6				10			8			7
4					1	3		6	2		5					11						10						8
8					1	4	3	6	2		5	9		7		11						10						9
8					1	4	3	6	2		5			7		11						10					9	10
8					1	4	3	5	2	6		9		7		11						10						11
8					1	7	3	4	2	6	5					11						10					9	12
					1	8	3	6	2	4	5	9		7		11						10						13
					1	8	3		2	4	6	7				11	5					10					9	14
					1	8	3		2	4	6	5				11								7	10		9	15
					1	8	3	6	2		5	9				11						10		7	4			16
					1	6	3		2		5	9				11		4				10			8			17
					1	7	3		2		5	9				11		4				10			8	6		18

Totals (Matches 1–18) — appearances: 11 18 14 16 5 2 12 13 6 15 11 2 3 2 18 4 2 2 2 15 2 7 3 6
Totals (Matches 1–18) — goals: 6 1 2 18 15 1 9 1 6   opp.og 1

Bentham S	Boothway J	Boyes W	Burnett G	Catterick H	Grant J	Greenhalgh N	Hallard W	Humphreys J	Jackson G	Jones J E	Jones S	Jones T G	Lawton T	Linaker J	Lowe W	McDonnell M	McIntosh	Mercer J	Mutch G	Scott	Steele E	Stevenson A	Tatters C	Turner P	Wainwright E	Watson T	Wyles T	No.
					1	7	3		2		5	9				11		4				10			8	6		19
	9				1	4	3		2		5					11						10		7	8	6		20
	7				1	4	3		2		5	9				11						10			8	6		21
	7				1	4	3		2		5	9				11						10			8	6		22
					1	4			2	3	5	9				11						10			8	6	7	23
					1	4			2	3	5	9				11		6				10			8		7	24
					1	4	3		2		5	9				11						10			8	6		25
		8		9	1	4	3		2		5					11						10				6		26
	9				1	4	3	7	2		5					11						10			8	6		27
					1	7	3		2		5	9				11		4				10				6		28
	7				1	4	3		2		5	9				11						10			8	6		29
		8		9	1	4	3	7	2		5					11						10				6		30
	10				1	4	3	7	2		5	9				11									8	6		31
	10				1	4	3	7	2		5	9				11									8	6		32
8					1	4	3	7	2		5					11						10				6	9	33
8					1	4	3	7	2		5	9				11						10				6		34
	10				1	7	3		2		5	9				11										6		35
8					1	4	3	7	2		5	9				11						10				6		36
	10				1	4	3		2		5					11										6	9	37
		4			1	8	3		2	5						11						10					9	38
	10				1	4	3	7	2							11									8	6	9	39
8					1	4	3	7	2		5	9				11										6		40

Totals (Matches 1–40) — appearances: 11 3 3 22 2 22 20 21 13 1 18 14 1 22 3 12 2 15 20 6
Totals (Matches 1–40) — goals: 2 2 1 2 3 3 22 14 13 8 3

T.Astbury played number 8 in Match 37; C.Britton played number 4 in Match 35;
J.Caskie played number 8 in Match 8; R.Doyle played number 6 in Match 38;
T.Gillick played number 8 in Match 35; D.Glidden played number 10 in Match 40;
J.Hall played number 7 in Match 25; A.Higgins played number 7 in Match 26;
F.Jones played number 7 in Match 38; N.Law played number 5 in Match 39;
G.Makin played number 7 in Match 17; Morley played number 4 in Match 5;
G.Murphy played number 9 in Match 8; A.Roberts played number 7 in Match 8;
E.Rogers played number 7 in Match 37; N.Sharp played number 10 in Match 6;
A.Smith played number 7 in Match 2; L.Wootton played number 8 in Match 28.

1944-45

1	Aug 26	(h)	Manchester U	L	1-2	Rawlings	0	
2	Sep 2	(a)	Manchester U	W	3-1	Boyes, Peters, Rawlings	2	
3	9	(a)	Bury	W	2-1	Wainwright, Wyles	4	
4	16	(h)	Bury	W	4-1	Wyles 2, Rawlings, Stevenson	6	
5	23	(h)	Chester	W	6-2	Lawton 2, Makin 2, Rawlings, Wainwright	8	
6	30	(a)	Chester	W	6-2	Wyles 3, Wainwright 2, Stevenson	10	
7	Oct 7	(a)	Tranmere R	W	4-1	Lawton 3, Wainwright	12	
8	14	(h)	Tranmere R	W	2-1	Stevenson, Wainwright	14	
9	21	(h)	Liverpool	L	0-2		14	
10	28	(a)	Liverpool	D	0-0		15	
11	Nov 4	(a)	Manchester C	W	3-1	Lawton, Stevenson, opp.og	17	
12	11	(h)	Manchester C	W	4-1	Catterick 3, Stevenson	19	
13	18	(h)	Crewe A	L	3-5	T.G.Jones, Lawton, Stevenson	19	
14	25	(a)	Crewe A	W	5-1	Lawton 5	21	
15	Dec 2	(a)	Wrexham	L	0-1		21	
16	9	(h)	Wrexham	D	2-2	Catterick, Makin	22	
17	16	(h)	Stockport C	W	6-1	Lawton 2, Stevenson 2, T.G.Jones, Makin	24	
18	23	(a)	Stockport C	W	7-0	T.G.Jones 3, Lawton 2, Wainwright 2	26	5
							Appearances Goals	
19	25	(h)	Tranmere R	L	2-4	Lawton 2	0	
20	26	(h)	Liverpool	D	2-2	Stevenson, Wainwright	1	
21	30	(a)	Tranmere R	W	4-0	T.G.Jones 3, Wainwright	3	
22	Jan 6	(h)	Bolton W	W	2-1	Lawton 2	5	
23	13	(a)	Bolton W	W	3-1	Lawton, Rawlings, Stevenson	7	
24	20	(a)	Stockport C	W	3-0	Bentham 2, Catterick	9	
25	27	(h)	Stockport C	W	9-2	Lawton 4, Bentham 2, McIntosh, Rawlings, Stevenson	11	
26	Feb 3	(h)	Liverpool	W	4-1	Bentham, McIntosh, Rawlings, Wyles	13	
27	10	(a)	Liverpool	L	1-3	Lawton	13	
28	17	(h)	Southport	W	6-0	Rawlings 2, Wyles 2, Bentham, Stevenson	15	
29	24	(a)	Southport	W	5-3	Wyles 2, Bentham, Mercer, Stevenson	17	
30	Mar 3	(h)	Chester*	W	4-1	Lawton 2, Bentham, Stevenson	19	
31	10	(a)	Chester*	L	4-6	Bentham 2, Wyles 2	19	
32	17	(h)	Preston N E	W	3-0	Wyles 3	21	
33	24	(a)	Liverpool**	L	0-1		21	
34	31	(h)	Liverpool**	L	0-1		21	
35	Apr 2	(a)	Liverpool***	W	3-1	Grant, Jackson, Wyles	23	
36	7	(a)	Wrexham	W	2-1	Wyles 2	25	
37	14	(h)	Wrexham	W	5-3	Stevenson 2, Wyles 2, Bentham	27	
38	21	(a)	Southport*	W	5-0	Catterick 3, Boyes, Stevenson	29	
39	28	(h)	Southport*	D	1-1	Wyles	30	
40	May 5	(a)	Accrington S*	D	1-1	Rawlings	31	
41	9	(a)	Tranmere R***	W	3-0	Bentham, Catterick, Rawlings	33	
42	12	(h)	Accrington S*	L	0-2		33	
43	19	(a)	Stoke C	L	1-5	Catterick	33	
44	21	(h)	Tranmere R***	W	4-1	Wyles 2, Bentham, Boyes	35	
45	26	(h)	Stoke C	W	3-2	Wyles 2, Bentham	37	2
							Appearances Goals	

Matches 1 to 18 inclusive were played in the League North (First Period).

Matches 19 to 45 inclusive were played in the League North (Second Period). There were 54 and 60 teams respectively in the competitions and no team played all the others.

Matches 19 to 28 inclusive were in the League War Cup Qualifying Competition. Matches marked thus* were in the Lancashire Cup; matches marked thus** were in the League War Cup KO Competition; matches marked thus*** were in the Liverpool Cup. All cup matches counted towards the League North (Second Period).

Ashley A	Bentham S	Boyes W	Burnett G	Catterick H	Doyle R	Gillick T	Grant J	Greenhalgh N	Hill	Humphreys J	Jackson G	Jones F	Jones T G	Lawton T	Lindley	McDonnell M	McIntosh	Makin G	Mercer J	Peters T	Rawlings	Sharp N	Stevenson A	Wainwright E	Watson T	Wootton L	Wyles T	Match
			1					4	3		2			9	5		11				7		10	8	6			1
		11	1					4	3		2			9	5				10	7					8	6			2
		11	1					4	3		2				5				10	7					8	6		9	3
		11	1					4	3		2				5						7		10	8	6		9	4
			1					4	3		2			9	5		11				7		10	8	6			5
			1					4	3		2				5		11				7		10	8	6		9	6
			1	6				4	3		2			9	5		11				7		10	8				7
			1	6				4	3		2				5		11				7		10	8			9	8
			1					4	3		2				5		11				7		10	8	6		9	9
			1	9				4	3		2		11		5						7		10	8	6			10
			1	11				4	3		2			9	5						7		10	8	6			11
			1	9				4	3		2	8			5						7		10		6	11		12
			1	7				4	3		2	8		9	5								10		6	11		13
			1	8				4	3		2			9	5		11				7		10		6			14
	8	11	1					4	3		2			9	5						7		10		6			15
			1	9				4	3		2		8		5		11				7		10		6			16
			1					4	3		2		8	9	5		11				7		10		6			17
			1					4	3		2		8	9	5		11	10						7		6			18

Sub-totals (first half): 1 4 18 6 2 · 18 18 · 18 1 · 5 10 17 1 · 9 1 3 16 · 15 12 16 2 5
1 4 · 5 16 · 4 1 4 · 8 8 · 6 opp.og 1

Ashley A	Bentham S	Boyes W	Burnett G	Catterick H	Doyle R	Gillick T	Grant J	Greenhalgh N	Hill	Humphreys J	Jackson G	Jones F	Jones T G	Lawton T	Lindley	McDonnell M	McIntosh	Makin G	Mercer J	Peters T	Rawlings	Sharp N	Stevenson A	Wainwright E	Watson T	Wootton L	Wyles T	Match
			1					4	3		2			9	5		11				7		10	8	6			19
			1			7		4	3		2			9	5		11						10	8	6			20
			1					4	3		2			9	5		11		8				10	7	6			21
	5		1					4	3		2	8		9			11				7		10		6			22
	5		1	8				4	3		2			9			11				7		10		6			23
	8		1	9				4	3		2		5				11				7		10		6			24
	8		1					4	3		2		5	9			11				7		10		6			25
	8		1					4	3		2		5				11				7		10		6		9	26
	8	7	1					4	3		2			9	5		11						10		6			27
	8		1					4	3		2		5								7	11	10		6		9	28
	8		1						3		2	5							4		7	11	10		6		9	29
	8	11	1					4	3	5	2			9								7		10		6			30
	8	11	1					4	3	5	2										7	10		6		9	31
	8	11	1					4	3		2										7	10		6		9	32
	8	11	1	7				4	3		2											10		6		9	33
			1		8			4	3		2			9		11			5				10	7	6			34
			1		8			4	3		2					11			5				10	7	6		9	35
7			1					4	3	5	2					11						10		6		9	36
	8	11	1					4	3	5	2									7		10		6		9	37
	8	11	1	9				4		5	2											10		6	7		38
	8	11	1	9				4	3	5	2											10		6	7		39
10	11		1	8				4	3	5	2									7				6		9	40
	8	10	1	9				4	3	5	2							11		7				6			41
	8	10	1	9				4	3	5	2									7				6	11		42
8	10	11	1	9				4	3	5	2							7						6			43
	8	11	1					4	3	5								7						6		9	44
8	10		1					4	3	5	2					11								6		9	45

Totals: 2 22 13 27 9 · 2 · 26 26 · 2 11 26 · 7 7 5 · 10 6 4 · 12 5 21 · 5 27 · 15
14 2 · 6 · 1 · 1 3 12 · 2 1 · 7 9 2 · 20

Curwen played number 5 in Match 32;   G.Dugdale played number 3 in Match 38;
C.Heath played number 7 in Match 45; J.Hedley played number 2 in Match 44;
T.King played 8 in Match 36; J.Logan played number 10 in Match 44; J. Morris
played number 5 in Match 33.

1945-46

						Scorers	Apps	Goals
1	Aug 25	(h)	Bolton W	W	3-2	Bentham, Catterick, Mercer	2	
2	Sep 1	(a)	Bolton W	L	1-3	Boyes	2	
3	8	(a)	Preston N E	W	2-0	Mercer, Wainwright	4	
4	12	(a)	Liverpool	L	1-2	Wyles	4	
5	15	(h)	Preston N E	D	1-1	Wyles	5	
6	22	(h)	Leeds U	L	0-2		5	
7	29	(a)	Leeds U	W	3-2	Boyes 2, Wainwright	7	
8	Oct 6	(a)	Manchester U	D	0-0		8	
9	13	(h)	Manchester U	W	3-0	Catterick, Fielding, Rawlings	10	
10	20	(h)	Sunderland	W	4-0	Lawton 3, Jones	12	
11	27	(a)	Sunderland	W	4-0	Catterick 2, Fielding, Wainwright	14	
12	Nov 3	(a)	Sheffield U	L	0-4		14	
13	10	(h)	Sheffield U	W	1-0	Catterick	16	
14	17	(h)	Middlesbrough	D	1-1	Catterick	17	
15	24	(a)	Middlesbrough	D	0-0		18	
16	Dec 1	(a)	Stoke C	W	3-2	Catterick 2, Rawlings	20	
17	8	(h)	Stoke C	W	6-1	Wainwright 3, Catterick 2, Rawlings	22	
18	15	(h)	Grimsby T	W	2-1	Catterick, Wainwright	24	
19	22	(a)	Grimsby T	W	2-1	Bentham 2	26	
20	25	(a)	Blackpool	L	2-5	Boyes, Jones	26	
21	26	(h)	Blackpool	W	7-1	Catterick 3, Wainwright 3, Boyes	28	
22	29	(h)	Liverpool	D	2-2	Boyes, Catterick	29	
23	Jan 1	(h)	Bury	W	3-1	Boyes, Catterick, Elliott	31	
24	12	(a)	Blackburn R	L	1-2	Catterick	31	
25	19	(h)	Blackburn R	W	4-1	Catterick 3, Fielding	33	
26	Feb 2	(h)	Bradford	D	0-0		34	
27	9	(h)	Manchester C	W	4-1	Bell 2, Bentham, Boyes	36	
28	16	(a)	Manchester C	W	3-1	Catterick, Mercer, Wainwright	38	
29	23	(a)	Newcastle U	W	3-1	Wainwright 2, Catterick	40	
30	Mar 2	(h)	Newcastle U	W	4-1	Boyes, Catterick, Wainwright, opp.og	42	
31	9	(h)	Sheffield W	D	2-2	Catterick, Stevenson	43	
32	16	(a)	Sheffield W	D	0-0		44	
33	23	(a)	Huddersfield T	W	1-0	Higgins	46	
34	30	(h)	Huddersfield T	W	5-2	Wainwright 3, Higgins, Watson	48	
35	Apr 3	(a)	Bradford	W	2-1	Boyes, Grant	50	
36	6	(h)	Chesterfield	W	4-0	Boyes 2, Jones 2	52	
37	13	(a)	Chesterfield	D	1-1	Stevenson	53	
38	19	(a)	Barnsley	L	0-2		53	
39	20	(h)	Burnley	W	2-0	Catterick, Greenhalgh	55	
40	22	(h)	Barnsley	L	0-4		55	
41	27	(a)	Burnley	L	0-1		55	
42	May 4	(a)	Bury	L	1-3	Bentham	55	2
						League Appearances		
						League Goals		
43	Jan 5	(a)	Preston N E	L	1-2	Catterick	FA Cup 1st leg Rd 3	
44	9	(h)	Preston N E	D	2-2	Elliott, Mercer	2nd leg	
						FA Cup Appearances		
						FA Cup Goals		

Matches 1 to 42 inclusive were in the Football League North which contained 22 teams.
The programme was a normal peacetime fixture list with each club playing each other
club home and away.

The FA Cup was resumed with matches up to and including the sixth round being played
on a two-legged home and away basis.

Bell R	Bentham S	Bond T	Boyes W	Burnett G	Catterick H	Cookson J	Elliott T	Fielding W	Grant J	Greenhalgh J	Higgins W	Humphreys J	Jackson G	Johnson A	Jones T G	Lawton T	Lowe W	McIlhatton J	Makin G	Mercer J	Rawlings J	Stevenson A	Wainwright E	Watson T	Wyles T	
	8		10	1	9				7	3		5	2							4				6	11	1
			10	1	8				7	3		5	2	9					11	4				6		2
	4		11	1				10		3			2	7		9				5		8		6		3
5	4	7	10	1						3			2						11			8		6	9	4
5	4		10	1						3			2			7			11			8		6	9	5
	8		10	1				11		3		5	2			7				4				6	9	6
	4		10	1	9					3			2						11	5	7	8		6		7
	8		10	1					4	3			2		9	7			11	5				6		8
	4		11	1	9			10	8	3			2		5						7			6		9
	4		11	1				10		3			2		5	9					7		8	6		10
	4		11	1	9			10		3			2		5						7		8	6		11
	8		11	1				10		3			2		5	9				4	7			6		12
			11	1	9		8	10	4	3			2		5						7			6		13
			11	1	9		8	10	4	3			2		5						7			6		14
	6		11	1	9			10	4	3			2		5					5	7	8				15
	6		11	1	9	4	8	10		3			2		5						7					16
	6		11	1	9			10		3		5	2							4	7	8				17
	4		11	1	9			10		3			2		5						7		8	6		18
	8		11	1	9			10		3			2		5					4	7			6		19
	6		11	1	9			10		3			2		5					4	7	8				20
	4		11	1	9			10		3			2		5						7		8	6		21
	4		11	1	9			10		3			2							5	7	8		6		22
8	4		11	1	9			7		3			2							5		10		6		23
	3		11	1	9			10	4	3			2							5	7	8		6		24
	4		11	1	9			10		3		5	2								7	8	6			25
	6		11	1	9			10		3		5	2							4	7	8				26
9	8		11	1				10		3		5	2							4			7	6		27
			11	1	9			10		3		5	2							4		7	8	6		28
			11	1	9			10		3		5	2							4		7	8	6		29
			11	1	9			10		3		5	2							4		7	8	6		30
			11	1	9			10		3		5	2							4		7	8	6		31
			11	1				10		3	9	5	2							4		7	8	6		32
			11	1				10		3	9	5	2							4		7	8	6		33
			11	1				10		3	9	5	2		7					4			8	6		34
	4		11	1				10	7	3	9	5	2										8	6		35
	4		11	1				10		3		5	2		9							7	8	6		36
9	4		11	1				10		3		5	2									7	8	6		37
	4		11	1	9			10		3		5	2									7	8	6		38
	4		11	1	9			10		3		5	2									7	8	6		39
	4		11	1	9			10		3		5	2									7	8	6		40
	4		11	1	9			10		3		5	2			7							8	6		41
	4		11	1	9			10		3		5	2										8	6		42
5	32	1	42	42	28	1	4	34	10	41	4	22	42	2	10	5	3	1	5	25	17	18	27	37	4	
2	5		12		25		1	3	1	1		2				4	3			3	3	2	17	1	2	opp.og 1
	4		11	1	9		8	10		3		5	2							6	7					43
	4		11	1	9		8	10		3		5	2							6	7					44
	2		2	2	2		2	2		2		2	2							2	2					
			1					1												1						

1946-47

1	Aug 31	(h)	Brentford	L	0-2		0	
2	Sep 2	(a)	Aston Villa	W	1-0	Boyes	2	
3	7	(a)	Blackburn R	L	1-4	Boyes	2	17
4	11	(h)	Arsenal	W	3-2	Livingstone 2, Bentham	4	13
5	14	(h)	Portsmouth	W	1-0	Bentham	6	10
6	21	(a)	Liverpool	D	0-0		7	8
7	28	(a)	Huddersfield T	L	0-1		7	14
8	Oct 5	(h)	Wolves	L	0-2		7	13
9	12	(a)	Sunderland	L	1-4	Eglington	7	18
10	19	(h)	Bolton W	W	2-1	Higgins, Stevenson	9	16
11	26	(a)	Charlton A	L	1-4	Stevenson	9	18
12	Nov 2	(h)	Grimsby T	D	3-3	Dodds, Jones, Stevenson	10	18
13	9	(a)	Leeds U	L	1-2	Dodds	10	18
14	16	(h)	Manchester U	D	2-2	Dodds 2	11	16
15	23	(a)	Stoke C	L	1-2	Dodds	11	17
16	30	(a)	Middlesbrough	W	2-1	Eglington, Wainwright	13	17
17	Dec 7	(a)	Chelsea	D	1-1	Dodds	14	17
18	14	(h)	Sheffield U	L	2-3	Dodds, Jones	14	17
19	21	(a)	Preston N E	L	1-2	Jones	14	17
20	25	(h)	Derby C	W	4-1	Wainwright 2, Boyes, Dodds	16	17
21	26	(a)	Derby C	L	1-5	Fielding	16	18
22	28	(a)	Brentford	D	1-1	Wainwright	17	18
23	Jan 1	(h)	Aston Villa	W	2-0	Dodds, Stevenson	19	17
24	4	(h)	Blackburn R	W	1-0	Wainwright	21	15
25	18	(a)	Portsmouth	L	1-2	opp.og	21	15
26	29	(h)	Liverpool	W	1-0	Wainwright	23	13
27	Feb 1	(h)	Huddersfield T	W	1-0	Bentham	25	12
28	15	(h)	Sunderland	W	4-2	Wainwright 3, Eglington	27	10
29	22	(a)	Bolton W	W	2-0	Stevenson, Wainwright	29	10
30	Mar 8	(a)	Grimsby T	D	2-2	Wainwright 2	30	10
31	22	(a)	Manchester U	L	0-3		30	12
32	29	(h)	Stoke C	D	2-2	Eglington, Fielding	31	12
33	Apr 4	(h)	Blackpool	D	1-1	Stevenson	32	12
34	5	(a)	Middlesbrough	L	0-4		32	13
35	7	(a)	Blackpool	W	3-0	Dodds 2, Stevenson	34	13
36	12	(h)	Chelsea	W	2-0	Dodds 2	36	11
37	19	(a)	Sheffield U	L	0-2		36	13
38	26	(h)	Preston N E	W	2-0	Dodds, Fielding	38	11
39	May 10	(a)	Wolves	W	3-2	Dodds, Fielding, McIlhatton	40	10
40	24	(h)	Charlton A	D	1-1	Wainwright	41	11
41	26	(h)	Leeds U	W	4-1	Dodds 2, Grant, Stevenson	43	10
42	31	(a)	Arsenal	L	1-2	Eglington	43	10
							League Appearances	
							League Goals	
43	Jan 11	(h)	Southend U	W	4-2	Fielding, Jones, McIlhatton, Wainwright	FA Cup Rd 3	
44	25	(a)	Sheffield W	L	1-2	Wainwright		4
							FA Cup Appearances	
							FA Cup Goals	

Bentham S	Boyes W	Burnett G	Catterick H	Davis J	Dodds E	Eglington T	Farrell P	Fielding W	Finnis H	Grant J	Greenhalgh N	Higgins W	Humphreys J	Jackson G	Johnson A	Jones T G	Livingstone A	McIlhatton J	Mercer J	Sagar E	Saunders G	Stevenson A	Wainwright E	Watson T	
	11	1	9					10			3			2		5		7	4			8	6		1
	11	1	9					10			3			2		5	8	7	4				6		2
	11	1	9	2				10			3					5		7	4			8	6		3
8		1				11					3					5	9	7	4		2	10	6		4
8		1				11					3					5	9	7	4		2	10	6		5
6		1				11		8			3	9				5		7	4		2	10			6
6		1				11		8			3	9				5		7	4		2	10			7
9		1				11		8	6		3					5		7	4		2	10			8
6		1				11		8			3					5	9	7	4		2	10			9
6		1				11		8			3	9	5					7	4		2	10			10
6		1				11		8			3	9				5		7	4		2	10			11
		1			9	11		8	6		3			2		5			4			10	7		12
4					9	11					3		5	2				7		1		10	8	6	13
4					9	11					3			2		5		7		1		10	8	6	14
4					9	11	6				3		5	2				7		1		10	8		15
4					9	11	6	10			3		5	2				7		1			8		16
4					9	11	6				3		5	2				7		1		10	8		17
4					9	11	6				3		5	2				7		1		10	8		18
4	11				9		6	10			3					5		7		1	2		8		19
4	11				9		6	10			3					5		7		1	2		8		20
4	11				9		6	10			3		5					7		1	2		8		21
4	11				9		6	10			3		5					7		1	2		8		22
4	11				9		6	10			3					5		7		1	2		8		23
4						11	6	10			3	9	5					7		1	2		8		24
4		1				11	6	10			3	9	5					7			2		8		25
4						11	6	10			3	9	5	2				7		1		8	9		26
4						11	6	10			3		5	2				7		1		8	9		27
4						11	6	10			3		5	2				7		1		8	9		28
4						11	6	10			3		5	2				7		1		8	9		29
4	6					11		10			3		5	2				7		1		8	9		30
4						11	6	10			3		5	2				7		1		8	9		31
4						11	6	10			3			2		5		7		1		8	9		32
4						11	6	10			3			2		5		7		1		8	9		33
4					9	11	6	10			3		5					7		1	2	8			34
					9	11	6			4	3		5	2				7		1		10	8		35
4					9	11	6	10			3		5					7		1	2		8		36
4					9	11	6	10			3		5					7		1	2		8		37
4					9	11	6	10			3		5					7		1	2		8		38
4					9	11	6				3		5					7		1	2	10	8		39
4					9	11	6				3		5					7		1	2	10	8		40
4					9	11	6	8			3		5					7		1	2	10			41
4					9	11	6	8			3		5					7		1	2	10			42
37	9	13	3	1	21	34	27	31	1	5	38	7	21	15	3	22	4	37	12	29	23	30	27	12	
3	3				17	5		4			1		1			3		2	1		1	8	13		opp.og 1
4					9	11	6	10			3		5					7		1	2		8		43
4					9	11	6	10			3		5	2		5		7		1			8		44
2					2	2	2	2			2		1	1		1		2		2	2	1	2		
					1						1					1							2		

1947-48

#	Date		Opponent	Res	Score	Scorers	Apps	Goals
1	Aug 23	(a)	Blackburn R	W	3-2	Dodds, Eglington, Wainwright	2	
2	27	(h)	Manchester C	W	1-0	Fielding	4	
3	30	(h)	Blackpool	L	1-2	Wainwright	4	7
4	Sep 3	(a)	Manchester C	W	1-0	Stevenson	6	5
5	6	(a)	Derby C	L	0-1		6	10
6	8	(a)	Aston Villa	L	0-3		6	11
7	13	(h)	Huddersfield T	D	1-1	Wainwright	7	12
8	17	(h)	Aston Villa	W	3-0	Fielding 2, opp.og	9	7
9	20	(a)	Chelsea	L	1-3	Catterick	9	10
10	27	(h)	Liverpool	L	0-3		9	12
11	Oct 4	(h)	Wolves	D	1-1	Boyes	10	12
12	11	(a)	Middlesbrough	W	1-0	Wainwright	12	10
13	18	(h)	Charlton A	L	0-1		12	16
14	25	(a)	Arsenal	D	1-1	Wainwright	13	15
15	Nov 1	(h)	Sheffield U	W	2-0	Dodds, Fielding	15	12
16	8	(a)	Stoke C	D	1-1	Stevenson	16	10
17	15	(h)	Burnley	L	0-3		16	12
18	22	(a)	Manchester U	D	2-2	Dodds, Fielding	17	12
19	29	(h)	Preston N E	W	2-1	Fielding, Wainwright	19	10
20	Dec 6	(a)	Portsmouth	L	0-3		19	12
21	13	(h)	Bolton W	W	2-0	Catterick, Wainwright	21	10
22	20	(h)	Blackburn R	W	4-1	Fielding 2, Farrell, Grant	23	9
23	25	(a)	Sunderland	L	0-2		23	11
24	26	(h)	Sunderland	W	3-0	Grant 2, Wainwright	25	8
25	Jan 3	(a)	Blackpool	L	0-5		25	11
26	17	(h)	Derby C	L	1-3	Wainwright	25	14
27	Feb 21	(a)	Wolves	W	4-2	Dodds 3, Eglington	27	13
28	28	(h)	Middlesbrough	W	2-1	Lello 2	29	12
29	Mar 6	(a)	Charlton A	W	3-2	Dodds 2, Eglington	31	11
30	13	(h)	Arsenal	L	0-2		31	12
31	20	(a)	Sheffield U	L	1-2	Farrell	31	13
32	26	(a)	Grimsby T	L	0-3		31	13
33	27	(h)	Stoke C	L	0-1		31	15
34	29	(h)	Grimsby T	W	3-1	Grant, Higgins, Jones	33	13
35	Apr 3	(a)	Burnley	W	1-0	Dodds	35	14
36	10	(h)	Manchester U	W	2-0	Dodds, Stevenson	37	13
37	14	(h)	Chelsea	W	2-3	Higgins 2	37	13
38	17	(a)	Preston N E	L	0-3		37	14
39	21	(a)	Liverpool	L	0-4		37	14
40	24	(h)	Portsmouth	L	0-2		37	15
41	28	(a)	Huddersfield T	W	3-1	Dodds 3	39	13
42	May 1	(a)	Bolton W	D	0-0		40	14
							League Appearances	
							League Goals	
43	Jan 10	(a)	Grimsby T	W	4-1	Wainwright 2, Dodds, Farrell	FA Cup Rd 3	
44	24	(a)	Wolves	D	1-1	Catterick	4	
45	31	(h)	Wolves	W	3-2	Fielding 2, Grant	Replay	
46	Feb 7	(a)	Fulham	D	1-1	Eglington	5	
47	14	(h)	Fulham	L	0-1		Replay	
							FA Cup appearances	
							FA Cup Goals	

Bentham S	Boyes W	Catterick H	Dodds E	Dugdale G	Eglington T	Farrell P	Fielding W	Gardner T	Grant J	Greenhalgh N	Hedley J	Higgins W	Humphreys J	Jackson G	Johnson A	Jones T G	Lello C	Lindley W	McIlhatton J	Pinchbeck C	Sagar E	Saunders G	Stevenson A	Wainwright E	Watson T	#
4		9		11	6	10				3		5							7		1	2		8		1
4		9		11	6	10				3		5							7		1	2	8			2
4		9		11	6	10				3		5							7		1	2		8		3
4		9		11	6					3		5							7		1	2	8	10		4
		9		11	6					3		5						4	7		1	2	10	8		5
4		9		11	6	10				3		5							7		1	2		8		6
4		9		11	6	10				3		5							7		1	2		8		7
4		9		11	6	10				3	2	5							7		1			8		8
4		9		11	6	10				3	2	5							7		1			8		9
		9		11	6				7	3		5									1	2	10	8	4	10
	11	9		3			10		7			5						4			1	2		8	6	11
	11	9		3		4						5							7		1	2	10	8	6	12
	11	9		3		4						5							7		1	2	10	8	6	13
4	11			3			10									5			7		1	2	8	9	6	14
			9	3	11	4	10									5			7		1	2		8	6	15
			9		11	4	10			3					7	5					1	2		8	6	16
			9		11	4	10			3					7	5					1	2		8	6	17
			9	3	11	4	10								7	5					1	2		8	6	18
			9	3	11	4	10								7	5					1	2		8	6	19
			9	3	11	4	10							2	7	5					1			8	6	20
			9	3	11	4	10								7	5					1	2		8	6	21
			9	3	11	4	10		7							5					1	2		8	6	22
			9	3		4	10		7				11			5					1	2		8	6	23
			9	3		4	10		7				11			5					1	2		8	6	24
			9	3		4	10		7				11			5					1	2		8	6	25
4				11	6	10			7							5				9	1	2	8		3	26
			9	3	11	6	8		7							5	10	4			1	2				27
			9	3	11	6	8		7							5	10	4			1	2				28
			9	3	11	6	8		7							5	10	4			1	2				29
				3	11	6	8		7							5	10	4		9	1	2				30
				3	11	6	8		7							5	10	4			1	2	9			31
			9	3	11	6	8									5	10	4			1	2		7		32
			9			6	8		7		3		11			5	10	4			1	2				33
			9			6	8		7		3		11	2		5		4			1		10	8		34
			9			6	8		7		3		11			5		4			1	2	10			35
			9			6	8		7		3		11			5		4			1	2	10			36
			9			6	8		7		3		11			5		4			1	2	10			37
						6	10		7		3		11			5		4		9	1	2		8		38
					11		6				3		7			5	9				1	2	10	8		39
			9		11	4					3		7	2		5	10				1			8	6	40
			9		11		6				3		7			5		4			1	2	10	8		41
			9		11						3		7		8	5		4			1	2	10			42
10	4	9	27	19	29	38	33	1	18	12	13	13	18	2	6	24	9	17	13	3	42	37	17	30	18	
	1	2	13		3	2	8		4				3			1	2							3	9	opp.og 1
4		9		11	6	10			7							5					1	2		8	3	43
4		9		3	11		10		7							5					1	2		8	6	44
4		9		3	11		10		7							5					1	2		8	6	45
4		9		3	11	6	10		7							5					1	2		8		46
8		9		3	11	4	10		7							5					1	2			6	47
5		4	1	4	5	3	5		5			5				5					5	5		4	4	
		1	1		1	1	2		1																2	

1948-49

1	Aug 21	(h)	Newcastle U	D	3-3	Dodds 2, Powell	1	
2	25	(a)	Portsmouth	L	0-4		1	
3	28	(a)	Middlesbrough	L	0-1		1	22
4	Sep 1	(h)	Portsmouth	L	0-5		1	22
5	4	(h)	Birmingham C	L	0-5		1	22
6	8	(h)	Stoke C	W	2-1	Juliussen, Powell	3	22
7	11	(a)	Chelsea	L	0-6		3	22
8	13	(a)	Stoke C	L	0-1		3	22
9	18	(h)	Liverpool	D	1-1	Dodds	4	22
10	25	(h)	Preston N E	W	4-1	Dodds 3, Stevenson	6	21
11	Oct 2	(a)	Burnley	L	0-1		6	22
12	9	(a)	Blackpool	L	0-3		6	22
13	16	(h)	Derby C	L	0-1		6	22
14	23	(a)	Arsenal	L	0-5		6	22
15	30	(h)	Huddersfield T	W	2-0	Catterick 2	8	22
16	Nov 6	(a)	Manchester U	L	0-2		8	22
17	13	(h)	Sheffield U	W	2-1	Bentham, Corr	10	21
18	20	(a)	Aston Villa	W	1-0	Catterick	12	19
19	27	(h)	Sunderland	W	1-0	opp.og	14	18
20	Dec 4	(a)	Wolves	L	0-1		14	20
21	11	(h)	Bolton W	W	1-0	Eglington	16	18
22	18	(a)	Newcastle U	L	0-1		16	19
23	25	(h)	Manchester C	D	0-0		17	19
24	27	(a)	Manchester C	D	0-0		18	19
25	Jan 1	(h)	Middlesbrough	W	3-1	Eglington 2, Stevenson	20	18
26	22	(h)	Chelsea	W	2-1	Wainwright 2	22	17
27	Feb 5	(a)	Liverpool	D	0-0		23	17
28	12	(a)	Birmingham C	D	0-0		24	17
29	19	(a)	Preston N E	L	1-3	Wainwright	24	17
30	26	(h)	Burnley	W	2-1	Eglington 2	26	16
31	Mar 5	(h)	Blackpool	W	5-0	Wainwright 4, McIntosh	28	16
32	12	(a)	Derby C	L	2-3	Fielding, McIntosh	28	16
33	19	(h)	Aston Villa	L	1-3	Wainwright	28	18
34	26	(a)	Sunderland	D	1-1	McIntosh	29	18
35	Apr 2	(a)	Charlton A	L	1-3	Wainwright	29	18
36	9	(a)	Sheffield U	D	1-1	McIntosh	30	18
37	16	(h)	Arsenal	D	0-0		31	18
38	18	(h)	Charlton A	D	1-1	Eglington	32	18
39	23	(a)	Huddersfield T	D	1-1	Powell	33	18
40	27	(h)	Manchester U	W	2-0	McIntosh, Wainwright	35	17
41	May 4	(h)	Wolves	W	1-0	Eglington	37	16
42	7	(a)	Bolton W	L	0-1		37	18

League Appearances
League Goals

| 43 | Jan 8 | (h) | Manchester C | W | 1-0 | Higgins | | FA Cup Rd 3 |
| 44 | 29 | (a) | Chelsea | L | 0-2 | | | 4 |

FA Cup Appearances
FA Cup Goals

Bentham S	Boyes W	Burnett G	Cameron D	Catterick H	Clinton T	Corr P	Dodds E	Dugdale G	Eglington T	Farrell P	Fielding W	Grant J	Greenhalgh N	Hedley J	Higgins W	Humphreys J	Jones T G	Juliussen A	Lello C	Lindley W	McCormick H	McIlhatton J	McIntosh J	Powell A	Sagar E	Saunders G	Stevenson A	Wainwright E	Watson T	#
							9	3	11	6	10						5		4		7			8	1	2				1
							9	3	11	6	10						5		4		7			8	1	2				2
							9	3	11	6	10	4			5				8		7				1	2				3
		5					9	3		6		4						10		11		7			1	2		8		4
								3		6	10	4			7	5	5	9		11					1	2		8		5
									4				6	3	2	7	5	9		11				8	1		10			6
									4				6	3	2	7	5	9		11				8	1		10			7
						7			11	4	8			3	9		5		10						1	2			6	8
4	11			9							8			3			5							7	1	2	10		6	9
4	11			9							8			3	5									7	1	2	10		6	10
4	11			9						7	8			3	5										1	2	10		6	11
4									11	6	8			3			5	9						7	1	2	10			12
4	1								11	6	8			3			5	9						7		2	10			13
4				9					11	6	8			3	7		5								1	2	10			14
4				9					11	6				3			5		10			7			1	2		8		15
4				9					11	6				3	7		5		10						1	2		8		16
8				9		7			11	6	10			3			5		4						1	2				17
8				9		7			11	6	10			3			5		4						1	2				18
8						7			11	6	10			3			5	9	4						1	2				19
8				9		7			11	6	10			3			5		4						1	2				20
						7			11	6	10			3			5	9	4						1	2		8		21
						7			11	6	10			3			5	9	4						1	2		8		22
4						7			11	6	10			3			5	9							1	2		8		23
									11	6	10			3	9		5		4			7		8	1	2				24
						7			11	6	10			3	9		5		4						1	2		8		25
				9					11	6	10			3			5		4						1	2	7	8		26
		9							11	4	10			3			5		6					7	1	2		8		27
			9						11	4	10			3			5		6					7	1	2		8		28
				9		7			3	11	4	10					5		6						1	2		8		29
					2				3	11	4	10				9	5		6					7	1			8		30
					2				3	11	4	10				7	5		6				9		1			8		31
					2				3	11	4	10				7	5		6				9		1			8		32
									3	11	4	10				7	5		6				9		1	2		8		33
					2				3	11	4	10					5		6				9	7	1			8		34
	1								3	11	4	10					5		6				9	7		2		8		35
									3	11	4	10				7	5		6				9		1	2	8			36
									3	11	4	10				7	5		6				9		1	2		8		37
									3	11	4	10					5		6				9		1	2	7	8		38
									3	11	4	10					5		6				9	7	1	2		8		39
									3	11	4	10					5		6				9	7	1	2		8		40
									3	11	4	10					5		6				9	7	1	2		8		41
									3	11	4						5		6				9	7	1	2	10	8		42
13	4	2	1	10	4	10	7	19	34	38	36	7	2	23	14	4	37	10	20	11	4	5	12	19	40	36	19	17	4	
1								3		1	6						1		1					5	3		2	10		opp.og 1
								3	11	6	10	7			2	9	5		4						1			8		43
		9							11	4	10			3			5		6			7			1	2		8		44
		1						1	2	2	2	1		2	1		2	1	1	1			1		2	1	1	1		

1949-50

1	Aug 20	(a)	Middlesbrough	W	1-0	Wainwright	2	
2	24	(h)	Newcastle U	W	2-1	McIntosh, Wainwright	4	
3	27	(h)	Liverpool	L	0-0		5	2
4	31	(a)	Newcastle U	L	0-4		5	9
5	Sep 3	(h)	Huddersfield T	W	3-0	Wainwright 3	7	5
6	7	(a)	Manchester U	D	0-0		8	5
7	10	(a)	Portsmouth	L	0-7		8	8
8	17	(h)	Wolves	L	1-2	Corr	8	11
9	24	(a)	Aston Villa	D	2-2	Higgins, Powell	9	12
10	Oct 1	(h)	Charlton A	L	0-1		9	17
11	8	(a)	Arsenal	L	2-5	Higgins, McIntosh	9	18
12	15	(h)	Bolton W	D	0-0		10	18
13	22	(a)	Birmingham C	D	0-0		11	17
14	29	(h)	Derby C	L	1-2	Powell	11	19
15	Nov 5	(a)	West Brom A	L	0-4		11	21
16	12	(h)	Manchester U	D	0-0		12	20
17	19	(a)	Chelsea	L	2-3	Buckle, Higgins	12	21
18	26	(h)	Stoke C	W	2-1	Buckle, McIntosh	14	20
19	Dec 3	(a)	Burnley	L	1-5	Wainwright	14	21
20	10	(h)	Sunderland	L	0-2		14	21
21	17	(h)	Middlesbrough	W	3-1	Buckle 2, Grant	16	20
22	24	(a)	Liverpool	L	1-3	Farrell	16	21
23	26	(h)	Fulham	D	1-1	Farrell	17	19
24	27	(a)	Fulham	D	0-0		18	19
25	31	(h)	Huddersfield T	W	2-1	Catterick, Wainwright	20	18
26	Jan 14	(h)	Portsmouth	L	1-2	Grant	20	19
27	21	(a)	Wolves	D	1-1	Buckle	21	18
28	Feb 4	(h)	Aston Villa	D	1-1	Catterick	22	19
29	18	(a)	Charlton A	L	0-2		22	19
30	25	(h)	Arsenal	L	0-1		22	19
31	Mar 8	(a)	Bolton W	W	2-1	Catterick, Higgins	24	19
32	11	(h)	Chelsea	D	1-1	Catterick	25	19
33	18	(a)	Stoke C	L	0-1		25	20
34	29	(h)	West Brom A	L	1-2	Wainwright	25	20
35	Apr 1	(a)	Manchester U	D	1-1	Grant	26	19
36	7	(h)	Blackpool	W	3-0	Wainwright 2, Buckle	28	19
37	8	(h)	Birmingham C	D	0-0		29	19
38	10	(a)	Blackpool	W	1-0	Catterick	31	19
39	15	(a)	Derby C	L	0-2		31	19
40	22	(h)	Burnley	D	1-1	Catterick	32	19
41	29	(a)	Sunderland	L	2-4	Catterick, Wainwright	32	20
42	May 6	(h)	Manchester C	W	3-1	Catterick 2, Eglington	34	18
							League Appearances	
							League Goals	
43	Jan 7	(a)	Q.P.R.	W	2-0	Buckle, Catterick	FA Cup Rd 3	
44	28	(a)	West Ham U	W	2-1	Catterick 2		4
45	Feb 11	(h)	Tottenham H	W	1-0	Wainwright		5
46	Mar 4	(a)	Derby C	W	2-1	Buckle, Wainwright		6
47	25	(n)	Liverpool	L	0-2		(Maine Road) SF	
							FA Cup Appearances	
							FA Cup Goals	

Buckle E	Burnett G	Catterick H	Corr P	Dugdale G	Eglington T	Falder D	Farrell P	Fielding W	Grant J	Hedley J	Higgins W	Hold O	Humphreys J	Jones T G	Lello C	Lindley W	McIntosh J	Moore E	Powell A	Sagar E	Saunders G	Wainwright E	No.
			7	3	11		4	10						5	6		9		1	2		8	1
	1		7	3	11		4	10						5	6		9			2		8	2
	1		7	3	11		4	10						5	6		9			2		8	3
	1		7	3	11		4	10						5	6		9			2		8	4
			7	3	11		4	10						5	6		9		1	2		8	5
		9	7	3	11		4	10						5	6				1	2		8	6
		9	7	3	11		4	10						5	6				1	2		8	7
			7	3	11		4	9					5		6		10		1	2		8	8
			7	3			4				9			5	6	11	10		1	2		8	9
			7	3			4				9			5	6	11	10		1	2		8	10
			7	3			4		4		9			5	6	11	10		1	2		8	11
			7	3	11		4	8					5		6		10		1	2		9	12
			7	3	11		4	8			9		5		6		10		1	2			13
			7	3	11		4	9					5		6		10		1	2		8	14
				3	11		4	9			7		5		6		10		1	2		8	15
11				3			4	9			7		5		6		10		1	2		8	16
11				3			4	9			7		5		6		10		1	2		8	17
7				3	11		4				9		5		6		10		1	2		8	18
7				3	11		4				9		5		6		10		1	2		8	19
7				3	11		4				9		5		6		10		1	2		8	20
7	1				11		4		10		9			5	6			2			3	8	21
7	1				11		4	8	10					5	6			2			3	9	22
7	1	9			11		4		10					5	6			2			3	8	23
7	1	9			11	5	4		10	3					6			2				8	24
7	1	9			11	5	4		10	3					6			2				8	25
7	1	9			11	5	4		10	3					6			2				8	26
7	1	9			11	5	4		10	3					6			2				8	27
	1	9			11	5	4		10	3	7				6			2				8	28
7	1	9			11	5	4		10	3					6			2				8	29
7	1	9			11	5	4		10	3					6			2				8	30
7	1	9			11	5	4		10	3					6			2				8	31
7	1	9			11	5	4		10	3					6			2				8	32
7	1				11	5	4		10	3		9			6			2				8	33
7	1				11	5	4		10		9				6			2			3	8	34
11	1	9				5	4		10	3					6			2	7			8	35
7	1	9			11	5	4		10	3					6			2				8	36
7	1	9			11	5	4		10	3					6			2				8	37
7	1	9			11	5	4		10	3					6			2				8	38
7	1	9			11	5	4		10	3					6			2				8	39
7	1	9			11	5	4		10	3					6			2				8	40
7	1	9			11	5	4		10	3					6			2				8	41
7		9			11	5	4		10	3					6			2	1			8	42
26	24	20	14	20	34	19	41	14	23	18	14	1	9	14	35	2	17	22	16	18	24	37	
6		9	1	1		2		3	4						3			2				11	
7	1	9			11	5	4		10	3					6			2				8	43
7	1	9			11	5	4		10	3					6			2				8	44
7	1	9			11	5	4		10	3					6			2				8	45
7	1	9			11	5	4		10	3					6			2				8	46
7	1	9			11	5	4		10	3					6			2				8	47
5	5	5			5	5	5	3	5	5					5			2				5	
2		3																				2	

1950-51

1	Aug 19	(h)	Huddersfield T	W	3-2	Buckle 2, Grant	2	
2	23	(a)	Middlesbrough	L	0-4		2	
3	26	(a)	Newcastle U	D	1-1	Catterick	3	13
4	30	(h)	Middlesbrough	W	3-2	Eglington 2, McIntosh	5	9
5	Sep 2	(h)	West Brom A	l	0-3		5	13
6	6	(a)	Arsenal	L	1-2	Farrell	5	16
7	9	(a)	Stoke C	l	0-2		5	19
8	13	(h)	Arsenal	D	1-1	Hold	6	17
9	16	(h)	Liverpool	L	1-3	Eglington	6	19
10	23	(h)	Portsmouth	L	1-5	Catterick	6	21
11	30	(a)	Chelsea	L	1-2	Eglington	6	21
12	Oct 7	(a)	Fulham	W	5-1	Catterick 3, Buckle, Fielding	8	20
13	14	(h)	Bolton W	D	1-1	Buckle	9	20
14	21	(a)	Charlton A	L	1-2	Eglington	9	20
15	28	(h)	Manchester U	L	1-4	McIntosh	9	21
16	Nov 4	(a)	Blackpool	L	0-4		9	22
17	11	(h)	Tottenham H	L	1-2	Buckle	9	22
18	18	(a)	Wolves	L	0-4		9	22
19	25	(h)	Sunderland	W	3-1	Eglington, Hold, Potts	11	22
20	Dec 2	(a)	Aston Villa	D	3-3	Fielding, McIntosh, Potts	12	22
21	9	(h)	Derby C	L	1-2	Wainwright	12	22
22	16	(a)	Huddersfield T	W	2-1	McIntosh 2	14	21
23	23	(h)	Newcastle U	W	3-1	Fielding, Hold, Potts	16	20
24	25	(h)	Burnley	W	1-0	McIntosh	18	17
25	26	(a)	Burnley	D	1-1	Eglington	19	17
26	30	(a)	West Brom A	W	1-0	Eglington	21	16
27	Jan 13	(h)	Stoke C	l	0-3		21	17
28	20	(a)	Liverpool	W	2-0	McIntosh 2	23	16
29	Feb 3	(a)	Portsmouth	L	3-6	Hold, McIntosh, Potts	23	18
30	17	(h)	Chelsea	W	3-0	Farrell, Grant, Hold	25	16
31	28	(h)	Fulham	W	1-0	McIntosh	27	15
32	Mar 3	(a)	Bolton W	L	0-2		27	16
33	10	(h)	Charlton A	D	0-0		28	17
34	17	(a)	Manchester U	l	0-3		28	17
35	24	(h)	Blackpool	L	0-2		28	18
36	26	(h)	Sheffield W	D	0-0		29	18
37	31	(a)	Tottenham H	L	0-3		29	19
38	Apr 7	(h)	Wolves	D	1-1	Farrell	30	20
39	14	(a)	Sunderland	L	0-4		30	20
40	21	(h)	Aston Villa	L	1-2	McIntosh	30	21
41	28	(a)	Derby C	W	1-0	Potts	32	20
42	May 5	(a)	Sheffield W	L	0-6		32	22
							League Appearances	
							League Goals	
43	Jan 6	(a)	Hull C	L	0-2		FA Cup Rd 3	
							FA Cup Appearances	
							FA Cup Goals	

	Buckle E	Burnett G	Catterick H	Clinton T	Eglington T	Falder D	Farrell P	Fielding W	Gibson D	Grant J	Hampson A	Harris J A	Hold O	Humphreys J	Jones T E	Lindley W	Lindsay J	McIntosh J	Moore E	O'Neill J	Parker J	Potts H	Rankin G	Sagar E	Saunders G	Wainwright E	
	7	1	9		11	5	6	10		4									2						3	8	1
	7		9		11	5	6	10		4									2	1					3	8	2
	7		9		11	5	6	10		4									2	1					3	8	3
	7				11	5	6	10		4			8	9					2	1					3		4
	7		9		11	5	6	10		4									2	1					3	8	5
	7		9	2	11		6	10		4					5					1					3	8	6
	7		9	2	11		6	10		4					5					1					3	8	7
	7			2	11		6	10		4			9		5					1					3	8	8
	7		3		11		6	10		4			9		5				2	1						8	9
	7		9	3	11	5		8		4					6		10		2	1							10
	7		9	2	11		6	10		4					5					1			3			8	11
	7		9	2	11		6	10		4					5								3	1		8	12
	7	1		2	11		6	8		4			10		5			9	3								13
	7	1		2	11		6	8		4					5			9	3			10					14
	7	1		2	11		6	8		4					5			9	3			10					15
	7	1		2	11		6	8		4					5			9	3			10					16
	7	1		2	11		6	8		4					5			9	3			10					17
	7	1		2	11		6	8		4					5			9	3			10					18
				2	11		6	7		4			8		5			9	3			10	1				19
				2	11		6	7		4			8		5			9	3			10	1				20
					11		6	7		4	10				5			9	2				3	1		8	21
					11		6	7		4			8		5			9	2			10	3	1			22
					11		6	7		4			8		5			9	2			10	3	1			23
					11		6	7		4			8		5			9	2			10	3	1			24
					11		6	7		4			8		5			9	2			10	3	1			25
					11		6	7		4			8		5			9	2			10	3	1			26
					11		6	7		4			8		5			9	2			10	3	1			27
					11		6	7		4			8		5			9	2			10	3	1			28
					11		6	7		4			8		5			9	2			10	3	1			29
					11		6	7		4			8		5			9	2			10	3	1			30
	7				11		6			4			8		5			9	2			10	3	1			31
	7				11		6			4			8		5			9	2			10	3	1			32
					11		6	7		4			8		5			9	2			10	3	1			33
	7		9		11		6			4			8		5		3	11	2			10		1			34
							6	7		4			8		5		3	9	2		11	10		1			35
								10		4		7			5	6		9	2		11	0	3	1			36
			9		11		6	7		4					5				2		10	8	3	1			37
					11		6	7		4					5			9	2		10	8	3	1			38
					11		6	7		4					5			9	2		10	8	3	1			39
	7				11		6			4			8		5			9	2			10	3	1			40
			9		11		6		7	4					5	3						10	8	1	2		41
		1	9		11		6	7		4					5	3						10	8		2		42
	22	8	13	15	39	6	42	34	1	42	1	1	21	1	30	8	4	29	37	10	7	28	18	24	10	11	
	5	5	8			3	3			2					5			11				5			1		
					11		6	7		4			8		5			9	2			10	3	1			43
					1		1	1		1			1		1			1	1			1	1	1			

1951-52

#	Date		Opponent	Res	Score	Scorers	App	Goals
1	Aug 18	(a)	Southampton	L	0-1		0	
2	22	(h)	Brentford	W	1-0	Buckle	2	
3	25	(h)	Sheffield W	D	3-3	Buckle 2, Eglington	3	12
4	27	(a)	Brentford	L	0-1		3	17
5	Sep 1	(a)	Leeds U	W	2-1	Eglington 2	5	12
6	5	(h)	Nottingham F	W	1-0	Parker	7	6
7	8	(h)	Rotherham U	D	3-3	Hickson, McNamara, Potts	8	7
8	12	(a)	Nottingham F	L	0-2		8	9
9	15	(a)	Cardiff C	L	1-3	Buckle	8	15
10	22	(h)	Birmingham C	L	1-3	Buckle	8	18
11	29	(a)	Leicester C	W	2-1	Buckle, McNamara	10	14
12	Oct 6	(h)	Blackburn R	L	0-2		10	18
13	13	(a)	Q.P.R.	D	4-4	Buckle 2, Eglington, Parker	11	17
14	20	(h)	Notts Co	l	1-5	Parker	11	18
15	27	(a)	Luton T	D	1-1	Parker	12	19
16	Nov 3	(h)	Bury	D	2-2	Buckle 2	13	18
17	10	(a)	Swansea T	W	2-0	Buckle, Fielding	15	16
18	17	(h)	Coventry C	w	4-1	Hickson 2, McNamara, Parker	17	15
19	24	(a)	West Ham U	D	3-3	Fielding, Hickson, Parker	18	14
20	Dec 1	(h)	Sheffield U	W	1-0	Parker	20	12
21	8	(a)	Barnsley	L	0-1		20	13
22	15	(h)	Southampton	W	3-0	Hickson 2, Parker	22	11
23	22	(a)	Sheffield W	L	0-4		22	13
24	25	(a)	Doncaster R	L	1-3	Buckle	22	14
25	26	(h)	Doncaster R	D	1-1	Hickson	23	14
26	29	(h)	Leeds U	W	2-0	Eglington 2	25	13
27	Jan 5	(a)	Rotherham U	D	1-1	Hickson	26	13
28	19	(h)	Cardiff C	W	3-0	Clinton, Hickson, McNamara	28	11
29	26	(a)	Birmingham C	W	2-1	Hickson 2	30	10
30	Feb 9	(h)	Leicester C	W	2-0	Hickson, Mcnamara	32	9
31	16	(a)	Blackburn R	L	0-1		32	10
32	Mar 1	(h)	Q.P.R.	W	3-0	Clinton, Fielding, Parker	34	8
33	8	(a)	Notts Co	D	0-0		35	8
34	15	(h)	Luton T	L	1-3	Parker	35	10
35	22	(a)	Bury	L	0-1		35	11
36	29	(h)	Swansea T	W	2-1	Lello, Parker	37	9
37	Apr 5	(a)	Coventry C	L	1-2	Parker	37	12
38	11	(h)	Hull C	W	5-0	Parker 3, Fielding, Hickson	39	8
39	12	(h)	West Ham U	W	2-0	Clinton, Hickson	41	7
40	14	(a)	Hull C	L	0-1		41	8
41	19	(a)	Sheffield U	W	2-1	Clinton, Eglington	43	7
42	26	(h)	Barnsley	D	1-1	Eglington	44	7

League Appearances
League Goals

#	Date		Opponent	Res	Score	Scorers		
43	Jan 12	(a)	Leyton O	D	0-0		FA Cup Rd 3	
44	16	(h)	Leyton O	L	1-3	Parker	Replay	

FA Cup Appearances
FA Cup Goals

#	Buckle E	Catterick H	Clinton T	Cummins G	Donovan D	Eglington T	Farrell P	Fielding W	Gibson D	Grant J	Hickson D	Jones T E	Lello C	Lewis G	Leyland H	Lindley W	Lindsay J	McNamara A	Moore E	O'Neill J	Parker J	Potts H	Rankin G	Sagar E	Saunders G
1	7	9				11	4	10				5	6				3		2		8			1	
2	7	9				11	4	8				5	6				3		2		10			1	
3	7	9			4	11	6	8				5					3		2		10			1	
4	7	9			4	11	6	8				5					3		2		10			1	
5					4	11	6	8			9	5					3	7	2		10			1	
6					4	11	6	8			9	5					3	7	2		10			1	
7					4	11	6	8			9	5					3	7	2		10			1	
8					4	11	6	8			9	5					3	7	2		10			1	
9	10				4	11	6	8			9	5					3	7	2					1	
10	10				4	11	6	8			9	5					3	7	2					1	
11	10				4	11	6	8			9	5		1			3	7	2						
12	10				4	11	6	8			9	5			1		3	7						2	
13	10				4	11		8			9	5	6		1		3	7						2	
14	10				4	11		8			9	5	6		1		3	7						2	
15	10				4	11	6	8			9	5		1			3	7	2						
16	10				4	11	6	8			9	5		1			3	7	2						
17	10		2		4	11	6	8			9	5		1				7					3		
18			2		4	11	6	8			9	5		1			3	7			10				
19			2		4	11	6	8			9	5		1			3	7			10				
20			2		4	11	6	8			9	5					3	7		1	10				
21			2		4	11	6	7			9	5					3			1	10	8			
22			2		4	11	6	8			9	5					3	7		1	10				
23			2		4	11	6	8	7		9	5					3			1	10				
24	8		2		10		4	6			9	5					3	7		1	11				
25	7		2		10	11	4	8			9	5	6				3			1					
26			2		4	11	6	8			9	5					3	7		1	10				
27			2		4	11	6	8			9	5					3	7		1	10				
28			2			11	4	8			9	5	6				3	7		1	10				
29			2			11	4	8			9	5	6				3	7		1	10				
30			2			11	4	8			9	5	6				3	7		1	10				
31			2			11	4	8			9	5	6				3	7		1	10				
32			2		10	11	4	7			9	5	6				3			1		8			
33			2		10	11	4	7			9	5	6				3			1		8			
34			2		10	11	4				9	5	6				3	7		1		8			
35			2		10	11	4	8			9	5	6					7		1					3
36			2			11	4	8			9	5	6				3	7		1	10				
37			2			11	4	8			9	5	6				3	7		1	10				
38			2			11	4	8			9	5	6				3	7		1	10				
39			2			11	4	8			9	5	6				3	7		1	10				
40			2			11	4	8			9	5	6				3	7		1	10				
41			2			11	4	8			9	5	6				3	7		1	10				
42			2			11	4	8			9	5	6				3	7		1	10				
Apps	15	4	26	5	22	38	40	37	2	5	31	37	21	1	12	13	40	33	5	20	36	4	2	10	3
Goals	12	4				8		4			14	1						5			15	1			
43			2		4	11	6	8			9	5					3	7		1	10				
44	7		2		4	11	6	8			9	5					3			1	10				
Cup	1		2		2	2	2	2			2	2					2	1		2	2				
Cup goals											1														

1952-53

#	Date		Opponent	Res	Score	Scorers	App	Goals
1	Aug 23	(h)	Hull C	L	0-2		0	
2	25	(a)	Sheffield U	L	0-1		0	
3	30	(a)	Blackburn R	L	1-3	Fielding	0	22
4	Sep 3	(h)	Sheffield U	D	0-0		1	22
5	6	(h)	Nottingham F	W	3-0	Parker 2, Fielding	3	20
6	10	(a)	Barnsley	W	3-2	Farrell, Harris, Hickson	5	14
7	13	(a)	Southampton	D	1-1	Harris	6	13
8	20	(a)	Brentford	W	4-2	Parker 2, Potts 2	8	14
9	27	(h)	Doncaster R	W	7-1	Eglington 5, Parker 2	10	10
10	Oct 4	(a)	Swansea T	D	2-2	Hickson 2	11	11
11	11	(h)	Notts Co	W	1-0	Fielding	13	8
12	18	(a)	Leicester C	L	2-4	Harris, Parker	13	10
13	25	(h)	West Ham U	W	2-0	Eglington, Harris	15	7
14	Nov 1	(a)	Fulham	L	0-3		15	9
15	8	(h)	Rotherham U	l	0-1		15	11
16	15	(a)	Plymouth A	L	0-1		15	12
17	22	(h)	Leeds U	D	2-2	Eglington, Potts	16	13
18	29	(a)	Luton T	L	2-4	Parker 2	16	14
19	Dec 6	(h)	Birmingham C	D	1-1	Potts	17	15
20	13	(a)	Bury	W	5-0	Potts 3, Eglington, Wainwright	19	13
21	20	(a)	Hull C	L	0-1		19	13
22	26	(a)	Lincoln C	D	1-1	Potts	20	13
23	Jan 1	(h)	Barnsley	W	2-1	Parker, Wainwright	22	13
24	3	(a)	Blackburn R	L	0-3		22	14
25	17	(a)	Nottingham F	D	3-3	Eglington, Fielding, Wainwright	23	14
26	24	(h)	Southampton	D	2-2	Eglington, Wainwright	24	14
27	Feb 7	(h)	Brentford	W	5-0	Hickson 3, Buckle, Eglington	26	13
28	18	(a)	Doncaster R	L	0-3		26	14
29	21	(h)	Swansea T	D	0-0		27	13
30	Mar 5	(a)	Notts Co	D	2-2	Lewis 2	28	13
31	7	(h)	Leicester C	D	2-2	Buckle, Hickson	29	13
32	14	(a)	West Ham U	L	1-3	Lewis	29	15
33	25	(h)	Fulham	D	3-3	Parker 2, Fielding	30	15
34	28	(a)	Rotherham U	D	2-2	Hickson, Parker	31	15
35	Apr 4	(h)	Plymouth A	W	2-0	Eglington 2	33	15
36	6	(h)	Huddersfield T	W	2-1	Buckle 2	35	14
37	7	(a)	Huddersfield T	L	2-8	Hickson 2	35	14
38	11	(a)	Leeds U	L	0-2		35	14
39	15	(h)	Bury	W	3-0	Mayers 2, Hickson	37	14
40	18	(h)	Luton T	D	1-1	Buckle	38	13
41	22	(h)	Lincoln C	L	0-3		38	13
42	25	(a)	Birmingham C	L	2-4	Eglington, Hickson	38	16

League Appearances
League Goals

#	Date		Opponent	Res	Score	Scorers	
43	Jan 10	(h)	Ipswich T	W	3-2	Hickson 2, Fielding	FA Cup Rd 3
44	31	(h)	Nottingham F	W	4-1	Parker 2, Clinton, Eglington	4
45	Feb 14	(h)	Manchester U	W	2-1	Eglington, Hickson	5
46	28	(a)	Aston Villa	W	1-0	Hickson	6
47	Mar 21	(n)	Bolton W	L	3-4	Parker 2, Farrell	(Maine Road) SF

FA Cup Appearances
FA Cup Goals

Buckle E	Clinton T	Cummings G	Donovan D	Easthope J	Eglington T	Farrall A	Farrell P	Fielding W	Grant J	Harris J A	Hickson D	Jones T E	Lello C	Lewis G	Leyland H	Lindsay J	McNamara A	Mayers D	Moore E	O'Neill J	Parker J	Potts H	Rankin G	Sagar E	Tansey J	Wainwright E	Woods M	
	2				11		4	8			9	5	6			3	7			1	10							1
	2				11		4	8	6	7	9	5				3			2	1	10							2
	2				11		4	8	6	7	9	5				3			2	1	10							3
	2				11		4	8	6	7	9	5				3			2	1	10							4
	2				11		4	8	6	7	9	5				3			2	1	10							5
	2				11		4	8	6	7	9	5				3			2	1	10							6
	2				11		4	8	6	7	9	5				3			2	1	10							7
					11		4	10	6	7		5				3			2	1	9	8						8
					11		4	10	6	7		5							2	1	9	8	3					9
					11		4		6	7	9	5							2	1	10	8	3					10
					11		4	10	6	7		5				3			2	1	9	8						11
					11		4	10	6	7		5				3			2	1	9	8						12
					11		4	8	6	7	9	5				3			2	1	10							13
					11		4	8	6	7	9	5				3			2	1	10							14
7	2				11		4	10	6			5								1	9	8	3					15
11	2	10	4									5	6			7					9	8	3	1				16
	2	10	4		11							5	6			7				1	9	8	3					17
	2	10			11		4		6			5				3	7			1	9	8						18
	2	10			11		4		6			5				3	7			1	9	8						19
	2				11		4	10			9	5	6			3				1	8					7		20
	2	10			11		4				9	5	6			3				1	8					7		21
	2	10			11		4					5	6			3				1	9	8				7		22
	2	10			11		4					5	6			3				1	9	8				7		23
	2	10			11				4			5	6			3				1	9	8				7		24
	2	10			11		4	8			9	5	6			3				1						7		25
	2	10			11		4				9	5	6			3				1	8					7		26
7	2	8			11		4				9	5	6			3				1	10							27
	2	8			11		4	10				5	6			3	7			1	9							28
7	2	8			11		4				9	5	6							1	10	3						29
	2				11		4	10				5	6	9		7				1	8	3						30
7	2	8	4		11				6		9	5	3							1	10							31
7	2	8	3		11		4					5	6	9						1	10							32
7			4		11			8			9	2	6		1						10	3				5		33
7	2				11		4	8			9	5	6		1						10	3						34
7	10	2			11		4	8			9	5	6			3				1								35
7	10				11		4	8			9	5	6			3				1					2			36
7					11		4	8			9	5	6			3				1		10			2			37
7					11		4	8			9	5	6			2				1	10	3						38
	2	8			11		4				9	5	6		1	3	7				10							39
7	2				11		4	8			9	5	6		1	3					10							40
		8			11	10	4				9	5	6		1	3	7	2										41
7	2				11		4	8			9	5	6		1						10	3						42
14	22	19	7	2	39	1	38	26	17	13	27	42	26	2	6	30	7	2	14	35	32	19	10	1	3	7	1	
5					14		1	5	4	12			3					2		13	8		4					
	2	10			11		4	7			9	5	6			3				1	8							43
7	2	8			11		4				9	5	6			3				1	10							44
7	2	8			11		4				9	5	6			3				1	10							45
7	2	8			11		4				9	5	6			3				1	10							46
7	2	8			11		4				9	5	6			3				1	10							47
4	5	5			5		5	1			5	5	5			5				5	4	1						
	1				2		1	1			4										4							

1953-54

1	Aug 19	(a)	Nottingham F	D	3-3	Parker 2, Eglington	1	
2	22	(a)	Luton T	D	1-1	Buckle	2	
3	24	(a)	Hull C	W	3-1	Fielding, Hickson, Parker	4	7
4	29	(h)	Oldham A	W	3-1	Parker 3	6	2
5	Sep 2	(h)	Hull C	W	2-0	Buckle, Fielding	8	2
6	5	(a)	Bury	D	2-2	Eglington, Parker	10	4
7	10	(a)	Notts Co	W	2-0	McNamara, Parker	11	2
8	12	(h)	Doncaster R	W	4-1	Eglington 2, Parker 2	13	2
9	19	(a)	Blackburn R	D	0-0		14	3
10	23	(h)	Notts Co	W	3-2	Hickson 2, Eglinton	16	2
11	26	(h)	Derby Co	W	3-2	Eglington, Lello, Parker	18	1
12	Oct 3	(a)	Brentford	L	0-1		18	1
13	10	(a)	Plymouth A	L	0-4		18	3
14	17	(h)	Swansea T	D	2-2	Parker 2	19	4
15	24	(a)	Rotherham U	W	2-1	Fielding, Hickson	21	2
16	31	(h)	Leicester C	L	1-2	Eglington	21	4
17	Nov 7	(a)	Stoke C	W	4-2	Hickson 3, Parker	23	4
18	14	(h)	Fulham	D	2-2	Hickson, Parker	24	3
19	21	(a)	West Ham U	D	1-1	Lewis	25	3
20	28	(h)	Leeds U	W	2-1	Buckle, Hickson	27	3
21	Dec 5	(a)	Birmingham C	L	1-5	Parker	27	3
22	12	(h)	Nottingham F	D	3-3	Hickson 2, Parker	28	3
23	19	(h)	Luton T	W	2-1	Eglington, Parker	30	3
24	25	(h)	Bristol R	W	4-0	Hickson 2, Eglington, Wainwright	32	2
25	28	(a)	Bristol R	D	0-0		33	2
26	Jan 16	(h)	Bury	D	0-0		34	2
27	23	(a)	Doncaster R	D	2-2	Hickson, Wainwright	35	1
28	Feb 6	(h)	Blackburn R	D	1-1	Hickson	36	2
29	13	(a)	Derby C	W	6-2	Wainwright 3, Hickson, Lindsay, Parker	38	2
30	24	(h)	Brentford	W	6-1	Hickson 2, Parker 2, Fielding, Wainwright	40	2
31	27	(h)	Plymouth A	W	8-4	Parker 4, Hickson 2, Lello, Lindsay	42	2
32	Mar 6	(a)	Swansea T	W	2-0	Hickson, Parker	44	2
33	13	(h)	Rotherham U	W	3-0	Parker 3	46	1
34	20	(a)	Leicester C	D	2-2	Hickson 2	47	1
35	27	(h)	West Ham U	L	1-2	Wainwright	47	1
36	Apr 3	(a)	Leeds U	L	1-3	Wainwright	47	3
37	10	(h)	Stoke C	D	1-1	Eglington	48	3
38	16	(h)	Lincoln C	W	3-1	Farrell, Fielding, Lewis	50	3
39	17	(a)	Fulham	D	0-0		51	3
40	19	(a)	Lincoln C	D	1-1	Eglington	52	3
41	24	(h)	Birmingham C	W	1-0	Hickson	54	3
42	29	(a)	Oldham A	W	4-0	Parker 2, Hickson, Jones	56	2
							League Appearances	
							League Goals	
43	Jan 9	(h)	Notts Co	W	2-1	Eglington, Hickson	FA Cup Rd 3	
44	30	(h)	Swansea T	W	3-0	Parker 2, Hickson		4
45	Feb 20	(a)	Sheffield W	L	1-3	Hickson		5
							FA Cup Appearances	
							FA Cup Goals	

Buckle E	Clinton T	Donovan D	Eglington T	Farrall A	Farrell P	Fielding W	Grant J	Hickson D	Jones T E	Lello C	Lewis G	Leyland H	Lindsay J	McNamara A	Mayers D	Moore E	O'Neill J	Parker J	Potts H	Rankin G	Wainwright E	#
7	2	3	11		4	8		9	5	6							1	10				1
7	2	3	11		4	8		9	5	6		1						10				2
	2	3	11		4	8		9	5	6		1	7					10				3
7	2	5	11		4	8		9		6		1						10		3		4
7		3	11		4	8		9	5	6		1				2		10				5
7		3	11	10	4	8			5	6		1				2		9				6
	2		11		4	8		9	5	6		1	3	7				10				7
	2		11		4	8		9	5	6		1	3	7				10				8
	2		11			8	4	9	5	6		1	3	7				10				9
7	2		11		4	8		9	5	6		1	3					10				10
7	2		11		4	8		9	5	6		1	3					10				11
11	2					8	4	9	5	6		1	3	7				10				12
7	2		11		4	8		9	5	6		1	3					10				13
7	2		11		4	8		9	5	6			3				1	10				14
7	2		11		4	8		9	5	6		1	3					10				15
7	2		11		4	8		9	5	6		1	3					10				16
7	2		11		4			9	5	6			3				1	10			8	17
7	2		11		4			9	5	6			3				1	10			8	18
7	2		11		4				5	6	9		3				1	10			8	19
7	2	5	11			10	4	9		6			3				1				8	20
7	2	5	11		4	8		9		6			3				1	10				21
7		5	11		4	8		9		6			3			2	1	10				22
		5	11		4	8		9		6			3			2	1	10			7	23
	2		11		4	8		9	5	6			3				1	10			7	24
	2		11		4	8		9	5	6			3				1	10			7	25
	2		11		4	8		9	5	6			3				1	10			7	26
	2		11		4	8		9	5	6			3				1	10			7	27
	2		11		4	8		9	5	6			3				1	10			7	28
	2		11		4	8		9	5	6			3				1	10			7	29
	2		11		4	8		9	5	6			3				1	10			7	30
	2		11		4	8		9	5	6			3				1	10			7	31
	2		11		4	8		9	5	6			3				1	10			7	32
	2		11		4	8		9	5	6			3				1	10			7	33
	2		11		4	8		9	5	6			3				1	10			7	34
	2		11		4	8		9	5	6			3				1	10			7	35
	2		11		4	8		9	5	6			3				1	10			7	36
	2		11		4	8		9	5	6			3				1	10			7	37
		3	11		4	8		9	5	6	10					2	1				7	38
		3	11		4	8		9	5	6						2	1		10		7	39
7		3	11		4	8		9	5	6	10					2	1					40
		3	11		4	8		9	5	6						2	1	10			7	41
		3	11		4	8		9	5	6						2	1	10			7	42
19	6	42	41	1	39	39	3	40	37	42	3	14	31	4	1	9	28	38	1	1	23	
3			11	1	5	25		1	2	2			2					31			8	
	2		11		4	8		9	5	6			3				1	10			7	43
			11		4	8		9	5	6			3			2	1	10			7	44
	2		11		4	8		9	5	6			3				1	10			7	45
	2	3			3	3		3	3	3			3			1	3	3			3	
			1					3										2				

1954-55

#	Date		Opponent		Score	Scorers	App	Goals
1	Aug 21	(a)	Sheffield U	W	5-2	Parker 2, Wainwright 2, Eglington	2	
2	25	(h)	Arsenal	W	1-0	Eglington	4	
3	28	(h)	Preston N E	W	1-0	Lello	6	1
4	31	(a)	Arsenal	L	0-2		6	2
5	Sep 4	(a)	Burnley	W	2-0	Eglington, Parker	8	1
6	8	(h)	West Brom A	L	1-2	Jones	8	5
7	11	(h)	Leicester C	D	2-2	Hickson, Lewis	9	6
8	15	(a)	West Brom A	D	3-3	Parker 2, Hickson	10	7
9	18	(a)	Chelsea	W	2-0	Eglington, Parker	12	5
10	25	(h)	Cardiff C	D	1-1	Parker	13	7
11	Oct 2	(a)	Manchester C	L	0-1		13	8
12	9	(a)	Aston Villa	W	2-0	Hickson, McNamara	15	6
13	16	(h)	Sunderland	W	1-0	McNamara	17	2
14	23	(a)	Huddersfield T	L	1-2	Hickson	17	6
15	30	(h)	Manchester U	W	4-2	Jones 2, Eglington, Hickson	19	3
16	Nov 6	(a)	Portsmouth	L	0-5		19	7
17	13	(h)	Blackpool	L	0-1		19	9
18	20	(a)	Charlton A	L	0-5		19	13
19	27	(h)	Bolton W	D	0-0		20	12
20	Dec 4	(a)	Tottenham	W	3-1	Parker 2, opp.og	22	10
21	11	(h)	Sheffield W	W	3-1	Parker 2, Hickson	24	8
22	18	(h)	Sheffield U	L	2-3	Eglington, Parker	24	9
23	25	(a)	Wolves	W	3-1	Hickson 2, Wainwright	26	9
24	27	(h)	Wolves	W	3-2	Fielding, Hickson, Potts	28	9
25	Jan 1	(a)	Preston N E	D	0-0		29	8
26	15	(h)	Burnley	D	1-1	Fielding	30	6
27	Feb 5	(h)	Chelsea	D	1-1	McNamara	31	5
28	12	(a)	Cardiff C	l	3-4	Parker 2, Lello	31	8
29	23	(h)	Manchester C	W	1-0	Hickson	33	7
30	Mar 5	(a)	Sheffield W	D	2-2	Eglington, Parker	34	8
31	19	(a)	Manchester U	W	2-1	Eglington, Parker	36	6
32	23	(h)	Huddersfield T	W	4-0	Hickson, McNamara, Parker, opp.og	38	4
33	26	(h)	Portsmouth	L	2-3	Jones, Parker	38	6
34	Apr 2	(a)	Blackpool	L	0-4		38	7
35	8	(h)	Newcastle U	L	1-2	Fielding	38	8
36	9	(h)	Tottenham H	W	1-0	Fielding	40	7
37	11	(a)	Newcastle U	L	0-4		40	8
38	16	(a)	Bolton W	L	0-2		40	9
39	20	(a)	Leicester C	D	2-2	Eglington, Hickson	41	8
40	23	(h)	Charlton A	D	2-2	Parker, Wainwright	42	8
41	30	(a)	Sunderland	L	0-3		42	11
42	May 4	(h)	Aston Villa	L	0-1		42	11

League Appearances
League goals

#	Date		Opponent		Score	Scorers		
43	Jan 8	(h)	Southend U	W	3-1	Fielding, Hickson, Potts	FA Cup Rd 3	
44	29	(h)	Liverpool	L	0-4			4

FA Cup Appearances
FA Cup Goals

Buckle E	Donovan D	Eglington T	Farrall A	Farrell P	Fielding W	Grant J	Hickson D	Jones T E	Lello C	Lewis G	Leyland H	McNamara A	Moore E	O'Neill J	Parker J	Potts H	Rankin G	Saunders R	Tansey J	Wainwright E	Woods M	
	3	11		4	8		9	5	6				2	1	10					7		1
	3	11		4	8		9	5	6				2	1	10					7		2
	3	11		4	8		9	5	6				2	1	10					7		3
	3	11		4	8		9	5	6				2	1	10					7		4
	3	11		4	8		9	5	6				2	1	10					7		5
	3	11		4	8		9	5	6				2	1	10							6
	3	11		4	8		9	5	6	10		7	2	1								7
	3	11		4	8		9	5	6			7	2	1	10							8
	3	11		4	8		9	5	6			7	2	1	10							9
	3	11		4	8		9	5	6			7	2	1	10							10
	3	11	8	4			9	5	6	10		7	2	1								11
	3	11		4			9	5	6			7	2	1	10					8		12
	3	11		4			9	5	6			7	2	1	10					8		13
	3	11		4			9	5	6			7	2	1	10					8		14
	3	11		4			9	5	6			7	2	1	10					8		15
11				4			9	5	6		1	7	2		10		3				8	16
	3	11		4			9	5	6			7	2	1	10					8		17
	3	11		4	8		9	5	6				2	1	10					7		18
	3	11		4	8		9	5	6				2	1	10					7		19
	3	11		4	8		9	5	6				2	1	10					7		20
	3	11		4	8		9	5	6				2	1	10					7		21
	3	11		4	8		9	5	6				2	1	10					7		22
	3	11		4	8		9	5	6				2	1		10				7		23
	3	11		4	8		9	5	6				2	1		10				7		24
		11		4	8		9	5	6				2	1		10	3			7		25
		11		4	8		9	5	6				2	1		10	3			7		26
	3	11		4	8		9	5	6			7	2	1	10							27
	3	11		4	8			5	6			7	2	1	10			9				28
	3	11		4	8		9	5	6			7	2	1	10							29
	3	11		4	8		9	5	6			7	2	1	10							30
	3	11		4	8		9	5	6			7	2	1	10							31
	3	11		4	8		9	5	6			7	2	1	10							32
	3	11		4	8		9	5	6			7	2	1	10							33
	2	11		4	8		9		6			7		1	10			3	5			34
	3	11		4	8		9	5	6			7	2	1	10							35
		11		4	8			5	6			7	2	1	10			9	3			36
		11		4	8			5	6			7	2	1	10			9	3			37
		11		4	8		9	5	6			7	2	1	10				3			38
		11		4	8		9	5	6			7	2	1	10				3			39
	3	11		4			9	5	6			7	2	1	10					8		40
	3	11		4			9	5	6	10		7	2	1						8		41
	3	11		4			9	5	6			7	2	1						8		42
1	35	41	1	41	33	1	39	41	42	3	1	27	41	41	34	4	3	3	5	24	1	
	9			4			12	4	2	1		4			19	1				4		opp.og 2
		11		4	8		9	5	6				2	1		10	3			7		43
		11		4	8		9	5	6				2	1		10	3			7		44
		2		2	2		2	2	2				2	2		2	2			2		
					1		1									1						

1955-56

#	Date	V	Opponent	Res	Score	Scorers	App	Gls
1	Aug 20	(h)	Preston N E	L	0-4		0	
2	24	(a)	West Brom A	L	0-2		0	
3	27	(a)	Burnley	W	1-0	Jones	2	19
4	31	(h)	West Brom A	W	2-0	Fielding, J.Harris	4	12
5	Sep 3	(h)	Luton T	L	0-1		4	18
6	7	(a)	Manchester U	L	1-2	Wainwright	4	19
7	10	(a)	Charlton A	W	2-0	J.Harris, Wainwright	6	15
8	14	(h)	Manchester U	W	4-2	Parker 2, Eglington, Wainwright	8	9
9	17	(h)	Tottenham H	W	2-1	Eglington, Parker	10	7
10	24	(a)	Portsmouth	L	0-1		10	10
11	Oct 1	(a)	Newcastle U	W	2-1	Eglington, J.Harris	12	7
12	8	(h)	Arsenal	D	1-1	Wainwright	13	7
13	15	(a)	Bolton W	D	1-1	J.Harris	14	7
14	22	(h)	Aston Villa	W	2-1	J.Harris 2	16	6
15	29	(a)	Sunderland	D	0-0		17	6
16	Nov 5	(h)	Huddersfield T	W	5-2	Mayers 2, Eglington, Lello, Woods	19	6
17	12	(a)	Cardiff C	L	1-3	J.Harris	19	6
18	19	(h)	Manchester C	D	1-1	J.Harris	20	7
19	26	(a)	Wolves	L	0-1		20	8
20	Dec 3	(h)	Chelsea	D	3-3	Eglington, J.Harris, Jones	21	10
21	10	(a)	Blackpool	L	0-4		21	11
22	17	(a)	Preston N E	W	1-0	J.Harris	23	9
23	24	(h)	Burnley	D	1-1	McNamara	24	9
24	26	(a)	Birmingham C	L	2-6	B.Harris, J.Harris	24	10
25	27	(h)	Birmingham C	W	5-1	J.Harris 2, Wainwright 2, Eglington	26	9
26	31	(a)	Luton T	D	2-2	J.Harris, Parker	27	7
27	Jan 14	(h)	Charlton A	W	3-2	Fielding, J.Harris, Lello	29	7
28	21	(a)	Tottenham H	D	1-1	Wainwright	30	7
29	Feb 4	(h)	Portsmouth	L	0-2		30	10
30	11	(h)	Newcastle U	D	0-0		31	9
31	21	(a)	Arsenal	L	2-3	Eglington, J.Harris	31	10
32	25	(h)	Bolton W	W	1-0	Eglington	33	7
33	Mar 3	(a)	Manchester C	L	0-3		33	8
34	10	(h)	Sunderland	L	1-2	J.Harris	33	14
35	17	(a)	Huddersfield T	L	0-1		33	15
36	24	(h)	Cardiff C	W	2-0	McNamara, Wainwright	35	13
37	30	(h)	Sheffield U	L	1-4	Donovan	35	14
38	31	(a)	Aston Villa	L	0-2		35	16
39	Apr 2	(a)	Sheffield U	D	1-1	J.Harris	36	16
40	7	(h)	Wolves	W	2-1	Fielding, B.Harris	38	13
41	14	(a)	Chelsea	L	1-6	J.Harris	38	15
42	21	(h)	Blackpool	W	1-0	Farrell	40	15

League Appearances
League Goals

#	Date	V	Opponent	Res	Score	Scorers	FA Cup
43	Jan 7	(h)	Bristol C	W	3-1	Eglington, J.Harris, Wainwright	Rd 3
44	28	(a)	Port Vale	W	3-2	Eglington, B.Harris, Wainwright	4
45	Feb 18	(h)	Chelsea	W	1-0	Farrell	5
46	Mar 3	(a)	Manchester C	L	1-2	J.Harris	6

FA Cup Appearances
FA Cup Goals

K.Birch	Donovan D	Eglington T	Farrall A	Farrell P	Fielding W	Harris A	Harris B	Harris J	Hickson D	Jones T E	Kirby G	Lello C	Lewis G	Leyland H	McNamara A	Mayers D	Moore E	O'Neill J	Parker J	Payne J	Potts H	Rankin G	Tansey J	Wainwright E	Williams G	Woods M	No.
3		11		4	8				9	5		6					2	1	10					7			1
		11		4	8				9	5		6	10				2	1					3	7			2
		11		4	10		7	9		5		6					2	1			8		3				3
		11		4	10		7	9		5		6					2	1			8		3				4
		11		4	10		7	9		5		6					2	1			8		3				5
		11		4	8			9		5		6					2	1	10				3	7			6
		11		4	8			9		5		6					2	1	10				3	7			7
		11		4	8			9		5		6					2	1	10				3	7			8
		11		4	8			9		5		6					2	1	10				3	7			9
		11		4	8		7	9		5		6					2	1	10				3				10
		11		4			7	9		5		6					2	1	10				3	8			11
		11		4			7	9		5		6					2	1	10				3	8			12
		11		4				9		5		6				7	2	1	10				3	8			13
		11		4				9				6				7	2	1	10				3	8	5		14
		11		4				9				6				7	2	1	10				3	8	5		15
		11		4				9				6				7	2	1	10				3	8	5		16
				4	7			9		5		6		11			2	1	10				3	8			17
		11		4				9		5		6				7	2	1	10				3	8			18
		11		4				9		5		6				7	2	1	10				3	8			19
		11		4				9		5		6			7		2	1	10				3	8			20
		11		4				9		5		6			7		2	1	10				3	8			21
		11		4	10			9		5		6			7		2	1					3	8			22
		11		4	10			9		5		6			7		2	1					3	8			23
				4	10		7	9		5		6					2	1	11				3	8			24
		11		4	10		7	9		5		6					2	1				3		8			25
		11		4			7	9		5		6					2	1	10			3		8			26
		11		4	10		7	9		5		6					2	1					3	8			27
		11		4	10		7	9		5		6					2	1					3	8			28
		11		4	10		7	9		5		6		1			2						3	8			29
				4	10		11	9		5		6		1	7		2						3	8			30
		11		4	10		7	9		5		6		1			2						3	8			31
		11		4	10		7	9		5		6					2	1					3	8			32
		11		4	10		7	9		5		6					2	1					3	8			33
		8		4	10		7	9		5		6					2	1	10				3		11		34
4		11	6	8				9		5							2	1	10				3	7			35
	8	11		4				9		5		6			7		2	1					3	10			36
	8	11		4				9		5		6			7		2	1					3	10			37
	8	11		4	10	1	7	9		5		6					2						3				38
4	8	11		6	10	1	7	9		5							2						3				39
4	8	11		6	10	1	7	9		5							2						3				40
4	8	11		6	8	1		9		5							2		10				3				41
4		11		6	8	1		9		5							2		10	7			3				42
4	8	38	1	42	29	5	20	40	2	39	2	37	1	3	7	7	42	34	20	1	3	2	39	31	2	3	
1		8	1	3	2			19	2	2					2	2			4					8	1		
		11		4	10		7	9		5		6					2	1					3	8			43
		11		4	10		7	9		5		6		1			2						3	8			44
		11		4	10		7	9		5		6		1			2						3	8			45
		11		4	10		7	9		5		6					2	1					3	8			46
		4		4	4		4	4		4		4		2			4	2					4	4			
		2		1	1			2		2														2			

1956-57

#	Date		Opponent	Res	Score	Scorers	App	Goals
1	Aug 18	(a)	Leeds U	L	1-5	Farrell	0	
2	22	(h)	Blackpool	L	2-3	Farrell, Llewellyn	0	
3	25	(h)	Bolton W	D	2-2	Llewellyn, McNamara	1	20
4	27	(a)	Blackpool	L	2-5	McNamara 2	1	20
5	Sep 1	(a)	Wolves	L	1-2	Kirby	1	21
6	3	(a)	Burnley	L	1-2	McNamara	1	21
7	8	(h)	Aston Villa	L	0-4		1	21
8	12	(h)	Burnley	W	1-0	Jones	3	20
9	15	(a)	Luton T	L	0-2		3	21
10	22	(h)	Sunderland	W	2-1	Kirby, Mayers	5	21
11	29	(a)	Charlton A	W	2-1	Fielding, Mayers	7	19
12	Oct 6	(a)	Preston N E	D	0-0		8	18
13	13	(h)	Chelsea	L	0-3		8	18
14	20	(a)	Manchester U	W	5-2	Kirby 2, Donovan, Eglington, McNamara	10	18
15	27	(h)	Arsenal	W	4-0	Farrell, Fielding, Jones, Kirby	12	16
16	Nov 3	(a)	West Brom A	L	0-3		12	16
17	10	(h)	Portsmouth	D	2-2	Fielding, Gauld	13	15
18	17	(a)	Newcastle U	D	0-0		14	18
19	24	(h)	Sheffield W	W	1-0	Kirby	16	16
20	Dec 1	(a)	Cardiff C	L	0-1		16	18
21	8	(h)	Birmingham C	W	2-0	Jones, Kirby	18	15
22	15	(h)	Leeds U	W	2-1	Gauld 2	20	14
23	25	(a)	Tottenham H	L	0-6		20	15
24	26	(h)	Tottenham H	D	1-1	Eglington	21	15
25	29	(h)	Wolves	W	3-1	McNamara 2, J.Harris	23	12
26	Jan 12	(a)	Aston Villa	L	1-3	J.Harris	23	14
27	19	(h)	Luton T	W	2-1	Gauld, Mayers	25	13
28	Feb 2	(a)	Sunderland	D	1-1	Fielding	26	13
29	9	(h)	Charlton A	W	5-0	J.Harris 2, Fielding, Gauld, Payne	28	11
30	23	(a)	Arsenal	L	0-2		28	12
31	27	(h)	Preston N E	L	1-4	Payne	28	14
32	Mar 6	(h)	Manchester U	L	1-2	Fielding	28	14
33	9	(a)	Birmingham C	W	3-1	Thomas 2, Williams	30	14
34	16	(h)	West Brom A	L	0-1		30	15
35	23	(a)	Portsmouth	L	2-3	Kirby, McNamara	30	16
36	30	(h)	Newcastle U	W	2-1	Gauld, McNamara	32	15
37	Apr 6	(a)	Sheffield W	D	2-2	McNamara, Temple	33	15
38	13	(h)	Cardiff C	D	0-0		34	13
39	19	(a)	Manchester C	W	4-2	Birch, Gauld, Haughey, Williams	36	13
40	20	(a)	Chelsea	L	1-5	Williams	36	14
41	22	(h)	Manchester C	D	1-1	Temple	37	14
42	27	(a)	Bolton W	D	1-1	Temple	38	15

League Appearances
League Goals

43	Jan 5	(h)	Blackburn R	W	1-0	J.Harris	FA Cup 3	
44	26	(h)	West Ham U	W	2-1	Farrell, Gauld		4
45	Feb 16	(a)	Manchester U	L	0-1			5

FA Cup Appearances
FA Cup Goals

Birch K	Donovan D	Dunlop A	Eglington T	Farrall A	Farrell P	Fielding W	Gauld J	Glazzard J	Harris B	Harris J	Haughey W	Jones T E	Kirby G	Lello C	Llewellyn H	McNamara A	Mayers D	Moore E	O'Neill J	Payne J	Rea K	Sutherland J	Tansey J	Temple D	Thomas E	Tomlinson J	Williams G	Woods M	#
	8	11	4							7	9	5	6				10	2	1				3						1
		11	4		10						9	2		6	8	7			1				3					5	2
		11	4		10						9	2		6	8	7			1				3					5	3
		11	4		10						9	2		6	8	7			1				3					5	4
		11	4		10							5	9		8	7			1		6	2	3						5
		11	4		10		8					5	9			7			1		6	2	3						6
		11	4			9	8					5	10			7			1		6	2	3						7
	2		4		10					7		5	9		8	11			1		6		3						8
	2		4		10					11		5	9		8	7			1		6		3						9
4	2				10							5	9		8	7	11		1		6		3						10
4	2				10							5	9		8	7	11		1		6		3						11
4	2				10							5	9		8	7	11		1		6		3						12
4	2				10							5	9		8	7	11		1		6		3						13
4	2	1	11		6	10	8					5	9			7							3						14
4	2	1	11		6	10	8					5	9			7							3						15
4	2	1	11		6	10	8					5	9			7							3						16
4	2	1	11		6	10	8					5	9			7							3						17
4	2	1	11		6	10	8					5	9										3			7			18
4	2	1	11		6	10	8					5	9			7							3						19
4	2	1	11		6	10	8					5	9			7							3						20
4	2	1	11		6	10	8					5	9			7							3						21
4	2	1	11		6	10	8					5	9			7							3						22
4	2	1	11		6	10	8					5	9			7							3						23
4	2	1	11			10	8					5	9			7					6		3						24
4	5	1	11			10	8						9			7					6	2	3						25
4	2	1	11		6	10	8					5	9										3			7			26
	5	1	11		4	10	8						9			7					6	2	3						27
	5	1	11		4	10	8						9							7	6	2	3						28
	2	1	11		4	10	8					5	9							7	6		3						29
4	2	1	11		6	10	8					5	9							7			3						30
4	2	1	11		6	10	8					5	9							7			3						31
	2	1	11		4	10						5	9			7					6		3		8				32
4	2	1			6	10						5	9			7							3		8		11		33
4	2	1			6	10						5	9			7							3		8		11		34
4	2	1	11		6	10						5	9			7							3		8				35
4	2	1			6	10	8					5				7							3	9			11		36
4	2	1			6	10						5				7							3	9	8		11		37
4	2	1		10	6							5				7							3	9	8		11		38
4	2	1			6		8	10				5				7							3	9			11		39
4	2	1			6	10						5				7							3	9	8		11		40
4	2	1			6		8	10				5				7							3	9			11		41
4	2	1			6		8	10				5				7							3	9			11		42
29	36	29	27	1	36	34	23	3	3	13	3	39	22	5	10	32	8	1	13	4	15	6	42	7	7	2	9	3	
1	1		2		3	6	7					4	1		3	8	2				10	3		3	2		3		
4	5	1	11			10	8						9			7					6	2	3						43
	5	1	11		4	10	8						9			7					6	2	3						44
	2	1	11		4	10	8					5	9			7					6		3						45
1	3	3	3		2	3	3					2	1	1	1	1					1	3	2	3					
					1		1					1																	

1957-58

1	Aug 24 (h)	Wolves	W	1-0	J.Harris		2	
2	28 (a)	Manchester U	L	0-3			2	
3	31 (a)	Aston Villa	W	1-0	Temple		4	9
4	Sep 4 (h)	Manchester U	D	3-3	Temple 2, J.Harris		5	7
5	7 (h)	Chelsea	W	3-0	Fielding, Hickson, Temple		7	5
6	10 (a)	Arsenal	W	3-2	Fielding, J.Harris, Hickson		9	3
7	14 (h)	Sunderland	W	3-1	Hickson 2, Meagan		11	2
8	21 (a)	Luton T	W	1-0	Fielding		13	3
9	Oct 5 (a)	Leicester C	D	2-2	Fielding, Hickson		14	6
10	12 (h)	Newcastle U	W	3-2	B.Harris, Hickson, opp.og		16	5
11	16 (h)	Arsenal	D	2-2	B.Harris, Thomas		17	5
12	19 (h)	Burnley	D	1-1	Temple		18	3
13	26 (a)	Preston N E	L	1-3	J.Harris		18	3
14	Nov 2 (h)	West Brom A	D	1-1	J.Harris		19	5
15	9 (a)	Tottenham H	L	1-3	Temple		19	6
16	16 (h)	Birmingham C	L	0-2			19	9
17	20 (h)	Blackpool	D	0-0			20	8
18	23 (a)	Portsmouth	L	2-3	Temple, Thomas		20	9
19	30 (h)	Sheffield W	D	1-1	Temple		21	8
20	Dec 7 (a)	Manchester C	L	2-6	J.Harris 2		21	12
21	14 (h)	Nottingham F	D	1-1	J.Harris		22	13
22	21 (a)	Wolves	L	0-2			22	14
23	25 (h)	Bolton W	D	1-1	Kirby		23	14
24	26 (a)	Bolton W	W	5-1	B.Harris 2, J.Harris, Hickson, Keeley		25	11
25	28 (h)	Aston Villa	L	1-2	J.Harris		25	11
26	Jan 11 (a)	Chelsea	L	1-3	J.Harris		25	13
27	18 (a)	Sunderland	D	1-1	Thomas		26	14
28	Feb 1 (h)	Luton T	L	0-2			26	14
29	15 (h)	Leicester C	D	2-2	J.Harris, Thomas		27	14
30	22 (h)	Newcastle U	L	1-2	Thomas		27	14
31	Mar 1 (a)	Burnley	W	2-0	Thomas 2		29	13
32	8 (h)	Preston N E	W	4-2	Thomas 4		31	13
33	15 (a)	West Brom A	L	0-4			31	14
34	22 (h)	Portsmouth	W	4-2	Thomas 2, Williams 2		33	13
35	29 (a)	Birmingham C	L	1-2	Thomas		33	14
36	Apr 4 (h)	Leeds U	L	0-1			33	14
37	5 (h)	Tottenham H	L	3-4	Hickson 2, Thomas		33	15
38	7 (a)	Leeds U	L	0-1			33	15
39	12 (a)	Sheffield W	L	1-2	J.Harris		33	17
40	19 (h)	Manchester C	L	2-5	Ashworth 2		33	17
41	23 (a)	Blackpool	W	1-0	Ashworth		35	16
42	26 (a)	Nottingham F	W	3-0	B.Harris 2, J.Harris		37	16
						League Appearances		
						League Goals		
43	Jan 4 (a)	Sunderland	D	2-2	Hickson 2	FA Cup Rd 3		
44	8 (h)	Sunderland	W	3-1	Keeley 2, Hickson	Replay		
45	29 (h)	Blackburn R	L	1-2	J.Harris	4		
						FA Cup Appearances		
						FA Cup Goals		

Ashworth A	Birch K	Donovan D	Dunlop A	Fielding W	Harris B	Harris J	Haughey W	Hickson D	Jones T E	Keeley J	King J	Kirby G	Labone B	Leeder F	Llewellyn H	McNamara A	Meagan M	O'Neill J	Rea K	Sanders A	Tansey J	Temple D	Thomas E	Williams G	No.
	4	2	1	10		7		9	5								6				3	8		11	1
	4	2	1	10		7		9	5								6				3	8		11	2
	4	2	1	10	11	7		9	5								6				3	8			3
	4	2	1	10	11	7		9	5								6				3	8			4
	4	2	1	10	11	7		9	5								6				3	8			5
		2	1	10	11	7		9	5								6		4		3	8			6
		2	1	10	11	7		9	5								6		4		3	8			7
		2	1	10	11	7		9	5								6		4		3	8			8
		2	1	10	11	7		9	5								6		4		3	8			9
	4	2	1		11	7		9	5							7	6				3	8	10		10
	4	2	1		11	7		9	5								6				3	8	10		11
	4	2	1	10	11	7		9	5								6				3	8			12
		2	1	10	11	7		9	5	4							6				3	8			13
		2	1	10	11	7		9	5								6		4		3	8			14
		5	1	10	11	7		9									6		4	2	3	8			15
		5	1	10	11	7		9									6		4	2	3	8			16
		5	1		11	7		9			4						6			2	3	8	10		17
		5	1		11	7		9									6		4	2	3	8	10		18
			1		11	7		9	5								6		4	2	3	8	10		19
		4	1			7		9	5								6			2	3	8	10	11	20
		4	1	10	11	7			5				9				6			2	3	8			21
		4	1	10	11	7						9					6			2	3	8			22
		4	1		11	7		9	5		10						6			2	3		8		23
			1		11	7		9	5		10						6		4	2	3		8		24
			1		11	7		9	5		10						6		4	2	3		8		25
			1			7		9	5		10		3				6		4	2			8	11	26
	4	3	1			7			5		10						6			2		9	8	11	27
	4	3	1			7	9		5	10							6			2			8	11	28
		2	1		11	7		9	5								6		4		3	10	8		29
		2	1		11	7		9	5								6		4		3	10	8		30
			1	10	11	7		9	5								6	1	4	2	3	8			31
			1	10	11	7		9	5								6	1	4	2	3	8			32
			1	10	11	7		9	5								6	1	4	2	3	8			33
			1	10		7		9	5								6	1	4	2	3	8		11	34
		1	1	10		7		9					5				6		4	2	3	8		11	35
		1	1	10		7							5				6		4	2	3	9	8	11	36
			1			7		9					5				6		4	2	3	10	8	11	37
		5	1			7		9									6		4	2	3	10	8	11	38
10		5	1			7		9									6		4	2	3		8	11	39
10		5	1			7		9					4				6			2	3		8	11	40
10			1	8	11	7				4			5				6	1		2	3		9		41
10			1	8	11	7				4			5				6	1		2	3		9		42
4	10	29	36	24	30	41	1	35	31	4	5	2	4	1	1	1	38	6	27	26	39	28	26	13	
3				4	6	14		9			1		1				1				8	15	2		opp.og 1
		1	1		11	7		9	5		10						6		4	2	3	8			43
		1	1		11	7		9	5		10						6		4	2	3	8			44
	4	3	1		11	7			5		10						6			2		9	8		45
	1	1	3		3	3		2	3	3							3		2	3	2	1	3		
						1		3	2																

1958-59

#	Date		Opponent	Res	Score	Scorers		
1	Aug 23	(a)	Leicester C	L	0-2		0	
2	27	(h)	Preston N E	L	1-4	Harburn	0	
3	30	(h)	Newcastle U	L	0-2		0	22
4	Sep 1	(a)	Preston N E	L	1-3	Hickson	0	22
5	6	(h)	Arsenal	L	1-6	Temple	0	22
6	9	(a)	Burnley	L	1-3	Hickson	0	22
7	13	(a)	Manchester C	W	3-1	Collins, Fielding, J.Harris	2	22
8	17	(h)	Burnley	L	1-2	J.Harris	2	22
9	20	(h)	Leeds U	W	3-2	Jones, King, opp.og	4	22
10	27	(a)	West Brom A	W	3-2	Hickson 2, Fielding	6	22
11	Oct 4	(h)	Birmingham C	W	3-1	Hickson 2, J.Harris	8	20
12	11	(a)	Tottenham	L	4-10	J.Harris 3, Collins	8	22
13	18	(h)	Manchester U	W	3-2	Thomas 2, J.Harris	10	20
14	25	(a)	Blackpool	D	1-1	O'Hara	11	19
15	Nov 1	(h)	Blackburn R	D	2-2	J.Harris, Hickson	12	18
16	8	(a)	Aston Villa	W	4-2	Jones 2, O'Hara, Thomas	14	16
17	15	(h)	West Ham U	D	2-2	J.Harris, Thomas	15	16
18	22	(a)	Nottingham F	L	1-2	Collins	15	20
19	29	(h)	Chelsea	W	3-1	Hickson 2, Collins	17	17
20	Dec 6	(a)	Wolves	L	0-1		17	18
21	13	(h)	Portsmouth	W	2-1	Thomas 2	19	16
22	20	(h)	Leicester C	L	0-1		19	16
23	26	(h)	Bolton W	W	1-0	Hickson	21	15
24	27	(a)	Bolton W	W	3-0	J.Harris, Hickson, Williams	23	13
25	Jan 1	(a)	Newcastle U	L	0-4		23	15
26	17	(a)	Arsenal	L	1-3	Collins	23	17
27	31	(h)	Manchester C	W	3-1	J.Harris, Hickson, Jones	25	14
28	Feb 7	(a)	Leeds U	l	0-1		25	16
29	18	(h)	West Brom A	D	3-3	Hickson, Laverick, Temple	26	15
30	21	(a)	Birmingham C	L	1-2	J.Harris	26	17
31	28	(h)	Tottenham H	W	2-1	Collins, Thomas	28	14
32	Mar 7	(a)	Manchester U	L	1-2	opp.og	28	14
33	14	(h)	Blackpool	W	3-1	Hickson, Laverick, Thomas	30	14
34	21	(a)	Blackburn R	L	1-2	B.Harris	30	15
35	27	(a)	Luton T	W	1-0	opp.og	32	14
36	28	(h)	Aston Villa	W	2-1	Hickson, Parker	34	13
37	30	(h)	Luton T	W	3-1	J.Harris 2, Thomas	36	12
38	Apr 4	(a)	West Ham U	L	2-3	Hickson, Laverick	36	12
39	11	(h)	Nottingham F	L	1-3	Hickson	36	13
40	15	(a)	Portsmouth	W	3-2	Collins, Laverick, Thomas	38	14
41	18	(a)	Chelsea	L	1-3	Laverick	38	14
42	25	(h)	Wolves	L	0-1		38	16

League Appearances
League Goals

#	Date		Opponent	Res	Score	Scorers		
43	Jan 10	(h)	Sunderland	W	4-0	Hickson 2, J.Harris, Thomas	FA Cup Rd 3	
44	24	(a)	Charlton A	D	2-2	Collins, Thomas		4
45	28	(h)	Charlton A	W	4-1	Collins 2, Hickson 2	Replay	
46	Feb 14	(h)	Aston Villa	L	1-4	Hickson		5

FA Cup Appearances
FA Cup Goals

Ashworth A	Bramwell J	Collins R	Dunlop A	Fielding W	Griffiths B	Harburn P	Harris B	Harris J	Hickson D	Jones T E	King J	Labone B	Laverick R	Meagan M	O'Hara E	O'Neill J	Parker A	Rea K	Sanders A	Tansey J	Temple D	Thomas E	Williams G	No.
10			1			9		7		5				6	11				4	2	3	8		1
10			1			9		7		5				6	11				4	2	3	8		2
				10		9		7		5	4			6		1			2		3	8	11	3
				10	3	9		7	8	5	4			6	11	1			2					4
				10	3		4	7	9	5				6	11	1			2			8		5
	3			10			6	7	9	5	4				11	1			2			8		6
	3	8		10			6	7	9	5	4				11	1			2					7
	3	8		10			6	7	9	5	4				11	1			2					8
10	3					7	6	8	9	5	4			11		1			2					9
	3					7	6	8	9	5	4				11	1			2		10			10
	3	10				7	6	8	9	5	4				11	1			2					11
	3	10	1			7	6	8	9	5	4				11				2					12
10	3		1				6	7	9	5	4				11				2			8		13
	3	10	1				6	7	9	5	4				11				2			8		14
	3	10	1				6	7	9	5	4				11				2			8		15
	3	10	1				6	7	9	5	4				11		2					8		16
	3	10	1				6	7	9	5	4				11		2					8		17
	3	10	1				6	7	9	5	4				11		2					8		18
	3	10	1				6	7	9	5	4				11		2					8		19
	3	10	1				6	7	9	5	4				11		2					8		20
	3	10	1				6	7	9	5							2		4			8	11	21
	3	10	1				6	7	9	5							2		4			8	11	22
	3	10	1				6	7	9	5							2		4			8	11	23
	3	10	1				6	7	9	5							2		4			8	11	24
	3	10	1				6	7	9	5							2		4			8	11	25
	3	10	1				6	7	9	5							2		4			8	11	26
	3	10	1					7	9	5				6	11		2		4			8		27
	3	10	1					7	9	5				6	11		2		4			8		28
	3	10	1					7	9	5			11	6			2		4		8			29
	3	10	1					7	9	5			11	6			2		4		8			30
	3	10	1				4	7	9	5			11	6			2					8		31
	3	10	1				4	7	9	5			11	6			2					8		32
	3	10	1				4	7	9	5			11	6			2					8		33
	3	10	1				11	7	9	5				6			2	4				8		34
	3	10	1				11	7	9	5				6			2	4				8		35
11	3	10	1				4	7	9	5				6			2					8		36
	3	10	1				4	7	9	5			11	6			2					8		37
	3	10	1				4	7	9	5			11	6			2					8		38
10	3		1				4	7	9	5			11	6			2					8		39
	3	10	1				4	7	9	5			11	6			2					8		40
	3	10	1				4	7	9	5			11	6			2					8		41
	3	10	1				4	7	9	5			11	6			2					8		42
6	37	32	33	10	2	4	35	42	39	38	17	4	11	21	21	9	26	4	25	3	4	32	7	
	7			2		1	1	14	17	4	1		5		2		1				2	10	1	opp.og 3
	3	10	1				6	7	9	5							2		4			8	11	43
	3	10	1				6	7	9	5							2		4			8	11	44
	3	10	1				6	7	9	5			11				2		4			8		45
	3	10	1				6	7	9	5			11				2		4			8		46
	4	4	4				4	4	4	4			2				4		4			4	2	
	3							1	5													2		

1959-60

#	Date		Opponent		Score	Scorers		
1	Aug 22	(h)	Luton T	D	2-2	J.Harris, Hickson	1	
2	25	(a)	Burnley	L	2-5	Thomas, opp.og	1	
3	29	(a)	Bolton W	L	1-2	Hickson	1	20
4	Sep 2	(h)	Burnley	L	1-2	Wignall	1	22
5	5	(h)	Fulham	D	0-0		2	22
6	12	(a)	Nottingham F	D	1-1	opp.og	3	21
7	16	(h)	Blackburn R	W	2-0	Hickson 2	5	21
8	19	(h)	Sheffield W	W	2-1	Shackleton 2	7	17
9	21	(a)	Blackburn R	L	1-3	Collins	7	19
10	26	(a)	Wolves	L	0-2		7	21
11	Oct 3	(h)	Arsenal	W	3-1	Collins, Laverick, Thomas	9	15
12	10	(a)	Leeds U	D	3-3	Hickson 2, Collins	10	16
13	17	(h)	West Ham U	L	0-1		10	18
14	24	(a)	Chelsea	L	0-1		10	20
15	31	(h)	Leicester C	W	6-1	Thomas 2, Collins, B.Harris, Parker, Shackleton	12	15
16	Nov 7	(a)	Newcastle U	L	2-8	Thomas 2	12	19
17	14	(h)	Birmingham C	W	4-0	Shackleton 3, J.Harris	14	16
18	21	(a)	Tottenham H	L	0-3		14	17
19	28	(h)	Manchester U	W	2-1	Collins, Thomas	16	17
20	Dec 5	(a)	Preston N E	D	0-0		17	17
21	12	(h)	West Brom A	D	2-2	Shackleton, Thomas	18	16
22	19	(a)	Luton T	L	1-2	J.Harris	18	17
23	26	(h)	Manchester C	W	2-1	Collins, Shackleton	20	16
24	28	(a)	Manchester C	L	0-4		20	17
25	Jan 2	(h)	Bolton W	L	0-1		20	19
26	16	(a)	Fulham	L	0-2		20	20
27	23	(h)	Nottingham F	W	6-1	Thomas 3, Collins, Parker, Shackleton	22	20
28	Feb 6	(a)	Sheffield W	D	2-2	Shackleton, Thomas	23	20
29	13	(a)	Wolves	L	0-2		23	20
30	20	(a)	Arsenal	L	1-2	Vernon	23	20
31	27	(h)	Preston N E	W	4-0	Vernon 2, J.Harris, Lill	25	19
32	Mar 5	(a)	West Ham U	D	2-2	Vernon 2	26	18
33	12	(h)	Chelsea	W	6-1	Ring 2, Collins, J.Harris, Lill, Vernon	28	16
34	19	(a)	West Brom A	L	2-6	Collins, J.Harris	28	17
35	25	(h)	Newcastle U	L	1-2	Collins	28	19
36	Apr 2	(a)	Birmingham C	D	2-2	J.Harris, Vernon	29	18
37	9	(h)	Tottenham H	W	2-1	Collins, J.Harris	31	17
38	15	(h)	Blackpool	W	4-0	Vernon 2, Collins, J.Harris	33	17
39	16	(a)	Leicester C	D	3-3	Collins 2, Lill	34	17
40	18	(a)	Blackpool	D	0-0		35	16
41	23	(h)	Leeds U	W	1-0	Tyrer	37	14
42	30	(a)	Manchester U	L	0-5		37	16

League Appearances
League Goals

| 43 | Jan 9 | (a) | Bradford C | L | 0-3 | | FA Cup Rd 3 |

FA Cup Appearances
FA Cup Goals

Ashworth A	Bramwell J	Collins R	Dunlop A	Gabriel J	Godfrey B	Harris B	Harris J	Hickson D	Jones T E	King J	Labone B	Laverick R	Lill M	Meagan M	O'Hara E	O'Neill J	Parker A	Ring T	Sanders A	Shackleton A	Tansey J	Thomas E	Tyrer A	Vernon R	Wignall F	
		10	1			4	7	9	5					6	11		2			3	8					1
	3	10	1			4	7	9	5					6	11		2				8					2
		10	1			4	7	9	5					6	11		2			3	8					3
		10	1			6	7	9	5	4					11		2		3						8	4
		10	1			6	7	9	3	4	5				11		2								8	5
		10	1			6	7		3	4	5				11		2			9					8	6
		10	1			6	7	9	3	4	5						2	11							8	7
		10	1			6	7	9	3	4	5						2	11							8	8
10		7	1			6		9	3	4	5						2	11							8	9
		10	1			6		9	3	4	5	11					2			7		8				10
		10	1			6	7		3	4	5	11					2			9		8				11
	3	10	1			6	7	9	5	4							2	11				8				12
	3	10	1			6	7	9	5	4							2	11				8				13
	3	10	1			6	7	9	5	4							2	11				8				14
	3	10	1			6	7		5	4		11					2			9		8				15
	3	10	1			6	7		5	4		11					2			9		8				16
		10	1			6	7		3	4	5	11					2			9		8				17
		10	1			6	7		3	4	5	11					2			9		8				18
		10	1			6	7		3	4	5	11					2			9		8				19
		10	1			6	7		3	4	5	11					2			9		8				20
		10	1			6	7		3	4	5	11					2			9		8				21
		10	1			6	7		3	4	5	11					2			9		8				22
	3	10	1			6	7		5	4		11					2			9		8				23
	3	10	1			6	7		5	4		11					2			9		8				24
8		10	1			6	7		3	4	5	11					2			9						25
		10							3	4	5	11		6		1	2			9		8	7			26
		10					7		3	4	5			6		1	2	11		9		8				27
		10					7		3	4	5			6		1	2	11		9		8				28
	3	8					7			4	5			6		1	2	11		9				10		29
	3	8		4			7				5			6		1	2	11		9				10		30
	3	8	1	4							5		7	6			2	11		9				10		31
	3	8	1	4							5		7	6			2	11		9				10		32
	3	8	1	4							5		7	6			2	11		9				10		33
	3	8	1	4							5		7	6			2	11		9				10		34
	3	8	1	4							5		7	6			2	11		9				10		35
		8	1	4					3		5		7	6			2	11		9				10		36
		8	1	4					3		5		7	6			2	11		9				10		37
		8	1	4					3		5		7	6			2	11		9				10		38
		10	1	4					3		5		7	6			2	11		9		8				39
		8	1	4					3		5		7	6			2	11		9				10		40
		10	1	4					3		5		7	6			2	11		9			8			41
		8	1	4	6				3		5						2	11		9			7	10		42
2	15	42	37	8	1	32	36	12	35	26	31	11	12	19	8	5	38	16	5	26	2	21	4	12	6	
	14					1	9	6				1	3				2	2		10		12	1	9	1	opp.og 2
		10	1			6	7		3	4	5	11					2			9		8				43
	1	1				1	1		1	1	1	1					1			1				1		

1960-61

#	Date		Opponent	Res	Score	Scorers		
1	Aug 20	(a)	Tottenham H	L	0-2		0	
2	24	(h)	Manchester U	W	4-0	Collins 2, Lill 2	2	
3	27	(h)	Leicester C	W	3-1	Ring 2, Collins	4	4
4	31	(a)	Manchester U	L	0-4		4	11
5	Sep 3	(a)	Aston Villa	L	2-3	Temple, Vernon	4	13
6	5	(a)	Blackpool	W	4-1	Collins, J.Harris, Temple, Vernon	6	8
7	10	(h)	Wolves	W	3-1	Vernon 2, J.Harris	8	7
8	14	(h)	Blackpool	W	1-0	Lill	10	5
9	17	(a)	Bolton W	W	4-3	Lill 2, Collins, Vernon	12	4
10	24	(h)	West Ham U	W	4-1	Vernon 2, Lill, Ring	14	3
11	Oct 1	(a)	Chelsea	D	3-3	Collins, Lill, Ring	15	3
12	8	(h)	Preston N E	D	0-0		16	4
13	15	(a)	Fulham	W	3-2	J.Harris 2, Vernon	18	4
14	24	(h)	Manchester C	W	4-2	Vernon 2, Collins, Temple	20	4
15	29	(a)	Nottingham F	W	2-1	Bingham, B.Harris	22	3
16	Nov 5	(h)	West Brom A	D	1-1	opp.og	23	3
17	12	(a)	Cardiff C	D	1-1	Bingham	24	3
18	19	(h)	Newcastle U	W	5-0	Collins 3, Vernon, Wignall	26	3
19	26	(a)	Arsenal	L	2-3	Collins, Vernon	26	3
20	Dec 3	(h)	Sheffield W	W	4-2	Vernon 2, J.Harris, opp.og	28	2
21	10	(a)	Birmingham C	W	4-2	Wignall 2, Bingham, Tyrer	30	2
22	17	(h)	Tottenham H	L	1-3	Wignall	30	3
23	26	(a)	Burnley	W	3-1	Bingham, Collins, B.Harris	32	3
24	27	(h)	Burnley	L	0-3		32	5
25	31	(a)	Leicester C	L	1-4	B.Harris	32	5
26	Jan 21	(a)	Wolves	L	1-4	Bingham	32	5
27	Feb 4	(h)	Bolton W	L	1-2	Collins	32	5
28	11	(a)	West Ham U	l	0-4		32	5
29	18	(h)	Chelsea	D	1-1	Vernon	33	5
30	25	(a)	Preston N E	L	0-1		33	6
31	Mar 4	(h)	Fulham	W	1-0	Gabriel	35	5
32	11	(a)	Manchester C	L	1-2	Vernon	35	5
33	18	(h)	Nottingham F	W	1-0	Bingham	37	5
34	22	(h)	Aston Villa	L	1-2	Wignall	37	5
35	25	(a)	West Brom A	L	0-3		37	6
36	31	(a)	Blackburn R	W	3-1	Young 2, Vernon	39	5
37	Apr 1	(h)	Birmingham C	W	1-0	Temple	41	5
38	3	(h)	Blackburn R	D	2-2	Bingham, Young	42	5
39	8	(a)	Newcastle U	W	4-0	Bingham 2, Vernon, Wignall	44	5
40	15	(h)	Cardiff C	W	5-1	Collins 3, Young 2	46	4
41	22	(a)	Sheffield W	W	2-1	Wignall 2	48	4
42	29	(h)	Arsenal	W	4-1	Vernon 3, Young	50	5

League Appearances
League Goals

#	Date		Opponent	Res	Score	Scorers		
43	Jan 7	(h)	Sheffield U	L	0-1		FA Cup Rd 3	
44	Oct 12	(h)	Accrington S	W	3-1	Wignall 2, J.Harris	League Cup Rd 1	
45	31	(h)	Walsall	W	3-1	Collins, Vernon, Webber		2
46	Nov 23	(h)	Bury	W	3-1	Wignall 2, J.Harris		3
47	Dec 21	(a)	Tranmere R	W	4-0	Wignall 3, Bingham		4
48	Feb 15	(a)	Shrewsbury	L	1-2	Young		5

Cup Appearances
Cup Goals

Bentley J	Bingham W	Collins R	Dunlop A	Fell J	Gabriel J	Green C	Harris B	Harris J	Jones T E	Kavanagh P	Labone B	Lill M	Meagan M	Parker A	Parnell R	Ring T	Sharples G	Temple D	Thomson G	Tyrer A	Vernon R	Webber K	Wignall F	Young A		
		8	1		4			9	3		5	7	6	2		11					10					1
		8	1		4			9	3		5	7	6	2		11					10					2
		8	1		4			9	3		5		6	2		11		7			10					3
		8	1		4			9	3		5		6	2		11		7			10					4
		8	1		4		6	9	3		5			2		11		7			10					5
		8	1		4	3	6	9			5			2		11		7			10					6
		8	1		4	3	6	9			5			2		11		7			10					7
		8	1		4		6	9	3		5	7		2		11					10					8
		8	1		4		6	9	3		5	7		2		11					10					9
		8	1		4		6	9	3		5	7		2		11					10					10
		8	1		4		6	9	3		5	7		2		11					10					11
		8	1		4		6	9	3		5	7		2						11	10					12
	7	8	1		4	3	6	9			5	11		2							10					13
	7	8	1		4	3	6	9			5			2				11			10					14
	7	8	1		4	3	6	9			5			2				11			10					15
	7	8	1			3	6	9			5			2			4	11			10					16
	7	8	1		4	3	6	9			5			2				11			10					17
	7	8	1		4		6		3		5			2				11			10		9			18
	7	8	1		4		6	11			5			2					3		10		9			19
	7	8	1		4		6	11			5			2					3		10		9			20
	7	10	1		4		6				5			2				11	3	8			9			21
	7	10	1		4		6				5			2				11	3				8	9		22
	7	8	1		4		6				5			2				11	3		10		9			23
	7	8	1		4		6				5			2				11	3		10		9			24
	7	8	1		4		6				5			2				11	3		10		9			25
	7	8	1		4		11		3		5				2		6				10		9			26
7		8	1		4		6		3		5			2				11			10			9		27
	7		1		4		11				5			2			6		3		10		9	8		28
		8	1		4		6			11	5			2					3		10	9		7		29
			1		4		6			11	5			2				7	3		10		8	9		30
	7	8	1		4		6			11	5			2					3		10			9		31
	7	8	1		4		6			11	5			2					3		10			9		32
	7	8	1		4		6			11	5			2					3		10			9		33
	7	10	1	11	4						5			2			6		3	8			9			34
	7	8	1				4			11	5			2			6		3		10		9			35
	7	8	1	11	4						5		6	2					3		10			9		36
	7	8	1		4						5		6	2				11	3		10			9		37
	7	8	1	11	4						5		6	2					3		10			9		38
	7	8	1		4						5		6	2				11	3		10		9			39
	7	8	1	11	4						5		6	2					3		10			9		40
	7	8	1	11	4						5		6	2					3		10		9			41
		8	1	11	4						5		6	2				7	3		10			9		42
1	26	40	42	6	40	7	30	19	13	6	42	8	11	41	1	11	5	20	22	3	39	1	15	13		
	9	16			1		3	5				7				4		4		1	21		8	6	opp,og 2	
	11	8	1		4		6		3		5			2						7	10		9			43
		8	1		4		6	7	3		5	11		2							10		9			44
	7	8	1		4	3	6		5					2				11			10	9				45
	7	10	1		4		6	8	3		5			2				11					9			46
	7	8	1		4		6				5			2				11	3		10		9			47
		8	1		4		11				5			2			6		3		10	9		7		48
	4	6	6		6	1	6	2	4		5	1		6			1	3	2	1	5	2	4	1		
	1	1						2													1	1	7	1		

1961-62

1	Aug 19	(h)	Aston Villa	W	2-0	Bingham, Young	2	
2	23	(a)	West Brom A	L	0-2		2	
3	26	(a)	Fulham	L	1-2	Temple	2	15
4	30	(h)	West Brom A	W	3-1	Bingham, Lill, Vernon	4	8
5	Sep 2	(h)	Sheffield W	L	0-4		4	16
6	6	(h)	Manchester C	L	0-2		4	19
7	9	(a)	Leicester C	L	0-2		4	19
8	16	(h)	Ipswich T	W	5-2	Temple 3, Bingham, Young	6	17
9	20	(a)	Manchester C	W	3-1	Temple, Wignall, Young	8	12
10	23	(a)	Burnley	L	1-2	Thomson	8	14
11	30	(h)	Arsenal	W	4-1	Vernon 2, Bingham, Gabriel	10	11
12	Oct 7	(h)	Nottingham F	W	6-0	Fell 2, Vernon 2, Gabriel, Young	12	10
13	14	(a)	Wolves	W	3-0	Gabriel, Young, opp.og	14	5
14	21	(h)	Sheffield U	W	1-0	Vernon	16	3
15	28	(a)	Chelsea	D	1-1	Vernon	17	3
16	Nov 4	(h)	Tottenham H	W	3-0	Wignall 2, Bingham	19	2
17	11	(a)	Blackpool	D	1-1	Fell	20	2
18	18	(h)	Blackburn R	W	1-0	Vernon	22	2
19	25	(a)	West Ham U	L	1-3	Vernon	22	3
20	Dec 2	(h)	Manchester U	W	5-1	Vernon 2, Collins, Fell, Young	24	3
21	9	(a)	Cardiff C	D	0-0		25	2
22	16	(a)	Aston Villa	D	1-1	Collins	26	5
23	23	(h)	Fulham	W	3-0	Collins 2, Vernon	28	3
24	26	(h)	Bolton W	W	1-0	Bingham	30	3
25	Jan 13	(a)	Sheffield W	L	1-3	Vernon	30	4
26	20	(h)	Leicester C	W	3-2	Collins, Green, Vernon	32	3
27	Feb 3	(a)	Ipswich T	L	2-4	Bingham, B.Harris	32	5
28	10	(h)	Burnley	D	2-2	Vernon 2	33	4
29	24	(a)	Nottingham F	L	1-2	Vernon	33	6
30	Mar 3	(h)	Wolves	W	4-0	Vernon 2, Wignall 2	35	4
31	14	(a)	Sheffield U	D	1-1	Bingham	36	4
32	17	(h)	Chelsea	W	4-0	Young 2, Temple, Vernon	38	3
33	24	(a)	Tottenham H	L	1-3	Temple	38	4
34	30	(h)	Blackpool	D	2-2	Young 2	39	4
35	Apr 4	(a)	Bolton W	D	1-1	Vernon	40	4
36	7	(a)	Blackburn R	D	1-1	Stevens	41	5
37	14	(h)	West Ham U	W	3-0	Stevens, Temple, Vernon	43	3
38	20	(h)	Birmingham C	W	4-1	Gabriel, Temple, Vernon, Young	45	4
39	21	(a)	Manchester U	D	1-1	Stevens	46	4
40	24	(a)	Birmingham C	D	0-0		47	4
41	28	(h)	Cardiff C	W	8-3	Vernon 3, Bingham, Gabriel, Stevens, Temple, Young	49	4
42	May 1	(a)	Arsenal	W	3-2	Young 2, Gabriel	51	4
						League Appearances		
						League Goals		
43	Jan 6	(h)	King's Lynn	W	4-0	Bingham, Collins, Fell, Vernon	FA Cup Rd 3	
44	27	(h)	Manchester C	W	2-0	Lill, Vernon		4
45	Feb 17	(a)	Burnley	L	1-3	Collins		5
						FA Cup Appearances		
						FA Cup Goals		

Bingham W	Collins R	Dunlop A	Fell J	Gabriel J	Gannon M	Green C	Harris B	Jones T E	Labone B	Lill M	Meagan M	Parker A	Parnell R	Stevens D	Temple D	Thomson G	Tyrer A	Vernon R	Webber K	West G	Wignall F	Young A	No.
7	8	1	11	4					5		6	2				3		10				9	1
7	8	1	11	4					5		6	2				3		10				9	2
9		1	11	4					5	7	6	2			8	3		10					3
7		1		4					5	11	6	2				3	8	10	9				4
7		1		4					5	11	6	2				3	8	10				9	5
7		1		4				5		11	6	2				3		10	9			8	6
7		1		4					5	11	6	2			10	3					9	8	7
7		1	11	4			6		5			2			10	3					9	8	8
		1	11	4			6		5	7		2			10	3					9	8	9
7		1	11	4			6		5			2			10	3					9	8	10
7	8	1	11	4			6		5			2				3		10				9	11
7	8	1	11	4			6		5			2				3		10				9	12
7	8	1	11	4			6		5			2				3		10				9	13
	8	1	11	4			6		5	7		2				3		10				9	14
	8	1	11	4			6		5			2				3		10			7	9	15
7		1	11	4			6		5			2				3		10			9	8	16
7		1	11	4	2		6		5							3		10			9	8	17
7		1	11	4	2		6		5							3		10			9	8	18
7	8	1	11	4			6		5			2				3		10				9	19
7	8	1	11	4			6		5			2				3		10				9	20
7	8	1	11	4			6		5			2				3		10				9	21
7	8	1	11	4			6		5			2				3		10				9	22
7	8	1	11	4			6		5			2				3		10				9	23
7	8	1	11	4			6		5			2				3		10				9	24
7	11	1		4		3	6		5			2						10			8	9	25
7	8	1		4		3	6		5			2						10				9	26
7	8	1		4		3	6		5	11		2						10				9	27
7	8	1		4		3	6		5	11		2						10				9	28
	8	1		4		3	6		5	7		2						10			9	11	29
7	8			4		3	6		5			2						10		1	9	11	30
7				4		3			5		6	2		8	9			10		1		11	31
7				4		3			5		6	2		8	11			10		1		9	32
7				4			6		5		3	2		8	11			10		1		9	33
7				4			6		5			2		8	11	3		10		1		9	34
7				4			6		5			2		8	11	3		10		1		9	35
7				4		3	6		5			2		8	11				9	1		10	36
7		1		4			6		5			2		8	11	3		10				9	37
7				4			6		5			2		8	11	3		10		1		9	38
				4			6		5	7		2		8	11	3		10		1		9	39
7				4			6		5			2		8	11	3		10		1		9	40
7				4			6		5			2		8	11	3		10		1		9	41
7				4			6		5			2		8	11	3		10		1		9	42
37	19	30	21	42	3	8	33	1	41	11	18	31	1	12	17	32	2	37	3	12	11	40	
9	5		4	6		1	1		1					4	10	1		26			5	14	opp.og 1
7	8	1	11	4			6		5			2				3		10				9	43
7	8	1		4		3	6		5	11		2						10				9	44
7	8	1		4		3	6		5	11		2						10				9	45
3	3	3	1	3		2	3		3	2		3				1		3				3	
1	2			1					1									2					

1962-63

1	Aug	18	(a)	Burnley	W	3-1	Bingham, Vernon, Young	2	
2		22	(h)	Manchester U	W	3-1	Young 2, Parker	4	
3		25	(h)	Sheffield W	W	4-1	Vernon 2, Stevens, Young	6	3
4		29	(a)	Manchester U	W	1-0	Vernon	8	1
5	Sep	1	(a)	Fulham	L	0-1		8	2
6		5	(h)	Leyton O	W	3-0	Bingham, Gabriel, Vernon	10	1
7		8	(h)	Leicester C	W	3-2	Stevens, Vernon, Young	12	1
8		12	(a)	Leyton O	L	0-3		12	2
9		15	(a)	Bolton W	W	2-0	Bingham, Gabriel	14	2
10		22	(h)	Liverpool	D	2-2	Morrissey, Vernon	15	2
11		29	(h)	West Brom A	W	4-2	Morrissey 3, Young	17	2
12	Oct	6	(a)	Wolves	W	2-0	Bingham, Young	19	1
13		13	(h)	Aston Villa	D	1-1	Vernon	20	1
14		27	(h)	Ipswich T	W	3-1	Morrissey 2, Vernon	22	2
15	Nov	3	(a)	Manchester C	D	1-1	Wignall	23	2
16		10	(h)	Blackpool	W	5-0	Young 2, Bingham, Gabriel, Stevens	25	2
17		13	(a)	Nottingham F	W	4-3	Vernon 2, Gabriel, Veall	27	1
18		17	(a)	Blackburn R	L	2-3	Harris, Stevens	27	2
19		24	(h)	Sheffield U	W	3-0	Vernon 2, Stevens	29	1
20	Dec	1	(a)	Tottenham H	D	0-0		30	1
21		8	(h)	West Ham U	D	1-1	Stevens	31	1
22		15	(h)	Burnley	W	3-1	Stevens, Vernon, Young	33	1
23		22	(a)	Sheffield W	D	2-2	Young, opp.og	34	1
24	Feb	12	(a)	Leicester C	L	1-3	Vernon	34	2
25		23	(h)	Wolves	D	0-0		35	3
26	Mar	9	(h)	Nottingham F	W	2-0	Parker, Young	37	3
27		19	(a)	Ipswich T	W	3-0	Young 2, opp.og	39	3
28		23	(h)	Manchester C	W	2-1	Morrissey, Young	41	3
29		26	(a)	Arsenal	L	3-4	Kay, Vernon, Young	41	3
30		30	(a)	Sheffield U	L	1-2	Scott	41	3
31	Apr	1	(a)	Aston Villa	W	2-0	Gabriel, Young	43	3
32		6	(h)	Blackburn R	D	0-0		44	3
33		8	(a)	Liverpool	D	0-0		45	3
34		13	(a)	Blackpool	W	2-1	Scott, Young	47	3
35		15	(h)	Birmingham C	D	2-2	Scott, Young	48	3
36		16	(a)	Birmingham C	W	1-0	Vernon	50	3
37		20	(h)	Tottenham H	W	1-0	Young	52	1
38		24	(h)	Arsenal	D	1-1	Vernon	53	1
39		27	(a)	West Ham U	W	2-1	Temple, Vernon	55	1
40	May	4	(h)	Bolton W	W	1-0	Vernon	57	1
41		7	(a)	West Brom A	W	4-0	Young 2, Vernon, opp.og	59	1
42		11	(h)	Fulham	W	4-1	Vernon 3, Scott	61	1

		League Appearances
		League Goals

43	Jan	15	(a)	Barnsley	W	3-0	Harris, Stevens, Vernon	FA Cup Rd 3
44		29	(a)	Swindon T	W	5-1	Vernon 2, Bingham, Gabriel, Morrissey	4
45	Mar	16	(a)	West Ham U	l	0-1		5

		FA Cup Appearances
		FA Cup Goals

Everton played in the Inter-City Fairs Cup (see Everton in Europe section).

Bingham W	Dunlop A	Gabriel J	Harris B	Heslop G	Kay A	Labone B	Meagan M	Morrissey J	Parker A	Scott A	Sharples G	Stevens D	Temple D	Thomson G	Veall R	Vernon R	West G	Wignall F	Young A	
7		4	6			5	2					8		3	11	10	1		9	1
7		4	6			5			2			8		3	11	10	1		9	2
7			6			5		11	2		4	8		3		10	1		9	3
7		4	6			5		11	2			8		3		10	1		9	4
7		4	6			5		11	2			8		3		10	1		9	5
7		4	6			5	2	11				8		3		10	1		9	6
7		4	6			5	2	11				8		3		10	1		9	7
7			6			5	2	11			4	8		3		10	1		9	8
7		4	6			5	2	11				8		3		10	1		9	9
7		4	6			5	2	11				8		3		10	1		9	10
7		4	6			5	2	11				8		3		10	1		9	11
7		4	6			5	2	11				8		3		10	1		9	12
7		4	6			5	2	11				8		3		10	1		9	13
7		4	6			5	3	11	2			8				10	1		9	14
		4	6			5	3	7	2			8			11		1	10	9	15
7		4	6			5	3		2			8			11	10	1		9	16
7		4	6			5	3		2			8			11	10	1		9	17
7		4	6			5	3		2			8			11	10	1		9	18
7		4	6			5	3		2			8			11	10	1		9	19
7		4	6			5	3		2			8			11	10	1		9	20
7		4	6			5	3		2			8			11	10	1		9	21
7		4	6			5	3		2			8			11	10	1		9	22
7		4	6			5	3		2			8			11	10	1		9	23
		4			6	5	3	11	2	7		8				10	1		9	24
		4			6	5	3	11	2			8	7			10	1		9	25
		4			6	5	3	11	2	7		8				10	1		9	26
		4			6	5		11	2	7		8		3		10	1		9	27
		4			6	5		11	2	7		8		3		10	1		9	28
7		4			6	5		11	2			8		3		10	1		9	29
		4			6	5		11	2	7		8		3		10	1		9	30
		4			6	5		11	2	7		8		3		10	1		9	31
		4			6	5		11	2	7		8		3		10	1		9	32
		4			6	5	3	11	2	7		8				10	1		9	33
		4			6	5	3	11	2	7		8				10	1		9	34
		5	4		6		3	11	2	7		8				10	1		9	35
		4		5	6		3	11	2	7		8				10	1		9	36
		4			6	5	3	11	2	7		8				10	1		9	37
		4			6	5	3	11	2	7		8				10	1		9	38
	1	4			6	5	3		2	7		8	11			10			9	39
	1	4			6	5	3		2	7		8	11			10			9	40
	1	4			6	5	3		2	7		8	11			10			9	41
	1	4			6	5	3		2	7		8	11			10			9	42
23	4	40	24	1	19	40	32	28	33	17	2	42	5	19	11	41	38	1	42	
5		5	1		1			7	2	4		7	1		1	24		1	22	opp.og 3
7		4	6			5	3	11	2			8				10	1		9	43
7		4			6	5	3	11	2			8				10	1		9	44
7		4			6	5	3	11	2			8				10	1		9	45
3		3	1		2	3	3	3	3			3				3	3		3	
1		1	1					1								1			3	

1963-64

1 Aug	24	(h)	Fulham	W	3-0	Scott, Temple, opp.og	2	
2	31	(a)	Manchester U	L	1-5	Vernon	2	
3 Sep	4	(a)	Bolton W	W	3-1	Young 2, Temple	4	9
4	7	(h)	Burnley	L	3-4	Gabriel, Hill, Scott	4	16
5	11	(h)	Bolton W	W	2-0	Stevens, Young	6	15
6	14	(a)	Ipswich T	D	0-0		7	13
7	21	(h)	Sheffield W	W	3-0	Stevens, Vernon, Young	9	11
8	28	(a)	Liverpool	L	1-2	Vernon	9	12
9 Oct	2	(h)	Arsenal	W	2-1	Temple, Young	11	11
10	5	(a)	Birmingham C	W	2-0	Kay, Temple	13	16
11	7	(a)	Aston Villa	W	1-0	Vernon	15	6
12	15	(h)	Sheffield U	W	4-1	Young 2, Stevens, Temple	17	6
13	19	(a)	West Ham U	L	2-4	Kay, Rees	17	9
14	26	(h)	Tottenham H	W	1-0	Temple	19	5
15 Nov	2	(a)	Blackpool	D	1-1	Vernon	20	5
16	9	(h)	Blackburn R	L	2-4	Temple, Young	20	8
17	16	(a)	Nottingham F	D	2-2	Harris, Vernon	21	7
18	23	(h)	Stoke C	W	2-0	Kay, Temple	23	6
19	30	(a)	Wolves	D	0-0		24	5
20 Dec	7	(h)	Chelsea	D	1-1	Vernon	25	7
21	10	(a)	Arsenal	L	0-6		25	9
22	14	(a)	Fulham	D	2-2	Harris, Young	26	8
23	21	(h)	Manchester U	W	4-0	Harris, Stevens, Temple, Vernon	28	6
24	26	(a)	Leicester C	L	0-2		28	8
25	28	(h)	Leicester C	L	0-3		28	10
26 Jan	11	(a)	Burnley	W	3-2	Gabriel, Morrissey, Scott	30	7
27	18	(h)	Ipswich T	D	1-1	Scott	31	8
28 Feb	1	(a)	Sheffield W	W	3-0	Gabriel, Scott, Vernon	33	5
29	8	(h)	Liverpool	W	3-1	Vernon 2, Gabriel	35	6
30	18	(h)	Birmingham C	W	3-0	Rees, Stevens, Vernon	37	4
31	22	(a)	Sheffield U	D	0-0		38	5
32	28	(h)	Aston Villa	W	4-2	Scott, Stevens, Vernon, Young	40	3
33 Mar	7	(a)	Tottenham H	W	4-2	Vernon 2, Temple, Young	42	4
34	14	(h)	Nottingham F	W	6-1	Pickering 3, Stevens 2, Vernon	44	2
35	21	(a)	Blackburn R	W	2-1	Scott, Temple	46	1
36	27	(h)	West Brom A	D	1-1	opp.og	47	1
37	28	(h)	Blackpool	W	3-1	Pickering 2, Young	49	1
38	31	(a)	West Brom A	L	2-4	Vernon 2	49	2
39 Apr	4	(a)	Stoke C	L	2-3	Gabriel, Pickering	49	2
40	11	(h)	Wolves	D	3-3	Pickering, Stevens, Temple	50	2
41	18	(a)	Chelsea	L	0-1		50	4
42	25	(h)	West Ham U	W	2-0	Pickering 2	52	3
							League Appearances	
							League Goals	
43 Jan	4	(a)	Hull C	D	1-1	Scott	FA Cup Rd 3	
44	7	(h)	Hull C	W	2-1	Harris, Scott	Replay	
45	25	(a)	Leeds U	D	1-1	Vernon	4	
46	28	(h)	Leeds U	W	2-0	Gabriel, Vernon	Replay	
47 Feb	15	(a)	Sunderland	l	1-3	Harris	5	
							FA Cup Appearances	
							FA Cup Goals	

Everton played in the European Cup (see Everton in Europe section).

Brown A	Gabriel J	Harris B	Harvey C	Heslop G	Hill J	Kay A	Labone B	Meagan M	Morrissey J	Parker A	Parnell R	Pickering F	Rankin A	Rees B	Scott A	Sharples G	Stevens D	Temple D	Vernon R	West G	Young A	No.
	4					6	5	3	11	2					7		8	10		1	9	1
	4					6	5	3		2					7		8	11	10	1	9	2
	4			10		6	5	3		2					7		8	11		1	9	3
3	4			10		6	5			2					7		8	11		1	9	4
3	6			10		4	5			2					7		8	11		1	9	5
	6						5			2	3				7	4	8	11	10	1	9	6
3	4					6	5			2					7		8	11	10	1	9	7
3	6					4	5		11	2					7		8	9	10	1		8
3	4					6	5			2					7		8	11	10	1	9	9
	4	3				6	5			2					7		8	11	10	1	9	10
	4	3				6	5			2					7		8	11	10	1	9	11
	4	3				6	5			2					7		8	11	10	1	9	12
	4	3				6	5			2				9	7		8	11	10	1		13
	4					6	5	3		2					7		8	11	10	1	9	14
	4					6	5	3		2					7		8	11	10	1	9	15
	4					6	5	3		2					7		8	11	10	1	9	16
	4					6	5	3		2			1		7		8	11	10		9	17
2	4	5				6		3					1		7		8	11	10		9	18
2	4	5				6		3					1		7		8	11	10		9	19
2	4	5						3					1		7	6	8	11	10		9	20
2	4	5						3					1		7	6	8	11	10		9	21
2	6	5	8					3					1		7		4	11	10		9	22
2	4	6	5					3					1		7		8	11	10		9	23
2	4	3	5			6							1		7		8	11	10		9	24
2	4	6	8					3					1		7		0	11	10		0	25
2	4	6		10			5	3	11				1		7		8	9				26
2	4	3		10		6	5		11				1		7		8	9				27
2	9	4				6	5	3							7		8	11	10	1		28
2	9	4				6	5	3							7		8	11	10	1		29
2	4					6	5	3						9	7		8	11	10	1		30
2	4			10		6	5	3	11					9	7		8			1		31
2	4					6	5	3							7		8	11	10	1	9	32
2	4					6	5	3							7		8	11	10	1	9	33
2	4	3				6	5					9	1		7		8	11	10			34
2	4	3		10		6	5					9	1		7		8	11				35
2	4	6		10			5	3				9	1		7		8	11				36
2	4	6					5	3	11			9	1				8	7		10		37
2	4					6	5	3				9	1				8	11	10	7		38
2	4	3				6	5					9	1		7		8	11	10			39
2	4	3				6	5		11			9	1		7		8	10				40
2	4	6					5	3				9	1		7		8	11	10			41
2	4	6					5	3				9	1		7		8	11	10			42
30	33	28	2	8	7	31	34	26	7	17	1	9	20	3	40	3	42	41	31	22	27	
	5	3			1	3			1			9		2	7		9	12	18		12	opp.og 2
2	4	6	5					3					1		7		8	11	10		9	43
2	4	6					5	3					1		7		8	11	10		9	44
2	4	3				6	5								7		8	11	10	1	9	45
2	9	4				6	5	3							7		8	11	10	1		46
2	9	4				6	5	3							7		8	11	10	1		47
5	5	5	1			3	4	4					2		5		5	5	5	3	3	
	1	2													2			2				

1964-65

1	Aug 22	(a)	Stoke C	W	2-0	Temple, Vernon	2	
2	25	(h)	Nottingham F	W	1-0	Pickering	4	
3	29	(h)	Tottenham H	W	4-1	Pickering 3, Young	6	1
4	Sep 1	(a)	Nottingham F	L	1-3	Brown	6	2
5	5	(a)	Burnley	D	1-1	Brown	7	2
6	8	(h)	Manchester U	D	3-3	Pickering 2, Young	8	3
7	12	(h)	Sheffield U	D	1-1	Brown	9	5
8	16	(a)	Manchester U	L	1-2	Pickering	9	7
9	19	(a)	Liverpool	W	4-0	Harvey, Morrissey, Pickering, Temple	11	5
10	26	(a)	Birmingham C	E	5-3	Pickering 2, Scott 2, Morrissey	13	3
11	Oct 3	(h)	West Ham U	D	1-1	Harris	14	4
12	5	(a)	Aston Villa	W	2-1	Gabriel, Scott	16	3
13	10	(h)	Sheffield W	D	1-1	Scott	17	3
14	17	(a)	Blackpool	D	1-1	Scott	18	3
15	24	(h)	Blackburn R	L	2-3	Pickering, Young	18	4
16	31	(a)	Arsenal	L	1-3	Pickering	18	8
17	Nov 7	(h)	Leeds U	L	0-1		18	10
18	14	(a)	Chelsea	L	1-5	Gabriel	18	11
19	21	(h)	Leicester C	D	2-2	Gabriel, Pickering	19	11
20	28	(a)	Sunderland	L	0-4		19	12
21	Dec 5	(h)	Wolves	W	5-0	Pickering 2, Temple 2, Brown	21	10
22	12	(h)	Stoke C	D	1-1	Pickering	22	8
23	19	(a)	Tottenham H	D	2-2	Pickering 2	23	9
24	26	(h)	West Brom A	W	3-2	Pickering, Scott, Temple	25	9
25	Jan 2	(h)	Burnley	W	2-1	Pickering, Temple	27	8
26	16	(a)	Sheffield U	D	0-0		28	9
27	Feb 6	(h)	Birmingham C	D	1-1	Harvey	29	10
28	13	(a)	West Ham U	W	1-0	Temple	31	9
29	20	(a)	Sheffield W	W	1-0	Pickering	33	5
30	27	(h)	Blackpool	D	0-0		34	6
31	Mar 6	(a)	Blackburn R	W	2-0	Harris, Pickering	36	5
32	13	(h)	Aston Villa	W	3-1	Vernon 2, Morrissey	38	5
33	20	(a)	Leeds U	L	1-4	Temple	38	6
34	23	(a)	West Brom A	L	0-4		38	8
35	31	(h)	Chelsea	D	1-1	Gabriel	39	6
36	Apr 3	(a)	Leicester C	L	1-2	Temple	39	7
37	10	(h)	Sunderland	D	1-1	Pickering	40	6
38	12	(h)	Liverpool	D	2-1	Morrissey, Temple	42	5
39	16	(h)	Fulham	W	2-0	Pickering, Temple	44	6
40	17	(a)	Wolves	W	4-2	Brown, Harris, Morrissey, Pickering	46	4
41	19	(a)	Fulham	D	1-1	Pickering	47	4
42	24	(h)	Arsenal	Q	1-0	Pickering	49	4
							League Appearances	
							League Goals	
43	Jan 9	(h)	Sheffield W	D	2-2	Pickering, opp.og	FA Cup Rd 3	
44	13	(a)	Sheffield W	W	3-0	Harvey, Pickering, Temple	Replay	
45	30	(a)	Leeds U	D	1-1	Pickering	4	
46	Feb 2	(h)	Leeds U	L	1-2	Pickering	Replay	
							FA Cup Appearances	
							FA Cup Goals	

Everton played in the Inter-Cities Fairs Cup (see Everton in Europe section).

Brown A	Gabriel J	Glover G	Harris B	Harvey C	Husband J	Labone B	Morrissey J	Parker A	Pickering F	Rankin G	Rees B	Scott A	Shaw S	Stevens D	Temple D	Vernon R	West G	Wilson R	Wright T	Young A	#
			6			5	2	9	1			7		4	11	10		3		8	1
			6			5	2	9	1			7		4	11	10		3		8	2
3			6			5	2	9	1			7		4	11	10				8	3
3	4		6			5	2	9	1			7			11	10				8	4
3	4		6			5	2	9	1			7			11	10				8	5
3	4		6			5	2	9	1			7			11	10				8	6
3	4		6			5	2	9	1			7			11	10				8	7
3	4		2	10		5		9	1			7		6	11					8	8
3	4		2	8		5	11	9	1			7		6	10						9
3	4		2	8		5	11	9	1			7		6	10						10
3	9		6	8		5	11	2	1			7		4	10						11
3	10		6	8		5	2	9	1			7		4	11						12
3			6	10		5	2	9	1			7		4	11					8	13
3	4			8		5		9	1			7		6	11				2	10	14
	4	3		10		5	2	9	1				7	6	11					8	15
3	4					5	11	2	9	1		7		6	10					8	16
3	4					5	11	9	1		2			6	7	10				8	17
3	4		6	10		5	11	9	1					2	7					8	18
3	4					5	11	9	1			7		6	10				2	8	19
3	4		6	10		5	11	9	1					2	7					8	20
3	4		6	8		5	11	9	1					7	10				2		21
2	4		6	8		5		9	1			7		11	10			3			22
	4		6			5	11	9				7				10	1	3	2	8	23
	4		6			5	11	9				7				10	1	3	2	8	24
2	4		6			5	11	9				7				10	1	3		8	25
	4		6	8		5	11	9				7				10	1	3	2		26
	4		6	8		5	11	9				7					1	3	2	10	27
	4			8		5		9				7		6	11	10	1	3	2		28
	4			8		5		9				7		6	11	10	1	3	2		29
	4		6	8		5		9				7			11	10	1	3	2		30
	4		6	8		5		9				7			11	10	1	3	2		31
	4		6	8		5	11	9				7			10		1	3	2		32
	4		6	8		5	11	9				7			10		1	3	2		33
	4		6	8		5	11	9				7			10		1	3	2		34
6	4			8		5	11	9				7			10		1	3	2		35
6	4			8		5	11	9				7			10		1	3	2		36
3	4		6	8		5	11	9				7			10		1		2		37
3	4		6	8		5	11	9				7			10		1		2		38
3	4		6	8		5	11	9				7			10		1		2		39
3	4		6	8		5	11	9				7			10		1		2		40
3	4		6	8	10	5	11	9				7					1		2		41
3	4		6	8		5	11	9				7			10		1		2		42
28	37	1	31	32	1	42	25	12	41	22	1	36	1	18	39	16	20	17	22	20	
5	4		3	2		5			27			6			11	3				3	
2	4		6			5	11	9				7			10		1	3		8	43
	4		6	8		5	11	9				7			10		1	3	2		44
	4			8		5	11	9				7		6	10		1	3	2		45
	4			8		5	11	9				7		6	10		1	3	2		46
1	4		1	4		4	4		4			4		2	4		4	4	3	1	
				1					4						1						

opp.og 1

1965-66

1	Aug 21	(h)	Northampton T	W	5-2	Pickering 2, Temple 2, Young	2	
2	25	(a)	Sheffield W	L	1-3	Scott	2	
3	28	(a)	Stoke C	D	1-1	Pickering	3	13
4	31	(h)	Sheffield W	W	5-1	Young 3, Pickering 2	5	2
5	Sep 4	(h)	Burnley	W	1-0	Temple	7	3
6	7	(h)	West Brom A	L	2-3	Harvey, Scott	7	7
7	11	(a)	Chelsea	L	1-3	Temple	7	9
8	15	(a)	West Brom A	D	1-1	Young	8	11
9	18	(h)	Arsenal	W	3-1	Harris, Pickering, Temple	10	9
10	25	(a)	Liverpool	L	0-5		10	12
11	Oct 5	(h)	Blackburn R	D	2-2	Gabriel, Labone	11	12
12	9	(h)	Tottenham h	W	3-1	Gabriel 2, Pickering	13	9
13	16	(a)	Fulham	L	2-3	Pickering 2	13	11
14	23	(h)	Blackpool	D	0-0		14	11
15	30	(a)	Blackburn R	W	2-1	Pickering, Scott	16	11
16	Nov 6	(h)	Leicester C	L	1-2	Morrissey	16	13
17	13	(a)	Sheffield U	L	0-2		16	13
18	20	(h)	Leeds U	D	0-0		17	11
19	27	(a)	West Ham U	L	0-3		17	12
20	Dec 4	(h)	Sunderland	W	2-0	Hurst, Pickering	19	11
21	11	(a)	Aston Villa	L	2-3	Hurst, Pickering	19	13
22	16	(a)	Manchester U	L	0-3		19	13
23	18	(h)	Fulham	W	2-0	Temple, Young	21	10
24	27	(a)	Nottingham F	L	0-1		21	12
25	Jan 1	(a)	Tottenham H	D	2-2	Pickering, Temple	22	13
26	8	(h)	Aston Villa	W	2-0	Pickering, Trebilcock	24	13
27	11	(h)	West Ham U	D	2-2	Pickering, Scott	25	11
28	15	(a)	Blackpool	L	0-2		25	11
29	29	(a)	Northampton T	W	2-0	Scott, Temple	27	11
30	Feb 5	(h)	Stoke C	W	2-1	Pickering, Young	29	11
31	19	(a)	Burnley	D	1-1	Labone	30	11
32	26	(h)	Chelsea	W	2-1	Harris, Temple	32	9
33	Mar 12	(a)	Arsenal	W	1-0	Pickering	34	8
34	15	(h)	Nottingham F	W	3-0	Gabriel, Morrissey, Pickering	36	7
35	19	(h)	Liverpool	D	0-0		37	7
36	Apr 8	(a)	Newcastle U	D	0-0		38	7
37	9	(h)	Sheffield U	L	1-3	Gabriel	38	9
38	11	(h)	Newcastle U	W	1-0	Gabriel	40	7
39	16	(a)	Leeds U	L	1-4	Trebilcock	40	9
40	25	(h)	Manchester U	D	0-0		41	10
41	30	(a)	Sunderland	L	0-2		41	10
42	May 4	(a)	Leicester C	L	0-3		41	11

League Appearances
League Sub Appnces
League Goals

43	Jan 22	(h)	Sunderland	W	3-0	Pickering, Temple, Young	FA Cup Rd 3
44	Feb 12	(a)	Bedford T	W	3-0	Temple 2, Pickering	4
45	Mar 3	(h)	Coventry C	W	3-0	Pickering, Temple, Young	5
46	26	(a)	Manchester C	D	0-0		6
47	29	(h)	Manchester C	D	0-0		Replay
48	Apr 5	(n)	Manchester C	W	2-0	Pickering, Temple	(Molineux) Replay
49	23	(n)	Manchester U	W	1-0	Harvey	(Burnden Park) SF
50	May 14	(n)	Sheffield W	W	3-2	Trebilcock 2, Temple	(Wembley) F

FA Cup Appearances
FA Cup Goals

Everton played in the Inter-Cities Fairs Cup (see Everton in Europe section).

Barnett G	Brown A	Darcy F	Gabriel J	Glover G	Harris B	Harvey C	Heslop G	Humphreys G	Hurst J	Husband J	Labone B	Morrissey J	Pickering F	Rankin A	Royle J	Scott A	Shaw S	Smith D	Stevens D	Temple D	Trebilcock M	West G	Wilson R	Wright T	Young A	
			4		6	10					5		9			7				11		1	3	2	8	1
			4		6	10					5		9			7				11		1	3	2	8	2
					6	10			12		5		9*			7			4	11		1	3	2	8	3
					6	10				4	5		9			7				11		1	3	2	8	4
					6	10				4	5		9			7				11		1	3	2	8	5
					6	10				4	5		9			7				11		1	3	2	8	6
					6	10	5			4			9			7				11		1	3	2	8	7
			4		6	10					5		9				7			11		1	3	2	8	8
			4		6	10					5		9				7			11		1	3	2	8	9
			4	12	6	10					5*	11	9			7				11		1	3	2	8	10
	3		4		6*	8		12	10		5		9			7			2	11		1				11
	2		4			8		6	10		5		9			7				11		1	3			12
	5		4		6	8						11	9	1		7				10			3	2		13
	5		4		6	8						11	9	1		7				10			3	2		14
	12		4*		6	8					5	11	9	1		7				10			3	2		15
					6	8					5	11	9	1		7			4	10			3	2		16
	3				6	8					5	11	9	1		7			4	10				2		17
					6	4					5	11	9	1					10	7			3	2	8	18
					6	4					5	11	9	1					10	7			3	2	8	19
1					6	4		10			5		9			7				11			3	2	8	20
1					6	4		10			5		9			7				11			3	2	8	21
1	8				6	4		10			5		9			7				11			3	2		22
1					6	4		10			5		9			7				11			3	2	8	23
1					6	4		10			5		9			7				11			3	2	8	24
1					6	4		8			5		9			7				11	10		3	2		25
1					6	4		8			5		9			7				11	10		3	2		26
1					6	4		8			5		9			7				11			3	2	10	27
1	3				6	4		10			5	12	9		8	7				11				2*		28
			4		6	10					5		9			7				11		1	3	2	8	29
			4		6	10					5		9			7				11		1	3	2	8	30
			4		6	10					5		9			7				11		1	3	2	8	31
			4		6	10					5		9			7				11		1	3	2	8	32
	2		4		6	10					5		9			7				11		1	3		8	33
	3		4		6	10					5	11	9			7						1		2	8	34
	2		4		6	10					5		9*			7				11		1	3	12	8	35
	2		4		6	10		9	7		5									11	8	1	3			36
	12		4		6	10					5					7				11		1	3*	2	8	37
	3		4		6	10		9			5					7				11	8	1		2		38
	2	3			6			8	4	7		11		1	9		5			10						39
	2		4		6			8			5		9			7				11	10	1	3			40
			4		6	10							9					5		11	7	1	3	2	8	41
	3		4		6	10				11	8	5	9	1		7								2		42
9	14	1	24	1	40	40	1	2	19	4	37	10	39	9	2	35	2	2	6	38	7	24	35	35	26	
	2			1				2				1												1		
		6			2	1			2		2	2	18			5				9	2				7	
			4		6	10					5		9			7				11		1	3	2	8	43
			4		6	10					5		9			7				11		1	3	2	8	44
	2		4		6	10					5		9			7				11		1	3		8	45
	4				6	10					5	11				7				9		1	3	2	8	46
	4				6	10					5		9			7				11		1	3	2	8	47
			4		6	10					5		9			7				11		1	3	2	8	48
	2		4		6	10					5					7				11	8	1	3	2	9	49
			4		6	10					5					7				11	8	1	3	2	9	50
	4		6		8	8					8	1	5			8				8	2	8	8	6	8	
						1					4		6							2					2	

1966-67

#	Date		Opponent	Res	Score	Scorers		
1	Aug 20	(a)	Fulham	W	1-0	Ball	2	
2	23	(h)	Manchester U	L	1-2	Temple	2	
3	27	(h)	Liverpool	W	3-1	Ball 2, Brown	4	6
4	31	(a)	Manchester U	L	0-3		4	14
5	Sep 3	(h)	Stoke C	L	0-1		4	15
6	6	(h)	Burnley	D	1-1	Young	5	14
7	10	(a)	Sheffield U	D	0-0		6	14
8	17	(h)	West Brom A	W	5-4	Ball 2, Morrissey, Temple, Young	8	12
9	24	(a)	Leeds U	D	1-1	Temple	9	12
10	Oct 1	(h)	Newcastle U	D	1-1	Gabriel	10	13
11	8	(a)	West Ham U	W	3-2	Temple 2, Young	12	10
12	15	(h)	Sheffield W	W	2-1	Gabriel, Temple	14	8
13	25	(a)	Southampton	W	3-1	Ball 2, Temple	16	6
14	29	(h)	Leicester C	W	2-0	Scott, Temple	18	3
15	Nov 5	(a)	Sheffield W	W	2-1	Ball, Temple	20	3
16	12	(h)	Arsenal	D	0-0		21	4
17	19	(a)	Manchester C	L	0-1		21	5
18	26	(h)	Blackpool	L	0-1		21	7
19	Dec 3	(a)	Chelsea	D	1-1	Young	22	7
20	17	(h)	Fulham	W	3-2	Temple 2, Ball	24	7
21	23	(h)	Nottingham F	L	0-1		24	8
22	26	(a)	Nottingham F	L	0-1		24	11
23	31	(a)	Liverpool	D	0-0		25	11
24	Jan 7	(a)	Stoke C	L	1-2	Young	25	12
25	14	(h)	Sheffield U	W	4-1	Ball 2, Gabriel, Husband	27	9
26	21	(a)	West Brom A	L	0-1		27	10
27	Feb 4	(h)	Leeds U	W	2-0	Gabriel, Husband	29	9
28	11	(a)	Newcastle U	W	3-0	Ball, Husband, Morrissey	31	9
29	25	(h)	West Ham U	W	4-0	Husband, Morrissey, Temple, Young	33	7
30	Mar 4	(a)	Leicester C	D	2-2	Hurst, Young	34	7
31	18	(h)	Southampton	L	0-1		34	8
32	22	(h)	Tottenham H	L	0-1		34	8
33	25	(a)	Sunderland	W	2-0	Husband, opp.og	36	7
34	27	(a)	Tottenham H	L	0-2		36	7
35	Apr 1	(h)	Aston Villa	W	3-1	Ball, Young, opp.og	38	7
36	19	(h)	Chelsea	W	3-1	Royle 2, Hurst	40	7
37	22	(a)	Blackpool	W	1-0	Royle	42	7
38	25	(a)	Arsenal	L	1-3	Gabriel	42	7
39	29	(h)	Manchester C	D	1-1	Ball	43	6
40	May 6	(a)	Aston Villa	W	4-2	Pickering 2, Gabriel, Husband	45	6
41	13	(a)	Burnley	D	1-1	Ball	46	6
42	16	(h)	Sunderland	W	4-1	Morrissey 3, Harvey	48	6

League Appearances
League Sub Appnces
League Goals

#	Date		Opponent	Res	Score	Scorers	
43	Jan 28	(a)	Burnley	D	0-0		FA Cup Rd 3
44	31	(h)	Burnley	W	2-1	Young 2	Replay
45	Feb 18	(a)	Wolves	D	1-1	Ball	4
46	21	(h)	Wolves	W	3-1	Husband 2, Temple	Replay
47	Mar 11	(h)	Liverpool	W	1-0	Ball	5
48	Apr 8	(a)	Nottingham F	L	2-3	Husband 2	6

FA Cup Appearances
FA Cup Sub Appncès
FA Cup Goals

Everton played in European Cup-winners Cup (see Everton in Europe section).

Ball A	Brown A	Gabriel J	Harris B	Harvey C	Hurst J	Husband J	Kendall H	Labone B	Morrissey J	Pickering F	Rankin A	Royle J	Scott A	Smith D	Temple D	Trebilcock M	West G	Wilson R	Wright T	Young A	
8		4		6				5		9			7		11		1	3	2	10	1
8		4		6				5		9			7		11		1	3	2	10	2
8	12	4		6				5	11	9*			7				1	3	2	10	3
8		4		6				5					7		11	10	1	3	2	9	4
8*	9	4		6	12			5					7		11		1	3	2	10	5
		4		6	8			5	11				7		10		1	3	2	9	6
8		4		6	9			5					7		11		1	3	2	10	7
8		4		6	12			5	11	9*			7				1	3	2	10	8
8		4		6				5	11				7		10		1	3	2	9	9
8		4	10	6				5	11				7				1	3	2	9	10
8		4		6				5	11				7		10		1	3	2	9	11
8	12	4		6				5	11*				7		10		1	3	2	9	12
8		4		6				5	11				7		10		1	3	2	9	13
8		4		6				5	11				7		10		1	3	2	9	14
8		4		6				5	11				7		10		1	3	2	9	15
8		4		6				5	11*				7	12	10		1	3	2	9	16
8		4		6	11			5					7		10		1	3	2	9	17
8	10	4		6				5					7		11		1	3	2	9	18
8	3	4		6				5	11				7		10		1		2	9	19
8	3	4		6				5	11				7		10		1		2	9	20
8	3	4		6				5	11				7		10		1		2	9	21
8	3	4		6	7			5	11						10		1		2	9	22
8	3	4		6	7			5	11						10		1		2	9	23
8	3	4		6	7	11		5							10		1		2	9	24
8	3	7		6	4	10		5	11						12		1		2*	9	25
8		7		6	4	10		5	11								1	3	2	9	26
8	9			6	4	10		5	11								1	3	2	7	27
8	5	9		6	4	10			11								1	3	2	7	28
8	12			6	4	10		5	11							9*	1	3	2	7	29
8				6	4	10		5	11	9							1	3	2	7	30
8		10	4	9	6			5	11								1	3	2	7	31
8		10	4	6				5	11	9							1	3	2	7	32
8		10	4	9	6			5	11								1	3	2	7	33
8	12			6	4	10		5	11	9			7				1	3*	2		34
8	3			6	4	9		5	11		1		7						2	10	35
7	3	12		10	4	9	6*	5	11		1	8							2		36
7	3			6	10	4	9	5	11		1	8							2		37
7	3			6	10	4	9	5			1	8			11				2		38
7	3			6	10	4	9	5			1	8			11				2		39
7		10		6	4	8		5	11	9							1	3	2		40
7		10		6	4	8		5	11	9							1	3	2		41
7	12	10		6	4	8*		5	11								1	3	2	9	42
41	**15**	**31**	**4**	**42**	**23**	**19**	**4**	**40**	**31**	**8**	**6**	**4**	**21**	**1**	**27**	**2**	**36**	**30**	**42**	**35**	
	5	1				2									1	1					
15	1	6		1	2	6			6	2			3	1	12					8	opp.og 2
8	12	7		6	4	10		5	11							9*	1	3	2		43
8	12	9		6	4	10		5*	11								1	3	2	7	44
8		9		6	4	10		5	11								1	3	2	7	45
8	12			6	4	10		5	11							9*	1	3	2	7	46
8				6	4	10		5	11							9	1	3	2	7	47
8	9			6	4	10		5	11		1							3	2	7	48
6	**1**	**3**		**6**	**6**	**6**		**6**	**6**		**1**					**3**	**5**	**6**	**6**	**5**	
	3																				
2						4										1				2	

1967-68

#	Date		Venue	Opponent	Res	Score	Scorers		
1	Aug	19	(h)	Manchester U	W	3-1	Ball 2, Young	2	
2		23	(a)	Tottenham H	D	1-1	opp. og	3	
3		26	(a)	Sunderland	L	0-1		3	10
4		29	(h)	Tottenham H	L	0-1		3	12
5	Sep	2	(h)	Wolves	W	4-2	Ball 2, Brown, Royle	5	8
6		5	(h)	West Ham U	W	2-0	Kendall, Young	7	4
7		9	(a)	Fulham	L	1-2	Young	7	8
8		16	(h)	Leeds U	L	0-1		7	13
9		23	(a)	Liverpool	L	0-1		7	15
10		30	(a)	Leicester C	W	2-0	Ball 2	9	15
11	Oct	7	(h)	Southampton	W	4-2	Ball, Hunt, Kendall, opp.og	11	9
12		14	(a)	Chelsea	D	1-1	Ball	12	11
13		24	(h)	West Brom A	W	2-1	Hunt, Kendall	14	7
14		28	(a)	Newcastle U	L	0-1		14	12
15	Nov	4	(h)	Manchester C	D	1-1	Hunt	15	12
16		11	(a)	Arsenal	D	2-2	Hurst, Husband	16	11
17		18	(h)	Sheffield U	W	1-0	Young	18	10
18		25	(a)	Coventry C	W	2-0	Husband, Royle	20	7
19	Dec	2	(h)	Nottingham F	W	1-0	Royle	22	6
20		9	(a)	Stoke C	L	0-1		22	6
21		16	(a)	Manchester U	L	1-3	Young	22	8
22		23	(h)	Sunderland	W	3-0	Ball, Husband, Royle	24	5
23		26	(h)	Burnley	W	2-0	Ball, Royle	26	5
24		30	(a)	Burnley	L	1-2	Husband	26	7
25	Jan	6	(a)	Wolves	W	3-1	Royle 2, Trebilcock	28	5
26		20	(a)	Leeds U	L	0-2		28	7
27	Feb	3	(h)	Liverpool	W	1-0	Kendall	30	6
28		26	(a)	Southampton	L	2-3	Ball, Royle	30	7
29	Mar	2	(h)	Coventry C	W	3-1	Royle 2, Ball	32	7
30		16	(a)	West Brom A	W	6-2	Ball 4, Morrissey, Royle	34	6
31		23	(h)	Newcastle U	W	1-0	Kendall	36	6
32	Apr	6	(h)	Arsenal	W	2-0	Royle 2	38	6
33		9	(h)	Leicester C	W	2-1	Morrissey, Royle	40	5
34		13	(a)	Sheffield U	W	1-0	Ball	42	5
35		15	(h)	Sheffield W	W	1-0	Hurst	44	5
36		16	(a)	Sheffield W	D	0-0		45	5
37		20	(h)	Chelsea	W	2-1	Hurst, Kendall	47	5
38		22	(a)	Nottingham F	L	0-1		47	5
39		29	(a)	Manchester C	L	0-2		47	5
40	May	4	(h)	Stoke C	W	3-0	Ball 2, Royle	49	5
41		11	(a)	West Ham U	D	1-1	Husband	50	5
42		21	(h)	Fulham	W	5-1	Hurst 2, Ball, Morrissey, Royle	52	5

League Appearances
League Sub Appnces
League Goals

#	Date		Venue	Opponent	Res	Score	Scorers		
43	Jan	27	(a)	Southport	W	1-0	Royle	FA Cup Rd	3
44	Feb	17	(a)	Carlisle U	W	2-0	Husband, Royle		4
45	Mar	9	(h)	Tranmere R	W	2-0	Morrissey, Royle		5
46		30	(a)	Leicester C	W	3-1	Husband 2, Kendall		6
47	Apr	27	(n)	Leeds U	W	1-0	Morrissey	(Old Trafford)	SF
48	May	18	(n)	West Brom A	L	0-1		(Wembley)	F
49	Sep	13	(a)	Bristol City	W	5-0	Kendall 2, Brown, Hurst, Royle	League Cup Rd	2
50	Oct	11	(h)	Sunderland	L	2-3	Young 2		3

Cup Appearances
Cup Sub Appnces
Cup Goals

Ball A	Barnett G	Bennett H	Brindle W	Brown A	Darcy F	Darracott T	Harvey C	Humphreys G	Hunt E	Hurst J	Husband J	Jackson T	Kendall H	Kenyon R	Labone B	Maher A	Morrissey J	Owen L	Royle J	Temple D	Trebilcock M	Turner D	West G	Whittle A	Wilson R	Wright T	Young A	
8							6			10			4	5			11		9				1		3	2	7	1
8*		12					6			10			4	5			11		9				1		3	2	7	2
		12					6			10	8		4	5			11*		9				1		3	2	7	3
		12					6			10			4	5			11		9	8			1		3	2*	7	4
8							3		6	10	12		4	5					9*11				1			2	7	5
8							3		6	10			4	5					9	11			1			2	7	6
8							3		6	9 10			4	5					9	11			1			2	7	7
7			3						6	8 10			4	5					9	11			1			2		8
7							3		6	8 10			4	5			11						1			2	9	9
7	12						3		6	8 10			4	5*			11						1			2	9	10
7							3		6	8 10			4	5			11						1			2	9	11
8							7		6	4 10				5			11						1		3	2	9	12
7							12		6*	8 10			4	5			11						1		3	2	9	13
7							12		6	8 10			4	5			11*						1		3	2	9	14
7							2		6	8*10			4		5 11				12				1		3		9	15
							11		6	10	8		4*12	5					7				1		3	2	9	16
7							2*		6	10	8		4 12	5					11				1		3		9	17
7									6	10	8		4	5					11				1		3	2	9	18
8									6	10 11			4	5					9				1		3	2	7	19
8									6	10 11			4	5					9				1		3	2	7	20
8									6	10			4	5		11			9				1		3	2	7	21
8							10			6 11			4	5					9				1		3	2	7	22
8									6	12 10			4*	5		11			9				1		3	2	7	23
8*		12							6	7 10 11			4	5					9				1		3	2		24
7		12							6	8 10			4	5					9		11		1		3	2*		25
8									6	10 7			4*12	5				9		11		1		3	2		26
8*		12							6	10 7 11			4	5				9				1		3	2		27
8		12							6	10 7			4	5		11		9				1		3*	2		28
8							3		6*	12 10 7			4	5		11		9				1		3	2		29
8										6 7			4	5		11		9				1	10	3	2		30
8		12								6 7			4	5		11		9				1	10*	3	2		31
8				3						10			4	6	5		11		9				1	7		2		32
8				3						10			4	6	5		11		9				1	7		2		33
8				3						10			4	6	5		11		9				1	7		2		34
		12	3							7*	10	8	4	6	5		11		9				1			2		35
		12	3*							10			4	6	5		11	8	9				1			2	7	36
				6 10						8	7		4 12	5		11			9			2*	1	3				37
	2	4								11	10		8	6	5		7*		9				1		3		12	38
8									6			7*12	4 10	5		11			9				1		3	2		39
8									6				4 10	5		11			9				1	7	3	2		40
	1			3					6	7			10 8	4	5		11									2	9	41
8	6	12							6	10 7			4	5		11			9				1		3*	2		42
34	1	2	1	12	4	1	34	4	12	40	19	1	38	12	40	1	26	2	33	5	2	1	41	6	28	38	24	
				13															1								1	
20		1					3	5	5	6			3		16	1			3								5	opp.og 2
7		12							6	10 11			4	5					9				1		3*	2	8	43
8									6	10 7			4	5		11		9				1		3	2		44
		12								10 6 7*			4	5		11		9				1		3	2	8	45
8										10 7*			4 6	5		11		9				1		3	2 12		46
									6		7*	4 10	8	5		11		9				1		3	2 12		47
8									6	10 7			4	5		11		9				1		3	2		48
8							3		6	10			4	5					9	11			1			2	7	49
7							3		6	8 10			4	5		11							1			2	9	50
6				2			2		6	2 7	6 1		8	2 8			6		7 1				8		6	8	4	
				2																							2	
				1						1 3			3						2	4							2	

1968-69

#	Date		Opponent	Res	Score	Scorers		
1	Aug 10	(a)	Manchester U	L	1-2	Ball	0	
2	13	(h)	Burnley	W	3-0	Ball, Husband, Royle	2	
3	17	(h)	Tottenham H	L	0-2		2	14
4	19	(a)	West Ham U	W	4-1	Ball, Harvey, Husband, Royle	4	7
5	24	(a)	Newcastle U	D	0-0		5	8
6	27	(h)	Liverpool	D	0-0		6	8
7	31	(h)	Nottingham F	W	2-1	Hurst, Royle	8	6
8	Sep 7	(a)	Chelsea	D	1-1	Morrissey	9	7
9	14	(h)	Sheffield W	W	3-0	Humphreys, Husband, Morrissey	11	6
10	21	(a)	Coventry C	D	2-2	Hurst, Husband	12	7
11	28	(h)	West Brom A	W	4-0	Ball 3, Harvey	14	5
12	Oct 5	(h)	Manchester C	W	2-0	Ball, Royle	16	4
13	8	(a)	Liverpool	D	1-1	Ball	17	4
14	12	(a)	Southampton	W	5-2	Husband 2, Ball, Royle, Wright	19	4
15	19	(h)	Stoke C	W	2-1	Harvey, Hurst	21	3
16	26	(a)	Wolves	W	2-1	Ball, Royle	23	2
17	Nov 2	(h)	Sunderland	W	2-0	Ball, Morrissey	25	1
18	9	(a)	Ipswich T	D	2-2	Royle 2	26	2
19	16	(h)	Q.P.R.	W	4-0	Harvey, Husband, Morrissey, Royle	28	2
20	23	(a)	Leeds U	l	1-2	Royle	28	2
21	30	(h)	Leicester C	W	7-1	Royle 3, Ball, Humphreys, Hurst, Husband	30	2
22	Dec 7	(a)	Arsenal	L	1-3	Ball	30	3
23	14	(h)	Southampton	W	1-0	Hurst	32	3
24	21	(a)	Stoke C	D	0-0		33	3
25	26	(a)	Manchester C	W	3-1	Husband 2, Royle	35	4
26	Jan 11	(a)	Sunderland	W	3-1	Royle 2, Kendall	37	4
27	18	(h)	Ipswich T	D	2-2	Brown, Husband	38	3
28	28	(h)	Wolves	W	4-0	Royle 2, Husband, Morrissey	40	3
29	Feb 1	(a)	Q.P.R.	W	1-0	Husband	42	3
30	8	(a)	Tottenham H	D	1-1	Royle	43	3
31	Mar 10	(h)	Manchester U	D	0-0		44	3
32	29	(h)	Chelsea	L	1-2	Royle	44	4
33	Apr 1	(h)	West Ham U	W	1-0	Husband	46	4
34	5	(a)	West Brom A	D	1-1	Ball	47	4
35	8	(a)	Burnley	W	2-1	Ball, Husband	49	4
36	12	(h)	Coventry	W	3-0	Hurst, Husband, Royle	51	4
37	14	(h)	Newcastle U	D	1-1	Husband	52	3
38	19	(a)	Sheffield W	D	2-2	Hurst, Husband	53	4
39	22	(h)	Leeds U	D	0-0		54	4
40	25	(a)	Nottingham F	L	0-1		54	4
41	29	(h)	Arsenal	W	1-0	Husband	56	3
42	May 14	(a)	Leicester C	D	1-1	Ball	57	3

League Appearances
League Sub Appnces
League Goals

#	Date		Opponent	Res	Score	Scorers		
43	Jan 4	(h)	Ipswich T	W	2-1	Hurst, Royle	FA Cup Rd 3	
44	25	(h)	Coventry C	W	2-0	Hurst, Royle	4	
45	Feb 12	(h)	Bristol C	W	1-0	Royle	5	
46	Mar 1	(a)	Manchester U	W	1-0	Royle	6	
47	22	(n)	Manchester U	L	0-1		(Villa Park) SF	
48	Sep 3	(h)	Tranmere R	W	4-0	Whittle 2, Ball, Royle	League Cup Rd 2	
49	24	(h)	Luton T	W	5-1	Royle 2, Ball, Husband, Morrissey	3	
50	Oct 16	(h)	Derby C	D	0-0		4	
51	23	(a)	Derby	L	0-1		Replay	

Cup Appearances
Cup Sub Appnces
Cup Goals

Ball A	Brown A	Darcy F	Darracott T	Harvey C	Humphreys G	Hurst J	Husband J	Jackson T	Kendall H	Kenyon R	Labone B	Morrissey J	Royle J	West G	Whittle A	Wilson R	Wright T	
8	3			6		10	7		4		5	11	9	1			2	1
8	3			6		10	7		4		5	11	9	1			2	2
8	3			6		10	7		4		5	11	9	1			2	3
8	3			6		10	7		4		5	11	9	1			2	4
8	3			6		10	7		4		5	11	9	1			2	5
8	3			6		10	7		4		5	11	9	1			2	6
8	3			6		10		7	4		5	11	9	1			2	7
8	3			6		10			4		5	11	9	1	7		2	8
8		3		6	11	10	7		4		5		9	1			2	9
8	3			6		10	7		4		5	11	9	1			2	10
8	3			6		10	7		4		5	11	9	1			2	11
8	3			6		10	7		4		5	11	9	1			2	12
8	3			6		10	7		4		5	11	9	1			2	13
8	3			6		10	7		4		5	11	9	1			2	14
8	3			6		10			4		5	11	9	1	7		2	15
8	3	12		6	7	10			4		5	11*	9	1			2	16
8	3			6	7	10			4		5	11	9	1			2	17
8	2			6	7	10			4		5	11	9	1	3			18
8	3		4	6		10	7				5	11	9	1			2	19
8	3			6		10	7		4		5	11*	9	1	12		2	20
8	3			6	11	10	7		4		5		9	1			2	21
8	3			6		10	7		4		5	11	9	1			2	22
	3			6		10	7		4	8	5	11	9	1			2	23
8	3			6		10	7		4		5	11	9	1			2	24
8	3			6		10	7		4		5	11	9	1			2	25
8	3					10	7		4	6	5	11	9	1			2	26
8	3					10	7		4	6	5	11	9	1			2	27
8	6					10	7		4		5	11	9	1	3		2	28
8	6					10	7		4*12		5	11	9	1	3		2	29
8	3					10	7	4		6	5	11	9	1			2	30
8	3			6			7	4		6	5	11	9	1	10		2	31
8	3			6		10	7	4	12		5	11	9	1			2*	32
8	3			6		10	7	4			5	11	9	1			2	33
8	3	12		6		10	7	4			5	11	9*	1			2	34
8	3			6*		10	7	4			5	11	9	1	12		2	35
	3			6		10	7	4	12		5	11	9	1	8*		2	36
8				6		10	7	4			5	11	9	1	3		2	37
8	3			6		10	7	4	12		5	11	9*	1			2	38
8	3			6		10	7	4			5	11	9	1			2	39
8	3			6		10	7	4			5	11	9	1			2	40
8	3			6		10	7	4			5	11	9	1			2	41
8	3			6		10	7	4			5	11	9	1			2	42
40	40	1	1	36	5	42	36	14	28	4	42	40	42	42	4	4	41	
	2										1	3			2			
16	1			4	2	7	19	1				4	22				1	
8	3			6		10	7		4		5	11	9	1			2	43
8	6					10	7		4		5	11	9	1	3		2	44
8	4	12		6*		10	7				5	11	9	1	3		2	45
8	3			6*		10	7	4	12		5	11	9	1			2	46
8	3			6		10	7	12	4*		5	11	9	1			2	47
8	3			6		10			4		5	11	9	1	7		2	48
8	3			6		10	7		4*12		5	11	9	1			2	49
8	3			6		10	7*		4	12	5	11	9	1			2	50
8	3			6	7*	10			4		5	11	9	1	12		2	51
9	9			8	1	9	7	1	7		9	9	9	9	1	2	9	
		1						1	3						1			
2							2	1				1	7		2			

1969-70

1	Aug	9	(a)	Arsenal	W	1-0	Hurst	2	
2		13	(a)	Manchester U	W	2-0	Ball, Hurst	4	
3		16	(h)	Crystal P	W	2-1	Morrissey, Royle	6	1
4		19	(h)	Manchester U	W	3-0	Ball, Morrissey, Royle	8	1
5		23	(a)	Manchester C	D	1-1	Morrissey	9	1
6		26	(h)	Sheffield W	W	2-1	Ball, Royle	11	1
7		30	(h)	Leeds U	W	3-2	Royle 2, Husband	13	1
8	Sep	6	(a)	Derby C	L	1-2	Kendall	13	2
9		13	(h)	West Ham U	W	2-0	Ball, Husband	15	3
10		17	(a)	Newcastle U	W	2-1	Husband 2	17	1
11		20	(a)	Ipswich T	W	3-0	Ball, Harvey, Royle	19	1
12		27	(h)	Southampton	W	4-2	Royle 3, Hurst	21	1
13	Oct	4	(a)	Wolves	W	3-2	Harvey, Morrissey, Royle	23	1
14		8	(a)	Crystal P	D	0-0		24	1
15		11	(h)	Sunderland	W	3-1	Kendall, Morrissey, Royle	26	1
16		18	(h)	Stoke C	W	6-2	Morrissey 2, Royle 2, Ball, Husband	28	1
17		25	(a)	Coventry C	W	1-0	Royle	30	1
18	Nov	1	(h)	Nottingham F	W	1-0	Wright	32	1
19		8	(a)	West Brom A	L	0-2		32	1
20		15	(a)	Chelsea	D	1-1	Husband	33	1
21		22	(h)	Burnley	W	2-1	Hurst, Royle	35	1
22	Dec	6	(h)	Liverpool	L	0-3		35	1
23		13	(a)	West Ham U	W	1-0	Whittle	37	1
24		20	(h)	Derby C	W	1-0	Ball	39	1
25		23	(h)	Manchester C	W	1-0	Whittle	41	1
26		27	(a)	Leeds U	L	1-2	Whittle	41	1
27	Jan	10	(h)	Ipswich T	W	3-0	Royle 2, Kendall	43	1
28		17	(a)	Southampton	L	1-2	Morrissey	43	2
29		24	(h)	Newcastle U	D	0-0		44	2
30		31	(h)	Wolves	W	1-0	Royle	46	2
31	Feb	14	(h)	Arsenal	D	2-2	Whittle 2	47	2
32		21	(h)	Coventry C	D	0-0		48	2
33		28	(a)	Nottingham F	D	1-1	Royle	49	2
34	Mar	7	(a)	Burnley	W	2-1	Ball, Hurst	51	2
35		11	(a)	Tottenham H	W	1-0	Whittle	53	1
36		14	(h)	Tottenham H	W	3-2	Ball, Royle, Whittle	55	1
37		21	(a)	Liverpool	W	2-0	Royle, Whittle	57	1
38		28	(h)	Chelsea	W	5-2	Royle 2, Ball, Kendall, Whittle	59	1
39		30	(a)	Stoke C	W	1-0	Whittle	61	1
40	Apr	1	(h)	West Brom A	W	2-0	Harvey, Whittle	63	1
41		4	(a)	Sheffield W	W	1-0	Morrissey	65	1
42		8	(a)	Sunderland	D	0-0		66	1

								League Appearances	
								League Sub Appnces	
								League Goals	

43	Jan	3	(a)	Sheffield U	L	1-2	Ball	FA Cup Rd 3	
44	Sep	3	(a)	Darlington	W	1-0	Ball	League Cup Rd 2	
45		24	(a)	Arsenal	D	0-0		3	
46	Oct	1	(h)	Arsenal	W	1-0	Kendall	Replay	
47		15	(a)	Manchester C	L	0-2		4	

								Cup Appearances	
								Cup Sub Appnces	
								Cup Goals	

Ball A	Bennett H	Brindle W	Brown A	Darcy F	Harvey C	Humphreys G	Hurst J	Husband J	Jackson T	Kendall H	Kenyon R	Labone B	Morrissey J	Newton K	Royle J	West G	Whittle A	Wright T	
			3		6		10	7	8	4*	12	5	11		9	1		2	1
8			3		6		10	7	4			5	11		9	1		2	2
8			3		6		10	7	4			5	11		9	1		2	3
8*			3	12	6		10	7	4			5	11		9	1		2	4
8			3		6		10	7	4			5	11		9	1		2	5
8			3		6		10	7	4			5	11		9	1		2	6
8			3		6		10	7	4			5	11		9	1		2	7
8			3		6		10	7		4		5	11		9	1		2	8
8			3		5		10	7		4		5	11		9	1		2	9
8			3		6		10	7		4		5	11		9	1		2	10
8			3		6		10	7		4		5	11		9	1		2	11
8			3		6		10	7		4		5	11		9	1		2	12
8			3		6		10	7		4		5	11		9	1		2	13
8			3		6		10	7		4		5	11		9	1		2	14
8			3		6		10	7		4		5	11		9	1		2	15
8			3		6		10	7		4		5	11		9	1		2	16
8			3		6		10	7		4		5	11		9	1		2	17
8			3		6		10	7		4		5	11		9	1		2	18
8			3		6		10	7		4		5	11		9	1		2	19
8			3		6		10	7		4		5	11		9	1		2	20
8			3	12			10	7*	6	4		5	11		9	1		2	21
8			3				10		6	4		5	11		9	1	7	2	22
8			3	12			10		6	4		5	11		9	1	7	2*	23
8				12			10	7*	6	4		5	11	3	9	1		2	24
8				12		11*	10		6	4		5		3	9	1	7	2	25
8							10		6	4		5	11	3	9	1	7	2	26
8							10	7	6	4		5	11	3	9	1		2	27
10					6*		8	7	12	4		5	11	3	9	1		2	28
				12	6		10	7		4		5	11	3	9	1	8	2*	29
				12	6*		10	7		4		5	11	3	9	1	8	2	30
					6		10	7		4		5	11	3	9	1	8	2	31
8					6		10	7		4		5	11	3	9	1		2	32
8					6		10	7		4		5	11	3	9	1		2	33
8					6		10			4		5	11	3	9	1	7	2	34
8				12	6		10			4	5		11	3*	9	1	7	2	35
8			3		6		10			4	5		11		9	1	7	2	36
8			3		6		10			4	5		11		9	1	7	2	37
8			3		6		10			4	5		11		9	1	7	2	38
8			3		6		10			4	5		11		9	1	7	2	39
8			3		6		10			4	5		11		9	1	7	2	40
8			3	12	6		10			4*	5		11		9	1	7	2	41
8			3	12	6		10	7		4*	5		11		9	1		2	42
37			31		35	1	42	30	14	36	8	34	41	12	42	42	15	42	
	5	5							1					1					
10			3					5	6	4			9		23		11	1	
8				12			10		6	4		5	11	3	9	1	7	2*	43
8			3		6		10	7		4		5	11		9	1		2	44
8			3		6		10			4	12	5	11		9	1	7	2*	45
8			3		6		10	7		4		5	11		9	1		2	46
	10	8	3			11			6	4		5			9	1	7	2	47
4	1	1	4		3	1	4	2	2	5		5	4	1	5	5	3	5	
				1										1					
2									1										

1970-71

1	Aug	15	(h)	Arsenal	D	2-2	Morrissey, Royle	1	
2		18	(h)	Burnley	D	1-1	Morrissey	2	
3		22	(a)	Leeds U	L	2-3	Brown, Husband	2	15
4		26	(a)	Chelsea	D	2-2	Husband, Royle	3	14
5		29	(h)	Manchester C	L	0-1		3	18
6	Sep	2	(a)	Manchester U	L	0-2		3	18
7		5	(a)	West Ham U	W	2-1	Husband, Royle	5	17
8		12	(h)	Ipswich T	W	2-0	Kendall, Whittle	7	14
9		19	(a)	Blackpool	W	2-0	Husband, Morrissey	9	10
10		26	(h)	Crystal P	W	3-1	Harvey, Morrissey, Royle	11	8
11	Oct	3	(a)	Coventry C	L	1-3	Hurst	11	12
12		10	(h)	Derby C	D	1-1	Morrissey	12	11
13		17	(a)	Arsenal	L	0-4		12	13
14		24	(h)	Newcastle U	W	3-1	Kendall, Royle, Whittle	14	10
15		31	(a)	West Brom A	L	0-3		14	12
16	Nov	7	(h)	Nottingham F	W	1-0	Whittle	16	11
17		14	(a)	Stoke C	D	1-1	Hurst	17	11
18		21	(a)	Liverpool	L	2-3	Royle, Whittle	17	13
19		28	(h)	Tottenham H	D	0-0		18	13
20	Dec	5	(a)	Huddersfield T	D	1-1	Ball	19	12
21		12	(h)	Southampton	W	4-1	Royle 2, Morrissey, Whittle	21	12
22		19	(h)	Leeds U	L	0-1		21	12
23		26	(a)	Wolves	L	0-2		21	14
24	Jan	9	(a)	Burnley	D	2-2	Johnson, H.Newton	22	13
25		16	(h)	Chelsea	W	3-0	Husband, H.Newton, Royle	24	12
26		30	(a)	Tottenham H	L	1-2	Royle	24	13
27	Feb	6	(h)	Huddersfield T	W	2-1	Royle 2	26	12
28		16	(a)	Southampton	D	2-2	Harvey, Wright	27	12
29		20	(h)	Liverpool	D	0-0		28	12
30		23	(h)	Manchester U	W	1-0	Wright	30	10
31		27	(h)	West Brom A	D	3-3	Husband, K.Newton, Royle	31	10
32	Mar	13	(h)	Stoke C	W	2-0	Royle, Whittle	33	9
33		17	(a)	Newcastle U	L	1-2	Royle	33	9
34		20	(a)	Nottingham F	L	2-3	Hurst, Lyons	33	10
35		30	(h)	West Ham U	L	0-1		33	10
36	Apr	3	(a)	Manchester C	L	0-3		33	12
37		6	(a)	Ipswich T	D	0-0		34	11
38		10	(h)	Wolves	L	1-2	H.Newton	34	13
39		12	(h)	Coventry C	W	3-0	Royle 2, Ball	36	10
40		17	(a)	Derby C	L	1-3	Whittle	36	13
41		24	(h)	Blackpool	D	0-0		37	13
42	May	1	(a)	Crystal P	L	0-2		37	14

League Appearances
League Sub Appnces
League Goals

43	Jan	2	(h)	Blackburn R	W	2-0	Husband 2	FA Cup Rd 3
44		23	(h)	Middlesbrough	W	3-0	Harvey, H.Newton, Royle	4
45	Feb	13	(h)	Derby C	W	1-0	Johnson	5
46	Mar	6	(h)	Colchester U	W	5-0	Kendall 2, Ball, Husband, Royle	6
47		27	(n)	Liverpool	L	1-2	Ball	(Old Trafford) SF

FA Cup Appearances
FA Cup Sub Appnces
FA Cup Goals

Everton played in the European Cup (see Everton in Europe section).

Ball A	Brown A	Darcy F	Darracott T	Davies D	Harvey C	Hurst J	Husband J	Jackson T	Johnson D	Jones G	Kendall H	Kenny W	Kenyon R	Labone B	Lyons M	Morrissey J	Newton H	Newton K	Rankin A	Royle J	West G	Whittle A	Wright T	No.
8					6	10					4			5		11		3		9	1	7	2	1
8	12				6*	10					4			5		11		3		9	1	7	2	2
8	6					10	7				4			5		11		3		9	1		2	3
8	6					10	7				4		5			11		3		9	1		2	4
8	12				6	10	7				4*			5				3		9	1	11	?	5
8					6	10	7				4			5		11		3		9	1		2	6
8	12				6	10	7				4			5		11*		3		9	1		2	7
8					6	10					4			5		11		3		9	1	7	2	8
8	12				6	10	7*				4			5		11		3	1	9			2	9
8*	12				6	10					4			5		11		3	1	9		7	2	10
8	12				6	10					4			5		11		3	1	9		7	2*	11
			2		6	10	8				4			5		11		3	1	9		7		12
8					6						4			5		11	10	3	1	9		7	2	13
8					6	10					4			5		11		3	1	9		7	2	14
8					6	10					4			5		11		3	1	9		7	2	15
8	12				6*	10					4		5			11	3		1	9		7	2	16
8	3					10					4		5			11	6		1	9		7	2	17
8					6	10					4*		5			11	3	12	1	9		7	2	18
8					6	10			11		4		5				3		1	9		7	2	19
8					6	10					4		5			11	3		1	9		7	2	20
8					6	10					4		5			11	3		1	9		7	2	21
8					6	10					4		5			11	3		1	9		7	2	22
8					6	10					4		5			11	3		1	9		7	2	23
8					6	10	7		9		4		5			11	3		1				2	24
8					6	10	7				4		5			11	3		1	9			2	25
8					6	10	7				4		12	5*		11	3		1	9			2	26
8					6	10	7				4		5			11	3		1	9			2	27
	9				6	10	7		11		4		5			8	3		1				2	28
8					6	10	7				4		5			11	3			9	1		2	29
8					6	10			11		4		5			7	3			9	1		2	30
8					6	10	7				4		5			11	3			9	1		2	31
8					6	10			11		4			5			3		1	9		7	2	32
8	4			1	6	10								5		7	3			9		11	2	33
	12			1		10					4	8*	7	5	6	11	3			9			2	34
8					6	10			11		4		5				3		1	9		7	2	35
8	6					10			12		4		5			11	3		1	9		7	2*	36
8	2	6				10	7				4		5			11	3		1	9				37
8	12				6	10	7				4*		5			11	3		1	9			2	38
8	4				6	10	7		11				5			12	3		1	9*			2	39
8					6	10			11		4		5				3		1	9		7	2	40
8					6	10			11		4		5				3		1	9		7	2	41
8					6		7				4		10	5		11	3		1	9			2	42
39	**6**	**2**	**2**	**2**	**36**	**40**	**15**	**1**	**10**	**1**	**40**	**1**	**28**	**16**	**1**	**34**	**23**	**21**	**28**	**40**	**12**	**24**	**40**	
	8	1					1							1				1						
2	1				2	3	6		1		2		1			6	3	1		17		7	2	
8					6	10	7				4			5		11	3		1	9			2	43
8					6	10	7				4			5		11	3		1	9			2	44
8					6	10	7		11		4		5				3			9	1		2	45
8	12				6	10	7				4		5			11	3		1	9			2*	46
8	12				6	10					4			5*		11		3	1	9		7	2	47
5	**2**				**5**	**5**	**4**		**1**		**5**		**2**	**3**		**4**	**4**	**1**	**4**	**5**	**1**	**1**	**5**	
2					1	3	1				2					1				2				

1971-72

1	Aug 14	(a)	Ipswich T	D	0-0		1	
2	18	(a)	West Brom A	L	0-2		1	
3	21	(h)	Sheffield U	L	0-1		1	21
4	24	(h)	Chelsea	W	2-0	Harvey 2	3	11
5	28	(a)	West Ham U	L	0-1		3	19
6	31	(h)	Manchester U	W	1-0	Johnson	5	14
7	Sep 4	(h)	Derby C	L	0-2		5	20
8	11	(a)	Wolves	D	1-1	Royle	6	19
9	18	(h)	Arsenal	W	2-1	Johnson, Royle	8	14
10	25	(a)	Crystal P	L	1-2	opp.og	8	15
11	Oct 2	(h)	Coventry C	L	1-2	Lyons	8	17
12	9	(a)	Manchester C	L	0-1		8	17
13	16	(h)	Ipswich T	D	1-1	Royle	9	19
14	23	(a)	Leeds U	L	2-3	Ball, Royle	9	19
15	30	(h)	Newcastle U	W	1-0	Ball	11	17
16	Nov 6	(a)	Tottenham H	L	0-3		11	18
17	13	(h)	Liverpool	W	1-0	Johnson	13	17
18	20	(h)	Southampton	W	8-0	Royle 4, Johnson 3, Ball	15	15
19	27	(a)	Leicester C	D	0-0		16	15
20	Dec 4	(h)	Stoke C	D	0-0		17	15
21	11	(a)	Nottingham F	L	0-1		17	15
22	18	(a)	Derby C	L	0-2		17	18
23	27	(h)	Huddersfield T	D	2-2	Johnson, Scott	18	16
24	Jan 1	(a)	Arsenal	D	1-1	Kendall	19	16
25	8	(h)	West Ham U	W	2-1	Harvey, Johnson	21	14
26	22	(h)	West Brom A	W	2-1	Husband, Kendall	23	13
27	29	(a)	Chelsea	L	0-4		23	15
28	Feb 12	(h)	Leeds U	D	0-0		24	16
29	19	(a)	Newcastle U	D	0-0		25	14
30	Mar 1	(h)	Tottenham H	D	1-1	H.Newton	26	14
31	4	(a)	Liverpool	L	0-4		26	14
32	8	(a)	Manchester U	D	0-0		27	14
33	11	(h)	Manchester C	L	1-2	Lyons	27	14
34	18	(a)	Sheffield U	D	1-1	B.Wright	28	15
35	21	(h)	Crystal P	D	0-0		29	13
36	25	(h)	Wolves	D	2-2	Kendall, Lyons	30	14
37	Apr 1	(a)	Huddersfield T	D	0-0		31	15
38	4	(a)	Coventry C	L	1-4	Johnson	31	15
39	8	(a)	Southampton	W	1-0	Buckley	33	15
40	15	(h)	Leicester C	D	0-0		34	15
41	22	(a)	Stoke C	D	1-1	Kendall	35	14
42	May 2	(h)	Nottingham F	D	1-1	Royle	36	15

League Appearances
League Sub Appnces
League Goals

43	Jan 15	(a)	Crystal P	D	2-2	Harvey, Whittle	FA Cup Rd 3
44	18	(h)	Crystal P	W	3-2	Hurst, Kenyon, Scott	Replay
45	Feb 5	(h)	Walsall	W	2-1	Johnson, Whittle	4
46	26	(h)	Tottenham H	L	0-2		5
47	Sep 7	(a)	Southampton	L	1-2	Johnson	League Cup Rd 2

Cup Appearances
Cup Sub Appnces
Cup Goals

	Ball A	Buckley M	Connolly J	Darracott T	Harvey C	Hurst J	Husband J	Johnson D	Jones G	Kendall H	Kenny W	Kenyon R	Labone B	Lyons M	McLaughlin J	Morrissey J	Newton H	Newton K	Royle J	Scott P	Seargeant S	West G	Whittle A	Wilson A	Wright B	Wright T
1	8				10	7				4	12	5			11		3		9	6		1			2*	
2	8	6			10	7	11			4		5					3		9	2		1				
3	8	6			10	7				4		5			11		3		9	2		1				
4	8	6			10	7	9			4		5*	12		11		3			2		1				
5	8				6*10	7	9			4	12	5			11		3			2		1				
6	8	6			10	7	9			4		5			11		3			2		1				
7	8	6			10	7	9			4*		5			11		3	12		2		1				
8	8	6			10		9			4		5					3		7	2		1	11			
9		6			10		9			8		5		4			3		7	2		1	11			
10		6			10		9	12		8*		5		4			3		7	2		1	11			
11		6			10		9					5	12		11		4	3		2		1	7	8*		
12		6			10		9			8*		5	12				4	3	7	2		1	11			
13					10	8	9	6				5	12				4	3	7	2		1	11*			
14	8				6*10		9					5			3	11	4	2	7	12		1				
15	8	6			10		9					5			3	11	4		7			1			2	
16	8	6			10		9					5			3	11	4		7			1			2	
17	8	6			10		9	7	11	4		5			3		2					1				
18	8				10	7				4		5			3		9	6				1	11		2	
19	8				10	7				4		5			3		9	6				1	11		2	
20	8				6*10	12	7			4		5			3		9					1	11		2	
21	8				10	7				4		5			3		6		9			1	11		2	
22	8				10	7				4		5			3		6		9			1	11		2	
23		6			10	7	8	11		4		5		12	3				9*	2		1				
24		6				11	7			4		5		8	3				9	2		1	10			
25		6	8*			7				4	12	5		10	3				9	2		1	11			
26		6	8			9*				4		5		3				12		2	10	1	11			
27		6	12		8	7				4*		5		10			3		9	2		1	11			
28	8				10	7	9			4		5			3			6				1	11		2	
29					10	7	9	11		4		5			3			6				1	8		2	
30		6				12	7	11*	4			5		10	3		8		9	2		1				
31	8	6				7	9*		4			5		10	3							1	11	12	2	
32	8	6							4	7		5		9	3					2		1	11	10		
33	8	6							4	7		5		9			3			2		1	12	11	10*	
34		6							4			5		10	3	11	8		9	2		1			7	
35		6							4			5		10	3	11	8		9	2		1			7	
36		8							4			5		10	3	11	6		9	2		1			7	
37		8			10	7			4			5		9	3		6			2		1	11			
38		8					7		4			5		10	3	11	6			2		1	9			
39		8			12	7	9		4			5		10	3	11*	6					1			2	
40		8	9			7	11		4			5		10	3		6					1			2	
41		8				7	11		4			5		10	3		6		9			1			2	
42		11			8	7			4			5		10	3		6		9			1			2	
	17	6	2	16	17	28	25	27	5	34	6	34	4	20	27	15	24	15	26	28	1	42	18	1	7	17
		1				1	2			1	1	2		4		1			2	1			1	1		
	3	1			3		1	9		4				3			1		9	1		1				opp.og 1
43					6	8				7		4	5	10	3				9	2		1	11			
44					6	8*12	7	9		4		5		10	3					2		1	11			
45		8			10	7			4			5			3		6		9			1	11		2	
46				12		7	11		4			5		10	3		6		9	2		1	8*			
47	8	6			10		9					5	4		3				7	2		1	11			
	1	3			3	2	1	5	1	4		4	1	4	4		2	1	4	4		5	5		1	
							2																			
						1	1			2				1						1			2			

1972-73

1	Aug 12 (a) Norwich C	D	1-1	Royle	1	
2	16 (a) Manchester C	W	1-0	Connolly	3	
3	19 (h) Manchester U	W	2-0	Connolly, Royle	5	3
4	22 (h) Crystal P	D	1-1	Royle	6	3
5	26 (a) Stoke C	D	1-1	Royle	7	4
6	29 (h) Derby C	W	1-0	Royle	9	2
7	Sep 2 (h) West Brom A	W	1-0	Royle	11	1
8	9 (a) Leicester C	W	2-1	Connolly, opp.og	13	1
9	16 (h) Southampton	L	0-1		13	1
10	23 (a) Birmingham C	L	1-2	Newton	13	3
11	30 (h) Newcastle U	W	3-1	Connolly, Johnson, Royle	15	3
12	Oct 7 (a) Liverpool	L	0-1		15	4
13	14 (h) Leeds U	L	1-2	Whittle	15	8
14	21 (a) Sheffield U	W	1-0	Whittle	17	5
15	28 (h) Ipswich	D	2-2	Kenyon, Whittle	18	6
16	Nov 4 (a) Crystal P	L	0-1		18	7
17	11 (h) Manchester C	L	2-3	Belfitt, Kenyon	18	10
18	18 (a) Arsenal	L	0-1		18	12
19	25 (h) West Ham U	L	1-2	B.Wright	18	14
20	Dec 2 (a) Coventry C	L	0-1		18	15
21	9 (h) Wolves	L	0-1		18	15
22	16 (h) Tottenham H	W	3-1	Kendall 2, Hurst	20	15
23	23 (a) Chelsea	D	1-1	Harper	21	15
24	26 (h) Birmingham C	D	1-1	Harper	22	13
25	Jan 6 (a) Stoke C	W	2-0	Buckley, Connolly	24	13
26	24 (a) Manchester U	D	0-0		25	13
27	27 (h) Leicester C	L	0-1		25	14
28	Feb 10 (a) Southampton	D	0-0		26	14
29	24 (a) Tottenham H	L	0-3		26	14
30	Mar 3 (h) Liverpool	L	0-2		26	15
31	10 (a) Leeds U	L	1-2	Lyons	26	16
32	17 (h) Sheffield U	W	2-1	Harper, Lyons	28	15
33	24 (a) Ipswich T	W	1-0	Harper	30	15
34	31 (a) West Ham U	L	0-2		30	17
35	Apr 3 (a) Norwich C	D	2-2	Belfitt, Kendall	31	15
36	7 (h) Coventry C	W	2-0	Harper 2	33	15
37	11 (a) West Brom A	L	1-4	Bernard	33	15
38	14 (a) Wolves	L	2-4	Connolly, Harper	33	17
39	17 (h) Chelsea	W	1-0	Kendall	35	15
40	21 (h) Arsenal	D	0-0		36	15
41	25 (a) Newcastle U	D	0-0		37	16
42	28 (a) Derby C	L	1-3	Connolly	37	17

					League Appearances	
					League Sub Appnces	
					League Goals	

43	Jan 13 (h) Aston Villa	W	3-2	Belfitt, Buckley, Harper	FA Cup Rd 3	
44	Feb 3 (h) Millwall	L	0-2		4	
45	Sep 5 (a) Arsenal	L	0-1		League Cup Rd 2	
					Cup Appearances	
					Cup Goals	

Belfitt R	Bernard M	Buckley M	Connolly J	Darracott T	Harper J	Harvey C	Hurst J	Husband J	Johnson D	Jones G	Kendall H	Kenyon R	Lawson D	Lyons M	McLaughlin J	Newton H	Royle J	Scott P	Seargeant S	Styles A	West G	Whittle A	Wilson A	Wright B	Wright T	No.
	8	11				10		7			4	5	1	6		3	9								2	1
	8	11*				10		7	12		4	5	1	6			9							3	2	2
	8	11				10		7			4		1	6		3	9	5						3		3
	8	11				10		7			4		1	6		3	9	5							2	4
	8	11				10			7		4	5	1			3	9								2	5
	8	11				10			7		4	5	1			3	9					6			2	6
	8	11				10			7		4	5	1			3	9		6						2	7
	8	11				10*			7		4	5	1		12	3	9		6						2	8
	8	11				10			7		4	5	1	6		3	9								2	9
	8	11				10			7		4	5	1	6		3	9								2	10
	8	11				10		7	12		4*	5	1			3	9		6						2	11
	8	11				10		7	6		4*	5	1		12	3	9								2	12
	8	11				10*		7	6		4	5	1			3	9						12		2	13
	8	11				10			6		4	5	1			3	9	2				7				14
	8	11				10			6	9	4	5	1			3		2				7				15
9	8	11				10			6		4	5	1			3		2				7				16
9		11	8			10			6	12	4	5	1			3		2				7*				17
9		11	8			10		7	6		4	5	1			3	12	2							2*	18
9		11	8			10			6		4	5	1			3		2				7				19
9	8	11	12			10					4	5	1		6*	3						7			2	20
9	12	11	8			10			6		4*	5	1						3			7				21
9	8	10*	11	7	12				6		4	5	1						3						2	22
9	8	11	7		10*				6		4	5	1		12				3						2	23
9	8	10	11		7				6		4	5	1		12				3						2*	24
9	8	10	11		7				6		4	5	1						3						2	25
9	8	10	11		7				6		4	5	1						3						2	26
9	8	10	11		7				6		4*	5	1		12				3						2	27
		11			9	10		6		7		5	1		4	8				3					2	28
	12	11			9	10	4*			7	8	5	1	6						3					2	29
		11	6		9		4			7	8	5	1	10						3					2	30
9		11	12		6*	4				7	8	5	1	10						3					2	31
	6	11	12	10	4	7	8*				5	1	9							3					2	32
		11	7	10	4				8	5	1	9	6*					12		3					2	33
12		7	11	6	10	4				8	5	1	9*						3					2	34
9*	8	11	12	10	6	7				4	5	1		3						3					2	35
	6	11	7	10	4			9	8	5	1								3						2	36
	10		6	9	4	7	11		8	5	1*	12							3						2	37
	6	11	12	10	4	7	8		5	9	3*	1													2*	38
	6	11	12	10	4	7	8		5	9	2	3*	1													39
	6	11	3	10	7	8		5	9	2		4	1													40
	6	11	3	10	12	7	8*		5	9	2		4	1												41
12	6	11	3*	10		7	5	1	9	2	4	8														42
14	**30**	**9**	**41**	**11**	**20**	**24**	**28**	**8**	**10**	**11**	**40**	**40**	**38**	**19**	**7**	**23**	**14**	**8**	**8**	**16**	**4**	**5**	**1**	**3**	**30**	
2	2		5		2	1	1	1	1						6				1		1		1			
2	1	1	7		7	1		1			4	2		2		1	7			3		1		opp.og 1		
9	8	10	11		7	6					4	5	1							3					2	43
9	8	10	11		7	6					4	5	1							3					2	44
	8	11				10		7			4	5	1	6		3	9								2	45
2	**3**	**2**	**3**		**2**	**1**	**2**		**1**		**3**	**3**	**3**	**1**		**1**	**1**		**2**						**3**	
1		1				1																				

1973-74

	Date		Opponent	Res	Score	Scorers		
1	Aug 25	(a)	Leeds U	L	1-3	Harper	0	
2	28	(h)	Leicester C	D	1-1	Kenyon	1	
3	Sep 1	(h)	Ipswich T	W	3-0	Connolly, Harper, Hurst	3	10
4	5	(a)	Stoke C	D	0-0		4	11
5	8	(a)	Derby C	L	1-2	Husband	4	11
6	11	(h)	Stoke C	D	1-1	Harper	5	12
7	15	(h)	Q.P.R.	W	1-0	Lyons	7	10
8	22	(a)	Wolves	D	1-1	Royle	8	11
9	29	(h)	Arsenal	W	1-0	McLaughlin	10	8
10	Oct 6	(a)	Coventry C	W	2-1	Connolly, Lyons	12	6
11	13	(h)	West Ham U	W	1-0	Harper	14	5
12	20	(h)	Burnley	W	1-0	Clements	16	4
13	27	(a)	Birmingham C	W	2-0	Connolly, Harper	18	2
14	Nov 3	(h)	Tottenham H	D	1-1	Connolly	19	3
15	10	(a)	Chelsea	L	1-3	Kenyon	19	5
16	17	(a)	Norwich C	W	3-1	Bernard, Clements, opp.og	21	4
17	24	(h)	Newcastle U	D	1-1	Lyons	22	4
18	Dec 1	(a)	Southampton	L	0-2		22	5
19	8	(h)	Liverpool	L	0-1		22	5
20	15	(h)	Sheffield U	D	1-1	Clements	23	4
21	22	(a)	Arsenal	L	0-1		23	7
22	26	(h)	Manchester U	W	2-0	Buckley, Hurst	25	4
23	29	(h)	Derby C	W	2-1	Buckley, Royle	27	4
24	Jan 1	(a)	Ipswich T	L	0-3		27	5
25	12	(a)	Q.P.R.	L	0-1		27	8
26	19	(h)	Leeds U	D	0-0		28	8
27	Feb 2	(a)	Sheffield U	D	1-1	Bernard	29	8
28	9	(h)	Wolves	W	2-1	Bernard, Lyons	31	5
29	16	(a)	West Ham U	L	3-4	Telfer 2, Harvey	31	6
30	23	(h)	Coventry C	W	1-0	Hurst	33	5
31	Mar 2	(a)	Leicester C	L	1-2	Latchford	33	7
32	9	(h)	Birmingham C	W	4-1	Latchford 2, Lyons 2	35	5
33	16	(a)	Burnley	L	1-3	Latchford	35	6
34	23	(a)	Chelsea	D	1-1	Bernard	36	6
35	30	(a)	Tottenham H	W	2-0	Connolly, Latchford	38	6
36	Apr 2	(a)	Manchester C	D	1-1	Lyons	39	6
37	6	(a)	Newcastle U	L	1-2	Latchford	39	6
38	13	(h)	Norwich C	W	4-1	Buckley, Latchford, Lyons, Telfer	41	7
39	15	(a)	Manchester U	L	0-3		41	7
40	20	(a)	Liverpool	D	0-0		42	8
41	23	(h)	Manchester U	W	1-0	Lyons	44	6
42	27	(h)	Southampton	L	0-3		44	7

							League Appearances
							League Sub Appnces
							League Goals

	Date		Opponent	Res	Score	Scorers		
43	Jan 5	(h)	Blackburn R	W	3-0	Clements, Harper, Hurst	FA Cup Rd 3	
44	27	(h)	West Brom A	D	0-0			4
45	30	(a)	West Brom A	L	0-1		Replay	
46	Oct 8	(h)	Reading	W	1-0	Buckley	League Cup Rd 2	
47	30	(h)	Norwich C	L	0-1			3

							Cup Appearances
							Cup Sub Appnces
							Cup Goals

Everton played in the Texaco Cup (see Other Matches section).

Bernard M	Buckley M	Clements D	Connolly J	Darracott T	Harper J	Harvey C	Hurst J	Husband J	Irving D	Jones G	Kendall H	Kenny W	Kenyon R	Latchford R	Lawson D	Lyons M	McLaughlin J	Newton H	Royle J	Seargeant S	Smith J	Styles A	Telfer G	#
	10		11	3	8	7	6						5		1	4	2		9					1
			11	2	10	7	6				4		5		1	12	3*	8	9					2
12			11	2	10	7*	6				4		5		1	8	3		9					3
8			11	2	10	7	6				4		5		1	9	3							4
8			11	2	10	7		4	12		6*		5		1	9	3							5
4			11	2	10		6						5		1	8	3	7	9					6
4*			11	2	10		6	12					5		1	8	3	7	9					7
	7	4	11	2	10		6						5		1	8			9	3				8
	8	4	11	2	10	7*	6		12				5		1	9	3							9
12	7	4	11	2	10		6				8*		5		1	9	3							10
7	8	4	11	2	10		6		12				5		1	9*	3							11
7	8	4	11	2	10		6		12				5		1	9*	3							12
7	8	4	11	2	10		6						5		1	9	3							13
7	8	4	11	2	10		6						5		1	9	3							14
8	10	4	11	2	7		6						5		1	9	3							15
7	8	4	11	2	10		6						5		1	9	3							16
7	10	4	11	2	8		6						5		1		3		9					17
7	10	4	11	2	8*		6		12				5		1		3		9					18
7	10	4	11	2	8		6						5		1		3		9					19
7	8	4	11	2			6						5		1	10			9	3				20
7	8*	4		2	12		6						5		1	10			9	3			11	21
7	8	4		2			6						5		1	10			9	3			11	22
7	8	4		2			6						5		1	10			9	3			11	23
7	8	4		2	12		6						5		1	10			9	3			11*	24
8		4		2	11		6			10			5*		1	12	3		9	7				25
7	8	4	11*	2	12		6			10			5		1		3		9					26
7	8	6*		2	12					10		4	5		1				9	3			11	27
6	8*			2		7				10	12	4	5		1	9	3						11	28
6	8			2		7				10		4	5	9	1		3						11	29
4	7*			2		8	6			10			5	9	1	12	3						11	30
4	8			2		7	6			10			5	9	1	12	3						11*	31
7	8	6	11	2								4	5	9	1	10	3							32
7	8	6	11	2								4	5	9	1	10	3							33
7	8	6	11	2						10		4	5		1	9	3							34
2	8	6	11		7					12		4	5	9*	1	10	3							35
2	8	6	11		7					12		4	5	9*	1	10	3							36
2	8	4			7		6						5	9	1	10	3						11	37
7	8	6		2								4	5	9	1	10	3						11	38
7	8*	6		2						12		4	5	9	1	10	3						11	39
2		4			7		6	8					5	9	1	10	3						11	40
2		4			7		6	8					5	9	1	10	3						11	41
2	8	3					6			10		4	5		1				9	7			11	42
35	33	31	26	36	20	15	39	1		10	7	1	36	13	42	37	21	6	18	12	2	6	15	
2		3	1					3	2	3	1					4				1				
4	3	3	5		5	1	3	1					2	7		9	1		2			3	opp.og 1	
7	8	4		2	11		6		12				5		1	10			9	3				43
7	8	4		2	11		6			10*			5		1		3		9			12		44
7	8			2			6			10		4	5		1				9	3			11	45
7	8	4	11	2	10								5		1	9	3							46
7	8	4		2	10		6	11*	12				5		1		3		9					47
5	5	4	1	5	4		5	1		2		1	3		5	4	3		4	2		1		
									1													1		
	1	1			1		1																	

1974-75

	Date		Opponent	Res	Score	Scorers	App	Gls
1	Aug 17	(h)	Derby C	D	0-0		1	
2	20	(h)	Stoke C	W	2-1	Royle 2	3	
3	24	(a)	West Ham U	W	3-2	Harvey, Latchford, Royle	5	5
4	28	(a)	Stoke C	D	1-1	Latchford	6	4
5	31	(h)	Arsenal	W	2-1	Latchford 2	8	3
6	Sep 7	(a)	Ipswich T	L	0-1		8	5
7	14	(h)	Wolves	D	0-0		9	6
8	21	(a)	Coventry C	D	1-1	Latchford	10	5
9	24	(a)	Q.P.R.	D	2-2	Latchford, Pearson	11	4
10	28	(h)	Leeds U	W	3-2	Clements, Lyons, Seargeant	13	4
11	Oct 5	(h)	Newcastle U	D	1-1	Buckley	14	4
12	12	(a)	Sheffield U	D	2-2	Buckley, Lyons	15	3
13	15	(h)	West Ham U	D	1-1	Lyons	16	5
14	19	(h)	Chelsea	D	1-1	Jones	17	4
15	26	(a)	Burnley	D	1-1	Jones	18	5
16	Nov 2	(h)	Manchester C	W	2-0	Connolly, Jones	20	3
17	9	(a)	Tottenham H	D	1-1	Connolly	21	3
18	16	(h)	Liverpool	D	0-0		22	3
19	30	(h)	Birmingham C	W	4-1	Connolly, Dobson, Jones, Lyons	24	4
20	Dec 7	(a)	Leicester C	W	2-0	Hurst, Telfer	26	2
21	14	(a)	Derby C	W	1-0	Latchford	28	1
22	21	(h)	Carlisle U	L	2-3	Latchford 2	28	4
23	26	(a)	Wolves	L	0-2		28	4
24	28	(h)	Middlesbrough	D	1-1	Latchford	29	4
25	Jan 11	(h)	Leicester C	W	3-0	Jones, Lyons, Pearson	31	2
26	18	(a)	Birmingham C	W	3-0	Latchford 2, opp.og	33	1
27	Feb 1	(h)	Tottenham H	W	1-0	Pearson	35	1
28	8	(a)	Manchester C	L	1-2	opp.og	35	1
29	22	(a)	Liverpool	D	0-0		36	3
30	25	(h)	Luton T	W	3-1	Dobson, Latchford, Telfer	38	1
31	Mar 1	(a)	Arsenal	W	2-0	Dobson, Lyons	40	1
32	8	(h)	Q.P.R.	W	2-1	Latchford, Lyons	42	1
33	15	(a)	Leeds U	D	0-0		43	1
34	18	(a)	Middlesbrough	L	0-2		43	1
35	22	(h)	Ipswich T	D	1-1	Lyons	44	1
36	29	(a)	Carlisle U	L	0-3		44	2
37	31	(h)	Coventry C	W	1-0	Dobson	46	1
38	Apr 4	(h)	Burnley	D	1-1	Latchford	47	1
39	9	(a)	Luton T	L	1-2	Latchford	47	3
40	12	(a)	Newcastle U	W	1-0	Dobson	49	3
41	19	(h)	Sheffield U	L	2-3	Jones, Smallman	49	3
42	26	(a)	Chelsea	D	1-1	Latchford	50	4

League Appearances
League Sub Appnces
League Goals

	Date		Opponent	Res	Score	Scorers		
43	Jan 4	(h)	Altrincham	D	1-1	Clements	FA Cup Rd 3	
44	7	(a)	Altrincham	W	2-0	Latchford, Lyons	(Old Trafford) Replay	
45	25	(a)	Plymouth A	W	3-1	Lyons 2, Pearson		4
46	Feb 15	(h)	Fulham	L	1-2	Kenyon		5
47	Sep 11	(a)	Aston Villa	D	1-1	Latchford	League Cup Rd 2	
48	18	(h)	Aston Villa	L	0-3		Replay	

Cup Appearances
Cup Sub Appncés
Cup Goals

Bernard M	Buckley M	Clements D	Connolly J	Darracott T	Davies D	Dobson M	Harvey C	Hurst J	Irving D	Jones G	Latchford R	Lawson D	Lyons M	Kenny W	Kenyon R	McLaughlin J	McNaught K	Marshall C	Pearson J	Royle J	Scott P	Seargeant S	Smallman D	Telfer G	No.
2	7	4	11				8	6			10	1			5					9	3				1
	7	4	11	2			8*	6			10	1	12		5					9	3				2
	7	4	11	2			8	6			10	1			5					9	3				3
	7	4	11	2			8	6			10	1			5					9	3				4
	7	4	11	2		8		6*			10	1	12		5					9	3				5
	7	4	11	2		8					10	1	6		5					9	3				6
2	7	4	11			8					10	1	6		5					9		3			7
2	6	11	12		1	8					10		4	7*	5				9			3			8
2	6	11	12		1	8					10		4	7*	5				9			3			9
2	7	6	11		1	8				12	10*		4		5				9			3			10
2	7	6	11		1	8					10		4		5				9			3			11
2	7	6	11		1	8				12	10*		4		5				9			3			12
2	7	6	11		1	8							4		5				9	10		3			13
2	7	6	11		1	8				12	10		4		5				9*			3			14
2	7*		11		1	8		6			9		4		5	12			10			3			15
2	7	4	11		1	8		6			10				5				9			3			16
2	7	4	11		1	8		6			10				5				9			3			17
2	7*	4	11		1	8		6			10				5				9	12		3			18
2		4	11		1	8		6		7	10				5				9			3			19
2		4	11		1	8*		6		7	10				5				9			3	12		20
2		4	11		1			6		7	10				5				9	12		3	8*		21
2	12	4	11		1			6		7	10				5				9			3	8*		22
2	8	4	11		1			6		7	10				5				9	12		3*			23
2	8	4	11		1				9	7	10		6		5*							3		12	24
		4			1					7	10		8		5	3	6		9			2		11	25
12	8*	3			1						10		4		5		6	7	9			2		11	26
		4			1	8					10		9		5		6	7*	12		3	2		11	27
12		4			1	8					10		9		5		6	7			3	2*		11	28
2		4			1	8		6		7	9		10		5				12			3		11*	29
2	12	4			1	8		6		7	10		9		5							3		11*	30
2	7	4			1	8		6		11	10		9		5							3			31
2	7*	4			1	8		6		11	10		9		5				12			3			32
2		4			1	8		6		7	10		9		5							3		11	33
2		4*			1	8		6		7	10		9		5				12			3		11	34
	7	4			1			6		11	10		9		5				8		2	3			35
	7	4*			1	8		6		11	10		9		5				12		2	3			36
2		4			1	8		6		7	9		10		5				12			3		11*	37
2		4	12		1	8		6		7	9		10		5				11			3*			38
2		4	3		1	8		6		7	9				5				11					10	39
2		4	3		1	8		6		7	9				5				11				10*	12	40
2		4	3		1	8		6		7	9				5				11*				10	12	41
2		4	3		1			6		7	9		8		5				11					10	42
31	**31**	**39**	**22**	**5**	**35**	**30**	**4**	**29**	**1**	**25**	**36**	**7**	**36**	**2**	**40**	**2**	**4**	**2**	**17**	**8**	**6**	**35**	**4**	**11**	Total
2	2	1	2					2		1			2			1			9				4		Sub
	2	1	3			5	1	1		6	17		8				3	3		1	1	2			Goals (opp.og 2)
2		4	11*		1			9		7	10		6		5	3			8					12	43
		4			1	8				7	10		6		5	3			9		2			11	44
12		4			1	8					10				5	6	7*	9			2	3		11	45
2		4			1	8		6		7	10*				5				9		3	11		12	46
2	7	4	11			8					10	1	6		5				9			3			47
2	7	4*	11			8					10	1	6		5		12		9			3			48
4	**2**	**6**	**3**		**4**	**5**		**1**	**1**	**3**	**5**	**2**	**6**		**4**	**2**	**3**	**1**	**4**	**2**	**2**	**4**		**2**	Cup Total
1						1					2		3		1				1						Cup Goals

1975-76

1	Aug 16	(h)	Coventry C	L	1-4	Kenyon	0	
2	19	(a)	Burnley	D	1-1	Smallman	1	
3	23	(a)	Birmingham C	W	1-0	Smallman	3	14
4	26	(h)	Sheffield U	W	3-0	Latchford, Lyons, Smallman	5	10
5	30	(h)	Derby C	W	2-0	Latchford, Lyons	7	4
6	Sep 6	(a)	Norwich C	L	2-4	Latchford, Pearson	7	10
7	13	(h)	Newcastle U	W	3-0	Clements, Latchford, Lyons	9	5
8	20	(a)	Arsenal	D	2-2	Buckley, Smallman	10	5
9	27	(h)	Liverpool	D	0-0		11	9
10	Oct 4	(a)	West Ham U	W	1-0	G.Jones	13	7
11	11	(a)	Q.P.R.	L	0-5		13	9
12	18	(h)	Aston Villa	W	2-1	G.Jones 2	15	8
13	25	(a)	Wolves	W	2-1	Dobson, G.Jones	17	7
14	Nov 1	(h)	Leicester C	D	1-1	Smallman	18	6
15	8	(a)	Stoke C	L	2-3	Pearson, Telfer	18	10
16	15	(h)	Manchester C	D	1-1	Telfer	19	10
17	22	(a)	Aston Villa	L	1-3	Telfer	19	10
18	29	(a)	Leeds U	L	2-5	Clements, Latchford	19	11
19	Dec 6	(h)	Ipswich T	D	3-3	Dobson 2, Latchford	20	10
20	10	(a)	Tottenham H	D	2-2	Latchford, Telfer	21	9
21	13	(h)	Birmingham C	W	5-2	Dobson, Hamilton, G.Jones, Latchford, Telfer	23	9
22	19	(a)	Coventry C	W	2-1	G.Jones, Latchford	25	9
23	23	(h)	Manchester U	D	1-1	Latchford	26	8
24	27	(a)	Middlesbrough	D	1-1	Latchford	27	9
25	Jan 10	(a)	Newcastle U	L	0-5		27	11
26	17	(h)	Norwich C	D	1-1	Dobson	28	11
27	31	(h)	Burnley	L	2-3	Hamiton 2	28	11
28	Feb 7	(a)	Sheffield U	D	0-0		29	12
29	21	(a)	Manchester C	l	0-3		29	15
30	24	(h)	Tottenham H	W	1-0	Lyons	31	10
31	28	(h)	Wolves	W	3-0	Telfer 2, Hamilton	33	8
32	Mar 6	(a)	Leicester C	L	0-1		33	10
33	13	(h)	Q.P.R.	L	0-2		33	12
34	20	(h)	Leeds U	L	1-3	Lyons	33	14
35	27	(a)	Ipswich T	L	0-1		33	16
36	Apr 3	(a)	Liverpool	L	0-1		33	16
37	7	(h)	Stoke C	W	2-1	Bernard, Hamilton	35	14
38	10	(h)	Arsenal	D	0-0		36	13
39	17	(a)	Manchester U	L	1-2	Telfer	36	16
40	19	(h)	Middlesbrough	W	3-1	Connolly, Latchford, Pearson	38	13
41	21	(a)	Derby C	W	3-1	King 2, Pearson	40	12
42	24	(h)	West Ham U	W	2-0	Bernard, Pearson	42	11

League Appearances
League Sub Appnces
League Goals

43	Jan 3	(a)	Derby C	L	1-2	G.Jones	FA Cup Rd 3
44	Sep 9	(h)	Arsenal	D	2-2	Lyons, Smallman	League Cup Rd 2
45	23	(a)	Arsenal	W	1-0	Kenyon	Replay
46	Oct 8	(h)	Carlisle U	W	2-0	Dobson, Latchford	3
47	Nov 11	(h)	Notts Co	D	2-2	Irving, G.Jones	4
48	25	(a)	Notts Co	L	0-2		Replay

Cup Appearances
Cup Sub Appnces
Cup Goals

Everton played in UEFA Cup (see Everton in Europe section).

Bernard M	Brand D	Buckley M	Clements D	Connolly J	Darracott T	Davies D	Dobson M	Goodlass R	Hamilton B	Hurst J	Irving D	Jones D	Jones G	Kenyon R	King A	Latchford R	Lawson D	Lyons M	McLaughlin J	McNaught K	Marshall C	Pearson J	Robinson N	Seargeant S	Smallman D	Telfer G	No.
2		4					8		6					5		9	1	7			11			3	10		1
2		4					8							5		9	1	6		7	11			3	10		2
		7	3		2		8			12				5		9	1	6		11*	4				10		3
2		7	3				8							5		9	1	6		11*	4				10	12	4
2		7	3				8							5		9	1	6		11*	4				10	12	5
2		7	3				8						11	5		9	1	6			4				10		6
2		7	12				8						11	5		9	1	6			4*			3	10		7
2		7					8						11	5		9	1	6			4			3	10		8
		7	3			1	8						11	5		9		6	2		4			3	10		9
		7	3			1	8						11	5		9		6		12	4*			2	10		10
2		7	10			1	8						11	5		9		6			4			3			11
2		7*	10			1	8						11			9		6		5	4			3	12		12
2		7				1	8						11	5*		9		6		12	4			3	10		13
		7				1	8					12	11*			9		6	2	5	4			3	10		14
		7*			2	1	8						11		9			6		5	4			3	10	12	15
		7			2		8								9*	11	1	6		5	4			3	10	12	16
		7			2*		8						11		4	9	1	6		5	12			3	10		17
	1	7*	4		2		8		10					5		9		6		12				3		11	18
4		3			2		8	7*					11	5		9	1	6		12					10		19
4		12			2	1	8	7					11	5		9		6						3*		10	20
2		7	3			1	8					4	11	5		9		6							10		21
2		7	3			1	8			4		12	11	5		9		6							10*		22
2			3			1	8		11			7	4	5		9		6							10		23
2			3*			1	8		7			4	11	5		9		6		12					10		24
2		12	3			1	8		7			4	11*	5		9		6							10		25
2		6			3		8		7			12	11	5		9	1	4							10*		26
		6					8		7				11	5		9	1	4		2				3	10		27
		6		10	2		8		7								1	4				5		9	3	11	28
2				10	3		8		7	6		9	12	5*			1	4								11	29
2		6		10	3		8		7				11				1	4				5				9	30
2		6			3		8		10	7			11				1	4				5				9	31
2		6		10			8		7			3	11				1	4				5				9	32
2		6		10*			8		12	7		3	11				1	4				5				9	33
2		6		10			8		7			3	11*				1	4				5		12		9	34
2		6		10			8		7			3					1	4				5	11			9	35
2		6		10		1	8		7			3	12			9		4				5*				11	36
2				10		1	8		7			3				6		4				5		9		11	37
2				10		1	8		7*			3	12			9		4				5		6		11	38
		7*		10	2	1	8		12			3	6			9		4				5				11	39
				10	2	1	8		7*	12		3		5		6	9	4								11	40
12				10	2	1	8					3		5*		6	9	4				7				11	41
2		7		10			8					3		6		9	1	4				5				11	42
29	**1**	**30**	**11**	**14**	**20**	**19**	**42**	**2**	**22**	**6**	**3**	**11**	**24**	**28**	**3**	**31**	**22**	**42**	**2**	**18**	**4**	**26**	**1**	**17**	**14**	**20**	
	1	1	1	1					1	1	3					2	1	2				1	2		3	1 1 4	
2		1	2	1			5		5				8	1	2	12		5				5			5	8	
2		12	3			1	8		7			4	11	5		9		6							10*		43
2		7	3				8						11	5		9	1	6			4				10		44
2		7				1	8						11	5		9		6			4			3	10		45
12		7	3			1	8						11	5		9		6			4			2		10*	46
		7	3*		2		8			4		9	11				1	6		5	10					12	47
		7	3				8						11	5		9	1	6			4*			2	12	10	48
3	**5**	**4**		**2**	**3**	**6**	**1**	**2**	**1**	**6**	**5**	**5**	**3**	**6**	**1**	**6**	**3**	**2**	**2**								
1		1			1		1			2	1			1		1								1			

1976-77

#	Date		Opponent	Res	Score	Scorers	App	Goals
1	Aug 21	(a)	Q.P.R.	W	4-0	Latchford 2, Bernard, opp.og	2	
2	24	(h)	Ipswich T	D	1-1	Telfer	3	
3	28	(h)	Aston Villa	L	0-2		3	10
4	Sep 4	(a)	Leicester C	D	1-1	Latchford	4	7
5	11	(h)	Stoke C	W	3-0	Telfer 2, Latchford	6	5
6	18	(a)	Arsenal	L	1-3	Telfer	6	9
7	25	(h)	Bristol C	W	2-0	Dobson, Latchford	8	6
8	Oct 2	(a)	Sunderland	W	1-0	Goodlass	10	5
9	5	(h)	Manchester C	D	2-2	Dobson, King	11	2
10	16	(a)	Liverpool	L	1-3	Dobson	11	6
11	23	(h)	West Ham U	W	3-2	King, Latchford, Lyons	13	4
12	30	(a)	Tottenham H	D	3-3	King, Latchford, McNaught	14	8
13	Nov 6	(h)	Leeds U	L	0-2		14	8
14	20	(h)	Derby C	W	2-0	King, Latchford	16	7
15	24	(a)	Newcastle U	L	1-4	Lyons	16	7
16	27	(a)	West Brom A	L	0-3		16	10
17	Dec 11	(a)	Coventry C	L	2-4	Kenyon, King	16	13
18	18	(h)	Birmingham C	D	2-2	McKenzie 2	17	13
19	27	(a)	Manchester U	L	0-4		17	14
20	29	(h)	Middlesbrough	D	2-2	Latchford, McNaught	18	13
21	Jan 15	(a)	Ipswich T	L	0-2		18	15
22	22	(h)	Q.P.R.	L	1-3	McKenzie	18	18
23	Feb 5	(a)	Aston Villa	L	0-2		18	18
24	12	(h)	Leicester C	L	1-2	Latchford	18	18
25	19	(a)	Stoke C	W	1-0	Dobson	20	16
26	Mar 1	(h)	Arsenal	W	2-1	Jones, Latchford	22	16
27	5	(a)	Bristol C	W	2-1	Latchford, opp.og	24	15
28	22	(h)	Liverpool	D	0-0		25	16
29	26	(h)	Tottenham H	W	4-0	Dobson, King, Latchford, Lyons	27	14
30	Apr 2	(a)	West Ham U	D	2-2	Goodlass, Pearson	28	14
31	5	(h)	Manchester U	L	1-2	Dobson	28	14
32	9	(a)	Middlesbrough	D	2-2	Latchford, Pearson	29	14
33	16	(a)	Derby C	W	3-2	Latchford, McKenzie, Pejic	31	14
34	19	(h)	Norwich C	W	3-1	King, McNaught, Pearson	33	13
35	30	(a)	Norwich C	L	1-2	Pearson	33	14
36	May 4	(a)	Leeds U	D	0-0		33	14
37	7	(h)	Coventry C	D	1-1	Rioch	35	13
38	10	(a)	Manchester C	D	1-1	Lyons	36	14
39	14	(a)	Birmingham C	D	1-1	Latchford	37	14
40	16	(h)	West Brom A	D	1-1	Dobson	38	12
41	19	(h)	Sunderland	W	2-0	Latchford, Rioch	40	12
42	24	(h)	Newcastle U	W	2-0	Dobson, McKenzie	42	9

League Appearances
League Sub Appnces
League Goals

#	Date		Opponent	Res	Score	Scorers		
43	Jan 8	(h)	Stoke C	W	2-0	Lyons, McKenzie	FA Cup Rd 3	
44	29	(h)	Swindon T	D	2-2	Latchford, McKenzie		4
45	Feb 1	(h)	Swindon T	W	2-1	Dobson, Jones	Replay	
46	26	(a)	Cardiff C	W	2-1	Latchford, McKenzie		5
47	Mar 19	(h)	Derby C	W	2-0	Latchford, Pearson		6
48	Apr 23	(n)	Liverpool	D	2-2	McKenzie, Rioch	(Maine Road)	SF
49	27	(n)	Liverpool	L	0-3		(Maine Road) Replay	
50	Aug 30	(a)	Cambridge U	W	3-0	Dobson, King, Latchford	League Cup Rd 2	
51	Sep 20	(a)	Stockport C	W	1-0	Latchford		3
52	Oct 26	(h)	Coventry C	W	3-0	King 2, Lyons		4
53	Dec 1	(a)	Manchester U	W	3-0	King 2, Dobson		5
54	Jan 18	(h)	Bolton W	D	1-1	McKenzie	1st leg SF	
55	Feb 15	(a)	Bolton W	W	1-0	Latchford	2nd leg	
56	Mar 12	(n)	Aston Villa	D	0-0		(Wembley)	F
57	16	(n)	Aston Villa	D	1-1	Latchford	(Hillsborough) Replay	
58	Apr 13	(n)	Aston Villa	L	2-3	Latchford, Lyons	(Old Trafford) Replay	

Cup Appearances
Cup Sub Appnces
Cup Goals

Bernard M	Brand D	Buckley M	Darracott T	Davies D	Dobson M	Goodlass R	Hamilton B	Higgins M	Jones D	Kenyon R	King A	Latchford R	Lawson D	Lyons M	McKenzie D	McNaught K	Pearson J	Pejic M	Rioch B	Robinson N	Seargeant S	Smallman D	Telfer G	No.
			2	1	8				3	5	7	9		4		6	10						11	1
			2	1	8					6	7	9		4		5	10				3		11	2
			2	1	8				3	6	7	9		4		5	10*				12		11	3
			2	1	8	10			3	6	7	9		4		5							11	4
			2	1	8	10			3	6	7	9		4		5							11	5
2*	12			1	8	10			3	6	7	9		4		5							11	6
			2	1	8	10	6		3		7	9		4		5							11	7
			2	1	8	10	6		3		7	9		4		5							11	8
				1	8	10	6		3	2	7	9		4		5							11	9
6*			2	1	8	10			3		7	9		4		5	12						11	10
			2	1	8*	10	6		3		7	9		4		5	12						11	11
2		12		1	8	10	6		3		7	9		4		5							11*	12
2		12		1	8	10			3	6	7	9		4		5							11*	13
			2	1	8	10			3	6	7	9		4		5							11	14
2		12		1	8	10			3	6	7*	9		4		5							11	15
			2	1	8	10	11		3	6	7	9		4*		5	12							16
			2	1	8	11			3	6	7	9			10	5			4					17
			2		8	11			3		7	9	1	4	10	5			6					18
			2		8	11			3		7	9	1	4	10	5			6					19
					8	11			2		7	9	1	4	10	5			6	3				20
					8	11			2		7	9	1	4	10	5			6	3				21
			2*		8	11	12		3		7	9	1	4	10	5			6					22
			2		8	11			3		7	9	1	4	10	5			6					23
			2		8	12	11		3		7*	9	1	4	10	5			6					24
					8	11	7		2			9	1	6	10	5			4	3				25
					8	11	7		2			9	1	4	10	5			6	3				26
					8	11	7		2	6		9	1	4	10	5				3				27
			2		8		7*			6		9	1	4	10	5	11		3		12			28
			2		8	11				6		9	1	4	10	5			7	3				29
6					8	11	7		2			9	1	4		5	12			3	10*			30
12			2		8	11			3*	6	7	9	1	4	10	5								31
			2		8	11				6	4*	9	1	12	10	5			7	3				32
12				1	8	11	7					9*		4	10	5		3	6	2				33
12				1	8	11	6*					9		4	10	5		3	7	2				34
		7	2	1		11*	12				8			4	10	5	9	3	6					35
		7	2	1	8	11								4	10	5	9	3	6					36
		7	2	1	8	11								4	10	5	9	3	6					37
		7	2	1	8	12								4	10	5	9	3	6		11*			38
12		7	2	1	8	11						9		4		5		3	6		10*			39
6		7	2	1	8	12	11							4		5	9	3			10*			40
		7		1	8	11						9		4	10	5		3	6	2				41
				1	8	11	4				7	9*			10	5	12	3	6	2				42
14	**1**	**7**	**20**	**26**	**40**	**29**	**16**	**2**	**28**	**14**	**36**	**36**	**15**	**39**	**20**	**42**	**12**	**17**	**22**	**4**	**4**	**1**	**17**	
1		4	3		2	2			1	1				4			4				1		2	
	1	8	2		1	1	7		17				4	5	3	4	1	2			.4			
		8	11		3		7	9	1		4	10	5			6	2							43
			2*		8	11	12		3		7	9	1	4	10	5			6					44
			2		8	11			3		7	9	1	4	10	5			6					45
					8	11	7		2			9	1	4	10	5			6	3				46
			2		8	11	8			6		9*	1	4	10	5		3	7		12			47
		7	2		8*	11	12						1	4	10	5	9	3	6					48
		7	2		8*	11	12						1	4	10	5	9	3	6					49
			2	1	8	11	12		3	6	7	9		4		5					10*			50
			2	1	8	10	6		3		7	9		4		5							11	51
			2	1	8	10	6		3		7	9		4		5							11	52
			2	1	8	10	12		3	6	7	9		4*		5							11	53
					8	11	6		3		7	9	1	4	10	5				2				54
			2		8	11	6		3		7	9	1	4	10	5								55
		3			8	11	7		2	6		9	1	4	10	5								56
2		3			8	11	7*			6		9	1	4	10	5					12			57
		3			8	11	7			6		9	1	4	10*	5				2	12			58
5		**2**	**9**	**4**	**14**	**16**	**8**		**11**	**4**	**13**	**14**	**12**	**16**	**10**	**16**	**4**	**4**	**7**	**3**	**1**		**3**	
						4									1				1		1	1		
						3			1		5	8			3	5			1	1				

opp. og 2

1977-78

#	Date		Opponent	Res	Score	Scorers	App	Goals
1	Aug 20	(h)	Nottingham F	L	1-3	Pearson	0	
2	23	(a)	Arsenal	L	0-1		0	
3	27	(a)	Aston Villa	W	2-1	McKenzie 2	2	15
4	Sep 3	(h)	Wolves	D	0-0		3	15
5	10	(a)	Leicester C	W	5-1	King 2, Latchford, McKenzie, Thomas	5	10
6	17	(h)	Norwich C	W	3-0	Dobson, McKenzie, Rioch	7	5
7	24	(a)	West Ham U	D	1-1	McKenzie	8	6
8	Oct 1	(h)	Manchester C	D	1-1	Latchford	9	8
9	4	(h)	West Brom A	W	3-1	Higgins, King, Latchford	11	5
10	8	(a)	Q.P.R.	W	5-1	Latchford 4, McKenzie	13	5
11	15	(h)	Bristol C	W	1-0	King	15	3
12	22	(a)	Liverpool	D	0-0		16	4
13	29	(h)	Newcastle U	D	4-4	Latchford 2, Lyons, Pejic	17	3
14	Nov 5	(a)	Derby C	W	1-0	Lyons	19	2
15	12	(h)	Birmingham C	W	2-1	Latchford 2	21	2
16	19	(a)	Ipswich T	D	3-3	Buckley, Lyons, Pearson	22	2
17	26	(h)	Coventry C	W	6-0	Latchford 3, Dobson, King, Pearson	24	2
18	Dec 3	(a)	Chelsea	W	1-0	Latchford	26	2
19	10	(h)	Middlesbrough	W	3-0	Latchford 2, Buckley	28	2
20	17	(a)	Birmingham C	D	0-0		29	2
21	26	(h)	Manchester U	L	2-6	Dobson, Latchford	29	2
22	27	(a)	Leeds U	L	1-3	Dobson	29	2
23	31	(h)	Arsenal	W	2-0	King, Latchford	31	2
24	Jan 2	(a)	Nottingham F	D	1-1	Ross	32	2
25	14	(h)	Aston Villa	W	1-0	King	34	2
26	21	(a)	Wolves	L	1-3	Ross	34	3
27	Feb 4	(h)	Leicester C	W	2-0	Latchford 2	36	2
28	18	(h)	West Ham U	W	2-1	McKenzie, Thomas	38	2
29	25	(a)	Manchester C	L	0-1		38	3
30	Mar 4	(h)	Q.P.R.	D	3-3	Dobson, King, Ross	39	3
31	11	(a)	Bristol C	W	1-0	Ross	41	2
32	15	(a)	Norwich C	D	0-0		42	2
33	24	(a)	Newcastle U	W	2-0	Latchford, McKenzie	44	2
34	25	(h)	Leeds U	W	2-0	Latchford, McKenzie	46	2
35	27	(a)	Manchester U	W	2-1	Latchford 2	48	2
36	Apr 1	(h)	Derby C	W	2-1	Dobson, Latchford	50	2
37	5	(h)	Liverpool	L	0-1		50	2
38	8	(a)	Coventry C	L	2-3	Latchford, Lyons	50	2
39	15	(h)	Ipswich T	W	1-0	Latchford	52	2
40	22	(a)	Middlesbrough	D	0-0		53	2
41	25	(a)	West Brom A	L	1-3	Telfer	53	2
42	29	(h)	Chelsea	W	6-0	Latchford 2, Dobson, Lyons, Robinson, Wright	55	3

League Appearances
League Sub Appnces
League Goals

#	Date		Opponent	Res	Score	Scorers	
43	Jan 7	(h)	Aston Villa	W	4-1	King, Latchford, McKenzie, Ross	FA Cup Rd 3
44	28	(a)	Middlesbrough	L	2-3	Lyons, Telfer	4
45	Aug 30	(a)	Sheffield U	W	3-0	King, Latchford McKenzie	League Cup Rd 2
46	Oct 25	(h)	Middlesbrough	D	2-2	King. Telfer	3
47	31	(a)	Middlesbrough	W	2-1	Lyons, Pearson	Replay
48	Nov 29	(a)	Sheffield W	W	3-1	Dobson, Lyons, Pearson	4
49	Jan 18	(a)	Leeds U	L	1-4	Thomas	5

Cup Appearances
Cup Sub Appnces
Cup Goals

Buckley M	Darracott T	Dobson M	Goodlass R	Higgins M	Jones D	Kenyon R	King A	Latchford R	Lyons M	McKenzie D	Pearson J	Pejic M	Rioch B	Robinson N	Ross T	Seargeant S	Telfer G	Thomas D	Wood G	Wright W	No.
	8*		12	6	2	5	7		4	10	9	3						11	1		1
	2		12			5*	7	9	4	10	8	3	6					11	1		2
	2					5	7	9	4	10	8	3	6					11	1		3
	2			6		5	7	9	4	10	8	3						11	1		4
	2*	8				5	7	9	4	10		3	6			12		11	1		5
	2	8				5	7	9	4	10		3	6*			12		11	1		6
	2	8				5	7	9	4	10		3	6			12		11*	1		7
	2	8				5	7	9	4	10		3	6					11	1		8
		8				5	7	9	4	10		3	6			2		11	1		9
		8				5	7	9	4	10		3	6			2		11	1		10
6*		8	12			5	7	9	4	10		3				2	11		1		11
		8				5	7	9	4	10		3	6			2		11	1		12
		8				5	7	9*	4	10		3	6			2	12	11	1		13
6		8				5	7	9	4	10		3		12		2*		11	1		14
6		8				5	7	9	4	10		3				2		11	1		15
6		8				5	7	9	4	10		3*		12		2		11	1		16
6		8				5	7	9	4	10		3				2		11	1		17
6		8				5	7	9	4	10		3				2		11	1		18
6		8				5	7	9	4	10		3				2		11	1		19
6		8				5	7	9	4	10		3				2		11	1		20
6		8				5	7	9	4	10*		3		12		2		11	1		21
		8				5	7	9	4	10		3			6	2		11	1		22
	2	8				5	7	9	4	10		3			6			11	1		23
	2	8	12			5*	7	9	4	10		3			6			11	1		24
	2	8				5	7	9	4	10		3			6			11	1		25
	2*		12			5	7	9	4	10	8	3			6			11	1		26
		8				5	7	9	4	10		3			6	2		11*	1	12	27
		8				5	7	9*	4	10		3			6	2	12	11	1		28
		8				5	7	9	4	10		3			6	2		11	1		29
		8			2*	5	7	9	4	10		3			6		12	11	1		30
		8			2	5	7	9	4	10		3			6			11	1		31
		8				5	7	9	4	10		3			6	2		11	1		32
	2	8				5	7	9	4	10*	12	3			6			11	1		33
		8				5	7	9	4	10		3			6	2		11	1		34
		8				5	7	9	4	10		3			6	2		11	1		35
		8				5	7	9	4	10		3			6	2		11	1		36
		8				5	7	9	4	10		3			6	2		11	1		37
		8				5	7	9	4	10		3			6	2		11	1		38
6		8					7	9	4	10		3		5		2		11	1		39
		8					7	9	4			3			6	2	10	11	1	5	40
6		8					7	9	4			3				2	10	11	1	5	41
6		8					7	9	4			3				2	10	11	1	5	42

League totals (as printed):

```
12 19 38   25 29   7 42 39 42 28 21 40  8  4 18   7 38 42  3
        1    1  1   5           2              1   3        1
 2  7  1    8 30   5  9  3  1  1  1     4              1  2  1
```

Buckley M	Darracott T	Dobson M	Goodlass R	Higgins M	Jones D	Kenyon R	King A	Latchford R	Lyons M	McKenzie D	Pearson J	Pejic M	Rioch B	Robinson N	Ross T	Seargeant S	Telfer G	Thomas D	Wood G	Wright W	No.
	2	8				5	7	9	4	10		3			6			11	1		43
		8				5*	7	9	4			3		12	6	2	10	11	1		44
	2					5	7	9	4	10	8	3			6		12	11*	1		45
		8				5	7	9*	4	10		3			6	2	12	11	1		46
6		8				5	7	9	4	10		3				2		11	1		47
6		8				5	7	9	4	10		3				2		11	1		48
6*	2	8				5	7	9	4	10		3					12	11	1		49

Cup totals (as printed):

```
 3  3  6    6  5   1  7  7  7  3  5  6  2  2  1  6  7
        1       1   1
 3  2  3    2  2   1           2     1
```

1978-79

#	Date		Opponent	Res	Score	Scorers		
1	Aug 19	(a)	Chelsea	W	1-0	King	2	
2	22	(h)	Derby C	W	2-1	King, Nulty	4	
3	26	(h)	Arsenal	W	1-0	Thomas	6	3
4	Sep 2	(a)	Manchester U	D	1-1	King	7	4
5	9	(h)	Middlesbrough	W	2-0	Dobson, Lyons	9	3
6	16	(a)	Aston Villa	D	1-1	Walsh	10	2
7	23	(h)	Wolves	W	2-0	King, Latchford	12	2
8	30	(a)	Bristol C	D	2-2	Latchford 2	13	2
9	Oct 7	(h)	Southampton	D	0-0		14	2
10	14	(a)	Ipswich T	W	1-0	Latchford	16	2
11	21	(a)	Q.P.R.	D	1-1	Latchford	17	2
12	28	(h)	Liverpool	W	1-0	King	19	2
13	Nov 4	(h)	Nottingham F	D	0-0		20	2
14	11	(h)	Chelsea	W	3-2	Dobson 2, King	22	2
15	18	(a)	Arsenal	D	2-2	Dobson, Ross	23	2
16	21	(h)	Manchester U	W	3-0	King, Latchford, Ross	25	2
17	25	(a)	Norwich C	W	1-0	Lyons	27	2
18	Dec 9	(a)	Birmingham C	W	3-1	Latchford, Ross, Todd	29	2
19	16	(h)	Leeds U	D	1-1	Ross	30	2
20	23	(a)	Coventry C	L	2-3	Latchford, Lyons	30	2
21	26	(h)	Manchester C	W	1-0	Wright	32	2
22	30	(h)	Tottenham H	D	1-1	Lyons	33	2
23	Jan 31	(h)	Aston Villa	D	1-1	Thomas	34	2
24	Feb 3	(a)	Wolves	L	0-1		34	3
25	10	(h)	Bristol C	W	4-1	King 3, Wright	36	1
26	17	(a)	Southampton	L	0-3		36	3
27	24	(h)	Ipswich T	L	0-1		36	3
28	Mar 3	(h)	Q.P.R.	W	2-1	Latchford, Telfer	38	2
29	6	(a)	Middlesbrough	W	2-1	Jack, Latchford	40	2
30	10	(h)	Nottingham F	D	1-1	Telfer	41	2
31	13	(a)	Liverpool	D	1-1	King	42	2
32	24	(a)	Derby C	D	0-0		43	2
33	30	(h)	Norwich C	D	2-2	Lyons 2	44	2
34	Apr 3	(a)	Bolton W	L	1-3	Ross	44	2
35	7	(a)	West Brom A	L	0-1		44	4
36	10	(h)	Coventry C	D	3-3	Kidd, Latchford, Ross	45	3
37	14	(a)	Manchester C	D	0-0		46	4
38	16	(h)	Bolton W	W	1-0	Higgins	48	3
39	21	(a)	Leeds U	L	0-1		48	4
40	28	(h)	Birmingham C	W	1-0	King	50	4
41	May 1	(h)	West Brom A	L	0-2		50	4
42	5	(a)	Tottenham H	D	1-1	Kidd	51	4

League Appearances
League Sub Appnces
League Goals

#	Date		Opponent	Res	Score	Scorers		
43	Jan 10	(a)	Sunderland	L	1-2	Dobson		FA Cup Rd 3
44	Aug 29	(h)	Wimbledon	W	8-0	Latchford 5, Dobson 3		League Cup Rd 2
45	Oct 3	(h)	Darlington	W	1-0	Dobson		3
46	Nov 7	(h)	Nottingham F	L	2-3	Latchford, opp.og		4

Cup Appearances
Cup Sub Appnces
Cup Goals

Everton played in the UEFA Cup (see Everton in Europe section).

Barton J	Darracott T	Dobson M	Eastoe P	Heard T	Higgins M	Jack R	Jones D	Kenyon R	Kidd B	King A	Latchford R	Lyons M	Nulty G	Pejic M	Robinson N	Ross T	Telfer G	Thomas D	Todd C	Walsh M	Wood G	Wright W	No.
	2	8			5					7	9	4	6	3			11		10		1		1
	2	8								7	9	4	6	3			11		10		1	5	2
	2	8								7	9	4	6	3			11		10		1	5	3
	2	8								7	9	4	6	3			11		10		1	5	4
	2	8								7	9	4	6	3			11		10		1	5	5
	2	8								7	9	4	6	3			11		10		1	5	6
		8								7	9	4		3		6	11	2	10		1	5	7
		8								7	9	4		3		6	11	2	10		1	5	8
		8								7	9	4		3		6	11	2	10		1	5	9
		8								7	9	4		3		6	11	2	10		1	5	10
		8								7	9	4*	6	3	12		11	2	10		1	5	11
		8						4		7	9		6	3			11	2	10		1	5	12
	2	8								7	9			3		6	11	2	10		1	5	13
		8								7	9			3	12	6	11	2	10*		1	5	14
		8								7	9	4	12	3		6	11	2	10		1	5*	15
		8								7	9	4	12	3		6	11	2	10*		1	5	16
		8							10	7	9	4		3		6	11	2			1	5	17
		8*							10	7	9	4		3		6	11	2			1	5	18
		8							10	7	9	4	12	3		6	11	2			1	5	19
		8						3	10	7	9	4				6	11	2			1	5	20
		8						3*	10	7	9	4	6		12	11		2			1	5	21
		8						3	10	7	9	4	6			10	11	2			1	5	22
		8					3			7	9	4				6	11	2	10		1	5	23
		8			12		3			7	9	4				6	11	2	10*		1	5	24
		8					3		10		9	4			2	6	11	7			1	5	25
		8			6		3		10	9	4				2		11	7			1	5	26
		8			6		3			7	9	4				10	11*	2	12		1	5	27
		8*					3			7	9	4			2	6	10	11	12		1	5	28
		8					3		2	7	9	4				6	10	11			1	5	29
		8					3		2	7	9	4				6	10*	11	12		1	5	30
		0					3			7	9	4				6	10	11	2		1	5	31
		8					3		9	7		4				6	10	11	2		1	5	32
12		8					3		9*	7		4				6	10	11	2		1	5	33
5		8					3			7	9	4				6	10	11	2		1		34
2		8	12				3		10	7	9	4				6	11*			5	1		35
2		8	11				3		10	7	9*	4				6		12			1	5	36
2		8	11				3*		10	7	9	4			12	6					1	5	37
2		8	11		5		3		10	7		4				6					1	9	38
2		8	11		5		3		10	7		4				6					1	9	39
2		8	11*		5		3		10	7	9				12					4	1	6	40
2		8	11		5		3		10	7	9									4	1	6	41
2		8	11		5		3		10	7	9									4	1	6	42
9	7	40	7	9	20	1	11	3	9	40	36	37	13	19	4	26	10	33	29	18	42	39	
1			1	1									4		3		2		2	1	1		
		4		1	1						2	12	11	6	1		6	2	2	1	1	2	
3		8								7	9	4				6	11	2	10		1	5	43
		8								7	9	4	6	3	2	12	11		10*		1	5	44
		8								7	9	4	11	3		6		2	10		1	5	45
	2	8								7	9			3		6	11	4	10		1	5	46
	2	4								4	4	3	2	3	1	3		3	3	4	4	4	
															1								
		5												6						opp.og 1			

1979-80

1	Aug	18	(h)	Norwich C	L	2-4	Nulty, Ross	0	
2		22	(a)	Leeds U	L	0-2		0	
3		25	(a)	Derby C	W	1-0	King	2	18
4	Sep	1	(h)	Aston Villa	D	1-1	Bailey	3	17
5		8	(a)	Stoke C	W	3-2	Bailey, Kidd, King	5	13
6		15	(h)	Wolves	L	2-3	Kidd, Ross	5	15
7		22	(a)	Ipswich T	D	1-1	Kidd	6	13
8		29	(h)	Bristol C	D	0-0		7	12
9	Oct	6	(a)	Coventry C	L	1-2	King	7	15
10		13	(h)	Crystal P	W	3-1	Kidd, King, Latchford	9	15
11		20	(a)	Liverpool	D	2-2	Kidd, King	10	17
12		27	(h)	Manchester U	D	0-0		11	17
13	Nov	3	(a)	Norwich C	D	0-0		12	18
14		10	(h)	Middlesbrough	L	0-2		12	17
15		13	(h)	Leeds U	W	5-1	Latchford 3, Kidd, opp.og	14	16
16		17	(a)	Arsenal	L	0-2		14	15
17		24	(h)	Tottenham H	D	1-1	Latchford	15	16
18	Dec	1	(a)	West Brom A	D	1-1	King	16	17
19		8	(h)	Brighton	W	2-0	Kidd, King	18	13
20		15	(a)	Southampton	L	0-1		18	16
21		22	(h)	Manchester C	L	1-2	Kidd	18	17
22		26	(a)	Bolton W	D	1-1	McBride	19	18
23		29	(h)	Derby C	D	1-1	King	20	17
24	Jan	1	(h)	Nottingham F	W	1-0	Kidd	22	16
25		12	(a)	Aston Villa	L	1-2	Eastoe	22	16
26	Feb	2	(a)	Wolves	L	0-0		23	16
27		9	(h)	Ipswich T	L	0-4		23	17
28		19	(a)	Bristol C	L	1-2	Ross	23	19
29		23	(a)	Crystal P	D	1-1	Eastoe	24	19
30	Mar	1	(h)	Liverpool	L	1-2	Eastoe	24	19
31		12	(a)	Manchester U	D	0-0		25	19
32		15	(h)	Coventry C	D	1-1	Eastoe	26	19
33		18	(h)	Stoke C	W	2-0	Eastoe, Latchford	28	18
34		22	(a)	Middlesbrough	L	1-2	Hartford	28	18
35		28	(h)	Arsenal	L	0-1		28	18
36	Apr	2	(a)	Manchester C	D	1-1	King	29	18
37		5	(h)	Bolton W	W	3-1	Eastoe, Kidd, Megson	31	18
38		19	(a)	Tottenham H	L	0-3		31	19
39		26	(h)	Southampton	W	2-0	Gidman, Stanley	33	19
40		28	(h)	West Brom A	D	0-0		34	18
41	May	3	(a)	Brighton	D	0-0		35	19
42		9	(a)	Nottingham F	L	0-1		35	19

League Appearances
League Sub Appnces
League Goals

43	Jan	5	(h)	Aldershot	W	4-1	Hartford, Kidd, King, Latchford	FA Cup Rd 3	
44		26	(h)	Wigan A	W	3-0	Kidd, Latchford, McBride		4
45	Feb	16	(h)	Wrexham	W	5-2	Eastoe 2, Latchford, Megson, Ross		5
46	Mar	8	(h)	Ipswich T	W	2-1	Kidd, Latchford		6
47	Apr	12	(n)	West Ham U	D	1-1	Kidd	(Villa Park)	SF
48		16	(n)	West Ham U	L	1-2	Latchford	(Elland Road) Replay	
49	Aug	28	(h)	Cardiff C	W	2-0	Kidd 2	League Cup 1st leg Rd 2	
50	Sep	5	(a)	Cardiff C	L	0-1		2nd leg	
51	Sep	25	(a)	Aston Villa	D	0-0			3
52	Oct	9	(h)	Aston Villa	W	4-1	Latchford 2, Kidd, King	Replay	
53		30	(a)	Grimsby T	L	1-2	Kidd		4

Cup Appearances
Cup Sub Appnces
Cup Goals

Everton played in the UEFA Cup (see Everton in Europe section).

Bailey J	Barton J	Eastoe P	Gidman J	Hartford A	Heard T	Higgins M	Hodge M	Kidd B	King A	Latchford R	Lyons M	McBride J	Megson G	Nulty G	O'Keefe E	Ratcliffe K	Ross T	Sharp G	Stanley G	Todd C	Varadi I	Wood G	Wright W	#
3	2	12		11*				10	9		4			7			6		8			1	5	1
3	2					5		10	9		4			7			6		8			1	11	2
3	2					5		10	9		4			7			6		8			1	11	3
3		11	7			5		10	9		4						6		8			1	2	4
3		11	7			5		10	9		4						6		8			1	2	5
3		12	7	11*		5		10	9		4						6		8			1	2	6
3	2	11	7			5		10			4	9					6					1	8	7
3	2*	11	7			5		10	9		4						6		8			1	12	8
3	2		7			5		10	11	9*	4						6		8		12	1		9
3				7*		5		10	11	9	4		12				6		8			1	2	10
3						5		10	11	9	4			7			6		8			1	2	11
3		11	2			5		10	9		4			7			6					1	8	12
3	2					5		10	11	9	4			7			6					1	8	13
3	2			7*		5		10	11	9			12				6		8			1	4	14
3	2		7			5	1	10	11	9*			12				6		8				4	15
3	2		7			5	1	10	11	9*			12				6		8				4	16
3	2		7			5	1	10	11	9							6		8				4	17
3	2		7			5	1	10	11	9							6		8				4	18
3	2		7			5	1	10	11	9							6		8				4	19
3		12	2	7		5	1	11	9*								6		8	10			4	20
3		2	7				1	10	11	9	5						6		8*	12			4	21
3		2	7				1	10			5	11					6		8	9			4	22
3		2	7				1	10	6	9	5	11							8				4	23
3		2	7				1	10	6	9	5	11							8				4	24
3		8	2	7			1	10		9	5	11	12		6*								4	25
3		8	2				1	10		9	5	11		7			6						4	26
3		8	2				1	10		9	5	11		7			6						4	27
3		8	2				1	9			5	11		7			6			10			4	28
3		8					1	9			5	11		7		4	6			10			2	29
3		12	2	7				10	9		5	11			4*		6		8			1		30
3		6					1	10	9		5	11		7		4			8				2	31
3		6	2				1	10	9		5	11		7					8				4	32
3		6	2				1	10	9		5	11		7					8				4	33
3		6	2				1	10	9		5	11		7					8				4	34
3		6	2				1	10	9		5	11	12	7*					8				4	35
3		6	2				1	10	9		5	11		7					8				4	36
3		6	2				1	10	9		5	11		7					8				4	37
3*		8		4			1	10	9		5	11	12	7			6						2	38
3		2	7					10	9		5	11					6		8			1	4	39
3		2	7					10	9		5	11					6		8			1	4	40
3		2	7					10	9*		5	11					6		8	12		1	4	41
3		2	7					10		9	5	11					6		8			1	4	42
42	**6**	**23**	**29**	**35**	**1**	**19**	**23**	**31**	**29**	**26**	**35**	**17**	**12**	**9**	**3**	**2**	**31**	**1**	**24**	**3**	**2**	**19**	**40**	
	1	0										3	1		1	1			1	1		2	1	*(subs)*
2	6	1	1						10	9	6			1	1	1			3			1		*(goals) — opp.og 1*
3		2	7				1	10	6	9	5	11							8				4	43
3		2	8	7			1	10		9	5	11					6						4	44
3		2	8				1	10		9	5	11		7			6						4	45
3		6	2					10		9	5	11		7					8			1	4	46
3		6	2				1	10	9		5	11	12	7*					8				4	47
3		2	7				1	10	9	8*	5	11					6			12			4	48
3	2					5		10	9		4			7			6		8			1	11	49
3	2	11	7			5		10	9		4						6		8			1		50
3	2	11	8			5		10	9*		4			7			6			12		1		51
3			7			5		10	11	9	4						6		8			1	2	52
3		11				5		10	9		4		12	7*			6		8			1	2	53

Cup/extra appearance totals:

11 3 8 6 8 5 5 9 8 7 11 4 3 4 1 7 6 6 9
2 1 8 2 7 1 1 1 1

1980-81

#	Date		Opponent		Score	Scorers		
1	Aug 16	(a)	Sunderland	L	1-3	Eastoe		0
2	19	(h)	Leicester C	W	1-0	Eastoe		2
3	23	(h)	Nottingham F	D	0-0			3	12
4	30	(a)	Ipswich T	L	0-4			3	17
5	Sep 6	(h)	Wolves	W	2-0	Eastoe, Wright		5	13
6	13	(a)	Aston Villa	W	2-0	Eastoe, Lyons		7	11
7	20	(a)	Crystal P	W	5-0	Latchford 3, Eastoe, Gidman		9	5
8	27	(a)	Coventry C	W	5-0	Latchford 2, McBride 2, Eastoe		11	3
9	Oct 4	(h)	Southampton	W	2-1	McBride 2		13	3
10	7	(a)	Brighton	W	3-1	Lyons, McBride, McMahon		15	3
11	11	(a)	Leeds U	L	0-1			15	4
12	18	(h)	Liverpool	D	2-2	Hartford, McBride		16	4
13	21	(h)	West Brom A	D	1-1	Eastoe		17	4
14	25	(a)	Manchester U	L	0-2			17	7
15	Nov 1	(h)	Tottenham H	D	2-2	Eastoe, McMahon		18	8
16	8	(a)	Norwich C	L	1-2	Latchford		18	8
17	12	(a)	Leicester C	W	1-0	Eastoe		20	6
18	15	(h)	Sunderland	W	2-1	Hartford, O'Keefe		22	4
19	22	(a)	Arsenal	L	1-2	Wright		22	7
20	29	(h)	Birmingham C	D	1-1	O'Keefe		23	7
21	Dec 6	(a)	Stoke C	D	2-2	McBride, Varadi		24	7
22	13	(h)	Brighton	W	4-3	Eastoe 2, McMahon, Varadi		26	5
23	26	(h)	Manchester C	L	0-2			26	7
24	27	(a)	Middlesbrough	L	0-1			26	9
25	Jan 10	(h)	Arsenal	L	1-2	O'Keefe		26	10
26	17	(h)	Ipswich T	D	0-0			27	10
27	31	(a)	Nottingham F	L	0-1			27	10
28	Feb 7	(h)	Aston Villa	L	1-3	Ross		27	12
29	21	(h)	Coventry C	W	3-0	Eastoe, McMahon, Ross		29	12
30	28	(a)	Crystal P	W	3-2	Eastoe, McMahon, Varadi		31	10
31	Mar 14	(h)	Leeds U	L	1-2	Varadi		31	12
32	17	(a)	Southampton	L	0-3			31	13
33	21	(a)	Liverpool	L	0-1			31	15
34	28	(h)	Manchester U	L	0-1			31	15
35	31	(a)	West Brom A	L	0-2			31	16
36	Apr 4	(a)	Tottenham H	D	2-2	Hartford, Varadi		32	15
37	11	(h)	Norwich C	L	0-2			32	15
38	18	(h)	Middlesbrough	W	4-1	Hartford 2, Eastoe, Megson		34	15
39	20	(a)	Manchester C	L	1-3	Varadi		34	15
40	25	(h)	Stoke C	L	0-1			34	16
41	May 2	(a)	Birmingham C	D	1-1	Eastoe		35	17
42	4	(a)	Wolves	D	0-0			36	15

League Appearances
League Sub Appnces
League Goals

#	Date		Opponent		Score	Scorers		
43	Jan 3	(h)	Arsenal	W	2-0	Lyons, opp.og		FA Cup Rd 3
44	24	(h)	Liverpool	W	2-1	Eastoe, Varadi		4
45	Feb 14	(a)	Southampton	D	0-0			5
46	17	(h)	Southampton	W	1-0	O'Keefe		Replay
47	Mar 7	(h)	Manchester C	D	2-2	Eastoe, Ross		6
48	11	(a)	Manchester C	L	1-3	Eastoe		Replay
49	Aug 26	(h)	Blackpool	W	3-0	Eastoe, Latchford, McBride	League Cup 1st leg Rd 2
50	Sep 3	(a)	Blackpool	D	2-2	Latchford 2		2nd leg
51	24	(h)	West Brom A	L	1-2	Gidman		3

Cup Appearances
Cup Sub Appnces
Cup Goals

Bailey J	Barton J	Eastoe P	Gidman J	Hartford A	Higgins M	Hodge M	Latchford R	Lodge P	Lyons M	McBride J	McDonagh J	McMahon S	Megson G	O'Keefe E	Ratcliffe K	Ross T	Sharp G	Stanley G	Telfer G	Varadi I	Wright W	No.
		12	2	10			9		5	11	1	7		6*	3	8					4	1
		8	2	10			9		5	11	1	7			3			6			4	2
		8	2	10			9		5	11	1	7			3			6			4	3
		10	2	8			9		5	11	1	7		12	3			6*			4	4
3		8	2	10			9*		5	11	1	7		12				6			4	5
3		8*	2	10			9		5	11	1	7		12				6			4	6
3		8	2	10			9		5	11	1	7						6			4	7
3		8	2	10*			9		5	11	1	7		12				6			4	8
3		8	2				9		5	11	1	7		10				6			4	9
3		8*	2	10			9		5	11	1	7		12				6			4	10
3		8	2	10			9		5	11	1	7		12				6*			4	11
3		8	2*	10			9		5	11	1	7		12				6			4	12
3		8		10			9		5	11	1	7			2			6			4	13
3		8	2	10			9		5	11	1	7		12				6*			4	14
3		8	2	10			9*		5	11	1	7		12				6			4	15
3		8	2	10			9		5*	11	1	7		12				6			4	16
3		8	2	10			9*			11	1	7		6				5			4	17
3		8	2	10			9*			11	1	7	12	6				5			4	18
3		8	2	10						11	1	7		6	9			5			4	19
3		8	2	10						11	1	7		6	9			5			4	20
3		8		10	5					11	1	7		6				4		9	2	21
3		8		10	5			12		11	1	7		6*				4		9	2	22
3		8	2	10				12		11*	1	7		6	5					9	4	23
3		8	2	10				12		11	1	7		5	6					9*	4	24
3		8		10							1	7		11	5	6				9	4	25
3		8		10					5	12	1	7		11*	2	6				9	4	26
3		8		10		1			5	12		7		11*	2	6				9	4	27
3		8		10		1		12	5			7		11*	2	6				9	4	28
		8	2*	10				12	5		1	7		11	3	6				9	4	29
		8	2	10				12	5		1	7		11	3	6*				9	4	30
3		8	2	10					5	11	1	7				6				9	4	31
		8	2	10					5*	12	1	7			3	11		6		9	4	32
3		8	2						10	12	1	7		11		6		5		9*	4	33
3*		8	2						10		1	7		11	12	6		5		9	4	34
		8	2	10						11	1	7*			3	6		5	9	12	4	35
3		8	2	10						11	6	1			7			5	12	9*	4	36
		8*	2	10					5	11	1	7	12		3	6*				9	4	37
		8	2	10					5	11	1	7			3			12	6*	9	4	38
		8*	2	10				6	5	11	1	7			3			12		9	4	39
3	2	8		10				6	5	11*	1	7			4			9			12	40
3	2	8	6	10					5		1				4	11				9	7	41
3	2	8*	6	10				12	5		1				4	11				9	7	42
31	**3**	**41**	**35**	**39**	**2**	**2**	**18**	**8**	**30**	**27**	**40**	**34**	**8**	**15**	**20**	**17**	**2**	**28**	**1**	**20**	**41**	
			1				1	3	3	4				2	10	1		2		1	2	
		15	1	5					6			2	7		5	1	3		2		6	2	

opp.og 1

1981-82

1	Aug	29	(h)	Birmingham C	W	3-1	Ainscow, Biley, Eastoe	3	
2	Sep	2	(a)	Leeds U	D	1-1	Biley	4	
3		5	(a)	Southampton	L	0-1		4	9
4		12	(h)	Brighton	D	1-1	Wright	5	11
5		19	(a)	Tottenham H	L	0-3		5	19
6		22	(h)	Notts Co	W	3-1	Eastoe, O'Keefe, Ross	8	9
7		26	(h)	West Brom A	W	1-0	Lyons	11	7
8	Oct	3	(a)	Stoke C	L	1-3	McBride	11	11
9		10	(a)	West Ham U	D	1-1	McMahon|	12	14
10		17	(h)	Ipswich T	W	2-1	Ferguson, Stevens	15	8
11		24	(a)	Middlesbrough	W	2-0	Ferguson 2	18	7
12		31	(h)	Manchester C	L	0-1		18	8
13	Nov	7	(a)	Liverpool	L	1-3	Ferguson	18	12
14		21	(h)	Sunderland	L	1-2	Eastoe	18	13
15		24	(a)	Notts Co	D	2-2	Biley, Sharp	19	13
16		28	(a)	Arsenal	L	0-1		19	15
17	Dec	5	(h)	Swansea C	W	3-1	O'Keefe 2, Sharp	22	13
18		19	(h)	Aston Villa	W	2-0	Eastoe, Lyons	25	11
19		28	(h)	Coventry C	W	3-2	Higgins 2, Sharp	28	8
20	Jan	6	(a)	Manchester U	D	1-1	Sharp	29	7
21		19	(h)	Southampton	D	1-1	Richardson	30	9
22		23	(a)	Wolves	W	3-0	Irvine 2, Richardson	33	5
23		30	(h)	Tottenham H	D	1-1	Sharp	34	8
24	Feb	6	(a)	Brighton	L	1-3	Heath	34	10
25		13	(h)	Stoke C	D	0-0		35	10
26		20	(a)	West Brom A	D	0-0		36	11
27		27	(h)	West Ham U	D	0-0		37	11
28	Mar	6	(a)	Ipswich T	L	0-3		37	11
29		13	(h)	Middlesbrough	W	2-0	Higgins, Sharp	40	11
30		20	(a)	Manchester C	D	1-1	Heath	41	12
31		27	(h)	Liverpool	L	1-3	Sharp	41	12
32	Apr	3	(a)	Nottingham F	W	1-0	McMahon	44	12
33		6	(a)	Birmingham C	W	2-0	Ainscow, Heath	47	12
34		10	(h)	Manchester U	D	3-3	Heath, Lyons, Sharp	48	11
35		13	(a)	Coventry C	L	0-1		48	12
36		17	(a)	Sunderland	L	1-3	Irvine	48	13
37		20	(h)	Nottingham F	W	2-1	Sharp 2	51	10
38		24	(h)	Arsenal	W	2-1	Heath, Wright	54	9
39	May	1	(a)	Swansea C	W	3-1	Sharp 2, Heath	57	8
40		4	(h)	Leeds U	W	1-0	Sharp	60	8
41		8	(h)	Wolves	D	1-1	Eastoe	61	8
42		15	(a)	Aston Villa	W	2-1	Sharp 2	64	8

League Appearances
League Sub Appnces
League Goals

43	Jan	2	(a)	West Ham U	L	1-2	Eastoe	FA Cup Rd 3	
44	Oct	6	(h)	Coventry C	D	1-1	Ferguson	League Cup 1st leg Rd 2	
45		27	(a)	Coventry C	W	1-0	Ferguson	2nd leg	
46	Nov	11	(h)	Oxford U	W	1-0	O'Keefe		3
47	Dec	15	(h)	Ipswich T	L	2-3	McMahon 2		4

Cup Appearances
Cup Sub Appnces
Cup Goals

Ainscow A	Arnold J	Bailey J	Biley A	Borrows B	Eastoe P	Ferguson M	Hartford A	Heath A	Higgins M	Irvine A	Kendall H	Lodge P	Lyons M	McBride J	McMahon S	O'Keefe E	Ratcliffe K	Richardson K	Rimmer S	Ross T	Sharp G	Southall N	Stevens G	Thomas M	Walsh M	Wright W	No.
7	1	3	9		8	10							5						11					6	4	2	1
11	1		9		8	10							5		7		3							6	4	2	2
11	1		9		8	12	10						5		7*		3							6	4	2	3
11	1		9		8	10							5		7		3							6	4	2	4
11	1		9		8	10							5		7*	12	3							6	4	2	5
11	1		9*		8	10							5			12	3			7				6	4	2	6
	1		9				10						5	12	8*	11	3			7				6	4	2	7
	1	3*	9										5	11	7	8				10	12			6	4	2	8
	1	3	8*					9	4				5	11	7	12				10			2	6			9
		3	12		9								5	11	7	8				10		1	2	6*	4		10
10*	1	3	12		9				4		6		5	11	7	8										2	11
10*	1	3			9				4		6		5	11	7	8					12					2	12
10*	1	3	12		9				4		6		5	11	7	8										2	13
10	1	3	9		8*						6		5	11	7			12					2			4	14
11*	1		10					8			6		5		7		3	12			9		2			4	15
	1		10								6		5		7		3	11		8	9		2			4	16
	1		10								6		5		7		3	11		8	9		2			4	17
			10						4	7	6	11	5				3			8	9	1	2				18
			10						4	11	6		5		7		3			8	9	1	2				19
			10						4		6	11	5		7		3	8			9	1	2				20
			10					8	4	7		11	5		6		3				9	1	2				21
			10					8	4	7		11	5		6		3				9	1	?				22
			10					8	4	7		11	5		6		3				9	1	2				23
			10					8	4	7		11	5		6		3				9	1	2				24
				2	10			8	4	7					6		3			11	9	1				5	25
		3	10	2				8	4	7					6					11	9	1				5	26
		3	10	2				8	4	7					6					11	9	1				5	27
		3	10*	2				8	4	7					6	12				11	9	1				5	28
12		3		2				8	4	7					6	10*				11	9	1				5	29
				2				8	4	7					6	10	3			11	9	1				5	30
				2				8	4	7					6	10	3			11	9	1				5	31
12		3		2	10			8	4	7					6		3			11	9*	1				5	32
			10	2	12			8	4	7					6		3			11	9	1				5*	33
			10	2				8	4	7		12	5		6		3			11	9	1*					34
			10	2				8	4	7			5		6		3			11	9	1					35
			10	2	9			8	4	7*		12			6		3			11		1				5	36
				2				8	4	7					6		3	10		11	9	1				5	37
								8	4	7					6			10		11	9	1	2		3	5	38
								8	4	7					6	10*		12		11	9	1	2		3	5	39
12								8	4	7					6	10*				11	9	1	2		3	5	40
			10	2				8	4	7					6					11	9	1			3	5	41
			10	2				8	4	7					6					11	9	1			3	5	42
15	16	12	16	15	17	7	7	22	29	25	4	12	26	7	31	8	25	15	2	27	27	26	19	10	18	24	
?		3		2	1							1	1	1	1	3		3					2				
2		3		5	4		6	3	3			3	1	2	3		2			1	15	1				2	
			10						4		6	11	5		12	3	7	8*			9	1	2				43
	1	3	9										5	11	7	8				10			2	6	4		44
10	1	3	9						4		6		5	11	7	8							2				45
12	1	3	10		9*				4		6		5	11	7	8							2				46
	1		10*		12						6		5		7		3	11		8	9		2			4	47
1	4	3	2		1			3	3	2	3	5	3	4	4	2	1	3		2	1	5	1	2			
1															1	1											
									1	2					2	1											

1982-83

#	Date		Venue	Opponent	Res	Score	Scorers		
1	Aug	28	(a)	Watford	L	0-2		0	
2		31	(h)	Aston Villa	W	5-0	Heath 2, Sharp 2, King	3	
3	Sep	4	(h)	Tottenham H	W	3-1	McMahon, Sheedy, Wright	6	5
4		8	(a)	Manchester U	L	1-2	King	6	10
5		11	(a)	Notts Co	L	0-1		6	14
6		18	(h)	Norwich C	D	1-1	Irvine	7	13
7		25	(a)	Coventry C	L	2-4	Heath, King	7	16
8	Oct	2	(h)	Brighton	D	2-2	Heath, Wright	8	17
9		9	(h)	Manchester C	W	2-1	King, McMahon	11	13
10		16	(a)	Swansea C	W	3-0	McMahon, Richardson, opp.og	14	10
11		23	(h)	Sunderland	W	3-1	Johnson, Richardson, Sharp	17	7
12		30	(a)	Southampton	L	2-3	King, Wright	17	11
13	Nov	6	(h)	Liverpool	L	0-5		17	13
14		13	(a)	Arsenal	D	1-1	King	18	11
15		20	(h)	West Brom A	D	0-0		19	14
16		27	(a)	West Ham U	L	0-2		19	15
17	Dec	4	(h)	Birmingham C	D	0-0		20	15
18		11	(a)	Ipswich T	W	2-0	Richardson, Sheedy	23	14
19		18	(h)	Luton T	W	5-0	Heath 2, Bailey, Curran, Sheedy	26	12
20		27	(a)	Stoke C	L	0-1		26	14
21		28	(h)	Nottingham F	W	3-1	Sharp 2, McMahon	29	11
22	Jan	1	(a)	West Brom A	D	2-2	Higgins, Sharp	30	11
23		3	(a)	Tottenham H	L	1-2	Sharp	30	13
24		15	(h)	Watford	W	1-0	Johnson	33	11
25		22	(a)	Norwich C	W	1-0	Ratcliffe	36	7
26	Feb	5	(h)	Notts Co	W	3-0	Heath, King, Sheedy	39	5
27		12	(a)	Aston Villa	L	0-2		39	7
28		26	(h)	Swansea C	D	2-2	King 2	40	7
29	Mar	2	(a)	Manchester C	D	0-0		41	7
30		5	(a)	Sunderland	L	1-2	Sharp	41	9
31		15	(h)	Southampton	W	2-0	Heath, Sheedy	44	6
32		19	(a)	Liverpool	D	0-0		45	8
33		26	(h)	Arsenal	L	2-3	Ainscow, Heath	45	11
34	Apr	2	(a)	Nottingham F	L	0-2		45	13
35		4	(h)	Stoke C	W	3-1	Sheedy 2, Sharp	48	10
36		9	(a)	Brighton	W	2-1	Sheedy 2	51	9
37		19	(h)	Manchester U	W	2-0	Heath, Sharp	54	8
38		23	(a)	Birmingham C	L	0-1		54	10
39		30	(h)	West Ham U	W	2-0	Sharp 2	57	7
40	May	2	(h)	Coventry C	W	1-0	Sharp	60	6
41		7	(a)	Luton T	W	5-1	Sharp 2, Sheedy 2, Johnson	63	6
42		14	(h)	Ipswich T	D	1-1	opp.og	64	7

League Appearances
League Sub Appnces
League Goals

#	Date		Venue	Opponent	Res	Score	Scorers		
43	Jan	8	(a)	Newport C	D	1-1	Sheedy	FA Cup Rd 3	
44		11	(h)	Newport C	W	2-1	King, Sharp	Replay	
45		30	(h)	Shrewsbury T	W	2-1	Heath, Sheedy	4	
46	Feb	19	(h)	Tottenham H	W	2-0	King, Sharp	5	
47	Mar	12	(a)	Manchester U	L	0-1		6	
48	Oct	5	(a)	Newport C	W	2-0	King, McMahon	League Cup 1st leg Rd 2	
49		27	(h)	Newport C	D	2-2	Johnson, King	2nd leg	
50	Nov	9	(h)	Arsenal	D	1-1	Stevens	3	
51		23	(a)	Arsenal	L	0-3		Replay	

Cup Appearances
Cup Sub Appnces
Cup Goals

Ainscow A	Arnold J	Bailey J	Borrows B	Curran T	Heath A	Higgins M	Irvine A	Johnson D	Keeley G	King A	McMahon S	Mountfield D	Ratcliffe K	Reid P	Richardson K	Ross T	Sharp G	Sheedy K	Southall N	Stevens G	Walsh M	Wright W	#
		3	2		6	4		8		10	7*				12		9	11	1			5	1
		3	2		8	4	7*			10	6				12		9	11	1			5	2
7		3	2		8	4				10	6						9	11	1			5	3
7*		3	2		8	4				10	6				12		9	11	1			5	4
7		3	2		8	4				10	6						9	11	1			5	5
			2		8		7*			10	6	4			12		9	11	1	3		5	6
					8	4		12		10	6		2			7*	9	11	1	3		5	7
		3	2		7	4		8		10	6						9	11	1			5	8
		3	2		7	4		8		10	6						9	11	1			5	9
		3	2			4		8		10	6				7		9	11	1			5	10
		3	2		7*	4		8		10	6				12		9	11	1			5	11
		3	2			4	12	8*		10	6				7		9	11	1			5	12
		3	2		7	4		8*		10	6				12		9	11	1			5	13
	1				7	4	12	8		10	6		3		11*		9			2		5	14
	1				7	4	11	8		10	6		3				9			2		5	15
	1				8*	4	7	12		10	6		3				9			2		5	16
	1	3			7	4		8		10	6						9	11		2		5	17
	1	3			7	8	5				9		6	4	10			11		2			18
	1	3			7	8	5				9*		6	4	10		12	11		2			19
	1	3			7	8	5				9		6	4	10		12	11		2*			20
	1	3			7		5				9		6	4	10		8	11		2			21
	1	3			7		5				9		6	4	10		8	11		2			22
	1	3			7		5				9		6	4	10		8	11		2			23
	1	3			7		5	12			9		6	4	10*		8	11		2			24
	1	3			8		5				7		6	4	10		9	11		2			25
	1	3			7*		5	12			9		6	4	10		8	11		2			26
	1	3			7		5	12			9		6	4	10*		8	11		2			27
	1	3			10		5	7*		12	8		6	4			9	11		2			28
	1	3			10		5	7			8		6	4			9	11		2			29
	1	3			10		5	12		7	8*		6	4			9	11		2			30
	1	3			10		5	7			8		6	4			9	11		2			31
12	1	3			10		5	7*			8		6	4			9	11		2			32
7	1	3			10		5	12			8		6	4			9	11		2*			33
7	1	3			10		5	12			8		6*	4			9	11		2			34
7	1	3			10		5				8		6	4	2		9	11					35
7	1	3			10		5				8		6	4			9	11		2			36
	1	3			10		5	8			7		6	4			9	11		2			37
12	1	3			10			8		7*	5		6	4			9	11		2			38
7		3			10		5	8					6	4			9	11	1	2			39
		3			10		5	12		8*	7		6	4			9	11	1	2			40
		3			10		5	8			7		6	4			9	11	1	2			41
7		3			10		5	12		8			6*	4			9	11	1	2			42
9	25	37	12	7	37	39	7	25	1	24	34	1	29	7	24	1	39	40	17	28	2	17	Apps
	2					7	6								5	1	2							Sub
	1				1	10	1	1		3	9		4	1	3		15	11			3		Gls

opp.og 2

Ainscow A	Arnold J	Bailey J	Borrows B	Curran T	Heath A	Higgins M	Irvine A	Johnson D	Keeley G	King A	McMahon S	Mountfield D	Ratcliffe K	Reid P	Richardson K	Ross T	Sharp G	Sheedy K	Southall N	Stevens G	Walsh M	Wright W	#
	1	3			7	5				9	6		4		10		8	11		2			43
	1	3			7	5				9	6		4		10		8	11		2			44
	1	3			7	5				9	6		4		10		8	11		2			45
	1	3			10	5		7		8			4		6		9	11		2			46
	1	3			10	5		7		8			4		6		9	11		2			47
		3	2		7*			8		10	6		4		12		9	11	1			5	48
		3	2		7*			8		10	6		4		12		9	11	1			5	49
	1				7	4	12	8*		10	6		3		11		9			2		5	50
	1				7	4		8		10	6		3				9	11		2		5	51
	7	7	2		9	7	2	4		8	8		9		3	3	9	8	2	7		4	Apps
					1			1			4		1							2			Sub
						1											2	2		1			Gls

1983-84

1	Aug 27	(h)	Stoke C	W	1-0	Sharp	3	
2	29	(h)	West Ham U	L	0-1		3	
3	Sep 3	(a)	Coventry C	D	1-1	Sheedy	4	12
4	6	(a)	Ipswich T	L	0-3		4	18
5	10	(h)	West Brom A	D	0-0		5	18
6	17	(a)	Tottenham H	W	2-1	Reid, Sheedy	8	15
7	24	(h)	Birmingham C	D	1-1	Sharp	9	14
8	Oct 1	(a)	Notts Co	W	1-0	Reid	12	13
9	15	(h)	Luton T	L	0-1		12	15
10	22	(h)	Watford	W	1-0	Johnson	15	13
11	29	(a)	Leicester C	L	0-2		15	15
12	Nov 6	(a)	Liverpool	L	0-3		15	17
13	12	(h)	Nottingham F	W	1-0	Heath	18	16
14	19	(a)	Arsenal	L	1-2	King	18	17
15	26	(h)	Norwich C	L	0-2		18	17
16	Dec 3	(a)	Manchester U	W	1-0	Sheedy	21	16
17	10	(h)	Aston Villa	D	1-1	Gray	22	14
18	17	(a)	Q.P.R.	L	0-2		22	16
19	26	(h)	Sunderland	D	0-0		23	16
20	27	(a)	Wolves	L	0-3		23	16
21	31	(h)	Coventry C	D	0-0		24	16
22	Jan 2	(a)	Birmingham C	W	2-0	King, Stevens	27	16
23	14	(a)	Stoke C	D	1-1	Heath	28	18
24	21	(h)	Tottenham H	W	2-1	Heath 2	31	14
25	Feb 4	(h)	Notts Co	W	4-1	Heath 3, Sheedy	34	14
26	11	(a)	West Brom A	D	1-1	Mountfield	35	13
27	25	(a)	Watford	D	4-4	Sharp 2, Gray, Heath	36	14
28	Mar 3	(h)	Liverpool	D	1-1	Harper	37	15
29	13	(a)	Nottingham F	L	0-1		37	15
30	17	(h)	Ipswich T	W	1-0	Mountfield	40	14
31	20	(h)	Leicester C	D	1-1	Richardson	41	13
32	31	(h)	Southampton	W	1-0	Gray	44	13
33	Apr 7	(a)	Luton T	W	3-0	Heath 2, Mountfield	47	11
34	9	(h)	Arsenal	D	0-0		48	10
35	17	(a)	Southampton	L	1-3	Richardson	48	11
36	21	(a)	Sunderland	L	1-2	Heath	48	14
37	23	(h)	Wolves	W	2-0	Gray, Steven	51	10
38	28	(a)	Norwich C	D	1-1	Gray	52	11
39	May 5	(h)	Manchester U	D	1-1	Wakenshaw	53	11
40	7	(a)	Aston Villa	W	2-0	Richardson, Sharp	56	10
41	12	(h)	Q.P.R.	W	3-1	Sharp 2, Heath	59	10
42	14	(a)	West Ham U	W	1-0	Richardson	62	7

League Appearances
League Sub Appnces
League Goals

43	Jan 6	(a)	Stoke C	W	2-0	Gray, Irvine	FA Cup Rd 3
44	28	(h)	Gillingham	D	0-0		4
45	31	(a)	Gillingham	D	0-0		Replay
46	Feb 6	(a)	Gillingham	W	3-0	Sheedy 2, Heath	Replay
47	18	(h)	Shrewsbury T	W	3-0	Irvine, Reid, opp.og	5
48	Mar 10	(a)	Notts Co	W	2-1	Gray, Richardson	6
49	Apr 14	(n)	Southampton	W	1-0	Heath	(Highbury) SF
50	May 19	(n)	Watford	W	2-0	Gray, Sharp	(Wembley) F
51	Oct 4	(a)	Chesterfield	W	1-0	Sharp	League Cup 1st leg Rd 2
52	26	(h)	Chesterfield	D	2-2	Heath, Steven	2nd leg
53	Nov 9	(h)	Coventry C	W	2-1	Heath, Sharp	3
54	30	(a)	West Ham U	D	2-2	Reid, Sheedy	4
55	Dec 6	(h)	West Ham U	W	2-0	King, Sheedy	Replay
56	Jan 18	(a)	Oxford U	D	1-1	Heath	5
57	24	(h)	Oxford U	W	4-1	Heath, Richardson, Sharp, Sheedy	Replay
58	Feb 15	(h)	Aston Villa	W	2-0	Richardson, Sheedy	1st leg SF
59	22	(a)	Aston Villa	L	0-1		2nd leg
60	Mar 25	(n)	Liverpool	D	0-0		(Wembley) F
61	28	(n)	Liverpool	L	0-1		(Main Road) Replay

Cup Appearances
Cup Sub Appnces
Cup Goals

Arnold J	Bailey J	Bishop I	Curran T	Gray A	Harper A	Heath A	Higgins M	Hughes D	Irvine A	Johnson D	King A	Mountfield D	Ratcliffe K	Reid P	Richardson K	Rimmer S	Sharp G	Sheedy K	Southall N	Steven T	Stevens G	Wakenshaw R	No.
1	3				2	8	5				10	4		6			9	11		7			1
1	3				2	8	5			12	10	4		6*			9	11		7			2
1	3				2	8*	5			12	10	4		6			9	11		7			3
1	3*		7		2		5				10	4	12	6			9	11		8			4
1	3		7*		2	8	5				10	4	12				9	11		6			5
1	3				2	8	5				10	4		6*	12		9	11		7			6
1	3				2	8	5				10	12	4	6			9	11		7*			7
	3				2	8	5				10	4		6			9	11	1	7			8
	3				2	8	5				10	4		6			9	11	1	7			9
	3				2		5	12	8		10	4		6			9	11	1	7*			10
	3				2	8	5			12	10	4		6			9	11*	1	7			11
	3				2	8	5		7		10	4					9	11	1	6			12
	3			9	2	8	5		7		10	4		6				11	1				13
	3			9	2	8			7		10	5	4	6				11	1				14
	3			9	2	8*			7		10	5	4	6				11	1	12			15
				10			5		7		8	5	3	6			9	11	1		2		16
	3			9	12	8			7		10*	5	4	6				11	1		2		17
	3					8			7	9	10	5	4	6				11	1		2		18
				9	3	8			7		10	5	4	6				11	1		2		19
				9	3				7			5	4	6	8		10	11*	1	12	2		20
	3			9		8*			7		10	5	4	6	12			11	1		2		21
	3			9		8			7		10	5	4	6				11	1		2		22
	3			10		8			7			5	4	6	2		9	11	1				23
	3					8			7			5	4	6	10		9	11			2		24
	3			9		8			7			5	4	6	10			11	1		2		25
	3			9		8			7			5	4	6	10			11	1		2		26
	3			10		8			7			5	4	6			9	11	1		2		27
	3			10	12	8						5	4	6			9	11	1	7*	2		28
	3			10	11				7			5	4	6	8		9		1		2		29
				10	3	8			7			5	4	6	11		9*		1	12	2		30
	3			9		8					10	5	4	6	11				1	7	2		31
	3			10	7*	8						5	4	6	11		9		1	12	2		32
	3		7		4	8						5		6	11		9		1	10	2		33
	3		7	10		8						5	4	6	11		9*		1	12	2		34
			7	9	3	8						5	4	6	11				1	10	2		35
	3		7	12		8						5	4	6*	11		9		1	10	2		36
	3		7	9		8						5	4	6	11				1	10	2		37
	3		7*	9		8						5	4	6	11		12		1	10	2		38
	3			12	4	8							5	6	11		9		1	10	2	7*	39
	3					8			7			5	4	6	11		9		1	10	2		40
				10	3	8						5	4	6	11		9		1	7	2		41
	3					8					10	5	4	6	11		9		1	7	2		42
7	33		8	23	26	36	14	1	19	7	19	31	38	34	25	1	27	28	35	23	26	1	
	1			3						2	2	1		1	3		1			4	1		
				5	1	12				1	2	3		2	4		7	4		1	1	1	
	3			10		8			7			5	4	6			9	11	1		2		43
				10	3	8			7			5	4	6			9	11	1		2		44
	3			12		8			7			5	4	6	10		9*	11	1		2		45
	3			9		8			7			5	4	6	10			11	1		2		46
	3			9		8*			7		10	5	4	6	12			11	1		2		47
	3			10		12			7			5	4	6	8		9	11*	1		2		48
	3			9		8			7			5	4	6	11		12		1	10*	2		49
	3			10		8						5	4	6	11		9		1	7	2		50
	3				2	8	5					4		6	10		9	11	1	7			51
	3				2	8	5					4		6			9	11	1	10			52
	3				2	8	5		7		10	4	12				9	11	1	6*			53
						8	5		7		10	4	3	6			9	11	1		2		54
						8	5		7		10	4	3	6			9	11	1		2		55
	3					8			7		10*	5	4	6	12		9	11	1		2		56
	3					8			7			5	4	6	10		9	11	1		2		57
	3					8			7			5	4	6	10		9	11	1		2		58
	3					8			7		10	5	4	6			9	11	1		2		59
	3			12		8			7			5	4	6	10		9	11*	1		2		60
	3			11		8			7*		12	5	4	6	10		9		1		2		61
	14			7	7	18	5		17	1	5	16	19	17	11		16	16	19	5	16		
				1	2						1		1	1							2		
				3		6					2	1		2	3		4	6		1			

opp.og 1

1984-85

#	Date		Opponent		Score	Scorers		
1	Aug 25	(h)	Tottenham H	L	1-4	Heath	0	
2	27	(a)	West Brom A	L	1-2	Heath	0	
3	31	(a)	Chelsea	W	1-0	Richardson	3	
4	Sep 4	(h)	Ipswich T	D	1-1	Heath	4	
5	8	(h)	Coventry C	W	2-1	Sharp, Steven	7	13
6	15	(a)	Newcastle U	W	3-2	Gray, Sheedy, Steven	10	6
7	22	(h)	Southampton	D	2-2	Mountfield, Sharp	11	6
8	29	(a)	Watford	W	5-4	Heath 2, Mountfield, Sharp, Steven	14	6
9	Oct 6	(a)	Arsenal	L	0-1		14	8
10	13	(h)	Aston Villa	W	2-1	Heath, Sharp	17	6
11	20	(a)	Liverpool	W	1-0	Sharp	20	4
12	27	(h)	Manchester U	W	5-0	Sheedy 2, Heath, Sharp, Stevens	23	2
13	Nov 3	(h)	Leicester C	W	3-0	Heath, Sheedy, Steven	26	1
14	10	(a)	West Ham U	W	1-0	Heath	29	1
15	17	(h)	Stoke C	W	4-0	Heath 2, Reid, Steven	32	1
16	24	(a)	Norwich C	L	2-4	Sharp, Sheedy	32	1
17	Dec 1	(h)	Sheffield W	D	1-1	Sharp	33	1
18	8	(a)	Q.P.R.	D	0-0		34	1
19	15	(h)	Nottingham F	W	5-0	Sharp 2, Reid, Sheedy, Steven	37	1
20	22	(h)	Chelsea	L	3-4	Sharp 2, Bracewell	37	3
21	26	(a)	Sunderland	W	2-1	Mountfield 2	40	2
22	29	(a)	Ipswich T	W	2-0	Sharp 2	43	2
23	Jan 1	(h)	Luton T	W	2-1	Steven 2	46	2
24	12	(h)	Newcastle U	W	4-0	Sheedy 2, Mountfield, Sharp	49	1
25	Feb 2	(h)	Watford	W	4-0	Stevens 2, Sheedy, Steven	52	1
26	23	(a)	Leicester C	W	2-1	Gray 2	55	1
27	Mar 2	(a)	Manchester U	D	1-1	Mountfield	56	1
28	16	(a)	Aston Villa	D	1-1	Richardson	57	1
29	23	(h)	Arsenal	W	2-0	Gray, Sharp	60	1
30	30	(a)	Southampton	W	2-1	Richardson 2	63	1
31	Apr 3	(a)	Tottenham H	W	2-1	Gray, Steven	66	1
32	6	(h)	Sunderland	W	4-1	Gray 2, Sharp, Steven	69	1
33	16	(h)	West Brom A	W	4-1	Sharp 2, Atkin, Sheedy	72	1
34	20	(a)	Stoke C	W	2-0	Sharp, Sheedy	75	1
35	27	(h)	Norwich C	W	3-0	Bracewell, Mountfield, Steven	78	1
36	May 4	(a)	Sheffield W	W	1-0	Gray	81	1
37	6	(h)	Q.P.R.	W	2-0	Mountfield, Sharp	84	1
38	8	(h)	West Ham U	W	3-0	Mountfield 2, Gray	87	1
39	11	(a)	Nottingham F	L	0-1		87	1
40	23	(h)	Liverpool	W	1-0	Wilkinson	90	1
41	26	(a)	Coventry C	L	1-4	Wilkinson	90	1
42	28	(a)	Luton T	L	0-2		90	1

League Appearances
League Sub Appnces
League Goals

#	Date		Opponent		Score	Scorers		
43	Jan 5	(a)	Leeds U	W	2-0	Sharp, Sheedy	FA Cup Rd 3	
44	26	(h)	Doncaster R	W	2-0	Steven, Stevens	4	
45	Feb 16	(h)	Telford U	W	3-0	Reid, Sheedy, Steven	5	
46	Mar 9	(h)	Ipswich T	D	2-2	Mountfield, Sheedy	6	
47	13	(h)	Ipswich T	W	1-0	Sharp	Replay	
48	Apr 13	(n)	Luton T	W	2-1	Mountfield, Sheedy	(Villa Park) SF	
49	May 18	(n)	Manchester U	L	0-1		(Wembley) F	
50	Sep 26	(a)	Sheffield U	D	2-2	Mountfield, Sharp	League Cup 1st leg Rd 2	
51	Oct 10	(h)	Sheffield U	W	4-0	Bracewell, Heath, Mountfield, Sharp	2nd leg	
52	30	(a)	Manchester U	W	2-1	Sharp, opp.og	3	
53	Nov 20	(h)	Grimsby T	L	0-1		4	

Cup Appearances
Cup Sub Appnces
Cup Goals

Everton won the European Cup-winners' Cup (see Everton in Europe section).

Atkin I	Bailey J	Bracewell P	Curran T	Danskin J	Gray A	Harper A	Heath A	Hughes D	Morrissey J	Mountfield D	Oldroyd D	Ratcliffe K	Reid P	Richardson K	Rimmer N	Sharp G	Sheedy K	Southall N	Steven T	Stevens G	Van Den Hauwe P	Wakenshaw R	Walsh D	Wilkinson P	#
	3	10			12		8			5		4	6	11*		9		1	7	2					1
	3					7	8			5		4	6	11		9		1	10	2					2
	3	10					8			5		4	6	11		9		1	7	2					3
	3	10			12		8			5		4	6	11*		9		1	7	2					4
	3	10			12		8			5		4	6	11*		9		1	7	2					5
	3	10				9	8			5		4	6				11	1	7	2					6
	3	10					8			5		4	6			9	11	1	7	2					7
	3	10			12		8			5		4	6			9	11*	1	7	2					8
		10					8			5		4	6	11		9		1	7	2	3				9
		10				11	8			5		4	6			9		1	7	2	3				10
		10				11	8			5		4	6			9		1	7	2	3				11
		10			12		8			5		4	6			9	11*	1	7	2	3				12
		10			12		8			5		4	6			9*	11	1	7	2	3				13
		10					8			5		4	6			9	11	1	7	2	3				14
		10					8			5		4	6			9	11	1	7	2	3				15
		10			12		8			5		4	6			9	11	1	7	2	3*				16
		10			12		8*			5		4	6			9	11	1	7	2	3				17
		10					8			5		4	6			9	11	1	7	2	3				18
		10			12		8*			5		4	6			9	11	1	7	2	3				19
	3	10					8			5		4	6			9	11	1	7	2					20
2	3	10					8			5		4	6			9	11	1	7						21
	3	10	8							5		4	6			9	11	1	7	2					22
	3	10	8							5		4	6			9	11	1	7	2					23
		10	8							5		4	6			9	11	1	7	2	3				24
		10	8							5		4	6			9	11	1	7	2	3				25
		10				9	8			5		4	6				11	1	7	2	3				26
		10				8	9			5		4	6				11	1	7	2	3				27
		10					9		11	5		4	6			8		1	7	2	3				28
		10					9			5		4	6	11		8		1	7	2	3				29
		10					9			5		4	6	11		8*		1	7	2	3	12			30
		10					9*		12	5		4	6			8	11	1	7	2	3				31
	3	10					9		12	5		4	6			8	11*	1	7	2					32
5		10					9					4	6			8	11	1	7	2	3				33
5		10					9					4	6			8	11	1	7	2	3				34
		10					9		11	5		4	6			8		1	7	2	3				35
		10					9			5		4	6			8	11	1	7	2	3				36
		10					9			5		4	6			8	11	1	7	2	3				37
4		10					9*			5			6	12		8	11	1	7	2	3				38
10							8*			5	12	4	6				11	1	7	2	3			9	39
10*	3						9		7			4	6				11	1		2	5	12		8	40
			10								2	4	6	12	5	8	11		7	2				9*	41
	3	10										4	6	12	5	8	11							9*	42

League totals:

- Appearances: 6 15 37 4 1 21 10 17 2 1 37 40 36 14 36 29 42 40 37 31 1 1 4
- Substitute appearances: 4 5 2 1 1 1 1 1
- Goals: 1 2 9 11 10 2 4 21 11 12 3 2

Atkin I	Bailey J	Bracewell P	Curran T	Danskin J	Gray A	Harper A	Heath A	Hughes D	Morrissey J	Mountfield D	Oldroyd D	Ratcliffe K	Reid P	Richardson K	Rimmer N	Sharp G	Sheedy K	Southall N	Steven T	Stevens G	Van Den Hauwe P	Wakenshaw R	Walsh D	Wilkinson P	#
12		10					8			5		4	6			9	11	1	7	2*	3				43
		10					8			5		4	6			9	11	1	7	2	3				44
		10					8		12	5		4	6			9*	11	1	7	2	3				45
		10				8	9			5		4	6				11	1	7	2	3				46
		10					9		11	5		4	6			8		1	7	2	3				47
		10					9			5		4	6			8	11	1	7	2	3				48
		10					9			5		4	6			8	11	1	7	2	3				49
	3	10					8			5		4	6			9	11	1	7	2					50
		10					8			5		4	6	11		9		1	7	2	3				51
		10				11	8			5		4	6			9		1	7	2	3				52
		10*			12		8			5		4	6			9	11	1	7	2	3				53

Cup totals:

- 1 11 1 7 2 4 11 11 11 1 10 8 11 11 11 10
- 1 1 1
- 1 2 1 4 1 5 4 2 1   opp.og 1

EVERTON IN EUROPE

European Cup

1963-4
18 Sep
Rd 1 1st leg v Inter Milan (h) 0-0
West, Parker, Harris, Gabriel, Labone, Kay, Scott, Stevens, Young, Vernon, Temple.
25 Sep
Rd 1 2nd leg v Inter Milan (a) 0-1 (aggregate 0-1)
West, Parker, Harris, Stevens, Labone, Kay, Scott, Harvey, Young, Vernon, Temple.

1970-71
16 Sep
Rd 1 1st leg v Keflavik (h) 6-2 *Ball 3, Royle 2, Kendall*
West, Wright, K.Newton, Kendall, Kenyon, Harvey, Husband(Whittle), Ball, Royle, Hurst, Morrissey.
30 Sep
Rd 1 2nd leg v Keflavik (a) 3-0 (aggregate 9-2) *Royle 2, Whittle*
Rankin, Wright, K.Newton, Kendall, Labone, Harvey(Brown), Whittle, Ball(Jackson), Royle, Hurst, Morrissey.
21 Oct
Rd 2 1st leg v Munchen Gladbach (a) 1-1 *Kendall*
Rankin, Wright, K.Newton, Kendall, Kenyon, Harvey, Whittle, Ball, Royle, Hurst, Morrissey.
4 Nov
Rd 2 2nd leg v Munchen Gladbach (h) 1-1 (aggregate 1-1; Everton won 4-3 on penalties). *Morrissey*
Rankin, Wright, K.Newton(Brown), Kendall, Kenyon, Harvey, Whittle(Husband), Ball, Royle, Hurst, Morrissey.
9 Mar
Rd 3 1st leg v Panathinaikos (h) 1-1 *Johnson*
Rankin, Wright, K.Newton, Kendall, Kenyon, Harvey, Husband(Johnson), Ball, Royle, Hurst, Morrissey.
24 Mar
Rd 3 2nd leg v Panathinaikos (a) 0-0 (aggregate 1-1; Panathinaikos won on away goals rule).
Rankin, Wright, K.Newton, Kendall, Labone, Harvey, Whittle, Ball, Royle, Hurst, Morrissey (Johnson).

European Cup-winners' Cup

1966-7
28 Sep
Rd 1 1st leg v Aalborg (a) 0-0
West, Wright, Wilson, Gabriel, Labone, Harvey, Temple, Ball, Young, Trebilcock, Morrissey.
11 Oct
Rd 1 2nd leg v Aalborg (h) 2-1 (aggregate 2-1) *Morrissey, Ball*
West, Wright, Wilson, Gabriel, Labone, Harvey, Temple, Ball, Young, Husband, Morrissey.
9 Nov
Rd 2 1st leg v Real Zaragoza (a) 0-2
West, Wright, Wilson, Gabriel, Labone, Harvey, Scott, Ball, Young, Temple, Morrissey.
23 Nov
Rd 2 2nd leg v Real Zaragoza (h) 1-0(aggregate 1-2) *Brown*
West, Wright, Wilson, Gabriel, Labone, Harvey, Scott, Ball, Young, Brown, Temple.

Kevin Sheedy is denied by the diving Bayern Munich goalkeeper Pfaff.

1984-5
19 Sep
Rd 1 1st leg v UC Dublin (a) 0-0
Southall, Stevens, Bailey, Ratcliffe, Mountfield, Reid, Steven(Curran), Heath, Sharp, Bracewell, Sheedy.
2 Oct
Rd 1 2nd leg v UC Dublin (h) 1-0 (aggregate 1-0) *Sharp*
Southall, Stevens, Bailey, Ratcliffe, Mountfield, Reid, Steven, Heath(Wakenshaw), Sharp, Bracewell, Curran.
24 Oct
Rd 2 1st leg v Bratislava (a) 1-0 *Bracewell*
Southall, Stevens, Bailey, Ratcliffe, Mountfield, Reid, Steven, Heath, Sharp, Bracewell, Harper.
7 Nov
Rd 2 2nd leg v Bratislava (h) 3-0 (aggregate 4-0) *Heath, Sharp, Sheedy*
Southall, Stevens, Bailey, Ratcliffe, Mountfield, Reid(Harper), Steven, Heath, Sharp, Bracewell, Sheedy(Morrissey).
6 Mar
Rd 3 1st leg v F Sittard (h) 3-0 *Gray 3*
Southall, Stevens, Van den Hauwe, Ratcliffe, Mountfield, Reid(Richardson), Steven, Curran, Gray, Bracewell, Sheedy.
20 Mar
Rd 3 2nd leg v F Sittard (a) 2-0 (aggregate 5-0) *Reid, Sharp*
Southall, Stevens, Van den Hauwe, Ratcliffe(Atkins), Mountfield, Reid, Steven, Curran, Sharp(Wakenshaw), Harper, Richardson.
10 Apr
SF 1st leg v Bayern Munich (a) 0-0
Southall, Stevens, Van den Hauwe, Ratcliffe, Mountfield, Reid, Steven, Harper, Sharp, Bracewell, Richardson.
24 Apr
SF 2nd leg v Bayern Munich (h) 3-1 (aggregate 3-1) *Gray, Sharp, Steven*
Southall, Stevens, Van den Hauwe, Ratcliffe, Mountfield, Reid, Steven, Sharp, Gray, Bracewell, Sheedy.
15 May
Final v Rapid Vienna (at Rotterdam) 3-1 *Gray, Sheedy, Steven*
Southall, Stevens, Van den Hauwe, Ratcliffe, Mountfield, Reid, Steven, Sharp, Gray, Bracewell, Sheedy.

Everton meet Fortuna Sittard in the European Cup-winners' Cup quarter-final and once more Andy Gray puts his head where few players would dare.

Inter-Cities Fairs' Cup

1962-3
24 Oct
Rd 1 1st leg v Dunfermline A (h) 1-0 *Stevens*
West, Parker, Thomson, Gabriel, Labone, Harris, Bingham, Stevens, Young, Vernon, Morrissey.
31 Oct
Rd 1 2nd leg v Dunfermline A (a) 0-2 (aggregate 1-2) West, Parker, Meagan, Gabriel, Labone, Harris, Bingham, Stevens, Young, Vernon, Morrissey.

1964-5
23 Sep
Rd 1 1st leg v Valerengen (a) 5-2 *Pickering 2, Harvey, Scott Temple*
Rankin, Harris, Brown, Gabriel, Labone, Stevens, Scott, Harvey, Pickering, Temple, Morrissey.
14 Oct
Rd 1 2nd leg v Valerengen (h) 4-2 (aggregate 9-4) *Young 2, Vernon, opp.og*
Rankin, Wright, Brown, Stevens, Labone, Harris, Scott, Young, Pickering, Vernon, Temple.
11 Nov
Rd 2 1st leg v Kilmarnock (a) 2-0 *Temple, Morrissey*
Rankin, Stevens, Brown, Gabriel, Labone, Harris, Temple, Young, Pickering, Vernon, Morrissey.
23 Nov
Rd 2 2nd leg v Kilmarnock (h) 4-1 (aggregate 6-1) *Pickering 2, Harvey, Young*
Rankin, Harris, Brown, Gabriel, Labone, Stevens, Temple, Young, Pickering, Harvey, Morrissey.
20 Jan
Rd 3 1st leg v Manchester U (a) 1-1 *Pickering*
West, Wright, Wilson, Gabriel, Labone, Stevens, Scott, Harvey, Pickering, Vernon, Temple.
4 Feb
Rd 3 2nd leg v Manchester U (h) 1-2 (aggregate 2-3) *Pickering*
West, Wright, Wilson, Gabriel, Labone, Stevens, Scott, Harvey, Pickering, Vernon, Temple.

1965-6
28 Sep
Rd 1 1st leg v IFC Nuremberg (a) 1-1 *Harris*
West, Wright, Wilson, Gabriel, Brown, Harris, Temple, Stevens, Pickering, Harvey, Morrissey.

12 Oct
Rd 1 2nd leg v IFC Nuremberg (h) 1-0 (aggregate 2-1) *Gabriel*
West(Rankin), Wright, Wilson, Gabriel, Labone, Harris, Scott, Harvey, Pickering, Young, Temple.
3 Nov
Rd 2 1st leg v Ujpest Dozsa (a) 0-3
Rankin, Wright, Wilson, Stevens, Labone, Harris, Scott, Harvey, Pickering, Temple, Morrissey.
16 Nov
Rd 2 2nd leg v Ujpest Dozsa (h) 2-1 (aggregate 2-4) *Harris, opp.og*
Rankin, Wright, Wilson, Harvey, Labone, Harris, Temple, Gabriel, Young, Husband, Morrissey.

UEFA Cup

1975-6
17 Sep
Rd 1 1st leg v AC Milan (h) 0-0
Lawson, Bernard, Seargeant, Pearson, Kenyon, Lyons, Buckley(Clements), Dobson, Latchford, Smallman(Hurst), G.Jones.
1 Oct
Rd 1 2nd leg v AC Milan (a) 0-1 (aggregate 0-1) Davies, Bernard, Seargeant, Pearson, Kenyon, Lyons, Buckley, Dobson, Latchford, Smallman, G.Jones.

1978-9
12 Sep
Rd 1 1st leg v Finn Harps (a) 5-0 *King 2, Latchford, Thomas, Walsh*
Wood, Darracott, Pejic, Lyons(Higgins), Wright, Nulty, King, Ross, Latchford, Walsh, Thomas.
26 Sep
Rd 1 2nd leg v Finn Harps (h) 5-0 (aggregate 10-0) *Dobson, King, Latchford, Ross, Walsh*
Wood, Darracott, Pejic, Lyons(Higgins), Wright, Ross, King, Dobson, Latchford, Walsh, Thomas(Nulty).
18 Oct
Rd 2 1st leg v Dukla Prague (h) 2-1 *King, Latchford*
Wood, Darracott(Robinson), Pejic, Lyons, Wright, Ross, King, Dobson, Latchford, Thomas, Walsh.
1 Nov
Rd 2 2nd leg v Dukla Prague (a) 0-1 (aggregate 2-2; Dukla Prague won on away goals). Wood, Darracott, Pejic, Kenyon, Wright, Nulty, Ross, Dobson, Latchford, Walsh, Thomas.

1979-80
19 Sep
Rd 1 1st leg v Feyenoord (a) 0-1
Wood, Barton, Bailey, Lyons, Higgins, Ross, Nulty, Wright, King, Kidd, Eastoe.
3 Oct
Rd 1 2nd leg v Feyenoord (h) 0-1 (aggregate 0-2)
Wood, Barton, Bailey, Lyons, Higgins, Nulty, McBride(Varadi), Wright, King, Kidd, Eastoe (Latchford).

Texaco Cup

1973-4
18 Sep
Rd 1 1st leg v Heart of Midlothian (h) 0-1
Lawson, Darracott, McLaughlin, Buckley, Kenyon, Hurst, H.Newton, Lyons, Belfitt(Bernard), Harper, Connolly.
3 Oct
Rd 1 2nd leg v Heart of Midlothian (a) 0-0 (aggregate 0-1)
Lawson, Darracott, McLaughlin, Clements, Kenyon, Hurst, Buckley, Husband, Lyons, Harper, Connolly.

Charity Shield

1928
24 Oct v Blackburn Rovers (at Old Trafford) 2-1 *Dean 2*
Davies, Cresswell, O'Donnell, Griffiths, Hart, Virr, Ritchie, Forshaw, Dean, Weldon, Troup.

1932
12 Oct v Newcastle United (a) 5-3 *Dean 4, Johnson*
Sagar, Williams, Cresswell, Britton, White, Thomson, Critchley, McGourty, Dean, Johnson, Stein.

1933
18 Oct v Arsenal (h) 0-3
Sagar, Cook, Bocking, Britton, Gee, Thomson, Geldard, Dunn, White, Johnson, Stein.

1963
17 Aug v Manchester United (h) 4-0 *Gabriel, Stevens, Temple, Vernon*
West, Parker, Meagan, Gabriel, Labone, Kay, Scott, Stevens, Young, Vernon, Temple.

1966
13 Aug v Liverpool (h) 0-1
West, Wright, Wilson, Gabriel, Labone, Glover, Scott, Young, Trebilcock, Harvey, Temple.

1970
8 Aug v Chelsea (a) 2-1 *Kendall, Whittle*
West, Wright, K.Newton, Kendall, Labone, Harvey, Husband, Ball, Royle, Hurst, Whittle.

1984
18 Aug v Liverpool (Wembley) 1-0 *opp.og*
Southall, Stevens, Bailey, Ratcliffe, Mountfield, Reid, Steven, Heath, Sharp, Bracewell, Richardson.

British Championship

1963
27 Nov v Glasgow Rangers (a) 3-1 *Scott, Temple, Young*
West, Brown, Meagan, Harris, Heslop, Kay, Scott, Stevens, Young, Vernon, Temple.
2 Dec v Glasgow Rangers (h) 1-1 (aggregate 4-2) *Young*
West, Brown, Meagan, Gabriel, Heslop, Harris, Scott, Stevens, Young, Vernon, Temple.

Dixie Dean (left) scored six Charity Shield goals for Everton, two against Blackburn and four against Newcastle.

THE GOODISON PARK STORY

Goodison Park as it looked in 1905.

GOODISON PARK was the first truly major football stadium in England, yet the magnificent soccer ground which the sporting world knows today would almost certainly not exist, had it not been for one man's dramatic change of heart, back in 1887.

It was then that George Mahon was converted to football. Mahon had professed a hatred for the game until he was enthralled by a match between Everton and Preston North End. Thereafter, he became an avid supporter and in 1892, when a furious row broke out within Everton's ranks, it was Mahon who guided the club towards a field on the north side of Stanley Park, near Goodison Road.

The disaffected Everton members left Anfield, which had staged an England-Ireland international in March that year, and turned their attentions to the job of transforming their new home into a ground good enough to stage League soccer.

The first tasks were to level the land, provide adequate drainage, build dressing rooms and stands in the close season of 1892 — and all before a penny in gate-money could be taken. There was a massive cash crisis before one club member, Dr James Clement Baxter, loaned an interest-free sum of £1,000.

Mere Green Field cost £8,090 and the total outlay of transforming overgrown wastelands into Goodison Park for 1892-3, and additions in the lease period, was £4,000.

The task of clearing the debris and laying drains was handed to a Mr Barton who charged the princely sum of fourpence-halfpenny for each of the 29,471 square yards.

Walton-based building firm, Kelly Brothers, erected two uncovered stands, each accommodating 4,000, and a covered stand for another 3,000, at a cost of £1,640. They also constructed outside enclosing hoardings for £150 and gates and sheds for £132 10s. Twelve turnstiles cost £7 15s each.

Goodison Park — the ground was renamed immediately — was officially opened by FA officials, Lord Kinnaird and Frederick Wall, on 24 August 1892, 12,000 people turning up to watch members of the Everton side compete in a variety of sports.

The first game played there was on 2 September when Everton beat Bolton Wanderers 4-2. One report stated: '...it appears to be one of the finest and most

Goodison Park in 1985.

complete grounds in the kingdom...'. Indeed, the authorities thought so highly of Everton's new home that the 1894 FA Cup Final between Notts County and Bolton was staged there.

There were more rapid improvements. In 1895 a new Bullens Road Stand was built at a cost of £3,407, and a further £403 was spent on covering the Goodison Road side.

Everton invariably prospered in their new surroundings and further improvements were undertaken after a profit of £3,718 5s 7d was made following the FA Cup success of 1906.

Some £13,000 was spent on building the Park End double-decker stand on the south side of Goodison Park, and in 1909 the club added the Main Stand, which also housed a suite of offices and players' quarters. It rose on the Goodison Road side at a cost of £28,000. This stand survived until 1971.   At the same time, Everton spent £12,000 on concreting the terraces and resurfacing the old cinder running-track. A 1909 edition of the *Athletic News* commented: 'Visitors to Goodison Park will be astonished at the immensity of the new double-decker stand'. The following year's FA Cup Final replay between Newcastle and Barnsley was staged at Goodison.

In 1913, Goodison Park became the first Football League ground to be visited by a reigning monarch when King George V and Queen Mary met Liverpool schoolchildren there.

During World War One, Goodison Park saw regular football as Everton played in the regional wartime league. The ground was also used for army drill, and there was even a baseball match between Chicago Giants and New York Whitesox.

In 1926, a double-decker stand was built by the Bullens Road at a cost of £30,000, and in the '30s Goodison Park saw probably the first trainers' 'dug-outs' in England. It was an idea copied from Aberdeen, whom Everton had visited for a friendly match.

In 1938 work was completed on the new £50,000 Gwladys Street stand, which now made Goodison Park the only British soccer ground to have four double-decker stands. Goodison Park inevitably suffered during German air raids on the city in World War Two. The club received £5,000 from the War Damage Commission for essential repair work. In 1948 the ground was sufficiently safe to hold a record attendance of 78,299 for the visit of Liverpool in a First Division match.

In 1971 came Goodison's latest and most spectacular improvement. The old Main Stand, a wonder in its day, was demolished and the present three-decker Main Stand was completed at a cost of £1 million. It provided seating for 10,000, modern dressing rooms, a treatment room, gymnasium, laundry and restaurant facilities.

The Goodison Park floodlighting system, which had been switched on for a game against Liverpool to mark the 75th anniversary of the Liverpool County FA on 9 October 1957, was also changed at this stage. The pylons were replaced by rows of ultra-powerful lights on the roof of the stands, the Bullens Road stand being re-roofed in the process.

The under-soil heating, which is now one of the finest in the country, has had its problems over the years. Electrical wiring was installed under the pitch in May 1958 at a cost of £16,000, but ultimately it was discovered that the drains could not cope with the melted ice and snow. The pitch was dug up and new drains laid. Further attempts at undersoil heating were tried and abandoned before the present system was introduced.

Everton received a shock when the local authority, acting under the 1975 Safety of Sports Grounds Act, announced that the official capacity of Goodison Park would have to be reduced from 56,000 to a mere 35,000. Work costing in excess of £250,000 was immediately carried out, pushing the limit back up to 52,800. The 1985 capacity was given as 53,091 with some 25,000 seated.

Goodison Park, a great 19th-century football stadium, has carried on that tradition. Graced by the likes of Pele and Eusebio during the 1966 World Cup, today it is one of the finest footballing theatres in Europe.

Everton 1922-3. Back row (l to r): J.Taylor, W.Brown, R.Irvine, D.Livingstone, J.Peacock, A.Jeffes, J. McGrae, E.Salt, W.Williams, R.Caddick, F.Forbes, H.Hart, S.Chedgzoy, G.Brewster, D.Raitt, J.MacDonald, T.Fern, H.Makepeace. Middle: J.Elliott, F.Alford, W.Jackson, W.Miller, W.Chadwick, D.Reid, G.Jones, G.Harrison. Front: A.Kemp, H.Spencer, H.Young, J.McGivney, A.Wall, A.Moffat.

PROGRAMME PARADE

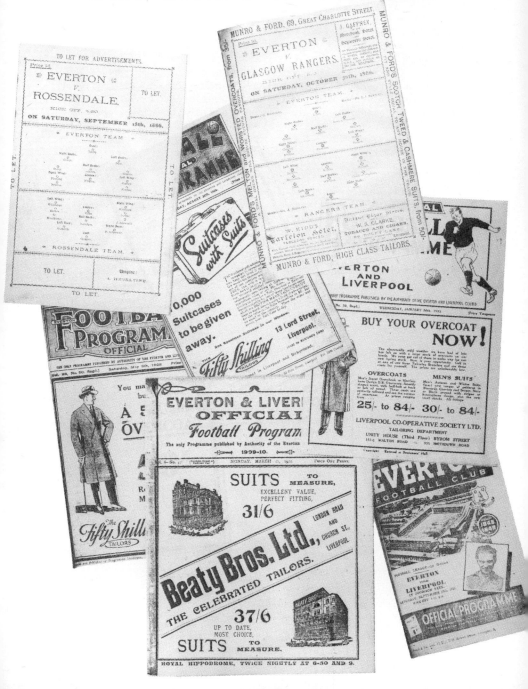

EVERTON MANAGERS

Theo Kelly
1939-1948

THEO Kelly was Everton's first ever manager. He was appointed at the end of the 1938-9 season, shortly after the club had secured the League title for the fifth time.

Everton were one of the last of the big name clubs to appoint a manager. Before Kelly took over the reins, team selection was a matter for senior coaches, prominent boardroom executives and specially appointed committees.

Kelly had been Everton club secretary for many years when it was decided to offer him the newly-created post. A superb organiser with a fine business brain, he was not particulary popular with the players, many finding it difficult to communicate with him.

But Harry Catterick, who played under Kelly, said of him: "He was the best public relations man I have ever known and any shortcomings he might have had with the players were compensated by his ability to open doors that were closed to other people."

His first seven years as manager found him in charge of a team playing in wartime regional football after the Football League had been suspended for the duration of hostilities. As peacetime soccer dawned, he angered many of Everton's loyal followers by selling Tommy Lawton to Chelsea in 1945, but in fairness to Kelly it has to be said that the free-scoring centre-forward had been restless for some time.

Joe Mercer, too, found it difficult to play for Kelly and the manager found himself selling another pre-war star to a London club, this time Arsenal.

Kelly rarely dipped into the transfer market during his time in charge, firmly believing that a manager should make do with what he has, unless an exceptional talent becomes available. Perhaps it was a philosophy which arose from the fact that, as secretary, he had spent so much time studying the administrative and financial problems of football.

The one big deal that he did line up turned sour on him. Constantly on the look-out for a forward to fill the gaping void left by Dixie Dean and Lawton, he pinned his hopes on Newcastle United's Albert Stubbins. But Liverpool chairman, Bill McConnell, got in first and even an increased offer of £12,500 was not good enough to bring Stubbins to Goodison.

In 1948, with Everton hovering just above the relegation zone, Kelly reverted to his old job of secretary when Cliff Britton returned to the club as manager.

Cliff Britton
1948-1956

WHEN Cliff Britton took charge of Everton in September 1948, he was, in effect, coming home.

As a wing-half of great style and polish he had enjoyed a memorable career with the club, culminating in an FA Cup winners' medal in 1933. For three years before rejoining Everton as manager he had been in charge of team matters at Burnley, enjoying great success. He took them from the Second Division to third place in the First, and to the FA Cup Final at Wembley. At Goodison he was handed the daunting task of restoring pride to a club which was struggling to regain the peak it had reached in the immediate pre-war days.

A fair-minded, easy-going man, he was well-liked by fans and players alike and managed to introduce some stability to a side which, although competent and confident, was never really good enough to live with the leading sides of the day.

He took Everton to an FA Cup semi-final with Liverpool at Maine Road in March 1950, but it was the old enemy from across Stanley Park who graced Wembley that season after a comfortable 2-0 win.

Britton paid £20,000 for Burnley's inside-forward, Harry Potts, who later returned to Turf Moor as manager; and in the fateful season of 1950-51 he spent a further £8,000 on Glasgow Rangers full-back, Jack Lindsay.

Things went dramatically wrong for Britton as the campaign reached its climax at the beginning of May. On the fifth day of that month, Everton found themselves with 32 points, with only Chelsea and Sheffield Wednesday, both on 30 points, below them in the table.

Everton, with a goal-average which was inferior to their fellow strugglers, needed one more point to guarantee First Division survival, but in the final matches Chelsea beat Bolton 4-0 — and Everton crashed 6-0 to Sheffield Wednesday.

Britton was naturally distraught, but the Everton board gave him a badly-needed vote of confidence and he diligently set about the task of winning back the club's First Division status. Everton finished seventh and 16th before he brought them back, as Division Two runners-up, in 1953-4.

But past glories still seemed a long way off and in 1956 Britton parted company with the club. It followed a dispute over Everton wanting to appoint an acting manager while Britton was abroad with the team.

He left, saying: "I want all managers to have the freedom to do the job for which they were appointed, which is to manage their clubs."

Ian Buchan
1956-58

THE appointment of Ian Buchan as team coach in succession to Cliff Britton was an ill-judged move on the part of the Everton board. Buchan, a former Scottish amateur international, was a courteous and intensely loyal man, but his position at Goodison was invidious and he never enjoyed the full trappings of manager.

His main influence during his time at the club was in the area of the players' fitness, and at a time when a few dozen laps of the pitch were all that was considered necessary, Buchan turned Everton into the fittest side in the First Division.

Unfortunately, he did not have players of sufficient quality to capitalise on that. He once said that his side, with its fast, first-time football, was a winning combination in the early months of the season when pitches were well-grassed, but that he yearned for players who could adapt to the mud and ice of an English winter.

He was a deep thinker and his commitment to Everton was unquestioned. But the club needed a big-name manager and Buchan was anything but that. He died in a motor accident in Glasgow in 1965, aged 45.

Johnny Carey
1958-1961

JOHNNY Carey was appointed Everton manager in October 1958, more than two years after Britton had departed. He took over from Ian Buchan, the club coach who never had the title of manager and who failed to drag Everton out of their ever deepening depression.

Carey, perhaps the best of Matt Busby's players during Manchester United's immediate post-war glory days, arrived not long after chairman Dick Seale had snapped up Celtic star, Bobby Collins.

Carey had been a calm, assured footballer and he brought those qualities to the manager's chair when he took over at Blackburn Rovers. He was at Ewood Park for five years and it was from there that he joined Everton.

At Goodison he inherited a promising squad. Apart from Collins, he had players of the calibre of Derek Temple, Mick Meagan, Brian Labone and Albert Dunlop.

He was also fortunate to arrive at the very moment that millionaire football fanatic and lifelong Everton supporter, John Moores, moved in to become the club's benefactor. With Moores' massive financial backing, Carey went into the transfer market to secure some of the most talented players ever seen at Goodison Park.

The job of transforming Everton into a team with a future as well as a past was handed to men like Roy Vernon, Billy Bingham, Alex Young and Jimmy Gabriel.

After two largely disappointing seasons, Carey took Everton to their highest position since the war when they finished fifth in 1960-61.

But, with the removal of the maximum players' wage, a new football age was dawning and club directors — and supporters — would soon be demanding championships and cups, and viewing anything less as failure.

At the end of the season Carey joined Moores, by now club chairman, at a Football League meeting in London. Rumours of Carey's impending dismissal were rife and the two men were besieged by journalists when they emerged from the meeting.

In the back of a taxi, Moores told Carey that he felt a change of manager was necessary and offered him a golden handshake. It was typical of Carey that, although stunned and saddened, he made no fuss, accepting the decision with great dignity.

Carey later took Leyton Orient to the First Division and spent five successful years as manager of Nottingham Forest.

Harry Catterick
1961-1973

HARRY Catterick was the man who transformed Everton into a great side once more, capable of living with the best. Indeed, he built two Championship-winning teams.

A tough taskmaster and strict disciplinarian, he ruled with a rod of iron while still managing to get the best from his players. He was appointed in 1961 to succeed Johnny Carey and was given a simple brief by Moores: to get Everton back to the very top by means of good, entertaining football.

Never afraid to back his own judgement and put his reputation on the line, Catterick proved adept when wheeling and dealing in the transfer market. He brought a succession of top-quality players to Goodison, including Gordon West, John Morrissey, Tony Kay, Fred Pickering and Ray Wilson.

When he was appointed manager, he was no stranger to Everton. Older fans remembered the centre-forward who scored 24 League and Cup goals for the club in 71 matches in the late '40s and early '50s.

In his first season in charge he guided Everton to fourth place in Division One as Liverpool reclaimed their top flight status by taking the Second Division title.

Twelve months later, the revival, which he had single-handedly sparked, reached its climax as a sixth Championship was taken with some stylish football.

Catterick's belief in the true values of sportsmanship were shattered in January 1965 when Kay was sent to prison and banned from football for life after being found guilty of fixing matches during his time with Sheffield Wednesday.

For a man who always believed that football was primarily a sport, not a business, it was a bitter pill to swallow. But, even without the influence of Kay at wing-half, Everton managed to walk hand in hand with success.

In 1966 they reached Wembley and Catterick's biggest gamble — the inclusion of unknown

Mike Trebilcock — paid off. The little Cornishman scored twice in one of the most exciting post-war FA Cup Finals.

Catterick signed Alan Ball from Blackpool at the same time as his youth policy began to pay dividends. Jimmy Husband, Joe Royle and John Hurst all fought their way through the ranks as a new side began to take shape.

In March 1967, Catterick signed Howard Kendall and took Everton back to Wembley in 1968, only to see West Brom snatch the Cup in extra-time.

More glory beckoned, but Manchester City ended dreams of a third Final in four years when they beat Everton in the semi-final. In the League, Everton finished third.

By the start of 1969-70, Catterick had built one of the finest sides of post-war English football. With Harvey, Kendall and Ball running the engine-room, and Royle hitting the target regularly, Everton swept to the title in glorious style.

But Catterick was unable to explain why his famous side then ran out of confidence and ideas and in only 12 months slumped to 14th place.

In January 1972, while driving home from Sheffield, Harry Catterick had a heart attack. In April 1973, with four years of his ten-year contract still to run, he was moved sideways into a senior executive role.

The man who restored pride to a famous club collapsed and died at Goodison Park after an FA Cup quarter-final match against Ipswich Town on 9 March 1985.

Billy Bingham
1973-1977

WHEN Billy Bingham took over in May 1973, he inherited a team badly in need of major reconstruction. A public who, just three years earlier, had grown used to watching superior football week after week, were fast becoming disillusioned as a slide in fortunes continued unchecked.

After playing in the club's 1963 Championship triumph, Bingham had set about learning the arts of management with such diverse teams as Southport and the Greek national side.

He took the job at Goodison with no illusions. The pressures were intense as Bill Shankly's Liverpool cast a giant shadow across Stanley Park.

A likeable man with a keen sense of humour, Bingham pushed the club to seventh spot in Division One in his first season, but he was the first to admit that it was not good enough. He bought Bob Latchford from Birmingham (Kendall moving to St Andrew's as part of the deal); Martin Dobson from Burnley and Jim Pearson from St Johnstone; and said farewell to men like Colin Harvey and Joe Royle.

The 1974-5 season proved to be the closest he would come to triumph during his short tenure at Goodison.

For long periods it seemed as if the League Championship would return to Everton. But, unable to sustain their form, they slipped to a disappointing fourth.

Convinced that the introduction of new faces would help the club turn the corner, Bingham bought Andy King, the enigmatic Duncan McKenzie and Bruce Rioch.

McKenzie and Rioch had played in only five matches for their new manager — two defeats, two draws and a win - before Bingham was sacked on 10 January 1977, as Everton slumped to 13th place.

With typical honesty and realism he said: "If you're with a top club, you expect to be shot down."

Three months later, he accepted a job in Greece as manager of Paok Salonika. Bingham, who played for Northern Ireland in the 1958 World Cup Finals, managed the national team when they next reached the World Finals, in 1982.

Gordon Lee
1977-1981

GORDON Lee arrived in January 1977 with a hard-earned reputation as a soccer troubleshooter.

Clubs in a mess often turned to Lee, and he would sort them out, usually sooner rather than later. He had spent 11 years as a defender with Aston Villa before becoming player-coach of Shrewsbury Town.

He took Port Vale up to the Third Division in his first managerial job, and won promotion to Division Two for Blackburn Rovers during their centenary year of 1974-5. He steered Newcastle United to the League Cup and into Europe.

When he took charge at Goodison he found the club at a crossroads. Although they were hovering perilously close to the relegation zone, they had battled through to the League Cup semi-finals, while the FA Cup campaign had got underway.

During the last four months of 1976-7, Lee proved a motivator of men. Everton lost only two of their remaining 18 League games to finish an encouraging ninth; and they won through to the League Cup Final and the FA Cup semi-finals.

His dreams of marking his first season with a trophy were shattered by Aston Villa after two replays, while it was Liverpool who won through to the FA Cup Final with two hotly-disputed goals.

Nevertheless, Lee built a side of considerable ability and, perhaps more importantly, one worth watching. In his first full season, Everton finished third and were the First Division's highest scorers with 76 goals.

The following season had an explosive start — 19 games without defeat and a rare victory over Liverpool. Midway through the campaign Lee was charged with bringing the game into disrepute after he criticised a referee for allowing a game to go ahead on a treacherous pitch at Southampton. He was later cleared by an FA disciplinary committee.

Everton went on to finish a disappointing fourth and storm clouds began to gather. Lee swooped into the transfer market on deadline day, in a bid to improve his side's fire-power. He signed Brian Kidd and Peter Eastoe, but they failed to revive the flagging fortunes.

As the 1979-80 season got underway, he spent money in a forlorn bid to buy success. Stanley, Hartford, Gidman and Megson were drafted in, but it was too late and confidence continued to sink, along with attendances.

On 11 April 1981, after an embarrassing 2-0 home defeat by Norwich, chairman Philip Carter gave the first indication that Lee's days as Everton manager were numbered.

Within an hour of the final whistle, Carter issued a statement saying that the positions of the manager and his staff were under review. After nearly a month of speculation, Lee was sacked on 6 May.

Gordon Lee was a dedicated hard-working man whose best was simply not good enough for a club which has always demanded success.

Howard Kendall
1981-

"Howard was our first choice. He is one of the finest players ever to come out of the club and we know he has always been an Everton man at heart," declared chairman Philip Carter on 8 May 1981, as one of Goodison's favourite sons returned to the scene of his greatest triumphs.

After two poor seasons (the club had finished 19th in 1979-80, avoiding relegation by only four points) a disgruntled Everton public, tired of being force-fed a diet of broken promises, badly needed a lift and who better to provide it than Kendall, a man idolised during his illustrious playing career with the club.

He had served his apprenticeship as a manager, having taken Blackburn Rovers from Division Three to the brink of Division One, and was ready for the big-time. Businesslike and ruthless when the occasion demanded, he immediately brought a feeling of stability and hope to the club, even though he was quick to discover that footballing miracles do not happen overnight.

Although he led the side to eighth place in Division One in his first season in charge, he struggled initially to come to grips with the enormity of the job, spending money on players who were simply not suited to football at the highest level.

Alan Biley, Mick Ferguson, Alan Ainscow and Mike Walsh came and went after making little or no impact. On the plus side, however, were the early buys of Neville Southall and Adrian Heath, two men who were destined to play leading roles in the well-documented revival.

Only days after his arrival, Kendall made his objectives perfectly clear — he wanted to win a trophy, something the club had failed to do since he himself was a key member of the 1970 Championship-winning side.

But, despite a significant and undeniable improvement in Everton's fortunes, the club's trophy cabinet was still bare two years later. In the 1982-3 season, the momentum had been maintained with seventh place and an FA Cup run ended by a late Manchester United goal in the quarter-finals.

The next season was make or break. Despite having the nucleus of a potentially superb side, things went from bad to worse. On 26 October 1983, only 8,067 people turned up to watch a Milk Cup-tie against Chesterfield. A fortnight later the figure was 9,080 for the visit of Coventry City in the same competition.

After a draw at Stoke on 14 January 1984 — Everton had beaten the Potters in the FA Cup third round a week earlier — the club plummeted to 18th place and the knives were out.

A small section of the crowd had made their feelings clear in the days leading up to that black Christmas, circulating leaflets which demanded the dismissal of both Kendall and his chairman.

And then it happened. A Milk Cup quarter-final match at Oxford was drifting away when

Heath latched on to a dreadful back-pass to snatch a late equaliser. Everton cantered to an easy win in the replay and were off and running.

A rejuvenated side strung together a series of impressive League results to climb to seventh place, won through to the first-ever all-Mersey Wembley meeting when they met Liverpool in the Milk Cup Final, and swept to the FA Cup Final against Watford.

With Philip Carter's backing, invaluable assistance from coaches Mick Heaton and Colin Harvey, and belief in his own ability to do the job, Kendall had dragged Everton back on to the glory trail.

The Milk Cup was lost after a replay, but the FA Cup came back to Goodison after an 18-year absence.

The 1984-5 season was simply glorious. A first League title in 15 years, a first European trophy in the shape of the Cup-winners' Cup, and glorious failure in the FA Cup Final against Manchester United.

Just 18 months after supporters had called for his resignation, Howard Kendall proudly accepted the Manager of the Year award.

Everton 1982-3. Back row (l to r): Ratcliffe, Wright, Walsh, Southall, Arnold, Higgins, Ferguson, Mountfield. Middle: Harvey, Johnson, Irvine, Richardson, Sharp, Borrows, King, Stevens, Heaton, Clinkard. Front: Sheedy, McMahon, Heath, Howard Kendall (manager), Ross, Bailey, Ainscow.

INTERNATIONAL BLUES

Many players won additional caps with other clubs, but the totals given here are solely for appearances made while Everton players. Before 1924 there was only one Ireland team. Then the Republic of Ireland began separate international matches. That position is reflected here. For some time, Northern Ireland could select, for the Home International Championship, players born in the Republic. Tommy Eglington and Peter Farrell were two such players who won caps with two countries. The date given for each match is the actual year in which that match was played.

ENGLAND

Abbott W. 1902 v Wales (1).
Baker B.H. 1921 v Belgium; 1925 v N.Ireland (2).
Ball A.J. 1966 v N.Ireland, Czechoslovakia, Wales; 1967 v Scotland, Spain, Austria, Wales, USSR; 1968 v Scotland, Spain twice), W.Germany, Yugoslavia, Romania; 1969 v Romania, N.Ireland, Wales, Scotland, Mexico, Uruguay, Brazil, Portugal; 1970 v Belgium, Wales, Scotland, Colombia, Ecuador, Romania, Brazil, Czechoslovakia (sub), W.Germany, E.Germany; 1971 v Malta, Greece, Malta (sub), N.Ireland, Scotland, Switzerland, Greece (39).
Balmer W. 1905 v Ireland (1).
Booth T. 1903 v Scotland (1).
Boyes W. 1938 v Wales, Rest of Europe (2).
Bracewell P. 1985 v W.Germany (sub), USA (2).
Britton C.S. 1934 v Wales, Italy; 1935 v N.Ireland, Scotland; 1936 v N.Ireland, Hungary, Scotland, Norway, Sweden (9).
Chadwick E. 1891 v Wales, Scotland; 1892 v Scotland; 1893 v Scotland; 1894 v Scotland; 1896 v Ireland; 1897 v Scotland (7).
Chedgzoy S. 1920 v Wales, Ireland; 1921 v Wales, Scotland, Ireland; 1923 v Scotland; 1924 v Wales, N.Ireland (8).
Cresswell W. 1929 v N.Ireland (1).
Cunliffe J.N. 1936 v Belgium (1).
Dean W.R. 1927 v Wales, Scotland, Belgium, France, Luxembourg, N.Ireland, Wales; 1928 v Scotland, France, Belgium, N.Ireland, Wales; 1929 v Scotland; 1931 v Scotland, Spain; 1932 v N.Ireland (16).
Dobson M. 1974 v Czechoslovakia (1).
Downs R.W. 1920 v Ireland (1).
Freeman B.C. 1909 v Wales, Scotland (2).
Geary F. 1890 v Ireland; 1891 v Scotland (2).
Gee C.W. 1931 v Wales, Spain; 1936 v N.Ireland (3).
Geldard A. 1933 v Italy, Switzerland; 1935 v Scotland; 1937 v N.Ireland (4).
Hardman H.P. 1905 v Wales; 1907 v Ireland, Scotland; 1908 v Wales (4).
Harrison G. 1921 v Belgium, Ireland (2).
Harvey J.C. 1971 v Malta (1).
Holt J. 1890 v Wales; 1891 v Wales, Scotland; 1892 v Ireland, Scotland; 1893 v Scotland; 1894 v Ireland, Scotland; 1895 v Scotland (9).
Howarth R.H. 1894 v Ireland (1). **Jefferis F.** 1912 v Wales, Scotland (2).
Johnson T.C.F. 1931 v Spain; 1932 v Scotland, N.Ireland (3).
Kay A.H. 1963 v Switzerland (1).
Labone B.L. 1963 v France, N.Ireland, Wales; 1967 v Spain, Austria; 1968 v Scotland, Spain, Sweden, W.Germany, Yugoslavia, USSR, Romania, Bulgaria; 1969 v N.Ireland, Scotland, Mexico, Uruguay, Brazil; 1970 v Belgium, Wales, Scotland, Colombia, Ecuador, Romania, Brazil, W.Germany (26).
Latchford R.D. 1977 v Italy; 1978 v Brazil, Wales, Denmark, Republic of Ireland, Czechoslovakia (sub); 1979 v Republic of Ireland, N.Ireland, Wales, Scotland, Bulgaria, Austria (12).
Lawton T. 1938 v Wales, Rest of Europe, Norway, N.Ireland; 1939 v Scotland, Italy, Yugoslavia, Romania (8).
Makepeace H. 1906 v Scotland; 1910 v Scotland; 1912 v Wales, Scotland (4).
Mercer J. 1938 v N.Ireland; 1939 v Scotland, Italy, Yugoslavia, Romania (5).
Milward A. 1891 v Wales, Scotland; 1897 v Wales, Scotland (4).

Newton K.R. 1970 v Holland, N.Ireland, Scotland, Colombia, Ecuador, Romania, Czechoslovakia, W.Germany (8).
Pickering F. 1964 v USA, N.Ireland, Belgium (3).
Reid P. 1985 v Mexico (sub), W.Germany, USA (sub) (3).
Royle J. 1971 v Malta; 1972 v Yugoslavia (2).
Sagar E. 1935 v N.Ireland; 1936 v Scotland, Austria, Belgium (4).
Settle J. 1902 v Ireland, Scotland; 1903 v Ireland (3).
Sharp J. 1903 v Ireland; 1905 v Scotland (2).
Steven T. 1984 v N.Ireland; 1985 v Republic of Ireland, Romania, Finland, Italy, USA (sub) (6).
Stevens G. 1985 v Italy, W.Germany (2).
Temple D.W. 1965 v W.Germany (1).
West G. 1968 v Bulgaria; 1969 v Wales, Mexico (3).
White T.A. 1933 v Italy (1).
Wilson R. 1965 v Scotland, Hungary, Yugoslavia, W.Germany, Sweden, Wales, Austria, N.Ireland, Spain; 1966 v Poland, W.Germany (sub); Yugoslavia, Finland, Denmark, Poland, Uruguay, Mexico, France, Argentina, Portugal, W.Germany, N.Ireland, Czechoslovakia, Wales; 1967 v Scotland, Austria, N.Ireland, USSR; 1968 v Scotland, Spain (twice), Yugoslavia, USSR (33).
Wolstenholme S. 1904 v Scotland (1).
Wright T.J. 1968 v USSR, Romania; 1969 v Romania, Mexico (sub), Uruguay, Brazil, Holland; 1970 v Belgium, Wales, Romania (sub), Brazil (11).

ENGLAND 'B'

Lyons M. 1979 v Czechoslovakia (1).
Wright W. 1979 v Austria; 1981 v Australia (2).

SCOTLAND

Bell J. 1896 v England; 1897 v England; 1898 v England; 1899 v Wales, Ireland, England; 1900 v Wales, England (8).
Brewster G. 1921 v England (1).
Collins R.Y. 1958 v Wales, N.Ireland; 1959 v England, W.Germany, Holland, Portugal (6).
Connolly J. 1973 v Switzerland (1).
Dunn J. 1928 v Wales (1).
Gabriel J. 1960 v Wales; 1963 v Norway (sub) (2).
Gillick T. 1937 v Austria, Czechoslovakia; 1938 v N.Ireland, Wales, Hungary (5).
Gray A. 1985 v Iceland (1).
Hartford A. 1979 v Peru, Belgium; 1981 v N.Ireland (sub), Israel, Wales, N.Ireland, England (7).
McBain N. 1923 v Ireland; 1924 v Wales (2).
Parker A. 1958 v Paraguay (1).
Rioch B.D. 1977 v Wales, N.Ireland, England, Chile, Brazil, Czechoslovakia (6).
Robertson J.T. 1898 v England (1).
Scott A.S. 1963 v Wales, Norway; 1964 v Finland; 1966 v Portugal, Brazil (5).
Sharp G. 1985 v Iceland (1).
Thomson J.R. 1932 v Wales (1).
Troup A. 1926 v England (1).
Wilson G.W. 1907 v England (1).
Wood G. 1979 v N.Ireland, England, Argentina (sub) (3).
Young A. 1961 v Republic of Ireland; 1966 v Portugal (2).
Young A. 1905 v England; 1907 v Wales (2).

WALES

Arridge S. 1894 v Ireland; 1895 v Ireland; 1896 v England (3).
Davies J. 1899 v Scotland, Ireland (2).
Davies S. 1921 v Scotland, England, Ireland (3).
Davies W.D. 1975 v Hungary, Luxembourg, Scotland, England, N.Ireland; 1976 v Yugoslavia, England, N.Ireland, Yugoslavia, W.Germany, Scotland; 1977 v Czechoslovakia, Scotland,

England, N.Ireland, Kuwait (16).
Griffiths T.P. 1927 v England, N.Ireland; 1928 v England; 1929 v England; 1931 v N.Ireland, Scotland, England, N.Ireland (8).
Hughes E. 1899 v Ireland, Scotland (2).
Humphreys J.V. 1947 v N.Ireland (1).
Jones R.S. 1894 v Ireland (1).
Jones T.G. 1938 v N.Ireland, England, Scotland; 1939 v N.Ireland; 1946 v Scotland, England; 1947 v England, Scotland; 1948 v N.Ireland, England; 1949 v N.Ireland, Portugal, Belgium, Switzerland, England, Scotland, Belgium (17).
Parry C.F. 1891 v England, Scotland; 1893 v England; 1894 v England; 1895 v England, Scotland (6).
Powell A. 1948 v England; 1949 v Belgium (2).
Ratcliffe K. 1981 v Czechoslovakia, Republic of Ireland, Turkey, Scotland, England, USSR; 1982 v Czechoslovakia, Iceland, USSR, Spain, England, Yugoslavia; 1983 v England, Bulgaria, Scotland, N.Ireland, Brazil, Norway, Romania, Bulgaria, Yugoslavia; 1984 v Scotland, England, N.Ireland, Norway, Israel, Iceland, Spain, Iceland; 1985 v Norway, Scotland, Spain (32).
Roose L.R. 1905 v Scotland, England (2).
Smallman D.P. 1975 v Hungary (sub), England, N.Ireland (sub), Austria (4).
Southall N. 1982 v N.Ireland, Norway; 1983 v England, Bulgaria, Scotland, N.Ireland, Brazil, Norway, Romania, Bulgaria, Yugoslavia; 1984 v Scotland, England, N.Ireland, Norway, Israel, Iceland, Spain, Iceland; 1985 v Norway, Scotland, Spain, Norway (23).
Thomas M. 1981 v Czechoslovakia (1).
Van den Hauwe P. 1984 v Spain (1).
Vernon T.R. 1960 v N.Ireland, Republic of Ireland, Scotland, England; 1962 v N.Ireland, Brazil (twice), Mexico, Scotland, Hungary, England; 1963 v England, Scotland (13).
Williams B.D. 1931 v N.Ireland, England; 1932 v Scotland, England, N.Ireland; 1935 v N.Ireland (6).

NORTHERN IRELAND (and Ireland before 1924)

Bingham W.P. 1960 v W.Germany, Scotland; 1961 v Italy, Greece, W.Germany, Greece, England; 1962 v Poland, England, Scotland, Poland; 1963 v Spain (12).
Clements D. 1973 v Bulgaria, Portugal; 1974 v Scotland, England, Wales, Norway; 1975 v Yugoslavia, England, Scotland, Wales, Sweden, Yugoslavia (12).
Cook W. 1935 v England, Scotland; 1936 v Wales, Scotland, England; 1937 v Wales, England, Scotland; 1938 v Wales, Scotland, England; 1939 v Wales (12).
Coulter J. 1934 v Scotland; 1935 v England, Wales; 1936 v Scotland; 1937 v Wales (5).
Eglington T.J. 1946 v Scotland; 1947 v Wales, Scotland, England; 1948 v Wales, Scotland (6).
Farrell P.D. 1946 v Scotland; 1947 v Wales, Scotland, England; 1948 v Wales, England; 1949 v Wales (7).
Hamilton B. 1976 v Israel, Scotland, England, Wales, Holland, Belgium; 1977 v W.Germany, England, Scotland, Wales, Iceland (11).
Harris V. 1909 v England, Scotland, Wales; 1910 v England, Scotland, Wales; 1911 v Wales, England, Scotland; 1912 v England; 1913 v England, Scotland; 1914 v Wales, Scotland (14).
Hill M.J. 1963 v Scotland, Spain, England (3).
Houston J. 1913 v England, Scotland; 1914 v Scotland (3).
Irvine R.W. 1922 v Scotland, England; 1923 v Wales, England; 1924 v Scotland, England; 1925 v England; 1926 v England; 1927 v Wales, England; 1928 v Scotland (11).
Jackson T. 1968 v Israel; 1969 v England, Scotland, Wales, USSR (twice, once as sub) (6).
Lacey W. 1909 v England, Scotland, Wales; 1910 v England, Scotland, Wales; 1911 v Wales, England, Scotland; 1912 v England (10).
Scott P.W. 1975 v Wales, Yugoslavia (2).
Scott W. 1905 v England, Scotland; 1907 v England, Scotland; 1908 v England, Scotland, Wales; 1909 v England, Scotland, Wales; 1910 v England, Scotland; 1911 v Wales, England, Scotland; 1912 v England (16).
Sheridan J. 1903 v England, Scotland, Wales; 1904 v England, Scotland (5).
Stevenson A.E. 1934 v Scotland; 1935 v England, Scotland; 1936 v Wales, England; 1937 v Wales, England; 1938 v Wales, Scotland, England; 1939 v Wales; 1946 v Scotland; 1947 v Wales, Scotland (14).

REPUBLIC OF IRELAND

Clinton T.J. 1951 v Norway; 1953 v France, Luxembourg (3).
Corr P.J. 1949 v Portugal, Spain, England, Sweden (4).
Donovan D. 1954 v Norway; 1955 v Holland, Norway, W.Germany; 1957 v England (5).
Eglington T.J. 1946 v England; 1947 v Spain, Portugal; 1948 v Portugal, Switzerland; 1949 v Portugal, Sweden; 1950 v Norway; 1951 v Argentina, W.Germany; 1952 v W.Germany, Austria, Spain, France; 1953 v Austria, France, Luxembourg, France; 1954 v Norway; 1955 v Holland, W.Germany, Spain (22).
Farrell P.D. 1947 v Spain, Portugal; 1948 v Portugal, Spain, Switzerland; 1949 v Portugal (sub), Spain, England, Finland, Sweden; 1951 v Argentina, Norway, West Germany; 1952 v W.Germany, Austria, Spain, France; 1953 v Austria, France (twice); 1954 v Norway; 1955 v Holland, W.Germany, Yugoslavia, Spain; 1957 v England (26).
McDonagh J. 1981 v Wales, Belgium, Czechoslovakia (3).
Meagan M.K. 1961 v Scotland; 1962 v Austria, Iceland; 1964 v Spain (4).
O'Keefe E. 1981 v Wales (1).
O'Neill J.A. 1952 v Spain, France; 1953 v Austria, France, Luxembourg, France; 1954 v Norway; 1955 v Holland, Norway, W.Germany, Yugoslavia, Spain; 1956 v Denmark; 1958 v Mexico, Poland; 1959 v Czechoslovakia (twice) (17).
Sheedy K. 1983 v Holland (sub), Malta; 1984 v Denmark; 1985 v Italy, Israel, Switzerland (6).
Walsh M.A. 1978 v N.Ireland (sub) (1).
Walsh M. 1982 v Chile, Brazil, Trinidad & Tobago, Spain (4).

VICTORY AND WARTIME INTERNATIONALS

1919 and 1946 Victory Internationals. 1939-45 Wartime Internationals. No caps were awarded for these matches.

ENGLAND

Britton C.S. 1941 v Wales (twice); 1942 v Scotland, Wales (twice); 1943 v Scotland (twice), Wales (three times); 1944 v Scotland, Wales (12).
Fleetwood T. 1919 v Scotland (twice) (2).
Greenhalgh N.H. 1939 v Scotland (1).
Grenyer A. 1919 v Wales (1).
Lawton T. 1939 v Scotland; 1941 v Scotland; 1942 v Scotland (three times), Wales (twice); 1943 v Scotland; 1944 v Scotland (three times), Wales (twice); 1945 v France, Scotland (twice), Wales, N.Ireland (18).
Mercer J. 1939 v Scotland; 1940 v Scotland; 1941 v Scotland (three times), Wales; 1942 v Scotland (twice), Wales; 1943 v Scotland (twice), Wales (twice); 1944 v Scotland (three times), Wales (twice); 1945 v Scotland (twice), Wales (twice), France, N.Ireland; 1946 v Belgium, Scotland (26).

SCOTLAND

Caskie J. 1939 v England; 1941 v England (three times); 1942 v England; 1944 v England (three times) (8).
Gillick T. 1941 v England; 1942 v England; 1943 v England (3).
Note: Although Jimmy Caskie is listed as an Everton player for wartime internationals, it should be noted that he made only four wartime appearances for the club.

WALES

Jones T.G. 1939 v England; 1940 v England (twice); 1941 v England (twice); 1942 v England (twice); 1943 v England (three times); 1946 v N.Ireland (11).

NORTHERN IRELAND

Stevenson A.E. 1946 v Scotland (1).

Match to Remember 1   8 September 1888

Everton 2   Accrington 1

MORE than 10,000 people, twice as many as had been expected, turned up to witness Everton's first match in the newly-formed Football League.

Cloudless skies brought even the most fickle Evertonians to Anfield despite the fact that seven days earlier Everton had been beaten by fierce local rivals, Bootle.

The match kicked off 20 minutes late, Accrington having lost their way to the ground. The visitors won the toss and surprisingly opted to kick into the sun.

The early pressure came from Everton. A fierce drive from Farmer brought the best out of Accrington goalkeeper, Horne, who gratefully conceded a corner.

The closest Accrington came to snatching a goal against the run of play was midway through the first-half when a huge clearance by Horne was headed against the Everton crossbar by Holden.

Lewis and Dobson both went close for the Merseysiders before the luckless Chadwick was guilty of the most glaring miss, two minutes before the interval. Fleming worked his way down the right before delivering an inch-perfect cross which the normally reliable inside-forward blasted high over the bar.

With the sun at their backs, Accrington were a different proposition. They pushed forward in great numbers and were unfortunate not to break the deadlock when Holden fired narrowly wide.

After 60 minutes Everton grabbed the lead after Horne conceded a corner on the left. Ross worked the ball to Waugh who neatly fed Farmer on the touchline. His cross was met perfectly by Fleming who headed firmly into the bottom corner from ten yards. The *Liverpool Daily Post* reported that the goal was greeted 'with tremendous cheering and waving of hats'.

Accrington came within a whisker of levelling affairs straight from the restart when Lewis cleared a Kirkham shot off the line with goalkeeper Smalley well beaten.

An incident 15 minutes from time virtually guaranteed an Everton victory. As Chadwick rose to meet a Waugh cross, Horne rushed off his goal-line and collided with the big forward before falling to the turf clutching his chest.

He had fractured a rib and was carried off in agony as McLennan took over in goal. Within two minutes Everton had made the most of their advantage, Fleming sweeping home a Farmer cross.

Accrington launched a furious late assault and Holden scored from close range after striking the crossbar with a header. In the last minute, Smalley came to Everton's rescue as he clawed away a dipping Holden volley.

Everton: Smalley, Dick, Ross, Holt, Jones, Dobson, Fleming, Waugh, Lewis, E. Chadwick, Farmer.
Accrington: Horne, Stevenson, McLennan, Haworth, Wilkinson, Pemberton, Lofthouse, Benar, Kirkham, Holden, Chippendale.

Referee: Mr J.J. Bentley (Bolton)   *Attendance: 10,000*

When Everton met Bootle in a local cup match in 1881 their opponents could muster only eight players. Bootle signed up three spectators and went on to win the tie.

Everton's record victory is their 11-2 FA Cup success over Derby County in 1889-90. Their record defeat is the 10-4 reverse at White Hart Lane in 1958-9.

Everton are one of only 14 League clubs never to have played below Division Two. Last promoted in 1954, the Blues completed 30 successive seasons in Division One by 1984-5. Only Arsenal (58) have played more.

Match to Remember 2   30 December 1893

Everton 7   West Bromwich Albion 1

JACK Southworth was one of the great goalscorers of 19th-century football. For one full season Everton enjoyed his services and he left a telling impression at Goodison Park. In one match alone he scored six goals for the club, a record which still stands in 1985.

Despite foggy weather, there was a crowd of some 25,000 people for the visit of West Brom to Goodison in the closing hours of 1893. Their interest was repaid when Jack Southworth achieved the biggest single scoring feat in the club's history.

Within a minute of the kick-off Everton were ahead through John Bell, and although Smart Arridge had to react quickly to prevent a rapid equaliser, it was the Merseysiders who went on to put the result beyond doubt — and Southworth was the hero of the hour.

Latta and Bell combined to give Southworth his first goal. His second came when Albion goalkeeper failed to hold a shot from Bell, and his hat-trick goal was a brilliant solo effort. From the half-way line the former Blackburn Rovers player dribbled through the Albion defence before shooting home.

Albion reached half-time trailing 4-0, and reflecting that it could have been more, had Chadwick not fired over the bar.

The second-half was not many minutes old when Bell laid on a fourth goal for Southworth, but the Midlanders battled on gamely and Williams was forced to make two fine saves. England star Billy Bassett was in particularly fine form, trying hard to salvage some pride for his team.

A mistake by Stewart allowed Norman through and at last West Brom opened their account. But any wild dreams of a sensational fightback were soon dashed. Bell beat three men to lay on Southworth's fifth, and then Latta wriggled his way through to give Southworth the chance of a sixth goal. The Everton man gratefully accepted it and wrote himself into the record book.

Everton: Williams, Parry, Arridge, Kelso, Holt, Stewart, Latta, Bell, Southworth, Chadwick, Milward.
West Bromwich Albion: Reader, Nicholson, Crone, Taggart, C.Perry, T.Perry, Bassett, Norman, McLeod, Williams, Pearson.

Attendance: 25,000

Jack Southworth (back row, fourth left) in the Football League team to meet the Scottish League in 1893. Everton's Fred Geary is second left on the middle row.

Match to Remember 3   31 March 1906

Everton 2   Liverpool 0

MERSEYSIDE took over Villa Park for the day when Everton met Liverpool in the semi-final of the FA Cup. Long before midday, the centre of Birmingham was a sea of red, white and blue as thousands of supporters arrived for the big game.

The teams enjoyed a more leisurely journey, Liverpool staying overnight in Tamworth, while Everton, after a morning train journey from Merseyside, arrrived in time for lunch at the Grand Hotel.

It was the game everyone wanted to see and there were 50,000 people present when Parkinson kicked off for Liverpool. It was Everton who had the first attempt at goal, through Settle, but it was Liverpool who applied early pressure with Scott making some fine saves in the Everton goal.

Abbott stopped an attack by Dunlop and Bradley, then Hewitt rounded Walter Balmer and put in a dangerous cross which Scott did well to fist away.

Parkinson went close for Liverpool but the flustered Everton defence held on and towards the end of an absorbing first-half, it was the Goodison men who might have taken the lead and were denied only by a last-ditch clearance from Parry.

As the second-half progressed, Everton asserted themselves, although not before Jack Crelley had been momentarily knocked-out during a fierce Liverpool raid.

Eventually the deadlock was broken when Abbott found the back of the Liverpool net with a rasping drive from just inside the penalty area.

A second goal, from Harold Hardman, made the match safe for Everton and took them through to their third FA Cup Final appearance. The following month Liverpool were crowned League Champions while Everton went to the Crystal Palace to meet Newcastle United. These were good times for Merseyside football followers.

Everton: Scott, R.Balmer, Crelley, Makepeace, Taylor, Abbott, Sharp, Bolton, Young, Settle, Hardman.
Liverpool: Hardy, West, Dunlop, Parry, Raisbeck, Bradley, Goddard, Robinson, Parkinson, Carlin, Hewitt.

Attendance: 50,000

Everton 1906. Top row (l to r): Makepeace, Young, Settle, Boulton, Hardman. Bottom: Fayton, Sharp, Abbott, Scott, W.Balmer, R.Balmer.

Match to Remember 4   21 April 1906

Everton 1   Newcastle United 0

MIGHTY Newcastle United were firm favourites to lift the FA Cup in 1906, having been surprisingly beaten 2-0 by Aston Villa 12 months earlier to be denied a League and Cup double.

Yet Everton were quietly confident that, after the disappointment of seeing the trophy snatched from their grasp in 1893, and again four years later, it would be a case of third time lucky.

Seventy-five thousand people filled the Crystal Palace stadium on a bright, breezy April afternoon, many of them having made the long journey south from Merseyside and Tyneside.

Both clubs were so determined to name full-strength line-ups that they were each fined for fielding weakened teams in games the week before the Final.

The first-half was a dull affair. Chances were created, then subsequently squandered at both ends as over-wary forwards met firm, unrelenting resistance from well-drilled defenders.

The game certainly failed to live up to the expectations of tens of thousands of fans. Everton and Newcastle effectively cancelled each other out as they battled for midfield supremacy.

In the days leading up to the match, United's much-vaunted half-back line had promised to make mincemeat out of the Goodison forwards but, while clear-cut openings were few, Everton supporters pinned their hopes on players of the calibre of Sandy Young and Jimmy Settle.

Settle saw a fierce header well saved by Lawrence after 15 minutes, but generally the penetration which had hallmarked Everton's route to the Crystal Palace was sadly missing.

United were restricted to two chances in the goalless first-half, Gosnell and Rutherford both firing wide.

Eight minutes after the restart, with Everton in total command, the deadlock appeared to have been broken when Lawrence failed to hold Sharp's cross. Settle passed across goal and Young turned the ball home — only to be ruled offside.

Frustrated at the prospect of a second successive Cup Final defeat, Newcastle cut up rough and the referee stopped the game to warn the Magpies about their ungentlemanly conduct.

With 13 minutes remaining, Taylor, sole playing survivor of Everton's last Cup Final appearance, found Sharp who evaded the lunging tackles of two United defenders before sending a low centre to Young. This time there was no waving linesman's flag as Young fired beyond Lawrence to give Everton the FA Cup for the first time.

Everton: Scott, Balmer (W), Crelley, Makepeace, Taylor, Abbott, Sharp, Bolton, Young, Settle, H.P. Hardman.
Newcastle United: Lawrence, McCombie, Carr, Gardner, Aitken, McWilliam, Rutherford, Howie, Veitch, Orr, Gosnell.

Referee: Mr F.Kirkham (Preston)   *Attendance: 75,000*

Everton press during the 1906 FA Cup Final against Newcastle United at the Crystal Palace. Note that goalkeepers did not wear distinguishing jerseys in those days.

Match to Remember 5   5 May 1928

Everton 3   Arsenal 3

EVERTON had already clinched the League Championship when they faced Arsenal on the final Saturday of the season.

Sixty thousand people crowded into Goodison Park, not so much to pay homage to the newly-crowned kings of the English game, as to witness one man's attempt to rewrite the record book. That man was Dixie Dean who stood on the threshold of a unique and quite astonishing personal triumph.

In the space of 90 minutes he needed three more goals to become the first player ever to notch 60 League goals in one season. It was a daunting task, particularly against a side which had already signalled their intentions to spoil the party.

Arsenal, a methodical side, held the early advantage and after only two minutes they went ahead when Everton goalkeeper Davies made the first of several mistakes by failing to hold a hopeful drive by Shaw.

Exactly 60 seconds later Everton were level and the scorer, almost inevitably, was Dean. Critchley swung over one of his famous drifting corners and the powerful centre-forward bundled the ball over the line with Gunners' goalkeeper Patterson well beaten.

Three minutes later, as Everton began to get into their stride, Dean was upended in the penalty area by Butler. It was Dean who ambled forward to drive the penalty low into the bottom corner, leaving himself one goal short of the magical figure.

Everton's overwhelming desire to give Dean the ball every time they ventured forward, allowed Arsenal time and space, and they equalised ten minutes from the interval when O'Donnell, under pressure from four opponents, mis-cued to send the ball spinning past his goalkeeper.

The second-half was played at a frantic pace as the massive crowd, sensing that time was running out for their hero, transformed Goodison into a seething cauldron.

With only eight minutes to play, Patterson palmed a fierce Martin drive for a corner. Troup, the man who had served as Dean's main provider throughout the season, took the flag-kick. Dean rose magnificently to outjump his markers and head powerfully home for his 60th goal of the season.

Joy was mixed with relief as 60,000 people stood to acknowledge a great player's finest hour. Even a late equaliser by Shaw could not dampen the enthusiasm as Arsenal players took advantage of stoppages to shake Dean's hand.

Everton: Davies, Cresswell, O'Donnell, Kelly, Hart, Virr, Critchley, Martin, Dean, Weldon, Troup.
Arsenal: Patterson, Parker, John, Baker, Butler, Blythe, Hulme, Buchan, Shaw, Brain, Peel.

Attendance: 60,000

Dean climbs high to meet Troup's corner and head his 60th goal of the season.

Match to Remember 6   12 October 1932

Newcastle United 3   Everton 5

EVERTON travelled to St James' Park as First Division champions, determined to land a piece of early-season silverware by lifting the Charity Shield at the expense of FA Cup-holders Newcastle.

Everton, urged on by a small but vociferous travelling army of fans in the 10,000 crowd, began well, carving out several excellent early openings. Dixie Dean went close before Ted Critchley hit the crossbar to underline the visitors' growing superiority.

Against the run of play, United snatched the opening goal when McMenemy broke free to comfortably beat Ted Sagar from ten yards.

Undaunted, Everton continued to sweep forward and they were rewarded when Dean rose unchallenged to head home. The goal deflated Newcastle and what followed was a display of vintage football from the League Champions.

With the irrepressible Dean acting as a human battering ram, and Cliff Britton and his defensive colleagues mopping up with great precision at the back, Everton took the North-Easterners apart.

Tommy Johnson added a second just before half-time and Dean headed another to give Everton a 3-1 interval lead.

That advantage would have been halved had Sagar not brilliantly saved a 44th minute penalty from Weaver, controversially awarded when Britton was adjudged to have upended Richardson.

Two minutes into the second half, Dean put the game beyond Newcastle's reach by completing his hat-trick from close range after an inspired piece of midfield play by the industrious Britton.

Dazed but defiant, United, fearing that they were now on the verge of a humiliating drubbing, hit back with a neat goal from Boyd. But it was the remarkable Dean who was to have the last say.

With two minutes remaining he turned sharply in the penalty area and smashed home his fourth goal, and Everton's fifth. McMenemey scored Newcastle's third.

Newcastle United: Burns, Nelson, Fairhurst, Bell, Higson, Weaver, Boyd, Richardson, Allen, McMenemy, Lang.
Everton : Sagar, Williams, Cresswell, Britton, White, Thomson, Critchley, McGourty, Dean, Johnson, Stein.

Attendance: 10,000

Ted Sagar made a brilliant penalty save to keep Everton two goals ahead.

Match to Remember 7 **29 April 1933**

Everton 3   Manchester City 0

THE clash between between royal blue and sky blue in the 1933 FA Cup Final meant that neutral strips had to be found. Everton and Manchester City were given the choice of red or white shirts. City preferred red.

The game's place in football history was assured, even before the kick-off, because it was the first time that players in a Final had been numbered. It was decided to employ a strict sequence, so Everton wore 1-11 and City were numbered through to 22, which meant that Eric Brook was the first man to wear number 12 in a Wembley Cup Final.

Many Everton supporters were dismayed at the decision to play Albert Geldard on the right wing in preference to Ted Critchley who, despite losing his regular place seven months earlier, had been brought back to score the winning goal in the semi-final defeat of West Ham.

Everton had no proper manager so the decision to omit Critchley from the Wembley team was almost certainly taken after lengthy consultations with skipper Dixie Dean, a man whom few questioned and no-one argued with.

City had their problems too. Centre-forward Freddie Tilson was ruled out and Marshall came in at inside-right with Herd moving to centre-forward. Veteran Jimmy McMullan played inside-left in his last game before retirement.

City took only 15 seconds to get into their stride, Toseland flinging over a high, searching far-post cross which Sagar did well to hold. Although hardly overworked, Sagar's calm assurance when he handled the ball had a noticeable effect on his teammates.

His confidence spread through the ranks and within 20 minutes Everton were in complete control, forcing City to defend furiously.

With Dean in tremendous form it was only a matter of time before City's defence crumbled and in the 41st minute the floodgates were opened when Langford, under a fierce challenge from Dean, dropped a Britton cross which winger Stein side-footed home from close range.

The hapless Langford was guilty of another dreadful error seven minutes into the second-half when he failed to hold another Britton cross and Dean headed powerfully home.

Ten minutes from time Everton took advantage of City's dejection, Jimmy Dunn heading a third goal from Geldard's looping centre.

Sheffield referee Mr E. Wood ended the first-ever FA Cup meeting between Everton and Manchester City. Everton climbed the steps to the royal box and collected the trophy.

Everton: Sagar, Cook, Cresswell, Britton, White, Thomson, Geldard, Dunn, Dean, Johnson, Stein.
Manchester City: Langford, Cann, Dale, Busby, Cowan, Bray, Toseland, Marshall, Herd, McMullan, Brook.

Referee: Mr E. Wood (Sheffield) *Attendance: 92,950*

Above left: Dean bundles the ball into the net for Everton's second goal in the 1933 FA Cup Final. Below left: Dean, the proud Everton skipper, parades the FA Cup at Wembley after the Blues' triumph over Manchester City.

Match to Remember 8   30 January 1935

Everton 6 Sunderland 4

AFTER a 1-1 draw at Roker Park, two of English football's finest sides met again four days later to continue their fight for a place in the fifth round of the FA Cup.

Nearly 60,000 people crammed inside Goodison Park for a match which was later described as 'the game of a life-time'. Unlike the first encounter which had been reported as an over-cautious affair, it was a full-blooded cup-tie with enough excitement and passion to fill a dozen lesser games.

Even so, it was far from the frantic hammer-and-tongs clash which the goal-laden scoreline suggests. Both sides performed with efficiency and flair; the football was, for the most part, quite breathtaking.

Left-winger Jackie Coulter opened the scoring after 14 minutes when he cut inside to unleash a powerful drive which Thorpe in the Sunderland goal was unable to hold. After half an hour he doubled Everton's lead to climax a spell of sustained pressure by the home side.

Sunderland were not a team to surrender easily and they hit back four minutes before the interval when Davies drove home from close range. As the Wearsiders searched for an equaliser, Everton slipped into their familiar defensive role, never looking likely to loosen their stranglehold.

Victory seemed assured when Stevenson broke through the middle to restore Everton's two-goal advantage.

The goal served only to spur on Sunderland who threw caution to the wind, attacking down both flanks and firing in shots from all angles. Their reward came when Connor picked up a back pass and shot beneath Sagar's diving body.

The drama was not over. This extraordinary game had more twists. Gurney scored a memorable goal with only seconds remaining, and the tie went into extra-time.

Within two minutes of the extra period, Coulter completed his hat-trick to put his side back in front. Back came Sunderland, equalising with a well-taken goal by Connor.

With a second replay looking increasingly likely, Everton winger Albert Geldard took matters into his own hands. He raced upfield to smash home a stunning goal with nine minutes to play. Eight minutes later he collected another as leg-weary Sunderland accepted defeat.

Everton: Sagar, Cook, Jones, Britton, Gee, Thomson, Geldard, Cunliffe, Dean, Stevenson, Coulter.
Sunderland: Thorpe, Murray, Hall, Thompson, Johnston, Hastings, Davis, Carter, Gurney, Gallacher, Connor.

Referee: Mr Pinkeston (Birmingham)   *Attendance: 59,213*

Albert Geldard (left) whose extra-time goals gave Everton victory. Dean (right) surprisingly failed to score, despite the goal feast.

Match to Remember 9   21 March 1953
Everton 3   Bolton Wanderers 4

EVERTON had travelled to Manchester to contest an FA Cup semi-final on three previous occasions — and each time had returned home with the bitter taste of defeat in their mouths.

In 1953, however, they were expected to dispose comfortably of a Bolton side which, although workmanlike, was not brimming with talent. The one exception was centre-forward Nat Lofthouse who, ten months earlier, had been dubbed 'Lion of Vienna' after his two goals in Austria had won England a famous victory.

It was to be Everton's misfortune that they would encounter this exceptional footballer on a day when he would again be in quite irresistable form.

Yet if the final glory was to be Bolton's, then the medals for courage and commitment were Everton's. They launched one of the most memorable fight-backs in the history of the FA Cup to come within a whisker of earning a replay.

The prospect of the Merseysiders winning a reprieve were unthinkable as they trooped off dejectedly at half-time, 4-0 down. Bolton deserved their impressive lead, not simply because they took their chances, but because they were so far ahead of Everton individually and tactically.

Everton had collapsed in the face of a furious onslaught. It took Bolton only seven minutes to break open a defence which had been creaking from the first whistle. Hassall, Langton and Lofthouse combined superbly to set up Doug Holden who scored from ten yards.

Ten minutes later Willie Moir took a long throw from Hassall, raced clear and struck the ball beyond the reach of the stranded O'Neill. Worse was to follow for Everton as Lofthouse scored from Moir's pass and then blasted home a brilliant solo effort.

Everton's cause had not been helped by the loss of Dave Hickson, with a head injury, for 15 minutes midway through the first-half.

And right on half-time, Clinton missed a penalty after Hartle had handled Parker's shot. The Everton right-back fired wide from the spot.

Two minutes into the second half, Everton pulled a goal back when Parker headed home Buckle's corner. It was the signal for Everton to launch their revival and they poured forward.

They had to wait until the 76th minute for another goal, when Peter Farrell drove home a twice-taken free-kick. With less than a quarter of an hour remaining, Everton saw a glimmer of hope.

Hope turned to belief that they could snatch a replay when, with six minutes left, Hickson rose at the far post to knock the ball back across the face of the goal and Parker headed their third.

But, although they threw everything at Bolton in the closing stages, Everton could not complete what would have been an epic recovery.

Everton: O'Neill, Clinton, Lindsay, Farrell, Jones, Lello, Buckle, Cummins, Hickson, Parker, Eglington.

Bolton Wanderers: Hanson, Hartle, Higgins, Wheeler, Barrass, Bell, Holden, Moir, Lofthouse, Hassall, Langton.

Attendance: 72,213

Eglington gets in a header in the 1953 FA Cup semi-final but Hartle is back to guard the Bolton goal.

Brian Labone (left) and Brian Harris carry the FA Cup at Wembley in 1966.

Everton 1966, with the FA Cup. Back row (l to r): Harris, Labone, West, Gabriel, Wright, Eggleston (trainer).
Front: Scott, Trebilcock, Young, Harry Catterick (manager), Harvey, Temple, Wilson.

Match to Remember 10   14 May 1966

Everton 3   Sheffield Wednesday 2

MANAGER Harry Catterick dropped a pre-match bombshell when he announced that Goodison favourite Fred Pickering was being left out of the side for the 1966 FA Cup Final.

His replacement was a young Cornishman, Mike Trebilcock, a relatively unknown striker signed for £20,000 from Plymouth Argyle the previous New Year's Eve.

Trebilcock had played only one previous FA Cup match for Everton — the semi-final against Manchester United — and only seven League games.

"Fred was popular and could score goals," said Catterick later, "but he'd been injured and had gone off the boil a bit. Trebilcock was a first-rate goal-poacher. I always felt his sharpness would show."

Catterick, astute as ever, was right. Trebilcock emerged as the unlikely hero of a day which will never be forgotten by those who saw one of the best of all FA Cup Finals, with its superior football and heart-stopping climax.

Wednesday opened in sensational style, taking the lead after only four minutes when a shot by Jim McCalliog took a wicked deflection off Ray Wilson and flew into the net past the helpless Gordon West.

The Owls dominated the game for the best part of an hour. Everton, meanwhile, toiled manfully in midfield, but the service to the strikers was virtually non-existent.

Everton felt they should have had a penalty when Ron Springett appeared to bring down Alex Young, but it was Wednesday who edged further in front when David Ford drove powerfully home in the 57th minute, after West had parried Fantham's shot.

What followed was one of the greatest Cup Final fightbacks of them all, as Everton dragged themselves off the floor and set about snatching an improbable victory.

Two minutes after Ford had struck, Trebilcock ran into a purple patch. Shaking off his markers he tore into the Owls' defence and threw his side a life-line when he drove past Springett after Temple's header had been blocked.

Five minutes later Everton were level. Alex Scott's free-kick was headed hesitatingly down by Sam Ellis and Trebilcock fired home, low and hard.

Now in command for the first time, Everton mounted pressure and with ten minutes to play, Gerry Young failed to control a bouncing ball and Temple collected and was off upfield. He drew Springett from his goal before scoring the goal which gave Everton perhaps their most famous victory.

Everton: West, Wright, Wilson, Gabriel, Labone, Harris, Scott, Trebilcock, A.Young, Harvey, Temple.
Sheffield Wednesday: Springett, Smith, Megson, Eustace, Ellis, G.Young, Pugh, Fantham, McCalliog, Ford, Quinn.

Referee: Mr J.F. Taylor (Wolverhampton)   *Attendance: 100,000*

Match to Remember 11   30 August 1969

Everton 3   Leeds United 2

WHEN League Champions Leeds United visited Goodison Park in the early stages of 1969-70, they could have had no idea that they were being entertained by the heirs-apparent to their throne.

Mighty Leeds arrived at Goodison with an unbeaten run of 34 League games behind them, but with designs of making up some of the ground they had lost because of a series of drawn matches in the first weeks of the new season.

Don Revie's ultra-professional side were always difficult opponents but Everton performed marvellously. It was the afternoon on which winger Johnny Morrissey turned in perhaps his finest performance in an Everton shirt.

Morrissey ran riot against the normally reliable Paul Reaney to provide numerous chances for the game's other outstanding player, big Joe Royle.

Twenty-year-old Royle gave Jack Charlton an afternoon which the England centre-half would soon want to forget, constantly beating him in the air and leaving him behind on the ground, thanks to sheer pace. But for the sterling work of Billy Bremner and Norman Hunter, Leeds would have found themselves on the end of a rare drubbing.

Leeds' otherwise rigid defensive pattern was at its most vulnerable early in the game and, after Jimmy Husband squandered a good chance in the opening minute, Everton went ahead three minutes later when Brown rolled a free-kick to Husband who let fly from just outside the penalty area. The ball cannoned off the defensive wall and this time Husband found his spot perfectly.

With Brian Labone and John Hurst snuffing out Leeds' dual strikers, Allan Clarke and Mick Jones, Everton held the upper hand and increased their lead after 21 minutes.

Morrissey floated over a cross from the left and Royle rose magnificently to send a fierce header thumping against the bar. As the ball bounced back, Royle was the quickest to react, darting forward again to head home.

Leeds, run ragged by this point, went further behind four minutes after half-time when Hurst and Husband linked to set up Royle who fired in from 20 yards.

Typically, Leeds refused to surrender and in the 62nd minute Bremner nipped between Brown and Jackson to chest home an inswinging corner from Giles.

West pawed to safety an overhead kick from Bremner, before that magnificent poacher of goals, Allan Clarke, struck with 15 minutes remaining. Cooper's cross from the right was missed by substitute Lorimer, but Clarke was on hand, swooping to force the ball over the line.

Leeds had fought back to set up a thrilling finale, but Everton held on to pick up two points. They were on their way to the title.

Everton: West, Wright, Brown, Jackson, Labone, Harvey, Husband, Ball, Royle, Hurst, Morrissey.
Leeds United: Sprake, Reaney, Cooper, Bremner, Charlton, Hunter, Madeley, Giles, Jones, Clarke, Gray (Lorimer).

Referee: Mr G.Hill (Leicester)   *Attendance: 51,797*

Dixie Dean was 23 years and 290 days old when he scored his 200th senior goal. It was a record which stood alone until Jimmy Greaves equalled it, netting his 200th goal at exactly the same age.

Everton have provided the four home nations with more international players than any other club.

Everton are the only club to win the Second and First Division Championships and the FA Cup in successive seasons (1931-3).

In 1889-90 Everton, along with Bolton, scored in every League match, a feat never repeated in the First Division.

Match to Remember 12   4 November 1970

Everton 1   Munchen Gladbach 1
(Everton won on penalties)

AFTER sweeping majestically to the League Championship seven months earlier, Everton entered their European Cup second round match against West German champions, Borussia Munchen Gladbach, with a huge question-mark hanging over their heads.

Since the start of the new season, Everton had failed miserably to recapture the form which had seen them hailed as the potential 'team of the '70s'. They were now desperate to prove, on the European stage, that their problems were short-term and not terminal.

They secured a commendable 1-1 draw in the first-leg of their match with the Germans, giving a fine display of defensive football after Kendall had scored a vital goal. Now Harry Catterick's team were confident of moving into the last eight of the great club competition.

Despite pouring rain more than 42,000 fans were present. They were rewarded with a match of nail-biting intensity and high drama.

Everton felt that they needed an early goal and they found it, though perhaps even they were astonished at the speed of its arrival. Only 23 seconds had elapsed when Morrissey flighted over a cross which appeared to pose no threat as the German goalkeeper, Wolfgang Kleff, rose unchallenged to meet it.

Unbelievably Kleff, who was to go on to give a brilliant display, allowed the greasy ball to slip through his fingers. It skidded off the wet turf and over the line to give Everton a sensational lead.

A second Everton goal would surely prove decisive, yet although the Merseysiders mounted an onslaught on Borussia's goal, Kleff redeemed himself with a series of world-class saves.

At the other end, Andy Rankin had been little more than a spectator. But in the 34th minute, he could only parry a shot by Laumen and the German picked himself up to net the rebound.

In the dying stages, Everton unleashed a furious barrage but Kleff defiantly stood his ground and the game went into extra-time.

Koppel hit the woodwork in the first period but the unwelcome prospect of a cruel penalty shoot-out became a harsh reality as legs tired and heads dropped.

The tension was almost unbearable as Joe Royle stepped forward to take the first kick. It was saved and the pendulum swung back in the Germans' favour.

Sielhoff and Ball both found the back of the net before Laumen missed. Morrissey was on target to nose Everton in front at 2-1. Heynckes levelled matters, then Kendall restored Everton's lead.

Koppel and Brown each converted their kicks leaving Everton 4-3 in front with one kick remaining.

Rankin's moment had arrived. Muller struck the kick hard and to Rankin's right. It was a well-taken penalty but the Everton goalkeeper dived to make a brilliant save and Everton were through.

Everton: Rankin, Wright, K.Newton(Brown), Kendall, Kenyon, Harvey, Whittle(Husband), Ball, Royle, Hurst, Morrissey.
Munchen Gladbach: Kleff, Vogts, Wittmann, Muller, Sielhoff, Deitrich, Le Fevre, Laumen, Koppel, Netzer, Heynckes.

Referee: A. Sbardella (Italy)   *Attendance: 42,744*

Everton are the only club to have played over 3,000 First Division matches, and they were the first to 5,000 goals, closely followed by Aston Villa.

Dixie Dean's 37 First Division hat-tricks are still a record.

Everton's record of most consecutive First Division wins (12) spanned the end of 1893-4 and the start of the following season.

Alan Irvine and Liverpool's Ronnie Whelan tussle in the 1984 Milk Cup Final.

Liverpool's Mark Lawrenson chases Kevin Richardson in the 1984 Milk Cup Final.

Match to Remember 13   24 March 1984

Liverpool 0   Everton 0

FOR so many years it had been the impossible dream — a Wembley Cup Final between the great Merseyside rivals.

In the weeks leading up to the Milk Cup Final, it had been suggested by people outside Liverpool that the famous stadium would be home to a less than capacity attendance. The sceptics, who still fail to grasp the enormous passions aroused by Merseyside derby matches, could see no way that a city racked by unemployment and economic gloom could dispose of their full quotas of expensive Wembley tickets.

How wrong they were. It was estimated that some 25,000 people were disappointed and had to join tens of thousands of other Merseysiders who watched the game on television.

The occasion itself in many ways overshadowed the match. Both sets of supporters behaved impeccably, and the relieved — and somewhat startled — Metropolitan Police labelled it the 'Friendly Final'.

While no classic, the match was an intriguing encounter between a side which had dominated English soccer for nearly two decades, and a team which was emerging dramatically from the shadows to challenge for that crown.

Everton shrugged off their lack of Wembley experience, tearing into Liverpool's rearguard. It was during this early period that the game's one controversial incident occurred.

After six minutes John Bailey pumped a high ball forward; Graeme Sharp outjumped his marker to flick it on, leaving Adrian Heath in the clear. Inevitably, Bruce Grobbelaar raced off his line, but too late to prevent Heath's drive.

The shot hit Alan Hansen's knee before he appeared to scoop the ball away with his left hand. Referee Robinson waved play on, but the arguments about the 'penalty that never was' will rage for years.

The first half belonged almost exclusively to Everton; the second period was Liverpool's. Shaken by the ferocity of their closest rivals, the Reds took some time to settle down before launching a series of telling raids.

Kennedy, Dalglish and Johnston all went close, but the best chances fell to ace marksman Ian Rush. Three times the normally lethal Welshman squandered great opportunities, thus guaranteeing extra-time.

One could almost sense that both teams were ready to settle for a replay as the sun took its toll on bodies that had already endured a hard season.

Both sides had the chance to snatch a late victory, but a draw was the perfect end to a remarkable day. As the players trooped off, blue mingled with red and the chant, 'Merseyside, Merseyside, Merseyside,' echoed around Wembley.

Four days later at Maine Road, a Graeme Souness volley from 25 yards was enough to give Liverpool the trophy for the fourth consecutive year.

Everton Southall, Stevens, Bailey, Ratcliffe, Mountfield, Reid, Irvine, Heath, Sharp, Richardson, Sheedy (Harper).
Liverpool: Grobbelaar, Neal, Kennedy, Lawrenson, Whelan, Hansen, Dalglish, Lee, Rush, Johnston (Robinson), Souness.

Referee: Mr A. Robinson (Portsmouth)   *Attendance: 100,000*

Andy Gray scores Everton's second goal in the 1984 FA Cup Final.

Adrian Heath shows off the FA Cup as Everton drive through the streets of Merseyside in May 1984.

Match to Remember 14   19 May 1984

Everton 2   Watford 0

AFTER the bitter disappointment of going so close to ending neighbours Liverpool's astonishing Milk Cup monopoly, Howard Kendall's Everton had a second Wembley appointment, this time with Graham Taylor's Watford.

Everton desperately needed victory and if ever there was an instance of the result being of far greater importance than the manner in which it was achieved, then it was here. Everton's maxim down the years has been that the performance is more important than the spoils themselves. But now everyone at Goodison Park needed tangible proof that a revival had begun.

The outcome was highly satisfactory to Goodison. Both the purists and the success-starved Everton supporters were well pleased. Everton duly won the FA Cup, and won it in some style.

It was a memorable day not just on the field, but on the terraces also, where northerner and southerner applauded their teams and gave no hint of trouble.

Taylor's enthusiastic but largely inexperienced side were comprehensively beaten by an Everton side on the threshold of a new golden age for the club.

Watford were outplayed for long spells, yet never once did they give the impression of capitulating in the face of a near-ceaseless barrage. They had their chances and, despite their inability to match the tireless midfield play of Peter Reid and Adrian Heath, they might have gone to the dressing room to contemplate a half-time lead.

As early as the second minute George Reilly flicked on Lee Sinnott's massive throw, only for John Barnes to mis-cue his shot with only Neville Southall blocking his route.

Les Taylor saw a 25-yard drive deflected just wide of an upright by John Bailey's outstretched leg, and Mo Johnston went close with a header, but it was Everton who held the greater initiative.

Graeme Sharp headed Trevor Steven's raking cross fractionally wide and Kevin Richardson hit the side-netting before Watford's defence was made to pay for a moment of slackness.

Richardson hooked a vague cross in from the left and as the Watford's defenders looked on, thinking that there was no danger, Gary Stevens fired in low and hard. Sharp stopped the ball dead before turning to lash a drive into the bottom corner via a post.

One goal would probably have been enough but Everton wanted a more comfortable margin. Six minutes after the interval, Andy Gray rose superbly to head home Steven's deep cross. Television slow-motion replays showed that the fearless Scot had made contact with the back of goalkeeper Sherwood's hands before heading the ball home, but referee Hunting's decision to let the goal stand found no-one at Goodison arguing.

Everton: Southall, Stevens, Bailey, Ratcliffe, Mountfield, Reid, Steven, Heath, Sharp, Gray, Richardson. Sub: Harper.
Watford: Sherwood, Bardsley, Price (Atkinson), Taylor, Perry, Sinnott, Callaghan, Johnston, Reilly, Jackett, Barnes.

Referee: Mr J.Hunting (Leicester)   *Attendance: 100,000*

Everton's ten consecutive First Division victories in 1984-5 is a club record for one season. In that campaign they also established a club record of 28 consecutive matches without defeat (18 League, six FA Cup, four European Cup-winners' Cup).

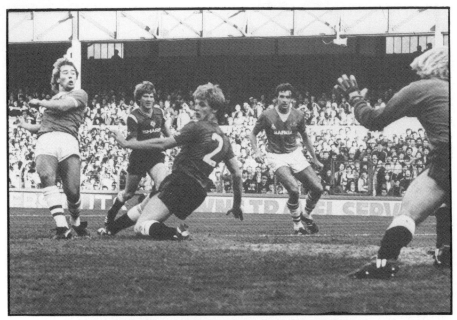

Adrian Heath scoring in Everton's 5-0 hammering of Manchester United.

Kevin Sheedy scores one of Everton's five goals in their crushing defeat of Manchester United in October 1984.

Match to Remember 15   27 October 1984

Everton 5   Manchester United 0

RON Atkinson's multi-million pound side arrived at Goodison Park as favourites to succeed Liverpool as League Champions. They had been beaten only once that season and saw this as the perfect opportunity to halt the Everton revival in its infancy.

In many respects, however, this was the day that Howard Kendall's team came of age; the day when the Goodison men proved conclusively that Everton was once again a name to rank with the best in British football.

With a staggering virtuoso performance which personified everything that is best about modern football, Kevin Ratcliffe and his colleagues put United to flight.

From the first whistle, Everton never once looked like relinquishing their stranglehold. Someone remarked that, if this had been a boxing match, it would have been stopped after ten minutes, so groggy were United at that point.

Kendall's blue-shirted terriers destroyed United in a manner which reminded many of the halcyon days of the 1969-70 Championship season; others felt it was the best single performance of the last two decades.

Joe Mercer, watching from the stand, went further. He said it was the best performance he had ever seen by an Everton side.

The pattern was set in the opening two minutes as Derek Mountfield fired just over Bailey's crossbar. Three minutes later there was no such escape for United. Kevin Sheedy, not famed for his aerial prowess, outjumped Moran to glide home a beautiful header. The young Everton star needed stitches to a head wound but bravely carried on.

After 23 minutes Sheedy made it 2-0 after Heath had put him clear. Everton's dazed hero hammered the ball into the bottom corner from 12 yards.

Unable to halt the swirling blue tide, United found themselves 3-0 down after 34 minutes when Heath rammed the ball home from close range.

Everton were hungry for more goals and they surged forward again in the second half. Albiston cleared Heath's header off the line before Stevens almost casually moved into position to lash a fierce drive into the United net via a post.

United's humiliation was complete with four minutes left when Sharp marked his own magnificent performance with the fifth goal of the afternoon.

Everton: Southall, Stevens, Van den Hauwe, Ratcliffe, Mountfield, Reid, Steven, Heath, Sharp, Bracewell, Sheedy (Gray).
Manchester United: Bailey, McQueen, Albiston, Moses(Stapleton), Moran, Hogg, Robson, Strachan, Hughes, Brazil, Olsen.

Referee: Mr G. Tyson (Sunderland)   *Attendance: 40,769*

Match to Remember 16   **15 May 1985**

Everton 3   Rapid Vienna 1

EVERTON arrived in Rotterdam for the European Cup-winners' Cup Final at the end of a long, hard season. There were many who feared that this might be the night they were made to pay for their relentless pursuit of a much-vaunted 'treble'.

Having already clinched their first League Championship for 15 years, they had to face the tough-tackling Austrians, controversial conquerors of Celtic in an earlier round. Four days later, they had to walk out at Wembley in a bid to retain the FA Cup.

Manager Howard Kendall had watched Rapid Vienna in action the previous week. He knew that if Everton could maintain the form they had shown week after week in the League, they would be more than capable of taking their first-ever European title.

Vienna's pre-match declaration that they would attack Everton from the start proved to be nonsense as they sat back and tamely soaked up the mounting pressure.

Aware that Rapid had publicly expressed reservations about their ability to cope with the aerial power of Scotsmen Andy Gray and Graeme Sharp, Everton pumped in high crosses from all angles.

Rapid were unsettled by this, but somehow they managed to hold firm. Everton thought that their long-overdue breakthrough had arrived in the 39th minute when a superbly-worked free-kick was climaxed by Gray.

Sheedy swung the ball over, Mountfield headed it down, and there was Gray to sweep it home. But Mountfield was adjudged to have been offside although millions back home saw television replays appear to prove that he was not.

It was not until the 57th minute that Everton eventually broke the deadlock. Graeme Sharp easily beat goalkeeper Konsel to an under-hit backpass. Sharp had time to turn and look up before chipping deftly across goal where Gray raced in to force the ball home, unchallenged, from eight yards.

Everton's victory was sealed in the 72nd minute when Trevor Steven found himself on the end of a Sheedy corner which had eluded the lunging boots of three defenders. Steven thumped the ball home at the far post before turning to begin the celebrations.

Astonishingly, Rapid managed to claw their way back into the game when veteran Hans Krankl beat Neville Southall from close range.

It was a minor and very temporary setback. Straight from the restart Sheedy hammered home a third goal, brilliantly from 25 yards.

Krankl summed up the game: "Everton were just too good for us. It's been a long time since we played against anyone of their class. They are possibly the best side in the whole of Europe."

Everton: Southall, Stevens, Van den Hauwe, Ratcliffe, Mountfield, Reid, Steven, Sharp, Gray, Bracewell, Sheedy.
Rapid Vienna: Konsel, Lainer, Brauneder, Weber, Garger, Kranjcar, Kienast, Hrstick, Pacuit (Gross), Krankl, Winhofer (Panenka).

Referee: Paolo Casarin (Italy)   *Attendance: 45,000*

Peter Reid proudly displays the European Cup-winners' Cup in Rotterdam.

274

Everton's 1931-2 Championship team. Back (l to r): H.Cooke (trainer), Clark, Williams, Sagar, Gee, Cresswell, Britton. Front: Critchley, White, Dean, Johnson, Stein, Thomson.

Everton skipper Kevin Ratcliffe puts in a bruising challenge on Liverpool's Craig Johnston.

Peter Reid and Manchester United's Bryan Robson tussle for the ball but England's captain cannot prevent the Everton man from getting in his shot.

A-Z OF EVERTON STARS

WALTER ABBOTT

	LEAGUE		FA CUP		TOTAL	
	App	Gls	App	Gls	App	Gls
1899-1900	25	1	1		26	1
1900-01	34	5	2		36	5
1901-02	31	4	2		33	4
1902-03	33	4	3	2	36	6
1903-04	32	4	1		33	4
1904-05	28	4	6		34	4
1905-06	27	5	5	1	32	6
1906-07	26	4	7	1	33	5
1907-08	21	1	7	1	28	2
	257	32	34	5	291	37

Walter Abbott joined Everton in the close season of 1899 because club officials were impressed with the form he had shown as an inside-left with Small Heath where his hard-shooting had brought him 33 goals in 1898-9. But it was as an equally hard-shooting left-half that Abbott flourished at Goodison Park, and where he made the bulk of his 250-plus League appearances before moving on to Burnley in the summer of 1908. Abbott had abundant stamina and he seemed to cover every inch of the pitch, urging on colleagues. Strangely, Abbott's one England cap came at centre-half, a position he never played in the League. He was drafted into the team against Wales at Wrexham in 1902, at a time when England were constantly changing their pivot. He played well enough in the goalless draw but was never invited to represent his country again. He played in Everton's FA Cup Finals of 1906 and 1907 and also represented the Football League. After Burnley he returned briefly to Small Heath, by now renamed Birmingham, and retired through injury in 1910. Later he worked in the early motor industry in Birmingham.

	LEAGUE		FA CUP		TOTAL	
	App	Gls	App	Gls	App	Gls
1893-94	2				2	
1894-95	3				3	
1895-96	23		2		25	
1896-97	23		3		26	
	51		5		56	

The unusually-named Smart Arridge started his football career with the Welsh club, Bangor, and after they had converted him to full-back he began to attract the attentions of leading clubs of the day. It was Second Division Bootle who landed his signature but inevitably a First Division club, Everton, soon lured him away. Yet, having signed for the Goodison club in 1893, he had to wait until the 1895-6 season before he could establish a place at left-back in the League side. He had two full seasons in the Everton first team, but his run did not extend to a place in the 1897 FA Cup Final team. After appearing in the first three rounds he missed the semi-final and Final. Disappointed and not a little bitter, he wanted to get away and in the close season signed for New Brighton Tower. A full-back who could play on either flank, Arridge was renowned for his fearsome shoulder-charges 'which are events to be thought over long after the person has been the recipient of such a favour'. Though born in Sunderland, his Welsh boyhood meant that, when he was good enough, he was selected for Wales and won eight full caps.

SMART ARRIDGE

	LEAGUE		FA CUP		FL CUP		EUROPE		TOTAL	
	App	Gls	App	Gls	App	Gls	App	Gls	App	Gls
1979-80	42	2	6		5				53	2
1980-81	31	4			1/1		2		38/1	
1981-82	12				3				15	
1982-83	37		5		2				44	
1983-84	33		7		7				47	
1984-85	15	1			1		4		20	1
	170	3	22		19/1		6		217/1	3

JOHN BAILEY

Although he lost his regular full-back berth in October 1984, following the arrival of Pat Van den Hauwe from Birmingham City, John Bailey is still very much the joker in Everton's pack. A local lad with a typically cutting Scouse sense of humour, Bailey is still an invaluable member of Howard Kendall's squad, more than capable of lifting spirits and morale when things are not going quite right. He was signed from Blackburn Rovers in July 1979 for £300,000, and within 12 months had forced his way on to the international scene by being called up for England 'B'. A clever defender who loves to push forward, Bailey remains a firm favourite with the Goodison crowd. The crowning moment of his career to date came at Wembley in May 1984, when he helped Everton to their first FA Cup success in 18 years, but just months later he found himself out of the picture. After a clear-the-air meeting with manager Howard Kendall in March 1985, Bailey was placed on the transfer list but changed his mind a month later and signed a new one-year contract.

	LEAGUE		FA CUP		FL CUP		EUROPE		TOTAL	
	App	Gls	App	Gls	App	Gls	App	Gls	App	Gls
1966-67	41	15	6	2			4	1	51	18
1967-68	34	20	4		2				40	20
1968-69	40	16	5		4	2			49	18
1969-70	37	10	1	1	3	1			41	12
1970-71	39	2	5		2	1	6	3	51	7
1971-72	17	3							17	3
	208	66	21	5	10	3	10	4	249	78

Alan Ball was one of the greatest players ever to pull on an Everton — and England — shirt. The flame-haired fire-brand who inspired his country to World Cup triumph in 1966, and who played a major role in Everton's Championship success in 1970, was never out of the spotlight as he walked a tightrope between fame and infamy. Constantly at odds with the authorities, Ball insisted on playing the game his way; he asked for no favours and although his hell-for-leather approach to football won him few friends on the field, he was immensely popular with supporters. His greatest asset was his extraordinary appetite for work. The ultimate competitor, he refused to accept defeat and ensured that anyone playing alongside him was of the same mind. Ball's work-rate more than made up for his temperamental outbursts and he will forever be remembered for his grim determination and defence-splitting passes. Ball was born in Farnworth, Lancashire, and was on the books of nearby Bolton Wanderers but signed professional for Blackpool. He joined Everton in August 1966 for a then British record fee of £110,000. He clocked up more than 200 League games in five years at Goodison. With Howard Kendall and Colin Harvey, he was part of the celebrated midfield trio which swept Everton to the title in 1969-70. For no apparent reason, that side broke up within two years and Harry Catterick sensationally transferred Ball to Arsenal in 1971 for another record fee, £220,000. After a successful career at Highbury, Ball moved to Southampton for £60,000 in 1976, then to Blackpool as manager in 1980. After weeks of boardroom discontent, he resigned in March 1981 and returned to Southampton. Ball played his last game in the top flight in October 1982, against Everton.

ALAN BALL

ROBERT BALMER

	LEAGUE		FA CUP		TOTAL	
	App	Gls	App	Gls	App	Gls
1902-03	1				1	
1903-04	3				3	
1904-05	11		3		14	
1905-06	20		2		22	
1906-07	25		8		33	
1907-08	26		7		33	
1908-09	35		2		37	
1909-10	20				20	
1910-11	23		1		24	
1911-12	1				1	
	165		23		188	

The younger brother of Walter Balmer, by four years, Robert was an extremely effective full-back who partnered his brother in the 1907 FA Cup Final against Sheffield Wednesday at the Crystal Palace. Born in Liverpool, he was of much slighter build than Walter, standing 5ft 7in and weighing 10st 2lbs. He made his League debut in the 3-0 win over Middlesbrough at Goodison Park on 3 January 1903 and he became a regular member of the side in 1905-06. After his brother's departure, Robert formed another good partnership with the stylish Scottish full-back, John Maconnachie. While Maconnachie liked to play his way out of trouble, Robert Balmer's technique was more traditional — the big clearance to relieve pressure — but their contrasting styles combined effectively and they had a good understanding with goalkeeper Billy Scott.

	LEAGUE		FA CUP		TOTAL	
	App	Gls	App	Gls	App	Gls
1897-98	12		5		17	
1898-99	23		2		25	
1899-1900	32	1	1		33	1
1900-01	31		2		33	
1901-02	28		2		30	
1902-03	28		3		31	
1903-04	32		1		33	
1904-05	30		3		33	
1905-06	18		5		23	
1906-07	33		8		41	
1907-08	26		6		32	
	293	1	38		331	1

Liverpool-born Walter Balmer served Everton well for more than a decade. A thick-set full-back, he signed as a 20-year-old in 1897 and played over 250 League games for the club as well as appearing in two FA Cup Finals and winning an England cap. Balmer made his League debut against West Bromwich Albion at The Hawthorns in November 1897 and played his last game at home to Sunderland in April 1908. He had the major attributes of a full-back of the day, a crunching tackle and a hefty clearance which sent the ball way out of the danger area. He could play on either flank and formed a good partnership with Jack Crelley, another locally-born defender who found his way to Goodison via Millwall. For some time he also partnered his younger brother, Robert, in Everton's rearguard. Balmer played in consecutive Cup Finals, collecting a winners' medal in 1906. He made his England appearance against Ireland in 1905, playing right-back in the 1-1 draw at Middlesbrough. He also represented the Football League before moving to Croydon Common, then a Southern League side. After World War One he was appointed Huddersfield Town coach. His nephew, Jack Balmer, had a few games with Everton before World War Two before joining Liverpool where he made his name.

WALTER BALMER

JOHN BELL

	LEAGUE		FA CUP		TOTAL	
	App	Gls	App	Gls	App	Gls
1892-93	3				3	
1893-94	24	9	1		25	9
1894-95	27	15	3	3	30	18
1895-96	27	9	3	1	30	10
1896-97	27	15	5	2	32	17
1897-98	22	4	5		27	4
1901-02	24	5	2		26	5
1902-03	23	5	3	2	26	7
	177	62	22	8	199	70

The sight of John Bell wriggling his way down the right flank was a familiar one around the turn of the century. A masterful dribbler who played as though he had the ball glued to the inside of his right foot at times, he was a member of Dumbarton's 1891-2 Scottish League championship side before signing for Everton in 1892. Regarded as one of the most inventive forwards of his day, Bell was an undoubted sporting craftsman who spent the best part of a decade thrilling audiences at Goodison Park. He played in the 1897 FA Cup Final, and although Everton were beaten 3-2 by Aston Villa, it was Bell who won the plaudits, universally praised for a heroic performance which nearly swung the game the Merseysiders' way. He left Everton to serve Spurs and Glasgow Celtic before returning to Goodison via New Brighton Tower FC, and later played for Preston where he became player coach. He was chairman of the first attempt at a players' union. In one First Division match he is alleged to have saved the life of a fellow player when he repositioned his dislocated neck with one firm wrench of his massive hands. Bell made 10 appearances for Scotland between 1890 and 1900. .

	LEAGUE		FA CUP		TOTAL	
	App	Gls	App	Gls	App	Gls
1935-36	7	4	1		8	4
1936-37	2				2	
1938-39	41	9	5		46	9
1945-46			2		2	
1946-47	37	3	2		39	3
1947-48	10		5		15	
1948-49	13	1			13	1
	110	17	15		125	17

STANLEY BENTHAM

Stan Bentham spent the best years of his life at Everton, first as a player and then as a key member of the backroom staff. Born in Leigh, he played most of his early football with a church team, Lowton St Mary's, before attracting the attention of Bolton Wanderers with whom he had a series of trials. In December 1933 he turned professional with Wigan Athletic and within a matter of months found himself the target of several top clubs. In February 1934 he threw in his lot with Everton, along with Springfield Park teammate Terry Kavanagh. Bentham made a dream League debut in November 1935. Everton claimed their first away success of the season with a superb 4-0 win at Grimsby and Bentham netted twice. He was an honest, hard-working inside-right and a pioneer of the roving midfield role which is so popular today. In 1938-9, when Everton won the Championship, Bentham missed only one match. He left Goodison in 1962 to take up a coaching post with Luton Town.

	LEAGUE		FA CUP		FL CUP		EUROPE		TOTAL	
	App	Gls	App	Gls	App	Gls	App	Gls	App	Gls
1972-73	30/2	1	2		1				33/2	1
1973-74	35/2	4	3		2				40/2	4
1974-75	31/2		2/1		2				35/3	
1975-76	29/1	2	1		2/1	2			34/2	2
1976-77	14/1	1	1		4				19/1	1
	139/8	8	9/1		11/1	2			161/10	8

Mike Bernard was a solid and reliable defender who was rather unfortunate not to make a bigger name for himself during his time with Everton. Highly competitive and a superb ball-winner, he reached his own footballing peak when the club were hardly enjoying the best of fortunes. He began his career with Stoke City. Sir Alf Ramsey gave him the first of his England Under-23 caps in 1970, and he was a member of the Stoke side which ended a 108-year wait for success when, in March 1972, they lifted the League Cup by defeating Chelsea. Harry Catterick signed Bernard for Everton in May of that year for £140,000. He arrived as a midfielder but was later converted into a defender where he made the vast majority of his appearances. After losing his place in early 1977, Bernard was linked with a return to Stoke, but eventually settled for a move to Oldham Athletic. He took over a pub in the Dee Valley after he was forced to quit the game because of injury in early 1979.

MIKE BERNARD

BILLY BINGHAM

	LEAGUE		FA CUP		FL CUP		EUROPE		TOTAL	
	App	Gls	App	Gls	App	Gls	App	Gls	App	Gls
1960-61	26	9	1		3	1			30	10
1961-62	37	9	3	1					40	10
1962-63	23	5	3	1			2		28	6
	86	23	7	2	3	1	2		98	26

Billy Bingham, the man who was to move into Goodison Park's managerial hot-seat in 1973, was a compelling outside-right who was partly instrumental in the club's successful assault on the League Championship in 1962-3. A superb dribbler and crosser of the ball, Bingham loved nothing better than to face an opponent in a one-to-one situation. In the title-winning side he made 23 appearances, scoring five goals, alongside such luminaries as Alex Young and Roy Vernon. He started his illustrious career with Irish League club Glentoran before joining Sunderland in October 1950. In 1958, after establishing himself as a firm favourite in the North-East, Bingham was transferred to Luton Town and played for them in the 1959 FA Cup Final. He joined Everton in 1960 and left for Port Vale in 1963. His playing days ended when he broke a leg two years later. Bingham made 56 appearances for Northern Ireland and later became Irish team manager as well as boss at Goodison Park.

	LEAGUE		FA CUP		TOTAL	
	App	Gls	App	Gls	App	Gls
1900-01	31		2		33	
1901-02	34	1	2		36	1
1902-03	29	2	3	1	32	3
1903-04	34	4	1		35	4
1904-05	8				8	
1905-06	17		2	1	19	1
1906-07	14	1			14	1
1907-08	8	1			8	1
	175	9	10	2	185	11

Tom Booth was unlucky to miss Everton's 1906 FA Cup Final, and to be disappointed when the club reached the Final again a year later. Injury in the days leading up to the 1906 semi-final ruled him out and there was no room for him 12 months later. Born in Manchester, Booth played for the Rest of Lancashire against Nelson in 1896 and his form as a strong half-back alerted Blackburn Rovers officials who claimed his signature. He moved from right-half to centre-half, the position in which he was first capped, against Wales in 1898. He joined Everton in April 1900, because Blackburn needed the cash, and went on to captain a side that challenged for the League title in the early days of this century. Although he continued to live in Manchester, no-one could doubt his commitment to Merseyside and when Everton met Manchester City in a vital end-of-the-season clash in 1905, Booth and his City namesake, Frank, were both cautioned in what became an infamous off-the-ball incident. He left Everton in 1908, for Preston, but was soon on his way to Carlisle United without playing a League game at Deepdale. He retired in 1909.

TOM BOOTH

	LEAGUE		FA CUP		TOTAL	
	App	Gls	App	Gls	App	Gls
1937-38	13	3			13	3
1938-39	36	4	5	4	41	8
1945-46			2		2	
1946-47	9	3			9	3
1947-48	4	1			4	1
1948-49	4				4	
	66	11	7	4	73	15

Wally Boyes was a tiny winger who linked up with another diminutive player, Alex Stevenson, to form one of the most impudent flank combinations ever to grace Goodison Park. Standing only 5ft 3ins tall, he overcame the additional handicap of having one leg shorter than the other, and scored some crucial goals in Everton's 1938-9 Championship season. As a schoolboy prodigy in Sheffield he once scored 17 goals in one game. His side won 31-2 and even then Boyes fell foul of the referee by demanding a late penalty, such was his basic enthusiasm for football. Boyes was the clever type of winger; some felt he was far too intricate and would have preferred him to be more direct, but on his day there were few full-backs who could master him. After scoring the first goal for West Brom in the 1935 FA Cup Final against Sheffield Wednesday, he joined Everton in February 1938. He made three appearances for England before leaving to join Notts County, later moving to Scunthorpe United. He was also player-manager of Retford, manager of Hyde United and trainer at Swansea Town.

WALLY BOYES

	LEAGUE		FA CUP		TOTAL	
	App	Gls	App	Gls	App	Gls
1892-93	25		7		32	
1893-94	21	1			21	1
1894-95	30	2	4		34	2
1895-96	30	3	3		33	3
1896-97	29		5	1	34	1
1897-98	22				22	
1898-99	34	1	2		36	1
1899-1900	29				29	
1900-1901	2				2	
	222	7	21	1	243	8

Another of Everton's famous Scottish imports, Richard Boyle came to Goodison Park in 1890 after spells with Dumbarton Episcopalians, Dumbarton Union and Dumbarton. He made an immediate impact on the English game and within four years he was appointed club captain. He was a sturdy half-back who led by example. Strong in the tackle and renowned for his ability to deliver a pin-point pass over any distance, Boyle was the kingpin in a side which, at the time, was built for stability rather than mobility. There was said to be no more stirring sight than Boyle robbing a forward and then proceeding to canter half the length of the field before releasing one of his own front men with a simple, yet incisive pass. In the days when the centre-half was no mere stopper, he often took it upon himself to push forward in search of goals and he scored many, particularly from free-kicks.

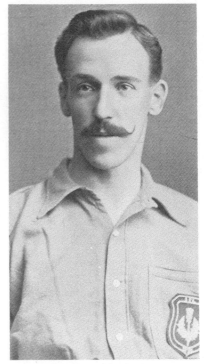

RICHARD BOYLE

	LEAGUE		FA CUP		FL CUP		EUROPE		TOTAL	
	App	Gls	App	Gls	App	Gls	App	Gls	App	Gls
1984-85	37	2	7		4	1	8	1	56	4
	37	2	7		4	1	8	1	56	4

Paul Bracewell holds the rare distinction of making his Everton debut at Wembley Stadium. After signing from Sunderland for £250,000 at the end of 1983-4, the talented midfielder was thrown in at the deep end in the Charity Shield showpiece against Liverpool three months later. It was perhaps the ultimate baptism of fire, but the Heswall-born youngster came through with flying colours as Howard Kendall's men tuned up for what was to be their Championship-winning season with a deserved 1-0 win. Bracewell had been high on Kendall's wanted list for two years. Indeed, he nearly moved to Goodison Park in 1983 while at Stoke City, but eventually decided to try his luck in the North-East. Things did not really work out for him at Roker Park and he jumped at the chance to return south. While not the quickest of players, he is a superb passer of the ball and has formed a telling partnership at the heart of the midfield alongside Peter Reid. He played a major part in Everton's success during 1984-5 and won his first full England cap when he came on as substitute for Bryan Robson against West Germany on the summer tour to Mexico.

PAUL BRACEWELL

GEORGE BREWSTER

	LEAGUE		FA CUP		TOTAL	
	App	Gls	App	Gls	App	Gls
1919-20	5				5	
1920-21	29		4		33	
1921-22	25	3			25	3
1922-23	5	1			5	1
	64	4	4		68	4

George Brewster was a tall, influential centre-half whose form while he was at Goodison led to him being capped for Scotland. Yet he could never be certain of a regular place in the Everton first team. He was born at Culsalmond, near Aberdeen, and played Scottish junior soccer with Mugiemoss before signing for Aberdeen in 1913. During World War One he guested for Falkirk before returning to Aberdeen. Everton heard of the 6ft centre-half who was playing a commanding role with the Dons and they brought him to England in January 1920 for £1,500. He played a handful of games in the second half of that season and the following campaign saw him as a regular, though he played all his games when Tom Fleetwood was switched to right-half. He caught the eye of the Scottish selectors and was capped in the 3-0 win over England in April that season. The following season he again covered for Fleetwood in the Everton team when that player was required to switch roles. But Brewster was unhappy at not being the first-choice centre-half. In November 1922, after playing in the first five games of the season before being dropped, he signed for Wolverhampton Wanderers. From there he moved to Lovells' Athletic and Wallasey United, coached Brooklands Athetic in New York, then became player-manager of Inverness.

	LEAGUE		FA CUP		TOTAL	
	App	Gls	App	Gls	App	Gls
1930-31	10				10	
1932-33	36		6		42	
1933-34	42		1		43	
1934-35	36		5		41	
1935-36	25	2	1		26	2
1936-37	40		4	1	44	1
1937-38	31		2		33	
1938-39	1				1	
	221	2	19	1	240	3

CLIFF BRITTON

Cliff Britton was a footballing genius who was later to turn his considerable talents to the even more demanding task of management. Extraordinarily gifted, he was a cultured wing-half whose passing ability was second to none. He began his lengthy and hugely successful career in local football in his native Bristol. He signed professional forms for Bristol Rovers in 1926 and was transferred to Everton four years later. On his arrival at Goodison Park he was considered too lightweight to deal with the rough and tumble of a central position and was played at outside-right in the Central League side. Once he made the breakthrough into League football he never looked back and he was in the side in 1933 when the FA Cup was lifted at the expense of Manchester City. He made his England debut in 1934, against Wales, and went on to win nine full caps. He appeared only once in the 1938-9 title-winning side but was a player, and something of an advisor, to the reserve squad. During World War Two his career enjoyed something of a revival and he won 12 wartime caps, forming a fine England half-back line with Joe Mercer and Stan Cullis.

	LEAGUE		FA CUP		Fl. CUP		EUROPE		TOTAL	
	App	Gls	App	Gls	App	Gls	App	Gls	App	Gls
1963-64	30		5						35	
1964-65	28	5	1				4		33	5
1965-66	14/2		4				1		19/2	
1966-67	15/5	1	1/3				1	1	17/8	2
1967-68	12/13	1	0/2		2	1			14/15	2
1968-69	40	1	5		4				49	1
1969-70	31/5		0/1		4				35/6	
1970-71	6/8	1	0/2				0/2		6/12	1
	176/33	9	16/8		10	1	6/2	1	208/43	11

SANDY BROWN

Alex 'Sandy' Brown was brought to Goodison in the wake of the 1963 Championship win. He had impressed Harry Catterick with a series of sterling displays for Partick Thistle and the Everton boss was quick to snap him up for £38,000 when the opportunity arose in September of that year. He was a real utility man, a defender who could move forward to stamp his authority on midfield. He could even play in goal and his versatility led to him being named substitute in no less than 33 League games. During the opening minutes of a bad-tempered encounter with Leeds United at Goodison in the mid-60s, he was sent off and the referee was later forced to lead both teams from the field for a cooling-down period. Brown played in four ties in Everton's FA Cup-winning year of 1966 but missed the Final itself. He made 36 appearances (five as sub) as a full-back in the Championship year, 1969-70. After joining Shrewsbury in 1971 he moved to Southport and played in their 1972-3 Fourth Division Championship side. In the summer of 1973 he signed for Northern Premier League club Fleetwood.

	LEAGUE		FA CUP		TOTAL	
	App	Gls	App	Gls	App	Gls
1914-15	4				4	
1919-20	20		1		21	
1920-21	10				10	
1921-22	16		1		17	
1922-23	8		2		10	
1923-24	37		2		39	
1924-25	20		3		23	
1925-26	28				28	
1926-27	25				25	
1927-28	2				2	
	170		9		179	

WILLIAM BROWN

William Brown was a product of a famous Scottish nursery, Cambuslang. He was a member of Everton's classic half-back line of the early 1920s and won national recognition for his cultured, patient displays. By trade he was an engineer's fitter but he had always dreamt of a career in football and did not hesitate to sign when offered a contract in 1913. He was only 17 when he made his First Division debut against Manchester City in December the following year. He was transferred to Nottingham Forest for what was diplomatically described as a 'nominal fee' in May 1928. Even in his later years he proved a useful wing-half with a flair for goalscoring. In August 1930 he was appointed player-coach of Liverpool Cables FC.

	LEAGUE		FA CUP		TOTAL	
	App	Gls	App	Gls	App	Gls
1949-50	26	6	5	2	31	8
1950-51	22	5			22	5
1951-52	15	12	1		16	12
1952-53	14	5	4		18	5
1953-54	19	3			19	3
1954-55	1				1	
	97	31	10	2	107	33

Ted Buckle was a Londoner who joined Everton from Manchester United in November 1949. A brash, bold winger with a lightning turn of speed, he quickly developed into a player of real class and quality. Less than 18 hours after completing his move from Old Trafford he made his debut — against United. His compelling flank play was one of the main reasons for Everton's remarkable FA Cup run in 1953. Inspired by his greyhound-like pace, the side reached the semi-finals only to be beaten, rather unfortunately, 4-3 by Bolton Wanderers at Maine Road. He was transferred to Exeter City in June 1955 after 107 League and Cup games. In the 1960s, at the age of 35, he took over as player-manager at Welsh League club Prestatyn. He was forced to resign less than 12 months later due to business commitments.

TED BUCKLE

	LEAGUE		FA CUP		FL CUP		EUROPE		TOTAL	
	App	Gls	App	Gls	App	Gls	App	Gls	App	Gls
1971-72	6	1							6	1
1972-73	9	1	2	1					11	2
1973-74	33	3	3		2	1			38	4
1974-75	31/2	2			2				33/2	2
1975-76	30/1	1			5		2		37/1	1
1976-77	7/4		2						9/4	
1977-78	12	2			3				15	2
	128/7	10	7	1	12	1	2		149/7	12

Mick Buckley had the football world very much at his feet during the early days of his career. A schoolboy star in his hometown of Manchester, he received offers from both City and United but surprised everyone by opting for Everton. His small frame belied his naturally aggressive instincts and he developed into a terrier-like midfielder, respected throughout the game for his totally professional attitude. Buckley fought his way through the ranks to claim a first-team spot in 1971-2 at the age of 18. He made two appearances for England Under-23s and was a member of the England Youth side that carried off the 'Little World Cup' in Spain in 1972. He lost his Everton place to Trevor Ross in 1977 after injury and was loaned to Queen's Park Rangers for a month, along with full-back Neil Robinson, at the start of the following season. He was transferred to Sunderland in 1978 but, despite his 100 per cent efforts, the going was far from smooth in the North-East. He recovered from a bad start at Roker Park to rescue the Wearsiders from relegation when he scored a vital goal against Manchester City on 15 May 1982. Shortly afterwards he left Sunderland and joined Carlisle.

MICK BUCKLEY

286

	LEAGUE		FA CUP		TOTAL	
	App	Gls	App	Gls	App	Gls
1888-89	22	6			22	6
1889-90	22	9	2		24	9
1890-91	22	10	1		23	10
1891-92	25	10	1	1	26	11
1892-93	27	10	7	3	34	13
1893-94	24	13			24	13
1894-95	28	11	4	3	32	14
1895-96	28	11	3	1	31	12
1896-97	28	7	5	2	33	9
1897-98	22	8	5	2	27	10
1898-99	22	2	2	1	24	3
	270	97	30	13	300	110

EDGAR CHADWICK

A native of Blackburn, Edgar Chadwick was one of the great names of football in the 1890s. His first senior club was Blackburn Olympic and he had one season with Blackburn Rovers before signing for Everton in the summer of 1888, in time for the Football League's inaugural season. An inside-left of enormous talent, he was quick and cunning and he passed the ball accurately and shot hard and often. His left-wing partnership with Alf Milward was probably the best in the League, with both men able to read the other's game with uncanny accuracy. Chadwick was a lightweight — he stood 5ft 6ins and weighed 10st 7lbs — but that never stopped him from being in the thick of the action. He won seven England caps, scoring after 30 seconds against Scotland in 1892. He won a League Championship medal with Everton, and a Southern League Championship medal with Southampton, but played on the losing side in three FA Cup Finals (with Everton in 1893 and 1897, and Southampton in 1902). He played for the Football League against the Scottish League and the Football Alliance and was reputed to be the first Englishman to coach abroad when he worked with teams in Holland and Germany before pursuing his trade as a baker in Blackburn. His cousin, Arthur Chadwick, lived in his shadow at Goodison and managed only five League games in five years before moving to Portsmouth where his career finally blossomed and he was capped for England.

Everton have enjoyed more seasons in Division One than any other club. Since becoming founder-members of the Football League in 1888 they have spent all but four seasons in the top-flight.

Everton were only the second club (Liverpool were the first) to win the Second and First Division Championships in successive seasons (1930-31 and 1931-2). Since then only Spurs and Ipswich have equalled that feat.

Everton's eighth Championship success, which came in 1984-5, put them joint second, with Arsenal, in the list of First Division title winners. Liverpool lead the list with 15.

Everton hold the record for the number of FA Cup semi-final appearances. They reached the last four for the 20th time in 1985.

	LEAGUE		FA CUP		TOTAL	
	App	Gls	App	Gls	App	Gls
1910-11	3				3	
1912-13	1				1	
1913-14	7	1			7	1
1914-15	30	2	5	1	35	3
1919-20	18	3	1		19	3
1920-21	35	5	5		40	5
1921-22	35	5	1		36	5
1922-23	36	3	2	1	38	4
1923-24	38	5	2	1	40	6
1924-25	38	2	3		41	2
1925-26	38	7	2		40	7
	279	33	21	3	300	36

SAM CHEDGZOY

Sam Chedgzoy was the man directly responsible for a major change in the game's laws. An intelligent man who was never scared to challenge authority, he discovered a glaring loophole in the laws and proceeded to exploit it during a match at White Hart Lane in 1924. A new rule had been introduced so that a goal could be scored direct from a corner. Chedgzoy took a corner by dribbling along the by-line as members of both sides looked on in astonishment. They saw Chedgzoy hammer the ball into the net and score a goal which led to a rule change. Twelve months later football's embarrassed hierarchy introduced a rule whereby the taker of a corner could only play the ball once before a second player had touched it. Chedgzoy was born in Ellesmere Port and initially played for Burnell's Ironworks alongside Joe Mercer's father. His lengthy career as an industrious outside-right saw him win a League Championship medal in 1914-15. On retirement, he went to America where he died. He made eight appearances for England between 1920 and 1925 and he had a son, also called Sam, who also joined Everton.

DAVE CLEMENTS

	LEAGUE		FA CUP		FL CUP		EUROPE		TOTAL	
	App	Gls	App	Gls	App	Gls	App	Gls	App	Gls
1973-74	31	3	2	1	2				35	4
1974-75	39/1	1	4		1	2			45/1	2
1975-76	11/1	2				4	0/1		15/2	2
	81/2	6	6	2	8		0/1		95/3	8

Dave Clements was one of Everton's most intelligent and erudite footballers. He became Billy Bingham's first signing when he joined from Sheffield Wednesday for £60,000 in September 1973. He won the great majority of his Northern Ireland caps as a midfield player, though he began as a winger in Wolves' reserve team. He moved to Coventry City for £1,000 in 1964 in what proved to be Stan Cullis' last deal, and it was while at Highfield Road that he was developed into a half-back of some consequence. He played 227 League games for Coventry, scoring 26 goals, before moving to Hillsborough in August 1971 in a £100,000 deal involving Brian Joicey. The Yorkshire side moved him to the full-back berth, but it was at Goodison that he matured into an influential midfielder with a game based on accurate passing. On 18 March 1975, while playing for Everton at Middlesbrough, he learned that he had been appointed manager of Northern Ireland. While still in charge of the national side he joined the star-studded New York Cosmos in January 1976 and went on to play with the legendary Pele. His decision to play in America cost him his job as manager of Northern Ireland.

	LEAGUE		FA CUP		TOTAL	
	App	Gls	App	Gls	App	Gls
1913-14	12	4			12	4
1914-15	36	14	5	3	41	17
1919-20	18	12	1		19	12
1920-21	1				1	
1921-22	1				1	
	68	30	6	3	74	33

When Everton signed Joe Clennell from Blackburn Rovers in January 1914 they found the balance that had for some time been lacking in their attack. He scored on his debut, against Aston Villa, and showed supporters enough skill to help them understand why he had been bought. Thereafter he was a regular fixture in the League side and on the opening day of the following season he netted a hat-trick as Everton began with a 3-1 win at White Hart Lane. It was the signal for a successful assault on the League Championship and Clennell continued to play a full part. He was one of several new signings which were to help Everton to their first title success for 24 years and, with Sam Chedgzoy and George Harrison, he threatened to run riot as Everton headed towards a possible League and Cup double. They failed in the Cup semi-final but Clennell could still be well pleased with his efforts. In wartime football he really excelled, scoring 114 goals in only 104 games. When the League resumed in 1919 he continued to score regularly until he was injured. The following season he played only once before moving to Cardiff City in October 1921. Clennell played for the Football League in 1920.

JOE CLENNELL

THOMAS CLINTON

	LEAGUE		FA CUP		TOTAL	
	App	Gls	App	Gls	App	Gls
1948-49	4				4	
1950-51	15				15	
1951-52	26	4	2		28	4
1952-53	22		5	1	27	1
1953-54	6				6	
	73	4	7	1	80	5

Thomas Clinton was the man who signed for Everton under perhaps the most unusual circumstances in the club's history. The young Irishman had been recommended by a local scout, and secretary Theo Kelly travelled to Ireland to discuss terms. As they chatted on the platform at Dundalk station, Clinton's train began to move out and he actually put pen to paper while hanging out of a lowered carriage window. He was the rugged type of full-back when he eventually landed at Goodison Park and Central League wingers soon found that they bred them tough in Eire. He made his League debut against Burnley on 26 February 1949, staying for a further seven years. He missed a penalty in the 1953 FA Cup semi-final against Bolton at Maine Road. In 1955 he was transferred to Blackburn.

	LEAGUE		FA CUP		TOTAL	
	App	Gls	App	Gls	App	Gls
1922-23	15	9			15	9
1923-24	35	15	2	2	37	17
1924-25	19	5	1		20	5
	69	29	3	2	72	31

It was once said of Jack Cock that he was far more interested in fashion than football, a conclusion easily reached after seeing this sophisticated socialite strutting around the streets of downtown Liverpool. A naturally gifted centre-forward who always gave the impression that he was playing the game for laughs, he was regarded as the snappiest dresser of the day and was known to lose his cool if confronted by someone wearing a similar outfit. Thankfully, his flamboyant taste extended only to clothes and on the field he proved to be a typically robust target-man with a lust for goalscoring. Born in Cornwall, he was one of a family of 10, one of his brothers going on to play for Notts County. Jack himself played for Brentford before joining Huddersfield just before the outbreak of World War One. He was reported killed in action but re-emerged after peace had been restored to join Chelsea. Cock made his England debut against Ireland in October 1919 and scored. He scored again when England fought back from 4-2 down to beat Scotland 5-4 at Sheffield in April 1920. He moved to Everton from Stamford Bridge in January 1923. He transferred to Plymouth Argyle in March 1925, and five years later was signed up to make a major film. He played for several leading amateur clubs before being appointed Millwall manager in 1944.

JACK COCK

	LEAGUE		FA CUP		TOTAL	
	App	Gls	App	Gls	App	Gls
1929-30	6				6	
1930-31	42		5		47	
1931-32	1				1	
1933-34	2				2	
	51		5		56	

Billy Coggins joined Everton from Bristol City in 1930 and made his debut in the crushing defeat by Grimsby Town, a reversal which condemned the Goodison side to Second Division football. When he arrived at the club, the only other goalkeeper on the books was Ted Sagar, then nothing more than another teenage hopeful. Coggins played in every game as Everton swept majestically to the Second Division title in 1931 but the following season Sagar stepped out of the shadows to launch his famous career. After sitting disconsolately on the sidelines for the best part of 12 months, Coggins left to play for Queen's Park Rangers and Bath City before retiring to his native Bristol. He died, aged 58, in August 1958.

BILLY COGGINS

	LEAGUE		FA CUP		FL CUP		TOTAL	
	App	Gls	App	Gls	App	Gls	App	Gls
1958-59	32	7	4	3			36	10
1959-60	42	14	1				43	14
1960-61	40	16	1		5	1	46	17
1961-62	19	5	3	2			22	7
	133	42	9	5	5	1	147	48

Without any doubt Bobby Collins was one of the finest inside-forwards of the last 50 years. This diminutive man — he stood only 5ft 4ins and weighed 10st 3lbs — was the heartbeat of every side he played for, fully justifying his nickname 'the Little General'. He joined Everton straight from Scottish junior soccer during the reign of Theo Kelly, but returned north to sign for Celtic after confessing that he was desperately homesick. In 1951 he made his international debut against Wales and seven years later he rejoined Everton, for £39,000. He made his debut only hours after signing, scoring a goal in the 3-1 win at Maine Road. He scored seven League goals in his first season and in the next he was top marksman with 14 in 42 games and continued to find the net throughout his Everton career. Many experts thought his career had taken a nosedive when he surprisingly signed for Leeds United for £30,000, but in many respects it was only the beginning. He helped steer a side which seemed destined to drop into Division Three back on to the straight and narrow, and by 1965 the Yorkshire club had won promotion and dramatically missed out on a League and Cup double. Collins won a recall to the Scotland side but broke a thigh bone in a bruising Fairs Cup match in Turin. It was typical of the man that he fought back to play first-team football again. He left Elland Road to join Bury on a free transfer in 1967 and from there moved to Morton. He travelled the world as a coach, taking up appointments in Australia and South Africa. In October 1972, at the age of 41, he joined Oldham Athletic as player-coach. He went on to manage Hull City before moving to Blackpool as coach in 1978. Collins also managed Huddersfield Town and Barnsley. He left Oakwell in 1985.

BOBBY COLLINS

JOHN CONNOLLY

	LEAGUE		FA CUP		FL CUP		TOTAL	
	App	Gls	App	Gls	App	Gls	App	Gls
1971-72	2						2	
1972-73	41	7	2		1		44	7
1973-74	26	5			1		27	5
1974-75	22/2	3	1		2		25/2	3
1975-76	14/1	1	0/1				14/2	1
	105/3	16	3/1		4		112/4	16

A talented if inconsistent winger, John Connolly twice fought his way back from the heartbreak of a broken leg. He cost Everton £75,000 when Harry Catterick raised himself from his sick-bed to complete a hastily-arranged deal with St Johnstone in March 1972. He was a direct sort of player, more than willing to take on a full-back. He never really hit it off with Catterick's successor, Billy Bingham, and was placed on the transfer list at his own request before the start of the 1976-7 season. He finally won his battle to leave Goodison in September 1976 when he joined up with former teammates Howard Kendall and Gary Jones at Birmingham City in a £90,000 deal. He did not last long at St Andrew's and was transferred to Newcastle United.

	LEAGUE		FA CUP		TOTAL	
	App	Gls	App	Gls	App	Gls
1932-33	20		6		26	
1933-34	35		1		36	
1934-35	29		5		34	
1935-36	25		1		26	
1936-37	41		4		45	
1937-38	35		2		37	
1938-39	40	5	5	1	45	6
	225	5	24	1	249	6

Billy Cook is one of the elite band of players to have won both a Scottish Cup winners' medal (with Celtic in 1931) and an FA Cup winners' medal (Everton 1933). An Irish international right-back, he joined Everton from Celtic for £3,000 in December 1932. In a Goodison career which spanned eight years he played nearly 250 senior games and was described at the time as a 'grand and wholehearted' player. He joined Wrexham in October 1945, and after inconclusive talks with Ellesmere Port moved to Rhyl as player-manager 12 months later. In February 1948 he was appointed Sunderland coach and four years later moved to, of all places, Peru after being appointed coach to the Peruvian FA in Lima. He spent a considerable amount of time coaching in Norway before being appointed Wigan Athletic manager in succession to Ron Suart in late 1966. By the turn of the decade he was at Norwich as player-coach.

BILLY COOK

	LEAGUE		FA CUP		TOTAL	
	App	Gls	App	Gls	App	Gls
1933-34	3				3	
1934-35	24	11	5	6	29	17
1936-37	21	5	3	2	24	7
1937-38	2				2	
	50	16	8	8	58	24

Jackie Coulter was a winger of undoubted craft and skill, a born footballer. He was completely unorthodox when in possession and used to enjoy toying with opposition full-backs before speeding past them on his way to the by-line. He was far more adventurous than the vast majority of wingers of the day and amassed a very respectable goal tally. He was born and raised in Belfast, learning his football with Clifton-ville before joining the highly-rated Belfast Celtic. It was from there he joined Everton in 1934 for £3,000. He became established immediately, along with players like Dixie Dean and Billy Cook, and proved a crowd-pleaser. He was a first-team regular until he broke a leg playing for Northern Ireland against Wales at Wrexham. He never fully recovered and was transferred to Grimsby Town late in 1937. He went on to play for Swansea and non-League Chelmsford before retiring. He died in Belfast in January 1981.

JACKIE COULTER

JACK CRELLEY

	LEAGUE		FA CUP		TOTAL	
	App	Gls	App	Gls	App	Gls
1899-1900	1				1	
1900-01	1				1	
1902-03	18		1		19	
1903-04	29		1		30	
1904-05	26		6		32	
1905-06	23		3		26	
1906-07	15				15	
1907-08	3				3	
	116		11		127	

Though a Liverpool man, John Crelley was signed from Millwall Athletic in 1899, one of many young North-West footballers recruited by Southern League clubs. Crelley was a sturdy defender and he formed a fine full-back partnership with Walter Balmer. He played left-back in the successful 1906 FA Cup Final team, but missed out a year later when Robert Balmer was selected to partner his elder brother in another Final. Even then, Crelley might have played because there were doubts about Walter Balmer until just before the game at the Crystal Palace. Crelley was a strong-tackling full-back who stood 5ft 9½ and weighed 12st. His stay at Millwall was a short one and he played his best football at Everton. He made 127 first-team appearances before moving to Exeter City in 1907.

WARNEY CRESSWELL

	LEAGUE		FA CUP		TOTAL	
	App	Gls	App	Gls	App	Gls
1926-27	15				15	
1927-28	36		2		38	
1928-29	32	1	1		33	1
1929-30	30				30	
1930-31	42		5		47	
1931-32	40				40	
1932-33	41		6		47	
1933-34	25		1		26	
1934-35	25		1		26	
1935-36	4				4	
	290	1	16		306	1

Warney Cresswell was one of the classiest defenders ever to pull on a pair of football boots. He was the forerunner of the modern style of full-back play with a superb sense of both position and timing. He was a fast mover and thinker who could quickly marshall the men in front of him. When he kicked the ball forward, it usually landed exactly where he wanted it. He had the gift of anticipation, constantly astounding forwards by turning up in crucial positions even before the ball had been delivered. Defensively he was not for the full-blooded tackle but preferred to jockey his opponents into impossible positions. His move from South Shields to Sunderland in 1922 for £5,500 was a British record. Strangely, he played for England only seven times in a career which spanned nine years and three clubs. He joined Everton in February 1927, staying with the club until 1936. In all, he made more than 500 appearances for South Shields, Sunderland and Everton. After his playing days were over, he moved into management with Port Vale and Northampton. He died in his native North-East in 1973.

	LEAGUE		FA CUP		TOTAL	
	App	Gls	App	Gls	App	Gls
1926-27	15				15	
1927-28	40	6	2		42	6
1928-29	25	1			25	1
1929-30	30	4	2	2	32	6
1930-31	37	13	4	2	41	15
1931-32	37	8	1		38	8
1932-33	17	2	2	1	19	3
1933-34	16	3	1		17	3
	217	37	12	5	229	42

Ted Critchley was the flamboyant outside-right who provided much of the ammunition for Dixie Dean. He was discovered playing in junior football in his native Stockport and transferred to Everton from Stockport County for a nominal fee in 1926. He succeeded Sam Chedgzoy wide on the right and proved to be an admirable replacement with his deft control and quick turn of speed. He was a key member of the 1927-8 Championship-winning side and was instrumental in helping Dean set his unsurpassable record of 60 League goals in one season. In an Everton career which spanned eight years, he had two quite remarkable FA Cup experiences. He was ruled out of the 1931 semi-final against West Brom through injury and, when the club reached the last four two years later, he had been dropped in favour of Albert Geldard. At the last minute Geldard was forced to drop out and in stepped Critchley. With just minutes remaining and the game deadlocked at 1-1, he forced West Ham defender Jim Barnett into conceding an own goal to set up a Wembley showdown with Manchester City. Geldard was fit for the Final, which Everton won 3-0, so Ted missed out. One year later he signed for Preston.

TED CRITCHLEY

CHARLIE CROSSLEY

	LEAGUE		FA CUP		TOTAL	
	App	Gls	App	Gls	App	Gls
1920-21	35	15	5	3	40	18
1921-22	15	3			15	3
	50	18	5	3	55	21

Signed from Sunderland in 1920, Charlie Crossley had only one full season in the Everton first-team, but he made his mark by being leading scorer with 15 League goals and forming, with George Harrison, a dynamic left-wing pairing. Crossley, who was born in Walsall, had an unusually 'top-heavy' build with broad shoulders but generally of small stature. A foraging inside-left, his star waned after that first season and in 1921-2 he was in and out of the team. In June 1922, Everton sold him to West Ham United and he played 14 times in their side which won promotion to Division One in 1922-3. But he could not find a place in the Hammers team which reached the first Wembley FA Cup Final that same season.

	LEAGUE		FA CUP		TOTAL	
	App	Gls	App	Gls	App	Gls
1932-33	2	1			2	1
1933-34	27	9	1		28	9
1934-35	39	15	5	2	44	17
1935-36	37	23	1		38	23
1936-37	28	9	4	1	32	10
1937-38	34	13	2		36	13
1938-39	7	3			7	3
	174	73	13	3	187	76

James 'Nat' Cunliffe will forever be remembered as the man who played alongside the legendary Dixie Dean. But for the great Dean and his all-encompassing brilliance, the youngster from Blackrod, Lancashire, would almost certainly have made an even bigger impact in the famous Everton side of the early '30s. He arrived at Goodison from Adlington FC in 1930 after quitting his job as an apprentice plater. After three years in the 'A' and Central League sides he finally got his big break in 1933 when he played two senior games, against Aston Villa (scoring on his debut) and Middlesbrough. His chance to stake a regular first-team spot came in his second season when he stood in at centre-forward for the injured Dean. When the fearsome striker returned to the side Cunliffe kept his place, being moved to inside-right. An exceptional ball-player with two good feet, he proved to be extremely versatile and filled every forward position except outside-right. He twice scored four goals in a game, against Stoke and West Brom. His most memorable contribution to the Everton cause was in 1935 when he snatched a dramatic equaliser in a Cup-tie at Roker Park. Everton went on to win the replay against Sunderland 6-4 with Cunliffe producing a virtuoso performance which went a long way to winning his solitary England cap against Belgium.

JIMMY CUNLIFFE

Spurs goalkeeper Hall smothers the ball as Dean waits for a slip during the 1937 FA Cup replay at White Hart Lane.

TERRY DARRACOTT

	LEAGUE		FA CUP		FL CUP		EUROPE		TOTAL	
	App	Gls	App	Gls	App	Gls	App	Gls	App	Gls
1967-68	1								1	
1968-69	1								1	
1970-71	2								2	
1971-72	16/1		2		1				19/1	
1972-73	11/5								11/5	
1973-74	36		3		2				41	
1974-75	5								5	
1975-76	20		1		1				22	
1976-77	20/3		4		5				29/3	
1977-78	19/1		1		2				22/1	
1978-79	7		1		1		4		13	
	138/10		12		12		4		166/10	

Terry Darracott is one of the most genuine and well-loved characters Merseyside football has ever produced. Although he never really hit the heights as a player, he was worth his presence for the sheer impact of his personality on the players around him. A local lad, he first experienced Division One life against Arsenal while still an apprentice. The date was 6 April 1968 and the youngster was drafted into the Everton defence at the last minute. After struggling to hold down a regular place, he was offered the post of youth team coach by Gordon Lee in 1979 but turned it down in preference to a move to NASL club Tulsa Roughnecks. From there he moved to Wrexham and on to Prescot as player-coach in February 1984. His overwhelming desire to return to the big time was rewarded when he was appointed reserve team coach at Everton three months later.

	LEAGUE		FA CUP		FL CUP		EUROPE		TOTAL	
	App	Gls	App	Gls	App	Gls	App	Gls	App	Gls
1970-71	2								2	
1974-75	35		4						39	
1975-76	19		1		2		1		23	
1976-77	26				4				30	
	82		5		6		1		94	

Dai Davies was a natural successor to Gordon West when he signed from Swansea City in a deal worth £20,000 in late December 1970. The only thing the genial six-footer valued more than his ability to thwart opposing forwards was his Welsh heritage. He had never played on the losing side as a professional before his move to Merseyside (he made nine appearances for Swansea) but, despite his near-perfect goal-keeping physique and his undoubted talent, he found the going tough. After spending four years in the shadow of West and his understudy David Lawson, during which time he made only two first-team appearances, Davies went back to Swansea on loan. The deal would almost certainly have been made permanent had the Welsh club been able to meet Everton's asking price. Davies eventually returned to Goodison and went on to make 94 first-team appearances before signing for Wrexham in September 1977 for £8,000. In his first season at the Racecourse, Wrexham suffered the lowest number of defeats in their history. In the 1978-9 Second Division campaign, Davies helped establish the club's best-ever League defensive record of only 42 goals conceded. He again returned to Swansea before joining Tranmere Rovers in June 1983. He played 52 times for Wales, breaking Jack Kelsey's long-standing record of 41 Welsh goalkeeping caps in May 1981 when he appeared in a British Championship match against Scotland.

DAI DAVIES

	LEAGUE		FA CUP		TOTAL	
	App	Gls	App	Gls	App	Gls
1924-25	7	2			7	2
1925-26	38	32	2	1	40	33
1926-27	27	21	4	3	31	24
1927-28	39	60	2	3	41	63
1928-29	29	26	1		30	26
1929-30	25	23	2	2	27	25
1930-31	37	39	5	9	42	48
1931-32	38	45	1	1	39	46
1932-33	39	24	6	5	45	29
1933-34	12	9			12	9
1934-35	38	26	5	1	43	27
1935-36	29	17			29	17
1936-37	36	24	4	3	40	27
1937-38	5	1			5	1
	399	349	32	28	431	377

Dixie Dean was arguably the greatest goalscoring machine that football has ever known. A larger than life, 'Roy of the Rovers' character, Dean carved for himself a very special niche in Merseyside sporting folklore. A positive giant of a man in both physique and application, Dean was years ahead of his time and, in many respects, the complete footballer. Typifying the robust, single-minded centre-forward of the day, he struck sheer terror into the hearts of defenders who were handed the unenviable task of stopping the man with the no-nonsense, never-say-die attitude. Arguably the most lethal header of a ball in the history of the game, Dean could achieve absolutely anything in the air when provided with the right service. After making his League debut for Tranmere Rovers in January 1924, he notched up 27 goals in 27 games for the Prenton Park club the following season before being lured across the River Mersey to Goodison Park. His scoring feats while wearing the royal blue of Everton are legendary. In his first full season he scored 32 goals in 38 appearances, but the pinnacle of his career was reached in 1927-8 when he logged the insurpassable total of 60 League goals in only 39 games. A measure of his indomitable spirit was his recovery from a bad road accident in 1926. In June that year he fractured his skull and jaw in a motor-cycle accident, yet on 23 October he returned to score at Leeds and help Everton to only their second win of the season. He severed his ties with Everton in 1938 when he moved to Notts County where he played only nine games, scoring three goals. He signed for Irish club Sligo in 1939 and, between January and May, played in 11 matches and scored 11 goals, thus maintaining the consistency he applied to goalscoring throughout his illustrious career in whatever standard of football he played. When he was demobbed after the war, Dean took over a pub in Chester called the Dublin Packet. Here he quite literally hung up his boots, together with his many trophies, and stayed for 15 years. Christened 'William Ralph', he disliked the nickname 'Dixie'. He was later a popular after-dinner speaker, filling halls and clubs wherever he appeared. Dean, who scored 349 goals for Everton and won 16 England caps, had his right leg amputated in 1976 after a long illness. It was somewhat fitting that he died at his beloved Goodison Park in March 1980, minutes after the final whistle of an Everton-Liverpool derby match.

DIXIE DEAN

MARTIN DOBSON

	LEAGUE		FA CUP		FL CUP		EUROPE		TOTAL	
	App	Gls	App	Gls	App	Gls	App	Gls	App	Gls
1974-75	30	5	3		2				35	5
1975-76	42	5	1		5	1	2		50	6
1976-77	40	8	6	1	8	2			54	11
1977-78	38	7	2		4	1			44	8
1978-79	40	4	1	1	3	4	3	1	47	10
	190	29	13	2	22	8	5	1	230	40

When he moved to Goodison Park in August 1974 for £300,000, Martin Dobson set a new British transfer record. After making 200 appearances for Burnley and picking up three England caps, he opted for a move into the big time, choosing Everton from a whole pack of would-be buyers. It took him a considerable length of time to settle into his new role — one of the major reasons being the enormous price tag which weighed heavily around his shoulders. He started his career as a centre-forward and went to Bolton as a professional but was eventually handed a free transfer. He considered giving up the game but was persuaded to continue by his father. He joined Burnley as a front runner but eventually switched to midfield where he won massive acclaim and continued international recognition. Hugely skilful and with the ability to drift forward to create openings and goals out of next to nothing, he was an integral part of the Everton set-up between 1974 and 1979. He stunned the football world after five years at Goodison by returning to Burnley for £100,000. Tired of the pressures which inevitably envelope every top-flight club, he yearned for the more tranquil surroundings of Turf Moor. After failing to halt the club's slide towards lower division obscurity, Dobson took over as Bury's player-manager in 1984.

	LEAGUE		FA CUP		TOTAL	
	App	Gls	App	Gls	App	Gls
1946-47	21	17	2		23	17
1947-48	27	13	1	1	28	14
1948-49	7	6			7	6
	55	36	3	1	58	37

EPHRAIM DODDS

Ephraim Dodds, known to everyone as simply 'Jock', was an enormous, no-nonsense centre-forward who led the line with his own distinctive brand of robust football. He was so good in the air that centre-halves used to dread being handed the task of marking him. His career covered the pre-World War Two and post-war periods and although he was never to win a full Scottish cap he did play eight times for his country in wartime internationals. He was born at Grangemouth in 1915 and played junior football in Lanarkshire and Durham before joining the staff at Huddersfield Town at the age of 15. He joined Sheffield United on a free transfer two years later and topped the scoring list in four seasons with the Blades. He played in the 1936 FA Cup Final against Arsenal and was transferred to Blackpool for £10,000 in March 1939. Everton, with no Dean or Lawton, nor 'Bunny' Bell, struggled to find a centre-forward immediately after the war and they signed Dodds in November 1946. He served them with 36 goals in 55 League games before moving to Lincoln City in October 1948. By the time he retired he had scored well over 200 League goals.

	LEAGUE		FA CUP		TOTAL	
	App	Gls	App	Gls	App	Gls
1905-06	8				8	
1906-07	13		2		15	
1907-08	16				16	
1908-09	3				3	
1919-20	16				16	
	56		2		58	

JOE DONNACHIE

One of an elite band of players who enjoyed two spells at Goodison Park. A tricky winger with a deceptive turn of speed, Joe Donnachie was widely acknowledged in his heyday as the finest far-post crosser of the ball in the English game. Quick into the tackle and difficult to dispossess, he was famous for his jinking runs down the flanks. A versatile player with a flair for the unusual, he played at both outside-left and outside-right for Scotland in three internationals between 1913 and 1915. Before World War One he played with Newcastle United, Everton and Oldham, but returned to Glasgow Rangers after the hostilities. He rejoined Everton and moved on to Blackpool before ending his playing days with Chester. He became a publican after retirement from football, running the Mariners' Arms Inn near Sealand Road. His son, Joe, was on Liverpool's books before he was killed in a World War Two flying accident.

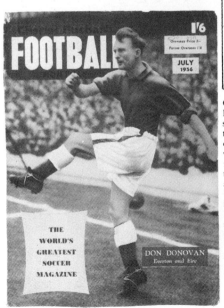

DON DONOVAN

	LEAGUE		FA CUP		TOTAL	
	App	Gls	App	Gls	App	Gls
1951-52	22		2		24	
1952-53	7				7	
1953-54	42		2		44	
1954-55	35				35	
1955-56	8	1			8	1
1956-57	36	1	3		39	1
1957-58	29		1		30	
	179	2	8		187	2

One of Everton's famous Irish 'colony' during the early '50s, Don Donovan was discovered purely by chance during the summer of 1949 when the club were enjoying a close-season tour of Eire. Manager Cliff Britton and a small band of directors took an evening stroll in Cork and ended up watching a local amateur cup-tie. Donovan, whose first name, Donal, was shortened to Don by his Goodison Park teammates, was playing at inside-right for Maymount Rovers and did enough to impress the watching English contingent. Britton immediately contacted the youngster's family and invited their talented son to join Everton's junior school. He began as an inside-forward with the 'B' team but developed at such pace that he soon graduated to the senior side. He was tried at wing-half and took to the new position like a natural. Exceptionally good in the air and commanding on the ground, he helped Everton gain promotion in 1953-4. He scored a quite spectacular goal from 35 yards when Everton, fighting against relegation in 1956, defeated Manchester United 5-2 at Old Trafford and so halted United's astonishing run of 26 League games without defeat. He was a full Republic of Ireland international and succeeded fellow countryman Peter Farrell as captain of Everton.

DICKY DOWNS

	LEAGUE		FA CUP		TOTAL	
	App	Gls	App	Gls	App	Gls
1919-20	12				12	
1920-21	40		5		45	
1921-22	28				28	
1922-23	9				9	
1923-24	3				3	
	92		5		97	

Because of his ability at overhead kicks and other acrobatic feats, Dicky Downs was known as the 'India Rubber Man' during his three years with Everton. A very small man, he developed into one of the most influential full-backs of his day. He joined the club from Barnsley with whom he played in the 1910 and 1912 FA Cup Finals. In 1912, West Brom were firm favourites but the first game, at the Crystal Palace, ended in a goalless draw. Against all the odds, the Second Division side from South Yorkshire won the replay 1-0 after extra-time. Downs was one of the Barnsley stars but it was not until March 1920 that Everton secured his signature, for £3,000. He made the transition into a big-time player look remarkably easy, holding down a first-team spot until his departure for Brighton in 1923. He made one international appearance for England, against Northern Ireland in 1920. Some claim that he was the inventor of the sliding tackle.

	LEAGUE		FA CUP		TOTAL	
	App	Gls	App	Gls	App	Gls
1947-48	19		4		23	
1948-49	19		1		20	
1949-50	20				20	
	58		5		63	

One of the unluckiest men ever to play professional football at the highest level, Gordon Dugdale was a brilliant left-back who seemingly had the world at his feet as his career reached its climax in the late '40s. A superb ball-winner and distributor, he looked a certainty for England's 1950 World Cup team when he was compelled to give up the game he loved. A heart complaint, which had developed during his service in the Far East as a pilot in the Fleet Air Arm, suddenly recurred. Dugdale was deceptively fast and, at a time when full-backs were supposed to stay back, he constantly defied tradition by making sudden forays into attack. He joined Everton in 1947 on his demob from the Royal Navy. He was described at the time as looking 'more like a solicitor's clerk than a sportsman' because of his light build. He had played with Linacre School, Bootle Schoolboys and Lancashire Schoolboys. He once incurred the wrath of the legendary Ted Sagar when, in a game against Middlesbrough, he tried to chip the ball back but only succeeded in scoring an own-goal. In three seasons he managed only 58 League games. In 1952 he became a director of South Liverpool FC and 18 months later he stood as the Conservative candidate for the Low Hill ward but failed to unseat the Labour member.

GORDON DUGDALE

	LEAGUE		FA CUP		FL CUP		TOTAL	
	App	Gls	App	Gls	App	Gls	App	Gls
1956-57	29		3				32	
1957-58	36		3				39	
1958-59	33		4				37	
1959-60	37		1				38	
1960-61	42		1		5		48	
1961-62	30		3				33	
1962-63	4						4	
	211		15		5		231	

ALBERT DUNLOP

A dependable and reliable goalkeeper who never really managed to fulfil his rich potential, Dunlop joined Everton in 1949 at the age of 17 but had to wait seven years for his League debut. Then he endured a baptism of fire when he was thrust into the club's desperate fight to avoid relegation. He made his debut in front of more than 50,000 people at Old Trafford when Everton claimed the shock result of the season by ending Manchester United's unbeaten run of 26 League games with a conclusive 5-2 victory. His main attributes were a safe pair of hands and good vision. He managed to instil confidence into his defenders in much the same way Neville Southall does. While prone to the occasional error as a direct result of lack of concentration, he was an effective last line of defence and a larger-than-life character off the pitch. His personal life became something of a disaster after he quit the game in the late '60s. In 1979 he was put on probation for two years after being found guilty of three charges of deception.

JIMMY DUNN

	LEAGUE		FA CUP		TOTAL	
	App	Gls	App	Gls	App	Gls
1928-29	24	4	1		25	4
1929-30	12		1		13	
1930-31	28	14	5	3	33	17
1931-32	22	10			22	10
1932-33	25	10	6	4	31	14
1933-34	23	4	1		24	4
1934-35	6				6	
	140	42	14	7	154	49

Watching Jimmy Dunn play football was said to be an emotional experience. He was a hugely gifted inside-forward with the passion and pace to leave experienced defenders rooted to the spot. He joined Everton from Hibernian in 1928, along with his right-wing partner Harry Ritchie, both players making their debut at Bolton in the opening game of the 1928-9 season. He won a Second Division Championship medal, League Championship medal and FA Cup winners' medal in successive seasons. He scored the third goal in the 1933 FA Cup Final triumph over fancied Manchester City. Dunn remained at Goodison Park until 1935 when he was transferred to Exeter City. He later joined Cheshire County League side, Runcorn. He had three footballing sons, the most famous of which was Jimmy Dunn junior, who was an England and Liverpool schoolboy player and who also won an FA Cup winners' medal with Wolves against Leicester in 1949. Dunn senior made six appearances for Scotland and played in the famous 'Wembley Wizards' team of 1928 when Scotland trounced England 5-1.

PETER EASTOE

	LEAGUE		FA CUP		FL CUP		EUROPE		TOTAL	
	App	Gls	App	Gls	App	Gls	App	Gls	App	Gls
1978-79	7/1								7/1	
1979-80	23/3	6	5	2	3		2		33/3	8
1980-81	41/1	15	6	3	3	1			50/1	19
1981-82	17/2	5	1		1				18/2	6
	88/7	26	12	6	6	1	2		108/7	33

As a youngster Peter Eastoe looked set for great things. Born in Tamworth, he was given an apprenticeship by Wolverhampton Wanderers and did so well that he won a string of England youth caps. But Wolves were well off for strikers with Derek Dougan, John Richards and Alan Sunderland all in the squad. That left little room for Eastoe and after only four League games he was allowed to join Swindon Town for £80,000. He realised his rich potential there, scoring an impressive 43 goals in 91 matches, before he was transferred to Queen's Park Rangers for £100,000 in March 1976. He was a member of the QPR side which went agonisingly close to taking the League Championship, but frequently found himself to be the odd man out. When he moved to Everton in an exchange deal involving Mick Walsh in 1979, he had managed only 56 League appearances in three years at Loftus Road. He was Everton's leading scorer in 1980-81 but moved to West Bromwich in a straight swop for Andy King in August 1982.

	LEAGUE		FA CUP		TOTAL	
	App	Gls	App	Gls	App	Gls
1946-47	34	5	2		36	5
1947-48	29	3	5	1	34	4
1948-49	34	7	2		36	7
1949-50	34	1	5		39	1
1950-51	39	8	1		40	8
1951-52	38	8	2		40	8
1952-53	39	14	5	2	44	16
1953-54	41	11	3	1	44	12
1954-55	41	9	2		43	9
1955-56	38	8	4	2	42	10
1956-57	27	2	3		30	2
	394	76	34	6	428	82

Tommy Eglington was one of Everton's greatest-ever servants, making more than 400 appearances in a Goodison career which spanned 11 years. He signed along with Peter Farrell from Shamrock Rovers in 1946 for a joint fee of £10,000, the deal proving to be one of the finest strokes of business Everton ever pulled off. He was widely recognised as the greatest match-winning left-winger in the British game and was seen by many as the natural successor to Billy Liddell in terms of poise and grace. The very mention of his name sent shivers of apprehension down the spines of right-backs the country over and he repaid the Everton board for putting their faith in him with an illustrious and golden career. He guaranteed himself a place in the pages of Everton history when, on 27 September 1952, he single-handedly demolished Doncaster Rovers at Goodison Park with five goals in a 7-1 win. He offset his devastating speed with intricate close control and stunning shooting power. He appeared alongside Farrell in the historic game at Goodison Park in 1949 when Eire defeated mighty England 2-0 to become the first 'overseas' nation to win on English soil. He gained his first international recognition the year he joined Everton and went on to win 24 Eire caps and make six appearances for Northern Ireland when that country could select Eire-born players for the Home International Championship. He was transferred to Tranmere Rovers in 1957 and now runs a butcher's shop in his native Dublin.

TOMMY EGLINGTON

	LEAGUE		FA CUP		TOTAL	
	App	Gls	App	Gls	App	Gls
1946-47	27		2		29	
1947-48	38	2	3	1	41	3
1948-49	38		2		40	
1949-50	41	2	5		46	2
1950-51	42	3	1		43	3
1951-52	40		2		42	
1952-53	38	1	5	1	43	2
1953-54	39	1	3		42	1
1954-55	41		2		43	
1955-56	42	1	4	1	46	2
1956-57	36	3	2	1	38	4
	422	13	31	4	453	17

Peter Farrell helped to make history when he scored one of the goals for Eire that defeated the star-studded and seemingly invincible England side in 1949. Fittingly, the venue for an Irish triumph which sent shock waves spinning around the football world was Goodison Park, a ground which Farrell graced for more than a decade. Strangely, the man who built an enviable reputation as a sturdy wing-half was forced to play out of position that day, figuring at inside-right. He joined Everton from Shamrock Rovers in 1946 along with his long-time friend Tommy Eglington. The package deal cost the Goodison board just £10,000, making it arguably the best double signing the club ever made. A resilient player who never shirked a tackle, Farrell was popular on the field and something of a hero off it, mixing freely with supporters in his down-to-earth manner. He captained the side for many years before, in October 1957 at the age of 33, he agreed to join Tranmere Rovers as player-manager for a fee of £2,500. He was later to become manager until leaving in December 1960. The following season he took over as player-boss of Welsh League club Holyhead Town but eventually returned to Ireland to continue in management. He played 28 times for Eire and represented Northern Ireland seven times when they could select players born in the Republic for the Home International Championship.

PETER FARRELL

	LEAGUE		FA CUP		TOTAL	
	App	Gls	App	Gls	App	Gls
1913-14	21		1		22	
1914-15	36		4		40	
1919-20	34		1		35	
1920-21	40		5		45	
1921-22	38		1		39	
1922-23	25				25	
1923-24	25				25	
	219		12		231	

Measham-born Tom Fern was the man who succeeded where others had failed, filling the gap left by the departure of goalkeeper Billy Scott. Fern was signed from Lincoln City in 1913 and his goalkeeping was a vital ingredient of revitalised Everton's 1914-15 League Championship success. That same season Everton reached the FA Cup semi-final but Fern missed the game against Chelsea at Villa Park because of injury. Indeed, injury was never far away — not suprising for a goalkeeper who was always in the thick of the action — and in the infamous 6-0 thrashing by Crystal Palace in the 1921-2 FA Cup, Fern kept goal with a damaged hand while his opposite number, Palace goalkeeper Jack Alderson, was eating oranges at the other end. Fern's career spanned World War One, but for which he would have added to his 219 League appearances for Everton. Fern, who stood 5ft 11in, moved to Port Vale in June 1924.

TOM FERN

	LEAGUE		FA CUP		TOTAL	
	App	Gls	App	Gls	App	Gls
1945-46			2		2	
1946-47	31	4	2	1	33	5
1947-48	33	8	5	2	38	10
1948-49	36	1	2		38	1
1949-50	14		3		17	
1950-51	34	3	1		35	3
1951-52	37	4	2		39	4
1952-53	26	5	1	1	27	6
1953-54	39	5	3		42	5
1954-55	33	4	2	1	35	5
1955-56	29	3	4		33	3
1956-57	34	6	3		37	6
1957-58	24	4			24	4
1958-59	10	2			10	2
	380	49	30	5	410	54

Alfred Walter Fielding was the little Londoner who travelled north to find sporting fame with Everton. He was at the centre of a row when he signed professional forms at Goodison in 1945. Before joining the army he was on Charlton's books as an amateur. He went to the Middle East where his form as an inside-forward was good enough to get him into army representative sides. When Fielding returned to England he was immediately offered terms by Charlton who naturally assumed they had first refusal. But despite the attentions of numerous other leading clubs of the day, he opted for Everton and started a furious debate which lasted many months. He was a brilliant ball player and strategist who ran the Everton engine-room with cool authority. Although he proved to be lethal when within striking distance of goal, he was regarded as a supplier rather than a striker. Despite his all-round ability he made only one appearance in the white shirt of England, the Bolton Disaster Fund match against Scotland at Manchester in 1946, a game that did not count as an official full cap.

WALLY FIELDING

	LEAGUE		FA CUP		TOTAL	
	App	Gls	App	Gls	App	Gls
1910-11	8	1			8	1
1911-12	34	1	5		39	1
1912-13	28	1	2	1	30	2
1913-14	27	1	1		28	1
1914-15	35	2	5		40	2
1919-20	37	1	1		38	1
1920-21	39	1	4		43	1
1921-22	33	1	1		34	1
1922-23	23		2		25	
	264	9	21	1	285	10

Tom Fleetwood had a disappointing finale to an Everton career that eventually realised well over 200 senior appearances in a 12-year span interrupted by World War One. When he was awarded a benefit match, against Sheffield United in 1921-2, Everton were playing badly. They narrowly missed relegation and were humiliated 6-0 in the Cup by Second Division Crystal Palace. The result for Fleetwood was that the attendance was far less than might have been hoped for by a player who had given the club such splendid service as a versatile half-back. He could perform equally well at left-half, or in the centre, and he had even tried his luck at centre-forward when emergency measures were needed. Indeed, he had joined Everton as a forward from Rochdale. Some of his best football was played in the Lancashire Section which prevailed between 1915 and 1919 and he was rewarded with two appearances for England in Victory internationals. Both games were against Scotland, one draw and a 4-3 victory when he did the bulk of the defensive work while his right-half colleague Arthur Grimsdell of Spurs found time to go forward and score twice. Fleetwood, who was born in Liverpool but joined Everton from Rochdale, signed for Oldham Athletic in August 1923.

TOM FLEETWOOD

	LEAGUE		FA CUP		TOTAL	
	App	Gls	App	Gls	App	Gls
1907-08	4	1			4	1
1908-09	37	36	1		38	36
1909-10	34	22	7	4	41	26
1910-11	11	2			11	2
	86	61	8	4	94	65

Bertie Freeman was a man who always scored goals regardless of what level of football he was involved in. After playing with Aston Villa and Arsenal he came to Everton and replaced Sandy Young — a feat in itself. A tenacious front-runner with good aerial ability and a lethal shot, he created a First Division record in 1908-09 when he scored 36 goals. After three impressive seasons with the club, he was transferred to Burnley and played at centre-forward against Liverpool in the 1914 FA Cup Final, scoring the winning goal. He played in the North v South England trial at Fulham in 1909, with Jack Sharp, and scored four goals for the Football League against the Irish League in the same year.

BERTIE FREEMAN

	LEAGUE		FA CUP		FL CUP		EUROPE		TOTAL	
	App	Gls	App	Gls	App	Gls	App	Gls	App	Gls
1959-60	8								8	
1960-61	40	1	1		5				46	1
1961-62	42	6	3						45	6
1962-63	40	5	3	1			2		45	6
1963-64	33	5	5	1			1		39	6
1964-65	37	4	4				5		46	4
1965-66	24	6	6				3	1	33	7
1966-67	31/1	6	3				4		38/1	6
	255/1	33	25	2	5		15	1	300/1	36

A powerhouse of a right-half, Jimmy Gabriel became one of the most expensive teenagers in British football when he arrived from Dundee for £30,000 in March 1960. He made his Everton debut against West Ham United only 72 hours after putting pen to paper and went on to make eight senior appearances in his first full season at Goodison. He was capped by Scotland at Youth, Under-23 and full international levels, making his first senior appearance against Wales in October 1960. In his youth days he played alongside Denis Law. While Gabriel was struggling to find his feet in English football, in only his third game for Everton he came up against big Derek Kevan, the West Brom 'bomber', on an afternoon he will never forget. Kevan hammered five goals, but Gabriel shrugged off the experience and went on to build a fine career. His strong, forceful style, particularly effective in defence, made him the near-perfect foil for the more adventurous wanderings of Brian Harris on the opposite flank. He played a major part in the title success of 1962-3 and was a member of the 1966 FA Cup-winning side. The date 18 March 1967 marked the beginning of the end of his Everton career. On that day he was sent to Blackpool with the reserves while a newcomer, Howard Kendall, was making his League debut against Southampton. After more than 300 senior appearances Gabriel moved to The Dell and after a spell with another south coast club, Bournemouth, he moved to North America where he played for Seattle Sounders.

JIMMY GABRIEL

	LEAGUE		FA CUP		TOTAL	
	App	Gls	App	Gls	App	Gls
1914-15	32	2	4	2	36	4
	32	2	4	2	36	4

Jimmy Galt, who captained Everton when they won the League Championship and reached the FA Cup semi-finals in 1914-15, was a classic example of a footballer whose career was ruined by war. After only one season with Everton he found that the road to more triumphs had been barred by events in Europe. It was the end of his Everton days, before they had barely started. Born in Ayrshire in 1885, Galt started as a left-half but moved into the centre of the half-back line with equal success. He signed for Rangers in January 1906 and won Scottish League Championship medals at Ibrox (1911-13 inclusive) and a Scottish Cup runners-up medal (1909). He won two Scottish caps in 1908 and played four times in the prestigious Glasgow versus Sheffield fixture. He joined Everton in the 1914 close season and looked set to lead the club to great heights when war was declared. He was officially transferred to Third Lanark in October 1920, though he rarely played for Everton after 1915. After retirement from football he became a motor engineer. He died in November 1935.

JIMMY GALT

	LEAGUE		FA CUP		TOTAL	
	App	Gls	App	Gls	App	Gls
1889-90	18	21	2	4	20	25
1890-91	22	20	1		23	20
1891-92	10	6			10	6
1892-93	24	19	3	4	27	23
1893-94	9	8			9	8
1894-95	8	4	1		9	4
	91	78	7	8	98	86

It would be fair to say that Fred Geary was the Dixie Dean of his day, leading the Everton forward line with his own particular and distinctive brand of robust front-running. Born in Nottingham, and once with Notts County, he was brought to Everton's attention while playing for Notts Rangers. He went to Grimsby and was eventually signed by Everton in 1889, quickly establishing himself as an indispensable member of a side which firmly believed attack was the best form of defence. He scored twice on his League debut for the club. He was capped for England against Ireland in 1890 (scoring a hat-trick in Belfast) and against Scotland the following year. He picked up one of the first gold medals struck in recognition of international service when he played in the inter-League fixture against Scotland three years later. At that time the payment to professionals in such representative games was two guineas and the side expressed a desire to have a more tangible souvenir to commemorate the occasion. Famed for his penetrating runs, he once said that he was lucky to have played alongside Chadwick and Milward in the Everton team. He signed for Liverpool in 1894 and ended his playing days at Anfield. His last six seasons of League soccer saw him make only 56 appearances due to injury and loss of form.

FRED GEARY

	LEAGUE		FA CUP		TOTAL	
	App	Gls	App	Gls	App	Gls
1930-31	20	2	5		25	2
1931-32	38		1		39	
1932-33	7				7	
1933-34	29				29	
1934-35	37		5		42	
1935-36	9				9	
1936-37	40		4		44	
1937-38	14				14	
1938-39	2				2	
	196	2	15		211	2

CHARLIE GEE

When Charlie Gee was called up to play for England against Wales at Anfield on 18 November 1931, he completed an astonishing rise to international stardom. Less than 12 months previously he had still been waiting to make his First Division debut for Everton. Born in Stockport, he began with Reddish Gren Wesleyans and signed for Stockport County in 1928. Everton bought him in July 1930 and he began his big-time apprenticeship in the reserve team. When Tommy Griffiths was injured, Gee stepped in for his League debut on New Year's Day 1931 and never looked back, helping Everton to promotion that year as well as the FA Cup semi-final. Then came his England call-up when, ironically, he found that his opposite number on the Welsh side was Griffiths, the man he had displaced from the Everton side. Gee was an uncomplicated centre-half who was always striving for something better than his best. A deep thinker with an ambitious vein, he gave his all and was consequently loved by the Goodison crowd. His progress was halted by a cartilage operation in 1932, and although he reclaimed his place, he was never quite the same player. His last appearance for Everton was at Fulham in May 1940, in the fourth round of the War League Cup, after which he retired.

ALBERT GELDARD

	LEAGUE		FA CUP		TOTAL	
	App	Gls	App	Gls	App	Gls
1932-33	26	5	4		30	5
1933-34	24	5			24	5
1934-35	31	5	5	5	36	10
1935-36	39	7	1	1	40	8
1936-37	13	3	1		14	3
1937-38	34	6	1		35	6
	167	31	12	6	179	37

Albert Geldard was the youngest footballer ever to play in a peacetime League match. At the tender age of 15 years 156 days he turned out for Bradford at Millwall in September 1929. Regarded as a schoolboy prodigy — he once scored 22 goals in a match — Geldard signed for Everton as an 18-year-old in November 1932. He made his debut against Middlesbrough the same month, scoring once in a 2-0 win. He was discovered by another famous outside-right, Jack Sharp, who was correct when he forecast an international future for the youngster labelled by Tommy Lawton as 'the fastest thing on two legs over ten yards'. Geldard won four England caps while at Goodison and he laid on the pass which enabled Jimmy Dunn to score the third goal in the 1933 FA Cup Final win over Manchester City. He was exceptionally fast, controlled the ball well and was not slow to cut inside and deliver a telling shot. His chief hobby outside football was conjuring and he was a member of the Magic Circle. In 1938 he joined Bolton for £4,500 and ended his career with them in 1946-7.

	LEAGUE		FA CUP		FL CUP		TOTAL	
	App	Gls	App	Gls	App	Gls	App	Gls
1979-80	29	1	6				35	1
1980-81	35	1	5		3	1	43	2
	64	2	11		3	1	78	3

An attacking full-back famous for his fearsome tackles, John Gidman has sustained and overcome a series of injuries which would have forced lesser men into premature retirement. A Garston lad, he was with Liverpool as an apprentice but joined Aston Villa after the Anfield club discarded him. He enjoyed ten years in the Midlands before being brought back to Merseyside when Everton paid a then club record fee of £650,000 in October 1979. He spent less than two years at the club. In July 1981, while lying on a Spanish beach, he discovered that Manchester United had made a substantial bid for him. He became Ron Atkinson's first signing in a deal which brought Welsh winger Mickey Thomas to Goodison. After four injury-plagued years at Old Trafford, he has now established himself as a first-team regular and was in the side which denied Everton their glorious treble by winning the 1985 FA Cup Final. During a Milk Cup-tie at Old Trafford in October 1984, he scored a sensational own-goal two minutes from time to send his old club Everton through to the fourth round.

JOHN GIDMAN

TORRY GILLICK

	LEAGUE		FA CUP		TOTAL	
	App	Gls	App	Gls	App	Gls
1935-36	23	9	1		24	9
1936-37	42	14	4	2	46	16
1937-38	16	3	2		18	3
1938-39	40	14	5	2	45	16
	121	40	12	4	133	44

Torrance Gillick was a man who helped to maintain the tradition of top-class Scottish players at Everton. A stockily-built winger and natural entertainer, he was an exhilarating sight when in full flight down the flanks. His major problem was his attitude to the game. Far too often he played it strictly for laughs, so annoying the more studious members of the side. Sometimes he was brilliant, sometimes woefully ineffective, but no matter what the circumstances, he was always entertaining. Sadly the Merseyside public never really saw the best of him for, like so many others, his peak years came and went during the course of World War Two. He joined Everton from Rangers in December 1935 in an £8,000 deal. He played on either wing, and very occasionally at inside-right, and won five Scotland caps. He rejoined Rangers in November 1945. He died in 1971.

RONNIE GOODLASS

	LEAGUE		FA CUP		FL CUP		TOTAL	
	App	Gls	App	Gls	App	Gls	App	Gls
1975-76	2/1						2/1	
1976-77	29/2	2	7		9		45/2	2
1977-78	0/1						0/1	
	31/4	2	7		9		47/4	2

Ronnie Goodlass achieved a life's ambition when he joined the club in 1968. He was born just down the road from Goodison Park and despite attracting the attentions of several leading sides after his impressive displays for England Schoolboys, he was always determined to play for Everton. He was a winger in the old-fashioned sense, always willing to take on defenders and wend his way to the by-line. His craft and skill made him a firm favourite with the Gwladys Street fans but his tendency to drift in and out of the game led to him being dropped on several occasions. He was a key man in the 1976-7 side which reached the League Cup Final and the FA Cup semi-finals. His chances were strictly limited after the arrival of Dave Thomas from Queen's Park Rangers and he was transferred to leading Dutch club, Breda, for £75,000 in October 1977. Two years later he moved to Den Haag for £80,000 but became homesick and signed for Fulham. From there he drifted to Scunthorpe, Hong Kong, and came back to Merseyside to join Tranmere Rovers in 1983.

JACKIE GRANT

	LEAGUE		FA CUP		TOTAL	
	App	Gls	App	Gls	App	Gls
1946-47	5	1			5	1
1947-48	18	4	5	1	23	5
1948-49	7		1		8	
1949-50	23	3	5		28	3
1950-51	42	2	1		43	2
1951-52	5				5	
1952-53	17				17	
1953-54	3				3	
1954-55	1				1	
	121	10	12	1	133	11

Jackie Grant was signed in December 1942 and although he was a first-team regular for just one season, in 1950-51 when he played in all 42 League games, he was a popular player who possessed great flair. Small, yet highly competitive, he played in no fewer than seven different positions in his Everton career. When Joe Mercer left for the army, Grant took his place in wartime soccer. He was the star man in the club's 3-2 FA Cup fourth round replay win over Wolves at Goodison in 1947-8. After failing to hold down a regular place he became an integral part of Everton's Central League side, captaining them to numerous successes. He severed his ties with Everton, after 133 senior appearances, in June 1956 when he was signed by the then Rochdale manager Harry Catterick. He made over 100 appearances for Rochdale before ending his League career with Southport.

ANDY GRAY

	LEAGUE		FA CUP		FL CUP		EUROPE		TOTAL	
	App	Gls	App	Gls	App	Gls	App	Gls	App	Gls
1983-84	23	5	7/1	3					30/1	8
1984-85	21/5	9	7		0/1		3	5	31/6	14
	44/5	14	14/1	3	0/1		3	5	61/7	22

Andy Gray is the first to admit that he can be his own worst enemy at times, going in where it hurts, pushing himself through the pain barrier, and then suffering the consequences. Arguably the bravest striker of his generation, his determination to win the ball at all costs is near-legendary. For a man who is not particularly tall, his heading ability is quite outstanding. Allied to his brilliant aerial skills are deft and incisive flicks on the ground which so often transform half-chances into goals, if not for Gray himself, then for one of his colleagues. A total professional both on and off the field, he breathed new life into a club which appeared to be going nowhere when he completed a hurriedly arranged £250,000 transfer from ailing Wolves in November 1983. Using his vast experience in the dressing room and on the pitch he lifted the youngsters around him and was largely instrumental in steering Everton back on to the trophy trail. He joined Aston Villa from Dundee United for £100,000 in 1975 and four years later moved to Wolves for a British record fee of £1.5 million. He scored the second goal in the 1984 FA Cup Final win over Watford, and the first in the 3-1 European Cup-winners' Cup triumph over Rapid Vienna in May 1985. His remarkable resurrection as a quality striker was capped when he was dramatically recalled into the Scotland side at the end of 1984-5, at the age of 29. In July 1985 he rejoined Aston Villa for £150,000.

	LEAGUE		FA CUP		TOTAL	
	App	Gls	App	Gls	App	Gls
1937-38	12				12	
1938-39	42	1	5		47	1
1945-46			2		2	
1946-47	38		2		40	
1947-48	12				12	
1948-49	2				2	
	106	1	9		115	1

Like so many others, Norman Greenhalgh had to move away from his home town to find fame. A Bolton lad he graduated in the hard school of Division Three North where, apart from knocking football sense into the minds of young hopefuls, they also instilled a measure of toughness into the physical frame. In 1935 New Brighton, desperate to secure a rugged half-back, persuaded Bolton Wanderers to let them have him. After a while he dropped to full-back before appendix trouble ruled him out for several months. After his return he had a spell up front before reverting to his more familiar duties and began to interest several leading clubs. He chose Everton and made his League debut for them in 1937-8, forming a formidable partnership with the equally ferocious Willie Cook. Stanley Matthews once said that Greenhalgh was the opponent he least enjoyed playing against. He made over 100 senior appearances and was an ever-present when Everton won the League Championship in 1938-9. He also represented the Football League. Greenhalgh had a good season in the first post-war campaign but then quickly lost his place. His last appearance for Everton was in the 6-0 hammering at Stamford Bridge in September 1948. He was given a free transfer and moved to Bangor City. After retiring he became a licensee.

NORMAN GREENHALGH

	LEAGUE		FA CUP		TOTAL	
	App	Gls	App	Gls	App	Gls
1910-11	1				1	
1911-12	3				3	
1912-13	26		4		30	
1913-14	22				22	
1914-15	14	1			14	1
1919-20	33	5	1		34	5
1920-21	23	1	1		24	1
1921-22	13	1			13	1
1922-23	7	1			7	1
	142	9	6		148	9

ALAN GRENYER

Alan Grenyer had to wait for two seasons after joining Everton before he could stake a first-team place. Everton bought him from his home town club, South Shields, in 1910, but in his first two years at Goodison Park he managed only four appearances because Harry Makepeace had made the left-half position his own. Slowly he began to establish a place on the fringes of selection, and in the Championship-winning season of 1914-15, he managed 14 games and one goal. It was an important goal too, helping Everton to a 2-1 win at Bradford's Park Avenue ground. There were only two League games to play after that and the success helped Everton to the top of the table for the first time that season. Like so many players, Grenyer played his best football in wartime soccer. It earned him a place in the England side for a Victory international against Wales but that was an unhappy experience. It was December 1919 and Grenyer allowed the great Billy Meredith to escape him. Meredith's shot-cum-centre slid through the hands of England goalkeeper Williamson and Wales were home 2-1. In January 1922 Grenyer selected the Aston Villa game for his benefit match which Everton won 3-2 with a hat-trick from Irvine. In November 1924 he returned home and signed for North Shields.

TOM GRIFFITHS

	LEAGUE		FA CUP		TOTAL	
	App	Gls	App	Gls	App	Gls
1926-27	1				1	
1928-29	26	2	1		27	2
1929-30	26	4	1		27	4
1930-31	23	3			23	3
	76	9	2		78	9

Tom Griffiths' footballing philosophy was basic. A tall, rangy centre-half, he was of the opinion that all defenders should relieve themselves of the ball as quickly as possible. He based his strategy on the simplistic premise that if you do not have the ball at your feet, then you cannot be dispossessed — and against all odds it proved remarkably successful. He began his career with Wrexham and succeeded the immortal Fred Keenor as the regular Welsh centre-half until he in turn was succeeded by another Everton star, T.G. Jones. In 1929-30 he was a regular member of the side that suffered the indignity of being relegated for the first time in the club's history. He played for the first half of the following season before losing his place, through injury, to Charlie Gee. He was transferred to Bolton Wanderers, moving to Middlesbrough shortly afterwards. In 1935 he joined Aston Villa for £5,000 but despite his heroic efforts, the Midlands club were still relegated. He became a publican in Wrexham and died on Christmas Day 1981.

	LEAGUE		FA CUP		FL CUP		TOTAL	
	App	Gls	App	Gls	App	Gls	App	Gls
1975-76	22/1	5	1				23/1	5
1976-77	16/2		1/2		7/2		24/6	
	38/3	5	2/2		7/2		47/7	5

Bryan Hamilton will always be remembered for scoring 'the goal that never was'. In an evenly-balanced FA Cup semi-final against the old enemy Liverpool at Maine Road in 1977, the teams were deadlocked at 2-2 and the minutes ticking away when Hamilton hammered the ball beyond the outstretched fingers of Ray Clemence to apparently clinch a place at Wembley. For no obvious reason, controversial referee Clive Thomas ruled out the effort and Liverpool went on to win the replay 3-0. A terrier-like midfielder, Hamilton spent two years with Everton after signing for £40,000 from Ipswich Town in 1975. He had made nearly 200 first-team appearances for the East Anglian club after moving there from Linfield. He made 41 League appearances (including three as a substitute) for Everton and played in the 1977 League Cup Final against Aston Villa before moving to Millwall, then Swindon. Capped 50 times for Northern Ireland, he became player-manager of Tranmere Rovers in October 1980 but was sacked in February 1985. He took over the reins at Wigan Athletic and led them to Wembley glory in the Freight Rover Trophy Final at the end of 1984-5.

BRYAN HAMILTON

HAROLD HARDMAN

	LEAGUE		FA CUP		TOTAL	
	App	Gls	App	Gls	App	Gls
1903-04	26	5			26	5
1904-05	32	8	6	1	38	9
1905-06	31	6	6	2	37	8
1906-07	19	3	7	1	26	4
1907-08	22	3	7		29	3
	130	25	26	4	156	29

A pint-sized winger of great flair, and one of the leading amateur footballers of his day, Harold Hardman went on to become one of the game's great adminstrators when he retired from playing. He was a stylish forward who played for Everton, Manchester United and Northern Nomads. He appeared in FA Cup Finals in consecutive years, in 1906 when Everton defeated Newcastle United, and 12 months later when they lost to Sheffield Wednesday. The 1906 success meant that he was one of only three amateurs this century to take an FA Cup winners' medal, joining Manchester City's S.B. Ashworth (1904) and Wolves' Rev K.R.G. Hunt (1908). Manchester-born Hardman joined Everton from Blackpool in 1903 and left for United in 1908, the year he won an Olympic Games soccer gold medal with Great Britain. He had already won four full England caps with Everton. A solicitor with offices in the centre of Manchester, he was a Manchester United director for 50 years, 17 years as chairman in the immediate post-war era. He was also an FA councillor and president of the Lancashire FA.

JOE HARPER

	LEAGUE		FA CUP		FL CUP		TOTAL	
	App	Gls	App	Gls	App	Gls	App	Gls
1972-73	20	7	2	1			22	8
1973-74	20/3	5	2	1	2		24/3	6
	40/3	12	4	2	2		46/3	14

Joe Harper was hailed as one of the new breed of strikers when he joined Everton in December 1972. His gift was sharpness in and around the penalty area, the quick eye and lightning reaction needed to take full advantage of split-second situations. At 5ft 6ins he simply did not have the physical ability to bustle around in the old-style centre-forward way. He relied on positional sense and timing. He came to Goodison at a time of crisis when it was learned that Joe Royle had been ruled out for the season which still had five months to run. Harry Catterick paid Aberdeen £180,000 for him — a Scottish League club record incoming fee — and his early form was encouraging. He made his League debut against Tottenham Hotspur a week after signing and although he missed a penalty, his immense potential was clear for all to see. After only 14 months with Everton he announced that he wanted to return to Scotland and was transferred to Hibernian for £120,000. He hit the headlines in 1975 when he was one of five Scotland stars banned from international football after an incident in Copenhagen. He moved back to Aberdeen for £50,000 in April 1976.

	LEAGUE		FA CUP		FL CUP		EUROPE		TOTAL	
	App	Gls	App	Gls	App	Gls	App	Gls	App	Gls
1955-56	20	2	4	1					24	3
1956-57	3								3	
1957-58	30	6	3						33	6
1958-59	35	1	4						39	1
1959-60	32	1	1						33	1
1960-61	30	3	1		5				36	3
1961-62	33	1	3						36	1
1962-63	24	1	1	1			2		27	2
1963-64	28	3	5	2			2		35	5
1964-65	31	3	1				4		36	3
1965-66	40	2	8				4	2	52	4
1966-67	4								4	
	310	23	31	4	5		12	2	358	29

Bebington-born Brian Harris was a winger when he joined Everton from Port Sunlight in January 1954, but his classy play and subtle skills could adapt to almost every position. Indeed, in the 11 years after making his League debut in August 1955, he played in every position except goal for the first team. And in the 1960s, when Everton could afford to compete at the top of the transfer market, Harris could still hold his place. Although he cost only a £10 signing-on fee, he ranked alongside expensive purchases and only once lost his place, briefly to Tony Kay. Perhaps best remembered as a defensive wing-half, he played 24 times in the 1962-3 Championship-winning team (before losing his number-six shirt to Kay) and he was a star of the 1966 FA Cup Final over Sheffield Wednesday. In the October following the Cup Final victory he went to Cardiff City for £15,000. No stranger to European soccer (he played in Everton's early European Cup and Fairs' Cup games), Harris appeared in all nine of Cardiff's European Cup-winners' Cup matches in 1967-8 when they narrowly missed the Final. Later he played for, and managed, Newport County. His League career totalled 541 games (plus three as a substitute).

BRIAN HARRIS

	LEAGUE		FA CUP		FL CUP		TOTAL	
	App	Gls	App	Gls	App	Gls	App	Gls
1955-56	40	19	4	2			44	21
1956-57	13	4	2	1			15	5
1957-58	41	14	3	1			44	15
1958-59	42	14	4	1			46	15
1959-60	36	9	1				37	9
1960-61	19	5			2	2	21	7
	191	65	14	5	2	2	207	72

Jimmy Harris was a pacey centre-forward whose greatest asset was his appetite for sheer hard work. Birkenhead-born and a member of the district's successful schoolboy side, he joined Everton as an amateur before making the transition to full-time professional. He made his debut at Burnley on 27 August 1955, replacing local hero Dave Hickson, and was to succeed the great man on a permanent basis when Hickson was transferred to Aston Villa a month later. Once established in the side, his form was a revelation. Within five months he had forced his way into the England Under-23 side for an international against Scotland at Hillsborough. When Hickson returned to Goodison Park in the 1957 close season, Harris switched to outside-right where his speed and power-shooting made him one of the finest and most dangerous wingers in the First Division. He holds the rare distinction of scoring a hat-trick and still finishing up on the losing side. It happened in October 1958 when Tottenham defeated Everton 10-4 at White Hart Lane. He moved to Birmingham City in December 1960 for a 'substantial' fee. He also represented the Football League.

JIMMY HARRIS

VAL HARRIS

	LEAGUE		FA CUP		TOTAL	
	App	Gls	App	Gls	App	Gls
1907-08	3		1		4	
1908-09	36		2		38	
1909-10	31		7		38	
1910-11	32		3		35	
1911-12	34		5		39	
1912-13	28	1	5	1	33	2
1913-14	26		1		27	
	190	1	24	1	214	2

Everton signed Dublin-born Valentine Harris from Shelbourne in 1907 and the Irishman proved to be one of their most consistent and effective players over the next six years. Harris was already an Irish international when he went to Goodison, winning his first cap at centre-forward. Thereafter he played at inside-forward, wing-half and centre-half for his country. He was wonderfully light on his feet and during his time at Everton he managed to steer clear of injuries, clocking up 214 senior appearances. Though Ireland made more use of his versatility than did Everton, Harris still turned out in six different positions for the Goodison club, though the vast majority of his appearances were at right-half. In 1914 he completed his 20th international appearance, playing in two of the three matches which gave Ireland their first outright Home International Championship title. He returned to Shelbourne the same year.

GEORGE HARRISON

	LEAGUE		FA CUP		TOTAL	
	App	Gls	App	Gls	App	Gls
1913-14	35	1	1		36	1
1914-15	26	4	4		30	4
1919-20	25		1		26	
1920-21	38	8	5		43	8
1921-22	40	2	1		41	2
1922-23	12	2	1		13	2
1923-24	1				1	
	177	17	13		190	17

George Harrison was a stocky player for a conventional winger. He weighed nearly 13st and that made him a difficult man to shake off the ball in the day's when the shoulder-charge was a full-back's chief weapon. He was born in Church Gresley, Derbyshire, in 1891 and began his senior career with Leicester Fosse who signed him in the close season of 1910. Three years later he joined Everton and was their regular outside-left the following season. He had one of the hardest shots in football, and was a notable penalty-taker, although his strike-rate at Everton — 17 goals in 190 League and Cup games — suggests that he was not all that successful in the role of out-and-out scorer. Yet he made plenty of goals for other people, notably Bobby Parker when Everton won the Championship in 1914-15. He played wartime football with Everton and was a regular when the League resumed. His form in the immediate post-war era led to him winning two England caps. Midway through 1923-4 he signed for Preston North End, joined Blackpool in 1931, and retired the following year to become a licensee in Preston.

	LEAGUE		FA CUP		TOTAL	
	App	Gls	App	Gls	App	Gls
1921-22	17				17	
1922-23	40	1	2		42	1
1923-24	42	2	1		43	2
1924-25	24				24	
1925-26	26				26	
1926-27	39	1	3		42	1
1927-28	41	1	2		43	1
1928-29	40		1		41	
1929-30	20		2		22	
	289	5	11		300	5

Glasgow-born Hunter Hart was signed by Everton from Airdrie for £4,000 in 1922 and arrived in time to make his debut against Bolton Wanderers that month. Everton lost 1-0 at Burnden Park but Hart, who had signed professional forms for Airdrie when the war ended, impressed and retained his place. He made most of his appearances at left-half, though towards the middle and end of his career at Goodison he switched to centre-half. He was a member of the team which helped Dixie Dean to his record-breaking 60 League goals in 1927-8, and for a time he skippered Everton. Sadly, the latter part of his career coincided with Everton's fall from grace. When he arrived at Goodison Park, the club were struggling to avoid relegation and they needed his strength in defence; when he played his final few games, in 1929-30, the club were again in trouble and this time his powers were waning and he could not help them. As the side plunged into Division Two for the first time, so the powerful half-back of earlier days was unable to hold his place. Just after Christmas he played his last game in Everton's first team and retired shortly afterwards.

HUNTER HART

ASA HARTFORD

	LEAGUE		FA CUP		FL CUP		TOTAL	
	App	Gls	App	Gls	App	Gls	App	Gls
1979-80	35	1	5	1	3		43	2
1980-81	39	5	6		3		48	5
1981-82	7						7	
	81	6	11	1	6		98	7

Asa Hartford was a midfield purist in the mould of Colin Harvey and Howard Kendall. A tough-tackling pocket dynamo, in the late '70s he was involved in two transfer deals worth a total of £1 million in the space of 63 turbulent days midway through his chequered career. He made his name with West Brom before Don Revie lured him to Leeds in November 1971. The £170,000 deal was sensationally called off 24 hours later after a routine medical revealed that Hartford had a heart condition. He underwent exhaustive tests and was quickly given the go-ahead to resume his career. He moved to Manchester City for £250,000 in August 1974. After five years at Maine Road he chose Nottingham Forest in preference to Everton, but he never took to Brian Clough and two months and three games later he was on his way to Goodison in another £500,000 deal. He quickly became the hub of Everton's vastly improved midfield and was voted Player of the Year by supporters. His stay lasted two years and he moved back to Maine Road in October 1981 for £350,000. He went on to Norwich City and picked up a Milk Cup winners' medal at Wembley in 1985. In July 1985 he joined Bolton Wanderers.

	LEAGUE		FA CUP		FL CUP		EUROPE		TOTAL	
	App	Gls	App	Gls	App	Gls	App	Gls	App	Gls
1963-64	2						1		3	
1964-65	32	2	4	1			4	2	40	5
1965-66	40	1	8	1			4		52	2
1966-67	42	1	6				4		52	1
1967-68	34		4		2				40	
1968-69	36	4	4		4				44	4
1969-70	35	3			3				38	3
1970-71	36	2	5	1			6		47	3
1971-72	17		3	3	1				20	4
1972-73	24/2				1				25/2	
1973-74	15/1	1			0/1				15/2	1
1974-75	4	1							4	1
	317/3	18	34	4	10/1		19	2	380/4	24

Colin Harvey was a classical type of midfield player. At his best he managed to pack into his tiny frame every attribute needed for the testing role. Liverpool-born, he made a dramatic first-team debut for Everton as an 18-year-old when he was thrown into a European Cup clash with mighty Inter Milan in the famous San Siro stadium in 1963. It took time for the ultra-critical scrutineers of Goodison to accept him, but they ultimately realised that he was a player of genuine quality and style. He showed class in everything he did, linking it with colossal workrate, skill on the ball, excellent positional play and passing ability — the lot. Many would argue that he trained and performed with such vigour that he pushed his body beyond its limits, so cutting perhaps one or two years from what was an extraordinarily successful career. When he hit his peak he was a treat to watch, delighting football purists with his uncanny passing ability. He made only one England appearance, against Malta in 1971. With Howard Kendall and Alan Ball he formed the famous midfield triangle which steered Everton to the League Championship in 1970. After a superb Goodison career covering more than 380 first-team games, he was transferred to Sheffield Wednesday in 1974. His career was brought to an abrupt and untimely end by a niggling hip injury. He returned to Everton in 1976 to work behind the scenes with the club's youngsters. His promotion to first-team coach in 1983 helped spark Everton's much vaunted revival.

COLIN HARVEY

	LEAGUE		FA CUP		FL CUP		EUROPE		TOTAL	
	App	Gls	App	Gls	App	Gls	App	Gls	App	Gls
1981-82	22	6							22	6
1982-83	37	10	5	1	4				46	11
1983-84	36	12	7	2	11	4			54	18
1984-85	17	11			4	1	4	1	25	13
	112	39	12	3	19	5	4	1	147	48

ADRIAN HEATH

Adrian Heath became Everton's record signing when Howard Kendall paid struggling Stoke City a massive £700,000 for his services on 7 January 1982, just four days before Heath's 21st birthday. He arrived with a reputation as a powerhouse midfielder, more than capable of using his considerable talents up front when required. Something of a pocket dynamo, he was talked about as a natural successor to two diminutive stars of the past, Alan Ball and Bobby Collins. A natural ball-player with a superb turn of speed, he has an aggressive and competitive streak which belies his frail frame. He struggled in his early days at Goodison, often trying too hard to justify the enormous price tag. He alternated between two or three different roles and despite flashes of brilliance rarely suggested that he was on the verge of becoming an inspirational driving-force behind the long overdue Everton revival. In 1983-4, four minutes from the end of a Milk Cup match at Oxford, he scored the goal which many people regard as the turning point in the club's fortunes. Everton went on to the Final and a first-ever Wembley showdown with neighbours Liverpool. He also scored the FA Cup semi-final winner against Southampton in the same season. He hit peak form at the start of 1984-5 and had scored 13 goals in 25 games when he was ruled out for the remainder of the season after severely damaging knee ligaments during a game against Sheffield Wednesday.

DAVE HICKSON

	LEAGUE		FA CUP		TOTAL	
	App	Gls	App	Gls	App	Gls
1951-52	31	14	2		33	14
1952-53	27	12	5	4	32	16
1953-54	40	25	3	3	43	28
1954-55	39	12	2	1	41	13
1955-56	2				2	
1957-58	35	9	2	3	37	12
1958-59	39	17	4	5	43	22
1959-60	12	6			12	6
	225	95	18	16	243	111

Dave Hickson will always be remembered on Merseyside as a talented and forceful centre-forward with tremendous heading ability. Off the field he was a quiet, retiring man who craved privacy, but as soon as he pulled on a football strip he was transformed into an aggressive, robust player who often fell foul of referees. He was initially with his local club Ellesmere Port before signing professional forms for Everton in May 1948 as an 18-year-old. After losing his place to Jimmy Harris in September 1955 he was transferred to Aston Villa for £17,500. He moved to Huddersfield Town for £16,000 only two months later, and back to Everton in a deal worth £7,500 in July 1957. Sadly, little went right for him after his return. In November 1959 Liverpool took him across Stanley Park for £12,000. Weeks later, Bill Shankly, who had been Hickson's boss at Huddersfield, joined Liverpool. In January 1960 Hickson was sent off for the third time in his stormy career during a game against Sheffield United. A bitter war of words followed which ended with Hickson found 'guilty of mis-conduct during the match'. The FA report continued: 'However the commission is not satisfied that Hickson was guilty of deliberate violent conduct.' Twelve months later he left Anfield and went into non-League football with Cambridge United. He later joined Tranmere Rovers and spent two years as player-manager of Irish League club Ballymena United.

	LEAGUE		FA CUP		FL CUP		EUROPE		TOTAL	
	App	Gls	App	Gls	App	Gls	App	Gls	App	Gls
1976-77	2								2	
1977-78	25/1	1	1		5				31/1	1
1978-79	20	1					0/2		20/2	1
1979-80	19				5		2		26	
1980-81	2								2	
1981-82	29	3	1		2				32	3
1982-83	39	1	5		2				46	1
1983-84	14				5				19	
	150/1	6	7		19		2/2		178/3	6

MARK HIGGINS

Mark Higgins took over the mantle of 'Mr Everton' when Mike Lyons left Goodison to pursue a career with Sheffield Wednesday. An Evertonian through and through, Higgins was on the verge of a call-up to the full England squad when his career was tragically cut short at the age of 26 by a potentially crippling pelvic injury. Born in Buxton, he quickly followed in the footsteps of his father, John, who was a giant centre-back with Bolton Wanderers. He joined Everton straight from school, registered as an apprentice in April 1975 and made his senior debut 18 months later in the 2-2 draw against Manchester City at Goodison Park. Exceptionally good in the air, he matured at an astonishing rate under the careful guidance of Lyons. He was a strong, brave centre-back who quickly showed he had great qualities of leadership. After partnering Billy Wright at the heart of Howard Kendall's defence he teamed up with Kevin Ratcliffe and was appointed captain. His injury problems began in December 1983 after a Milk Cup replay against West Ham. What was initially diagnosed as a simple groin injury turned out to be a serious pelvic disorder. Sadly, despite two operations and numerous attempts at a comeback, there was to be no reprieve. Higgins, who won a record 19 England Schoolboy caps, was told that he would never play again.

JOHNNY HOLT

	LEAGUE		FA CUP		TOTAL	
	App	Gls	App	Gls	App	Gls
1888-89	17				17	
1889-90	21	1	2		23	1
1890-91	21	1	1		22	1
1891-92	21		1		22	
1892-93	26		7		33	
1893-94	26		1		27	
1894-95	27		3		30	
1895-96	14		2		16	
1896-97	25	1	5	1	30	2
1897-98	27		5		32	
	225	3	27	1	252	4

Johnny Holt was a fine centre-half nicknamed the 'Little Everton Devil' by supporters who worshipped the ground he walked upon. Enormously powerful in the air, he was one of the best one-to-one markers in the business, relying on his muscular physique to subdue rival centre-forwards. He was an expert at last-ditch tackles and made a habit of appearing from nowhere to scoop the ball to safety. He played ten times for England but his finest moment came against Scotland at Ibrox in 1892. He was part of the side dubbed the Old Crocks' because Old Etonian Arthur Dunn, who had been centre-forward in 1884, was recalled as captain and full-back. Scottish journalists had a positive field-day in the weeks leading up to the international, predicting that their star man, Sandy McMahon, would lead Holt a merry dance. In fact the Everton defender marked him out of the game. The official history of the club tells how Holt was 'an artist in the perpetuation of clever minor fouls. When they were appealed for, his shocked look of innocence was side-splitting'. He joined Everton from Bootle in 1888, in time for the League's first season, and played regularly for ten years before moving to Reading.

JOHN HURST

	LEAGUE		FA CUP		FL CUP		EUROPE		TOTAL	
	App	Gls	App	Gls	App	Gls	App	Gls	App	Gls
1965-66	19/2	2							19/2	2
1966-67	23/2	2	6						29/2	2
1967-68	40	5	5		2	1			47	6
1968-69	42	7	5	2	4				51	9
1969-70	42	5	1		3				46	5
1970-71	40	3	5				6		51	3
1971-72	28/1		1/2	1	1				30/3	1
1972-73	28/1	1	2						30/1	1
1973-74	39	3	3	1	2				44	4
1974-75	29/2	1	1						30/2	1
1975-76	6/3		1		1		0/1		8/4	
	336/11	29	30/2	4	13	1	6/1		385/14	34

John Hurst was the sort of player every manager dreams of having in his side. A dedicated club man, he arrived at Everton in a blaze of publicity as a 14-year-old England Schoolboy international in May 1962. Blackpool-born, he was largely a product of Everton's hugely successful youth policy. After learning his trade in the Central League, he forced his way into the senior squad in August 1965 when he was named, alongside such greats as Brian Labone and Fred Pickering, for a game against newly-promoted Northampton Town. However, he had to wait for a substitute appearance against Stoke for his debut. He was originally a striker but manager Harry Catterick transformed him into one of the finest wing-halves in the country. A solid tackler with an eye for an opening up front, he quickly established himself and went on to play 385 games in a career which spanned 11 years. In 1968 he confounded medical experts who told him that he would not play again that season after contracting hepatitis on the eve of the FA Cup semi-final against Leeds United. Against all the odds he recovered in time to play in the Final against West Brom which Everton lost 1-0. He won England Under-23 honours, and an FA Youth Cup winners' medal in 1965.

	LEAGUE		FA CUP		FL CUP		EUROPE		TOTAL	
	App	Gls	App	Gls	App	Gls	App	Gls	App	Gls
1964-65	1								1	
1965-66	4						1		5	
1966-67	19	6	6	4			1		26	10
1967-68	19/1	5	6	3					25/1	8
1968-69	36	19	5		2	1			43	20
1969-70	30	6			2				32	6
1970-71	15	6	4	3			2/1		21/1	9
1971-72	25/2	1	1						26/2	1
1972-73	8/1								8/1	
1973-74	1/3	1			1				2/3	1
	158/7	44	22	10	5	1	4/1		189/8	55

Jimmy Husband was a likeable and talented Geordie, nicknamed 'Skippy' by supporters because of his distinctive running style. He was signed from North-East side Shields in July 1963 and went on to become one of the most exciting strikers in the country. Unorthodox and totally unpredictable, he was capable of moments of genuine brilliance. He was fast, skilful on the ball, with a superb swerve and dribble and was deadly when presented with a half-chance. He became a full-time professional in October 1964 and made his debut towards the end of that season, altogether playing 158 full League matches and scoring 44 goals. He won a Fairs Cup place against the Hungarian side Ujpest Dozsa as a 17-year-old in 1965-6. He was a regular member of Everton's title-winning side of 1970 and also picked up an FA Cup runners-up medal in 1968. He won England Under-23 honours but, despite being on the fringes for a couple of seasons, never managed to force his way into the full international side. In 1984 he was tempted out of retirement to play for a Bedfordshire village side. Perhaps their name appealed to him. It was Everton.

JIMMY HUSBAND

	LEAGUE		FA CUP		FL CUP		TOTAL	
	App	Gls	App	Gls	App	Gls	App	Gls
1981-82	25	3					25	3
1982-83	7/1	1	2		0/1		9/8	1
1983-84	19/2		7	2	10		36/2	2
	51/9	4	9	2	10/1		70/10	6

Alan Irvine is an 'old-fashioned' winger who arrived at Everton at a time when such players were most definitely not in vogue. A natural crowd-pleaser with superb close control and tremendous dribbling ability, he was signed as an amateur from Queen's Park in May 1981 after helping them to the Scottish Second Division Championship. Manager Howard Kendall made several largely unsuccessful attempts to introduce him into a struggling side but he was never able to hold down a senior place with any degree of regularity. Nevertheless, he did play in the historic Milk Cup Final and subsequent replay against Liverpool. Frustrated at playing Central League football, he asked for a transfer in September 1983 and eventually moved to Steve Coppell's Crystal Palace for £50,000.

ALAN IRVINE

	LEAGUE		FA CUP		TOTAL	
	App	Gls	App	Gls	App	Gls
1921-22	25	11	1		26	11
1922-23	32	8	1		33	8
1923-24	40	9	2		42	9
1924-25	28	4	3	1	31	5
1925-26	31	8	2		33	8
1926-27	34	11	4	1	38	12
1927-28	9	3	2	1	11	4
	199	54	15	3	214	57

Lisburn-born Bobby Irvine played at both centre-forward and inside-right. He was a magical dribbler, a brave forward who thrilled the crowd with his foraging runs. He won his first Ireland cap, against Scotland, in March 1922 and as an Everton player he collected 11 altogether. He played twice in teams that beat England (1923 and 1927) and he scored in the 3-3 draw with England at Liverpool in 1926. He joined Everton from Dunmurry in September 1921 and was transferred to Portsmouth in March 1928, one short of 200 League appearances for Everton. He made only nine appearances in the 1927-8 Championship season before signing for Pompey. On his departure from Goodison it was written of him: 'There is no man who takes harder knocks and squeals less than Irvine.' But injury robbed him of a place in the 1929 FA Cup Final after he had played in the earlier rounds. In two years Irvine made only 35 League appearances for Portsmouth. He went to Connah's Quay, then Derry City, where he won the last of his 15 caps, almost ten years after his first.

BOBBY IRVINE

	LEAGUE		FA CUP		TOTAL	
	App	Gls	App	Gls	App	Gls
1934-35	8		1		9	
1935-36	18				18	
1936-37	26				26	
1937-38	4				4	
1938-39	2				2	
1945-46			2		2	
1946-47	15		1		16	
1947-48	2				2	
	75		4		79	

George 'Stonewall' Jackson was a full-back who served Everton well in the inter-war years. Born within a stone's throw of Goodison Park, he began his football apprenticeship with Arnott Street School which turned out many notable players shortly before World War Two. He was spotted by Everton while playing for Walton Parish Church and while working his way through the ranks he was loaned to Crosby side, Marine. He played with the Mariners through their memorable FA Amateur Cup bid when they met Dulwich Hamlet in the Final at Upton Park. Tough in the tackle and with a fine turn of speed, he made his senior debut against Wolverhampton Wanderers in February 1935. In seven seasons he totalled 75 League appearances before transferring to Caernarvon Town in 1949.

GEORGE JACKSON

FRANK JEFFERIS

	LEAGUE		FA CUP		TOTAL	
	App	Gls	App	Gls	App	Gls
1910-11	5	2			5	2
1911-12	36	7	5	1	41	8
1912-13	27	5	5	2	32	7
1913-14	27	3	1		28	3
1914-15	18	4			18	4
1919-20	12	1	1		13	1
	125	22	12	3	137	25

Frank Jefferis was a first-rate tactician and the driving force behind the Everton forward line in the years leading up to World War One. He was born in Hampshire in 1887 and joined Southampton, his local Southern League club, in the close season of 1905. After 171 appearances for the Saints he moved to Goodison in March 1911 and won a Championship medal in 1914-15, although injury ruled him out of the latter part of the season. At Goodison he created goals for players like Browell and Bradshaw. He was capped twice for England shortly after arriving on the First Division scene, playing as a scheming inside-forward against Wales and Scotland in 1912. After wartime football with Everton he managed half a season when League soccer resumed. He moved to Preston in January 1920 and two years later was a member of their beaten FA Cup Final side. In 1923 he was appointed Southport player-coach and retired in the close season of 1925. In 1927 he was forced back into action and played two League games when Southport were short of players.

	LEAGUE		FA CUP		FL CUP		EUROPE		TOTAL	
	App	Gls	App	Gls	App	Gls	App	Gls	App	Gls
1970-71	10/1	1	1		1		0/2	1	11/3	3
1971-72	27	9	4	1	1	1			32	11
1972-73	10/1	1			1				11/1	1
1982-83	25/6	3			4	1			29/6	4
1983-84	7/2	1			1				8/2	1
	79/10	15	5	2	7	2	0/2	1	91/12	20

Striker David Johnson's colourful career came full-circle
when he signed for Everton in August 1982. Howard
Kendall's surprise decision to bolster his shot-shy forward
line with the 30-year-old former England international came
ten years after he had left Goodison Park for Ipswich Town.
Johnson, who was nothing like as skilful as many of his
contemporaries, was nevertheless a natural goalscorer who
could amble through a game seemingly uninterested before
switching up a gear to carve out the decisive opening. He
joined Everton in 1969 but despite his success was transferred
to Ipswich three years later. In 1976 Bob Paisley brought him
to Anfield as a replacement for John Toshack and during a
distinguished Anfield career he scored 78 goals and won eight
full England caps. He missed the European Cup triumphs in
Rome and at Wembley but was a key member of the side
which won the trophy for the third time in Paris in 1981. His
second spell with Everton was little short of a disaster, the
goal touch which had at one time made him one of the most
feared strikers in Europe sadly missing. He spent a month on
loan to Barnsley in February 1984 before moving to Manchester
City. He then had a brief spell with Tulsa Roughnecks in the
NASL before being transferred to Preston North End.

DAVID JOHNSON

TOMMY JOHNSON

	LEAGUE		FA CUP		TOTAL	
	App	Gls	App	Gls	App	Gls
1929-30	10	4			10	4
1930-31	36	14	5	4	41	18
1931-32	41	22	1		42	22
1932-33	40	13	6	4	46	17
1933-34	19	3	1		20	3
	146	56	13	8	159	64

Tommy Johnson was a member of the famous Everton side
that raced away with the Second Division Championship in
1930-31 when they clinched a return to the top-flight
immediately after being relegated for the first time in the
club's history. He was a tricky inside-left who could turn a
game on its head with one flash of brilliance. Technically
superb, he was the perfect foil to the stunning power of Dixie
Dean. Born near Barrow, he was playing for his local team,
Dalton Casuals, when Manchester City discovered him and
gave him his chance in wartime football. He played for City in
the 1926 FA Cup Final against Bolton and signed for Everton
in March 1930, the season after he had helped the Maine
Road side destroy Everton 6-2 at Goodison Park. That
season Johnson scored 38 League goals for City and when he
left for Everton he had netted 158 altogether, both records
which still stand. He went back to Wembley with Everton in
1933 and helped them to a 3-0 victory — ironically over City.
He joined Liverpool shortly afterwards and finished his
career with a total of 222 League goals.

	LEAGUE		FA CUP		FL CUP		EUROPE		TOTAL	
	App	Gls	App	Gls	App	Gls	App	Gls	App	Gls
1970-71	1								1	
1971-72	5	1							6	
1972-73	11/1								11/1	
1973-74	10/3		2/1						12/4	
1974-75	25/1	6	3						28/1	6
1975-76	24/1	6	1	1	5	1	2		32/1	8
	76/6	12	7/1	1	5	1	2		90/7	14

GARY JONES

Gary Jones was one of the most talented yet controversial players to wear an Everton shirt during the mid-'70s. On his day he was a mercurial forward, the sort of player who could change the course of a game with one devastating piece of skill. Huyton-born, he was robbed of a dramatic debut as a 19-year-old when illness prevented him from playing in a European Cup-tie against Keflavick in 1970. He then had to endure a seven-month wait on the sidelines before making his League debut at Coventry. Although he made 90 appearances for Everton, he never quite fulfilled his rich potential and controversy dogged the final days of what should have been a long and illustrious Goodison career. Following a defeat at Manchester City in February 1976, he submitted a transfer request which was turned down by a board all too aware of his immense popularity on the terraces. A month later he was suspended for a fortnight and fined two weeks' wages by manager Billy Bingham for making a gesture to the bench when substituted during a match against Leeds United, and for subsequently airing his grievances in public. At the end of that season he moved to Birmingham City for £110,000 and made 33 appearances there before joining Fort Lauderdale in America. He now runs the Albert pub in Liverpool's trendy Lark Lane.

JACK JONES

	LEAGUE		FA CUP		TOTAL	
	App	Gls	App	Gls	App	Gls
1933-34	5				5	
1934-35	10		3		13	
1935-36	34		1		35	
1936-37	16		4		20	
1937-38	33		2		35	
	98		10		108	

Through sheer hard work Jack Jones developed into one of the most astute and reliable full-backs of his day. After playing for Bebington in numerous boys' representative games he enjoyed a spell with Bromborough Pool before switching his allegiance to Ellesmere Port Town. He was with Town at the same time as Joe Mercer. He was snapped up by Everton in 1933 and was an automatic choice during 1935-6 when he made 34 appearances. Like so many other defenders he started his career as a centre-forward before deciding that it was a far simpler task to stop goals than to score them. His first reserve team appearance at Goodison came quite by chance. In early 1933 he had been selected to play for the third team at Whiston and was on his way to the match when he literally bumped into second-team manager Bill Gibbins who found himself one man short for a fixture at Stockport. Jones filled the vacancy and was so impressive that he held his place. His one moment of controversy came in 1937 when he was sent off during the final match of Everton's tour of Denmark. Eventually he moved to Sunderland.

TOMMY E. JONES

	LEAGUE		FA CUP		FL CUP		TOTAL	
	App	Gls	App	Gls	App	Gls	App	Gls
1950-51	30		1				31	
1951-52	37						37	
1952-53	42		5				47	
1953-54	37	1	3				40	1
1954-55	41	4	2				43	4
1955-56	39	2	4				43	2
1956-57	39	3	1				40	3
1957-58	31		3				34	
1958-59	38	4	4				42	4
1959-60	35		1				36	
1960-61	13		1		3		17	
1961-62	1						1	
	383	14	25		3		411	14

Liverpool-born Tommy E. Jones was Everton's first-choice centre-half through the '50s. Although for many years regarded exclusively as a stopper, he was originally a full-back. He signed professional forms in January 1948 after successfully captaining the England and Liverpool County FA youth teams. It was manager Cliff Britton who recognised his potential as a pivot and guided him into a new career. He made his senior debut against Arsenal at Highbury on 6 September 1950 and went on to make over 400 appearances for the club. Cool, unruffled and a most gentlemanly player, his consistency spoke for itself down the years. Although full international honours surprisingly passed him by, he played for an England XI against the British Army at Maine Road, and was captain of the FA side that toured Ghana and Nigeria in the summer of 1958. A smashed knee-cap sustained in a Central League game at Barnsley ended his career and he left Britain to coach Italian club Montreal.

	LEAGUE		FA CUP		TOTAL	
	App	Gls	App	Gls	App	Gls
1936-37	1				1	
1937-38	28		2		30	
1938-39	39		5		44	
1946-47	22	3	1	1	23	4
1947-48	24	1			24	1
1948-49	37		2		39	
1949-50	14				14	
	165	4	10	1	175	5

Tommy G. Jones was always regarded as one of the footballing 'scientists' of his day. He was never the battering-ram stopper of centre-forwards, but a thoughtful, neat player who read his opponents' intentions superbly before stepping in with great nonchalance to sweep the ball away and use it to good advantage. He signed for Everton from Wrexham in March 1936 for £3,000 and picked up the first of his 17 Welsh caps two years later. He was appointed club captain in August 1949, succeeding Peter Farrell. In 1948 he might have become a trailblazer to Europe when Italian giants Roma made desperate and prolonged attempts to sign him. Everton initially accepted a considerable fee but the deal fell through after a row over the currency transaction. Towards the end of his career he upset the Everton board by publicly expressing his concern at the way the club was being run. He eventually moved to Pwllheli where he was appointed player-manager.

TOMMY G. JONES

	LEAGUE		FA CUP		FL CUP		EUROPE		TOTAL	
	App	Gls	App	Gls	App	Gls	App	Gls	App	Gls
1962-63	19	1	2						21	1
1963-64	31	3	3				2		36	3
	50	4	5				2		57	4

Tony Kay was at the centre of football's greatest-ever scandal when, in 1965, he was banned for life — and imprisoned — after the infamous soccer bribes trial. It was a sad end to the career of a man who was one of the most talented wing-halves of his day. A small, flame-haired tiger of a footballer, he was hard-tackling and a superb passer of the ball who cost Everton £55,000 — then a British record for a wing-half — when he signed from Sheffield Wednesday in late December 1962. He had spent nine years at Hillsborough and was on the verge of a call-up to the full England squad when he arrived at Goodison. He was appointed captain during Harry Catterick's reign and was to play a leading role in the Championship success of 1962-3. Despite his qualities as a leader and his considerable skill, he won only one full cap, against Switzerland in 1963.

TONY KAY

	LEAGUE		FA CUP		TOTAL	
	App	Gls	App	Gls	App	Gls
1888-89	1				1	
1891-92	23	2	1		24	2
1892-93	14	1	7		21	1
1893-94	26	1	1		27	1
1894-95	19	1	4		23	1
1895-96	6		1		7	
	89	5	14		103	5

Bob Kelso came from the famous Scottish football breeding-ground of the 1880s and he first made his name with Renton when they were a prominent force in football north of the border. He moved to Newcastle West End in the close season of 1888. Kelso made one appearance for Everton in the League's first season of 1888-9, at right-half against Preston North End, and the following season was a member of the Preston side which won the League again. Eventually he threw in his lot with Everton and they persuaded him to convert to full-back with good effect. Strong-tackling and hard-kicking, he was in the Everton team which lost the 1893 FA Cup Final to Wolves at Fallowfield, and also played in the side which came second in the First Division two seasons later. In the 1896 close season Kelso moved to Dundee where he won another Scottish cap. In those days the Scots did not select players with English clubs and 10 years had elapsed between Kelso's last two international appearances.

BOB KELSO

HOWARD KENDALL

	LEAGUE		FA CUP		FL CUP		EUROPE		TOTAL	
	App	Gls	App	Gls	App	Gls	App	Gls	App	Gls
1966-67	4								4	
1967-68	38	6	6	1	2	2			46	9
1968-69	28/1	1	3		4				35/1	1
1969-70	36	4	1		4	1			41	5
1970-71	40	2	5	2			6	2	51	6
1971-72	34/1	4	4						38/1	4
1972-73	40	4	2		1				43	4
1973-74	7		1						8	
1981-82	4		1		1				6	
	231/2	21	23	3	12	3	6	2	272/2	29

Few people with a basic knowledge of the modern game would argue with the sentiment that Howard Kendall was the finest player never to win full international honours. The stylish, competitive midfielder who has put pride back ito a great club since moving into the Goodison managerial hot-seat, was a positive inspiration during his seven-year playing career with the club. He became the youngest player ever to appear in an FA Cup Final when he played at left-half for Preston North End against West Ham United in 1964 — just 20 days before his 18th birthday. After 104 appearances for Preston he was signed for £80,000 in March 1967 and went on to be part of the most influential midfield combination Everton has ever known. Along with Colin Harvey and Alan Ball, he ran the side's engine-room as Everton swept to an emphatic Championship success in 1969-70. It is one of football's great unsolved mysteries as to why that superb team faltered so badly in following seasons. After playing over 250 games for the club Kendall departed to Birmingham City in February 1974 as part of a complicated £350,000 deal which brought striker Bob Latchford to Goodison. In August 1977 he was transferred to Stoke City for a mere £40,000 and despite being tempted by an offer from North American side, Minnesota Kicks, he became club coach under Alan Durban in 1978.

Howard Kendall is pictured with an England squad in 1972, but Everton's talented midfielder never won a full international cap.

	LEAGUE		FA CUP		FL CUP		EUROPE		TOTAL	
	App	Gls	App	Gls	App	Gls	App	Gls	App	Gls
1967-68	12/4		2						14/4	
1968-69	4/3		0/1		0/2				4/6	
1969-70	8/1				0/1				8/2	
1970-71	28/1		2				4		34/1	
1971-72	34/2		3	1	1				38/2	1
1972-73	40	2	2		1				43	2
1973-74	36	2	1		2				39	2
1974-75	40		2	1	2				44	1
1975-76	28/2	1	1		4	1	2		35/2	2
1976-77	14	1	1		3				18	1
1977-78	7		1						8	
1978-79	3						1		4	
	254/13	6	15/1	2	13/3	1	7		289/17	9

Roger Kenyon was a reliable and consistent centre-half who was handed the unenviable task of following Brian Labone into the heart of Everton's defence. He was substitute, but did not play, in the 1968 FA Cup Final against West Bromwich Albion and was called into the side to help clinch the League Championship two years later. Seen as the natural successor to Labone, he earned a long series of glowing write-ups in the closing weeks of the 1970 title campaign. Mystifyingly that famous team went into decline, Kenyon's progress being badly interrupted by a car accident in 1974. He was dogged by a series of niggling injuries but, every time he fought his way back to full fitness, he proved conclusively that he had lost none of his speed or superb timing. He was an England substitute for the European Championship games against West Germany, Cyprus and Wales at Wembley in 1975. He stayed with Everton for around 15 years before moving to the west coast of Canada to join Vancouver Whitecaps. In 1979 he helped steer them to the North American Soccer League title.

ROGER KENYON

	LEAGUE		FA CUP		FL CUP		EUROPE		TOTAL	
	App	Gls	App	Gls	App	Gls	App	Gls	App	Gls
1978-79	9	2							9	2
1979-80	31	10	4	4	5	4	2		42	18
	40	12	4	4	5	4	2		51	20

When Everton signed Brian Kidd they acquired not only a man with a proven goalscoring record, but also someone who cherished the traditional values of football. In Kidd's book, qualities like loyalty, hard work and respect had a high rating. An exhilarating forward when playing to the peak of his form, he hit the heights of his career when it had barely started. On his 19th birthday in 1968 he lined up alongside such greats as Bobby Charlton and George Best to score a goal in Manchester United's famous European Cup Final victory over Portuguese aces Benfica at Wembley. He arrived at Everton 11 years later, for £150,000 in March 1979. By that point he had picked up England caps at Schoolboy, Youth, Under-23 and full international levels. He started at Old Trafford, breaking into the League side after a tour of Australia in 1967. After playing more than 200 games for United he moved to Arsenal for £110,000 and was top scorer for the Gunners in each of his two seasons at Highbury. But he was anxious to return north and in June 1976 he jumped at the chance of joining Manchester City for £100,000. He finished his first season at Maine Road as top scorer with 21 goals and topped the charts 12 months later with 16. Although his time at Goodison was a happy one he never really recaptured the stunning form which made him a household name in the '70s and was transferred to Bolton for £150,000 in May 1980.

BRIAN KIDD

ANDY KING

	LEAGUE		FA CUP		FL CUP		EUROPE		TOTAL	
	App	Gls	App	Gls	App	Gls	App	Gls	App	Gls
1975-76	3	2							3	2
1976-77	36/1	7	4/1		9	5			49/2	12
1977-78	42	8	2	1	5	2			49	11
1978-79	40	12	1		3		3	4	47	16
1979-80	29	9	4	1	4	1	2		39	11
1982-83	24	9	4	2	4	2			32	13
1983-84	19/1	2	1		4/1	1			24/2	3
	193/2	49	16/1	4	29/1	11	5	4	243/4	68

Andy King was the man who simply could not live without Everton. A hugely gifted yet erratic and inconsistent player, he enjoyed two spells at Goodison Park and would almost certainly have gone on to full England honours had he been capable of matching his undoubted skill with a degree of self-discipline. A thoughtful midfield general who could score goals, he was a magnificent ball-player on his day. Sadly he was unable to maintain his best form when it really mattered and far too often found himself the odd man out. He was originally signed by Billy Bingham from Luton Town for £35,000 in 1976. He was idolised by the fans who appreciated his flair for the unusual. He joined Tommy Docherty's QPR in a £450,000 deal in September 1980, but was unhappy at Loftus Road and moved to West Brom for a similar fee only 12 months later. He encountered problems both on and off the field and was on the verge of ending up on football's scrapheap when Howard Kendall rescued his career in July 1982. At the age of 25 he was brought back to Everton in a straight swop which took Peter Eastoe to The Hawthorns. At the time Kendall described him as a 'technically superb player and finisher' but he failed to realise his full potential and after around 50 senior games he was allowed to leave and went to Holland.

Everton 1976-7. Back row (l to r): G.Jones, D.Jones, Brand, Davies, Lawson, McNaught, Connolly. Middle: Burtenshaw (coach), Telfer, Latchford, Kenyon, Lyons, Pearson, Dobson, Smallman, Harrison (asst.coach). Front: Bernard, Buckley, Seargeant, Darracott, Billy Bingham (manager), Hamilton, King, Goodlass, Robinson.

	LEAGUE		FA CUP		FL CUP		EUROPE		TOTAL	
	App	Gls	App	Gls	App	Gls	App	Gls	App	Gls
1957-58	4								4	
1958-59	4								4	
1959-60	31	1							32	
1960-61	42	1			4				47	
1961-62	41	3							44	
1962-63	40	3					2		45	
1963-64	34	4					2		40	
1964-65	42	4					6		52	
1965-66	37	2	8				3		48	2
1966-67	40		6				4		50	
1967-68	40		6		2				48	
1968-69	42		5		4				51	
1969-70	34		1		4				39	
1970-71	16		3				2		21	
1971-72	4				1				5	
	451	2	45		15		19		530	2

BRIAN LABONE

One of the greatest players to wear the royal blue of Everton, Brian Labone was the model professional for both club and country. An exemplary character in the mould of Tom Finney and Bobby Charlton, he was booked only twice in a career which spanned 14 years. He started with Everton in 1957, several years before the maximum wage was abolished, and played the game as much for the love of it as for the money he took home. From being a schoolboy fan on the terraces Labone went on to captain the club he idolised and led them out at Wembley. He was a cultured and effective defender who made full use of his height. Unlike so many of his centre-back contemporaries, Labone had little interest in straying upfield in search of goals. He was a stopper pure and simple, and managed to find the net only twice in his lengthy career. Altogether he made 533 first-team appearances and his League tally — 451 — was only 12 short of the record held by Ted Sagar whose career was nine years longer than Labone's. He won two League Championship medals and FA Cup winners' and runners-up medals. He was a key member of England's 1970 World Cup squad and altogether won 26 full caps. He injured an achilles tendon in a reserve game in September 1971 and was forced to quit the following year.

Brian Labone (front, fourth from right) is one of several Everton men with the 1968 England squad. Others are Tommy Wright (back, fourth from right), Ray Wilson (back, extreme right), and Alan Ball (front, extreme right).

	LEAGUE		FA CUP		FL CUP		EUROPE		TOTAL	
	App	Gls	App	Gls	App	Gls	App	Gls	App	Gls
1973-74	13	7							13	7
1974-75	36	17	3		2	1			41	19
1975-76	31	12	1		4	1	2		38	13
1976-77	36	17	5	3	9	5			50	25
1977-78	39	30	2	1	5	1			46	32
1978-79	36	11	1		3	6	4	3	44	20
1979-80	26	6	5/1	5	2	2	0/1		33/2	13
1980-81	18/1	6			3	3			21/1	9
	235/1	106	17/1	10	28	19	6/1	3	286/3	138

A big, bustling centre-forward in the traditional mould, Bob Latchford was one of the finest goal-getters ever to play for Everton. He made his name with Birmingham City before joining Everton for £350,000 in 1974. Initial doubts about whether he had the speed to match his instinctive ability in front of goal were soon dispelled as he made the transition from raw material to finished product within the space of two seasons. His greatest asset was his uncanny knack of turning half-chances into goals. He was devastating in the penalty area, firing home literally dozens of goals from seemingly impossible angles. Although not a particularly tall man, he was dangerous in the air. Latchford was top League scorer in his first four full seasons with the club, reaching his peak in 1977 8 when he became the first Division One player for six years to reach the 30 goals mark. He entered the final game of that season, against Chelsea at home, needing two to claim a national newspaper prize of £10,000, and a double blast in a comprehensive victory was enough to snatch the money and carve for himself a place in Merseyside football folklore. After a glittering career in which he picked up 12 full England caps, he was transferred to Swansea City for £125,000 in July 1981. He left as Everton's highest post-war League goalscorer with 106 from 235 games. He enjoyed mixed fortunes at Vetch Field but still managed 32 goals in 1982-3. He was given a free transfer in January 1984 and joined Dutch club, Breda. Five months later he returned to England, signing for Coventry City. In July 1985 he signed for Lincoln City.

BOB LATCHFORD

	LEAGUE		FA CUP		TOTAL	
	App	Gls	App	Gls	App	Gls
1889-90	19	9	2		21	9
1890-91	10	4	1		11	4
1891-92	25	17	1		26	17
1892-93	28	18	7	1	35	19
1893-94	29	9	1		30	9
1894-95	20	11			20	11
1895-96	5	1			5	1
	136	69	12	1	148	70

Alex Latta was Everton's regular outside-right during their early days in the Football League, forming a much-feared partnership with inside-forward Alex Brady. Latta was born in Dumbarton in 1867 and played for Dumbarton Athletic before joining Everton in 1889. He made his debut against Blackburn Rovers on 7 September 1889. Latta, who was tall for a winger, won two Scotland caps, against England and Wales, and played for Everton in the 1893 FA Cup Final. Two years earlier he had been a member of the Championship-winning team. A tee-totaller, Latta left for Liverpool in 1896 and when he retired from football began a yacht-making business. Later he worked for 20 years as manager of a boatbuilding yard. He died in August 1928.

ALEX LATTA

DAVID LAWSON

TOMMY LAWTON

	LEAGUE		FA CUP		FL CUP		EUROPE		TOTAL	
	App	Gls	App	Gls	App	Gls	App	Gls	App	Gls
1972-73	38		2		1				41	
1973-74	42		3		2				47	
1974-75	7				2				9	
1975-76	22				3		1		26	
1976-77	15		7		5				27	
	124		12		13		1		150	

David Lawson became Britain's most expensive goalkeeper when he joined Everton from Huddersfield Town for £80,000 in June 1972. A quietly-spoken Geordie, he had a rather topsy-turvy career which saw him both as a disillusioned reserve rooted at the bottom of the Fourth Division, and a player tasting the big-time with the Goodison club. When he arrived at Everton he was involved in a straight dog-fight with Dai Davies for the goalkeeping jersey. His career got off to a stuttering start when he joined Newcastle United as an apprentice. He was allowed to leave and joined now extinct Bradford, but even at Park Avenue he could not be guaranteed a place. He had a spell with Shrewsbury and trials with various other clubs, including Liverpool, before ending up at Huddersfield in 1969. It was not until regular-choice Terry Poole broke a leg that he was given an extended first-team run. He made his Everton debut on the opening day of 1972-3 at Norwich. He played in every game the following season, but after seven matches in 1974-5 he lost his place through injury. He was a fine, brave last line of defence with a very safe pair of hands and good positional sense. He was transferred to Luton Town for £15,000 in October 1978.

	LEAGUE		FA CUP		TOTAL	
	App	Gls	App	Gls	App	Gls
1936-37	10	3	1	1	11	4
1937-38	39	28	2		41	28
1938-39	38	34	5	4	43	38
	87	65	8	5	95	70

Many critics would argue that Tommy Lawton was a better footballer than the legendary Dixie Dean, if not a better goalscorer. Certainly the youngster who went on to international fame with England was a superlative athlete who stood head and shoulders above his contemporaries in terms of skill and determination to succeed. When he was in full flow he was simply too hot to handle and in the days when sides played with only one central defender, Lawton often found himself shadowed by a posse of attendants, desperately anxious to cut short his famous surging runs before he reached the edge of the penalty area. Despite his flat feet (he was forced to wear arch-supports in his boots) he was brilliant on the ground, spraying passes around with astonishing ease. His heading ability was second to none; they used to say that if the ball was in the air he would inevitably connect with it. He was born in Bolton and in three seasons of schoolboy football scored a staggering total of 570 goals. It was Burnley who snapped him up and he played his first League game for them just four days after his 17th birthday. It was a prophetic debut, for the youngster scored a hat-trick. He cost Everton £6,500 in March 1937 and repaid them with 65 goals in 87 games. He topped the Football League scorers list in 1937-8 with 28 (jointly with Roberts of Port Vale) and again in 1938-9 (with Mickey Fenton of Middlesbrough). In November 1945, he joined Chelsea for £11,500, then Notts County (who paid a British record £20,000 for him), Brentford and Arsenal before becoming manager of Notts County, ending a career in which he had scored 231 goals in 390 League games, and 22 goals in 23 full England matches. Taking his wartime and Victory internationals into account, his England figures were 46 goals in 45 games. On one memorable day in 1940 he played in two matches for different clubs within the space of a few hours. In 1972 a testimonial game which raised £6,300 was held for him at Goodison Park between Everton and Great Britain XI.

CYRIL LELLO

	LEAGUE		FA CUP		TOTAL	
	App	Gls	App	Gls	App	Gls
1947-48	9	2			9	2
1948-49	20		1		21	
1949-50	35		2		37	
1951-52	21	1			21	1
1952-53	26		5		31	
1953-54	42	2	3		45	2
1954-55	42	2	2		44	2
1955-56	37	2	4		41	2
1956-57	5				5	
	237	9	17		254	9

Signed from Shrewsbury Town in September 1947, Cyril Lello stayed with Everton for over nine years, serving them as a hard-working right-half, although he began his Goodison career as an inside-forward. A native of Shropshire, Lello played wartime football with Lincoln City — in December 1943 he scored seven goals in a League North match against Notts County — before joining the Shrews. When Everton were relegated from Division One in 1950-51, Lello was injured and did not play a single game. But he was an ever-present when Everton won promotion in 1953-4, and again during their first season back in the First Division. In 1953 he was a member of the side which reached the semi-final of the FA Cup before losing to Bolton Wanderers. In November 1956, Harry Catterick, who had played with Lello in the immediate post-war era, signed him for Rochdale but he made only 11 League appearances there before ending his first-class career.

	LEAGUE		FA CUP		TOTAL	
	App	Gls	App	Gls	App	Gls
1950-51	4				4	
1951-52	40		2		42	
1952-53	30		5		35	
1953-54	31	2	3		34	2
	105	2	10		115	2

Cast in the studious mould, Jack Lindsay was a thoughtful player who had great craft in his play. One of only two Scottish-born players on Everton's books in 1951, he was signed from Glasgow Rangers for £7,000 by Cliff Britton who saw him as a solid and reliable full-back with a flair for the unorthodox. He proved to be a useful acquisition, shoring up a defence which at the time was far from water-tight. He remained Everton's first choice until he fractured a leg in 1954. Two years later he stunned the board by demanding a transfer after making 115 senior appearances. In May 1956 he moved to Bury along with teammate John Parker but after only one season at Gigg Lane he left to join South Liverpool as a part-time professional.

JACK LINDSAY

	LEAGUE		FA CUP		TOTAL	
	App	Gls	App	Gls	App	Gls
1921-22	24		1		25	
1922-23	8		2		10	
1923-24	38		2		40	
1924-25	20				20	
1925-26	5				5	
	95		5		100	

Regarded as a model professional, Duggie Livingstone was said to have a 'schoolgirl complexion' when he joined Everton from his native Scotland in 1921. A former Celtic player, he earned great praise in his formative years for his cool and calculated play at full-back although many felt him too slow to play the game at the highest level. He became totally disillusioned with the Goodison heirarchy towards the end of 1925 and eventually opted for a move, joining Plymouth Argyle in February 1926. Within four years he was back on Merseyside with Tranmere Rovers, with whom he stayed until 1935. After ending his playing career at Prenton Park, he was appointed trainer at Exeter City before he moved on to fill a similar post at Sheffield United. After spending the best part of a decade learning the ropes, he moved into management with Sheffield Wednesday. Eventually he left Hillsborough to try his luck on the continent where he coached Sparta of Holland before offering his services to the Belgium national side. On New Year's Day 1955 he moved into the hot-seat at St James' Park, Newcastle, and looked on in horror as United conceded four goals in only seven minutes against his old club, Sheffield United. But by the end of the season Newcastle had won the FA Cup. Livingstone left the North-East after a furious row with the United board who took away his powers of team selection early in 1956.

DUGGIE LIVINGSTONE

	LEAGUE		FA CUP		FL CUP		EUROPE		TOTAL	
	App	Gls	App	Gls	App	Gls	App	Gls	App	Gls
1970-71	1/1	1							1/1	1
1971-72	20/4	3	4						24/4	3
1972-73	19/6	2			1				20/6	2
1973-74	37/4	9	3		1				41/4	9
1974-75	36/2	8	4	3	2				42/2	11
1975-76	42	5	1		5	1	2		50	6
1976-77	39/1	4	7	1	9	2			55/1	7
1977-78	42	5	2	1	5	2			49	8
1978-79	37	6	1		2		3		43	6
1979-80	35/3		6		5		2		48/3	
1980-81	30/3	2	0/1	1					30/4	3
1981-82	26/1	3	1		4				31/1	3
	364/25	48	29/1	6	34	5	7		434/26	59

To many supporters the world over, Mick Lyons will always be 'Mr Everton'. He was a player who once admitted that he would readily run through a brick wall to further the Everton cause, but for the most part he contented himself with halting opposition forwards in their tracks. He was born in Croxteth and joined the club as a striker, playing in the forward role in both youth and Central League teams. He was demoted to the 'A' team when David Johnson emerged from the shadows and it was during this period that Tommy Casey switched him to centre-back. He made his first-team debut in 1970-1 and went on to build a brilliant career which encompassed more than 450 senior appearances. He lost his regular place at the age of 30, early in 1982 when Billy Wright was brought into Howard Kendall's constantly-changing side to partner Mark Higgins. After waiting patiently for a recall which was never to come, he severed his ties with the club in August 1982, joining Sheffield Wednesday who he helped to steer into the First Division. Sadly, Lyons, who dedicated the best years of his life to a club he dearly loved, won nothing during his time at Goodison Park.

MICK LYONS

	LEAGUE		FA CUP		TOTAL	
	App	Gls	App	Gls	App	Gls
1922-23	15				15	
1923-24	37		2		39	
1924-25	35		4		39	
1925-26	10	1			10	1
	97	1	6		103	1

Neil McBain is the oldest player ever to appear in a Football League match. In March 1947, when he was manager of New Brighton, he found himself one player short — a goalkeeper — for a Third Division North match at Hartlepool. At the age of 52 years and four months he boldly placed himself between the posts and, for the record, Hartlepools won 3-0. He signed for Everton in early 1923 from Manchester United, a transfer which caused uproar at Old Trafford. When the deal was announced, more than a thousand supporters packed into a local hall to protest about his impending departure. McBain was a useful wing-half whose greatest strength was his heading ability. He was an elegant player, perhaps too elegant for his own good at times. He often forsook his defensive duties in favour of an over-adventurous approach. In a long and varied career he also played for Liverpool, St Johnstone and Watford. After hanging up his boots he turned to management with Watford, New Brighton, Luton and Leyton Orient. He was a full Scottish international, making three appearances between 1922 and 1924. After becoming disenchanted with the English game, he went to South America to coach the Argentinian club, Estudiantes de la Plata. He died, aged 78, in May 1974.

NEIL McBAIN

JOHN McDONALD

	LEAGUE		FA CUP		TOTAL	
	App	Gls	App	Gls	App	Gls
1920-21	39		5		44	
1921-22	26		1		27	
1922-23	29				29	
1923-24	24		2		26	
1924-25	29		4		33	
1925-26	37		2		39	
1926-27	24		2		26	
	208		16		224	

Everton signed full-back John McDonald from Airdrie in 1920 and he went straight into the League side for the start of 1920-21, making his debut in the 3-3 draw at Bradford Park Avenue on 28 August. McDonald missed only three games that season and in August 1921 he was appointed club captain. His inspiration was vital that season as Everton struggled against relegation, and although he missed some games through injury, he was a telling influence in the dressing room. A native of Dykehead, McDonald had appeared in Scottish representative football during World War One, but his move to Everton did not coincide with one of the more successful periods in the club's history. By the time the League Championship next came to Goodison Park (1927-8), McDonald was playing Third Division North football with New Brighton, for whom he signed in August 1927. He went on to give them several years valuable service.

	LEAGUE		FA CUP		FL CUP		TOTAL	
	App	Gls	App	Gls	App	Gls	App	Gls
1976-77	20	5	6	4	4	1	30	10
1977-78	28	9	1/1	1	2	1	31/1	11
	48	14	7/1	5	6	2	61/1	21

Duncan McKenzie was one of football's great enigmas. A player of unquestionable brilliance, he turned into a sporting nomad, constantly moving from club to club in a forlorn bid to find the right stage for his stunning skills. A tremendous showman, at one stage he seemed to spend more time amusing supporters by jumping over cars than actually playing football. A slight, wiry man, he was one of the game's most dazzling dribblers, the sort of player who could comfortably glide around four opponents in the space of ten yards. He started his career with Nottingham Forest and was loaned to Mansfield before moving to Leeds United where he witnessed first hand the sensational coming and going of Brian Clough. After a turbulent period at Elland Road he quit English football for the continent, joining Anderlecht. After only 30 games — and 16 goals — for the Belgian side, he was signed by Goodison boss Billy Bingham in December 1976. Shortly after his £200,000 signing, Bingham was sacked and replaced by Gordon Lee. McKenzie and Lee never got on and eventually the player left. He later played with Chelsea and Blackburn, and with Tulsa Roughnecks and Chicago Sting in the NASL. He returned to live on Merseyside and is often to be found proffering his expert opinion in the Goodison press box.

DUNCAN McKENZIE

	LEAGUE		FA CUP		FL CUP		TOTAL	
	App	Gls	App	Gls	App	Gls	App	Gls
1980-81	34	5	5		3		42	5
1981-82	31/1	2			4	2	35/1	4
1982-83	34	4	4		4	1	42	5
	99/1	11	9		11	3	119/1	14

Steve McMahon's burning desire to win trophies forced him to quit Goodison Park just months before Howard Kendall steered Everton back on the glory trail. A former Goodison ball-boy, he joined Everton as an apprentice in December 1977. He made his first-team debut at Sunderland in August 1980, and the following season was voted Player of the Year by supporters who appreciated his honest endeavour and total commitment. A bright future seemed assured when he was picked to play for the England Under-21 side against the Republic of Ireland. He continued to perform at a consistently high level even though he was not playing in a particularly good side. Eventually he came to the conclusion that the only way to further his career was to move away from the club he had always supported. His contract expired at the end of 1982-3 and he refused to sign another, even though manager Howard Kendall was adamant that he wanted McMahon to stay. Liverpool made a firm offer for him, but after discussions with his family he opted for a move to Aston Villa for £250,000 in May 1983. Ironically, less than 12 months later, Everton defeated Villa to reach the Milk Cup Final.

STEVE McMAHON

	LEAGUE		FA CUP		FL CUP		TOTAL	
	App	Gls	App	Gls	App	Gls	App	Gls
1974-75	4		3				7	
1975-76	18/2				1		19/2	
1976-77	42	3	7		9		58	3
	64/2	3	10		10		84/2	3

A tall, blond centre-half, Ken McNaught joined Everton as a 16-year-old apprentice before signing full professional forms in 1972. His greatest asset was his powerful heading which proved immensely valuable in both defence and up front. A tough, rugged Scot, he had set his heart on making the grade as a striker before the timely intervention of his father, Willie, a former Scottish international who played with Raith Rovers. He was persuaded to drop back and he made an immediate impression, being selected for the Scotland amateur youth side. The scouts were soon showing interest and McNaught decided to move to Goodison only after completing his school studies which yielded seven 'O' levels. He moved out of the 'A' team and into the reserves at the end of his first season in 1971 and made his big breakthrough in 1975. In 1976-7 he was Everton's only ever-present, appearing in all 58 League and Cup games, but less than three months later he was on his way to Aston Villa for £200,000.

KEN McNAUGHT

	LEAGUE		FA CUP		TOTAL	
	App	Gls	App	Gls	App	Gls
1907-08	21				21	
1908-09	38		2		40	
1909-10	31		7		38	
1910-11	22		2		24	
1911-12	31		5	1	36	1
1912-13	23	4	5		28	4
1913-14	35		1		36	
1914-15	28		3		31	
1919-20	16	2			16	2
	245	6	25	1	270	7

John Smith Maconnachie was a Scottish left-back, cool and polished, who joined Everton in April 1907 from Hibernian. Aberdeen-born Maconnachie made his Everton debut at centre-half, playing in the third game of 1907-08 against Preston North End at Goodison Park. Slowly he established himself in the side, settling down at left-back for the last few games of that season. The following year, as Everton pushed for the League Championship before settling for runners-up spot, Maconnachie was an ever-present and he played regularly until the outbreak of war eventually ended League soccer for the duration. Everton fans appreciated his cool, authoritative approach to the game and he seldom seemed ruffled, often playing his way out of tight situations in his own penalty area. In 1919-20 he completed 270 League and Cup appearances for Everton and then signed for Swindon Town at the start of the following season. He was one of the more skilful defenders to wear Everton's colours in an era when a full-back's main function was to punt the ball downfield as far as possible with little regard for its eventual destination. Maconnachie of Everton was too much of a footballer to settle for that.

JOHN MACONNACHIE

	LEAGUE		FA CUP		TOTAL	
	App	Gls	App	Gls	App	Gls
1902-03	3		1		4	
1904-05	19	5	6	2	25	7
1905-06	27	2	6	2	33	4
1906-07	23		8		31	
1907-08	31	2	7		38	2
1908-09	33		2		35	
1909-10	32	4	7	2	39	6
1910-11	33	1	3		36	1
1911-12	34	1	5	1	39	2
1912-13	10		1		11	
1913-14	16		1		17	
1914-15	23	1	5		28	1
	284	16	52	7	336	23

Harry Makepeace was a rare sporting talent. He represented England at both football and cricket — a distinction he shared with his Everton and Lancashire colleague, Jack Sharp. Although practically all his sporting life was spent west of the Pennines, he was born in Middlesbrough, moving to Liverpool when he was ten. He developed his cricketing ability with great success while playing with such sides as Clubmoor and Wavertree, but his football distinction came first. He signed for Everton in 1902 and made his debut in an FA Cup-tie against Manchester United in February 1903. He began life as a forward but was quickly switched to the half-back line where his fearsome tackling and excellent distribution were better employed. He was a regular member of the side between 1904 and 1914 and played in the FA Cup-winning team of 1906 and again in the 1907 Final. He was chosen as England's left-half against Scotland on three occasions (1906, 1910 and 1912) and against Wales (1912). He also played for the Football League in 1910. He was a quietly spoken and thoughtful man whose behaviour was exemplary both on and off the field. His connection with Everton resumed after World War One when he was appointed coach. Twelve years later he held a similar position with Crosby amateur side, Marine. An opening batsman, he played in four Tests, all of them abroad, and scored 117 in the 1920-21 Melbourne Test. He died, aged 70, at Bebington in December 1952.

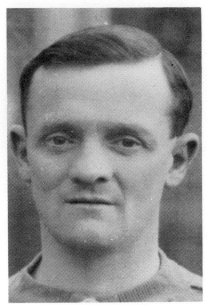

HARRY MAKEPEACE

GEORGE MARTIN

	LEAGUE		FA CUP		TOTAL	
	App	Gls	App	Gls	App	Gls
1927-28	10	3			10	3
1928-29	18	6			18	6
1929-30	40	15	1	1	41	16
1930-31	15	7			15	7
1931-32	2				2	
	85	31	1	1	86	32

George Martin was a man of many talents, not least of which was his considerable ability as a sharp-shooting inside-forward. A native of Lanarkshire, he spent a time with Bo'ness before joining Hull City in October 1922. Hull were later fined £50 for conducting the transfer incorrectly. He was fast, powerful and versatile, filling no fewer than five different positions during his time with the Yorkshire club. He was transferred to Everton in March 1928. Towards the end of 1927-8 he played several times alongside the legendary Dixie Dean as the great man completed his historic 60 League goals in a season. Martin enjoyed a spell at Middlesbrough before moving to Luton Town in 1933 where he spent the remainder of his playing days. At the end of the war he took over as manager. In 1947 he moved to Newcastle United as manager where he received wholesale criticism during his first year in office. Nevertheless his organising ability and sharp football brain helped take United from Second Division anonymity to fourth place in Division One within two seasons. He was a talented sculptor and a fine singer, making several records during the early '40s.

	LEAGUE		FA CUP		FL CUP		EUROPE		TOTAL	
	App	Gls	App	Gls	App	Gls	App	Gls	App	Gls
1957-58	38	1	3						41	1
1958-59	21								21	
1959-60	19								19	
1960-61	11								11	
1961-62	18								18	
1962-63	32		3				1		36	
1963-64	26		4						30	
	165	1	10	0	0	1			176	1

MICK MEAGAN

Born in Dublin on 19 May 1934, Mick 'Chick' Meagan began his career with Eire junior clubs, Rathfarnham and Johnville. A versatile competitor who firmly believed that no game was won or lost until the final whistle, he signed for Everton in September 1952. He turned full-time professional 18 months later and his League debut came in August 1957 against Wolves at Goodison. He went on to make 175 appearances for the club before he was effectively used as bait to lure Ray Wilson to Merseyside. The deal was struck in July 1964 with Meagan joining Huddersfield Town and Wilson coming in the other direction with a cash adjustment. He continued to play for Eire and was made captain of Huddersfield. He was transferred to Halifax Town in 1968, given a three-year contract and made skipper at The Shay.

Everton 1956-7. Back (l to r): Moore, Lello, Tansey, Donovan, O'Neill, Jones, Payne, Rea. Front: Fielding, B.Harris, J.Harris, Farrell, Mayers, Eglington, Meagan.

338

JOE MERCER

	LEAGUE		FA CUP		TOTAL	
	App	Gls	App	Gls	App	Gls
1932-33	1				1	
1934-35	8				8	
1935-36	33	1	1		34	1
1936-37	39		4		43	
1937-38	36		2		38	
1938-39	41		5		46	
1945-46			2	1	2	1
1946-47	12				12	
	170	1	14	1	184	2

One of the European game's all-time greats, Joe Mercer had a superb tactical brain and outstanding ability. He started as a junior with Everton in September 1932 and forced himself into the first team on a regular basis in 1935 when he took over in the half-back line from Jock Thomson. Developing quickly, he became England's left-half. The war came and went and Sergeant-Major Mercer, captain of his country and his appetite whetted by recent events, returned to Goodison, having won 26 wartime caps. But Everton had both a captain and a manager and Mercer became disconolate. It was the low-point of his career. For a fortnight after returning he rarely left his house. Mighty Arsenal heard about his disenchantment and had his signature on a transfer form within 24 hours, for £7,000. He captained the Gunners from his second season at Highbury onwards and won a League Championship medal in 1948 and an FA Cup winners' medal in 1950. Arsenal narrowly missed the double, in 1952, and then topped the League once more in 1953. During this time he continued to live on Merseyside, training at Anfield. That he was captain of the side that beat Liverpool at Wembley in 1950 was rather embarrassing; that he should sustain the double fracture of a leg (which ended his playing days) against them four years later was tragic. He stepped into management, serving a brief apprenticeship at money-concious Sheffield United before moving to Villa Park as manager, coach, chief scout and money-raiser. Villa won the Second Division Championship, reached the FA Cup semi-finals twice, won the League Cup, built a £120,000 stand and finished halfway up the First Division before Mercer's health gave way. In 1965 he came out of what many had assumed was permanent retirement to take charge of Manchester City. Together with a bright young man called Malcolm Allison he restored pride to a great club. In 1977 he took temporary charge of the England team after the resignation of Don Revie. He became a director of Coventry City but resigned in 1981 after nine years. Today, Joe Mercer still lives on his beloved Merseyside, and is as irrepressible as ever.

Everton's best start to a season came in 1978-9 when they were unbeaten in their first 19 League games (11 wins and eight draws).

As 1984-5 Canon League Champions, Everton collected a £50,000 prize. With 88 goals they also claimed a further £8,500 as leading scorers in Division One.

When Everton first won the League Championship, in 1890-91, they used 20 players in 22 matches. Only three players appeared in every game. Their 1984-5 success saw the Blues use 25 players in 42 matches, of whom only Neville Southall was ever-present.

	LEAGUE		FA CUP		TOTAL	
	App	Gls	App	Gls	App	Gls
1935-36	15	1	1		16	1
1936-37	1	1			1	1
	16	2	1		17	2

Everton had high hopes of landing a major find when they brought Willie Miller from Partick Thistle in 1935. Miller had made 38 appearances for Partick in the Scottish League the previous season and he went straight into the Everton team for the opening day of the 1935-6 campaign and helped his new club to score a resounding 4-0 success over Derby County. But Miller's personal fortunes at Goodison were not so happy. It was surprising that he never settled there, because he was an exciting inside-right who had plenty of dash and good close control. His spirited runs straight at the heart of a defence had been a feature of the Scottish game. In 1935 he had played for the Scottish League against the Football League, and that summer he had gone to the USA and Canada with the Scotland team. He played in six of the 12 games on that tour, but none of them counted as full internationals and he was never capped. He managed one goal for Everton, in the 5-1 thrashing of Chelsea in October 1935, then lost his place. After one game the following season he signed for Burnley in October 1936. He was a potentially brilliant player whose star flashed all too briefly across the Goodison sky.

WILLIE MILLER

	LEAGUE		FA CUP		TOTAL	
	App	Gls	App	Gls	App	Gls
1888-89	6	2			6	2
1889-90	22	10	2	4	24	14
1890-91	22	12	1		23	12
1891-92	26	6	1		27	6
1892-93	27	11	7	2	34	13
1893-94	24	8	1		25	8
1894-95	18	10	3		21	10
1895-96	29	17	3	2	32	19
1896-97	27	9	5	3	32	12
	201	85	23	11	224	96

Alfred Milward was one of five Everton players to line up for England against Scotland at Blackburn in 1891. He was a hard-working outside-left with a superior technical brain and tremendous vision. Although his angled crossfield passes were an integral part of his game, he was at his very best when rampaging down the flanks, leaving confused defenders trailing in his wake. Born at Great Marlow, he joined Everton in 1888 from Old Borlasians, and Marlow, and quickly established himself as a first-team regular. Perhaps his greatest attribute was that he never surrendered. Indeed, he lost his temper on more than one occasion with teammates who had opted to accept defeat long before the final whistle. He performed with great consistency for Everton between 1888 and 1897 and was rewarded with four full England caps. Both he and Edgar Chadwick were great players, but together they were devastating and it was their left-wing partnership for Everton that shattered many a defence. Milward joined New Brighton Tower in the close season of 1897, moved to Southampton two years later and finished his career with New Brompton (later Gillingham) before retiring in 1903.

ALFRED MILWARD

	LEAGUE		FA CUP		TOTAL	
	App	Gls	App	Gls	App	Gls
1949-50	22		5		27	
1950-51	37		1		38	
1951-52	5				5	
1952-53	14				14	
1953-54	9		1		10	
1954-55	41		2		43	
1955-56	42		4		46	
1956-57	1				1	
	171		13		184	

A product of Haydock, Eric Moore had his fair share of ups and downs during his eight years at Goodison Park. After a solid start in the Central League side, in which he figured at both centre-forward and right-half, he was transformed into a full-back, signing professional forms in February 1949. He made his first-team debut in December that year at right-back. From that point he was a regular for the best of part of 18 months but a troublesome knee injury sidelined him for long spells during the following two seasons. When he was fully fit again he missed only one game in two seasons, but in December 1956, unhappy at making only one First Division appearance that season, he asked for a transfer. He moved to Chesterfield in a deal worth £10,000 in January 1957, after nearly 200 outings for Everton. In July 1957 he was signed by Tranmere Rovers. Later he became a publican in Atherton.

ERIC MOORE

	LEAGUE		FA CUP		FL CUP		EUROPE		TOTAL	
	App	Gls	App	Gls	App	Gls	App	Gls	App	Gls
1962-63	28	7	3	1			2		33	8
1963-64	7	1							7	1
1964-65	25	5	4				4	1	33	6
1965-66	10/1	2	1				3		14/1	2
1966-67	31	6	6				3	1	40	7
1967-68	26	3	5	2	1				32	5
1968-69	40	4	5		4	1			49	5
1969-70	41	9	1		3				45	9
1970-71	34	6	4				6	1	44	7
1971-72	15/1								15/1	
	257/2	43	29	3	8	1	18	3	312/2	50

Johnny Morrissey was the man who guaranteed Everton's place in the 1968 FA Cup Final with a dramatic penalty winner against high-fliers Leeds United at Old Trafford. The tenacious and gutsy winger hammered the spot-kick beyond Gary Sprake to set up a Wembley showdown with West Bromwich Albion, a match Everton were to lose 1-0. Regarded as the 'pocket Hercules' of a side which won national acclaim for its cultured football, Morrissey arrived at Goodison from neighbours Liverpool for the bargain fee of £10,000 in 1962. His competitive style and fearsome shooting quickly saw him rise through the oft-crowded ranks and claim a regular first-team spot. He was instrumental in Everton's League Championship triumph in 1970 but shortly afterwards found his place threatened. He was transferred to Oldham Athletic in the summer of 1972 but was forced to retire from the game six months later because of injury.

JOHN MORRISSEY

	LEGUE		FA CUP		FL CUP		EUROPE		TOTAL	
	App	Gls	App	Gls	App	Gls	App	Gls	App	Gls
1982-83	1								1	
1983-84	31	3	8		8				47	3
1984-85	37	10	7	2	4	2	9		57	14
	69	13	15	2	12	2	9		105	17

A Merseyside-grown talent, Derek Mountfield arrived at
Goodison Park from Fourth Division Tranmere Rovers for
£30,000 in June 1982. As a schoolboy he used to stand on the
Goodison terraces and dream of emulating his sporting
heroes by one day playing for the club he has always
supported. A fine athlete with good pace and vision, his
greatest asset is his considerable heading ability which has
frustrated quality strikers the length and breadth of the
country since he made the number-five shirt his own. He
made his League debut against Birmingham City at St
Andrew's on 23 April 1983 and was given an unexpected
chance to press for a regular place when centre-back Mark
Higgins suffered the first of a series of cruel injuries which
ultimately led to his premature retirement. He grabbed his
golden opportunity with both hands and proved to be mature
beyond his years as the Everton revival got underway. An
added bonus during the magnificent 1984-5 season were the
goals he scored — 14, including the last-gasp equaliser
against Ipswich Town in the FA Cup quarter-final tie at
Goodison Park.

DEREK MOUNTFIELD

HENRY NEWTON

	LEAGUE		FA CUP		FL CUP		TOTAL	
	App	Gls	App	Gls	App	Gls	App	Gls
1970-71	23	3	4	1			27	4
1971-72	24	1	2				26	1
1972-73	23	1			1		24	1
1973-74	6						6	
	76	5	6	1	1		83	6

Henry Newton arrived at Goodison Park in October 1970
after doing what few players of the day had the courage to do
— turn down the ever-persuasive Brian Clough. As skipper of
Nottingham Forest, Newton had been pursued for the best
part of 18 months by then Derby County manager Clough,
but when he finally decided to quit the City Ground, he
surprisingly accepted the terms offered by Harry Catterick.
Everton paid £150,000, plus Irish international Tommy
Jackson, for his services, looking at Newton as a long-term
investment. Sadly, after making his debut in the nightmare 4-0
defeat at Highbury, his career was handicapped by a series
of long-term injuries. In three years with the club he played
only 83 League and Cup games, and would be the first to
admit that he never settled on Merseyside. Despite his
problems he proved an effective defender (he started as a
midfielder but switched to left-back when Keith Newton was
injured) when playing at his peak. In September 1973, Clough
at last got his man when Newton jumped at the chance to
return to the Midlands for £110,000.

KEITH NEWTON

	LEAGUE		FA CUP		FL CUP		EUROPE		TOTAL	
	App	Gls	App	Gls	App	Gls	App	Gls	App	Gls
1969-70	12		1						13	
1970-71	21/1	1	1				6		28/1	1
1971-72	15				1				16	
	48/1	1	2		1		6		57/1	1

Although Keith Newton was to spend only two and a half years at Everton, he will always be remembered as a fine, attacking full-back. He arrived at Goodison Park in December 1969 from Blackburn Rovers in a deal worth £80,000. After laying the foundations for what everyone presumed would be a lengthy and illustrious career, he was selected to play for England in the 1970 World Cup Finals in Mexico, along with teammate Tommy Wright. On his return, his career took a down-turn and he lost his place in the Everton team after 14 games of 1971-2, after a series of uncharacteristically poor performances. In June 1972 he was transferred to Burnley where he played a leading role in the Turf Moor club's promotion from the Second Division in 1972-3. After his departure, he attacked Harry Catterick in the press, claiming that his creative style and determination to play his way out of trouble led to friction. Newton made 27 appearances in the full England side.

	LEAGUE		FA CUP		FL CUP		EUROPE		TOTAL	
	App	Gls	App	Gls	App	Gls	App	Gls	App	Gls
1978-79	13/4	1			2		2/1		17/5	1
1979-80	9/1	1			4		2		15/1	1
	22/5	2			6		4/1		32/6	2

In March 1980 Geoff Nulty was stretchered away from a derby match against Liverpool at Goodison Park and out of football for good. A tackle by Jimmy Case caused extensive damage to the polished defender's left knee and he was told immediately that he would never play again. It was a shattering blow to a player who had worked so hard to prove his worth after a £40,000 move from Newcastle less than two years earlier. While he could never be described as world-beater, Nulty was a dedicated professional with a no-nonsense approach to the defensive arts. He was firm in the tackle and more than capable of delivering a telling pass when given the space. He made less than 40 appearances for Everton, and was approaching the 250-mark in his career when tragedy struck. As the holder of an Open University degree in social sciences he was better prepared than most players to face a life without football. In fact he stayed in the game and took a coaching job at Goodison under Gordon Lee, later following Lee to Preston. In February 1984 he announced that he was suing both Liverpool and Jimmy Case for substantial damages. In 1985 the case was still pending.

GEOFF NULTY

	LEAGUE		FA CUP		TOTAL	
	App	Gls	App	Gls	App	Gls
1950-51	10				10	
1951-52	20				20	
1952-53	35		5		40	
1953-54	28		3		31	
1954-55	41		2		43	
1955-56	34		2		36	
1956-57	13				13	
1957-58	6				6	
1958-59	9				9	
1959-60	5				5	
	201		12		213	

Goalkeeper Jimmy O'Neill's father was a leading golf professional in the '30s. Born in Dublin, Jimmy was spotted by an Everton scout while playing in local junior circles and invited to Goodison Park for a trial period. He was taken on at the end of 1948-9 and offered full professional terms. He made his debut in the Central League on 24 August 1949, and 364 days later made his full debut in a defeat at Middlesbrough. He enjoyed a successful career, becoming one of Britain's outstanding goalkeepers, forcing his way into the Eire side to win 17 caps. He was exceptionally safe when handling crosses and he utilised his speed well. Indeed, he was often seen halting opposing forwards in their tracks on the edge of the penalty area. He eventually lost his Everton place to Albert Dunlop. He was transferred to Stoke City for £5,000 in July 1960, before joining Darlington in March 1965. Later he played with Port Vale.

JIMMY O'NEILL

	LEAGUE		FA CUP		FL CUP		EUROPE		TOTAL	
	App	Gls	App	Gls	App	Gls	App	Gls	App	Gls
1958-59	26	1	4						30	1
1959-60	38	2	1						39	2
1960-61	41		1		5				47	
1961-62	31		3						34	
1962-63	33	2	3				2		38	2
1963-64	17						2		19	
1964-65	12								12	
	198	5	12		5		4		219	5

Alex Parker was a full-back in the classic mould. Fast, adventurous and very strong in the tackle, he became the latest in a long line of superb Everton defenders when he joined the club from Falkirk in 1958. Born in Irvine, Ayrshire, he began his career as a centre-forward but was switched to wing-half after joining Scottish junior club Kelso Rovers. Shortly after completing his move to Goodison he was posted to Cyprus with the Royal Scots Fusiliers, delaying his Everton debut until 8 November 1958. He won the first of 15 full international caps against Portugal in May 1955. He left Everton in September 1965 to join Southport where he finished his playing career. In 1968 he was released by the Haig Avenue club to become player-manager of Irish League side, Ballymena United. He returned to Southport in May 1970 to take over as manager.

ALEX PARKER

JOHN WILLIE PARKER

	LEAGUE		FA CUP		TOTAL	
	App	Gls	App	Gls	App	Gls
1950-51	7				7	
1951-52	36	15	2	1	38	16
1952-53	32	13	4	4	36	17
1953-54	38	31	3	2	41	33
1954-55	34	19			34	19
1955-56	20	4			20	4
	167	82	9	7	176	89

John Willie Parker spent more than four years in the shadows before establishing himself in the Everton side in the early '50s. He was a tall, stylish inside-forward with two good feet and the ability to score as well as make goals. He arrived as an amateur in 1947, from St Lawrence CYMS, and quickly graduated through the junior sides, signing professional forms in December 1948. Within 18 months he was a regular in the Central League side but he did not make his full debut until 24 March 1951 when he filled the outside-left berth against Blackpool at Goodison. He was a very deceptive player who was often criticised for being too casual in his approach to the game. He had his faults but was widely regarded as one of the more cultured performers of the day. He appeared in 176 League and Cup matches, scoring a highly creditable 89 goals before signing for Bury in May 1956.

	LEAGUE		FA CUP		TOTAL	
	App	Gls	App	Gls	App	Gls
1913-14	24	17	1		25	17
1914-15	35	36	5	2	40	38
1919-20	8	4			8	4
1920-21	17	11	2	1	19	12
	84	68	8	3	92	71

When Bobby Parker signed from Glasgow Rangers in November 1913, he immediately solved the Everton goalscoring problem, hammering 17 goals in 24 League games after Everton had sold Tommy Browell to Manchester City for £1,450. The next season Parker did even better. Equalling Freeman's Everton record of six years earlier, his 36 goals in 35 games established him as the First Division's leading scorer and, more importantly, helped Everton to take the League Championship. His goals were scored out of an Everton total of 76 for that season, and, like Freeman's, they came under the old offside law which was more restrictive, needing three players goalside of the attacker rather than two. It was said of Parker that he was 'a dandy of a player who likes to score them in twos and threes'. He moved to Nottingham Forest in May 1921.

BOBBY PARKER

	LEAGUE		FA CUP		TOTAL	
	App	Gls	App	Gls	App	Gls
1889-90	22	4	2		24	4
1890-91	13		1		14	
1891-92	1				1	
1892-93	10				10	
1893-94	11		1		12	
1894-95	27	1	4		31	1
1895-96	2				2	
	86	5	8		94	5

Welsh international Charlie Parry started his Everton career as a wing-half and finished it as a full-back. He signed from Welsh junior football in 1889 and made his debut on the opening day of the League's second season, scoring in Everton's home 3-2 win over Blackburn Rovers. Parry was a regular that season, but his appearances dwindled until he forced his way back into the League side at left-back. He was competent in all the defender's arts, having a sure kick with either foot, a fair turn of speed, a bone-crunching tackle and the ability to get high above the heads of opposing forwards when the ball came over from the wing. His positional sense was sound and one contemporary writer praised his ability to be up with his forwards one minute, and back helping out in defence the next. He made his Welsh international debut in 1891, at left-half against England, and won six caps while with Everton, and another seven after he left. He gained particular praise in 1894 game against England at the Queen's Club in London. The Welsh managed a 1-1 draw and Parry kept the English star forwards, Smith and Gosling, at bay with a sterling performance.

CHARLIE PARRY

	LEAGUE		FA CUP		TOTAL	
	App	Gls	App	Gls	App	Gls
1919-20	9	2			9	2
1920-21	28	3	2		30	3
1921-22	29	1	1		30	1
1922-23	39	4	2		41	4
1923-24	8	1	1		9	1
1924-25	17		1		18	
1925-26	18	1	2		20	1
1926-27	3		1		4	
	151	12	10		161	12

JOE PEACOCK

Born in Wigan in 1900, Joe Peacock joined Everton from Atherton in the close season of 1919 and proved an important part of the club's plans as they rebuilt after the war. After a couple of outings at right-half he was given the centre-forward berth and in his second match in that role, he scored a goal which helped Everton beat Sheffield United — their first home victory for two months. Peacock also played at inside-forward, but it was as a wing-half that he settled down and found international honours. They came after he had moved to Middlesbrough in 1927. He played in Boro's Second Division Championship side of 1928-9. In the summer of 1929 Peacock joined the England team which toured the continent. The former Everton man won his three caps against France, Belgium and Spain. Later he played with Sheffield Wednesday and Clapton Orient. From March 1933 he coached in Sweden and in July 1939 was appointed Wrexham trainer.

JIM PEARSON

	LEAGUE		FA CUP		FL CUP		EUROPE		TOTAL	
	App	Gls	App	Gls	App	Gls	App	Gls	App	Gls
1974-75	17/9	3	4	1	0/1				21/10	4
1975-76	26/3	5	1		5		2		34/3	5
1976-77	12/4	4	3	1	1/1				16/5	5
1977-78	21/1	3	1		4	2			26/1	5
	76/17	15	9	2	10/2	2	2		97/19	19

Jim Pearson was a highly-talented striker who never really settled at Goodison Park. Capable of moments of genuine brilliance he too often allowed his fiery Scottish temperament to disrupt both his form and his concentration. He arrived from St Johnstone in a £100,000 deal in July 1974 after scoring 39 goals in 96 League appearances north of the border. A Scottish Youth and Schoolboy international, he played for the Under-23 side against Wales and England in 1973-4 and was substitute for the Scottish League against the Football League the same season. He was brought to Goodison to score goals but they dried up whenever he was given an extended run in the first-team, and just three years after his arrival he was on the transfer list. Gordon Lee sold him to Newcastle United in August 1978 for £70,000. Pearson, who played in 93 League games for Everton, scoring 15 goals, made an immediate impact at St James' Park before losing his place through injury.

	LEAGUE		FA CUP		FL CUP		EUROPE		TOTAL	
	App	Gls	App	Gls	App	Gls	App	Gls	App	Gls
1976-77	17	1	4						21	1
1977-78	40	1	2		4				46	1
1978-79	19				3		4		26	
	76	2	6		7		4		93	2

Mike Pejic was regarded as the last piece in Gordon Lee's jigsaw as he fought to stave off relegation. Pejic joined Everton in February 1977 for £150,000 and took to Goodison arguably the fiercest tackle ever seen there. Pejic won a host of admirers with his rugged style and adventurous forward thrusts. Like so many of his contemporaries he was dogged by injury and was eventually forced to quit the game after losing a prolonged battle to overcome a severe pelvic disorder. The tragedy that ended in premature retirement in March 1981, started in December 1978 when he was very much in his prime and rightly rated as the finest English left-back in the game. He broke down in agony during a match at Leeds and never played for Everton in a League match again. Even though he returned to full match fitness and successfully completed a close-season tour of Egypt, the Goodison picture was changing. John Bailey had forced his way on to the scene and Pejic was on his way to Aston Villa for £250,000.

MIKE PEJIC

	LEAGUE		FA CUP		FL CUP		EUROPE		TOTAL	
	App	Gls	App	Gls	App	Gls	App	Gls	App	Gls
1963-64	9	9							9	9
1964-65	41	27	4	4			6	6	51	37
1965-66	39	18	5	4			3		47	22
1966-67	8	2							8	2
	97	56	9	8	0	0	9	6	115	70

Fred Pickering was one of Everton's finest post-war strikers. After beginning his turbulent career as a full-back with Blackburn Rovers he made the transition to front-runner in the early '60s before joining Everton for £85,000 in 1964. He soon demonstrated his immense power and pace. He was quickly blooded in the first team and went on to fulfil his rich promise with 56 goals in only 97 League games. He had a memorable international debut when he lined up against the USA in New York in 1964 and scored a hat-trick in the 10-0 win. He picked up two more caps, against Northern Ireland and Belgium, the same year. In 1966 many considered him unlucky to miss the FA Cup Final meeting with Sheffield Wednesday. He was transferred to Birmingham City for £50,000 in August 1967 and moved to Blackpool two years later for £45,000. In March 1971 he returned to his old hunting ground, Ewood Park, but left the club 11 months later after a series of rows with manager Ken Furphy.

FRED PICKERING

	LEAGUE		FA CUP		TOTAL	
	App	Gls	App	Gls	App	Gls
1922-23	36		2		38	
1923-24	19				19	
1924-25	20		4		24	
1925-26	30		2		32	
1926-27	11		1		12	
1927-28	6				6	
	122		9		131	

Dundee discovered full-back David Raitt playing army football during World War One. Born at Buckhaven, Fife, he was not quite the build one expected in a full-back during an era when the ability to knock an opponent off the ball was as important as tackling ability and positional sense. Raitt stood barely 5ft 9ins tall and weighed around 11st. He played Scottish League football with Dundee from 1919 until he signed for Everton in May 1922. Raitt came to Goodison at a particularly dismal time for the club who had struggled all season to avoid relegation while, across Stanley Park, Liverpool were celebrating their League Championship success. Raitt won an immediate place in a shaky Everton defence and his presence helped the club's rapid improvement to fifth place in his first season. Then Duggie Livingstone won a regular place at left-back, with McDonald switching flanks, so Raitt's chances were restricted. He fought to win back his place, only to find that Warney Cresswell had arrived at Goodison. It was clear that Cresswell was going to be a First Division star. Raitt managed only six games in the Championship season of 1927-8 and before the start of the next campaign he was a Blackburn Rovers player.

DAVID RAITT

ANDY RANKIN

	LEAGUE		FA CUP		FL CUP		EUROPE		TOTAL	
	App	Gls	App	Gls	App	Gls	App	Gls	App	Gls
1963-64	20		2						22	
1964-65	22						4		26	
1965-66	9						2/1		11/1	
1966-67	6		1						7	
1970-71	28		4				5		37	
	85		7		0	0	11/1		103/1	

Andy Rankin was a technically superb goalkeeper who was sadly plagued by misfortune and injury at crucial times during his 10 years with Everton. He was on the verge of quitting football for the police force when Harry Catterick took over at Goodison Park. After being gently persuaded to continue he was rewarded with his first-team chance at Nottingham Forest on 16 November 1963 when Gordon West was dropped. Despite his obvious talent he was never able to lay claim to a regular place and spent much of his time as West's understudy. He was out in the cold when Everton won the FA Cup in 1966, and again in 1968 when they lost to West Brom at Wembley. In the Championship-winning season of 1969-70 he did not manage a single game. Perhaps he will be best remembered for his performance against Munchen Gladbach in the 1970-71 European Cup. The match went to a penalty shoot-out and Rankin became the unlikely hero of the hour when he put Everton into the third round with a vital save. He was transferred to Watford for £20,000 in November 1971 after making 104 senior appearances.

KEVIN RATCLIFFE

KEVIN RATCLIFFE

349

	LEAGUE		FA CUP		FL CUP		EUROPE		TOTAL	
	App	Gls	App	Gls	App	Gls	App	Gls	App	Gls
1979-80	2		1						3	
1980-81	20/1		5		2				27/1	
1981-82	25		1		1				27	
1982-83	29	1	5		4				38	1
1983-84	38		8		11				57	
1984-85	40		7		4		9		60	
	154/1	1	27		22		9		212/1	1

At the age of 24, Kevin Ratcliffe is already the most successful captain in Everton's history. In the 12 months between May 1984 and May 1985, the quietly-spoken Welshman led his team forward to pick up the FA Cup, the Charity Shield, the Canon League Championship and the European Cup-winners' Cup. He was taken on as an apprentice professional straight from school in June 1977, after picking up schoolboy caps at Under-15 and Under-18 levels. Within 18 months he signed full forms and began a fairytale march through the ranks. After making his debut in the goalless draw at Old Trafford in March 1980 he found himself on the verge of leaving Everton in 1981 when Ipswich Town manager Bobby Robson expressed interest. Unhappy at being asked to play full-back, he struggled to find his true form and asked for a transfer when he was dropped for the home game against Birmingham City in December 1982. Manager Howard Kendall reluctantly agreed to circulate his name, but he soon was recalled in favour of Billy Wright. He formed a brilliant partnership at the heart of a revitalised defence, first alongside Mark Higgins, then Derek Mountfield. In December 1983 he was appointed Everton skipper and three months later captain of his country. He is superb in the air and is rated as the quickest defender in the First Division. Ratcliffe is now widely acknowledged as one of the best centre-backs in British football.

	LEAGUE		FA CUP		FL CUP		EUROPE		TOTAL	
	App	Gls	App	Gls	App	Gls	App	Gls	App	Gls
1982-83	7		3						10	
1983-84	34/1	2	8	1	9/1	1			51/2	4
1984-85	36	2	7	1	4		9	1	56	4
	77/1	4	18	2	13/1	1	9	1	117/2	8

Tenacious Peter Reid became one of the bargain buys of all time when Howard Kendall bought him from Bolton Wanderers for £60,000 in December 1982. That deal was struck just two and a half years after Everton, then managed by Gordon Lee, had agreed to pay ten times that amount for a player who was to overcome a potentially devastating catalogue of injuries on the road to international acclaim. At the age of 29, Reid has no right to be standing without support, never mind performing near miracles in the heart of Everton's impressive engine-room. In 1978 he broke his left kneecap; in 1979 he tore apart ligaments in his right leg; in 1980 he underwent a cartilage operation on his left knee; and in 1981 he broke his right leg. He was kept going through those dark days only by his appetite for a battle, and his perseverance was finally rewarded when he established himself in the senior side after a prolonged wait. What Reid lacks in pace he makes up in sheer enthusiasm. He is a no-holds-barred workaholic with an astonishing will to win. He was a member of the 1984 beaten Milk Cup Final team, but has since picked up an FA Cup winners' medal, Canon League Championship medal and European Cup-winners' Cup medal. In 1985 he was voted Player of the Year by the PFA, and the same year won his first full England cap during the summer tour to Mexico.

PETER REID

	LEAGUE		TOTAL	
	App	Gls	App	Gls
1888-89	19	5	19	5
	19	5	19	5

Though he played only one season for Everton — the League's inaugural campaign of 1888-9 — Nick Ross goes down as one of the greatest defenders ever to wear an Everton shirt. In July 1883, Ross, the 20-year-old captain of Hearts, was given work as a slater in Preston and signed for Preston North End. He was the subject of a furious debate over professionalism but, undaunted, Preston made him their captain, converting him from a forward to one of the best backs of any generation. In many ways he was an unlucky footballer. He was on the losing side when Preston were defeated by West Brom in the 1888 FA Cup Final; he missed the famous Preston double-winning season of 1888-9 because he had joined Everton; and he was never capped by Scotland who were ignoring players south of the border. He arrived at Everton on 30 July 1888 and within two weeks was made captain. His wage was reported to be £10 per month, nearly twice that of any most players. He stayed one season and then rejoined Preston, at last tasting success when they won the League again in 1889-90. In April 1891 he played in the first-ever Football League representative side, against the Football Alliance. He died of consumption when only 31. His brother, Jimmy, was also one of the League's earliest stars, playing for Preston, Liverpool, Burnley and Manchester City.

NICK ROSS

TREVOR ROSS

	LEAGUE		FA CUP		FL CUP		EUROPE		TOTAL	
	App	Gls	App	Gls	App	Gls	App	Gls	App	Gls
1977-78	18/2	4	2	1					20/2	5
1978-79	26	6	1		2/1		4	1	33/1	7
1979-80	31/1	3	3	1	4		1		39/1	4
1980-81	17	2	6	1					23	3
1981-82	27	1	1		2				30	1
1982-83	1/1								1/1	
	120/4	16	13	3	8/1	5		1	146/5	20

Trevor Ross joined Everton for £180,000 from Arsenal in November 1977. He was brought to Goodison to help stabilise a midfield which, at the time, was considered skilful but woefully lacking in bite and aggression. Initially he seemed the perfect solution to a problem which had dogged successive Everton managers, but in the final count it has to be said that he failed to make a major impression during his six years at the club. He was cool when on the ball, and capable of delivering telling passes with great accuracy, but he suffered long periods of inconsistency. He was in and out of the side before being give a free transfer in February 1983. He went to Portsmouth on loan, and to Sheffield United, also on loan, as Everton tried to tempt the Blades to part with Terry Curran. Eventually he was drawn to the leading Greek side AEK Athens. He spent only six months there and after describing the move as 'the worst mistake of my life', he rejoined Sheffield United on a permanent basis.

	LEAGUE		FA CUP		FL CUP		EUROPE		TOTAL	
	App	Gls	App	Gls	App	Gls	App	Gls	App	Gls
1965-66	2								2	
1966-67	4	3							4	3
1967-68	33/1	16	6	3	1	1			40/1	20
1968-69	42	22	5	4	4	3			51	29
1969-70	42	23	1		4				47	23
1970-71	40	17	5	2			6	4	51	23
1971-72	26/2	9	3		1				30/2	9
1972-73	14	7			1				15	7
1973-74	18	2	3		1				22	2
1974-75	8	3			2				10	3
	229/3	102	23	9	14	4	6	4	272/3	119

Joe Royle was widely acknowledged as Everton's finest post-war centre-forward. He became the youngest-ever player to wear the famous royal blue when, at the tender age of 16, he was thrown into a First Division match by Harry Catterick, against Blackpool in 1966. He enjoyed a rapid rise to stardom, utilising his massive physique to good effect. He was a tremendous header of the ball and capable of clinical finishing when presented with a scoring chance inside the penalty area. He won his first England cap against Malta in 1971 and went on to pick up five more, the last being against Luxembourg at Wembley in 1977. His power up front and his crucial goals made him a key member of the 1970 Championship-winning side. After more than 15 years in League football he was forced to retire in April 1982, the result of a painful knee injury sustained in a game four months earlier. At the time he was with Norwich City, and it proved to be the last of his 473 League games in a career which included spells at Manchester City and Bristol City. He was appointed manager of Second Division Oldham Athletic in July 1982.

JOE ROYLE

Liverpool v Everton at Anfield in October 1984 and Graeme Sharp scores the only goal of the match with a spectacular shot.

	LEAGUE		FA CUP		TOTAL	
	App	Gls	App	Gls	App	Gls
1929-30	8		1		9	
1931-32	41		1		42	
1932-33	42		6		48	
1933-34	40		1		41	
1934-35	35		4		39	
1935-36	37				37	
1936-37	29		4		33	
1937-38	26				26	
1938-39	41		5		46	
1946-47	29		2		31	
1947-48	42		5		47	
1948-49	40		2		42	
1949-50	18				18	
1950-51	24		1		25	
1951-52	10				10	
1952-53	1				1	
	463		32		495	

TED SAGAR

An Everton legend, Ted Sagar was one of the finest goalkeepers of all time, combining sheer athleticism with bravery and tremendous vision. His handling, particularly of crosses, was exemplary. He spent an astonishing 24 years and one month with the club between 1929 and 1953 — the longest spell any player has ever had professionally with one Football League club. He also holds the record for League appearances in Everton colours with 463 games (some record books give the erroneous figure of 465). Yet, but for a lack of foresight on the part of Hull City, Sagar would never have found his way to Goodison Park. As a lad he was playing with Thorne Colliery in the Doncaster Senior League when he was spotted by a Tigers' scout. He was given a trial, but the Yorkshire club were slow to offer him a contract, so allowing Everton to nip in and sign him from under their noses. He won his first England cap against Northern Ireland in October 1935 and was honoured on three further occasions in 1936, against Scotland, Austria and Belgium. He won two League Championship medals and an FA Cup winners' medal with the club. Slim and perhaps underweight for a goalkeeper in the days when it was legitimate for centre-forwards to bounce both 'keeper and ball into the back of the net, Sagar survived by skill alone. He had the uncanny ability to judge the high flight of a ball from the wings and he was completely without nerves. He was famous for launching himself headlong at the ball, regardless of the number of players blocking his path.

	LEAGUE		FA CUP		TOTAL	
	App	Gls	App	Gls	App	Gls
1946-47	23		1		24	
1947-48	37		5		42	
1948-49	36		1		37	
1949-50	24				24	
1950-51	10				10	
1951-52	3				3	
	133		7		140	

George Saunders was a product of Merseyside junior football, recommended to Everton by Dixie Dean. Alhough he was never to reach the same heights as his sponsor — few did — Saunders was a reliable, consistent defender, well respected both on the terraces and in the Goodison dressing room. His motto was 'safety first' and he adamantly refused to embroider his play with fancy touches. He was a firm believer that it was the first duty of any full-back to clear his lines as quickly and as clinically as possible. He was an expert in killing stone-dead an awkward, bouncing ball and he was very useful in the air, often outjumping taller opponents. He signed as a professional in February 1939, but before that had played for two seasons with the 'A' team. His debut was in wartime football, against Liverpool at Anfield on 2 December 1939. His first peacetime League match was against Arsenal at Goodison on 11 September 1946. He was also a fine golfer, and cousin of Ron Saunders who spent five years at Everton in the early '50s.

GEORGE SAUNDERS

	LEAGUE		FA CUP		FL CUP		EUROPE		TOTAL	
	App	Gls	App	Gls	App	Gls	App	Gls	App	Gls
1962-63	17	4							17	4
1963-64	40	7	5	2			2		47	9
1964-65	36	6	4				4	1	44	7
1965-66	35	5	8				2		45	5
1966-67	21	1					2		23	1
	149	23	17	2	0	0	10	1	176	26

Alex Scott pledged his immediate future to Everton in February 1963, only after one of the fiercest transfer battles of the decade. Already established as a Scotland regular while with Glasgow Rangers, he was pursued by a number of leading English clubs when it became known that he was keen to move south of the border. Everton and Tottenham Hotspur led the way with a long series of bids, offers and pledges. Ultimately it was a £40,000 bid by Harry Catterick which won the day, and the flamboyant outside-right was on his way to Merseyside. By the end of the season he had picked up a Championship medal, and was an integral part of the set-up. In 1966 he won an FA Cup winners' medal to add to his winners' medals from a Scottish League Championship, two Scottish League Cup Finals and a Scottish Cup Final. Never a man to shirk responsibilty, Scott, known as 'Chico' to the fans, enjoyed a thoroughly successful career with Everton before being transferred to Hibernian for £15,000 in September 1967.

ALEX SCOTT

	LEAGUE		FA CUP		TOTAL	
	App	Gls	App	Gls	App	Gls
1904-05	16				16	
1905-06	35		6		41	
1906-07	35		8		43	
1907-08	34		7		41	
1908-09	36		2		38	
1909-10	27		7		34	
1910-11	31		3		34	
1911-12	37		5		42	
	251		38		289	

Goalkeeper Billy Scott succeeded Dick Roose at Everton — and then recommended his younger brother, Elisha, to Liverpool. Billy was born in Belfast and joined Everton from Irish League club Linfield in 1904. He was already an Irish international with six caps to his credit and he continued his run in the Ireland team after arriving at Goodison. Indeed, there always seemed to be a Scott in the Ireland goal. Even after he left Everton, for Leeds City in 1912, Billy continued to win caps, taking his overall tally to 25 in an international career which lasted from 1903 to 1913. Elisha kept goal 30 times between 1920 and 1936. Billy was Everton's goalkeeper in their 1906 and 1907 FA Cup Finals and he won three League Championship runners-up medals with the club (1904-05, 1908-09, 1911-12). His departure for Yorkshire caused Everton some concern and until the emergence of Tom Fern, Billy Scott proved a difficult man to replace, so well had he guarded Everton's net in his eight years at Goodison.

BILLY SCOTT

JIMMY SETTLE

	LEAGUE		FA CUP		TOTAL	
	App	Gls	App	Gls	App	Gls
1898-99	1				1	
1899-1900	26	10	1		27	10
1900-01	30	10	2	1	32	11
1901-02	29	18			29	18
1902-03	20	5	2		22	5
1903-04	29	8	1		30	8
1904-05	32	9	6	4	38	13
1905-06	28	11	5	1	33	12
1906-07	21	6	8	4	29	10
1907-08	21	7	7	3	28	10
	237	84	32	13	269	97

Jimmy Settle was one of the English game's most instinctive finishers at the turn of the century. Although strictly an inside-forward, he was always on hand to help out up front and his goals, usually poached from inside the penalty area, were as vital to Everton as his classy, defence-splitting passes. Below average height, he was uncommonly fast and it was said that he would have made a first-class sprinter had he chosen athletics instead of football. He started with Bolton Wanderers before joining Bury, but it was while at Goodison that he hit peak form. It was written of him: "Few are more dangerous near goal, often scores when the goalkeeper isn't looking. This diminutive marvel has won the highest honours and deserves them all." Settle won six full England caps between 1899 and 1903 and he also played for the Football League. He played in the 1906 and 1907 FA Cup Finals before moving to Stockport County in the summer of 1908. He retired a year later.

	LEAGUE		FA CUP		FL CUP		EUROPE		TOTAL	
	App	Gls	App	Gls	App	Gls	App	Gls	App	Gls
1979-80	1/1								1/1	
1980-81	2/2								2/2	
1981-82	27/2	15	1		1				29/2	15
1982-83	39/2	15	5	2	4				48/2	17
1983-84	27/1	7	5/2	1	11	3			43/3	11
1984-85	36	21	6	2	4	3	8	4	54	30
	132/8	58	17/2	5	20	6	8	4	177/10	73

Graeme Sharp was a virtually unknown striker when Gordon Lee splashed out £120,000 to bring him to Goodison Park from Dumbarton in April 1980. A powerful header of the ball with an eye for an opening, he was bought as an investment for the future. He made his League debut as a substitute in a goalless draw at Brighton a month after his arrival and, although he took time to settle down, he won a host of admirers with a series of spectacular goals. After partnering numerous strikers, he hit form following the arrival of fellow Scot Andy Gray in November 1983. Under the veteran striker's influence he matured at an astonishing rate to become a key member of Howard Kendall's new-look side. He scored the first goal in the 1984 FA Cup Final success over Watford and found the back of the net 30 times in 1984-5. His meteoric rise to stardom was capped when Jock Stein gave him his first full Scottish outing in the World Cup qualifier against Iceland in May 1985. His value has now increased enormously and he is high on the wanted lists of several leading Italian clubs.

GRAEME SHARP

	LEAGUE		FA CUP		TOTAL	
	App	Gls	App	Gls	App	Gls
1899-1900	29	5	1		30	5
1900-01	25	7	2		27	7
1901-02	32	6	2	1	34	7
1902-03	27	6	2	1	29	7
1903-04	31	6	1		32	6
1904-05	21	8	6	2	27	10
1905-06	29	9	6	2	35	11
1906-07	27	7	6	3	33	10
1907-08	23	4	7		30	4
1908-09	31	7	2	1	33	8
1909-10	25	4	7	2	32	6
	300	69	42	12	342	81

JACK SHARP

Double-international Jack Sharp was Everton's regular outside-right for 11 seasons after signing from Aston Villa in 1899. Born in Hereford, he started out with Hereford Thistle before Villa signed him in 1897. Sharp could not fit in at Villa Park and made only 23 League appearances. But Everton had no reservations about signing him and he repaid them with a career which saw him play 300 League games before retiring in 1910. He was an ideal wingman, possessing a telling burst of speed and an accurate centre. He liked to cut inside his full-back too, and that brought him his fair share of goals. He was a short, stocky man and one writer described him as a 'pocket Hercules'. He played in Everton's two FA Cup Finals of 1906 and 1907 and won two England caps as well as representing the Football League. J.T. Howcroft, 30 years a referee, nominated Sharp the best outside-right he had ever seen, better even than Meredith or Matthews. His brother, Bert, played as a full-back with him at Villa and Everton. Jack Sharp was also a fine cricketer, good enough to win three Test caps and score 105 against the Australians at The Oval in 1909. He played for Lancashire from 1899 to 1925, captaining them for a time, and his first-class career brought him 22,715 runs (38 centuries). A fast-medium bowler, he took 440 wickets and held 223 catches. He was a particularly brilliant cover-point. He ran a thriving sports outfitters in Liverpool and both he and his son were Everton directors. He died in January 1938, aged 59.

356

	LEAGUE		FA CUP		FL CUP		EUROPE		TOTAL	
	App	Gls	App	Gls	App	Gls	App	Gls	App	Gls
1982-83	40	11	5	2	3				48	13
1983-84	28	4	6	2	10	4			44	10
1984-85	29	11	6	4	2		5	2	42	17
	97	26	17	8	15	4	5	2	134	40

KEVIN SHEEDY

An unwritten agreement stretching back nearly 20 years was broken when Kevin Sheedy joined Everton from Liverpool in June 1982. The young Irish midfield star, tired of waiting in the Anfield shadows, decided to throw in his lot with Everton, so breaking the barrier which had prevented players moving between the two clubs for almost two decades. He signed for Liverpool for £70,000 from Hereford United in June 1978, but despite his outstanding Central League form, he was restricted to only two League outings in four years. Bob Paisley, who recognised his immense potential, was reluctant to release him, and the deal went to a tribunal before the fee of £100,000 was fixed. Sheedy is undoubtedly one of the finest left-sided midfield players that Everton have ever had, combining accurate passing with deadly shooting. He is a free-kick expert, capable of flighting a shot in to the top corner from anywhere up to 30 yards away. Although he has struggled with injuries since establishing himself, he is a consistent performer. He scored the third goal in the 1985 European Cup-winners' Cup Final victory over Rapid Vienna and is now a regular member of the Republic of Ireland side.

	LEAGUE		FA CUP		FL CUP		EUROPE		TOTAL	
	App	Gls	App	Gls	App	Gls	App	Gls	App	Gls
1981-82	26		1						27	
1982-83	17				2				19	
1983-84	35		8		11				54	
1984-85	42		7		4		9		62	
	120		16		17		9		162	

Neville Southall is a goalkeeper of outstanding ability who is now rated alongside Peter Shilton. It was in July 1981 that he completed the remarkable two-year transformation from Llandudno hod-carrier to First Division footballer. He turned his back on the building site after an eventful career in Welsh non-League football. He was a centre-back in his teens and had unsuccessful trials with several clubs including Crewe and Bolton. He moved between the posts after joining Llandudno Swifts, then had short spells with Conway United and Bangor City before moving to Cheshire League side Winsford. Bury bought him for £6,000 in 1980, and then Howard Kendall moved in with a £150,000 bid. After claiming a first-team place, he was dropped in favour of Jim Arnold and in 1982-3 he was one of ten Everton players loaned out when he went to Port Vale. He returned to win back his place and proved so consistently brilliant that Kendall felt able to compare him with Gordon Banks. Southall is magnificent in the air and has the sort of cat-like reflexes that leave opposing forwards pounding the turf in disbelief. He is firmly established as first-choice for Wales and in 1985 he was voted Footballer of the Year by the Football Writers' Association.

NEVILLE SOUTHALL

JACK SOUTHWORTH

	LEAGUE		FA CUP		TOTAL	
	App	Gls	App	Gls	App	Gls
1893-94	22	27	1		23	27
1894-95	9	9			9	9
	31	36	1		32	36

Though illness and injury meant that he served Everton for only one full season, the impression Jack Southworth made at Goodison Park lasted long after his enforced retirement. He began with Blackburn Olympic, for whom he once scored six goals in a match against Leigh when he was 16, and moved to Blackburn Rovers where he won FA Cup winners' medals in 1890 and 1891. They thought so much of him at Blackburn that in 1892 Rovers arranged a floodlit testimonial match — white ball and all — for him against Darwen. Everton paid £400 for his signature in August 1893 and after a slow start he began to pile in the goals, scoring four against Sheffield Wednesday and six against West Brom in successive matches. By the end of the season he had rattled in 27 goals in 22 games. Nine goals in his first nine games the following season indicated that he would carry on this incredible scoring rate, but then injury forced him into premature retirement. Southworth had scored one goal for each of his 139 League appearances with the two clubs, yet he made only three appearances for England (inevitably scoring three goals). This talented centre-forward had the misfortune to play at the same time as other great English goalscorers like Lindley, Goodall, Bloomer and G.O. Smith. He became a professional violinist, good enough to play with the Halle Orchestra.

JIMMY STEIN

	LEAGUE		FA CUP		TOTAL	
	App	Gls	App	Gls	App	Gls
1928-29	4		1		5	
1929-30	29	10	2		31	10
1930-31	28	10	5	3	33	13
1931-32	37	9	1		38	9
1932-33	40	16	6	5	46	21
1933-34	42	8	1		43	8
1934-35	19	4			19	4
	199	57	16	8	215	65

Everton have had some exciting Scottish players on their books over the years, but they never had a better servant than Jimmy Stein. In eight years with the club he was a model professional, never once complaining or grumbling when he was left out of the side in favour of younger, less experienced players. He was a quiet man, but was anything but friendly to the opposition. His long stride ate up space and he was a winger who liked to adopt the now standard ploy of cutting inside to deliver telling shots. His link-up with his inside partners was near perfect. A native of Coatbridge, he helped Dunfermline to gain promotion in 1925-6 before joining Everton in 1928. He was part of the side which won the Second Division title, the League Championship and the FA Cup in successive seasons between 1930 and 1933. He scored the first goal in the Wembley triumph over Manchester City in 1933. He moved to Burnley in October 1936 before returning to Merseyside to help New Brighton.

TREVOR STEVEN

	LEAGUE		FA CUP		FL CUP		EUROPE		TOTAL	
	App	Gls	App	Gls	App	Gls	App	Gls	App	Gls
1983-84	23/4	1	2		3	1			28/4	2
1984-85	40	12	7	2	4		9	2	60	16
	63/4	13	9	2	7	1	9	2	88/4	18

Howard Kendall took on the role of marathon man in his dogged chase to land Burnley's brilliant young midfielder Trevor Steven. The Goodison boss was so sure of Steven's ability to shine in the big time that he carefully followed the progress of the Burnley starlet for two years before the Turf Moor club finally relented and agreed to a £300,000 deal in July 1983. One of the finest natural talents that Everton have ever had on their books, Steven has already established himself as a full England international and is being favourably compared to Steve Coppell. A brilliant dribbler with superb close control, he complements the more aggressive style of Peter Reid in the Everton midfield. Although regarded as a supplier rather than a finisher, he scored 16 goals in 1984-5 as the club came within one match of landing an unprecedented treble. He supplied the cross for Andy Gray's decisive goal in the 1984 FA Cup Final triumph over Watford and won his first England cap, against Northern Ireland, on 27 February 1985.

DENNIS STEVENS

	LEAGUE		FA CUP		FL CUP		EUROPE		TOTAL	
	App	Gls	App	Gls	App	Gls	App	Gls	App	Gls
1961-62	12	4							12	4
1962-63	42	7	3	1			2	1	47	9
1963-64	42	9	5				2		49	9
1964-65	18		2				6		26	
1965-66	6						2		8	
	120	20	10	1	0	0	12	1	142	22

When Everton strode so majestically to the First Division title in 1963, it was players like Alex Young and Roy Vernon who captured so many of the headlines. They commanded — and at times demanded — attention because they had abundant skill. But strength, courage and determination are also needed in a team with title aspirations and it was Dennis Stevens who provided these qualities in that famous Everton line-up, with his quiet yet effective midfield play. He came from Bolton Wanderers (for whom he had played outside-right in the 1958 FA Cup Final) in March 1962, just days before Bobby Collins left for Leeds United. He was a tireless worker who switched to wing-half in 1964. With the arrival of youngsters like Colin Harvey and John Hurst, he found it increasingly difficult to retain his place and was eventually transferred to Oldham Athletic for £20,000 in December 1965. Two years later, at the age of 32, he joined Tranmere Rovers on a free transfer. His last game for Tranmere was, ironically, against Everton.

GARY STEVENS

	LEAGUE		FA CUP		FL CUP		EUROPE		TOTAL	
	App	Gls	App	Gls	App	Gls	App	Gls	App	Gls
1981-82	19	1	1		4				24	1
1982-83	28		5		2	1			35	1
1983-84	26	1	8		8				42	1
1984-85	37	3	7	1	4		9		57	4
	110	5	21	1	18	1	9		158	7

In just over two years Gary Stevens has developed into one of the finest defenders in Britain. Born in Barrow-in-Furness, he joined Everton straight from school, signing as an apprentice in July 1979. He made an impact in the Central League and was given his first-team debut in the 1-1 draw at West Ham on 10 October 1981. Content to bide his time, he returned to the reserves before taking over from Brian Borrows in November 1982. After a short period of acclimatization, his form was a revelation. His natural sprinting ability and great composure when in possession led to him being called into Bobby Robson's England squad for the World Cup qualifier against Northern Ireland in February 1985. He made his full international debut in Mexico later that year, against World Cup holders Italy. Although only 22, he has already made more than 150 senior appearances for Everton.

	LEAGUE		FA CUP		TOTAL	
	App	Gls	App	Gls	App	Gls
1933-34	12	1			12	1
1934-35	36	15	5	3	41	18
1935-36	29	10			29	10
1936-37	41	19	3	2	44	21
1937-38	35	13	2	1	37	14
1938-39	36	11	5	2	41	13
1946-47	30	8			30	8
1947-48	17	3			17	3
1948-49	19	2	1		20	2
	255	82	16	8	271	90

Alex Stevenson was one of the finest ball-players of his generation. His control was near perfect, his stocky body able to withstand the sometimes ruthless tackling of his contemporaries. But it was his brain that made him a truly great player and he graced the Everton team either side of World War Two. Although born in Dublin — he won his first Eire caps while with the Dolphin club — he rose to stardom in Scotland with Glasgow Rangers. His love for Rangers was such that it took a good deal of coaxing before Everton persuaded him to leave Ibrox in 1934. He went on to score 90 goals in 271 games for the club — respectable figures for a man not employed primarily as a scorer. His partnership with fellow Irishman Jackie Coulter was a feature of the First Division before the war. The impish pair tore many defences to shreds with their speedy interplay and remarkable understanding of each other's intentions. Stevenson was capped 17 times for Northern Ireland and seven times for Eire, his last cap for the Republic coming in 1949, 17 years after the first.

ALEX STEVENSON

	LEAGUE		FA CUP		TOTAL	
	App	Gls	App	Gls	App	Gls
1893-94	29	1	1		30	1
1894-95	27	2	3		30	2
1895-96	28		3		31	
1896-97	29	3	4		33	3
1897-98	9		4		13	
	122	6	15		137	6

BILLY STEWART

Born in Arbroath, Billy Stewart first made his reputation playing with the Black Watch team which won the Army Cup. Preston North End bought him out of the army and he played for them for several years before joining Everton in 1893. One of the key features of his play was his exceptionally long throw-in, although his running and jumping technique was eventually outlawed. He formed part of a famous Everton half-back line with Holt and Campbell and he played left-half in the 1897 FA Cup Final. Once, when the Everton team were training at Hoylake, he was the victim of a typical footballers' practical joke. As he slept, string was attached to every piece of bedroom furniture; then out in the hotel corridor the rest of the team pulled on the strings as hard as they could. Stewart woke up with the biggest fright of his life. He signed for Bristol City in 1897.

	LEAGUE		FA CUP		TOTAL	
	App	Gls	App	Gls	App	Gls
1896-97	30	13	5	2	35	15
1897-98	30	3	5	3	35	6
1898-99	34	3	2	1	36	4
1899-1900	32	7	1		33	7
1900-01	25	11	2	1	27	12
1901-02	26	8	2		28	8
1902-03	33	3	3	1	36	4
1903-04	22	6	1	1	23	7
1904-05	34	4	6		40	4
1905-06	36	4	6	2	42	6
1906-07	34	1	8	2	42	3
1907-08	23	2	7		30	2
1908-09	27	1	1		28	1
1909-10	14		7	1	21	1
	400	66	56	14	456	80

JACK TAYLOR

One of the stars of his day, Jack Taylor was a versatile player who could be relied upon to give a good account of himself in almost any position. He was an inspirational footballer who coaxed the very best out of those around him. He played on the right wing in the 1897 FA Cup Final and was the sole playing survivor from that side when Everton returned to the Crystal Palace in 1906 and 1907, turning out at centre-half. He played first for Dumbarton Athletic, moved to St Mirren and then joined Everton in 1896. A freak accident in the 1910 FA Cup semi-final effectively brought his career to an end. Against Barnsley at Manchester, he was struck in the throat by a fierce shot and sustained severe damage to the larynx, an injury from which he never fully recovered. After 400 League games for Everton, he went into non-League football for the first time in his career, with South Liverpool. He was 77 when he died, in West Kirby in 1949, after a motoring accident.

GEORGE TELFER

	LEAGUE		FA CUP		FL CUP		EUROPE		TOTAL	
	App	Gls	App	Gls	App	Gls	App	Gls	App	Gls
1973-74	15	3	1/1						16/1	3
1974-75	11/4	2	2/2						13/6	2
1975-76	20/4	8			2/1		1		23/5	8
1976-77	17/2	4	0/1		3				20/3	4
1977-78	7/3	1	1	1	0/1	1			8/4	3
1978-79	10/2	2							10/2	2
1980-81	1/1								1/1	
	81/16	20	4/4	1	5/2	1	1		91/22	22

George Telfer was a speedy winger who scored some spectacular goals during his time with Everton. After making his debut in 1973 his form was so impressive that he was talked about as a future England international. An aggressive, robust striker with tremendous sprinting ability, he was lethal when presented with time and space in the penalty area. Things appeared to be going well for him until the arrival of Duncan McKenzie cost him his first-team place. His belief in his own ability was such that he decided to stay at Goodison and fight for a recall despite offers from other clubs. In November 1980 he turned down a move to Chester who were willing to pay £30,000 for him, to replace Ian Rush. Eventually Telfer tired of Central League football, however, and signed for NASL club San Diego. He returned to England to play for Scunthorpe United, where England cricket star Ian Botham cleaned his boots, and Preston. After spells in non-League football, with Runcorn and Barrow, he was appointed Football Development Officer for Merseyside Youth Association in October 1984.

	LEAGUE		FA CUP		FL CUP		EUROPE		TOTAL	
	App	Gls	App	Gls	App	Gls	App	Gls	App	Gls
1956-57	7	3							7	3
1957-58	28	8	1						29	8
1958-59	4	2							4	2
1960-61	20	4			3				23	4
1961-62	17	10							17	10
1962-63	5	1							5	1
1963-64	41	12	5				2		48	12
1964-65	39	11	4	1			6	2	49	14
1965-66	38	9	8	6			4		50	15
1966-67	27/1	12	3	1			4		34/1	13
1967-68	5				1				6	
	231/1	72	21	8	4		16	2	272/1	82

Derek Temple's place in Everton's 'Hall of Fame' was guaranteed when he scored the winning goal in the 1966 FA Cup Final against Sheffield Wednesday and so completed one of the great Wembley fightbacks. Not very tall, but powerfully built, Temple was a utility man who could fill a variety of roles. Born in Liverpool, he played for Lancashire and England Schoolboys during 1953-4 before joining Everton shortly after leaving school. His form with the Colts was astonishing. In one season alone he scored 70 goals, sometimes claiming five or six in a match. He made his senior debut against Newcastle at Goodison in March 1957 and went on to make 231 League appearances. After 11 seasons with Everton he was transferred to Preston for £35,000 in September 1967. Three years later he joined Wigan Athletic. Temple won one England cap, against West Germany in Nuremberg in 1965.

DEREK TEMPLE

362

	LEAGUE		FA CUP		FL CUP		EUROPE		TOTAL	
	App	Gls	App	Gls	App	Gls	App	Gls	App	Gls
1977-78	38	2	1		5	1			44	3
1978-79	33	2	1		2		4	1	40	3
	71	4	2		7	1	4	1	84	6

Dave Thomas had speed and the ability to cross the ball with unerring accuracy and that made him a key man in Gordon Lee's side. After making his name with Burnley, where he won England Under-23 honours, he surprisingly turned down the likes of Manchester United, Leeds and Everton for Second Division QPR. The London club paid £165,000 for his signature in October 1972 and provided him with an excellent stage on which to display his silky skills. He enjoyed five very successful years at Loftus Road, winning eight full international caps, before he decided to seek a move back north. Everton, desperately searching for a provider of ammunition for their shot-shy front line, headed a lengthy queue and completed his transfer, for £200,000, in August 1977. He performed with restrained brilliance during his days at Goodison before being sold to Wolves in October 1979, as part of a wholesale clear-out. He never settled at Molineux and jumped at the chance to join NASL side Vancouver Whitecaps, then managed by Johnny Giles. But the motivation was not there and after only 10 matches he returned to sign for Middlesbrough.

DAVE THOMAS

MICKEY THOMAS

	LEAGUE		FA CUP		FL CUP		TOTAL	
	App	Gls	App	Gls	App	Gls	App	Gls
1981-82	10				1		11	
	10				1		11	

Gifted Mickey Thomas had a brief and stormy stay with Everton. It was an unhappy relationship that began with smiles in July 1981, and ended in bitter recriminations a little over three months later. After sparkling with Wrexham, the club he joined as a boy, Thomas attracted several top clubs before Manchester United, under the managership of Dave Sexton, emerged from the pack to sign him in November 1978. The price paid by the Old Trafford club was £330,000, a huge fee for a youngster who had never played First Division football. Flamboyant and fiery, Thomas was an instant success with the fans, but not with the United management. He could take on and beat an opponent with apparent ease, but his skills were often overlooked as he tried to keep his temper in check. In the summer of 1981 he was transferred to Everton in the deal which saw John Gidman move to Old Trafford. After recovering from injury in November that year, Thomas refused to play in a Central League game at Newcastle, claiming that he should have been selected for the First Division game against Manchester City. After only 11 senior games, Thomas was placed on the transfer list. Brighton bought him for £400,000 and he has since served Stoke and Chelsea.

JOCK THOMSON

	LEAGUE		FA CUP		TOTAL	
	App	Gls	App	Gls	App	Gls
1929-30	9				9	
1930-31	41		5		46	
1931-32	39		1		40	
1932-33	41	3	6		47	3
1933-34	38		1		39	
1934-35	42	1	5		47	1
1935-36	25				25	
1936-37	2				2	
1937-38	9	1			9	1
1938-39	26		4		30	
	272	5	22		294	5

John Ross Thomson played for Everton in two League Championship sides, an FA Cup-winning team, and a Second Division title-winning side. Born in Thornton, Fifeshire, in 1906, he went from Scottish junior football to Dundee in 1925, and to Everton in March 1930 where he found himself in a side destined for relegation to the Second Division. Twelve months later Everton were back in the First as Thomson missed only one game, playing a key role in the promotion drive with his forceful play at left-half. One year on, Everton were League Champions, and a year after that they won the FA Cup. So, in a little over 36 months, Thomson had known the agony of relegation, the joy of promotion, the elation of a Championship medal and the ultimate ecstasy of Wembley triumph. In October 1932 he won his solitary Scotland cap, against Wales at Tynecastle, but by the late '30s he found his Everton place hard to come by after the emergence of the young Joe Mercer. There was one last triumph however. In the 1938-9 Championship year he played 26 times when Cliff Britton ended his career and Mercer switched to right-half. Thomson retired in 1939 and from 1947 to 1950 was Manchester City manager. Until his retirement in 1974 he ran a pub in Carnoustie. He died in 1979.

	LEAGUE		FA CUP		FL CUP		TOTAL	
	App	Gls	App	Gls	App	Gls	App	Gls
1978-79	29	1	1		2		32	1
1979-80	3						3	
	32	1	1		2		35	1

Colin Todd was that rare footballer — a defender who could excite spectators. As a sweeper, his ability to send a crossfield pass perhaps 60 yards to the feet of a colleague was breathtaking and he was undoubtedly one of the classiest defenders English football has ever produced. Todd, who also proved a resilient full-back — he played there for England as well as at sweeper — arrived at Goodison in the twilight of an illustrious career which yielded 27 full England caps. He was the England Under-23 skipper when Brian Clough astonished football by paying £170,000 for a defender, taking Todd to Derby in February 1971. He spent seven years at the Baseball Ground, winning two League Championship medals and being named PFA Player of the Year in 1975. Everton beat off Southampton and signed the 29-year-old football perfectionist for £300,000 in September 1978. Todd brought a calm assurance to an inconsistent side before losing his place after being laid low with a mystery stomach complaint. After falling out with Lee he was transferred to Birmingham City for £275,000, exactly one year and three days after moving to Goodison. In December 1982 he linked up with Clough again, at Nottingham Forest, and then signed for Oxford United. He also appeared in the NASL with Vancouver Whitecaps.

COLIN TODD

364

	LEAGUE		FA CUP		FL CUP		EUROPE		TOTAL	
	App	Gls	App	Gls	App	Gls	App	Gls	App	Gls
1965-66	7	2	2	2					9	4
1966-67	2						1		3	
1967-68	2	1							2	1
	11	3	2	2	0	0	1		14	5

Mike Trebilcock is the little Cornishman who won a permanent place in the hearts of all Evertonians when he took centre-stage in one of the most famous of all FA Cup Finals. It was only his second Cup match for the club but he brought about one of the greatest of all Wembley recovery stories. The player who never established himself at Goodison nevertheless left an indelible entry in the club's history. Virtually unknown, he signed from Plymouth Argyle for £20,000 on the last day of 1965. Less than four months later he was dramatically drafted into the FA Cup semi-final against Manchester United, replacing Fred Pickering. Surprisingly, he kept his place for the Final against Sheffield Wednesday. Though his name was not even on the Wembley programme, his moment of destiny came that afternoon, with Everton trailing 2-0 after 57 minutes. Within two minutes Trebilcock pulled a goal back. Soon afterwards he equalised, leaving Derek Temple to complete one of the great Cup Final fight-backs. It was Trebilcock's last Cup game for Everton. After two years on Merseyside — and only 11 League games — he joined Portsmouth before ending his career with Torquay. He now works as a storeman in Newcastle, Australia.

MIKE TREBILCOCK

	LEAGUE		FA CUP		TOTAL	
	App	Gls	App	Gls	App	Gls
1922-23	17	2			17	2
1923-24	41	1	2		43	1
1924-25	32	2			32	2
1925-26	38	6	2		40	6
1926-27	37	5	4	2	41	7
1927-28	42	10	2	1	44	11
1928-29	38	5			38	5
1929-30	4	1			4	1
	249	32	10	3	259	35

After Dixie Dean had completed his magnificent 60-goal haul in 1927-8, he said that the achievement would not have been possible but for the assistance of Alec Troup. The tiny Scottish winger — he stood 5ft 5ins — with the fantastic ball control was the man who supplied many of the pin-point crosses which Dean so regularly despatched into the net. Troup seemed able to make the ball 'hang' in the air while Dean found a suitable launching-pad. It was such a cross, in the final League game of that season, which enabled Dean to reach the 60-goal mark. Troup was born in Forfar in 1895 and played for Forfar Athletic and Dundee before joining Everton in January 1923. He made light of a weak collar-bone which had to be heavily strapped before every game. He won five full Scotland caps — the presence of the great Alan Morton denied him more — and rejoined Dundee in February 1930. He retired in 1933 to run a clothiers in Forfar. Troup died in 1951.

ALEC TROUP

	LEAGUE		FA CUP		FL CUP		EUROPE		TOTAL	
	App	Gls	App	Gls	App	Gls	App	Gls	App	Gls
1984-85	31	7			3		5		46	
	31	7			3		5		46	

Pat Van den Hauwe is a ferocious tackler who plays the game in the old-fashioned way, believing that a defender's first priority is to win the ball and then release it as quickly as possible. After a relatively low-key career with Birmingham City, he was signed from the recently-relegated Midlanders in late September 1984 when Howard Kendall paid £100,000 for his services. He immediately replaced John Bailey at left-back and retained his place for the rest of what was to become a famous season. Born in Belgium, he moved to London at an early age. After becoming an important link in Everton's defensive chain, he appeared to be on the verge of a call-up to the Belgium national side when manager Guy Thees flew to Old Trafford to watch him in March 1985. After being pencilled in as an over-age player for the under-21 match against Spain, he discovered that he had unwittingly signed away his birthright by opting out of national service. That led to much press speculation as to which of the British nations would pursue him. Eventually he joined Goodison colleagues Kevin Ratcliffe and Neville Southall in the Welsh team, making his debut in the splendid World Cup victory over Spain at Wrexham in April 1985.

PAT Van den HAUWE

IMRE VARADI

	LEAGUE		FA CUP		FL CUP		EUROPE		TOTAL	
	App	Gls	App	Gls	App	Gls	App	Gls	App	Gls
1979-80	2/2		0/1		0		0/1		2/4	
1980-81	20/2	6	6	1	0				26/2	7
	22/4	6	6/1	1	0		0/1		28/6	7

Imre Varadi was one of the game's most exciting new faces when he joined Everton early in 1979 after a handful of games for Sheffield United. A fast, tricky forward, he was an acknowledged goalscorer, despite having been 'sacked' by a non-League club in his formative days. London-born of Hungarian parents, his career appeared to be in tatters in 1978 when, while working as an asphalter, he was asked to leave Letchworth Town. Sheffield United spotted him in Sunday football and manager Harry Haslam offered him terms. He had played only 10 League games for the Bramall Lane club when Gordon Lee paid £80,000 for him. Although erratic, he proved a gifted front-runner with an exciting turn of speed and an explosive shot. He scored seven goals in 28 appearances in 1980-81, the highspot of his Goodison career coming when he netted the club's second goal in their 2-1 FA Cup win over Liverpool. After losing his place he looked set to join mighty Portuguese side, Benfica, in May 1981, but the deal fell through at the last moment. After becoming a free agent in 1981 he moved to Newcastle United for £125,000, and later Sheffield Wednesday and West Brom.

	LEAGUE		FA CUP		FL CUP		EUROPE		TOTAL	
	App	Gls	App	Gls	App	Gls	App	Gls	App	Gls
1959-60	12	9							12	9
1960-61	39	21	1		4	1			44	22
1961-62	37	26	3	2					40	28
1962-63	41	24	3	3			2		46	27
1963-64	31	18	5	2			2		38	20
1964-65	16	3					3	1	19	4
	176	101	12	7	4	1	7	1	199	110

Roy Vernon was an inside-forward, mature beyond his years, who revelled in producing the unexpected. He made his League debut for Blackburn Rovers as an 18-year-old in September 1955. On that day he played on the right wing against Liverpool and in direct opposition was his fellow countryman, Roy Lambert. Four days before his 20th birthday, Vernon won the first of 32 caps for Wales, against Northern Ireland. In February 1960, Johnny Carey, his former manager at Blackburn, lured him to Goodison Park in a £27,000 deal which took Eddie Thomas to Ewood Park in part-exchange. Yet Everton might have had him for nothing. He was once offered a trial but opted for a place on Blackburn's groundstaff. Three months after he eventually signed for Everton, Blackburn were at Wembley for the FA Cup Final. Vernon shook off that disappointment and went on to captain Everton. He scored 24 League goals when Everton won the Championship in 1962-3. An expert penalty-taker, he was regarded as one of the finest strikers of a dead ball. He moved to Stoke for £40,000 in March 1965 and in 1970 spent a short time playing in South Africa. In September that year he joined his former Blackburn colleagues Bryan Douglas and Ronnie Clayton at Great Harwood.

ROY VERNON

	LEAGUE		FA CUP		TOTAL	
	App	Gls	App	Gls	App	Gls
1924-25	1		1		2	
1925-26	16		2		18	
1926-27	32	1	4	1	36	2
1927-28	39	1	1		40	1
1928-29	24		1		25	
1929-30	5				5	
	117	2	9	1	126	3

Six-feet tall, long-legged Albert Virr was a local boy who succeeded in two vocations. After training as an engineer, he became a full-time footballer in the early '20s and was a vital member of Everton's Championship winning side of 1928. He was a colourful character, a half-back who liked to play the simple but effective way. Although there was probably no firmer tackler in the League, he was a scrupulously fair player. His career was wrecked by a serious knee injury sustained during an FA Cup match against Chelsea in January 1929. The damage was diagnosed as severe cartilage trouble and although he did attempt a come-back the following season, he was eventually forced into retirement. He became a schoolteacher, survived a major lung operation in 1954, but died, aged 57, in Sefton General Hospital in July 1959.

ALBERT VIRR

EDDIE WAINWRIGHT

	LEAGUE		FA CUP		TOTAL	
	App	Gls	App	Gls	App	Gls
1946-47	27	13	2	2	29	15
1947-48	30	9	4	2	34	11
1948-49	17	10	1		18	10
1949-50	37	11	5	2	42	13
1950-51	11	1			11	1
1952-53	7	4			7	4
1953-54	23	8	3		26	8
1954-55	24	4	2		26	4
1955-56	31	8	4	2	35	10
	207	68	21	8	228	76

Eddie Wainwright was one of Southport's major gifts to
football. He started with High Park in the resort's amateur
league before being spotted by Everton and signing amateur
forms in 1939. In his early days he was 'farmed out' to
Fleetwood to aid his development. He improved rapidly
during the early years of the war and played a great deal of
army representative football where he came under the eye of
Arthur Rowe, later to manage Spurs' famous 'push and run'
side. His goalscoring feats rekindled Everton's interest and in
September 1943 they gave him his first-team debut, in a
League North game against Manchester United when the
youngster played alongside pre-war internationals like Tommy
Lawton and Joe Mercer. An intelligent ball-player with a
fierce shot, Wainwright played a major role in Everton's
1949-50 FA Cup run which was ended in the semi-final by
Liverpool. The same year he toured the USA and Canada
with an FA party. He also played for the Football League
against the Irish League. The latter stages of his career were
ruined by injuries. In December 1950, a tackle by Derby's
Chick Musson broke his leg but he fought back and
eventually ran up 228 appearances and 76 goals.

	LEAGUE		FA CUP		TOTAL	
	App	Gls	App	Gls	App	Gls
1936-37	2				2	
1937-38	9	1			9	1
1938-39	16		1		17	
1946-47	12				12	
1947-48	18		4		22	
1948-49	4				4	
	61	1	5		66	1

Tommy Watson, who prefers the name 'Gordon', arrived
at Goodison Park in January 1933 and went on to become
one of Everton's greatest servants. He had been playing with
Blyth Spartans in his native North-East and quickly impressed
with his close control and fierce tackling. He made his League
debut in 1937 and appeared in 27 pre-war League games. He
was twelfth man on so many occasions during the 1938-9
Championship season that his teammates clubbed together to
buy him a special cushion so that he would have a comfortable
seat on the trainer's bench. He had an impish sense of humour
and took it all in good spirit, never once bemoaning the fact
that he was not in the team. After the war he was appointed
first-team trainer and in 1968 joined the club's promotions
department. By 1985 he had celebrated 52 years with Everton
and is now a part-time barman in the '300 Club'.

TOMMY (GORDON) WATSON

	LEAGUE		FA CUP		FL CUP		EUROPE		TOTAL	
	App	Gls	App	Gls	App	Gls	App	Gls	App	Gls
1961-62	12								12	
1962-63	38	3					2		43	
1963-64	22	3					2		27	
1964-65	20	4					2		26	
1965-66	24	8					2		34	
1966-67	36	5					4		45	
1967-68	41	6			2				49	
1968-69	42	5			4				51	
1969-70	42	1			4				47	
1970-71	12	1					1		14	
1971-72	42	4			1				47	
1972-73	4								4	
	335	40		11		13			399	

When he joined Everton from Blackpool in March 1962 for a then record fee for a goalkeeper of £27,000, Gordon West became the first signing made by new manager Harry Catterick. A superb athlete with a theatrical dash about him, West was a technically brilliant last line of defence. He immediately took over from Albert Dunlop and in just over 12 months won a Championship medal. His consistency brought him to the attention of Sir Alf Ramsey, but West staggered the football world when he refused to join the party for the 1970 World Cup Finals in Mexico, preferring to remain at home with his family. He was a regular choice at Goodison for four years before being dropped in favour of Andy Rankin in 1970-71. Typically, this exuberant character fought back and in 1971-2 he was ever-present. In June 1972, however, David Lawson arrived from Huddersfield and West made only four more League appearances and retired after nearly 400 appearances for Everton and three England caps. In 1975 he began a brief comeback with Tranmere.

GORDON WEST

TOMMY WHITE

	LEAGUE		FA CUP		TOTAL	
	App	Gls	App	Gls	App	Gls
1927-28	1	2			1	2
1928-29	21	6			21	6
1929-30	35	11			35	11
1930-31	10	10			10	10
1931-32	23	18	1		24	18
1932-33	34	2	6		40	2
1933-34	28	14	1		29	14
1934-35	5				5	
1935-36	35	3	1		36	3
1936-37	1				1	
	193	66	9		202	66

When Everton signed Tommy White from Southport in 1927 they bought a player of exceptional versatility. White could play almost anywhere and was guaranteed to give a good account of himself in whatever position he was asked to perform. As a schoolboy he was a centre-half, but he joined Everton as a goalscorer who could play anywhere in the forward line. His aggressive style won him many admirers and on occasions he stood in for Dixie Dean, which in itself was quite a daunting task. Towards the end of his Everton career he reverted to centre-half and he was a tower of strength in the 1935-6 season as Everton battled to avoid relegation. White made 193 League appearances for Everton, scoring 66 goals. He played centre-half for England against Italy in Rome in 1933. In October 1937 he signed for Northampton Town.

	LEAGUE		FA CUP		FL CUP		EUROPE		TOTAL	
	App	Gls	App	Gls	App	Gls	App	Gls	App	Gls
1967-68	6								6	
1968-69	4				1	2			5	2
1969-70	15	11	1		2				18	11
1970-71	24	7	1				4/1	1	29/1	8
1971-72	18/1		4	2	1				23/1	2
1972-73	5/1	3							5/1	3
	72/2	21	6	2	4	2	4/1	1	86/3	26

Harry Catterick described Alan Whittle as 'the greatest Everton discovery of all time'. Sadly, however, the gritty forward with a flair for goalscoring failed to live up to expectations. He was hailed as a 'new Denis Law' when, as a precocious 18-year-old, he helped Everton shatter West Brom 6-2 on his debut in March 1968, and he went on to win a League Championship medal in 1970. But, while nobody could dispute his commitment and determination, he was largely inconsistent and found himself out of the side on numerous occasions. After such a blistering start to his career, things did not work out and in December 1972 he was transferred to Crystal Palace for £100,000. The same day, Catterick paid Aberdeen £180,000 for Joe Harper. Whittle looked set to join Wrexham in 1975 but eventually found his way to Sheffield United on a free-transfer in July 1976. He went on to play for Bournemouth before trying his luck in Australia.

ALAN WHITTLE

	LEAGUE		FA CUP		TOTAL	
	App	Gls	App	Gls	App	Gls
1929-30	9		2		11	
1930-31	36		5		41	
1931-32	33		1		34	
1932-33	20				20	
1933-34	18				18	
1934-35	12				12	
1935-36	3				3	
	131		8		139	

Ben Williams was a strong full-back who captained Everton when the club marched back to the First Division in 1930-31. He was born in Penhriwceiber, South Wales, a fact which led to him being called Khyber by his teammates. As a schoolboy he was a good boxer and seriously considered a career in the ring before Swansea Town convinced him that his future lay in soccer. He signed for the Swans in 1923 and played 97 games for them before Everton took him to Goodison Park in December 1929. He formed a brilliant partnership with Warney Cresswell and won international recognition, playing ten times for Wales. In January 1933 his career received a serious blow when he underwent a cartilage operation. He never fully recovered and was transferred to Newport County in 1936. Twelve months later he was appointed club coach. He retired from football to pursue a business career.

BEN WILLIAMS

	LEAGUE		FA CUP		FL CUP		EUROPE		TOTAL	
	App	Gls	App	Gls	App	Gls	App	Gls	App	Gls
1964-65	17		4				2		23	
1965-66	35		8				4		47	
1966-67	30		6				4		40	
1967-68	28		6						34	
1968-69	4/2		2		0/1				6/3	
	114/2	26			0/1	10			150/3	

RAY WILSON

Ramon Wilson was one of the most cultured full-backs ever to play on Merseyside. Born near Mansfield, he joined Huddersfield Town from local amateur circles in 1951. He stayed at Leeds Road for 13 years before signing for Everton in July 1964. A tough tackler with superb tactical knowledge, he was widely regarded as the finest full-back in European football when he won a World Cup winners' medal with England in 1966. His career in the top flight ended in July 1968 when a knee injury sustained in training required surgery. He fought back, but although the finesse which had been the hallmark of his play was still evident, he had lost some of his old speed and confidence and he was given a free transfer. The experience of 18 years in the game, and 63 England appearances, made him an attractive proposition for several clubs. He joined Oldham Athletic in 1969 before moving to Bradford City as player-coach. He quit football in 1971 and is now an undertaker.

SAM WOLSTENHOLME

	LEAGUE		FA CUP		TOTAL	
	App	Gls	App	Gls	App	Gls
1897-98	1				1	
1898-99	15		2		17	
1899-1900	29		1		30	
1900-01	34	2	2		36	2
1901-02	27	1	2		29	1
1902-03	22	1	2		24	1
1903-04	32	4	1		33	4
	160	8	10		170	8

Sam Wolstenholme was still a current international when Everton surprisingly let him go to Blackburn Rovers in 1904. It may have been that they thought he was past his best — certainly his prematurely balding pate and bandy legs gave the impression that he was nearing the end of his career — but he was only 25 and enjoyed several more seasons at the top. Born at Little Lever, he joined Everton in late 1897 and made one appearance that season. Thereafter he soon forced his way into the side as a wing-half whose anticipation made up for any shortcomings he might have had in the tackle. In 1900-01 he was an ever-present. In April 1904 he made his England debut, against Scotland. By the time he played in the next two games, against Ireland and Wales, he was a Blackburn player. In 1908 he went to Croydon Common and helped them into the Southern League before moving to another Southern League club, Norwich City, before retiring in 1913. He was coaching in Germany when war was declared and was interned along with fellow England internationals Steve Bloomer and Fred Spikesley. Together they persuaded their camp commandant to allow them to organise a football league for prisoners' teams.

GEORGE WOOD

	LEAGUE		FA CUP		FL CUP		EUROPE		TOTAL	
	App	Gls	App	Gls	App	Gls	App	Gls	App	Gls
1977-78	42	2			5				49	
1978-79	42	1			3		4		50	
1979-80	19	1			5		2		27	
	103	4			13		6		126	

Gordon Lee had been searching for a goalkeeper for nearly six months before he landed George Wood in August 1977. Standing 6ft 3ins and weighing around 14st, Wood was surprisingly agile for such a big man. He proved capable of acts of great athleticism between the Everton posts. He was signed from Blackpool for £150,000, the same day that Dave Thomas came from QPR for £200,000. Born at Douglas, Wood joined Blackpool in 1971-2 from East Stirling and in his last season at Bloomfield Road he played in every League match for the Seasiders. In his first two seasons at Goodison Park he was also an ever-present, his displays winning him three full Scotland caps. But the inconsistency which had dogged his early days gradually returned and he lost his place to newcomer Martin Hodge. Wood made 103 League appearances for Everton before signing for Arsenal in August 1980 for £150,000 and after three seasons at Highbury he moved to Crystal Palace.

	LEAGUE		FA CUP		FL CUP		EUROPE		TOTAL	
	App	Gls	App	Gls	App	Gls	App	Gls	App	Gls
1964-65	22		3				3		28	
1965-66	35/1		6				4		45/1	
1966-67	42		6				4		52	
1967-68	38		6		2				46	
1968-69	41	1	5		4				50	1
1969-70	42	1	1		4				47	1
1970-71	40	2	5				6		51	2
1971-72	17		1						18	
1972-73	30		2		1				33	
	307/1	4	35		11		17		370/1	4

Tommy Wright was the classic case of local boy made good. He joined Everton straight from school as a talented inside-forward, but was converted to wing-half, then right-back. A former England Schoolboy international, he made his first-team debut in 1964, aged 19. He took over from Scottish international Alex Parker and in 1966 won an FA Cup winners' medal against Sheffield Wednesday. He added Under-23 honours to his caps before his first full appearance, against Russia in the 1968 European Championships third-place play-off. One of the most constructive back-four men in British football, he played in the 1970 World Cup Finals in Mexico. He was a solid defender who liked to force his way down the flanks when the opportunity arose. One of Everton's 1970 Championship side, Tommy Wright will be remembered as one of football's natural gentlemen.

TOMMY WRIGHT

	LEAGUE		FA CUP		FL CUP		EUROPE		TOTAL	
	App	Gls	App	Gls	App	Gls	App	Gls	App	Gls
1977-78	3/1	1							3/1	1
1978-79	39	2	1		3		4		47	2
1979-80	40/1		6		3		2		51/1	
1980-81	41	2	6		3				50	2
1981-82	24	2							24	2
1982-83	17	3			4				21	3
	164/2	10	13		13		6		196/2	10

BILLY WRIGHT

Billy Wright will be remembered as the towering centre-back who lost his Everton place because he was overweight. Only hours before a League game at Ipswich on 11 December 1982, manager Howard Kendall told his club captain that he was being left out as a disciplinary measure for weighing 8lbs more than the club decreed. Wright, a life-long Everton supporter, never recovered from the blow to his confidence and never played for Everton again. Within six months he was on his way to Birmingham City. A hard-working defender, Wright had proved a pillar of strength in Everton's back-four. He made 164 League appearances and was the club's longest-serving professional at the time he left Goodison. As he fought to trim down his frame, the makeshift central defensive partnership of Kevin Ratcliffe and Mark Higgins came good. That left Wright little alternative but to accept the free transfer in June 1983. He joined a Birmingham side destined for relegation, but in 1984-5 he helped them back to Division One. He is a nephew of Tommy Wright.

	LEAGUE		FA CUP		TOTAL	
	App	Gls	App	Gls	App	Gls
1901-02	30	6	2	1	32	7
1902-03	19	5	1		20	5
1903-04	22	10			22	10
1904-05	31	14	6		37	14
1905-06	30	12	5	2	35	14
1906-07	33	28	8	1	41	29
1907-08	33	16	6	5	39	21
1908-09	23	9	1		24	9
1909-10	24	2	7	3	31	5
1910-11	30	8	3	3	33	11
	275	110	39	15	314	125

ALEX YOUNG

Alex 'Sandy' Young — no ancestor of Everton's star of the '60s — was the man who scored the 75th-minute goal which won the 1906 FA Cup Final for the club when he converted a centre from Jack Sharp to sink Newcastle United. The reception which greeted Young's effort was likened by one newspaper to the San Francisco earthquake which had happened a week earlier. Born in Slamannan, Stirlingshire, in June 1880, Young's career took him to St Mirren and Falkirk before he joined Everton in the summer of 1901. A centre-forward who occasionally turned out at outside-left, he made his Everton debut at Villa Park on 28 September 1901, but it took him until the first week in December to score his first goal for the club, against Sheffield Wednesday at Goodison. In subsequent seasons Young showed Everton fans just why he had been bought. He scored 110 goals in 275 League games and topped the scoring charts in 1906-07 when his 28 goals included four against Manchester City as Everton romped home 9-1. In the close season of 1911 he moved to Tottenham Hotspur but was not at White Hart Lane long. A year later he began to wind down his career with Burslem Port Vale. He won two Scottish caps while at Everton, against England and Wales.

ALEX YOUNG

	LEAGUE		FA CUP		FL CUP		EUROPE		TOTAL	
	App	Gls	App	Gls	App	Gls	App	Gls	App	Gls
1960-61	13	6			1	1			14	7
1961-62	40	14	3						43	14
1962-63	42	22	3				2		47	22
1963-64	27	12	3				2		32	12
1964-65	20	3	1				3	3	24	6
1965-66	26	7	8	2			2		36	9
1966-67	35	8	5	2			4		44	10
1967-68	24/1	5	2/2		2	2			28/3	7
	227/1	77	25/2	4	3	3	13	3	268/3	87

Alex Young was one of the most talked-about players of his generation. His instinctive, flowing style combined with the on-field arrogance of a great performer to make him a sporting hero on Merseyside. The adulation which rolled down from the Goodison terraces when he touched the ball verged on unashamed hero-worship. In the eyes of a public which searched desperately for a focal point for their affection, the young Scotsman with the magic boots could do no wrong. In many respects he was an infuriating player, capable of seemingly impossible feats one minute, unable or unwilling to complete a far simpler task the next. Critics said that he 'disappeared' for lengthy periods when the going got tough. Certainly he was not built for a fight. He was a graceful, compact player who could turn a match with one flick of a spidery leg. He was so revered that he inspired a television play centred around Everton and entitled *The Golden Vision*, the nickname Young carries to this day. He arrived at Goodison in November 1960, along with Hearts colleague George Thomson. Within two years of establishing his place, he helped Everton to the Championship with a series of stunning solo displays. He played in the 1966 FA Cup-winning side, leaving Goodison in 1968 to become player-manager of Irish League club Glentoran. He stayed only a matter of weeks. He joined Stockport County but was forced to retire in August 1969 because of a knee injury.

Crowd's-eye view of the 1907 Cup Final between Everton and Sheffield Wednesday.

PLAYER	BIRTHPLACE	FROM	TO	LEAGUE		FA CUP		L. CUP		TOTAL	
				App	Gls	App	Gls	App	Gls	App	Gls
ABBOTT W.	Birmingham	Small Heath 1899	Burnley 1907	257	32	34	5	0	0	291	37
ADAMS J.	Edinburgh	Hearts 1894	Hearts 1895	40	1	3	0	0	0	43	1
ADAMSON H.		Lochgelly 1907	Bolton W. Dec 1909	25	0	0	0	0	0	25	0
AINSCOW A.	Bolton	Birmingham C. Aug 1981	# May 1983	24/4	3	0	0	1/1	0	25/5	3
ALFORD F.J.	Swindon	Swindon T. 1921	Barrow 1921	2	0	0	0	0	0	2	0
ALLAN J.	Carlisle	Carlisle U. 1909	Manchester C. Jun 1912	19	0	0	0	0	0	19	0
ANGUS J.A.		Sunderland A. 1888	retired 1890	16	0	1	0	0	0	17	0
ARCHER J.W.	Wednesbury	Walsall 1932	Coventry C. 1935	15	2	0	0	0	0	15	2
ARNOLD J.	Stafford	Blackburn R. Aug 1981	*	48	0	5	0	6	0	59	0
ARRIDGE S.	Sunderland	Bootle 1893	New Brighton 1896	51	0	5	0	0	0	56	0
ASHWORTH A.	Southport	**May 1957	Luton T. Oct 1960	12	3	0	0	0	0	12	3
ASHWORTH S.B.	Stoke	Manchester C. Sep 1904	Port Vale 1904	11	0	0	0	0	0	11	0
*ATKIN I.	Birmingham	Sunderland Nov 1984	*	6	1	0/1	0	0	0	6/1	1
ATTWOOD A.A.	Walsall	Walsall 1928	Bristol R. 1929	3	0	0	0	0	0	3	0
*BAILEY J.	Liverpool	Blackburn R. Jul 1979	*	170	3	22	0	19/1	0	211/1	3
BAIN D.	Rotherglen	Manchester U. 1924	Bristol C Nov 1928	38	3	5	0	0	0	43	3
BAKER B.H.	Liverpool	Blackburn R. 1920	Chelsea 1926	13	0	0	0	0	0	13	0
*BALL A.J.	Farnworth	Blackpool Aug 1966	Arsenal Dec 1971	208	66	21	5	10	3	239	74
BALMER R.	Liverpool	**1902	1911	165	21	23	0	0	0	188	21
BALMER W.	Liverpool	South Shore 1897	Croydon 1907	293	1	38	0	0	0	331	1
BANKS H.		Army 1896	Third Lanark 1896	2	0	0	0	0	0	2	0
BARBER E		**1938	1938	2	0	0	0	0	0	2	0
BARDSLEY J.C.	Southport	N.Nomads 1909	Manchester C Nov 1911	1	0	0	0	0	0	1	0
BARKER G		**1896	Bristol C. 1897	10	0	0	0	0	0	10	0
BARLOW G.H.		Preston N.E. 1908	Preston N.E. 1910	34	5	8	1	0	0	42	6
BARLOW J.	Prescot	**1897	Reading 1898	4	0	0	0	0	0	4	0
BARNETT G.C.	Northwich	**May 1964	Arsenal Oct 1969	10	0	0	0	0	0	10	0
*BARTON J.S.	Birmingham	Worcester C. Dec 1978	Derby C. Mar 1982	18/2	1	0	0	3	0	21/2	1
BATTEN H.G.	Bristol	Plymouth A. Feb 1926	Bradford C. Nov 1926	15	1	0	0	0	0	15	1
BEARE G.	Southampton	Blackpool 1910	Cardiff C. Jun 1914	104	18	14	1	0	0	118	19
BELFITT R.	Doncaster R.	Ipswich T. Nov 1972	Sunderland Oct 1973	14/2	2	2	1	0	0	16/2	3
BELL J.	Dumbarton	Dumbarton 1892 / New Brighton T. 1901	Tottenham H. 1898 / Preston N.E. 1903	177	62	22	8	0	0	199	70
BELL L.	Dumbarton	Sheffield W. Jul 1897	Bolton W. 1898	41	17	7	3	0	0	48	20
BELL R.C.	Birkenhead	Tranmere R. Mar 1936	1938	14	9	0	0	0	0	14	9
BENNETT H.	Liverpool	**Mar 1967	Aldershot Jan 1971	2	0	0	0	1	0	3	0
BENTHAM S.J.	Lawton St Mary's	Wigan A. Jan 1934	retired 1948	110	17	15	0	0	0	125	17
BENTLEY J.	Liverpool	**Nov 1959	Stockport C. May 1961	1	0	0	0	0	0	1	0
BERNARD M.P.	Shrewsbury	Stoke C. May 1972	Oldham A. Jul 1977	139/8	8	9/1	0	11/1	0	159/10	8

PLAYER	BIRTHPLACE	FROM	TO	LEAGUE App	Gls	FA CUP App	Gls	L. CUP App	Gls	TOTAL App	Gls
BERRY A.	Liverpool	Fulham 1909	Liverpool 1910	27	7	2	0	0	0	29	7
BERRY C.H.	Warrington	*1908	1911	3	0	0	0	0	0	3	0
BERWICK W.	Northampton	Glossop 1919	1919	1	0	0	0	0	0	1	0
BEVERIDGE R.	Polmuti	Nottingham F. 1900	Died Oct 1901	4	0	0	0	0	0	4	0
BILEY A.	Leighton Buzzard	Derby C. July 1981	Portsmouth Aug 1982	16/3	3	0	0	2	0	18/3	3
*BINGHAM W.P.	Belfast	Luton T. Oct 1960	Port Vale Aug 1963	86	23	7	2	3	1	96	26
BIRCH K.J.	Birkenhead	**Aug 1951	Southampton Mar 1958	43	1	2	0	0	0	45	1
BIRNIE A.		**1905	Norwich C. 1905	3	0	0	0	0	0	3	0
BISHOP I.	Liverpool	**Jun 1981	*	0/1	0	0	0	0	0	0/1	0
BLACK W.	Isle of Mull	Celtic 1905	1906	20	0	0	0	0	0	20	0
BLAIR J.E.	Liverpool	1919	Oldham A 1921	5	3	1	0	0	0	6	3
BLYTHE J.		Jarrow 1898	West Ham U. 1901	34	1	1	0	0	0	35	1
BOCKING W.	Stockport	Stockport C. Apr 1931	Apr 1931	15	0	1	0	0	0	16	0
BOLTON H.	Port Glasgow	Newcastle U. Jan 1906	Bradford Dec 1908	75	27	12	7	0	0	87	34
BONE J.		**1901	1901	2	0	0	0	0	0	2	0
BOOTH T.	Manchester	Blackburn R. May 1900	Preston N.E. 1907	175	9	10	2	0	0	185	11
BORROWS B.	Liverpool	**July 1977	Bolton W. Mar 1983	27	0	0	0	2	0	29	0
BORTHWICK J.		Hibernian 1907	Millwall 1910	25	0	0	0	0	0	25	0
BOWMAN A.		E.Stirling 1901	Blackburn R. 1902	9	3	2	0	0	0	11	3
BOYES W.E.	Sheffield	West Brom A. Feb 1938	Notts C. Jul 1949	66	11	7	4	0	0	73	15
BOYLE D.		New Brighton T. 1901	Dundee 1901	7	0	0	0	0	0	7	0
BOYLE R.H.	Dumbarton	Dumbarton 1890	Dundee Jun 1902	222	7	21	1	0	0	243	8
*BRACEWELL P.	Heswall	Sunderland May 1984	*	37	2	7	0	4	1	48	3
BRADSHAW F.	Sheffield	Northampton T. Nov 1911	Arsenal Aug 1914	66	19	8	2	0	0	74	21
BRADSHAW G.F.	Southport	New Brighton 1934	Arsenal 1934	2	0	1	0	0	0	3	0
BRADY A.		Sunderland Nov 1889	Celtic 1890	34	17	2	3	0	0	36	20
BRAMWELL J.	Ashton-in-Makerfield	** Apr 1958	Luton T. Oct 1960	52	0	4	0	0	0	56	0
BRAND D.S.	Edinburgh	**Nov 1975	Crewe A. Feb 1977	2	0	0	0	0	0	2	0
BRANNICK J.		1912	St.Mirren Apr 1914	3	2	0	0	0	0	3	2
BREARLEY J.	Liverpool	Middlesbrough 1902	Tottenham H. 1902	22	7	2	1	0	0	24	8
BREWSTER G.	Culsalmond	Aberdeen Jan 1920	Wolves Nov 1922	64	4	4	0	0	0	68	4
BRIGGS H.F.		Darwen 1895	1896	11	0	0	0	0	0	11	0
BRINDLE W.	Liverpool	**Aug 1967	Barnsley May 1970	1	0	0	0	1	0	2	0
BRISCOE W.		1888	1888	3	0	0	0	0	0	3	0
BRITTON C.S.	Bristol	Bristol R. June 1930	Burnley May 1945	221	2	19	1	0	0	240	3
BROAD J.	Stalybridge	Sittingbourne Nov 1924	New Brighton Dec 1925	18	8	3	0	0	0	21	8
BROMILOW W.	Liverpool	1912	1912	1	0	0	0	0	0	1	0
BROWELL A.	Walbottle	Hull C. 1912	West Stanley 1912	1	0	0	0	0	0	1	0
BROWELL T.	Walbottle	Hull C. Dec 1911	Manchester C. Oct 1913	50	26	10	11	0	0	60	37

PLAYER	BIRTHPLACE	FROM	TO	LEAGUE App	LEAGUE Gls	FA CUP App	FA CUP Gls	L. CUP App	L. CUP Gls	TOTAL App	TOTAL Gls
*BROWN A.D.	Grangemouth	Partick T. Sep 1963	Shrewsbury T. May 1971	176/33	9	16/8	0	10	1	202/41	10
BROWN W.		Stanley 1888	1888	6	2	0	0	0	0	6	2
BROWN W.	Cambuslang	Partick T. 1914	Nottingham F. May 1928	170	9	9	0	0	0	179	0
BUCK H.		Tranmere R. 1908	1908	1	0	0	0	0	0	1	0
BUCKLE E.W.	Southwark	Manchester U Nov 1949	Exeter C. Jul 1955	97	31	10	2	0	0	107	33
*BUCKLEY M.J.	Manchester	**June 1971	Sunderland Aug 1978	128/7	10	7	1	12	1	147/7	12
BURNETT G.G.	Liverpool	**1946	Oldham A. Oct 1951	47	0	7	0	0	0	54	0
BURTON A.D.	Lochgelly	Bristol C. 1911	Reading 1911	12	4	0	0	0	0	12	4
CAIN R.		Airdrie 1889	Bootle 1889	10	0	0	0	0	0	10	0
CAIN T.		Stoke C. 1894	Southampton 1894	11	0	1	0	0	0	12	0
CALDWELL J.H.	Carronshore	Reading 1912	Arsenal Jun 1913	31	0	5	0	0	0	36	0
CAMERON D.P.	Dublin	Shelbourne U. Jul 1948	Sligo R. Sep 1949	1	0	0	0	0	0	1	0
CAMERON J.	Ayr	Queen's Park Sep 1895	Tottenham H. 1897	42	12	6	2	0	0	48	14
CAMPBELL W.C.		Bootle 1890	Clyde 1896	20	2	0	0	0	0	20	2
CASKIE J.		St.Johnstone 1938	Rangers 1938	5	1	0	0	0	0	5	1
CATTERICK H.	Darlington	Stockport C. 1946	Crewe A. Dec 1951	59	19	12	5	0	0	71	24
CHADWICK A.	Church	**1888	Accrington 1892	5	0	0	0	0	0	5	0
CHADWICK E.W.	Blackburn	Blackburn R. 1888	Burnley May 1899	270	97	30	13	0	0	300	110
CHADWICK R.		Blackburn R. 1901	1907	21	0	1	0	0	0	22	0
CHADWICK W.	Bury	**Feb 1922	Leeds U. Nov 1925	102	50	7	5	0	0	109	55
CHEDGZOY S.	Ellesmere Port	**Dec 1910	USA May 1926	279	33	21	3	0	0	300	36
CLARK A.W.	Shoreham	Luton T. May 1931	Tranmere R. Mar 1936	41	1	1	0	0	0	42	1
CLARK C.		1901	Plymouth A. 1902	6	1	1	0	0	0	7	1
CLARKE H	Walsall	**1898	Portsmouth 1898	12	2	0	0	0	0	12	2
*CLEMENTS D.	Larne	Sheffield W. Sep 1973	#Feb 1976	81/2	6	6	2	8	0	95/2	8
CLENNELL J	Sunderland	Blackburn R. Jan 1914	Cardiff C. Oct 1921	68	30	6	3	0	0	74	33
CLIFFORD R.		Bolton W. Nov 1908	Fulham 1910	37	0	8	0	0	0	45	0
CLINTON T.J.	Dublin	Dundalk Mar 1948	Blackburn R. Apr 1955	73	4	7	1	0	0	80	5
COCK J.G.	Hayle	Chelsea Jan 1923	Plymouth A. Mar 1925	69	29	3	2	0	0	72	31
COGGINS W.H.	Bristol	Bristol C. Mar 1930	Q.P.R. 1933	51	0	5	0	0	0	56	0
COLEMAN J.G.	Kettering	Arsenal 1907	Sunderland 1909	69	30	2	1	0	0	71	31
COLLINS H.		1905	1905	3	0	0	0	0	0	3	0
COLLINS J.		Cambuslang 1891	1892	15	0	0	0	0	0	15	0
COLLINS R.Y.	Glasgow	Celtic Sep 1958	Leeds U. Mar 1962	133	42	9	5	5	1	147	48
COMMON E.W.	Seaton Delavel	Blyth Spartans Jan 1928	Preston N.E. Nov 1933	14	0	0	0	0	0	14	0
CONNOLLY J.	Glasgow	St.Johnstone Mar 1972	Birmingham C. Sep 1976	105/3	16	3/1	0	4	0	112/4	16
COOK H.E.		1905	1905	7	3	2	0	0	0	9	3
COOK W.		Celtic Dec 1932	Wrexham 1945	225	5	24	1	0	0	249	6
CORR P.J.	Dundalk	Preston N.E. Aug 1948	Bangor 1949	24	2	0	0	0	0	24	2

PLAYER	BIRTHPLACE	FROM	TO	LEAGUE App	Gls	FA CUP App	Gls	L. CUP App	Gls	TOTAL App	Gls
CORRIN T		1900	Southampton 1903	11	1	1	0	0	0	12	1
COSTLEY J.T.		Blackburn R. 1888	1888	6	3	3	0	0	0	6	3
COULTER J.	Co.Antrim	Belfast Celtic Feb 1934	Grimsby T. Oct 1937	50	16	8	8	0	0	58	24
COUPER G.		Hearts 1906	1907	4	1	0	0	0	0	4	1
COX W.		Burnley 1889	Nottingham F. 1889	4	0	0	0	0	0	4	0
COYNE		Gainsborough 1888	1888	2	1	0	0	0	0	2	1
CRELLEY J.	Liverpool	Millwall A. 1899	Exeter C. 1907	116	0	11	0	0	0	127	0
CRESSWELL W.	South Shields	Sunderland Feb 1927	Port Vale May 1936	290	1	16	0	0	0	306	1
CRITCHLEY E.	Ashton	Stockport C. Dec 1926	Preston N.E. Jun 1934	217	37	12	5	0	0	229	42
CROMPTON T.		1898	1898	3	1	1	0	0	0	4	1
CROSSLEY C.A.	Walsall	Sunderland 1920	West Ham U. Jun 1922	50	18	5	3	0	0	55	21
CUMMINS G.F.	Dublin	**Nov 1950	Luton T. Aug 1953	24	0	5	0	0	0	29	0
CUNLIFFE J.N.	Blackrod	Adlington May 1930	Rochdale Sep 1946	174	73	13	3	0	0	187	76
*CURRAN T.	Kingsley	Sheffield U. Sep 1983	*	19/4	1	1	0	0	0	20/4	1
DANSKIN J.	Winsford	**July 1984	*	1	0	0	0	0	0	1	0
DARCY F.J.	Liverpool	**Aug 1964	Tranmere R. Jul 1972	8/8	0	0/1	0	0	0	8/9	0
*DARRACOTT T.	Liverpool	**Jul 1968	#Feb 1979	138/10	0	12	0	12	0	162/10	0
DAVIDSON W.	Glasgow	Middlesbrough 1911	St Mirren Jun 1913	38	3	7	1	0	0	45	4
DAVIE	Renton	1888	1888	2	0	0	0	0	0	2	0
DAVIES A.L.	Wallasey	Flint Aug 1926	Exeter C. Aug 1930	90	0	3	0	0	0	93	0
DAVIES J.		1888	Chirk 1888	8	2	0	0	0	0	8	2
DAVIES J.W.	Denbigh	Cardiff C. 1946	Plymouth A. Feb 1947	1	0	0	0	0	0	1	0
DAVIES S.	Chirk	Preston N.E. Jan 1921	West Brom A. Nov 1921	20	9	2	1	0	0	22	10
*DAVIES W.D.	Ammanford	Swansea C. Dec 1970	Wrexham Sep 1977	82	0	5	0	6	0	93	0
DAWSON H.		Rossendale 1908	Blackpool Mar 1909	4	0	1	0	0	0	5	0
DEAN W.R.	Birkenhead	Tranmere R. Mar 1925	Notts C. Mar 1938	399	349	32	28	0	0	431	377
DEPLEDGE R.P.	Wallasey	**1906	1906	1	0	0	0	0	0	1	0
DEWAR J.		1892	1892	1	0	0	0	0	0	1	0
DICK A.		Kilmarnock 1888	1888	9	0	0	0	0	0	9	0
DICKINSON	Saltney	**1934	Port Vale 1934	1	0	0	0	0	0	1	0
DILLY T.	Arbroath	Hearts 1902	West Brom A. Mar 1906	9	2	0	0	0	0	9	2
DIVER J.		Celtic Apr 1897	Celtic 1898	30	11	2	0	0	0	32	11
DOBSON G.		Bolton W. 1888	1888	18	0	0	0	0	0	18	0
*DOBSON M.	Blackburn	Burnley Aug 1979	Burnley Aug 1974	190	29	13	2	22	8	225	39
*DODDS E.	Grangemouth	Blackpool Nov 1946	Lincoln C. Oct 1948	55	36	3	1	0	0	58	37
DOMINY A.A.	Southampton	Southampton May 1926	Gillingham Mar 1928	29	12	4	1	0	0	33	13
DONALDSON J.		**1905	Preston N.E. 1905	2	0	0	0	0	0	2	0
DONNACHIE J.	Kilmarnock	Newcastle U. Feb 1906	Oldham A. Oct 1908	56	0	2	0	0	0	58	0
		Rangers 1919	Blackpool Jun 1920								0

PLAYER	BIRTHPLACE	FROM	TO	LEAGUE App	LEAGUE Gls	FA CUP App	FA CUP Gls	L. CUP App	L. CUP Gls	TOTAL App	TOTAL Gls
DONOVAN D.	Cork	**May 1949	Grimsby T. Aug 1958	179	2	8	0	0	0	187	2
DOUGAL P.G.	Midridge	Arsenal Aug 1937	Bury Jun 1938	11	2	0	0	0	0	11	2
DOWNS R.W.	Paisley	Barnsley Mar 1920	Brighton Aug 1923	92	0	5	0	0	0	97	0
DOYLE D.	Liverpool	Bolton W. 1889	Celtic 1890	42	0	3	1	0	0	45	1
DUGDALE G.	Liverpool	**June 1947	Retired 1949	58	0	5	0	0	0	63	0
DUNLOP A.	Liverpool	**Aug 1949	Wrexham Nov 1963	211	0	15	0	5	0	231	0
DUNN J.	Glasgow	Hibernian Apr 1928	Exeter C. May 1935	140	42	14	7	0	0	154	49
EARP M.J.	Nottingham	Nottingham F. 1891	Nottingham F. 1891	9	0	1	0	0	0	10	0
EASTHOPE J.	Liverpool	**Apr 1950	Stockport C. Jun 1954	2	0	0	0	0	0	2	0
*EASTOE P.R.	Tamworth	Q.P.R. Mar 1979	West Brom A. Aug 1982	88/7	26	12	6	6	1	106/7	33
EASTON W.C.	Blyth	Blyth Spartans Mar 1927	Swansea T. Jan 1930	15	3	0	0	0	0	15	3
ECCLES G.S.	Newcastle	Wolves Apr 1898	West Ham U. May 1902	56	0	4	0	0	0	60	0
EGLINGTON T.	Dublin	Shamrock R. Jul 1946	Tranmere R. Jun 1957	394	76	34	6	0	0	428	82
ELLIOTT J.		1890	1895	14	1	1	0	0	0	15	1
ELLIOTT T.		1945	1945	0	0	2	1	0	0	2	1
EVANS W.B.	Llandiloes	1919	Swansea T. 1919	2	0	0	0	0	0	2	0
FALDER D.E.J.	Liverpool	Wigan A. 1949	Ellesmere Port 1950	25	0	5	0	0	0	30	0
FARMER G.		Oswestry 1888	1889	31	1	0	0	0	0	31	1
FARRALL A.	Hoylake	**Mar 1953	Preston N.E. May 1957	5	0	0	0	0	0	5	0
FARRELL P.D.	Dublin	Shamrock R. Aug 1946	Tranmere R. Oct 1957	422	13	31	4	0	0	453	17
FAZACKERLEY S.	Preston	Sheffield U. Nov 1920	Wolves Nov 1922	51	21	6	0	0	0	57	21
FELL J.I.	Grimsby	Grimsby T. Mar 1961	Newcastle U. Mar 1962	27	4	1	1	0	0	28	5
FERGUSON M.	Newcastle	Coventry C. Aug 1981	Birmingham C. Jun 1983	7/1	4	0	0	3/1	2	10/2	6
FERN T.E.	Measham	Lincoln C. 1913	Port Vale Jun 1924	219	0	12	0	0	0	231	0
FIELDING W.A.	Edmonton	Charlton A. 1946	Southport Jan 1959	380	49	30	5	0	0	410	54
FINNIS H.A.	Liverpool	**Jun 1946	Retired 1946	1	0	0	0	0	0	1	0
FLEETWOOD T.	Liverpool	Rochdale Mar 1911	Oldham A. Aug 1923	264	9	21	1	0	0	285	10
FLEMING G.		1888	1888	4	2	0	0	0	0	4	2
FLEWITT A.	Beeston	Lincoln C. 1895	West Brom A. 1895	3	1	0	0	0	0	3	1
FORBES F.J.	Edinburgh	Hearts 1922	Plymouth A. Mar 1925	14	4	0	0	0	0	14	4
FORSHAW R.	Widnes	Liverpool Mar 1927	Wolves Aug 1929	41	8	0	0	0	0	41	8
FREEMAN B.C.	Birmingham	Arsenal 1907	Burnley Apr 1911	86	61	8	4	0	0	94	65
*GABRIEL J.	Dundee	Dundee Mar 1960	Southampton Jul 1967	255/1	33	25	2	5	0	285/1	35
GALT J.	Saltcoats	Rangers May 1914	Third Lanark Oct 1920	32	2	4	2	0	0	36	4
GANNON M.J.	Liverpool	**Feb 1960	Scunthorpe U. May 1962	3	0	0	0	0	0	3	0
GARDNER T.		Jun 1947	1947	1	0	0	0	0	0	1	0
GAULD J.	Aberdeen	Charlton A. Oct 1956	Plymouth A. Oct 1957	23	7	3	1	0	0	26	8
GAULT W.E.	Wallsend	1912	Cardiff C. May 1920	29	13	1	0	0	0	30	13
GEARY F.	Hyson Green	Notts Co. 1889	Liverpool 1894	91	78	7	8	0	0	98	86

PLAYER	BIRTHPLACE	FROM	TO	LEAGUE App	LEAGUE Gls	FA CUP App	FA CUP Gls	L. CUP App	L. CUP Gls	TOTAL App	TOTAL Gls
GEE C.W.	Stockport	Stockport C. Jul 1930	Retired May 1940	196	2	15	0	0	0	211	2
GEE E.	Grassmoor	Chesterfield 1897	Notts C. 1899	31	0	1	0	0	0	32	0
GELDARD A.	Bradford	Bradford Nov 1932	Bolton W. Jul 1938	167	31	12	6	0	0	179	37
GIBSON D.J.	Runcorn	**Aug 1950	Swindon T. Nov 1954	3	0	0	0	0	0	3	0
GIDMAN J.	Liverpool	Aston Villa Oct 1979	Manchester U. Jul 1981	64	2	11	0	3	1	78	3
GILLICK T	Airdrie	Rangers Dec 1935	Rangers Nov 1945	121	40	12	4	0	0	133	44
GLAZZARD J.	Normanton	Huddersfield T. Aug 1956	Mansfield T. Dec 1955	3	0	0	0	0	0	3	0
GLOVER G.J.	Liverpool	**Aug 1964	Mansfield T. Sep 1967	2/1	0	0	0	0	0	2/1	0
GODFREY B.C.	Flint	**May 1958	Scunthorpe U. Jun 1960	1	0	0	0	0	0	1	0
GOLDIE H.		St.Mirren 1895	Celtic 1896	18	1	1	0	0	0	19	1
GOODLASS R.	Liverpool	**Jul 1971	# Oct 1977	31/4	2	7	0	9	0	47/4	2
GORDON P.		Renton 1890	Liverpool 1892	18	3	5	2	0	0	23	5
GOURLAY J.	Annbank	Port Glasgow 1909	Morton May 1913	54	8	4	1	0	0	58	9
GRACIE T.	Glasgow	Morton 1910	Liverpool Feb 1912	13	1	0	0	0	0	13	1
GRAHAM R.		Third Lanark 1906	Bolton W. 1906	2	0	1	0	0	0	3	0
GRANT J.A.	Gateshead	High Spon Ath. Aug 1942	Rochdale Jun 1956	121	10	12	1	0	0	133	11
*GRAY A.	Glasgow	Wolves Nov 1983	Aston Villa Jul 1985	44/5	14	14/1	3	0/1	0	58/7	17
GRAY R.		Partick 1899	Southampton 1900	20	1	1	0	0	0	21	1
GREEN C.R.	Wrexham	**Feb 1959	Birmingham C. Dec 1962	15	1	2	0	1	0	18	1
GREENHALGH N.	Bolton	New Brighton Jan 1938	Bangor C. 1948	106	1	9	0	0	0	115	1
GRENYER A.	North Shields	North Shields 1910	South Shields Nov 1924	142	9	6	0	0	0	148	9
GRIFFITHS B.	Liverpool	**Mar 1956	Southport Jun 1960	2	0	0	0	0	0	2	0
GRIFFITHS P.	Tylorstown	Port Vale 1931	West Brom A. 1932	8	3	0	0	0	0	8	3
GRIFFITHS T.	Wrexham	Wrexham Dec 1926	Bolton W. Dec 1931	76	9	2	0	0	0	78	9
GRUNDY H.		1905	Reading 1905	2	0	0	0	0	0	2	0
HAMILTON B.	Belfast	Ipswich T. Nov 1975	Millwall Jul 1977	38/3	5	2/2	0	7/2	0	47/7	5
HAMILTON H.	Wallasey	**1926	Preston N.E. May 1927	1	0	0	0	0	0	1	0
HAMMOND H.		1889	1889	1	0	0	0	0	0	1	0
HAMPSON A.	Prescot	**Aug 1949	Halifax T. Nov 1952	42	0	2	0	0	0	44	0
HANNAH A.B.	Renton	Renton 1889	Renton 1890	1	0	0	0	0	0	1	0
HANNAN J.		Celtic 1905	1905	1	0	0	0	0	0	1	0
HARBURN P.	Finsbury	Brighton & HA Aug 1958	Scunthorpe U. Jan 1959	4	1	0	0	0	0	4	1
HARDMAN H.P.	Manchester	Blackpool 1903	Manchester U. Aug 1908	130	25	26	4	0	0	156	29
HARDY H.J.	Stockport	Stockport C. Oct 1925	Bury Jul 1928	40	0	5	0	0	0	45	0
HARGREAVES F.	Ashton	Oldham A. 1924	Oldham A. May 1925	9	2	0	0	0	0	9	2
HARLAND A.I.	Crookstown	Linfield Oct 1922	Runcorn 1925	64	0	6	0	0	0	70	0
*HARPER A.	Liverpool	Liverpool June 1983	*	36/5	1	2/2	0	7/1	0	45/8	1
HARPER J.	Greenock	Aberdeen Dec 1972	Hibernian Feb 1974	40/3	12	4	2	2	0	46/3	14
HARRIS A.E.	Liverpool	**Jan 1955	Tranmere R. May 1957	5	0	0	0	0	0	5	0

PLAYER	BIRTHPLACE	FROM	TO	LEAGUE App	LEAGUE Gls	FA CUP App	FA CUP Gls	L. CUP App	L. CUP Gls	TOTAL App	TOTAL Gls
*HARRIS B.	Bebington	*Jan 1954	Cardiff C. Oct 1966	310	23	31	4	5	0	346	27
HARRIS J.	Birkenhead	*Sep 1951	Birmingham C. Dec 1960	191	65	14	5	2	2	207	72
HARRIS J.A.	Liverpool	**Jul 1950	Bangor C. 1952	14	4	0	0	0	0	14	4
HARRIS V.	Dublin	Shelbourne 1907	Shelbourne 1913	190	1	24	1	0	0	214	2
HARRISON G.	Church Gresley	Leicester F. Apr 1913	Preston N.E. Dec 1923	177	17	13	0	0	0	190	17
HART H.	Glasgow	Airdrie Jan 1922	Retired 1929	289	5	11	0	0	0	300	5
HARTFORD A.	Clydebank	Nottingham F. Aug 1979	Manchester C. Oct 1981	81	6	11	1	6	0	98	7
HARTILL W.J.	Wolverhampton	Wolves 1935	Liverpool 1935	5	1	0	0	0	0	5	1
HARTLEY A.		Dumbarton 1892	Liverpool Dec 1897	50	24	11	4	0	0	61	28
*HARVEY J.C.	Liverpool	**Oct 1962	Sheffield W. Sep 1974	317/3	18	34	4	10/1	0	361/4	22
HAUGHEY W.	Glasgow	*June 1956	Falkirk Jun 1958	4	1	0	0	0	0	4	1
HEARD P.	Hull	**Sep 1978	Aston Villa Oct 1979	10/1	0	0	0	0	0	10/1	0
*HEATH A.	Stoke	Stoke C. Jan 1982	*	112	39	12	3	19	5	143	47
HEDLEY J.R.	Wellington Quay	**1947	Sunderland Jul 1950	54	0	7	0	0	0	61	0
HENDERSON W.	Linlithgow	Southampton 1902	Reading 1903	15	0	2	0	0	0	17	0
HESLOP G.W.	Wallsend	Newcastle U. Mar 1962	Manchester C. Sep 1965	10	0	1	0	0	0	11	0
HICKSON D.	Ellesmere Port	**May 1948 Huddersfield T. Jul 1957	Aston Villa Sep 1955 Liverpool Nov 1959	225	95	18	16	0	0	243	111
HIGGINS M.		1888	1888	1	0	0	0	0	0	1	0
*HIGGINS M.N.	Buxton	**Aug 1976	Retired 1984	150/1	6	7	0	19	0	176/1	6
HIGGINS W.C.	Tranmere	Tranmere R. 1946	Bogota (Colombia) 1949	48	8	1	1	0	0	49	9
HIGHAM N.	Chorley	**1933	Middlesbrough 1934	14	6	0	0	0	0	14	6
HILL M.J.	Carrickfergus	Norwich C. Aug 1963	Port Vale Oct 1965	7	1	0	0	0	0	7	1
HILL P.		Southampton 1905	Manchester C. Nov 1906	14	0	2	0	0	0	16	0
HILLMAN J.	Tavistock	Burnley Feb 1895	Dundee 1895	35	0	3	0	0	0	38	0
HODGE M.	Southport	Plymouth A. July 1979	Sheffield W. Sep 1983	25	0	6	0	0	0	31	0
HODGE W.	Kilwinning	1912	1913	10	0	0	0	0	0	10	0
HOLBEM W.	Sheffield	Sheffield W. 1911	St Mirren Jul 1913	18	0	0	0	0	0	18	0
HOLD O.	Barnsley	Notts C. Feb 1950	Q.P.R. Feb 1952	22	5	1	0	0	0	23	5
HOLT J.	Blackburn	Bootle 1888	Reading Oct 1898	225	3	27	1	0	0	252	4
HOUGHTON H.	Liverpool	**1927	Exeter C. Jun 1928	1	0	0	0	0	0	1	0
HOUSTON J.	Belfast	Linfield Feb 1913	Linfield 1919	26	2	2	0	0	0	28	2
HOWARTH H.B.	Liverpool	1914	1919	8	2	0	0	0	0	8	2
HOWARTH R.H.	Preston	Preston N.E. Nov 1891	Preston N.E. 1893	59	0	9	0	0	0	68	0
HUGHES D.	Prescott	** Jul 1982	*	3	0	0	0	0	0	3	0
HUGHES D.	Ruabon	1898	Tottenham H. 1898	8	0	0	0	0	0	8	0
HUMPHREYS G.	Llandudno	**Sep 1963	Crystal P. Jun 1970	12	2	0	0	0	0	14	2
HUMPHREYS J.	Llandudno	1946	Llandudno T. 1950	53	0	8	0	0	0	61	0
HUNT E.	Swindon	Wolves Sep 1967	Coventry C. Mar 1968	12/2	3	1	0	1	0	14	3

PLAYER	BIRTHPLACE	FROM	TO	LEAGUE App	Gls	FA CUP App	Gls	L. CUP App	Gls	TOTAL App	Gls
HUREL E.	Jersey	St.Helier 1936	Northampton T. 1936	5	1	0	0	0	0	5	1
*HURST J.W.	Blackpool	**Oct 1964	Oldham A. Jun 1976	336/11	29	30/2	4	13	1	379/13	34
*HUSBAND J.	Newcastle	**Oct 1964	Luton T. Nov. 1973	158/7	44	22	10	5	1	185/7	55
IRVINE A.	Glasgow	Queen's Park May 1981	Crystal P. Nov 1984	51/9	4	9	2	10/1	0	70/10	6
IRVINE R.W.	Belfast	Dunmurry Sep 1921	Portsmouth Mar 1928	199	54	15	3	0	0	214	57
IRVING D.	Workington	Workington T. Jan 1973	Oldham A. Jun 1976	4/2	1	1	0	1	1	6/2	1
JACK R.	Avoch	**Feb 1977	Norwich C. Dec 1975	1	1	0	0	0	0	1	1
JACKSON G.	Liverpool	**1934	Retired 1947	75	0	4	0	0	0	79	0
*JACKSON T.	Belfast	Glentoran Feb 1968	Nottingham F. Oct 1970	30/2	0	3/1	0	1	0	34/3	0
JAMIESON J.		1889	Sheffield W. 1892	15	0	0	0	0	0	15	0
JARDINE D.		Bootle Nov 1890	Nelson 1893	37	0	0	0	0	0	37	0
JEFFERIS F.	Fordingbridge	Southampton Mar 1911	Preston N.E. Jan 1920	125	22	12	3	0	0	137	25
JOHNSON A.	Weaverham	**1946	Chesterfield Sep 1948	9	0	0	0	0	0	9	0
*JOHNSON D.E.	Liverpool	**Apr 1969	Ipswich T. Nov. 1972	79/10	15	5	2	7	2	91/10	19
JOHNSON T.C.	Dalton-in-Furness	Manchester C. Mar 1930	Liverpool Mar 1934	146	56	13	8	0	0	159	64
JOHNSTON L.		1913	1913	8	1	0	0	0	0	8	1
JOLIFFE C.		1888	1888	5	0	0	0	0	0	5	0
JONES D.R.	Liverpool	**May 1974	Coventry C. Jun 1979	79/7	1	5	1	11/1	0	95/8	2
*JONES G.K.	Liverpool	**Oct 1968	Birmingham C. Jul 1976	76/6	12	7/1	1	5	1	88/7	14
JONES G.W.	Crook	Gwersylt 1919	Wigan B. Jan 1923	36	2	0	0	0	0	36	2
JONES J.E.	Bromborough	Ellesmere Port 1933	Sunderland Dec 1945	98	0	10	0	0	0	108	0
JONES R.		1888	Manchester C. 1892	7	1	0	0	0	0	7	1
JONES R.H.	Liverpool	**1924	Southport 1924	3	0	0	0	0	0	3	0
JONES T	Liverpool	1905	Birmingham Sep 1910	15	5	0	0	0	0	15	5
JONES T.E.	Liverpool	**Jan 1948	Retired 1961	383	14	25	0	3	0	411	14
JONES T.G.	Queensferry	Wrexham Mar 1936	Pwllheli Apr 1950	165	4	10	1	0	0	175	5
JORDAN W.C.	Langley	West Brom A. 1911	Wolves Jul 1912	2	0	0	0	0	0	2	0
JULIUSSEN A.	Blyth	Portsmouth Sep 1948	Berwick R. Aug 1951	10	1	0	0	0	0	10	1
KAVANAGH P.J.	Romford	**Feb 1961	# Jun 1961	6	0	0	0	0	0	6	0
*KAY A.H.	Sheffield	Sheffield W. Dec 1962	Suspended sine die 1963	50	4	5	0	0	0	55	4
KERSLAKE J.G.	Scuthampton	1919	Wigan 1919	1	1	0	0	0	0	1	1
KERLEY J.	Liverpool	**May 1954	Accrington Jul 1959	4	1	3	2	0	0	7	3
KEELEY G.M.	Basildon	Blackburn R. Oct 1982	Blackburn R. Dec 1982	1	0	0	0	0	0	1	0
KEELEY S.		1897	Duncie 1897	1	1	2	0	0	0	1	0
KELLY J.	Hamilton	Ayr U. Feb 1927	Carlisle U. Aug 1929	81	1	2	0	0	0	83	1
KELSO R.	Renton	Newcastle U. 1888	Preston N.E. 1888	89	5	14	0	0	0	103	5
*KENDALL H.	Durham	Preston N.E. Mar 1967	Birmingham C. Feb 1974	231/2	21	23	3	12	3	266/2	27

PLAYER	BIRTHPLACE	FROM	TO	LEAGUE App	Gls	FA CUP App	Gls	L. CUP App	Gls	TOTAL App	Gls
KENDALL J.	Broughton	Lincoln C. Apr 1924	Preston N.E. May 1927	21	0	2	0	0	0	23	0
KENNEDY A.L.	Belfast	Arsenal 1928	Tranmere R. Jun 1930	1	0	0	0	0	0	1	0
KENNEDY F.	Bury	Manchester U. 1924	Middlesbrough May 1927	35	11	0	0	0	0	35	11
KENNEY W.	Liverpool	**Jul 1969	Tranmere R. Mar 1975	10/2	0	0	0	0	0	10/2	0
KENT J.		1891	1891	1	0	0	0	0	0	1	0
*KENYON R.N.	Blackpool	**Sep 1966	#Feb 1979	254/13	6	15/1	2	13/3	1	282/17	9
KERR J.	Burnbank	Bathgate Dec 1923	Preston N.E. Mar 1927	18	1	3	0	0	0	21	1
KEYS		1888	1888	1	0	0	0	0	0	1	0
*KIDD B.	Manchester	Manchester C. Mar 1979	Bolton W. May 1980	40	12	4	4	5	4	49	20
*KING A.	Luton	Luton T. Apr 1976 West Brom A. Jul 1982	Q.P.R. Sep 1980 #Jun 1984	193/2	49	16/1	4	29/1	11	238/4	64
KING F.O.	Radcliffe	Blyth Spartans Oct 1933	Derby C. 1936	13	0	1	0	0	0	14	0
KING J.A.	Marylebone	**Mar 1956	Bournemouth & BA Jul 1960	48	1	1	0	0	0	49	1
KIRBY G.	Liverpool	**Jun 1952	Sheffield W. Mar 1959	26	9	1	0	0	0	27	9
KIRKWOOD D.		1889	Broxburn 1891	35	1	3	1	0	0	38	2
KIRSOPP W.	Liverpool	**Apr 1914	Bury May 1921	58	28	5	1	0	0	63	29
KIRWAN J.	Wicklow	Southport Jul 1898	Tottenham H. 1898	24	5	2	0	0	0	26	5
KITCHEN G.W.	Fairfield	Stockport C. 1898	1903	87	0	3	0	0	0	90	0
*LABONE B.L.	Liverpool	**Jul 1957	Retired 1971	451	2	45	0	15	0	511	2
LACEY W.	Wexford	Shelbourne 1908	Liverpool Feb 1912	37	11	3	0	0	0	40	11
*LATCHFORD R.	Birmingham	Birmingham C. Feb 1974	Swansea C. Jul 1981	235/1	106	17/1	10	28	19	280/2	135
LATTA A.	Dumbarton	Dumbarton 1889	Liverpool 1895	136	69	12	1	0	0	148	70
LAVERICK R.	Castle Eden	Chelsea Feb 1959	Brighton & H A Jun 1960	22	6	1	0	0	0	23	6
*LAWSON D.	Newcastle	Huddersfield T. Jun 1972	Luton T. Oct 1978	124	0	12	0	13	0	149	0
LAWTON T.	Bolton	Burnley Jan 1937	Chelsea Nov 1945	87	65	8	5	0	0	95	70
LEE J.		1902	1902	2	0	0	0	0	0	2	0
LEEDER F.	Seaton Delavel	**Mar 1955	Darlington Jul 1958	1	0	0	0	0	0	1	0
LEIVESLEY W.		1919	Reading 1919	5	0	0	0	0	0	5	0
LELLO C.F.	Ludlow	Shrewsbury T. Sep 1947	Rochdale Nov 1956	237	9	17	0	0	0	254	9
LEWIS G.	Bangor	**May 1948	Rochdale Jun 1956	10	6	0	0	0	0	10	6
LEWIS T.H.	Wolverhampton	**1928	Wrexham Jun 1930	1	0	0	0	0	0	1	0
LEWIS W.		1888	1888	3	1	0	0	0	0	3	1
LEYFIELD C.	Chester	1934	Sheffield U. 1936	38	13	0	0	0	0	38	13
LEYLAND H.K.	Liverpool	**Aug 1950	Blackburn R. Aug 1956	36	0	4	0	0	0	40	0
LILL M.J.	Barking	Wolves Feb 1960	Plymouth A. Jun 1962	31	11	2	1	1	0	34	12
LINDLEY M.W.	Keighley	**Feb 1946	Swindon T. 1951	51	0	3	0	0	0	54	0
LINDSAY J.S.	Glasgow	Rangers Mar 1951	Bury May 1956	105	2	10	0	0	0	115	2
LINDSAY W.	Stockton	**1893	Grimsby T. 1893	9	0	0	0	0	0	9	0
LIVINGSTONE A.	Pencaithland	Bury May 1946	Southport Jun 1947	4	2	0	0	0	0	4	2

PLAYER	BIRTHPLACE	FROM	TO	LEAGUE App	Gls	FA CUP App	Gls	L. CUP App	Gls	TOTAL App	Gls
LIVINGSTONE D.	Dumbarton	Celtic Apr 1921	Plymouth A. Feb 1926	95	0	5	0	0	0	100	0
LLEWELLYN H.	Golborne	**May 1956	Crewe A. Jul 1958	11	2	0	0	0	0	11	2
LOCHHEAD A.	St.Johnstone	Third Lanark 1890	Third Lanark 1891	6	0	0	0	0	0	6	0
LODGE P.	Liverpool	**June 1977	Preston N.E. Feb 1983	20/4	0	6	0	5	0	31/4	0
LOWE H.	Skelmersdale	Southport 1930	Preston N.E. 1931	5	0	0	0	0	0	5	0
*LYONS M.	Liverpool	**Jul 1969	Sheffield W. Jul 1982	364/25	48	29/1	6	34	5	427/26	59
McBAIN N.	Campletown	Manchester U. Jan 1923	St Johnstone 1925	97	1	6	0	0	0	103	1
*McBRIDE J.	Glasgow	**Aug 1978	Rotherham U. Aug 1982	51/6	9	6	1	6	1	63/6	11
McCAMBRIDGE J.	Larne	Ballymena U. 1930	Cardiff C. 1930	1	0	0	0	0	0	1	0
McCLURE J.H.	Workington	**1925	Brentford Jun 1933	29	0	5	0	0	0	34	0
McCORMICK H.	Coleraine	Derby C. Jul 1948	Coleraine Sep 1949	4	0	0	0	0	0	4	0
McDERMOTT T.	Glasgow	Celtic 1903	Chelsea Oct 1905	64	15	7	4	0	0	71	19
McDONAGH J.	Rotherham	Bolton W. Jul 1980	Bolton W. Aug 1981	40	0	5	0	3	0	48	0
McDONALD A.		Jarrow 1899	Southampton 1900	23	6	0	0	0	0	23	6
McDONALD J.	Dykehead	Airdrie 1920	New Brighton Aug 1927	208	16	16	0	0	0	224	16
McFARLANE R.	Greenock	Third Lanark 1897	E.Stirling 1897	9	0	0	0	0	0	9	0
McGOURTY J.	Fauldhouse	Partick T. May 1932	Hamilton A. Aug 1934	15	2	0	0	0	0	15	2
McILHATTON J.	Arceer	Albion R. Apr 1946	Dundee 1948	55	1	3	1	0	0	58	2
McINNESS T.		Third Lanark 1894	Luton T. 1895	42	18	5	0	0	0	47	18
McINTOSH J.M.	Dunfries	Blackpool Mar 1949	Distillery May 1952	58	19	1	0	0	0	59	19
McKENZIE D.	Grimsby	Anderlecht Dec 1976	Chelsea Sep 1978	48	14	7/1	5	6	2	61/1	21
McKINNON A.		Hibernian 1888	1888	6	4	0	0	0	0	6	4
McLAUGHLIN J.	Stirling	Falkirk Oct 1971	#Apr 1976	59/2	7	7	0	2	0	68/2	7
McLAUGHLIN W.		Hamilton 1904	Plymouth A. 1905	15	5	0	0	0	0	15	5
McLEAN D.	Dumbarton	Renton Nov 1890	Liverpool 1891	25	0	1	0	0	0	26	0
McMAHON S.	Liverpool	**Dec 1977	Aston Villa May 1983	99/1	11	9	0	11	3	119/1	14
McMILLAN J.		1892	1892	7	5	0	0	0	0	7	5
McNAMARA A.	Birkenhead	**May 1950	Liverpool Dec 1957	111	22	2	0	0	0	113	22
McNAUGHT K.	Kirkcaldy	**May 1972	Aston Villa Aug 1977	64/2	3	10	0	10	0	84/2	3
McPHERSON L.	Glasgow	Swansea T Jan 1930	New Brighton Aug 1932	30	1	1	0	0	0	31	1
MACCONACHIE J.	Aberdeen	Hibernian Apr 1907	Swindon T. Aug 1920	245	6	25	1	0	0	270	7
MAGNER E.	Newcastle	Gainsborough T. 1910	St.Mirren Jan 1912	6	2	3	1	0	0	9	3
MAHER A.	Liverpool	**Dec 1964	Plymouth A. Oct 1968	1	0	0	0	0	0	1	0
MAKEPEACE H.	Middlesbrough	**1902	Retired 1914	284	16	52	7	0	0	336	23
MALEY W.		1896	1836	2	0	0	0	0	0	2	0
MARSDEN J.	Darwen	Darwen 1891	Retired 1891	1	0	0	0	0	0	1	0
MARSHALL C.	Liverpool	**Nov 1973	Southport Sep 1976	6	0	1	0	0	0	7	0
MARTIN G.S.	Bathgate	Hull C. Mar 1928	Middlesbrough May 1932	85	31	1	1	0	0	86	32
MAXWELL A.		Cambuslang Oct 1891	Darwen Nov 1893	43	13	7	3	0	0	50	16

PLAYER	BIRTHPLACE	FROM	TO	LEAGUE App	Gls	FA CUP App	Gls	L. CUP App	Gls	TOTAL App	Gls
MAYERS D.	Liverpool	**Aug 1952	Preston N.E. May 1957	18	7	1	0	0	0	19	7
MAYSON T.	Whitehaven	Grimsby T. 1919	Wolves May 1921	1	1	0	0	0	0	1	1
*MEAGAN M.K.	Dublin	**Sep 1952	Huddersfield T. Jul 1964	165	1	10	0	0	0	175	1
MEECHAM P.		Celtic 1896	Southampton 1897	24	0	4	0	0	0	28	0
MEGSON G.	Manchester	Plymouth A. Feb 1980	Sheffield W. Aug 1981	20/2	2	3	1	0	0	23/2	3
MEIKLEJOHN G.		1896	1896	1	0	0	0	0	0	1	0
MENHAM C.		1925	1925	3	0	0	0	0	0	3	0
MENHAM R.C.	North Shields	**Jan 1897	Wigan 1896	18	0	5	0	0	0	23	0
MERCER J.	Ellesmere Port	Ellesmere Port Sep 1932	Arsenal Dec 1946	170	1	14	1	0	0	184	2
MESTON S.W.	Southampton	Gillingham 1927	Tranmere R. Jul 1928	1	0	0	0	0	0	1	0
MEUNIER J.B.	Birmingham	Southport 1910	Lincoln C. Jun 1912	5	0	0	0	0	0	5	0
MICHAELS W.		1909	1909	3	0	0	0	0	0	3	0
MILLER H.J.	Preston	Leyland 1922	Preston N.E. 1922	2	0	0	0	0	0	2	0
MILLER J.	Tynemouth	Grimsby T. 1919	Coventry C. Dec 1920	8	1	0	0	0	0	8	1
MILLER W.R.	Bainsford	Partick T. Jul 1935	Burnley Oct 1936	16	2	1	0	0	0	17	2
MILLIGAN G.H.	Failsworth	Oldham A. May 1938	1938	1	0	0	0	0	0	1	0
MILLINGTON T.	Wrexham	Oswestry Mar 1925	Gillingham Mar 1928	13	0	1	0	0	0	14	0
MILWARD A.	Great Marlow	Great Marlow 1888	New Brighton 1896	201	85	23	11	0	0	224	96
MITCHELL F.W.	Elgin	Motherwell 1913	Liverpool 1919	23	0	1	0	0	0	24	0
MOFFATT A.		East Fife 1920	Wrexham 1920	1	0	0	0	0	0	1	0
MOFFATT H.		Luton T. 1926	Oldham A. 1926	2	0	1	0	0	0	3	0
MOLYNEUX G.	Liverpool	Wigan 1896	Southampton 1899	43	0	2	0	0	0	45	0
MOORE E.	St Helens	**Feb 1949	Chesterfield Jan 1957	171	0	13	0	0	0	184	0
MORRIS		1888	1888	1	0	0	0	0	0	1	0
*MORRISSEY J.	Liverpool	Liverpool Sep 1962	Oldham A. May 1972	257/2	43	29	3	8	1	294/2	47
MORRISSEY J.	Liverpool	**Mar 1983	Wolves Jul 1985	1/1	0	0	0	0	0	1/1	0
MORTON H.	Chadderton	Aston Villa Mar 1937	Burnley May 1939	27	0	2	0	0	0	29	0
*MOUNTFIELD D.	Liverpool	Tranmere R. Jun 1982	*	69	13	15	2	12	2	96	17
MOUNTFORD H.	Hanley	Burslem 1907	Burnley Apr 1911	25	5	0	0	0	0	25	5
MUIR W.	Ayr	Kilmarnock Apr 1897	Dundee May 1902	127	10	10	0	0	0	137	10
MURRAY D.B.		Rangers 1903	Liverpool 1903	2	0	0	0	0	0	2	0
MURRAY D.J.	South Africa	1925	Bristol C. Oct 1926	3	1	0	0	0	0	3	1
MURRAY J.J.		Rangers 1891	Swindon T. 1892	8	0	0	0	0	0	8	0
NEWTON H.A.	Nottingham	Nottingham F. Oct 1970	Derby C. Sep 1973	76	5	6	1	1	0	83	6
*NEWTON K.R.	Manchester	Blackburn R. Dec 1969	Burnley Jun 1972	48/1	1	2	0	1	0	51/1	1
*NULTY G.	Prescott	Newcastle U. Jul 1978	Retired 1979	22/5	2	0	0	6	0	28/5	2
NUTTALL T.A.	Manchester	Manchester U. 1913	St.Mirren 1914	19	7	0	0	0	0	19	7
O'DONNELL J.	Gateshead	Darlington Jan 1925	Blackpool Dec 1930	188	10	9	0	0	0	197	10
O'HARA A.E.	Glasgow	Falkirk Jun 1958	Rotherham U. Feb 1960	29	2	2	0	0	0	31	2

PLAYER	BIRTHPLACE	FROM	TO	LEAGUE App	Gls	FA CUP App	Gls	L. CUP App	Gls	TOTAL App	Gls
O'KEEFE E.	Manchester	Mossley Jul 1979	Wigan Jan 1982	26/14	6	4/1	1	4/2	1	34/17	8
O'NEILL J.A.	Dublin	**May 1949	Stoke C. Jul 1960	201	12	12	0	0	0	213	0
OLDHAM W.	Omskirk	1898	Blackburn R. 1899	22	11	0	0	0	0	22	11
OLDROYD D.	Omskirk	**Nov 1984	*	0/1	0	0	0	0	0	0/1	0
OLIVER F.	Southampton	Brentford 1905	Clapton O. 1905	4	4	1	0	0	0	5	4
ORR		1889	1889	1	1	0	0	0	0	1	1
OWEN L.T.	Liverpool	**Dec 1966	Bradford C. Jun 1970	2	0	0	0	0	0	2	0
OWEN W.	Liverpool	Wolves 1898	1898	13	3	0	0	0	0	13	3
PAGE J.	Liverpool	**1913	Cardiff C. May 1920	9	0	1	0	0	0	10	0
PAGE T.		Rochdale 1913	St.Mirren May 1914	7	2	0	0	0	0	7	2
PALMER J.		1896	1896	1	0	0	0	0	0	1	0
PALMER W.		Bristol R. May 1913	Bristol R. 1914	22	1	1	1	0	0	23	2
*PARKER A.H.	Irvine	Falkirk Jun 1958	Southport Sep 1965	198	5	12	0	5	0	215	5
PARKER J.W.	Birkenhead	**Dec 1948	Bury May 1956	167	82	9	7	0	0	176	89
PARKER R.N.	Possil Park	Rangers Nov 1913	Nottingham F. May 1921	84	68	8	3	0	0	92	71
PARKER T.	Blackrod	**1926	1926	6	0	1	0	0	0	7	0
PARKINSON H.		1888	1888	1	0	0	0	0	0	1	0
PARNELL R.	Birkenhead	**Oct 1960	Tranmere R. Aug 1964	3	0	0	0	0	0	3	0
PARRY C.F.		1889	Ardwick 1895	86	5	8	0	0	0	94	5
PARRY F.T.	Liverpool	**1922	Grimsby T. Jun 1926	12	0	1	0	0	0	13	0
PATRICK	Kilsyth	St.Mirren 1896	St.Mirren 1896	1	0	0	0	0	0	1	0
PATERSON		R.Albert 1901	1901	5	1	0	0	0	0	5	1
PAYNE J.B.	Liverpool	Liverpool Apr 1956	Retired 1956	5	2	1	0	0	0	6	2
PEACOCK J.	Wigan	Atherton 1919	Middlesbrough May 1927	151	12	10	0	0	0	161	12
*PEARSON J.F.	Falkirk	St.Johnstone Jul 1974	Newcastle U. Aug 1978	76/17	15	9	2	10/2	2	95/19	19
*PEJIC M.	Chesterton	Stoke C. Feb 1977	Aston Villa Sep 1979	76	2	6	0	7	0	89	2
*PICKERING F.	Blackburn	Blackburn R. Mar 1964	Birmingham C. Aug 1967	97	56	9	8	0	0	106	64
PINCHBECK C.B.	Grimsby T.	**Dec 1947	New Brighton Aug 1949	3	0	0	0	0	0	3	0
PINKNEY E.	Glasgow	W.Hartlepool 1909	Gillingham Jul 1913	8	1	0	0	0	0	8	1
PINNELL A.		1892	1892	3	0	0	0	0	0	3	0
POLLOCK		1888	1888	1	0	0	0	0	0	1	0
POTTS H.	Wetton-le-Hole	Burnley Oct 1950	Wolves Jul 1956	59	15	4	1	0	0	63	16
POWELL A.	Swansea	Leeds U. Jul 1948	Birmingham C. Aug 1950	35	5	5	0	0	0	35	5
PRATT C.		Barrow 1909	Exeter C. 1909	2	0	0	0	0	0	2	0
PROUDFOOT J.		Blackburn R. 1898	Watford 1901	84	30	5	1	0	0	89	31
RAFFERTY D.		1907	1909	7	0	0	0	0	0	7	0
RAITT D.	Buckhaven	Dundee May 1922	Blackburn R. Aug 1928	122	0	9	0	0	0	131	0
*RANKIN A.G.	Liverpool	**Oct 1961	Watford Nov 1971	85	0	7	0	0	0	92	0
RANKIN B.	Glasgow	**1901	West Brom A. 1905	37	7	1	0	0	0	38	7

PLAYER	BIRTHPLACE	FROM	TO	LEAGUE App	Gls	FA CUP App	Gls	L. CUP App	Gls	TOTAL App	Gls
RANKIN G.	Liverpool	**Aug 1948	Southport Jul 1956	36	0	3	0	0	0	39	0
*RATCLIFFE K.	Mancot	**Jul 1977	*	154/1	1	27	0	22	0	203/1	1
RAWLINGS J.	Wombwell	Millwall 1945	Plymouth A. May 1945	0	0	0	0	0	0	2	0
REA K.W.	Liverpool	**Jun 1952	Runcorn 1958	46	0	5	0	0	0	51	0
REAY H.		Newcastle U. 1893	Southampton 1893	1	1	1	0	0	0	2	1
REES B.G.	Rhyl	**Sep 1961	Brighton & H A Jan 1965	4	2	0	0	0	0	4	2
REID D.	Glasgow	Distillery May 1920	Distillery Feb 1927	97	11	4	0	0	0	101	11
*REID P.	Liverpool	Bolton W. Dec 1982	*	77/1	4	18	2	13/1	1	108/2	7
RENNIE A.		1892	1892	4	0	0	0	0	0	4	0
*RICHARDSON K.	Newcastle	**May 1979	*	78/12	13	8	1	8/3	2	94/15	16
RIGBY A.	Manchester	Blackburn R. Nov 1929	Middlesbrough May 1932	42	11	2	0	0	0	44	11
RIGSBY H.	Aintree	Southport 1919	Swansea T. 1919	14	5	0	0	0	0	14	5
RIMMER N.	Liverpool	**Apr 1984	*	0/1	0	0	0	0	0	0/1	0
RIMMER S.	Southport	**May 1981	*	3	0	0	0	0	0	3	0
RING T.	Glasgow	Clyde Jan 1960	Barnsley Nov 1961	27	6	0	0	0	0	27	6
RIOCH B.D.	Aldershot	Derby C. Dec 1976	Derby C. Nov 1977	30	3	7	1	2	0	39	4
RITCHIE H.M.	Perth	Hibernian Aug 1928	Dundee Feb 1930	28	5	1	0	0	0	29	5
ROBERTS J.		1888	1888	1	0	0	0	0	0	1	0
ROBERTS J.		1914	1914	1	0	0	0	0	0	1	0
ROBERTSON H.		Patrick T. 1890	Bootle 1892	29	1	2	1	0	0	31	2
ROBERTSON J.T.Dumbarton		Morton 1895	Southampton 1897	30	1	6	0	0	0	36	1
ROBINSON A.J. Birkenhead		1919	Tranmere R. 1919	1	0	0	0	0	0	1	0
*ROBINSON N.	Liverpool	**May 1974	Swansea C. Oct 1979	13/3	1	1	0	3/1	0	17/4	1
ROBINSON W.	Birkenhead	1919	Chester 1919	7	0	0	0	0	0	7	0
ROBSON T.	Morpeth	Blyth Spartans Apr 1929	Sheffield W. Oct 1930	27	0	2	0	0	0	29	0
ROCHE W.		1901	1901	1	0	0	0	0	0	1	0
ROONEY W.F.	Liverpool	1924	Wrexham 1929	14	0	4	0	0	0	18	0
ROOSE L.R.	Wrexham	Stoke C. Nov 1904	Stoke C. Aug 1905	18	0	6	0	0	0	24	0
ROSS N.J.		Preston N.E. Jul 1888	Preston N.E. Feb 1889	19	5	0	0	0	0	19	5
*ROSS T.	Ashton-under-Lyne	Arsenal Nov 1977	#1982	120/4	16	13	3	8/1	0	141/5	19
*ROYLE F.W.	Bracknell	Stoke C. 1906	Chelsea Oct 1907	9	2	1	0	0	0	10	2
*ROYLE J.	Liverpool	**Aug 1966	Manchester C. Dec 1974	229/3	102	23	9	14	4	266/3	115
RUSSELL J.		1902	West Ham U. 1902	3	0	0	0	0	0	3	0
SAGAR E.	Moorends	**Mar 1929	Retired May 1953	463	0	32	0	0	0	495	0
SALT E.	Walsall	1921	Accrington S. 1921	4	0	0	0	0	0	4	0
SANDERS A.	Salford	**Jul 1956	Swansea T. Nov 1959	56	0	7	0	0	0	63	0
SAUNDERS G.E. Birkenhead		**Feb 1939	1951	133	0	7	0	0	0	140	0
SAUNDERS R.	Birkenhead	Feb 1951	Tonbridge May 1957	3	0	0	0	0	0	3	0
SCHOFIELD A.	Liverpool	1895	Manchester U. 1899	13	2	0	0	0	0	13	2

PLAYER	BIRTHPLACE	FROM	TO	LEAGUE App	Gls	FA CUP App	Gls	L. CUP App	Gls	TOTAL App	Gls
*SCOTT A.S.	Falkirk	Rangers Feb 1963	Hibernian Sep 1967	149	23	17	2			166	25
SCOTT P.W.	Liverpool	**Jul 1970	York C. Dec 1975	42/2	1	5	1	1	1	48/2	2
SCOTT Walter	Worksop	Grimsby T. 1909	Sunderland Jul 1911	18	0	0	0	0	0	18	0
SCOTT William	Belfast	Linfield 1904	Leeds C. Aug 1912	251	38	38	0	0	0	289	0
* SEARGEANT S.	Liverpool	**Jul 1968	#Feb 1978	77/3	1	2	0	5/1	0	84/4	1
SETTLE J.	Millom	Bury Apr 1899	Stockport C. May 1908	237	84	32	13	0	0	269	97
SHACKLETON A.	Padiham	Leeds U. Sep 1959	Oldham A. Aug 1961	26	10	1	0	0	0	27	10
SHARP B.	Hereford	Aston Villa 1899	Southampton 1901	9	0	1	0	0	0	10	0
*SHARP G.	Glasgow	Dumbarton Apr 1980	*	132/8	58	17/2	5	20	6	169/10	69
SHARP J.	Hereford	Aston Villa 1899	Retired 1909	300	69	42	12	0	0	342	81
SHARPLES G.	Ellesmere Port	**Sep 1960	Blackburn R. Mar 1965	10	0	0	0	1	0	11	0
SHAW S.	Liverpool	**Dec 1961	Crystal P. Dec 1966	3	0	0	0	0	0	3	0
*SHEEDY K.	Builthwells	Liverpool Aug 1982	*	97	26	17	8	15	4	129	38
SHERIDAN J.		Cambuslang 1902	Stoke C. 1903	20	4	0	0	0	0	20	4
SIMMS S.		1912	Swindon T. Jun 1913	2	1	0	0	0	0	2	1
SIMPSON R.H.	Redcar	1912	1914	21	0	2	0	0	0	23	0
SIMPSON T.	Keyworth	Leicester F. 1903	Leicester F. 1903	1	0	0	0	0	0	1	0
SINGLETON		Bury 1901	Grimsby T. 1901	3	0	0	0	0	0	3	0
SLOAN D.	Llandudno	Linfield 1906	Liverpool 1907	6	0	0	0	0	0	6	0
SMALLEY R.E.		Preston N.E. 1888	1890	36	0	2	0	0	0	38	0
*SMALLMAN D.P.	Connah's Quay	Wrexham Mar 1975	Wrexham Jul 1980	19/2	6	0	0	3/1	1	22/3	7
SMITH D.L.	Liverpool	**Nov 1963	Tranmere R. Mar 1968	3/1	0	0	0	0	0	3/1	0
SMITH Joseph	West Stanley	Hull C. 1911	Bury Dec 1913	10	0	0	0	0	0	10	0
SMITH John	Liverpool	**Sep 1970	Carlisle U. Jun 1976	2	0	0	0	0	0	2	0
*SOUTHALL N.	Llandudno	Bury Jul 1981	*	120	0	16	0	17	0	153	0
SOUTHWORTH J.	Blackburn	Blackburn R. Aug 1893	Retired 1894	31	36	1	0	0	0	32	36
SPENCER H.G.	Burton-upon-Trent	**1921	Wigan 1921	9	2	0	0	0	0	9	2
STANLEY G.E.	Coatbridge	Chelsea Aug 1979	Swansea C. Oct 1981	52	1	2/1	0	7/1	0	61/2	1
STEIN J.		Dunfermline A. 1928	Burnley Oct 1936	199	57	16	8	0	0	215	65
STEPHENSON G.		1888	1888	1	0	0	0	0	0	1	0
*STEVEN T.	Berwick	Burnley Jul 1983	*	63/4	13	9	2	7	1	79/4	16
*STEVENS D.	Dudley	Bolton W. Mar 1962	Oldham A. Dec 1965	120	20	10	1	0	0	130	21
*STEVENS G.	Barrow	**Jun 1979	*	110/1	5	21	1	18	1	149/1	7
STEVENS G.L.	New Brighton	New Brighton 1932	Southend U. 1932	5	0	0	0	0	0	5	0
STEVENS T.		Clyde 1912	1912								
STEVENSON A.	Dublin	Rangers Jan 1934	Bootle 1948	255	82	16	8	0	0	271	90
STEVENSON W.	Accrington	Accrington S. 1907	1913	111	0	14	0	0	0	125	0
STEWART A.	Accrington	Burnley Dec 1892	Nottingham F. 1892	12	1	7	0	0	0	19	1
STEWART W.S.	Arbroath	Preston N.E. 1893	Bristol C. 1897	122	6	15	0	0	0	137	6

PLAYER	BIRTHPLACE	FROM	TO	LEAGUE App	LEAGUE Gls	FA CUP App	FA CUP Gls	L. CUP App	L. CUP Gls	TOTAL App	TOTAL Gls
STORRIER D.	Arbroath	Arbroath 1893	Celtic 1897	55	10	10	0	0	0	65	0
STRETTLE S.		1906	Exeter C. Aug 1913	4	0	0	0	0	0	4	0
STYLES A.	Liverpool	**Aug 1967	Birmingham C. Feb 1974	22/1	0	4	0	0	0	26/1	0
SUGG F.H.	Ilkeston	Derby C. 1888	Burnley 1889	10	0	0	0	0	0	10	0
SUTHERLAND J.	Cork	**May 1950	Chesterfield Jun 1957	6	0	2	0	0	0	8	0
SUTTON		1894	1894	1	0	0	0	0	0	1	0
TANSEY J.	Liverpool	**May 1948	Crewe A. Jun 1960	133	0	9	0	0	0	142	0
TAYLOR E.H.	Liverpool	Huddersfield T. Feb 1927	Wrexham Nov 1928	40	0	2	0	0	0	42	0
TAYLOR J.D.	Dumbarton	St.Mirren 1896	South Liverpool 1909	400	66	56	14	0	0	456	80
*TEFLER G.A.	Liverpool	**Aug 1972	Scunthorpe U. Jun 1981	81/16	20	4/4	1	5/2	1	90/22	22
*TEMPLE D.	Liverpool	**Aug 1956	Preston N.E. Sep 1967	231/1	72	21	8	4	0	256/1	80
THOMAS		1892	1892	1	0	0	0	0	0	1	0
*THOMAS D.	Liverpool	Q.P.R. Aug 1977	Wolves Oct 1979	71	4	2	0	7	1	80	5
*THOMAS E.	Newton-le-Willows	**Oct 1951	Blackburn R. Feb 1960	86	39	7	2	0	0	93	41
THOMAS M.	Mochdre	Manchester U. Jul 1981	Brighton & H.A. Nov 1981	10	0	0	0	1	0	11	0
THOMPSON R.		1892	1892	1	0	0	0	0	0	1	0
THOMPSON R.	Newcastle	Leicester F. Apr 1913	Millwall 1920	83	0	6	0	0	0	89	0
*THOMSON G.M.	Edinburgh	Hearts Nov 1960	Brentford Nov 1963	73	1	1	0	2	0	76	1
THOMSON J.R.	Thornton	Dundee Mar 1930	Retired Dec 1939	272	5	22	0	0	0	294	5
THOMSON S.		Wolves 1891	Accrington Oct 1891	3	1	0	0	0	0	3	1
TODD C.	Washington	Derby C. Sep 1978	Birmingham C. Sep 1979	32	1	1	0	2	0	35	1
TOMAN W.	Bishop Auckland	Burnley Apr 1899	Southampton 1901	29	10	0	0	0	0	29	10
TOMLINSON J.	Birkenhead	**Jun 1952	Chesterfield Jun 1957	2	0	0	0	0	0	2	0
*TREBILCOCK M.	Gunnislake	Plymouth A. Dec 1965	Portsmouth Jan 1968	11	3	2	2	0	0	13	5
TRENTHAM D.	Chirbury	** Dec 1936	Ellesmere Port Aug 1949	16	7	1	0	0	0	17	7
TROUP A.	Forfar	Dundee Jan 1923	Dundee Feb 1930	249	32	10	3	0	0	259	35
TURNER D.	Derby	**Oct 1966	Southport May 1970	1	0	0	0	0	0	1	0
TURNER G.	Mansfield	Luton T. 1932	Bradford C. 1932	2	0	0	0	0	0	2	0
TURNER J.H.	Burslem	Stoke C. 1898	Southampton Apr 1900	34	8	2	1	0	0	36	9
TURNER R.F.	Leicester	Leicester F. 1908	Preston N.E. 1910	34	1	0	0	0	0	34	1
TYRER A.	Liverpool	**Dec 1959	Mansfield T. Jul 1963	9	2	1	0	0	0	10	2
UREN H.J.	Bristol	Liverpool 1911	Wrexham 1912	24	3	0	0	0	0	24	3
*VAN d HAUWE P.	Dendermonde	Birmingham C. Sep 1984	*	31	0	7	0	3	0	41	0
*VARADI I.	Paddington	Sheffield U. Mar 1979	Newcastle U. Aug 1981	22/4	6	6/1	1	0	0	28/5	7
VAUGHAN A.		1898	1898	1	0	0	0	0	0	1	0
VEALL R.J.	Skegness	Doncaster R. Sep 1961	Preston N.E. May 1965	11	1	0	0	0	0	11	1
*VERNON T.R.	Ffynnongroew	Blackburn R. Feb 1965	Stoke C. Mar 1965	176	101	12	7	4	1	192	109
VIRR A.E.	Liverpool	**1924	Retired 1929	117	2	9	1	0	0	126	3
WAINWRIGHT E.	Southport	Southport Mar 1944	Rochdale Jun 1956	207	68	21	8	0	0	228	76

PLAYER	BIRTHPLACE	FROM	TO	LEAGUE		FA CUP		L. CUP		TOTAL	
				App	Gls	App	Gls	App	Gls	App	Gls
*WAKENSHAW R.	Ashington	**Jun 1982	*	2/1	1	0	0	0	0	2/1	1
WALKER J.*		Gainsborough 1893	Leicester F. 1893	3	1	0	0	0	0	3	1
WALL A.	Liverpool	1919	Swindon T. Jun 1925	16	3	1	0	0	0	17	3
WALSH D.	Hamilton	**Oct 1984	*	1	0	0	0	0	0	1	0
*WALSH M.A.	Chorley	Blackpool Aug 1978	Q.P.R. Mar 1979	18/3	1	1	0	3	0	22/3	1
WALSH M.T.	Manchester	Bolton Aug 1981	Fort Lauderdale May 1983	20	0	0	0	2	0	22	0
WAREING W.	Southport	Preston N.E. 1912	Swindon T. 1919	64	4	5	2	0	0	69	6
WARMBEY		1888	1888	1	0	0	0	0	0	1	0
WATSON J.		Dundee 1899	Tottenham H. 1901	44	0	0	0	0	0	44	0
WATSON J.G.	Wolsingham	Blyth Spartans 1932	Coventry C. 1933	2	0	0	0	0	0	2	0
WATSON R.		1888	Gorton Villa 1888	18	4	0	0	0	0	18	4
WATSON T.G.	Wolsingham	**Jan 1933	Retired 1948	61	1	5	0	0	0	66	1
WAUGH D.		Burnley 1888	Retired 1888	7	2	0	0	0	0	7	2
WEAVER W.	Birkenhead	Burnley 1924	Wolves Oct 1926	18	3	4	0	0	0	22	3
WEBBER K.J.	Cardiff	Feb 1960	Brighton & H.A. Apr 1963	4	0	0	0	2	1	6	1
WEIR J.		Hibernian 1888	1889	19	0	0	0	0	0	19	0
WELDON A.	Croy	Airdrie Mar 1927	Hull C. Jun 1930	70	13	3	0	0	0	73	13
WELLER L.C.	Stoke	Chesterfield 1909	1921	65	2	5	0	0	0	70	2
*WEST G.	Barnsley	Blackpool Mar 1962	Tranmere R. Oct 1975	335	0	40	0	11	0	386	0
WHITE T.A.	Manchester	Southport Feb 1927	Northampton T. Oct 1937	193	66	9	0	0	0	202	66
WHITE W.	Hurlford	Bolton W. Nov 1908	Fulham Oct 1910	43	10	9	3	0	0	52	13
WHITEHEAD-J.	Seacombe	1893	1893	2	0	0	0	0	0	2	0
WHITLEY J.	Liverpool	Aston Villa 1902	Leeds C. 1903	11	0	3	0	0	0	14	0
*WHITTLE A.	Liverpool	**Aug 1967	Crystal P. Dec 1972	72/2	21	6	2	4	2	82/2	25
WIGNALL F.	Blackrod	Horwich RMI May 1958	Nottingham F. Jun 1958	33	15	2	7	3	0	38	22
WILDMAN W.	Liverpool	1904	West Ham U. 1905	2	0	0	0	0	0	2	0
WILKINSON J.	Esh Winning	Newcastle U. 1929	Blackpool May 1931	11	2	1	0	0	0	12	2
WILKINSON P.	Louth	Grimsby T. Mar 1985	*	4/1	2	0	0	0	0	4/1	2
WILLIAMS B.D.	Penrhiwceiber	Swansea T. Dec 1929	Newport C. 1935	131	0	8	0	0	0	139	0
WILLIAMS G.G.	Wrexham	Bradford C. Mar 1956	Swansea T. Feb 1959	31	6	2	0	0	0	33	6
WILLIAMS O.	Holyhead	South Liverpool 1919	Wigan 1919	2	0	0	0	0	0	2	0
WILLIAMS R.		**1891	Luton T. 1894	58	0	12	0	0	0	70	0
WILLIAMS W.		1894	Blackburn R. 189?	23	4	1	1	0	0	24	5
WILLIAMS W.D.	Manchester	Darwen 1922	Blackpool Mar 1925	39	14	2	0	0	0	41	14
WILSON A.	Liverpool	**Jul 1970	Southport Jul 1975	2	0	0	0	0	0	2	0
WILSON D.	Lochgelly	Hearts 1906	Portsmouth Jun 1907	5	0	0	0	0	0	5	0
WILSON G.W.	Lochgelly	Hearts May 1906	Newcastle U. Nov 1907	28	3	6	1	0	0	34	4
*WILSON R.	Shirebrook	Huddersfield July 1964	Oldham A. Jul 1979	114/2	0	26	0	0/1	0	140/3	0
WILSON W.		1888	1888	1	0	0	0	0	0	1	0

PLAYER	BIRTHPLACE	FROM	TO	LEAGUE App	Gls	FA CUP App	Gls	L. CUP App	Gls	TOTAL App	Gls
WINTERHALDER A.		West Ham U. 1907	Preston N.E. 1907	4	0	0	0	0	0	4	0
WOLSTENHOLME S.	Little Lever	Horwich 1897	Blackburn R. 1903	160	8	10	0	0	0	170	8
*WOOD G.	Douglas	Blackpool Aug 1977	Arsenal Aug 1980	103	0	4	0	13	0	120	0
WOODHOUSE R.	Leyland	Preston N.E. 1926	Wrexham May 1927	2	0	0	0	0	0	2	0
WOODS L.G.		**1907	1907	4	0	0	0	0	0	4	0
WOODS M.	Skelmersdale	**Nov 1949	Blackburn R. Nov 1956	8	1	0	0	0	0	8	1
WRIGHT B.P.	Birmingham	Walsall Feb 1972	Walsall Jan 1973	10/1	2	0	0	0	0	10/1	2
WRIGHT R.		**1905	Burnley 1905	1	0	0	0	0	0	1	0
*WRIGHT T.J.	Liverpool	**Mar 1963	Retired 1972	307/1	4	35	0	11	0	353/1	4
*WRIGHT W.	Liverpool	**Aug 1974	Birmingham C. Jun 1983	164/2	10	13	0	13	0	190/2	10
WRIGHT W.P.		St-Mirren 1914	Tranmere R. 1914	2	0	0	0	0	0	2	0
WYLIE T.G.	Maybole	Rangers Dec 1890	Liverpool 1891	20	5	1	0	0	0	21	5
YOUNG A.	Slamannan	Falkirk 1901	Tottenham H. 1910	275	110	39	15	0	0	314	125
*YOUNG A.	Loanhead	Hearts Nov 1960	Glentoran Aug 1968	227/1	77	25/2	4	3	3	255/3	84
YOUNG R.	Swinhill	Middlesbrough 1910	Wolves Nov 1911	38	7	3	1	0	0	41	8

Eddie Wainwright beats Bert Trautmann in the 1955-6 FA Cup quarter-final, but Manchester City's Leivers is on the line to clear.

ATTENDANCE FIGURES

ONE huge problem facing football statisticians is the collection of attendance figures. In the earliest days of the Football League, attendances were given only in the vaguest terms ('about five thousand'), and even when newspapers began to print attendance figures with the classified results, they were still an approximation (ie. 10,000). The position improved during the latter part of the inter-war period, but only since 1946 have precise figures been available in the majority of cases.

However, using what information is available, football statistician Tony Matthews, who specializes in attendance figures, has been able to draw some interesting conclusions about the numbers of people who have watched Everton at Goodison (and at Anfield) since the League was founded in 1888.

Since that first League match, against Accrington on 8 September 1888, nearly 48 million people have watched 1,684 Everton home games in Divisions One and Two, up to the end of 1984-5. That figure gives an average attendance, since the League began, of well over 28,000.

Since World War Two — and figures are much more accurate here — 819 League games at Goodison have been watched by 31,043,543, which gives an average turnout of 37,904 at each League match.

Everton's best season in terms of crowds came in the Championship-winning campaign of 1962-3 when their 21 home League matches attracted 1,080,660 fans, giving an average of 51,460. The Goodison average easily beat Tottenham Hotspur (47,342) and Liverpool (42,957).

Everton have broken the one-million barrier three times since World War Two. In 1962-3, 1963-4 and not surprisingly, in 1969-70 when they won the League Championship again.

In comparison, the 1984-5 Championship-winning season attracted 687,225 spectators, a measure of how football attendances generally have declined in recent years.

The lowest post-war aggregate at Goodison Park came in 1983-4 (406,203). The club made a mediocre start and even Wembley appearances in the FA Cup and Milk Cup came too late to salvage interest in the League programme, which was won by Liverpool.

In football's boom years of the late '40s, Everton's average attendance never dropped below the 40,000 mark. Throughout the '60s, when the League title and the FA Cup came to Goodison, the average never fell below 38,000.

Based on the information available over the years, Everton stand sixth in the list of biggest average attendances, from the clubs' first matches in the Football League to the end of 1984-5. Ahead of Everton at the moment are Manchester United, Arsenal, Sunderland, Aston Villa and Wolverhampton Wanderers.

Everton's best-ever attendance is 78,299 (v Liverpool in a First Division match on 18 September 1948).

The lowest Everton home League attendance on record is 2,079 (v West Bromwich Albion, First Division, 23 February 1889, at Anfield).

Everton have enjoyed home League attendances of more than 70,000 on 12 occasions. They have topped the 60,000 mark 34 times, and Goodison Park has witnessed no less than 75 turnouts of 50,000 plus.

At the other end of the scale, Everton's home attendance has dropped below 10,000 on 40 occasions, most of which occured in the late 1880s.

Everton's home attendance figures since World War Two.

Season	Aggregate	Average
1946-7	848,463	40,403
1947-8	934,270	44,489
1948-9	947,017	45,096
1949-50	928,434	44,211
1950-51	634,368	30,208
1951-2	714,530	34,025
1952-3	613,768	29,227
1953-4	930,720	44,320
1954-5	972,595	46,314
1955-6	894,348	42,588
1956-7	730,300	34,776
1957-8	822,297	39,157
1958-9	822,570	39,170
1959-60	856,548	40,788
1960-61	912,513	43,453
1961-2	869,127	41,387
1962-3	1,080,660	51,460
1963-4	1,037,421	49,401
1964-5	883,302	42,062
1965-6	808,458	38,498
1966-7	894,936	42,616
1967-8	985,572	46,932
1968-9	965,580	45,980
1969-70	1,040,151	49,531
1970-71	862,895	41,090
1971-2	782,082	37,242
1972-3	723,896	34,471
1973-4	742,370	35,351
1974-5	840,420	40,020
1975-6	569,394	27,114
1976-7	630,973	30,046
1977-8	829,774	39,513
1978-9	744,571	35,456
1979-80	602,924	28,711
1980-81	548,211	26,105
1981-2	518,147	24,673
1982-3	426,510	20,310
1983-4	406,203	19,343
1984-5	687,225	32,725
39 Seasons	**31,043,543**	**37,904**

Everton's Progressive Record Attendance

18 Sep 1948	78,299 v Liverpool (Div 1).
22 Jan 1938	68,158 v Sunderland (FA Cup).
2 Mar 1935	66,865 v Bolton W (FA Cup).
15 Oct 1927	66,737 v Liverpool (Div 1).
24 Jan 1948	74,721 Man Utd v Liverpool (FA Cup).
28 Apr 1910	69,364 FA Cup Final Replay.

EVERTON AGAINST OTHER LEAGUE CLUBS

Everton have played 65 clubs in the Football League since 1888-9. Below is their record against each club. Some clubs have modified their names over the years (eg there was Woolwich Arsenal, Leicester Fosse, Leyton Orient). In all cases the last name used by each club covers all games under previous names. Since 1981-2 three points have been awarded for a win. A percentage success-rate is therefore shown instead of a points- won total.

	P	W	D	L	F	A	%
Accrington	10	5	3	2	21	16	65%
Arsenal	128	44	27	57	169	202	44%
Aston Villa	142	59	31	52	242	226	53%
Barnsley	6	3	2	1	12	8	66%
Birmingham City	102	52	27	23	194	133	64%
Blackburn Rovs	112	44	25	43	202	192	50%
Blackpool	46	20	11	15	66	55	55%
Bolton Wandrs	112	57	25	30	190	151	62%
Bradford	8	5	2	1	19	12	75%
Bradford City	22	8	8	6	32	29	54%
Brentford	16	7	2	7	29	22	50%
Brighton & H.A.	8	4	3	1	15	11	60%
Bristol City	20	12	3	5	34	22	67%
Bristol Rovers	2	1	1	0	4	0	75%
Burnley	98	41	28	29	161	147	56%
Bury	52	21	16	15	87	72	56%
Cardiff City	30	10	8	12	43	35	47%
Carlisle Utd	2	0	0	2	2	6	0%
Charlton Ath	24	8	5	11	44	41	44%
Chelsea	94	37	26	31	161	149	53%
Coventry City	38	17	8	13	68	53	53%
Crystal Palace	12	5	4	3	19	12	58%
Darwen	4	2	1	1	17	10	62%
Derby County	104	50	18	36	209	152	57%
Doncaster Rovs	6	2	2	2	15	11	50%
Fulham	26	12	8	6	46	29	61%
Glossop N.E.	2	1	1	0	5	2	75%
Grimsby Town	22	12	4	6	46	28	64%
Huddersfield T	56	22	13	21	80	81	51%
Hull City	6	3	0	3	10	5	50%
Ipswich Town	40	14	16	10	53	49	54%
Leeds United	76	21	18	37	100	119	40%
Leicester City	76	30	19	27	150	127	52%
Lincoln City	4	1	2	1	5	6	50%
Liverpool	132	46	40	46	167	179	49%
Luton Town	24	10	5	9	39	32	54%
Manchester City	118	40	32	46	165	175	47%
Manchester Utd	112	43	28	41	188	167	50%
Middlesbrough	82	40	19	23	142	111	61%
Millwall	2	2	0	0	5	1	100%

	P	W	D	L	F	A	%
Newcastle Utd	110	42	23	45	165	174	49%
Northampton T	2	2	0	0	7	2	100%
Norwich City	22	7	8	7	34	31	48%
Nottingham F	96	43	20	33	170	127	55%
Notts County	64	36	12	16	125	68	66%
Oldham Athletic	22	6	6	10	33	39	41%
Orient	2	1	0	1	3	3	50%
Plymouth Argyle	6	4	0	2	22	12	66%
Portsmouth	42	14	8	20	68	88	43%
Port Vale	2	1	0	1	5	4	50%
Preston N.E.	88	33	25	30	120	120	52%
Queens Park R	20	10	5	5	38	27	61%
Reading	2	2	0	0	5	2	100%
Rotherham Utd	6	2	3	1	11	8	58%
Sheffield Utd	110	46	27	37	175	142	54%
Sheffield Wed	100	46	29	25	185	153	60%
Southampton	36	15	7	14	59	48	50%
Stoke City	104	50	27	27	183	112	61%
Sunderland	130	55	19	56	215	223	49%
Swansea City	12	8	4	0	31	12	82%
Tottenham H	96	35	29	32	140	153	51%
Watford	6	4	1	1	15	10	72%
West Bromwich A	130	50	31	49	219	221	50%
West Ham United	70	32	14	24	114	95	55%
Wolverhampton W	114	54	20	40	195	162	56%
TOTAL	3368	1409	809	1150	5593	4914	57%

CONSOLIDATED COMPETITIVE RECORD 1884-1985						
	P	W	D	L	F	A
First Division	3200	1332	764	1104	5245	4657
Second Division	168	77	45	46	348	257
FA Cup	303	167	53	83	579	344
League/Milk Cup	74	35	19	20	126	73
European Cup	8	2	5	1	12	6
European CW Cup	13	9	3	1	19	5
UEFA Cup	8	3	1	4	12	5
Fairs Cup	12	7	2	3	22	15
Texaco Cup	2	0	1	1	0	1
Charity Shield	7	5	0	2	14	9
British Champ'nship	2	1	1	0	4	2
TOTAL	3797	1638	894	1265	6381	5374

Figures up to and including last match of 1984-5

SUBSCRIBERS

1   **Everton Football Club**
2   **The Football Association**
3   **The Football League**
4   **Association of Football Statisticians**

5	Gordon Smailes	53	L.A. Zammit	101	James Gwyther
6	Ian Ross	54	David Randles	102	S.G. Wilson
7	Mike Kenney	55	L. Davies	103	Raymond C.Wilcock
8	Richard Humphrey	56	Angela Woodward	104	Trevor M. Jones
9	Brian Joyce	57	Sydney Robinson	105	Robin J. Dickson
10	Garry & Shaun Anders	58	D.Fitzgerald	106	Tony Condron
11	Keith Tomlinson	59	D.A. Quaile	107	D. Lee
12	J. Gardiner	60	Ronald Hynds	108	Rory McKean
13	Ronald Symons	61	Paul Evans	109	S.C. Mahon
14	Stephen Williams	62	David Evans	110	Martin H. Mason
15	David Roche	63	Ian Mackenzie	111	Mrs L. Barnes
16	J. Plant	64	Paul Leamey	112	Don Cooper
17	A. Davies	65	R.A. Smith	113	Donald R. Catherall
18	John Treleven	66	Terence Nelson	114	David Whelan
19	D.J. Harrison	67	H.E. Mansley	115	Mark Warham
20	Nick Caine	68	Allan Harper	116	Leslie Warham
21	Ronald Deri	69	Mrs D. Bunting	117	Gary J.McFerran
22	Neil Hankey	70	Miss M. Rothwell	118	C.E. Wilson
23	Keith Moss	71	Paul Quigley	119	John F. Downey
24	Terry Fearn	72	Geo. A. Buckley	120	Terry Comish
25	David Thomson	73	Peter Fealey	121	Dermot Nealon
26	Leslie Mouzcr	74	Ian Kidd	122	Malcolm D. Glaister
27	Michael Saunders	75	John Worsley	123	G.C. Turner
28	David Fletcher	76	D.C. Wheatley	124	M. Swart
29	Gerard McAleavey	77	N. Green	125	Dominic Noviski
30	Paul Daw	78	John Waddington	126	Robert M. Blundell
31	Ralph Carson	79	David W. Hancock	127	Douglas W. Hayhurst
32	Kevin J. Mitchell	80	David Kelly	128	William T. Wright
33	John Whitby	81	Peter P. Rimmer	129	Peter J. Stewart
34	Stephen Dingsdale	82	M. Downey	130	T.G. Cornish
35	Robert Baker	83	Frank Keegan	131	Frank Johnson
36	Noel Davies	84	A. Brown	132	W.D. Johnson
37	Douglas Houghton	85	Joseph P. Cody	133	Thomas Fitzpatrick
38	Cyril George	86	John Shaw	134	Steven Mabbs
39	C.H. Parker	87	John A. Jones	135	Malcolm E. Murphy
40	Bert King	88	Robert Evason	136	Colin Thompson
41	Edward Gore	89	Karl B. Evason	137	Eric Thornton
42	Ronald G. Vickers	90	John Warburton	138	M.J. O'Connor
43	Charles Horne	91	James Connor	139	Harry Finney
44	Francis Tollitt	92	Gordon A. Fraser	140	Edward Jones
45	William T. Walker	93	Kenneth Ronson	141	Charles A. Shone
46	Eric Jones	94	Peter A. Howard	142	Michael Dyble
47	Robert P. Darby	95	Brian F. Jones	143	J.J. Howard
48	George Currie	96	Graham Jones	144	J. Henderson
49	Joseph Garner	97	Patrick McGuinness	145	J. Paul Chattle
50	Geoffrey Ormesher	98	James B. Harrison	146	Carl Stonall
51	Anthony Moloney	99	T.D. Culshaw	147	Paul Johnson
52	P.R. Silsby	100	M.R.P. Woods	148	Dennis Vickers

149	B.R. Phillips	206	Francis Johnson
150	K.R. Kelly	207	J.C. Parkin
151	Dixie Dean	208	Philip Mattison
152	Neil J. McNamara	209	Paul Burns
153	David Rigby	210	Joseph L. Carey
154	Mark Flannery	211	Stephen Heneghan
155	Michael Kelly	212	Stephen Follis
156	N.R. Hawthorne	213	Barry McBride
157	Thomas Riley	214	Neil B. Scott
158	Royston W. Fisher	215	Paul Bayliss
159	Michael P. McElhinney	216	Nigel Ogden
160	Bryan P. Allman	217	R.A. Butler
161	Tony Rowan	218	Robert A. Jordan
162	Kevin P. Kenneally	219	D.A. Earnshaw
163	K. Maddocks	220	Michael Driscoll
164	J. Jones	221	John Crosby
165	L. Fitzsimmons	222	Philip J. Cottrell
166	Thomas A. Murray	223	Miss L. Ainsworth
167	A.J. Bent	224	G.R. Finnis
168	C. Bent	225	Michael L. Purkiss
169	M. Murphy	226	George Bethell
170	Gavin Wadeson	227	Francis J. Byrne
171	Ronald A. Serridge	228	Alan Guy
172	Philip W. Duffy	229	Patrick T. Rooney
173	Frederick M. Heritage	230	Martin Wylie
174	Steve Daniels	231	David A. Roscoe
175	Sam Wildman	232	James Gibbons
176	Dennis Hughes	233	Philip R. Fabian
177	Paul E. Martin	234	David A. Winckles
178	Ronald A. Ryan	235	Steven Bowers
179	Edward Palmer	236	R.S. Sutton
180	J.L. Burton	237	Graham Blackwood
181	Karen Riley	238	George R. Brizell
182	David Motler	239	W.E. Pritchard
183	David N. Hood	240	Gary Gavan
184	M. Byrne	241	Eric Williams
185	Peter A. Yorke	242	George Bordessa
186	Michael P. Yorke	243	Garry Parkin
187	Andrew J.R. Cove	244	David Walsh
188	David Berrington	245	John Robinson
189	Joseph McChrystal	246	Clifford Evans
190	Gordon Jones	247	Angus W. Rodger
191	Antony Gaskell	248	John G. Hughes
192	Paul Molyneux	249	Philip Soar
193	John S. Teggin	250	David A. Porter
194	Alan Morris	251	Alan Young
195	Michael Featherstone	252	Colin J. Quinn
196	Tony Draper	253	David A. Wilsdon
197	George Lyon	254	Stanley Boughey
198	John A. McGee	255	Billy Evans
199	P.J. Sherry	256	Brian Leach
200	Jon Hankin	257	Alan Roughsedge
201	John H.B. Grace	258	Chris G. Nicholls
202	John Parkinson	259	Robert Jesson
203	Hugh J. McElroy	260	Alex Mattson
204	C.E. Hammond	261	John Roulston
205	W.C. Peters	262	Tom Hall

263	E.J. Jones
264	James P. Jones
265	William F. Hannon
266	Stephen Hickson
267	Joseph Collins
268	Andrew T. Beazley
269	Alan R. Burberry
270	Robert Stoddern
271	David C. Wright
272	Stephen J. Wright
273	Harry E. Povall
274	John Butler
275	C.H. Bolton
276	Anthony Spark
277	W.K. Stafford
278	Dave W. Roberts
279	Jean Caunce
280	David J. Whittaker
281	Richard A. Jones
282	K.G. Kendall
283	Francis A. Matulewicz
284	Rob Turbitt
285	J.O. Catterall
286	J.G. Kenny
287	Philip Danher
288	A.J. Woods
289	Andrew R. Conway
290	Clifford J. Hughes
291	R.J.O. Thompson
292	John D. O'Callaghan
293	David Kabluczenko
294	Gareth R. Jones
295	Philip Gordon
296	Alan G. Smithers
297	J.C. Sharkey
298	Keith J. Parkinson
299	Stuart Styles
300	R. Ivers
301	Thomas Laidlaw
302	Bobby Coakley
303	John McAllister
304	Joe Mercer
305	Ron Cain
306	Richard J. Boswarva
307	Terence McCabe
308	James Keary
309	David Keary
310	Alec Murt
311	Chris Murt
312	Ian Anderson
313	Anne Connolly
314	Robert Jex
315	Karl Reid
316	Gary A. Donnelly
317	Philip J. Vose
318	Stephen A. Watterson
319	Harry Booth

320 John W. Taylor	377 Steve Byrne	434 J.J. Fennell
321 Michael S. Hughes	378 Peter Lloyd	435 John Byrne
322 E.J. Aubrey	379 P.B. Collins	436 Peter Hayes
323 Paul J. Grisdale	380 G.W. Gannon	437 Darren J. Waterfield
324 Tom Goulding	381 Dr J. Rowlands	438 James K. Waterfield
325 David Hartley	382 William McDonald	439 David Wood
326 Chris Hartley	383 John F.G. Nicholls	440 J. Murray
327 Neil Brimage	384 Geoffrey Adie	441 Paul West
328 Alan Ruddock	385 Stephen Price	442 Ged Dwyer
329 Neil G. Hughes	386 Gavin McLean	443 D.W. Taylor
330 Frank Smith	387 Lawrence P. Connolly	444 James Walker
331 Charles V. Denty	388 Nick House	445 Philip Howard
332 Stephen Denty	389 K.N. Taylor	446 Leonard Howard
333 Keith A. Leonard	390 Paul Kennedy	447 Denise Miley
334 Thomas A. Tinsley	391 Dennis Crompton	448 C. Haselden
335 Tommy Coulton	392 William Collins	449 R.W. Dann
336 Edward Fortune	393 Mark Shaw	450 Brendan O'Neill
337 E. & J. O'Donovan	394 Ramon A. Creevy	451 James Rigby
338 Anthony McKenzie	395 Stephen Draper	452 Billy Williams
339 Lewis Eyles	396 Derek Checkland	453 D.F. Farrell
340 Peter J. Johnson	397 David C. Ashton	454 John Roberts
341 G. Evans	398 John Northcutt	455 J. Woods
342 David Chandler	399 David L. Rea	456 Thomas Ackerley
343 Martin Drake	400 K.E. Mawdsley	457 Peter Durgan
344 A. Howard	401 Stanley Sherwin	458 John McCormack
345 David Dickens	402 Karl L. Johansen	459 Nicholas Grundy
346 Philip Tideswell	403 Ray Johansen	460 Roy Durban
347 Mark Grogan	404 F.E. Robinson	461 Paul Slater
348 C.H. Roberts	405 J.J. Stott	462 Allan K. Bridger
349 Robert J. Parkinson	406 Clive Smith	463 E.W. Lyons
350 William Davies	407 Nicola A. Colley	464 Graham Bethell
351 Andrew H. Ray	408 John Qvarnberg	465 John Moorcroft
352 Gordon O'Rourke	409 Gerard Hughes	466 Antony Haselton
353 Alan J. Gadsden	410 Henry Jackson	467 Mark Harding
354 Roger Baker	411 John Bignall	468 J.P. Robinson
355 Alan Platt	412 M. Menard	469 J.F. Greig
356 Lawrence Dodd	413 Stephen J. Rogers	470 John Quigley
357 Sioban Daly	414 Jack Donovan	471 Jan R. Henriksen
358 Geoffrey Woods	415 John Donnelly	472 Paul Rigby
359 Peter Daly	416 J.E. Hanley	473 R.J. Gauntlett
360 Derek Thomas	417 John Murt	474 Edward Horan
361 Stephen E. Watson	418 Thomas G. Melia	475 Brian Garside
362 Alan Jackson	419 Debbie Cassidy	476 Peter B. Pearce
363 R.A. Vaughan	420 David Doran	477 Colette Duffy
364 W.A. Minshull	421 T.A. Dickinson	478 William Dunne
365 Paul Minett	422 Brian Patterson	479 Keith L. Newby
366 Kenneth E. Buckley	423 Paul Casey	480 Gordon Dugdale
367 Richard Auger	424 Owen W. Jones	481 Roy Johnstone
368 A.H. Tran	425 Ian Smith	482 Lionel Cooke
369 Les Gold	426 Arthur Ponting	483 Alan Robinson
370 Dale Slater	427 Tommy Davies	484 Kristina Judic
371 Steven Doherty	428 Paul Fawcett	485 Lennart Hylen
372 Kenneth S. Parker	429 Gerard Jones	486 Michael Johnston
373 Derek E. Bicknell	430 Nigel Bracewell	487 Colin Egan
374 G.E. Brien	431 John Eagleton	488 Francis J. Carolan
375 M.J. Brien	432 George H. Fitzjohn	489 Dorothy McDonnell
376 Mrs Beryl Owens	433 Leslie B. Maher	490 Colin S. Moore

491	David Purdie	548	Alan & Claire Ritchie	605	Barry Hewitt
492	Andrew P. Roberts	549	Ian J. Topping	606	John A. Hughes
493	Gordon Smailes	550	Michael Billington	607	Ronald E. Garvie
494	Jeremy B. Brewer	551	Kenneth J. Ireland	608	Robert Stevenson
495	G.P. Flavell	552	James M. Matthews	609	Stephen Friar
496	Christine Golder	553	Graham C. Edwards	610	John C. Lawless
497	Olle Netzell	554	Derek Lunt	611	Robert Kendrick
498	F. Alan Challinor	555	Mark Thompson	612	John Badger
499	K.P. Jones	556	Geoff Thorp	613	Graeme Crewe
500	M.W. Westhead	557	Charles C. Porteous	614	Richard Spencer
501	Ronald Lunt	558	Paul Blakey	615	Colin MacDonald
502	Paul T. Arnold	559	Peter L. Parry JP	616	Michael T. Gorman
503	Glyn Tickle	560	David Hirshman	617	Robert E. Nelson
504	Michael Earl	561	Ray Cunliffe	618	Thomas Clare
505	Tracey L. Andrus	562	Keith Jones	619	A. Kelly
506	Ray Campion	563	K.J. Rushton	620	Anthony W. Laywood
507	John F. McEwan	564	Gary J. Judge	621	Malcolm Cole
508	Richard Fazakerley	565	Stuart Atherton	622	T.J. Hargreaves
509	J.A. Bishop	566	Stephen Gerrard	623	Glyn Jones
510	George E. Wyles	567	Paul Gerrard	624	Paul Simpson
511	Philip J. Beals	568	Stephen L. Pearce	625	David F. Thompson
512	Shaun J. Brady	569	Ronald P. Thornton	626	David J. Appleton
513	K. & M. Ibbotson	570	Lee Fenney	627	Raymond Webb
514	Michael Dickinson	571	Gareth & David Lewis	628	Dr D.W. Pritchard
515	E. Roocroft	572	David Reid	629	Stephen Maloney
516	Bernard J. Flood	573	Paul M. Fearon	630	Stanley J. Lewis
517	P. Armstrong	574	Gary W. Bennett	631	Tony G. Hodge
518	Marie Rossiter	575	Ronald Daniels	632	Warren R. Halford
519	David Webb	576	R.J. Sherry	633	David Singleton
520	Jerry Burns	577	John McDonough	634	Andrew T. Craven
521	John Kennedy	578	Ernie Hewitt	635	Andrew Ellinson
522	Owen West	579	Raymond Mayes	636	Richard Battersby
523	Peter Carroll	580	Andrew Gosling	637	Michael Power
524	Barry Spencer	581	Gary Cunliffe	638	Tony Killen
525	David Hoggen	582	Brian Adams	639	Andrew McGill
526	Philip O'Rourke	583	Mark Davies	640	Keith Parsons
527	Mick Hampson	584	Christopher Collins	641	Frank Bowman
528	Alan Robinson	585	N. & E. Allen	642	N.J. Condliff
529	N.D. Jones	586	M.A. Willmore	643	Ian Robinson
530	Anthony P. Goulbourn	587	Mark A. Bailey	644	W.S. Cooper
531	Steve McNally	588	David E. Giles	645	Philip Pratt
532	David J. Brady	589	Tony Kildare	646	Paul W. Carr
533	Brian A. Arnot	590	J.J. Raftery	647	Eric Taylor
534	Francis Hunt	591	A. Barker	648	Ken Parkin
535	William S. Hayes	592	Allan Heron	649	Paul Carr
536	Eric J. Williams	593	Nick White	650	Tony Gallagher
537	Chris P. Kelly	594	Geoffrey Barnes	651	Stephen Brown
538	Derek Daly	595	Robert Davies	652	Ian J. Barton
539	Steven Baker	596	Gary Wood	653	Bill Peet
540	David I. Tickner	597	Derek Steel	654	John M. Appleyard
541	Mark Hyland	598	W.T. Jones	655	Mark W. Appleyard
542	Steve Dunbar	599	Ian Stewart	656	Philip G. Castle
543	Mark Randles	600	Myles Buckley	657	J. Trevor Gauntlett
544	Thomas Driscoll	601	David I. Swainston	658	L.F. Seddon
545	Alan Jones	602	Adrian Jackson	659	Mark Jones
546	R.D. Ellis	603	Roy Hampson	660	Alan D. Bacon
547	Stephan Richards	604	R.M. Taylor	661	A.K. Downing

662 G. Williamson	719 Ken I. Williams	776 Francis J. Mottram
663 Reginald Draper	720 David W. Cleverley	777 John M. Green
664 David Bickley	721 Terence Roulston	778 Michael D. Bates
665 Barry I. Jennings	722 Tom Chauveau	779 Stephen Chapman
666 Ian D. Riley	723 Eric Corlett	780 Philip J. Warwick
667 Stanley Bagot	724 Steve Jones	781 Lesley Jones
668 Andrew J. Clark	725 Joseph Somers	782 P. Dodsworth
669 Michael Jones	726 A.M. Owens	783 B. Worthington
670 H.G. Johnson	727 Ian Shingler	784 William A. Meichan
671 Phil Crilly	728 John Quinlan	785 John Ralphs
672 Neil Cox	729 Antony D. Jones	786 Timothy Cornes
673 Peter Phillip	730 Duff Fawcett	787 Daniel McKay
674 Patrick J. McGrath	731 Terry O'Hare	788 Ken Bowden
675 Lloyd J.C. Dunn	732 Richard Evans	789 Denis J. O'Meara
676 Ian Stewart	733 Barry Huelin	790 Ross Fennessey
677 Gordon A. Collins	734 Gareth M. Davies	791 Peter W. Richards
678 Stuart Robbins	735 J. Shortt	792 David Somerville
679 James Hastings	736 N.R. Inwood	793 John Borg
680 James Clift	737 Brian Hulme	794 Anthony M. Polak
681 Leslie Callan	738 S.A. Brown	795 David I. Hamilton
682 J. Ryan	739 Dominic R. Ward	796 Carl Yates
683 K. Harding	740 Paul Ward	797 Eric Edge
684 Philip A. Miles	741 John M. Jennings	798 Terence W. Edge
685 George Mayne	742 Stephen Dunn	799 L. Barry Cross
686 John Jeffery	743 Peter L. Weigh	800 Peter Johns
687 Louise C. Harley	744 Clive Fenwick	801 Reg Warriner
688 Andrew Maloney	745 Les O'Hare	802 Mr & Mrs E. Blything
689 David Starsky	746 John Grainger	803 Derek Hough
690 L.W. Scott	747 Anton Rippon	804 Bernard T. Dooley
691 Gary L. Smith	748 John M. Green	805 Tony J. Burns
692 John Cassidy	749 Edmund C. Owen	806 Arthur Giles
693 Douglas K.V. Bristow	750 Philip Guyers	807 Gary Burdett
694 Jane Goss	751 Gwynfor Hughes	808 Neil Burdett
695 Mike Jackson	752 Geoffrey Harper	809 Anthony G. Whitby
696 K.M. Rice	753 Kieron Sloan	810 Paddy Shennan
697 Peter Milsom	754 Steven Maddocks	811 M. & T.Lowry
698 Paul Lynch	755 John W. Owen	812 P.J. O'Hara
699 Andrew C. Baker	756 Gary West	813 Peter Rowlands
700 W. Hughes	757 Derek West	814 Mick Moore
701 Liam G. Walsh	758 P.N. Bradshaw	815 Paul Currie
702 Robert English	759 Micky Bretherton	816 Terje W. Pedersen
703 Michael G. Cardwell	760 A.R. Roscoe	817 Philip Mann
704 Philip R. Cardwell	761 N.C. Roscoe	818 Chris Lysaght
705 Fred Barton	762 C. Roscoe	819 Steve Watson
706 Tony Bowden	763 Jason Melling	820 John Drew
707 Jeffrey Parkinson	764 Paul Howard	821 James R. Costello
708 Peter D. Owen	765 R.A. Sadler	822 James T. Costello
709 Glyn Owen	766 G. Smyth	823 Graham Roberts
710 Leslie Cliff	767 C.M. Judge	824 Vincent Dahill
711 Peter E. Aspinall	768 Ralph Mortimer	825 Julian Maude
712 Dr Eamonn R. Maher	769 Victor Enon	826 Anthony Ferguson
713 J. Keith Park	770 Philip Roberts	827 Douglas W.Hayes
714 K.A. Pemberton	771 M. McLoughlin	828 Michael Lyth
715 A.C. Potter	772 Chrissie Doherty	829 I.R. Derbyshire
716 John T. Jordan	773 Tommy Lawton	830 Finn W. Fosen
717 Phil L. Roberts	774 A. Pigott	831 Stephen Bull
718 Peter Dunne	775 Ian Jarvis	832 Richard Healey

833	Ronald Ambage	889	Graham K. Barnes	945	A.G. Jennings
834	Barry Kirby	890	E.J. Houghton	946	David Prole
835	Peter Crawford	891	Stephen Beattie	947	Douglas Lamming
836	R.F. Rodgers	892	Jane Heptonstall	948	Michael Braham
837	Andrew McMaster	893	Gerard Scully	949	Maurice Golesworthy
838	Patrick J. Jones	894	Alan Williams	950	J. Ringrose
839	Stephen T. Farrell	895	Paul Boudler	951	Harry Thompson
840	Les Leedham	896	Ian Headen	952	Ian Griffiths
841	W.G. Harries	897	Steve Mather	953	Lars Lund-Hansen
842	Colin Wood	898	R.H. White	954	Claudio Pigoni
843	Paul L. Brayne	899	Martin Tyler	955	Roger Hudson
844	Philip Johnston	900	K.W. McCulloch	956	P.L.M. Lunn
845	James H. Weedon	901	Geoffrey Wright	957	W. Needs
846	Anthony Bell	902	Joe Waters	958	Malcolm Hartley
847	John Ashurst	903	N.J. Shields	959	R.D. King
848	Larry Leahy	904	Ken Dalton	960	Reidar Anensen
849	John Rowlinson	905	Richard Orritt	961	Alan Wheatley
850	Alan Booth	906	G.F. Watson	962	J. Musgrove
851	Paul Weigh	907	Derek Hyde	963	Duncan Watt
852	Colin Foreman	908	Dave Hillam	964	Mark Revell
853	Nigel French	909	R.J. Gamble	965	Roger Boyle
854	Julian French	910	Ian Cruddas	966	Peter Baxter
855	Paul N. Livingstone	911	John C. Jump	967	Keith Coburn
856	Bob Fleming	912	Richard Wells	968	Frederick J. Lee
857	J. Melling	913	Kelvin Dickinson	969	Michael Belshaw
858	Edward Gerrard	914	Richard Ainsley	970	A.J. Scanlon
859	Ellen Brown	915	Gavin P. Baldry	971	K.P. Wood
860	William Sapsford	916	Tony Brady	972	Gerald Hill
861	John T. Rigby	917	Graham Brady	973	Terry Axon
862	Tony Smith	918	S.B. Vick	974	Anthony K. Ambrosen
863	Colin E. Haworth	919	Peter Farrell	975	Dave Sauntson
864	John De Frece	920	Thomas S. Blythe	976	Ian Milan
865	Andrew McGlynn	921	J.F. Burrell	977	Alan Walker
866	Bob Roberts	922	Stewart Fell	978	S. Fenlon
867	Peter Marshall	923	David Keats	979	Roy N.L. Sheils
868	Geoff Dobson	924	Rodney Cottam	980	Gerald Appleby
869	John Shyne	925	P. Marks	981	Brian H. Hobbs
870	John R. Hickey	926	Gordon Small	982	Wallace Brown
871	Thomas Jennings	927	Phil Hollow	983	Geir Juvar
872	Paul Wyatt	928	B. Hourston	984	Paul Buttner
873	J.D. & D.M.Shaw	929	Ivor Gamble	985	N.P. Roche
874	John Lambert	930	A. & J. Waterman	986	David Morris
875	Graham Stringer	931	William Donnachie	987	R.G. Woolman
876	C.J.& P.A. Middlemiss	932	A.L. Higgins	988	Jack Mills
877	Joe Dummett	933	R.K. Shoesmith	989	B.H. Standish
878	Julian J. Wilson	934	J.A. Harris	990	Trevor Bull
879	Jennifer Ross	935	Margaret Statham	991	Caroline Evers
880	David Gordon	936	Stephen Laski	992	Alexander Wyness
881	Alan A. Dowd	937	Kenneth Park	993	Lars-Olof Wendler
882	Mrs Pat Gerrard	938	M.R.P. Woods	994	Jochen Ahle
883	David W. Pinder	939	David Downs	995	Colin Cameron
884	James Conway	940	Roy Shirley	996	Roderick J. Dean
885	A.W.S. Pinnington	941	John Motson	997	P.H. Scully
886	Stuart A. McIntosh	942	Jim Wattam	998	Peter P. Perree
887	David Croxall	943	M.F. Tuohey	999	William S. Hopkins
888	John Keith	944	M.S. Ball	1000	Gareth A. Yates